SCHMITTHOFF'S EXPOR

BY THE SAME AUTHOR

The English Conflict of Laws; 3rd ed., 1954.

The Sale of Goods; 2nd ed., 1966.

Legal Aspects of Export Sales; 3rd ed., 1978 (*First edition translated into Spanish*).

Palmer's Company Law; 22nd ed., 1976 (*Co-Editor*).

Charlesworth's Mercantile Law; 13th ed., 1977 (*Co-Editor*).

The Sources of the Law of International Trade; 1964 (*Editor*).

The Harmonisation of European Company Law; 1973 (*Editor*).

Commercial Law in a Changing Economic Climate (*1977*)

Agency Agreements in the Export Trade (*1980*).

AUSTRALIA
The Law Book Company Ltd.
Sydney : Melbourne : Brisbane

CANADA AND U.S.A.
The Carswell Company Ltd.
Agincourt, Ontario

INDIA
N. M. Tripathi Private Ltd.
Bombay
and
Eastern Law House Private Ltd.
Calcutta
M.P.P. House, Bangalore

ISRAEL
Steimatzky's Agency Ltd.
Jerusalem : Tel Aviv : Haifa

MALAYSIA: SINGAPORE: BRUNEI
Malayan Law Journal (Pte.) Ltd.
Singapore

NEW ZEALAND
Sweet & Maxwell (N.Z.) Ltd.
Auckland

PAKISTAN
Pakistan Law House
Karachi

SCHMITTHOFF'S
EXPORT TRADE

THE LAW AND PRACTICE OF INTERNATIONAL TRADE

BY

CLIVE M. SCHMITTHOFF

LL.M., LL.D. (London), Dr. jur. (Berlin), Dres. jur. h.c. (Marburg and Berne), D.Litt.h.c. (Heriot-Watt), F.I.Ex., Barrister, Hon. Professor of Law at the University of Kent at Canterbury, Visiting Professor of International Business Law at the City University, Hon. Professor of Law at the Ruhr-Universität Bochum, General Editor of the Journal of Business Law.

SEVENTH EDITION

What would this island be without foreign trade, but a place of confinement to the inhabitants, who (without it) could be but a kind of Hermites, as being separated from the rest of the world; it is foreign trade that renders us rich, honourable and great, that gives us a name and esteem in the world.

Charles Molloy,
De Jure Maritimo et Navale, 1676

LONDON

STEVENS & SONS

1980

First Edition	*1948*
Second Edition	*1950*
Third Edition	*1955 (translated into Russian 1958)*
Fourth Edition	*1962 (translated into Japanese 1968)*
Fifth Edition	*1969 (translated into French 1974)*
Sixth Edition	*1975*
Second Impression	*1977*
Seventh Edition	*1980*

Published by
Stevens & Sons Limited of
11 New Fetter Lane London
and printed in Great Britain
by Page Bros. (Norwich) Ltd

ISBN Hardback 0 420 45410 1
Paperback 0 420 45740 2

PREFACE

THE aim of this book is to give a concise account of the law and practice of international trade. We are told by economists and politicians that the promotion of exports is vital to the well-being of this country; this book endeavours to explain how modern export is transacted.

The book is intended for the use of businessmen and their professional advisers, and the growing number of students who study the law of international trade as part of their syllabuses in legal and business studies. The fact that this book is written for lawyers and laymen alike has not presented a serious difficulty. In my experience businessmen engaged in the promotion of foreign trade are able to appreciate the meaning of legal principles, if explained to them without undue stress on legal terms of art; they talk the same language as commercial lawyers, dealing with the same subject from a different angle. I have endeavoured to give guidance to the newcomer and the expert by describing the elements of legal institutions with which I have to deal, before treating their special functions in the practice of international trade.

In recent years great changes have taken place in the climate and atmosphere of the law of international trade. The United Nations have established the Commission on International Trade Law (UNCITRAL) and charged it with the task of promoting "the progressive harmonisation and unification of the law of international trade." These aims have thus received recognition by the highest international authority. They reflect the experience that the expansion of international trade is in the interest of all countries, industrialised and developing, of free market economy and of socialist state planning. That these aims are practically attainable in many fields of international trade law is shown by the almost world-wide acceptance of the rules relating to documentary credits. These rules were developed by the international business community; their customs have proved to be one of the most potent sources of the law of international trade, thus continuing the tradition and inspiration of the old law merchant.

The accession of the United Kingdom to the European Communities, has affected the pattern of trade in the United Kingdom. Whilst this book continues to treat international trade in its global setting, the effect of the membership of the United Kingdom of one of the great regional groupings of the world is also taken into account in this work. In particular, the Competition Law of the EEC is treated in a separate chapter, in which the Community legislation and the decisions of the European Court are considered, and the Part on Customs Law deals with the free movement of Community goods and export documentation in inter-Community transactions.

Account is taken of the major events in this lively and active branch of commercial law. Among the recent Acts to which reference is made are the Unfair Contract Terms Act 1977 (with its definition of international supply contracts), the Patents Act 1977, the State Immunity Act 1978, the Arbitration Act 1979, the Carriage by Air and Road Act 1979, and the Customs and Excise Acts 1979. A note is added on the Sale of Goods Bill, at present before Parliament. The Carriage of Goods by Sea Act 1971, to which are appended the Hague-Visby Rules relating to bills of Lading, came into operation in 1977. The Hamburg Rules on Bills of Lading, which will be considered by an international conference in 1980, are noted. Full attention is given to the legal problems of containerisation. The treatment includes the following new topics: fraud in documentary credit transactions, on demand guarantees and performance bonds, reservation of property clauses, the UNCITRAL Arbitration Rules 1976. Reference is made to the latest publications of the International Chamber of Commerce, such as the addition of the term "f.o.b. Airport" to Incoterms, and the pamphlets on Contract Guarantees, Adaptation of Contracts, and Extortion and Bribery. Approximately 100 new cases of English, Commonwealth and American courts and of the Court of the European Communities are noted.

It has become necessary to add a new Part which deals with Long Term Contracts. These are contracts which have as their object the construction of works and installations abroad. The topics treated in that section relate, among other subjects, to an analysis of the principal provisions of the FIDIC Contract Form, the Guidelines of the World Bank, the General Conditions of the European Development Fund of the EEC, the pre-contractual stage, tenders, tender bonds, hardship clauses, and third party interventions.

There have also been considerable developments in commercial practice. The activities of multinational enterprises extend to the field of export and new forms of joint ventures have emerged. The non-negotiable sea waybill, the forwarder's through bill of lading, and the data freight receipt have gained in popularity. The Institute of Freight Forwarders has published the 1978 edition of their Standard Trading Conditions. All these developments are noted and the new Standard Trading Conditions of the Freight Forwarders are reproduced in Appendix 4, by kind permission of the Institute.

It is my pleasant duty to record my sincere thanks to all who helped me in the preparation of this edition. The persons and organisations who willingly gave me help and information are too numerous to be listed here but the following should be mentioned. First, I wish to thank the readers and reviewers who drew my attention to changing trade practices and shortcomings of previous editions; I have learned much from their comment. Mr. Arnold W. G. Kean C.B.E., Secretary and Legal Adviser to the Civil Aviation Authority, helped with the revision of the sections on carriage by air and aviation insurance. Dr. Mary Vitoria, of the English Patent Bar, kindly revised the chapter on Patents and Trade Marks. Dr. Valentine Korah, Reader in Law at University College, London, read the chapters on Restrictive Trade Practices in the United Kingdom and The Competition Law of the European Community and made most helpful suggestions. The Export Credits Guarantee Department gave valuable assistance by bringing the chapter on Export Credit Guarantees up to date. Mr. A. H. J. Muirhead, Deputy Director of the British National Committee of the International Chamber of Commerce, kindly kept me posted of the latest developments planned by this important institution. I am especially indebted to my friend Mr. Peter Crowley, B.A., Barrister, who willingly agreed to read the proofs and to accept responsibility for the preparation of the index; he carried out these tasks with great care and competence and made some valuable suggestions for the improvement of the text. The following very kindly allowed the inclusion of copyright matter: H.M. Stationery Office, The London Court of Arbitration, The International Chamber of Commerce and the Institute of Freight Forwarders.

The law of the export trade is, as already observed, the most active branch of commercial law and changes and new developments occur constantly. It is, therefore, important that the reader should be in possession of the latest information as soon as possible. The present edition will be kept up to date by notes in the section on the Export Trade in the *Journal of Business Law* which is published by Messrs. Stevens & Sons Ltd. in London.

The law is stated as on September 1, 1979 unless another date is given.

C. M. S.

29 Blenheim Road,
Bedford Park,
London, W4 1ET
September 1, 1979

[*Note*]

1. The Sale of Goods Act 1979 received the Royal Assent on December 7, 1979 (see p. 7).

2. Exchange Control has been removed in the United Kingdom. The Exchange Control (Scheduled Territories) Orders have not been revoked (see pp. 71 *et seq.*).

December 13, 1979

CONTENTS

PART TWO

REPRESENTATIVES ABROAD

PART THREE

MATTERS INCIDENTAL TO EXPORTING

PART FOUR

LONG TERM CONTRACTS

PART FIVE

CUSTOMS LAW

APPENDICES

CASES

(*References in* **bold** *type indicate the page where the case is treated fully*)

Cases other than those decided by the European Court of Justice and the EEC Commission; for these see p. xxviii, post.

Cases

Decisions of the European Court of Justice and EEC Commission

STATUTES

International Conventions and other Formulations of International Trade Law

* A national formulation.

* A national formulation.

* A national formulation.

PART ONE

THE INTERNATIONAL SALE OF GOODS

Chapter 1

INTRODUCTION

The conduct of export transactions can be divided into two categories: transactions founded on the contract of export sale and those having as their object the construction of works and installations abroad.

Export transactions founded on the contract of sale

These transactions are carried out in two ways. An exporter may sell goods directly to an importer abroad or he may build up a sales organisation abroad and transact business through distributors, agents, branch offices or subsidiary companies.

Both forms of export sales have their justification: the former type is more appropriate to cases where the export of goods is secondary to the home trade or where export connections are so slender as not to warrant the establishment of a permanent representation abroad; the second type, which is particularly favoured by medium and large-scale enterprise, offers definite advantages where export trading assumes more than casual character. Considerable variety exists within these two categories; direct export sales may be transacted regularly or may be isolated ventures into the overseas markets; trading through representatives abroad may be carried out under the direct control of an enterprise in the United Kingdom, as in the case of overseas branch offices and subsidiaries, or may be transacted on the basis of loose arrangements, as in the case where the overseas representative is an independent distributor who represents other firms in addition to the United Kingdom principal; it may likewise be carried out by establishing a joint venture with an undertaking in the country to which the exports are directed.

Trading by means of sales contracts and through representatives abroad are not exclusive methods of export trading; they are, in fact, complementary. The exporter who has appointed permanent representatives abroad normally carries out individual export transactions with them, or through them, by virtue of contracts of sale. An exporter who has established a subsidiary company in Canada and granted exclusive sales rights to an importer in Sweden exports goods to those countries by selling them to the Canadian company and the Swedish importer.

It is intended, in this Part, to examine export trading which is based on the contract of sale and, in the following Part, to deal with export trading carried out through representatives resident overseas.

Export transactions for the construction of works and installations

These transactions are often major export projects involving a considerable amount of capital. They occur particularly frequently where organisations in the developing countries wish to procure the establishment of new industries in their own countries and, in that case, are a means of transferring technology from the industrialised to the developing countries. The construction contract proceeds often by invitation of tenders but there exist also other procurement methods.

Construction contracts and contracts founded on export sales are not mutually exclusive. Often the procurement contract provides that, when the construction is in progress or has been completed, machinery or other equipment shall be supplied by the contractor on the basis of export sales.

It is, therefore, appropriate to deal with transactions for the construction of works and installations abroad after those founded on export sales and their financial, insurance and transportation implications have been considered. Construction contracts will be discussed in Part 4.[1]

Export Merchants and Manufacturers; Bankers, Insurers, Carriers and Shipping Agents

The persons concerned with the export trade are chiefly export merchants and manufacturers.

Export merchants carry on their business under various descriptions, such as Export Houses, Confirming Houses or Merchant Shippers.[2] None of these descriptions has a definite legal or commercial meaning and it is important to ascertain in every instance whether the exporter who buys goods from a manufacturer in this country does so as a principal or as agent for his customer abroad.[3] In the former case his profit consists often[4] in the profit made on the turnover of the goods when reselling them to the importer abroad; in the latter case his profit is represented by the buying commission which the overseas principal has agreed to pay. A vast proportion of the export trade is handled by export houses, and it cannot be denied that the merchant system has been responsible to a large degree for the expansion and prosperity of British foreign trade during the last two centuries.

Today many manufacturers, particularly large business houses, sell direct to overseas customers and maintain their own export organisation. In particular, the multinational enterprise is often used in the export trade, both within the European Community and outside. A multinational enterprise consists of several national companies, connected by shareholdings, managerial control or contract and acting as one economic unit in world

---

[1] See p. 443, *post*.

[2] They have formed the British Export Houses Association, whose address is 69 Cannon Street, London, E.C.4.

[3] See p. 173, *post*.

[4] But not invariably; *e.g.* a confirming house may buy goods in this country in its own name or may make itself personally responsible to the seller and, yet, its profits may be the commission payable by its overseas customer; see *Rusholme & Bolton & Roberts Hadfield Ltd.* v. *S. G. Read & Co. (London) Ltd.* [1955] 1 W.L.R. 146; *Sobell Industries Ltd.* v. *Cory Brothers & Co. Ltd.* [1955] 2 Lloyd's Rep. 82; and p. 176, *post*.

trade. Usually there is the parent company in the home country and its subsidiaries in the host countries.

Other categories of persons closely connected with the export trade are bankers, finance houses, insurers, carriers and freight forwarders. The assistance which they give to the exporter will be surveyed later.[5]

EXPORTS AND THE NATIONAL INTEREST

The promotion of exports is a matter of national importance. The national interest is reflected in arrangements made by the government with a view to assisting the exporter and in statutory regulations. First, the Department of Trade has provided extensive information services for exporters. Secondly, the Export Credits Guarantee Department, a separate government department, under the Secretary of State for Trade, provides insurance facilities covering export risks not normally covered by commercial insurance. Thirdly, the government exercises some control over certain aspects of exporting, mainly by means of export licences, exchange control and customs regulations. Fourthly, the law relating to restrictive trade practices recognises the special importance of exports for the national economy by exempting exclusive export agreements from the duty of registration by the Director General of Fair Trading. Fifthly, company law requires in certain circumstances the disclosure of the export turnover in the directors' report, in order to enable the authorities and the public to form a view of the company's export performance. While the first four topics will be treated later on in their appropriate places,[6] the fifth topic calls for discussion here.

The Companies Act 1967 provides[7] that in certain circumstances a company or a group of companies has to disclose its export turnover in the directors' report which has to be attached to the annual balance sheet laid before the general meeting.[8] The circumstances in which such a disclosure is required are:

(1) the business of the company must consist in, or include, the supply of goods; and
(2) the total turnover of the company must exceed £250,000.[9]

Disclosure has to be given of—

(a) if in the relevant year goods have been exported by the company from the United Kingdom, a statement of the value of the goods so exported;
(b) if no goods have been exported, a statement of that fact.

[5] On finance of exports, p. 233, *post*; on credit insurance, p. 274, *post*; on other insurance of exports, p. 288, *post*; on carriage by sea and air, p. 329, *post*; on freight forwarders, p. 178, *post*.

[6] Government information services, p. 57, *post*; Export Credits Guarantees, p. 274, *post*; government regulation of exports, p. 461, *post*; Restrictive trade practices, p. 210, *post*.

[7] s. 20; see Palmer's *Company Law* (22nd ed.), para. 68–15.

[8] Companies Act 1948, s. 157(1).

[9] Companies (Accounts) Regulations 1971 (No. 2044).

Goods exported by the company as the agent of another person are disregarded[10] but it is irrelevant for the requirement of disclosure whether the exported goods were manufactured by the company or not. No information need be disclosed if the directors of the company can satisfy the Department of Trade that it would not be in the national interest to disclose the information.[11]

THE EXPORT TRANSACTION

The export transaction is normally founded on a contract of international sale of goods. From the legal point of view, it is essential to distinguish this contract which has as its object the exportation of goods from this country, from other contracts of sale relating to the same goods but not being the direct and immediate cause for the shipment of the goods. We are concerned only with the contract of sale under which the goods are actually shipped[12] from these shores; all other contracts of sale, though preparatory to the ultimate exportation of the goods, are home transactions and outside our purview. When an exporter in the United Kingdom buys, for the purpose of export, goods from a manufacturer in the same country, the contract of sale is a home transaction, but when he resells these goods to a buyer abroad that contract of sale has to be classified as an export transaction. When an overseas buyer orders goods direct, or through an agent, from a manufacturer in the United Kingdom, we deal, strictly speaking, with an export transaction although it makes a great difference in law whether the contract has to be performed by delivery of the goods ex works or the goods have to be sent free of charge to the address of the buyer. In practice, there is no difficulty in determining whether the contract of sale has as its objective the exportation of goods from this country because the terms of the export contract contain provisions dealing with the place of delivery of the goods and the mode of their transportation to the place of destination, and the buyer, or the person authorised by him to receive the goods, invariably resides abroad. It is evident that a bewildering variety of transactions has to be classified as export sales and that the rights and duties of the contracting parties vary greatly according to the arrangement which they make with respect to the place and method of delivery of the goods and the payment of the purchase price. Fortunately the custom of the merchants has developed a number of stereotyped trade clauses peculiar to the export transaction and it is possible, by a separate examination of these clauses, to reduce to order the numerous export arrangements which the exporter is at liberty to make with his overseas buyer.

Contracts for the international sale of goods exhibit a characteristic which is not present in contracts for the sale of goods in the home market. They are entwined with other contracts, in particular with the contract of carriage by sea, air or road under which the goods are exported, and the contract of insurance by which they are insured. In many export transactions

---

[10] Companies Act 1967, s. 20(3).

[11] *Ibid.* s. 20(4).

[12] The customary words "shipped" and "shipper" include "carried by air" and "consignor of air cargo" unless otherwise stated.

the delivery of the shipping documents to the buyer or his agent plays, as will be seen,[13] an important role in the performance of the contract of sale; the shipping documents consist normally of the bill of lading, the marine insurance policy and the invoice and thus represent elements of the three contracts referred to. The situation is even more involved when payment is made under a bankers' documentary credit because this frequent method of payment in the export trade requires the addition of two further contracts to the export transaction, namely the contracts of the bank with the buyer and seller respectively.[14] In short, the export transaction presents itself to the business man as a natural and indivisible whole[15] and he is apt to pay little attention to its constituent parts, like the motorist who thinks of the components of his car only when he notices a fault in them. We have to analyse the individual contracts which constitute the export transaction because this is the best method of appreciating the functioning of the machinery of exports as a whole. From this point of view, the contract for the sale of goods abroad is the principal and central legal arrangement involved in the export transaction, and all other contracts, such as contracts of carriage, insurance and credit, have a supporting and incidental character.[16]

The United Kingdom Sale of Goods Act

The enactment on which the law relating to the sale of goods is founded in the United Kingdom is, at the date of going to press,[17] the Sale of Goods Act 1893, amended by three Acts, *viz.* the Misrepresentation Act 1967, the Supply of Goods (Implied Terms) Act 1973, and the Unfair Contract Terms Act 1977. In July 1979 the Government introduced into Parliament a Bill, the object of which is the consolidation of the original Act with the relevant parts of the amending Acts into one enactment. The Bill, if accepted by Parliament, will become a new Sale of Goods Act, either of 1979 or of 1980.

The consolidating Sale of Goods Bill 1979 has retained the numbering of the sections of the 1893 Act, as amended, as far as possible, but there are some important changes.[18] The Bill provides[19] that, if enacted, the new Act shall apply to contracts of sale of goods made on or after (but not to those made before) January 1, 1894.

In this work reference to the sections of the Sale of Goods Act is to the present and future law where the sections are substantially identical, but where there are differences, the reference is to the Sale of Goods Act 1893, as amended, and the contemplated changes are indicated in a footnote.

---

[13] See p. 29, *post*.
[14] See p. 244, *post*.
[15] This concept underlies the treatment of export transactions in the U.S. Uniform Commercial Code; Soia Mentschikoff, "Highlights of the Uniform Commercial Code" (1964) 27 M.L.R. 167, 168.
[16] Matters incidental to the export transaction are dealt with in Part 3; p. 231, *post*.
[17] September 1, 1979.
[18] Particularly relating to ss. 24 to 26.
[19] In cl. 1(1).

CHAPTER 2

SPECIAL TRADE TERMS IN EXPORT SALES

EXPORT transactions based on the contract of sale usually embody trade terms which are not customary in the home trade. The most common of these terms are the f.o.b. and the c.i.f. clause, but there are other clauses which likewise call for attention.

These trade terms have been developed by international mercantile custom and have simplified, and to a certain extent standardised,[1] the sale of goods abroad. They are in universal use in international trade transactions, both in the countries which have founded their economy on the free market and in those of state-planned economy.[2] They are, however, sometimes interpreted differently in various countries and their meaning may be modified by agreement of the parties, the custom of a particular trade or the usage prevailing in a particular port.

The United Kingdom exporter, who wishes to avoid a misunderstanding with his overseas buyer, should make clear the meaning of a special trade clause which he intends to adopt. There are various ways of achieving this aim: he may insert a term into the contract to the effect that the contract shall in all respects be governed by the law of his own country[3]; or he may, when referring to a trade clause, add explicitly what he understands by it, a precaution which is often adopted, particularly in the commodity trade; or he may adopt one of the standard sets of export trade terms,[4] *e.g.*, the terms suggested by the International Chamber of Commerce in its publication *Incoterms*[5]; in that case he would quote "c.i.f. (Incoterms)," adding the locality appropriate to the clause. In the following, reference is made from time to time to the definitions of Incoterms.

The special trade terms are primarily designed to define the method of delivery of the goods sold. They are, however, often used for another purpose, namely to indicate the calculation of the purchase price and, in particular, the incidental charges included therein.[6] It is evident that the seller, when quoting f.o.b., will ask for a lower price than when quoting c.i.f. because in the latter case he would include insurance and freight in

---

[1] See p. 45, *post.*

[2] *The Sources of the Law of International Trade* (Clive M. Schmitthoff ed. 1964), p. 3.

[3] See pp. 53, 128, *post.*

[4] See p. 45, *post.*

[5] The Incoterms were first published in 1953 and became known as Incoterms 1953. In 1967 two further terms were added, *viz.* "Delivered at frontier" and "Delivered." In 1976 a further term was added, *viz.* "f.o.b. airport." In April 1977 all terms, including the added terms, were published under the title *Incoterms*. They can be obtained from the British National Committee of the International Chamber of Commerce, address on p. 46, *post.*

[6] See Roskill, L.J. in *The Albagero* [1975] 3 W.L.R. 491, 523, reversed [1971] A.C. 774 (H.L.).

the purchase price while he would not do so in the former case. The seller's price list or catalogue might quote ex works prices for the advertised goods, and the overseas buyer might order goods accordingly, but the parties might agree that the goods shall be dispatched by mail by the seller, who undertakes to pack, invoice, frank and insure them; here the term "ex works" refers to the calculation of the purchase price only, while the delivery of the goods is governed by other terms. In the British customs and excise practice, the export value is based on the f.o.b. value and the import value on the c.i.f. value, irrespective of the terms of delivery arranged by the parties. We shall now proceed to deal with clauses referring to the actual delivery of the goods and the attendant responsibilities of the parties, but these observations likewise cover, *mutatis mutandis*, clauses describing the elements of price calculation.

Ex Works, Ex Warehouse, or Ex Store (where the goods are situate)

This is the most favourable arrangement which can be obtained by a seller desirous of conducting an export transaction as closely as possible on the lines of an ordinary sale of goods in the home market. The clause denotes that the overseas buyer, or his agent, has to collect the goods at the locality at which the seller's works, factory, warehouse or store is situate.

The obligations of the parties under an ex works contract in the United Kingdom are described in detail in Incoterms as follows:

A. The seller must:

1. Supply the goods in conformity with the contract of sale, together with such evidence of conformity as may be required by the contract.
2. Place the goods at the disposal of the buyer at the time as provided in the contract, at the point of delivery named or which is usual for the delivery of such goods and for their loading on the conveyance to be provided by the buyer.
3. Provide at his own expense the packing, if any, that is necessary to enable the buyer to take delivery of the goods.[7]
4. Give the buyer reasonable notice as to when the goods will be at his disposal.[7]
5. Bear the cost of checking operations (such as checking quality, measuring, weighing, counting) which are necessary for the purpose of placing the goods at the disposal of the buyer.
6. Bear all risks and expense of the goods until they have been placed at the disposal of the buyer at the time as provided in the contract, provided that the goods have been duly appropriated to the contract, that is to say, clearly set aside or otherwise identified as the contract goods.
7. Render the buyer, at the latter's request, risk and expense, every assistance in obtaining any documents which are issued in the country of delivery and/or of origin and which the buyer may require for the purposes of exportation and/or importation (and, where necessary, for their passage in transit through another country).[7]

B. The buyer must:

1. Take delivery of the goods as soon as they are placed at his disposal at the place and at the time, as provided in the contract, and pay the price as provided in the contract.

---

[7] It is thought that in the British practice these obligations arise only if stipulated in the contract. On the duty of the seller under an ex works contract not specifying the locality of the seller's works to notify the buyer of that locality, see p. 10, *post*.

2. Bear all charges and risks of the goods from the time when they have so placed at his disposal, provided that the goods have been duly appropriated to the contract, that is to say, clearly set aside or otherwise identified as the contract goods.
3. Bear any customs duties and taxes that may be levied by reason of exportation.
4. Where he shall have reserved to himself a period within which to take delivery of the goods and/or the right to choose the place of delivery, and should he fail to give instructions in time, bear the additional costs thereby incurred and all risks of the goods from the date of the expiration of the period fixed, provided that the goods shall have been duly appropriated to the contract, that is to say, clearly set aside or otherwise identified as the contract goods.
5. Pay all costs and charges incurred in obtaining the documents mentioned in article A.7, including the cost of certificates of origin, export licence and consular fees.[7]

The purchase price becomes due on delivery of the goods unless other arrangements have been made. As the contract is both concluded and to be performed in this country, it is normally governed by English law.

In an ex works contract a dispute arises sometimes as to who has to bear the cost of packing. This question has to be decided by reference to the terms of the contract of sale between the parties, but, as stated in Article A3 of Incoterms, normally the seller is under an obligation to pack the goods, and in that case the customary method of packing has to be adopted. The seller has, however, only to provide the packing necessary to enable the buyer to take delivery; unless otherwise stipulated in the contract,[8] he is not bound to provide export packing or to bear the cost of such packing.

The ex works clause may either contain the address of the premises from which the goods are to be collected or refer only to the town where the sellers' works, factory, store or warehouse is situate. The latter form appears preferable when the seller's business is carried on at various premises in the same locality and it is desired that the sale shall not interfere with the disposition of the goods in the seller's business before they are collected. The seller is then bound to inform the buyer or his agent in time of the local address at which the goods are ready for collection; if he fails to give the buyer notice of the locality at which the goods are to be delivered he might lose his claim for damages for non-acceptance and be himself liable in damages. In one case[9] Brett J. said: "The words are 'ex quay or warehouse Liverpool.' Liverpool is a large place, and is there not, then, an implied condition for notice to be given?"

An ex works contract does not necessarily qualify as an international supply contract within the meaning of section 26 of the Unfair Contract Terms Act 1977,[10] even if the seller knows that the goods are destined for export. Consequently the consumer protection provisions of that Act may apply to an ex works contract in appropriate circumstances.[11]

---

[8] In *Commercial Fibres (Ireland) Ltd.* v. *Zabaida* [1975] 1 Lloyd's Rep. 27 the sellers undertook to provide export packing at the expense of the buyers.

[9] *Davies* v. *McLean* (1873) 21 W.R. 264, 265.

[10] See p. 65, *post*.

[11] See *Rasbora Ltd.* v. *J. C. L. Marine Ltd.* [1977] 1 Lloyd's Rep. 645. (This case was decided under the Sale of Goods Act 1893, s. 62(1), as amended, which provision was superceded by the Unfair Contract Terms Act 1977, ss. 26 and 31(4).)

The expressions "ex store" and "ex warehouse" are synonymous and denote the place for the storage of goods on land[12]; the terms do not normally include the storage of goods afloat, *e.g.* in a lighter, because in this case the goods, when insured, represent a marine risk, whereas goods stored on land are a land risk.[13] The term "ex store" may refer, in certain circumstances, to a particular kind of storage; if *e.g.* frozen meat is sold "ex store," the term might have to be construed as meaning "ex refrigerating store."

F.O.R. or F.O.T. (named point of departure)

These expressions mean "free on rail" and "free on truck."

In the United Kingdom, a distinction is drawn between these two clauses. "The interpretation of 'free on rail,' based on practice, includes the placing of the goods on British Railways' collecting vehicle. The definition of 'free on truck' means responsibility for all charges up to and including the loading of the goods"[14] on the railway wagon. The f.o.r. or f.o.t. clause offers the seller similar advantages to the ex store clause, so that he has little to do with the actual exportation of the goods and overseas risks. The main difference between these stipulations is that in the case of the f.o.r. or f.o.t. clause the goods are not collected at the seller's doorstep, but have to be delivered by him into the custody of the railway authority at the agreed locality.

According to Incoterms, the obligations of the parties under an f.o.r. or f.o.t. contract are:

A. The seller must:

1. Supply the goods in conformity with the contract of sale, together with such evidence of conformity as may be required by the contract.
2. In the case of goods constituting either a wagonload (carload, truckload) lot or a sufficient weight to obtain quantity rates for wagon loading, order in due time a wagon (car, truck) of suitable type and dimensions, equipped, where necessary, with tarpaulins, and load it at his own expense at the date or within the period fixed, the ordering of the wagon (car, truck) and the loading being carried out in accordance with the regulations of the dispatching station.
3. In the case of a load less than either a wagonload, (carload, truckload) or a sufficient weight to obtain quantity rates for wagon loading, deliver the goods into the custody of the railway either at the dispatching station or, where such facilities are included in the rate of freight, into a vehicle provided by the railway, at the date or within the period fixed, unless the regulations of the dispatching station shall require the seller to load the goods on the wagon (car, truck).
   Nevertheless, it shall be understood that if there are several stations at the point of departure, the seller may select the station which best suits his purpose, provided it customarily accepts goods for the destination nominated by the buyer, unless the buyer shall have reserved to himself the right to choose the dispatching station.
4. Subject to the provisions of article B.5 below, bear all costs and risks of the goods until such time as the wagon (car, truck) on which they are loaded shall have been

---

[12] *Fisher, Reeves & Co.* v. *Armour & Co.* [1920] 3 K.B. 614.

[13] The term "warehouse" has been interpreted in a case concerning burglary insurance as a building and not an enclosed yard (*Leo Rapp Ltd.* v. *McClure* [1955] 1 Lloyd's Rep. 292, 293). The same interpretation need not necessarily be given to the term in a contract of sale.

[14] *Trade Terms 1953* (3rd ed.), International Chamber of Commerce (I.C.C. Doc. No. 16, 1953).

delivered into the custody of the railway or, in the case provided for in article A.3, until such time as the goods shall have been delivered into the custody of the railway.

5. Provide at his own expense the customary packing of the goods, unless it is the custom of the trade to dispatch the goods unpacked.[15]
6. Pay the costs of any checking operations (such as checking quality, measuring, weighing, counting) which shall be necessary for the purpose of loading the goods or of delivering them into the custody of the railway.
7. Give notice, without delay, to the buyer that the goods have been loaded or delivered into the custody of the railway.
8. At his own expense, provide the buyer, if customary, with the usual transport document.[16]
9. Provide the buyer, at the latter's request and expense (see B.6), with the certificate of origin.
10. Render the buyer, at the latter's request, risk and expense, every assistance in obtaining the documents issued in the country of dispatch and/or of origin which the buyer may require for purposes of exportation and/or importation (and, where necessary, for their passage in transit through another country).

B. The buyer must:

1. Give the seller in time the necessary instructions for dispatch.
2. Take delivery of the goods from the time when they have been delivered into the custody of the railway and pay the price as provided in the contract.
3. Bear all costs and risks of the goods (including the cost, if any, of hiring tarpaulins) from the time when the wagon (car, truck) on which the goods are loaded shall have been delivered into the custody of the railway or, in the case provided for in article A.3, from the time when the goods shall have been delivered into the custody of the railway.
4. Bear any customs duties and taxes that may be levied by reason of exportation.
5. Where he shall have reserved to himself a period within which to give the seller instructions for dispatch and/or the right to choose the place of loading, and should he fail to give instructions in time, bear the additional costs thereby incurred and all risks of the goods from the time of expiration of the period fixed, provided, however, that the goods shall have been duly appropriated to the contract, that is to say, clearly set aside or otherwise identified as the contract goods.
6. Pay all costs and charges incurred in obtaining the documents mentioned in articles A.9 & 10 above, including the cost of certificates of origin and consular fees.

The seller under an f.o.r. or f.o.t. contract has normally to procure the railway wagons or other means of transportation. This means that he has to make the normal arrangements with the railway authority to obtain railway wagons or other means of transportation in good time. This should not be difficult as usually railway wagons are obtainable at non-competitive rates, railway transport being a state monopoly in most states or subject to strict state regulations. The seller is not, however, under an absolute duty; he does not warrant to the buyer that railway wagons will be available. He undertakes to use due diligence in the procurement of railway transport. If, in spite of this diligence, the transport is not available, *e.g.* because special wagons are required for the carriage of liquid chemicals, it depends on the terms of the contract between the seller and the buyer whether the duty to obtain these wagons falls on the former or the latter.

The seller is not obliged to obtain a waybill from the carrier and to forward it to the buyer unless this is agreed expressly or by implication, or is a custom of the trade. It is further essential that the seller should give

---

[15] On the question of export packing, see p. 68, *post*.

[16] It is thought that in British practice these obligations arise only if stipulated in the contract.

the buyer immediate notice of loading or delivery to the railway authority in order to enable him to make a claim on the authority within the time prescribed by its regulations, in the event of the goods going astray or being lost or damaged in transit; it is sufficient for the seller to send an invoice or an advice note relating to the goods promptly. The seller is further responsible for the loading of the goods and has to ascertain that the consignment is correctly addressed in accordance with the buyer's instructions. He is normally entitled to the purchase price when the goods are placed in the custody of the railway authority.

The British clause "f.o.r." corresponds to the French "*franco wagon*."[17]

DELIVERED AT CONTAINER COLLECTION DEPOT (named place of depot)

This clause means that the seller must pay all charges until the goods are accepted by the combined transport operator at the container depot named in the contract of sale.[18] Further, the risk of loss of, or damage to, the goods is on the seller until that point and he would be wise to cover the transportation to the depot by insurance. The liability of the seller ends when the goods reach the depot and the combined transport operator takes them into his possession; it is not necessary that the goods are placed into the container.

When the goods are taken into the possession of the combined transport operator at the depot, the buyer becomes liable for the further transportation to the overseas destination. He has to make arrangements to that effect with the combined transport operator. He is liable for freight, insurance and other charges and bears the risk of transport from the depot to the arrival of the goods at the overseas destination.

F.A.S. (named vessel in the port of shipment)

The clause "free alongside ship" embodies certain elements which are not to be found in a sale on the home market. The seller's responsibility and risk in respect of the goods is discharged when they are carried alongside the ship so that they can be placed on board either in the ship's tackle, or by a shore crane or some other means. The actual loading of the goods over the ship's rail is the buyer's and not the seller's responsibility. Where the ship is berthed alongside a wharf or quay, the goods have to be placed ashore near her anchorage; where the ship cannot enter the port or is anchored in the stream, the seller has to provide and pay for lighters which will take the consignment alongside the ship, unless the parties agree that delivery should be made "free on lighter," in which case the responsibility of the seller ends when the goods are delivered over the lighter's rail.

---

[17] In the U.S.A. the terms f.o.r. and f.o.t. are only used when the carrier is a railway (*Trade Terms 1953*, p. 31).

[18] On container transport, see p. 377, *post*.

According to Incoterms, the obligations arising under an f.a.s. contract [19] are the following:

A. The seller must:

1. Supply the goods in conformity with the contract of sale, together with such evidence of conformity as may be required by the contract.
2. Deliver the goods alongside the vessel at the loading berth named by the buyer, at the named port of shipment, in the manner customary at the port, at the date or within the period stipulated, and notify the buyer, without delay, that the goods have been delivered alongside the vessel.
3. Render the buyer at the latter's request, risk and expense, every assistance in obtaining any export licence, or other governmental authorisation necessary for the export of the goods.[20]
4. Subject to the provisions of articles B.3 and B.4 below, bear all costs and risks of the goods until such time as they shall have been effectively delivered alongside the vessel at the named port of shipment, including the costs of any formalities which he shall have to fulfil in order to deliver the goods alongside the vessel.
5. Provide at his own expense the customary packing of the goods, unless it is the custom of the trade to ship the goods unpacked.
6. Pay the costs of any checking operations (such as checking quality, measuring, weighing, counting) which shall be necessary for the purpose of delivering the goods alongside the vessel.
7. Provide at his own expense the customary clean document in proof of delivery of the goods alongside the named vessel.[21]
8. Provide the buyer, at the latter's request and expense (see B.5), with the certificate of origin.[21]
9. Render the buyer, at the latter's request, risk and expense, every assistance in obtaining any documents other than that mentioned in article A.8, issued in the country of shipment and/or of origin (excluding a bill of lading and/or consular documents) and which the buyer may require for the importation of the goods into the country of destination (and, where necessary, for their passage in transit through another country).

B. The buyer must:

1. Give the seller due notice of the name, loading berth of and delivery dates to the vessel.
2. Bear all the charges and risks of the goods from the time when they shall have been effectively delivered alongside the vessel at the named port of shipment, at the date or within the period stipulated, and pay the price as provided in the contract.
3. Bear any additional costs incurred because the vessel named by him shall have failed to arrive on time, or shall be unable to take the goods, or shall close for cargo earlier than the stipulated date, and all the risks of the goods from the time when the seller shall place them at the buyer's disposal provided, however, that the goods shall have been duly appropriated to the contract, that is to say, clearly set aside or otherwise identified as the contract goods.
4. Should he fail to name the vessel in time or, if he shall have reserved to himself a period within which to take delivery of the goods and/or the right to choose the port of shipment, should he fail to give detailed instructions in time, bear any additional costs incurred because of such failure and all the risks of the goods from the date of expiration of the period stipulated for delivery, provided, however, that the goods shall have been duly appropriated to the contract, that is to say, clearly set aside or otherwise identified as the contract goods.
5. Pay all costs and charges incurred in obtaining the documents mentioned in articles A.3, A.8 and A.9 above.

---

[19] On the definition of f.a.s. vessel in American law, see Uniform Commercial Code, s. 2–319(2).

[20] Under the agreement of the parties, the duty to obtain an export licence falls normally on the seller, see pp. 15 and 23, *post.*

[21] It is thought that in the British practice these obligations arise only if stipulated in the contract.

Port rates falling due when the goods are "exported," *i.e.* when the ship carrying them leaves port, as, *e.g.* port rates payable under the Port of London Acts 1968 and 1970 have to be paid under the f.a.s. clause by the export buyer, failing express stipulation to the contrary; there exists, however, a fairly extensive practice under which the export seller pays Port of London rates.[22] The Association of British Chambers of Commerce, when discussing the interpretation of the clause f.o.b. London, which in that respect is the same as that of f.a.s. London, recommends[23] that, in order to avoid any dispute as to the responsibility for the payment of port rates, that liability should be covered by express agreement of the parties; thus, a clause f.a.s. London (including port rates) would indicate that the export seller wishes to conform with the practice mentioned earlier.

Dock dues payable when the goods enter the docks, as well as wharfage, porterage, lighterage and similar charges, have to be borne by the seller,[24] in the absence of a contrary agreement or custom of the port. Where the parties agree that the goods are to be delivered "free to docks" or the phrase "delivery to docks" is used, these charges fall upon the buyer.

The seller need not provide a dock or wharfingers' receipt unless this is stipulated in the contract in terms or required by the custom of the trade.

Under the f.a.s. contract, as under the strict f.o.b. contract,[25] the duty to nominate an effective ship falls on the buyer unless the parties have made other arrangements.[26]

The question whether under an f.a.s. contract an export licence has to be obtained by the seller or the buyer is subject to the same considerations as are explained later with reference to the f.o.b. contract.[27] In the leading case of *M. W. Hardy & Co. Inc.* v. *A. V. Pound & Co. Ltd.*[28] (which dealt with an f.a.s. contract) Lord Goddard C.J. when examining this question said: "that in the present case the contract was f.a.s. and not f.o.b. is in my opinion immaterial."

In container transport, the letters f.a.s. have a meaning entirely different from that just discussed. They signify "free arrival station," meaning that the carrier undertakes to deliver the containers to the arrival station specified in the contract, ready for customs clearance and emptying by or on behalf of the importer.[29] This type of contract is, in effect, an arrival contract.[30]

---

[22] On Port Rates, see *Export Schedule*, published by the Port of London Authority (effective January 1, 1974, amended from time to time).

[23] In *F.O.B. Vessel* (1971 ed.).

[24] The seller has likewise normally to pay or refund to the buyer the "f.o.b. service charge" which freight forwarders often charge. It would appear to make no difference whether the forwarder was chosen by the seller or by the buyer.

[25] See p. 19, *post*.

[26] *Anglo-African Shipping Co. of New York Inc.* v. *J. Mortner* [1962] 1 Lloyd's Rep. 610.

[27] See p. 23, *post*.

[28] [1955] 1 Q.B. 499, 512; affirmed by the House of Lords [1956] A.C. 588.

[29] *Kuehne and Nagel Ltd.* v. *W. B. Woolley (Scotland) Ltd.* (1973) unreported. Westminster County Court, see p. 379, *post*.

[30] See p. 42, *post*.

F.O.B. (named port of shipment)

Definition

The seller when selling f.o.b. ("free on board") assumes still further responsibilities than in the preceding instances.[31] He undertakes to place the goods on board a ship that has been named to him by the buyer and that is berthed at the agreed port of shipment. All charges incurred up to and including the delivery of the goods over the ship's rail have to be borne by the seller while the buyer has to pay all subsequent charges, such as the stowage of the goods on board ship,[32] freight, marine insurance as well as unloading charges, import duties, consular fees and other incidental charges due on arrival of the consignment in the port of destination.[33] This transaction differs considerably from an ordinary sale in the home market where no dealings in a port have to be carried out, and yet it does not exhibit the foreign complexion which is a true characteristic of an export transaction.

The following meaning is attributed to the British f.o.b. clause[34]—

The charges and responsibilities falling on the seller are—

1. To make available at the port of loading and to ship free on board goods answering in all respects the description in the contract of sale.
2. To pay all handling and transport charges in connection with the above operation.
3. In case of delivery of goods from bond or under drawback to complete declarations required by H.M. Customs and Excise.
4. To meet all charges arising in connection with the goods up to the time of their passing over the ship's rail.

4A. To comply with section 32(3) of the Sale of Goods Act which provides—

"Unless otherwise agreed, where goods are sent by the seller to the buyer by a route involving sea transit, under circumstances in which it is usual to insure, the seller must give such notice to the buyer as may enable him to insure them during their sea transit, and, if the seller fails to do so, the goods shall be deemed to be at his risk during such sea transit.

4B. The seller has the onus of passing Customs entry and bears the cost and charges for it.[35]

The charges and responsibilities falling on the buyer are—

1. To advise the seller in good time on what ship at the port of loading agreed in the contract the seller has to put the goods free on board.
2. To secure shipping space in the designated vessel.

---

[31] On the history of f.o.b. and c.i.f., see David M. Sassoon, "The Origin of f.o.b. and c.i.f. Terms and the Factors influencing their Choice," in [1967] J.B.L. 32. See also Frank Wooldridge, "The Kinds of f.o.b. Contracts," in *Law and International Trade* (Festschrift für Clive M. Schmitthoff), Frankfurt, 1973, 383.

[32] The parties may, however, agree on "f.o.b. stowed" or "f.o.b. stowed/trimmed": *President of India* v. *Metcalfe Shipping Co.* [1970] 1 Q.B. 289 (C.A.); *David T. Boyd & Co. Ltd.* v. *Louis Louca* [1973] 1 Lloyd's Rep. 209; *The Filipinas I* [1973] 1 Lloyd's Rep. 349.

[33] The f.o.b. buyer under a strict f.o.b. contract has to pay the charges for obtaining the bills of lading. In any event, the f.o.b. buyer has to pay the costs for obtaining documents such as certificate of origin, consular documents or other documents which he may require for importation into his country or for transit through other countries.

[34] The definition in the text is suggested by the Institute of Export, except that clauses 4A and 4B are added: see Schmitthoff, *Legal Aspects of Export Sales* (3rd ed., 1978) pp. 33–34.

[35] Without doing so he is not allowed to place the goods on board the vessel. This is true in the case of entry as well as pre-entry; see p. 466, *post*. This view is taken in *F.O.B. Vessel* (revised ed., Jan. 1971), published by the Association of British Chambers of Commerce, but the Institute of Export, in its definition of f.o.b., takes a different view.

3. . . .[36]
4. To designate an effective ship in time to enable the seller to deliver within the period agreed in the contract.
5. . . .[37]
6. To make entry and meet charges arising from the upkeep and conservancy of waterways used by the ship in her passage out of port, *e.g.* London port rates.
7. In the event of breakdown of his arrangement with the ship to arrange for substitute vessel or vessels with the least possible delay and pay all additional costs of transport, rent, and other charges incurred on account of substitution and/or transfer.

The liabilities of the parties arising under a contract of sale on f.o.b. terms are sometimes defined by the custom prevailing in a particular trade or a particular port. These customs and practices are collected in the pamphlet *F.O.B. Vessel*, published by the Association of British Chambers of Commerce.[38] Thus the term "f.o.b. Liverpool," which has been adopted by members of the Liverpool Chamber of Commerce, denotes:

> The custom of the port of Liverpool is that under a Liverpool f.o.b. contract, the seller of the goods f.o.b. is responsible for the goods until placed on board the vessel; included in that responsibility is the payment of carriage to Liverpool, as also cartage, haulage and lighterage and wharf handling charges applied by certain conferences, according to the method of delivery employed. The seller is moreover responsible for the payment of Dock and Town Dues and (in the absence of agreement to the contrary) the service charge for passing of Customs Entries.

Where a contract is stated to be on f.o.b. terms, the presumption is that the parties intend to give it its established meaning; the seller's instructions to the shipping agents not to hand over the goods until payment has been secured, do not nullify the normal consequence that the seller has completed the delivery of the goods when they are placed on board ship in the port of despatch.[39]

The responsibilities of the parties for the payment of port rates, dock dues, wharfage, porterage and similar charges are the same as were explained in connection with a sale on f.a.s. terms on p. 15, *ante*.

American practice

In the United Kingdom and the Commonwealth "f.o.b." is understood as meaning "f.o.b. vessel." In the American practice "f.o.b." has become a general delivery term which, if used in the form "f.o.b. place of destination" even denotes free delivery at that place.[40] The equivalent to the

---

[36] Clause 3 of this part of the definition suggested by the Institute of Export—on which the definition in the text is founded—reads: "*To obtain an export licence when necessary*." This clause is omitted in the text because, as a result of the decision of the House of Lords in *Pound* v. *Hardy* [1956] A.C. 588, it can no longer be regarded as correct as a general proposition of law; on the responsibilities of the parties to an f.o.b. sale to obtain the export licence, see p. 23, *post*.

[37] Clause 5 of this part of the definition suggests that the duty to make and pay for Customs entry falls on the buyer. This can no longer be upheld; see above clause 4B.

[38] Revised ed., Jan. 1971.

[39] *Frebold and Sturznickel* (*Panda O.H.G.*) v. *Circle Products Ltd.* [1970] 1 Lloyd's Rep. 499, 504.

[40] In this sense the term was used by a Canadian company in *Northland Airliners Ltd.* v. *Dennis Ferranti Meters Ltd.* (1970) 114 S.J. 845.

English meaning of "f.o.b." is the American term "f.o.b. vessel." The American regulation can be gathered from the following provisions of the Uniform Commercial Code[41]:

> Unless otherwise agreed the term f.o.b. (which means "free on board") at a named place, even though used only in connection with the stated price, is a delivery term under which
> (a) when the term is f.o.b. the place of shipment, the seller must at that place ship the goods . . . and bear the expense and risk of putting them into the possession of the carrier; or
> (b) when the term is f.o.b. the place of destination, the seller must at his own expense and risk transport the goods to that place and there tender delivery of them . . .;
> (c) where under either (a) or (b) the term is also f.o.b. vessel, car or other vehicle, the seller must in addition at his own expense and risk load the goods on board. If the term is f.o.b. vessel the buyer must name the vessel and in an appropriate case the seller must comply with the provisions of this Article on the form of bill of lading. . . .

In the English practice the use of the term f.o.b. has begun to spread from maritime to air transport.[42] Further, the revolution in cargo transport resulting from the containerisation of transport favours the extension of the term f.o.b. as a general delivery term, *e.g.* in such phrases as f.o.b. inland port or inland place of shipment, but a better term is the term "Delivered at Container Collection Depot," which has already been considered.[43]

Types of f.o.b. clauses

The term f.o.b. is used in transactions of different character and the responsibilities which arise under the clause differ according to the nature of the transaction in which the clause occurs; the incidental obligations which the clause f.o.b. implies have to be ascertained by an analysis of the express or implied intention of the parties.[44]

The clause f.o.b. may be used by an exporter who buys from a manufacturer or merchant in the United Kingdom and who intends to resell the goods abroad; this supply transaction may, *e.g.* be concluded f.o.b. London. Further, an exporter may sell or resell goods to an overseas buyer f.o.b. London; in this case the f.o.b. clause is used in the export transaction. The exporter should be aware of the fact that the f.o.b. clause when used in the supply transaction may carry different incidental obligations from such a clause when used in the export transaction. This point was made clear by Singleton L.J. in *M. W. Hardy & Co. Inc.* v. *A. V. Pound & Co. Ltd.*,[45] who explained that this difference might be material for the decision whether an export licence had to be obtained by the seller or the buyer.[46]

---

[41] s. 2–319(1).
[42] On f.o.b. airport, see p. 24, *post*.
[43] See p. 13, *ante*.
[44] The different types of f.o.b. clauses and the incidents of the f.o.b. contract in general are analysed in Sassoon, *C.I.F. and F.O.B. Contracts* (*British Shipping Laws*, Vol. 5, 1975).
[45] [1955] 1 Q.B. 499, 508, 510; affirmed by the House of Lords [1956] A.C. 588.
[46] See p. 23, *post*.

A further difference of considerable practical importance is that between the *f.o.b. clause of the strict or "classic" type*[47] under which the buyer has to make arrangements for freight and insurance, and the *f.o.b. clause providing for additional services* under which the seller undertakes to make such arrangements at the expense of the buyer.[48] Devlin J. described the difference between these two types of f.o.b. contracts in *Pyrene Co. Ltd.* v. *Scindia Navigation Co. Ltd.* as follows[49]:

> The f.o.b. contract has become a flexible instrument. In . . . the classic type . . . for example, in *Wimble, Sons & Co. Ltd.* v. *Rosenberg & Sons*,[50] the buyer's duty is to nominate the ship, and the seller's to put the goods on board for account of the buyer and procure a bill of lading in terms usual in the trade. In such a case the seller is directly a party to the contract of carriage at least until he takes out the bill of lading in the buyer's name. Probably the classic type is based on the assumption that the ship nominated will be willing to load any goods brought down to the berth or at least those of which she is notified. Under present conditions, when space often has to be booked well in advance, the contract of carriage comes into existence at an earlier point of time. Sometimes the seller is asked to make the necessary arrangements; and the contract may then provide for his taking the bill of lading in his own name and obtaining payment against the transfer, as in a c.i.f. contract. Sometimes the buyer engages his own forwarding agent at the port of loading to book space and to procure the bill of lading; if freight has to be paid in advance this method may be most convenient. In such a case the seller discharges his duty by putting the goods on board, getting the mate's receipt and handing it to the forwarding agent to enable him to obtain the bill of lading.

In that case the plaintiffs, Pyrene Co. Ltd., sold a number of fire tenders to the Government of India for delivery f.o.b. London. The buyers nominated a ship belonging to the defendants and through their forwarding agents made all arrangements for the carriage of the goods to Bombay. While one of the tenders was lifted into the vessel by the ship's tackle the mast broke and the tender, which had not crossed the ship's rail, was dropped on the quay and damaged; it was repaired at the cost of £966 and later shipped in another vessel. The sellers claimed the cost of the repair from the defendants who admitted negligence but pleaded that being carriers, their liability was limited under the regulation then in force[51] to £200. Devlin J. held that the sellers although not parties to the contract of carriage by sea (which was concluded between the buyers and the defendants) participated in the contract so far as it affected them, and took the benefits of the contract which appertained to them subject to the qualifications imposed by the contract, *i.e.* subject to the maximum limits of liability. The learned judge held further that as far as the defendants as carriers were concerned the "loading" for which they were responsible was the whole loading operation undertaken by them, and not only that

[47] McNair J. in *N.V. Handel My. J. Smits Import-Export* v. *English Exporters (London) Ltd.* [1957] 1 Lloyd's Rep. 517, 519.

[48] See p. 20, *post*.

[49] [1954] 2 Q.B. 402, 424.

[50] [1913] 3 K.B. 743.

[51] That regulation was art. IV(5) of the Schedule to the Carriage of Goods by Sea Act 1924, as supplemented by the British Maritime Law Association Agreement of 1950; see p. 373, *post*. The 1924 Act is now superseded by the Carriage of Goods by Sea Act 1971; see p. 346, *post*.

stage of the loading occurring after the goods crossed the ship's rail. Devlin J. gave judgment for the sellers for £200.[52]

F.o.b. values

The f.o.b. clause is frequently taken as a basis for the calculation of the price of the goods sold and not as a term defining the method of delivery.[53] Thus in the practice of the United Kingdom customs and export licensing authorities, the export value of the goods is founded on an f.o.b. calculation, whatever the agreed terms of delivery.[54]

Arrangement of freight and marine insurance

When goods are sold on f.o.b. terms in the strict sense it is the duty of the buyer to arrange the freight and marine insurance cover, and these expenses have to be borne by the buyer.[55]

This arrangement is sometimes inconvenient because the seller who conducts his business in the country where the goods are situatc beforc dispatch has better facilities for arranging these items than the buyer. This has given rise to the *f.o.b. clause providing for additional services* by which the parties agree that the seller shall procure freight and marine insurance in respect of the goods sold.[56] He acts in that respect as the agent of the buyer and may take out the bill of lading and enter into the other contracts of additional service in that capacity in the buyer's name or in his own name[57] but will do so always for the buyer's account. In this case the seller is entitled to charge for these items and incidental expenses; and he further can charge a commission for having procured the contracts of carriage by sea and marine insurance unless the parties have agreed otherwise or there is a custom of the trade to the contrary. Where the f.o.b. seller undertakes to ship and insure the goods sold, he may make out two invoices, one invoice showing the f.o.b. values of the goods including all expenses up to the delivery of the goods over the ship's rail, and another invoice showing the additional services which he performed by request of the buyer, and

[52] It has been questioned whether *Pyrene Co. Ltd.* v. *Scindia Navigation Co. Ltd.* is still good law, in view of the decision of the House of Lords in *Midland Silicones Ltd.* v. *Scruttons Ltd.* [1962] A.C. 446. It is thought that this question has to be answered in the affirmative; see Viscount Simonds on p. 471. This view is supported by the fact that in U.S.A. where the Supreme Court in *Robert C. Herd & Co. Inc.* v. *Krawill Machinery Corpn.* (1959) 359 U.S. 297; [1959] 1 Lloyd's Rep. 305 decided similarly to *Midland Silicones*, a New York court gave later a decision similar to *Pyrene* in *Carle & Montanari Inc.* v. *American Export Isbrandtsen Lines Inc.* [1968] 1 Lloyd's Rep. 260; see also *New Zealand Shipping Co. Ltd.* v. *A. M. Satterthwaite & Co. Ltd.* [1975] A.C. 154; *The Mormaclynx* [1970] 1 Lloyd's Rep. 527, 536.

[53] See p. 8, *ante*.

[54] See p. 468, *post*.

[55] If the seller under a strict f.o.b. contract has given the buyer credit, it may be in his interest to take out a contingency insurance relating to the goods: see p. 305, *post*.

[56] *N.V. Handel My. J. Smits Import-Export* v. *English Exporters Ltd.* [1957] 1 Lloyd's Rep. 517, and Herring C.J. in *The Mafia* (*No.* 2) [1960] 1 Lloyd's Rep. 191, 198 (Sup.Ct., Victoria).

[57] See p. 163, *post*.

in particular the costs of prepaid freight and marine insurance and any commission which might be due to him.[58]

Responsibilities of the parties

Under the f.o.b. clause the cost of loading the goods into the ship has to be borne by the seller[59] but normally this is included in the freight which has to be paid by the buyer.[60] The risk with respect to the consignment passes from the seller to the buyer when the goods are shipped; normally this means when they are delivered over the ship's rail.[61] The property in the sold goods likewise passes at that moment unless the passing of the property is postponed by express or implied stipulation; thus, the seller may have reserved the right of disposal of the goods until the contract terms of payment have been performed; or the seller—and not the buyer—may have taken out the bill of lading in which case the passing of the property in the goods is postponed until the seller makes the bill available to the buyer.[62] When the seller has not, by express stipulation or implication of the law, retained the property in the goods sold after delivery to the carrier, he may in certain circumstances[63] be entitled to claim the rights of the unpaid seller, and in particular a lien on the goods or the right of stoppage *in transitu*. The buyer is not normally obliged to inspect the goods when they are shipped and, if he fails to examine them on that occasion, he will not lose his right of rejection if they do not conform to the stipulations in the contract. The place where the goods have to be examined depends on the circumstances of the case, usually "the only possible place of inspection would be on arrival of the goods at their place of destination."[64] If the goods are bought by the overseas buyer with a view to resale, the court might regard as sufficient an inspection which is carried out at the place where the ultimate buyer resides.

Naming an effective ship

The ship or line upon which the goods are to be delivered is sometimes specified in the contract; where this is not done, it is the duty of the buyer to inform the seller of the name of the effective ship which he has chartered or in which he has secured shipping space, and of the date when she will be available for loading. Lord Hewart C.J. defined this duty in the following

---

[58] In the certificate of value p. 67 the second invoice should be mentioned under "special arrangement."

[59] This distinguishes the f.o.b. contract from the f.a.s. contract under which the buyer has to pay the cost of loading.

[60] Exceptionally the parties may agree that the seller shall bear the cost of stowing goods in the ship's hold; this clause is sometimes referred to—rather ambiguously—as the f.i. ("free in") clause; see p. 16, *ante*.

[61] *Carlos Federspiel & Co. S.A.* v. *Charles Twigg & Co. Ltd.* [1957] 1 Lloyd's Rep. 240; see p. 77, *post*.

[62] See p. 79, *post*.

[63] On the rights of the unpaid seller, see p. 103, *post*.

[64] *Per* Atkin L.J. in *Boks & Co. Ltd.* v. *J. H. Rainer & Co. Ltd.* (1921) 37 T.L.R. 800, 801; on examination of the goods, see p. 92, *post*.

words[65]: "It was the duty of the purchasers to provide a vessel at the appointed place at such a time as would enable the vendors to bring the goods alongside the ship and to put them over the ship's rail so as to enable the purchasers to receive them within the appointed time . . . the usual practice under such a contract is for the buyer to nominate a vessel and to send notice of her arrival to the vendor, in order that the vendor may be in a position to fulfil his part of the contract." The seller is entitled to claim damages for the delay caused by the buyer's omission to name a ship or for the buyer's failure to do so, but it is doubtful whether he can claim the purchase price in the same manner as if he had placed the goods on an effective ship. It was held,[66] in a case where the buyer's failure to name a ship was due to a chain of unfortunate circumstances, that the seller could not claim the purchase price, but was only entitled to damages. In view of this uncertainty the seller is well advised to insist on a contract clause to the effect that the purchase price becomes due on a fixed date whether an effective ship has been named or not.

Where the f.o.b. clause is combined with a clause allowing a shipment period, *e.g.* shipment in August and September, it should be borne in mind that such a shipment period is provided for the benefit of the seller.[67] At his option he can ship any time between August 1 and September 30. To give business efficacy to this type of contract, a term has to be implied into the contract providing that, before the buyer need nominate an effective ship, the seller shall notify him when, or approximately when, the seller expects to load.[68]

In an f.o.b. contract the time to nominate an effective ship is normally of the essence of the contract and the seller is entitled to treat the contract as repudiated if the buyer fails to nominate the ship in the stipulated time or, if no time is stipulated, in a reasonable time.[69]

Where the nominated ship is withdrawn or the nomination fails for another reason the buyer is obliged to name a substitute vessel as soon as possible and to bear the additional expense caused by the substitution. This rule is, however, subject to a qualification: if the contract of sale provides that the buyer shall nominate a ship within a stated time or the goods shall be delivered to the ship within a stated time, it is thought that he can nominate a substitute ship only if he is within the contract time.[70] Unless a term can be implied into the contract allowing the substitution beyond

---

[65] In *J. and J. Cunningham Ltd.* v. *Robert A. Monroe & Co. Ltd.* (1922) 28 Com.Cas. 42, 45; see also Scrutton L.J. in *H. O. Brandt & Co.* v. *H. N. Morris & Co. Ltd.* [1917] 2 K.B. 784, 798. For a detailed nomination clause see *Bremer Handelsgesellschaft mbH* v. *J. H. Rayner & Co. Ltd.* [1978] 2 Lloyd's Rep. 73, 85–86.

[66] In *Colley* v. *Overseas Exporters* [1921] 3 K.B. 302.

[67] See p. 254, *post*.

[68] *Harlow & Jones Ltd.* v. *Panex (International) Ltd.* [1967] 2 Lloyd's Rep. 509, 526–527.

[69] *Olearia Tirrena S.p.A.* v. *N.V. Algemeene Oliehandel; The Osterbeck* [1972] 2 Lloyd's Rep. 341.

[70] *Agricultores Federados Argentinos Sociedad Cooperativa Limitada* v. *Ampro S.A. Commerciale Industrielle et Financiere* [1965] 2 Lloyd's Rep. 157, 167.

the contract time[71] or a trade custom or practice exists to that effect—which in any event would allow the substitution only within a reasonable time—the buyer would be in default if the second nomination carried him beyond the contract time.

Multi-port f.o.b. clauses

The contract provides sometimes for delivery at one of several ports which are defined regionally, *e.g.* "f.o.b. United Kingdom port," or "f.o.b. European continental port."[72]

Such a clause has to be interpreted according to the intention of the parties. Where the contract is a strict f.o.b. contract, the buyer's duty to nominate an effective ship normally includes his duty to elect the port of shipment within the range stipulated in the contract and to inform the seller accordingly in good time.[73] Where the contract is an f.o.b. contract providing for additional services, the duty to select the appropriate port falls on the seller. In short, the party responsible for the shipment has normally the choice of the port of shipment.

Duty to procure an export licence[74]

Normally the parties agree expressly or by implication that any export licence that may be required shall be procured by the seller. If the contract does not expressly provide for it[75] such implication is readily prompted when f.o.b. occurs in an export, and not a supply, transaction[76] and, to the knowledge of both parties, regulations requiring an export licence are in existence in the country of shipment at the date of the contract or according to those regulations the seller, or his local supplier, is the only party competent to apply for the licence. In *A. V. Pound & Co. Ltd.* v. *M. W. Hardy & Co. Inc.*[77] an American company agreed to buy from the sellers, an English company, 300 metric tons of Portuguese gum spirits of turpentine f.a.s. buyers' tank steamer at Lisbon. The sellers knew at the time they entered into the contract that the buyers contemplated a port in East Germany as the destination of the goods. The sellers then bought

---

[71] An express contract clause allowing substitution does not, it is thought, normally extend the shipment time; see *Finnish Government (Ministry of Food)* v. *H. Ford & Co. Ltd.* (1921) 6 Ll.L.R. 188. But such clause may in appropriate cases reveal that intention of the parties; see *Thomas Borthwick (Glasgow) Ltd.* v. *Bunge & Co. Ltd.* [1969] 1 Lloyd's Rep. 17 (however, this was a c.i.f. contract).

[72] *Fielding & Platt Ltd.* v. *Najjar* [1969] 1 W.L.R. 357.

[73] *David T. Boyd & Co. Ltd.* v. *Louis Louca* [1973] 1 Lloyd's Rep. 209; *Muller Brothers* v. *G. M. Power Plant Co.* [1963] C.L.Y. 3114.

[74] On export and import licences generally and frustration, see p. 116, *post*.

[75] Thus, in *Compagnie Continentale d'Importation Zurich S.A.* v. *Ispahani* [1962] 1 Lloyd's Rep. 213, the contract provided that export duties should be based on current rates and that "change of export duties [should be] for buyers' account." Export duties were abolished after part of the shipment was made. The Court of Appeal held that the buyers were entitled to recover from the sellers a sum equivalent to the export duties saved.

[76] See p. 18, *ante*.

[77] [1956] A.C. 588.

the goods from Portuguese suppliers subject to export licence which, however, was refused. The buyers had nominated a tank steamer which arrived in Lisbon in time and was ready to load but as they refused to name another destination and a licence for East Germany was not forthcoming, the goods were not loaded. It was proved that by Portuguese law only the Portuguese suppliers could obtain the export licence and the goods could not be put alongside and cleared through the Customs House before a licence was obtained. The House of Lords, treating the case as being subject to the same rules as apply to an f.o.b. contract, held that, in the circumstances of the case, the parties intended and impliedly agreed that it was the duty of the sellers, and not of the buyers, to obtain the export licence.[78]

Where the parties have neither expressly nor impliedly agreed that the f.o.b. seller should obtain the licence and where there is no trade custom to that effect the duty to obtain the export licence is on the f.o.b. buyer, and not the seller. This will normally be the case where the f.o.b. stipulation occurs in the supply transaction but will, in modern circumstances, be rarely so where it occurs in an export transaction proper. The reason for this rule is that the licence is normally required only for the actual exportation of the goods from the country in question and that that act is the buyer's responsibility after the seller has placed the goods on board ship. In *H. O. Brandt & Co.* v. *H. N. Morris & Co.*[79] the plaintiffs, Manchester merchants who acted as agents for an American firm, bought goods from a manufacturer in Manchester on f.o.b. terms; the contract was concluded shortly before the First World War when no export licence was required for the exportation of the goods, but before it could be performed war broke out and export licences were required. The plaintiffs sued for non-delivery of the goods and contended that it was the duty of the defendants, and not their own duty, to apply for the licence. This argument failed. Scrutton L.J. observed: "The buyers must provide an effective ship, that is to say a ship which can legally carry the goods. When the buyers have done that, the sellers have to put the goods on board the ship. If that is so, the obtaining of a licence to export is the buyer's concern. It is their concern to have the ship sent out of the country after the goods have been put on board."

F.o.b. airport[80]

The clause f.o.b. airport, sometimes expressed as f.o.a., was incorporated into Incoterms in 1976.[81] The obligations of the seller and the buyer under

---

[78] But there is a duty on both parties to co-operate reasonably in obtaining the licence: *A. V. Pound & Co. Ltd.* v. *M. W. Hardy & Co. Inc.* [1956] A.C. 588, 608, 611; see p. 118, *post*.

[79] [1917] 2 K.B. 784.

[80] For the history of this clause see p. 8, n. 5. See also "Air Trade Terms," by Leslie T. Pal, in [1973] J.B.L. 9.

[81] See p. 8, n. 5.

this clause are set out in Incoterms at great length. The main duties of the parties are stated therein as follows:

A. The seller must:

1. Supply the goods in conformity with the contract of sale, together with such evidence of conformity as may be required by the contract.
2. Deliver the goods into the charge of the air carrier or his agent or any other person named by the buyer, or, if no air carrier, agent or other person has been so named, of an air carrier or his agent chosen by the seller. Delivery shall be made on the date or within the period agreed for delivery, and at the named airport of departure in the manner customary at the airport or at such other place as may be designated by the buyer in the contract.
3. Contract at the buyer's expense for the carriage of the goods, unless the buyer or the seller gives prompt notice to the contrary to the other party. When contracting for the carriage as aforesaid, the seller shall do so, subject to the buyer's instructions as provided for under article B.1, on usual terms to the airport of destination named by the buyer, or, if no such airport has been so named, to the nearest airport available for such carriage to the buyer's place of business, by a usual route in an aircraft of a type normally used for the transport of goods of the contract description.

4.–14. . . .

B. The buyer must:

1. Give the seller due notice of the airport of destination and give him proper instructions (where required) for the carriage of the goods by air from the named airport of departure.
2. If the seller will not contract for the carriage of the goods, arrange at his own expense for said carriage from the named airport of departure and give the seller due notice of said arrangements, stating the name of the air carrier or his agent or of any other person into whose charge delivery is to be made.
3. Bear all costs payable in respect of the goods from the time when they have been delivered in accordance with the provisions of article A.2 above, except as provided in article A.5 above.

4.–9. . . .

Two points should be noted. First, in f.o.b. airport the legal frontier between the seller and the buyer is the point at which the air carrier takes delivery of the goods at the airport (clause A (2)). That will normally be the air carrier's transit shed at the airport. If the goods are lost or damaged between that point and before they are lifted into the aircraft, *e.g.* in the carrier's transit shed or on the tarmac, such loss or damage would fall on the buyer and he should insure against it. Secondly, Incoterms provide that, unlike under f.o.b. vessel, the seller shall be entitled to arrange for air carriage, of course at the buyer's expense, if he or the buyer has not given prompt notice to the contrary (clause A (3)). Whether in British practice the seller has that right is doubtful and depends on the intention of the parties.

The clause f.o.b. aircraft, under which the seller would be responsible until the goods are lifted into the aircraft, is unusual.

C.I.F. (named port of destination)

This is the most characteristic export clause which the custom of the merchants has evolved. Lord Wright[82] observed that the c.i.f. ("cost,

[82] In *T. D. Bailey, Son & Co.* v. *Ross T. Smyth & Co. Ltd.* (1940) 56 T.L.R. 825, 828.

insurance, freight"[83]) "is a type of contract which is more widely and more frequently in use than any other contract used for purposes of seaborne commerce. An enormous number of transactions, in value amounting to untold sums, is carried out every year under c.i.f. contracts," and Lord Porter[84] indicated the general characteristics of the c.i.f. stipulation in the following passage:

> The obligations imposed on a seller under a c.i.f. contract are well known, and in the ordinary case include the tender of a bill of lading covering the goods contracted to be sold and no others, coupled with an insurance policy in the normal form and accompanied by an invoice which shows the price and, as in this case, usually contains a deduction of the freight which the buyer pays before delivery at the port of discharge.[85] Against tender of these documents the purchaser must pay the price. In such a case the property may pass either on shipment or on tender, the risk generally passes on shipment or as from shipment, but possession does not pass until the documents which represent the goods are handled over in exchange for the price. In the result, the buyer, after receipt of the documents, can claim against the ship for breach of the contract of carriage and against the underwriters for any loss covered by the policy. The strict form of c.i.f. contract may, however, be modified. A provision that a delivery order may be substituted for a bill of lading or a certificate of insurance for a policy would not, I think, make the contract be concluded on something other than c.i.f. terms.

And Donaldson J. observed in one case[86]:

> The contract called for Chinese rabbits, c.i.f. Their obligation was, therefore, to tender documents, not to ship the rabbits themselves. If there were any Chinese rabbits afloat, they could have bought them . . .

The nature of the c.i.f. contract is best understood if its economic purpose is kept distinct from the strict legal effect of the transaction.

Definition

From the business point of view, it has been said that the purpose of the c.i.f. contract is not a sale of the goods themselves but a sale of the documents relating to the goods. "It is not a contract that goods shall arrive, but a contract to ship goods complying with the contract of sale, to obtain, unless the contract otherwise provides, the ordinary contract of carriage to the place of destination, and the ordinary contract of insurance of the goods on that voyage, and to tender these documents against payment

---

[83] T. S. Eliot's explanation (in Notes on *The Waste Land*, 1. 210) that c.i.f. denotes "carriage and insurance free", is by way of poetical licence.

[84] In *Comptoir d'Achat* v. *Luis de Ridder* [1949] A.C. 293, 309; Blackburn J. in *Ireland* v. *Livingston* (1872) L.R. 5 H.L. 395, 406; Sellers J. in *André et Cie S.A.* v. *Vantol Ltd.* [1952] 2 Lloyd's Rep. 282, 291.

[85] See p. 336, *post*.

[86] *P. J. van der Zijden Wildhandel N.V.* v. *Tucker & Cross Ltd.* [1975] 2 Lloyd's Rep. 240, 242.

of the contract price."[87] McNair J.[88] described the ordinary c.i.f. contract as a contract in which "the seller discharges his obligations as regards delivery by tendering a bill of lading covering the goods." The buyer's aim is to obtain, as early as possible, the right of disposal of the goods in order to resell them or to secure a bank advance on them, and to obtain either the goods or, if they are lost, the insurance money. The seller's aim is to accommodate the buyer and to secure for himself increased profits by providing carriage and insurance cover, to part with the right of disposal of the goods only against payment of the purchase price and not to be answerable for loss or damage to the goods during the voyage. The aims of both parties are attained when the buyer—or his agent—effects payment in the stipulated manner against delivery of the documents relating to the goods. The fact that the delivery of the shipping documents is, "in a business sense, the equivalent of the goods,"[89] is, as will be seen later,[90] of great importance when the goods are lost in transit but the shipping documents have been delivered to the buyer or can still be delivered to him.

The sale on c.i.f. terms involves the exporter in calculations and operations which, being different from those applied in the home market, require expert knowledge and experience. Export merchants and confirming houses naturally possess this expert knowledge and are often in a position to make favourable arrangements as regards freight and insurance; in particular, they will often secure reductions in these charges when engaged on subtantial or regular trade with the buyer's country, or they may be able to group several consignments to the same consignee or a number of consignments to various consignees in order to make the best use of the available shipping space[91]; in these cases the c.i.f. clause offers them distinct advantages.

From the legal point of view, the situation is complicated because the c.i.f. transaction embodies, by necessity, elements of three contracts, *viz.*, the contract of sale, the contract of carriage by sea and the contract of insurance; these complications have in the past often given rise to litigation, but most of them can now be regarded as settled by precedent.[92]

---

[87] *Per* Scrutton, J. in *Arnold Karberg & Co.* v. *Blythe, Green Jourdain & Co.* [1915] 2 K.B. 379, 388; the phraseology, but not the substance, of Scrutton J.'s observations has been subjected to certain criticism in the Court of Appeal: [1916] 1 K.B. 495. See also Diplock J. in *Tricerri Ltd.* v. *Crosfields and Calthrop Ltd.* [1958] 1 Lloyd's Rep. 236, 242.

[88] In *Gardano and Giampieri* v. *Greek Petroleum George Mamidakis & Co.* [1962] 1 W.L.R. 40, 52; further, Roskill J. in *Margarine Union GmbH* v. *Cambay Prince Steamship Co.* [1967] 2 Lloyd's Rep. 315, 332; and Lord Morris of Borth-y-Gest in *Kendall & Sons* v. *William Lillico & Sons Ltd., etc.*, appeals from *Hardwick Game Farm* v. *Suffolk Agricultural Poultry Producers' Association* [1969] 2 A.C. 31, 101.

[89] Lord Wright in *T. D. Bailey, Son & Co.* v. *Ross T. Smyth & Co. Ltd* (1940) 56 T.L.R. 825, 829.

[90] See p. 37, *post*.

[91] On groupage bills of lading and container shipment, see pp. 357 and 377, *post*.

[92] These problems form the subject-matter of Sassoon, *C.I.F. and F.O.B. Contracts* (*British Shipping Laws*, Vol. 5, 1975).

The seller's obligations under a c.i.f. contract have been defined as follows[93]:

1. To ship at the port of shipment goods of the description contained in the contract.[94]
2. To procure a contract of carriage by sea under which the goods will be delivered at the destination contemplated by the contract.
3. To arrange for an insurance upon the terms current in the trade which will be available for the benefit of the buyer.
4. To make out an invoice which normally will debit the buyer with the agreed price, or the actual cost, commission charges, freight, and insurance premium, and credit him for the amount of the freight which he will have to pay to the shipowner on delivery of the goods at the port of destination.[95]
5. To tender these documents to the buyer, so that he may know what freight he has to pay and obtain delivery of the goods, if they arrive, or recover for their loss, if they are lost on the voyage.

The duties of the buyer are defined by Incoterms as follows. The buyer must:

1. Accept the documents when tendered by the seller, if they are in conformity with the contract of sale, and pay the price as provided in the contract.
2. Receive the goods at the agreed port of destination and bear, with the exception of the freight and marine insurance, all costs and charges incurred in respect of the goods in the course of their transit by sea until their arrival at the port of destination, as well as unloading costs, including lighterage and wharfage charges, unless such costs and charges shall have been included in the freight or collected by the steam-ship company at the time freight was paid.
   If war insurance is provided, it shall be at the expense of the buyer . . .
   Note: If the goods are sold "CIF landed", unloading costs, including lighterage and wharfage charges, are borne by the seller.
3. Bear all risks of the goods from the time when they shall have effectively passed the ship's rail at the port of shipment.
4. In case he may have reserved to himself a period within which to have the goods shipped and/or the right to choose the port of destination, and he fails to give instructions in time, bear the additional costs thereby incurred and all risks of the goods from the date of the expiration of the period fixed for shipment, provided always that the goods shall have been duly appropriated to the contract, that is to say, clearly set aside or otherwise identified as the contract goods.
5. Pay the costs and charges incurred in obtaining the certificate of origin and consular documents.
6. Pay all costs and charges incurred in obtaining the documents mentioned . . . above.
7. Pay all customs duties as well as any other duties and taxes payable at the time of or by reason of the importation.
8. Procure and provide at his own risk and expense any import licence or permit or the like which he may require for the importation of the goods at destination.

Businessmen will adapt these legal definitions to the particular transaction which they wish to carry out, and will vary and supplement them whenever necessary. They will, in particular, define exactly in their contract the requirements of the shipping documents which the seller has to tender to the buyer, and the terms, time, place and currency of payment of the purchase price. They have, however, to take care that these amendments

---

[93] By Lord Sumner (then Hamilton J.) in *Biddell Brothers* v. *E. Clemens Horst Co.* [1911] 1 K.B. 214, 220. See, further, Sellers J. in *André et Cie S.A.* v. *Vantol Ltd.* [1952] 2 Lloyd's Rep. 282, 291.

[94] Or to procure and tender to the buyer goods afloat which have been so shipped. See p. 37, *post*.

[95] This definition is founded on the assumption that the parties have arranged "freight collect" and that the freight has not been prepaid by the seller; see p. 340, *post*.

and variations do not destroy the essential characteristics of the c.i.f. stipulation which are that as the result of the transfer of the shipping documents a direct relationship is established between the buyer on the one hand and the carrier and insurer on the other hand, so as to enable the buyer to make direct claims against these persons in case of loss of, or damage to, the goods. If the parties vary this quality of the shipping documents, *e.g.* by providing that the seller shall be at liberty to tender, instead of a bill of lading, a delivery order on his agent in the port of destination or the goods themselves, the contract ceases to be a true c.i.f. contract in the legal sense.[96]

The shipping documents

The shipping documents consist, on principle, of—

1. A clean bill of lading evidencing a contract of carriage by sea to the agreed place of destination.
2. A marine insurance policy covering the usual marine risks and any agreed additional risks.
3. The invoice in the stipulated form.

Two of these shipping documents, *viz.* the bill of lading and the insurance policy, provide a continuous cover from the port of shipment until the port of discharge, "so that the c.i.f. buyer, whatever happens to the goods, will have either a cause of action on the bill of lading against the ship or cause of action against underwriters on the policy."[97]

It is usual to send the buyer at least two sets of documents, one set by one airmail, and the other by a subsequent one, and it is advisable to arrange that both airmail letters should be sent by registered post.[98] The buyer's order may, *e.g.* provide—

Shipping documents—Originals by first airmail and duplicates by the following airmail.

The individual documents included in a set of shipping documents are examined later[99]; it is sufficient here to make the following observations. The *bill of lading*, which the seller has to procure, must be a clean bill, *i.e.* a bill which must not contain a qualification of the statement that the goods are shipped in apparent good order and condition.[1] It depends, in the absence of express agreement between the parties, on the custom prevailing in the particular trade whether a "received for shipment" bill or a delivery order on the ship may be substituted for a "shipped" bill.[2] Sometimes the seller will include in his conditions of sale an express clause to the effect that a "received for shipment bill of lading, if tendered, shall be accepted

---

[96] See p. 38, *post.*

[97] *Per* Roskill J. in *Margarine Union GmbH* v. *Cambay Prince Steamship Co. Ltd.* [1969] 1 Q.B. 219, 245.

[98] On sending a set of shipping documents in the ship's bag, see p. 333, *post.*

[99] On bills of lading, p. 345, *post*; on marine insurance policies, p. 299, *post*; on invoices, p. 66, *post.*

[1] On clean bills, see p. 352, *post.*

[2] On "shipped" and "received" bills, see p. 350, *post*; on delivery orders, see p. 357, *post.*

by the buyer." If the terms of the contract are silent and no contrary trade custom applies, the buyer is entitled to a "shipped" bill. The parties may further agree that the seller shall be entitled to substitute a delivery order for a bill of lading. Unless the parties have defined the delivery order differently, this means a ship's delivery order, *i.e.* a delivery order addressed to the ship and giving the buyer a direct right of action against the carrier to receive the goods from the ship.[3] A contract which provides that the seller may substitute a delivery order of different character, *e.g.* an order addressed to one of his agents or to a warehouseman, would not be a true c.i.f. contract.[4] The seller under a c.i.f. contract must ship the goods by the customary route, except if a particular route of shipment is stipulated in the contract, but if the customary route is blocked the seller is not relieved of his contractual obligation but must ship the goods by any reasonable and practicable route.[5]

The *marine insurance policy*, which the seller has to tender to the buyer, should provide cover against the risks which it is customary in the particular trade to cover with respect to the cargo and voyage in question,[6] but need not cover all risks included in the standard form of Lloyd's S.G. policy set out in Schedule I to the Marine Insurance Act 1906.[7] The parties should not place too much reliance on the custom of the trade, which sometimes varies at the ports of shipment and destination and may be differently interpreted by merchants and courts; they should, in appropriate cases, agree in the contract of sale on the nature of the insurance policy which the seller has to tender, *e.g.* whether the policy should be an "all risks" policy or should cover war risks. It has been held that a seller, who undertakes to insure "on usual Lloyd's conditions," has not discharged his obligations unless the insurance cover which he obtains is as comprehensive as that provided by the customary transit clause.[8] Another point which should be covered by agreement of the parties to the c.i.f. contract is the value of the insurance cover which the seller has to obtain. The parties often agree on the calculation of that value. Their contract normally provides that the insurable value shall be the invoice value of the goods plus incidental shipping and insurance charges plus a specified percentage of say 10 or 15 per cent. representing the buyer's anticipated profits.[9] It should be noted that the law requires the seller, in the absence of a clear custom of the trade to the contrary, to insure merely the reasonable value of the goods at the place of shipment. Normally this means the cost price

[3] *Colin & Shields* v. *W. Weddel & Co. Ltd.* [1952] W.N. 420; *Margarine Union GmbH* v. *Cambay Prince Steamship Co. Ltd.* [1969] 1 Q.B. 219; on the various types of delivery orders, see p. 358, *post*.

[4] See p. 38, *post*.

[5] *Tsakiroglou & Co. Ltd.* v. *Noblee Thorl GmbH* [1962] A.C. 93, 113 (Lord Simonds), 121–122 (Lord Radcliffe); see p. 115, *post*.

[6] *Reinhart Co.* v. *Joshua Hoyle & Sons Ltd.* [1961] 1 Lloyd's Rep. 346, 352.

[7] See p. 308, *post*, and App. 1, *post*.

[8] Which incorporates the "warehouse to warehouse" clause; see p. 311, *post*.

[9] See p. 292, *post*.

of the goods including commission, shipping charges and insurance premium but excluding any rise in the value of the goods, anticipated profits of the buyer and the freight (which, unless it is advance freight,[10] will not be payable if the goods fail to arrive). It is therefore necessary for a buyer, who wishes to obtain cover for any of these interests, to make express arrangements to that effect with the seller at the time when the contract of sale is concluded.[11] The seller will often have arranged an open cover[12] which covers an unspecified quantity of goods that are to be shipped within a fixed time, and describes the insurance in general terms only, and he then will effect the insurance of the ordered goods by sending the insurers a declaration relating to the details of the consignment in question; in this case he will not receive an insurance policy which he can tender to the buyer, but he will merely receive a broker's cover note or certificate or himself issue a certificate of insurance.[13] These documents are not regarded in law as equivalent to an insurance policy[14] and the seller will wisely insist on a contract clause to the effect that the buyer shall be obliged to accept a certificate of insurance in the place of an insurance policy. The requirement that an effective insurance policy has to be obtained to cover the goods when in transit is an essential condition of the contract, and the buyer under a c.i.f. contract would be entitled to refuse the acceptance of uninsured goods even when they arrived safely at the port of destination.[15] The American practice differs from the English practice: in the United States a certificate of insurance issued by an insurance company may invariably be tendered in lieu of a policy of insurance[16]; "the term 'certificate of insurance,' however, does not of itself include certificates or 'cover notes' issued by the insurance broker and stating that the goods are covered by a policy"[17]; as regards the latter the American practice is similar to the English practice.

The *invoice* must be completed in strict agreement with the terms of the contract; even the slightest variation may cause difficulties, in particular with the bank which will, in that case, be reluctant to make available the

---

[10] See pp. 339–340, *post*.

[11] On insurable value, see p. 291, *post*.

[12] See p. 297, *post*.

[13] See p. 300, *post*.

[14] *Wilson, Holgate & Co.* v. *Belgian Grain and Produce Co.* [1920] 2 K.B. 1. It was held in *Donald H. Scott & Co.* v. *Barclays Bank* [1923] 2 K.B. 1 that a certificate of insurance is not an "approved insurance policy"; and it was decided in *Harper & Co.* v. *Mackechnie & Co.* [1925] 2 K.B. 423 that, even where the buyer accepts a certificate of insurance, the seller impliedly warrants that the assertions in the certificate are correct and that he will produce the insurance policy referred to in the certificate. See also *Promos S.A.* v. *European Grain and Shipping Co.* [1979] 1 Lloyd's Rep. 375.

[15] *Orient Company Ltd.* v. *Brekke & Howlid* [1913] 1 K.B. 531; *Diamond Alkali Export Corp.* v. *Fl. Bourgeois* [1921] 3 K.B. 443; *Koskas* v. *Standard Marine Insurance Co. Ltd.* (1927) 32 Com.Cas. 160.

[16] Uniform Commercial Code, s. 2–320(2)(*c*).

[17] Comment to the section quoted in the preceding footnote, para. 9.

buyer's credit to the seller.[18] The legal requirements for the trading invoice have been described earlier[19]; they apply unless abrogated by the agreement of the parties or the custom of the trade. On occasion the invoice has to be given on an official form, or a consular invoice; we shall deal with these requirements later.[20]

The parties may further agree that, in addition to the three principal documents, *other documents* shall be included in the shipping documents, such as certificates of origin or of quality.[21] Failure to tender these documents in the proper form will normally have the same consequences as a failure to tender the appropriate principal documents.[22]

Refusal to accept the documents

In a c.i.f. contract the right to reject the documents is distinct from the right to reject the goods. Devlin J. observed in *Kwei Tek Chao* v. *British Traders and Shippers Ltd.*[23] that "the right to reject the documents arises when the documents are tendered, and the right to reject the goods arises when they are landed and when after examination they are not found to be in conformity with the contract."

In principle, the right to reject the documents is lost when the buyer or his agent, *e.g.* the bank, takes up the documents, even if inaccurate, and pays against them without objection. The documents are inaccurate if, when taken together,[24] they disclose a defect to a person who reads them or could have read them. Thus, in *Panchaud Frères S.A.* v. *Establissements General Grain Co.*,[25] a contract for the sale of a quantity of Brazilian maize, c.i.f. Antwerp, provided for shipment in June/July 1965. The goods were shipped on August 10 to 12 but the bill of lading was backdated to July 31, 1965. The superintendents who supervised the loading of the maize issued a certificate of quantity in which they stated that they had drawn samples on August 10 to 12. That certificate formed part of the shipping documents which were taken up and paid for by the buyers. Later the buyers sought to complain about the false dating of the bill of lading and the delayed shipment. The Court of Appeal rejected this claim. Lord Denning M.R. said[26]: "By taking up the documents and paying for them, they are precluded afterwards from complaining of the late shipment or of a defect in the bill of lading."

---

[18] See p. 248, *post*.
[19] See p. 28, *ante*.
[20] See p. 67, *post*.
[21] On certificates of quality, p. 85, *post*.
[22] *Re Reinhold & Co. and Hansloh* (1869) 12 T.L.R. 422.
[23] [1954] 2 Q.B. 459, 481. See in greater detail, p. 98, *post*.
[24] On the rule that all documents forming part of the shipping documents have to be read together, see p. 252, *post*.
[25] [1970] 1 Lloyd's Rep. 53 (C.A.).
[26] On p. 58. On the question of waiver see also *Bunge GmbH* v. *Alfred C. Toepfer* [1978] 1 Lloyd's Rep. 506 and *Bunge S.A.* v. *Schlesmo-Holsteinische etc.* [1978] 1 Lloyd's Rep. 480.

Exceptionally, however, where the buyer or his agent could not realise that the documents were inaccurate, he does not lose his right to claim damages for a breach of a condition relating to the documents on the ground that he has lost his right to reject the goods.[27] In *Kwei Tek Chao* v. *British Traders and Shippers Ltd.* London exporters sold goods to merchants in Hongkong c.i.f. Hongkong, shipment from continental port not later than October 31, 1951. Unknown to the sellers, the goods were shipped in Antwerp after that date but the bill of lading was forged and showed October 31 as the date of shipment. The buyers, who were unaware of it, accepted the documents and disposed of the goods after their arrival by placing them into a go-down and by pledging the go-down warrants with a bank by way of security. Later the buyers discovered the forgery of the bill of lading and sued the sellers for damages. Devlin J. held that, the two rights to reject the documents and to reject the goods being distinct in a c.i.f. contract, the disposal of the goods by the buyers did not result in the loss of their right to reject the documents as not being in accordance with the contract and that they were entitled to claim damages for being prevented from rejecting the documents; the amount of damages which they could recover was substantial; it consisted of the difference between the contract price of the goods and the value of the goods when the buyers discovered the breach of the sellers' obligation.[28]

Responsibilities of the parties

Under the c.i.f. clause, the seller's responsibility for the goods ends when he delivers them at the port of shipment on board ship into the shipowner's custody and the goods travel at the buyer's risk although the seller is responsible for the payment of the freight and the marine insurance premium. Despite the presumption of section 32(1) of the Sale of Goods Act, the goods are deemed to be delivered to the buyer when the bill of lading is delivered to him.[29] The property in the goods sold does not normally pass on shipment, and in so far as the two incidents of the passing of the risk and of the property are separated under the c.i.f. clause, are contrary to the provisions of the Sale of Goods Act 1893, s. 20.[30] The property usually passes when the bill of lading is delivered to the buyer or his agent, *e.g.* the correspondent bank if payment is arranged under a documentary credit and the buyer thereby acquires the right of disposal

---

[27] On the right to refuse acceptance of the goods, see pp. 89 and 97, *post*.

[28] [1954] 2 Q.B. 459.

[29] *Biddell Bros.* v. *E. Clemens Horst Co.* [1912] A.C. 18, 22. In exceptional cases, however, the goods may be released by the seller to the buyer before delivery of the bills of lading; such procedure may raise the presumption that property in the goods shall not pass to the buyer on such an anticipated delivery: *Cheetham & Co. Ltd.* v. *Thornham Spinning Co. Ltd.* [1964] 2 Lloyd's Rep. 17; *Ginzberg* v. *Barrow Haematite Steel Co. Ltd.* [1966] 1 Lloyd's Rep. 343. See p. 79, *post*.

[30] See p. 80, *post*.

of the goods,[31] but normally he acquires only conditional property, *viz.* property subject to the condition subsequent that the goods shall revert to the seller if, upon examination, they are found to be not in accordance with the contract.[32] The buyer's right to inspect the goods is governed by the same rules as apply to these incidents under the f.o.b. stipulation.[33]

Import duties and consular fees have to be paid, in the case of the c.i.f. contract, by the buyer while export licences have to be obtained by the seller who likewise would be responsible for export duties in the rare cases where they are levied; but these rules of law apply only where the parties have not agreed on another arrangement.[34]

A seller of feeding stuff under a c.i.f. contract who transfers the bills of lading and other shipping documents to his buyer in England, is liable to him under the warranty implied by what was then section 2(2) of the U.K. Fertilisers and Feeding Stuffs Act 1926[35] which provides that the goods must be suitable for their use as feeding stuff and not contain a prohibited ingredient.[36] The decisive feature here is that the transfer of the shipping documents takes place in England; the physical situation of the goods themselves at the date of transfer of the documents is irrelevant.

Payment of the price

In a c.i.f. contract, unless the parties have otherwise agreed, the payment of the price becomes due when documents conforming to the contract are tendered.

But delay in presenting the shipping documents may entitle the buyers to rescind the contract. Thus in a case[37] concerning the sale of Canadian rapeseed by German sellers to Dutch buyers on a contract form issued by the Oils, Seeds and Fats Association (FOSFA) the contract provided: "Payment: net cash against documents and/or delivery order on arrival of the vessel at port of discharge but not later than 20 days after date of bill of lading. . . ." The bills of lading were issued dated December 11, 1974 but the arrival of the ship, which had run aground and had to be repaired,

---

[31] Exceptionally the parties may make other arrangements concerning the passing of property. They may arrange that property shall pass on shipment (*per* Roskill L.J. in *The Albazero* [1975] 3 W.L.R. 491, 523, reversed by The House of Lords [1977] A.C. 774); David G. Powles, "Action without Loss; The Consignor's Right against the Carrier," [1977] J.B.L. 132, 137, or they may arrange for the property to remain in the seller (shipper) until he receives the purchase price in cash; see also p. 79, *post*.

[32] *Kwei Tek Chao* v. *British Traders and Shippers Ltd.* [1954] 2 Q.B. 459, 487. On defeasible property, see also *McDougall* v. *Aeromarine of Emsworth Ltd.* [1958] 1 W.L.R. 1126.

[33] See p. 21, *ante*; on examination of the goods, see p. 92, *post*.

[34] *Produce Brokers New Co. (1924) Ltd.* v. *British Italian Trading Co.* [1952] 1 Lloyd's Rep. 379. *Cf.* this case with *Compagnie Continentale d'Importation Zurich S.A.* v. *Ispahani* [1962] 1 Lloyd's Rep. 213; see p. 23, *ante*. See also *D. I. Henry Ltd.* v. *Wilhelm G. Clasen* [1973] 1 Lloyd's Rep. 159 (C.A.) ("Cape surcharge buyer's account").

[35] Now s. 72 of the Agriculture Act 1970.

[36] *Henry Kendall & Sons* v. *William Lillico & Sons Ltd., etc.*; appeals from *Hardwick Game Farm* v. *Suffolk Agricultural Producers' Association* [1969] 2 A.C. 31, 120–122, 127.

[37] *Alfred C. Toepfer (Hamburg)* v. *Verheijdens Veervoeder Commissiehandel Rotterdam The Times*, April 26, 1978.

was delayed without fault of the sellers, who received the bills in January 1975 and presented delivery orders on the ship in February 1975. The buyers rejected them on the ground that the presentation was out of time. Donaldson J. held that in a commodity contract provisions as to the time of shipment were prima facie conditions and that the payment clause imposed not only an obligation on the buyers to pay within the stipulated time but also an obligation on the sellers to present the documents within that time; these were correlative obligations and rights. The buyers had therefore rightly rejected the documents.

Port of shipment and port of destination

Stipulations in a c.i.f. contract as to the time and place of shipment are, as already observed, ordinarily conditions of the contract, a breach of which entitles the buyer to refuse to accept the documents when presented.[38] The contract may provide for shipment in a specified ship "or substitute."[39]

Where a c.i.f. contract provides for shipment from a specified port and prohibits the transhipment of the goods, the buyer is normally[40] entitled to a bill of lading evidencing the continuous carriage from the port of shipment to the port of destination; in this case the bill of lading should not contain a transhipment clause; if the goods are shipped from another port or are transhipped, contrary to the contract of sale, the buyer would be entitled to reject the bill of lading.[41] Where the contract of sale does not prohibit transhipment the buyer can claim a bill of lading issued by the ship carrying the goods to the port of destination because it is only on presentation of such bill that he will receive the goods; in this case indirect shipment or transhipment (under an appropriate and usual clause in the bill of lading) is admitted; if in such a case the goods are transhipped owing to an emergency, *e.g.* because the first ship cannot continue the voyage in consequence of a mishap, and the oncarrying ship does not issue a bill of lading but its master would deliver the goods on the presentation of a bill issued by the first ship, the tender of such bill is sufficient although it is not issued by the carrying ship.[42]

Where transhipment is prohibited by the contract of sale and payment is to be made under a banker's documentary credit, the instructions to the bank should state the prohibition expressly because the *Uniform Customs*

---

[38] Donaldson J. in *Aruna Mills Ltd.* v. *Dhanrajmal Gobindram* [1968] 1 Lloyd's Rep. 304, 311; *Thos. Borthwick (Glasgow)* v. *Bunge & Co.* [1969] 1 Lloyd's Rep. 17, 28; *Alfred C. Toepfer (Hamburg)* v. *Verheijdens Veervoeder Commissiehandel Rotterdam, The Times*, April 26, 1978.

[39] *Thos. Borthwick (Glasgow)* v. *Bunge & Co.* [1969] 1 Lloyd's Rep. 17. On the substitute clause see also p. 21, n. 71.

[40] Unless the contract makes special arrangements or a trade custom or practice exists to the contrary.

[41] *Continental Imes Ltd.* v. *H. E. Dibble* [1952] 1 Lloyd's Rep. 220, 226.

[42] *Holland Colombo Trading Society Ltd.* v. *Segu Mohamed Khaja Alawdeen* [1954] 2 Lloyd's Rep. 45.

and Practice for Documentary Credits 1974, which apply to most bankers' credits, provide in article 21[43]:

> Unless transhipment is prohibited by the terms of the credit, bills of lading will be accepted which indicate that the goods will be transhipped en route, provided the entire voyage is covered by one and the same bill of lading.
>
> Bills of lading incorporating printed clauses stating that the carriers have the right to tranship will be accepted notwithstanding the fact that the credit prohibits transhipment.

Where the tendered bill of lading or delivery order does not name as the terminus of the carriage the port stipulated in the contract as destination, it may be rejected by the buyer. In an import transaction in which hides were brought c. and f. Liverpool but were shipped to Manchester and were from there transhipped to Liverpool in a dumb barge, a delivery order addressed to the master porter of the hide berth in the North Carriers Dock of Liverpool was held to be rightly rejected by the buyers.[44]

Tender of goods afloat

Normally the seller under a c.i.f. contract has the option either to arrange the actual shipment of the goods in a ship chosen by him or to purchase goods which are already afloat; in either case the seller has to tender to the buyer the appropriate bills of lading.[45]

The buyer cannot compel the seller to adopt one or the other of these alternatives; the choice is with the seller. If, however, one alternative becomes impossible, in principle the seller is obliged to use the other one to perform; if, *e.g.*, the goods cannot be shipped at the contemplated port of shipment because the Government places an embargo on them the seller is bound to procure the goods afloat and to tender the buyer bills of lading relating to them.[46]

In practice, however, the situation will often be different and the seller will not be under an obligation to buy the goods afloat or to prove that he could not have bought them afloat, if the despatch of the goods from the contemplated port of shipment has become frustrated. The reason is that the c.i.f. contract will provide expressly or by necessary implication that the frustrating event shall absolve the seller from that obligation.[47] Commercial considerations may compel this interpretation of the contract. In

---

[43] On the Uniform Customs and Practice for Documentary Credits see p. 246, *post*.

[44] *Colin & Shields* v. *W. Weddel & Co. Ltd.* [1952] W.N. 420.

[45] *Vantol Ltd.* v. *Fairclough Dodd & Jones Ltd.* [1955] 1 W.L.R. 642, 646; *Pike (Joseph) & Sons (Liverpool)* v. *Cornelius (Richard) & Co.* [1955] 2 Lloyd's Rep. 747, 751; *P. J. van der Zijden Wildhandel N.V.* v. *Tucker & Cross Ltd.* [1975] 2 Lloyd's Rep. 240, 242.

[46] *Per* Lord Denning M.R. in *Tradex Export S.A.* v. *Andre & Cie S.A.* [1976] 1 Lloyd's Rep. 416, 423.

[47] *Vantol Ltd.* v. *Fairclough Dodd & Jones Ltd.* [1955] 1 W.L.R. 642, 647; *Lewis Emanual & Son Ltd.* v. *Sammut* [1959] 2 Lloyd's Rep. 62; *Tradex Export S.A.* v. *Andre & Cie S.A.* [1976] 1 Lloyd's Rep. 416; *Toepfer* v. *Schwarze* [1977] 2 Lloyd's Rep. 380, 390; *Exportelisa S.A.* v. *Rocco Giuseppe & Figli Soc. Coll.* [1978] 1 Lloyd's Rep. 433, 437; *Bremer Handelsgellschaft mbH* v. *Vanden Avenne-Izegem* P.V.B.A. [1978] 2 Lloyd's Rep. 109.

many circumstances buying afloat would be impracticable and commercially unsuitable. Lord Denning M.R. observed in one case[48]:

> Take the usual case of a string of contracts between the shipper and the receiver. If there were an obligation to buy afloat, who is to do the buying? Is each seller to do so in order to fulfil his obligation to the buyer? If that were so there would be . . . "large numbers of buyers chasing very few goods and the price would reach unheard of levels." Alternatively, is the first seller in the string to do so? Or the last seller? No one can tell. It seems to me that if there is prohibition of export or *force majeure*, the sellers are not bound to buy afloat in order to implement their contract.

On the other hand, the c.i.f. contract may expressly provide that the goods should be shipped "afloat," with or without reference to a particular ship.[49]

Loss of goods

It follows from the peculiar character of the c.i.f. contract that, if the goods are shipped and lost during the ocean transit, the seller is still entitled to tender proper shipping documents to the buyer and to claim the purchase price. "The contingency of loss is within and not outside the contemplation of the parties to a c.i.f. contract."[50] It has been held[50] that these rules apply even when the seller at the time when offering the shipping documents knows that the goods are lost. It is immaterial whether before the tender of the documents the property in the goods is vested in the seller or the buyer or a third person or whether the goods are unascertained or have been appropriated. "The seller must be in a position to pass the property in the goods by the bill of lading if the goods are in existence but he need not have appropriated the particular goods in the particular bill of lading to the particular buyer until the moment of the tender, nor need he have obtained any right to deal with the bill of lading until the moment of the tender."[51]

The buyer's remedy, in case of loss of the goods in transit, is normally a claim against the shipowner by virtue of the bill of lading or against the insurer by virtue of the marine insurance policy. When the documents are transferred to him he acquires the status of a consignee of the bill of lading[52] and assignee of the policy[53] and can, in his own name, sue the shipowner or insurer unless, of course, these persons prefer to settle his claim for damages voluntarily.

Cases may arise where the goods are lost in transit owing to causes which do not entitle the buyer to make a claim against the shipowner or insurer. In these cases the significance of the statement becomes evident that under a c.i.f. contract the buyer, and not the seller, bears the risk from the

---

[48] *Per* Lord Denning M.R. in *Tradex Export S.A.* v. *Andre & Cie S.A.* [1976] 1 Lloyd's Rep. 416, 423.

[49] See, *e.g. Mash & Murrell Ltd.* v. *Joseph I. Emanuel Ltd.* [1961] 1 W.L.R. 862, 863; [1962] 1 W.L.R. 16.

[50] MacCardie J. in *Manbre Saccharine Co.* v. *Corn Products Co.* [1919] 1 K.B. 198, 204.

[51] Atkin J. in *C. Groom Ltd.* v. *Barber* [1915] 1 K.B. 316, 324.

[52] See p. 352, *post*.

[53] See p. 307, *post*.

moment when the goods are delivered to the carrier. It means that, even in these cases, which sometimes involve hardship for the buyer, the buyer has to pay the purchase price upon delivery of the duly made out shipping documents or, if he has already paid, cannot recover the price on the ground that there was a total failure of consideration.

Contracts expressed to be c.i.f. but not being true c.i.f. contracts

These strict rules are peculiar to the c.i.f. contract and do not apply to other contracts, in particular not to arrival contracts[54] and other contracts which are not true c.i.f. contracts though they may be so described by the parties. It should be noted that the terminology employed by the parties is not always a safe guide to their real intentions. In *Comptoir d'Achat* v. *Luis de Ridder*[54] the sellers who sold on c.i.f. terms reserved the right to substitute a delivery order on their agents at the port of destination for the bill of lading; the buyers accepted the delivery order and paid the purchase price but the order could not be implemented because the ship carrying the goods had to be diverted owing to circumstances connected with the Second World War. The House of Lords held that the buyers were entitled to the return of the purchase price because an analysis of the customary course of trading of the parties showed, in the words of Lord Porter,[55] that "payment was not made for the documents but as an advance payment for a contract afterwards to be performed"; the contract was, thus, no true c.i.f. contract and the sellers' inability to deliver the goods at the port of destination resulted in a total failure of consideration for the payment of the purchase price by the buyers.

Where a contract expressed to be on c.i.f. terms provided that "any tender or delivery of the goods or of the bill of lading" should constitute a valid tender or deliver, the Judicial Committee of the Privy Council, on appeal from Ceylon, advised that the contract was not intended to be a true c.i.f. contract since the tender of the goods was admitted as an alternative to the tender of the documents.[56]

A contract using the term c.i.f. in connection with air transport is not a true c.i.f. contract, as Graham J. correctly held in a case[57] which provided for delivery of goods sent from Holland to purchasers in the United Kingdom "c.i.f. Gatwick."

---

[54] [1949] A.C. 293. See further, *Re Denbigh, Cowan & Co. and R. Atcherley & Co.* (1921) 90 L.J.K.B. 936; *The Parchim* [1918] A.C. 157, 163; *Colin & Shields* v. *W. Weddel & Co. Ltd.* [1952] W.N. 420; *John Martin of London* v. *A. E. Taylor* [1953] 2 Lloyd's Rep. 589; *Holland Colombo Trading Society Ltd.* v. *Segu Mohamed Khaja Alawdeen* [1954] 2 Lloyd's Rep. 45; *H. Glynn (Covent Garden) Ltd.* v. *Wittleder* [1959] 2 Lloyd's Rep. 409, 413; *Gardano and Giampieri* v. *Greek Petroleum George Mamidakis & Co.* [1962] 1 W.L.R. 40 ("Delivery ex Eleussinia Installation"); *Margarine Union GmbH* v. *Cambay Prince Steamship Co. Ltd.* [1969] 1 Q.B. 219 (delivery orders not on ship).

[55] [1949] A,C. 293, 310.

[56] *Holland Colombo Trading Society Ltd.* v. *Segu Mohamed Khaja Alawdeen, supra.*

[57] *Morton-Norwich Products Inc.* v. *Intercen Ltd.* [1976] F.S.R. 513; [1977] J.B.L. 182.

Refusal to accept the goods

The peculiar features of the c.i.f. contract do not prevent the buyer from rejecting the goods[58] when, on delivery and inspection, he finds that they are not in accordance with the terms of the contract, *e.g.* that they are of an inferior quality or damaged owing to insufficient packing. The payment of the purchase price on delivery of the shipping documents is conditional on the goods being in accordance with the terms of the contract of sale. If they fall short in that respect, the condition is discharged and the position is the same as in every other contract of sale. If the agreement of the parties as to the quality of the goods was a condition of the contract of sale and not merely a warranty,[59] as is normally the case, the buyer may rescind the contract and recover the purchase price.[60]

The buyer's right to inspect and examine the goods is similar to that of a buyer under an f.o.b. contract.[61]

Variants of the c.i.f. contract

Two variants of the contract, even if called by the parties "c.i.f.," do not, as already observed,[62] satisfy the essential legal requirements of the c.i.f. contract. First, if according to the intention of the parties the actual delivery of the goods is an essential condition of performance, the contract is not a c.i.f. contract. Secondly, if on transfer of the shipping documents no direct relation is constituted between the transferee, on the one hand, and the carrier and insurer, on the other, the contract lacks the essential legal features of a c.i.f. contract.

The following variants of the c.i.f. contract are admissible; they are reconcilable with the legal nature of that type of contract:

1. *c. and f.*; *c.i.f. and c.*; *c.i.f. and e.*; *c.i.f. and c. and i.* These variants are discussed in the following paragraphs.
2. *date of arrival of goods is mere determinant for payment of price.* The parties agree sometimes on c.i.f. terms, adding "payment on arrival of goods," or "payment x days after arrival of goods."

   This clause is ambiguous and its meaning has to be ascertained from the intention of the parties.

   The parties may have intended that the arrival of the goods shall be a condition for the payment of the price. In this case the contract is not a c.i.f. contract. The English practice was formerly inclined to interpret the clause in this manner,[63] but the better view is that this

[58] On the refusal to accept the documents, see p. 32, *ante*.
[59] On conditions and warranties in contracts of sale, see p. 90, *post*.
[60] See pp. 90–91, *post*.
[61] See p. 21, *ante*; on examination of the goods, see p. 92, *post*.
[62] See p. 38, *ante*.
[63] *Dupont* v. *British South Africa Co.* (1901) 18 T.L.R. 24; *Polenghi* v. *Dried Milk Co.* (1904) 10 Com.Cas. 42.

interpretation should only be adopted if that intention of the parties can clearly be gathered from the contract.[64]

Alternatively, the parties may have intended that the clause shall only refer to the time at which payment has to be made, in short that, if the goods do not arrive, payment shall be made on tender of the documents at the date at which the goods would normally have arrived. In this case the clause refers only to the incident of payment but not to that of delivery and the contract is a proper c.i.f. contract. The American practice is inclined to this interpretation, as appears from the Uniform Commercial Code, section 2–321(3):

> Unless otherwise agreed where the contract provides for payment on or after arrival of the goods the seller must before payment allow such preliminary inspection as is feasible; but if the goods are lost delivery of the documents and payment are due when the goods should have arrived.[65]

3. "*net landed weights*," "*delivered weights*," "*outturn*," *quantity or quality*. These or similar clauses are normally intended only to relate to the determination of the price.[66] They do not affect the character of the contract as a true c.i.f. contract.

   These clauses mean that after the goods are landed the seller must allow a price adjustment.[67] If the goods are lost and the buyer has already paid an estimated price on tender of the documents, he is not entitled to an adjustment unless he can prove that the shipped goods were less in quantity or quality than he paid for.
4. *a specified element of the charges to be borne by the buyer*. A clause such as "increase of export duties for buyer's account"[68] or "Cape surcharge buyer's account"[69] again refers only to the ascertainment of the charges and is entirely reconcilable with the character of the contract as a c.i.f. contract.

c. and f. (named port of destination)

C. and f. stands for "cost and freight." Under this clause the seller has to arrange the carriage of the goods to the named foreign port of destination at his expense but not at his risk (which ceases when he places the goods on board ship at the place of shipment), but he has not to arrange marine insurance which is the concern of the buyer and, if effected, has to be paid

---

[64] Sassoon, *C.I.F. and F.O.B. Contracts* (*British Shipping Laws*, Vol. 5, 1975), para. 14.

[65] The term "no arrival, no sale," under which the seller is not obliged to ship, appears to be used in the American practice (Uniform Commercial Code, s. 2–324) but is not customary in the English practice.

[66] Uniform Commercial Code, s. 2–321(1).

[67] See *Oleificio Zucchi S.p.A.* v. *Northern Sale Ltd.* [1965] 2 Lloyd's Rep. 496, 518, where a contract c.i.f. Genoa provided for allowances if the goods (Canadian rapeseed screenings in bulk) arrived damaged. Further: *Oricon Waren-Handels GmbH* v. *Intergraan N.V.* [1967] 2 Lloyd's Rep. 83, 94 ("gross delivered weight").

[68] *Produce Brokers New Co. (1924) Ltd.* v. *British Italian Trading Co.* [1952] 1 Lloyd's Rep. 379.

[69] *Henry (D. I.) Ltd* v. *Wilhelm G. Clascu* [1973] 1 Lloyd's Rep. 159 (C.A.).

by him.[70] In this respect the clause differs from the ordinary c.i.f. clause, but in all other respects the liabilities and duties of the parties are the same as under a c.i.f. contract.

The c. and f. seller should bear in mind the provisions of section 32(3) of the Sale of Goods Act.[71] If he fails to give the buyer such notice as may enable him to insure the goods,[72] the goods would, exceptionally, travel at the seller's, and not at the buyer's risk.

A c. and f. contract sometimes contains the words "insurance to be effected by buyer," or words to the same effect. It has been held[73] that these words are not merely declaratory but constitute a contractual obligation of the buyer to take out the usual insurance policy, *i.e.* a policy which, if the contract had been on c.i.f. terms, would have to be taken out by the seller.

The c. and f. clause is not frequently adopted by export merchants, except in the case of some countries which, for political reasons or owing to lack of foreign exchange, require their importers to insure at home rather than to buy on c.i.f. terms. The c. and f. clause leads to an artificial separation of the arrangements for insurance and freight, whereas the c.i.f. stipulation, like the f.o.b. clause, provides a natural division of responsibilities between the export merchant and the overseas buyer.

c.i.f. and c., c.i.f. and e., c.i.f. and c. and i.

Other variants of the ordinary c.i.f. stipulation are the clauses *c.i.f. and c., c.i.f. and e.,* and *c.i.f. and c. and i.* The first of these abbreviations stands for "cost, insurance, freight and commission," in the second the letter "e." means "exchange," and in the third the letters "c. and i." denote "commission and interest." These clauses should only be used when it is clear that the other party is acquainted with their meaning because they are often misunderstood; and, if there is any danger of a misunderstanding, it is advisable to state expressly the additional terms which it is desired to introduce into the conventional c.i.f. clause. The commission referred to in the c.i.f. and c. clause is the export merchant's commission which he charges when acting as buying agent for the overseas buyer; export houses claim this commission as a matter of course and quote their prices "c.i.f. and c." because they wish to inform their customers abroad that the prices include their commission. The expression "exchange" is ambiguous; it is sometimes said to refer to the banker's commission or charge, while others maintain that it refers to exchange fluctuations. In the former case it denotes that the banker's charges are included in the price calculation when "c.i.f. and e." prices are quoted; in the latter case it means that the purchase price is not affected by the subsequent rise or fall

[70] Where the c. and f. seller has given the buyer credit, it may be advisable for him to take out a contingency insurance covering the goods in transit, see p. 305, *post.*

[71] See p. 16, *ante.*

[72] And unless the parties have otherwise agreed.

[73] *Reinhart Co.* v. *Joshua Hoyle & Sons Ltd.* [1961] 1 Lloyd's Rep. 346, 354, 357, 359.

of the stipulated currency of payment against the pound sterling. It is thought that the former interpretation is more common and that arrangements about currency fluctuations are usually made explicitly. The clause "c.i.f. and c. and i." is used when goods are exported to distant places where some time elapses before the bill drawn on the customer abroad is settled. When the seller negotiates the bill to his bank, the latter charges him commission and interest until payment has been received on the draft in this country, and the seller, by adding, in his contract of export sale, the letter "i." to the clause, indicates to the buyer that the quoted price includes the bank's interest and commission; this arrangement is used in the export trade with India, Pakistan, Bangladesh, Burma and the Far East; if the buyer pays the bill before maturity he is often allowed a rebate by the eastern exchange banks.

ARRIVAL, OR EX SHIP (named ship and named port of arrival)

This clause has been defined by the Judicial Committee of the Privy Council as denoting that "the seller has to cause delivery to be made to the buyer from a ship which has arrived at the port of delivery and has reached a place therein which is usual for the delivery of goods of the kind in question."[74] The clause is also defined in Incoterms. Under this clause the seller has to pay the freight or otherwise to release the shipowner's lien, and the buyer is only bound to pay the purchase price if actual delivery of the goods is made to him at the stipulated port of delivery.

The difference between the arrival (or ex ship) contract and the c.i.f. contract is that in the former case the documents do not stand in the place of the goods, but that delivery has to be made *in specie*, *i.e.* the goods sold have to be delivered to the buyer at the named port of delivery. Consequently, if the goods are lost in transit, the buyer is not obliged to pay the purchase price upon tender of the documents, and can, in certain circumstances, claim return of the price he paid in advance. The delivery of the indorsed bill of lading from the seller to the buyer is not given with the intention of passing the property in the goods, but, unless otherwise agreed, the property will pass only when the goods are handed over to the buyer after arrival of the ship at the agreed port of destination. As the goods are not at the buyer's risk during the voyage, the seller is not under an obligation to the buyer to insure the goods. Where the seller actually insures them and they are lost or damaged in transit and the seller has not taken out insurance as agent of the buyer, the buyer cannot claim the insurance money from the insurance company because the seller, when effecting the insurance, does not act on behalf of the buyer, who has no insurable interest in the goods though he may have an insurable interest in the profits which he hoped to make on the goods.[75] The seller must

---

[74] *Yangtsze Insurance Association* v. *Lukmanjee* [1918] A.C. 585, 589. On the meaning of this clause in the American practice, see Uniform Commercial Code, s. 2–322.

[75] *Yangtsze Insurance Association* v. *Lukmanjee* [1918] A.C. 585, 589.

discharge all liens arising out of the carriage and, if he has not transferred the bill of lading to the buyer, must give him a delivery order on the ship.

The ex ship clause relates exclusively to the place of delivery of the goods and does not bring into play the special method of payment of the purchase price against delivery of the shipping documents. In the case of the clause the contract of sale remains isolated; its elements are not combined with those of the contracts of carriage and insurance in the manner characteristic of the c.i.f. contract.

The reference in a contract of sale to the goods being purchased "ex" or "afloat per" a particular ship is part of the description of the goods and if the goods are not shipped in that ship a condition of the contract of sale is broken.[76] Likewise the reference to the approximate date of arrival of the named ship is part of the description of the goods: "there is good commercial sense in that, inasmuch as a description of the goods being 'afloat per SS. *Morton Bay* due approximately 8th June' does give the buyers, not an absolute guarantee of arrival on June 8, but at least some indication of the date on which they may be expected in London."[77]

Ex Quay (named port of destination)

Under this clause, which should not be confused with the clause "free to docks" or "franco quay" combined with a named port of *shipment*,[78] the seller's duties are the same as under the arrival clause but, in addition, the seller accepts responsibility for import duties and unloading charges payable at the port of destination, such as lighterage, dock dues and porterage. "Ex quay" combined with the port of destination, which is also defined in Incoterms, is rarely used in British export practice because the seiler will not normally accept responsibilities arising from the landing of the goods unless he has a representative or agent at the port of destination who is acquainted with the local habits. The buyer remains, under this clause, liable for the carriage on and from the quay to the ultimate place of destination of the goods, which may be situate inland.[79]

Delivered at Frontier (named place of delivery at frontier)

This clause is frequently used in the Continental export trade where no sea or air carriage is involved. It is also defined in Incoterms.[80] United Kingdom importers of Continental vegetables and fruit sometimes buy "delivered

---

[76] s. 13 of the Sale of Goods Act 1893; see p. 90, *post*.

[77] *Per* McNair J. in *Macpherson Train & Co. Ltd.* v. *Howard Ross & Co. Ltd.* [1955] 1 W.L.R. 640, 642.

[78] On this clause, see p. 15, *ante*.

[79] In *Bunten & Lancaster (Produce)* v. *Kiril Mischeff* [1964] 1 Lloyd's Rep. 386 an import contract provided for "landed duty paid ex quay Liverpool." Also *Glass's Fruit Markets Ltd.* v. *A. Southwell & Son (Fruit) Ltd.* [1969] 2 Lloyd's Rep. 398.

[80] In the *General Conditions of Delivery of Goods* 1968 adopted by the U.S.S.R. and the other members of the Council of Mutual Economic Assistance (see p. 49, *post*) "delivered at frontier" is the standard arrangement for all deliveries by rail.

at frontier" also described as "franco frontier", of the country where the fruit originates.

The clause, when used in a contract of sale, should specify not only the frontier but also the named place of delivery, *e.g.* "Delivered at Franco-Italian frontier (Modena)." The clause does not oblige the seller to obtain an insurance policy for the buyer's benefit; the parties should lay down in the contract of sale the duties which they should assume with respect to insurance.

DELIVERED (named place of destination in the country of importation) DUTY PAID

This clause, sometimes expressed as "franco domicile" or "free delivery," represents the most favourable terms which the buyer can obtain and the most onerous arrangement for the seller. The clause is rarely found in the practice of the British export trade, except where the parties have agreed on delivery by ordinary parcel post, *e.g.* when goods of small size are exported to France, Belgium or other not too distant countries on the Continent. The obligations arising under this clause are stated in Incoterms.

Under this clause the goods have to be placed at the seller's risk and expense at the buyer's disposal at the named place of destination. The seller's obligation is to pay all charges up to the delivery of the goods at the buyer's address, including import duties and inland carriage in the buyer's country. An import licence has to be obtained by the seller.

In the absence of agreement to the contrary, the buyer is not obliged to pay the purchase price on presentation of the bill of lading or consignment note, but payment can only be demanded against delivery of the goods themselves. Quality and quantity of the goods are judged in accordance with the state of the goods on arrival and not, as under f.o.b. or c.i.f. terms, according to their state on loading.

The French equivalent to this clause is the clause *rendu . . . droits acquittés*.

CHAPTER 3

STANDARDISATION OF TERMS IN INTERNATIONAL SALES

THE trade terms used in export sales which were considered in the preceding chapter are not always interpreted in the same manner in all countries.[1] These differences may lead to misunderstandings and disputes amongst those engaged in international trade. To avoid them, frequent attempts have been made to standardise the terms in which export and import business is transacted.

These attempts can be classified into three groups[2]: *Uniform conditions of general character* have been issued which are intended to apply to all types of export goods. Sometimes the uniform terms have, or are intended to have, the force of law; sometimes they are intended to apply only if adopted by the parties to the contract. Further, in some types of business, mainly in the trade in commodities or in capital goods, *model contract forms applying to specified international transactions* are in existence which normally apply only if used by the parties to the contract. Thirdly, exporters and importers frequently embody *general terms of business* into their contracts. They are intended to apply to all transactions to which these persons become a party unless they are expressly excluded.

UNIFORM CONDITIONS OF EXPORT SALES

The most important sets of uniform conditions are noted in the following; some of them are the result of international agreement while others have, or are intended to have, the force of national law or are sponsored by national organisations interested in international trade. The use of uniform conditions is of increasing importance in the export trade.

United Nations Commission on International Trade Law

In 1966 the United Nations decided to take an interest in the progressive harmonisation of the law of international trade. They constituted the United Nations Commission on International Trade Law (UNCITRAL) which became operative on January 1, 1968.[3] The Commission consists of 36 states. Its object are "to further the progressive harmonisation and unification of the law of international trade." UNCITRAL has accorded priority to the study and consideration of the international sale of goods,

---

[1] See p. 8, *ante*.

[2] See Mario Matteuci, "The Unification of Commercial Law," in [1960] J.B.L. 137.

[3] Schmitthoff, "The Unification of the Law of International Trade," in [1968] J.B.L. 105; Paolo Contini, "The United Nations Commission on International Trade Law," in 16 Am. J. Comp. L. 666 (1968).

international payments, commercial arbitration and shipping law, but has extended its activities to the examination of multinational enterprises and other topics. The seat of UNCITRAL is in Vienna.

The most important publications of UNCITRAL are the *Register of Texts of Conventions and other Instruments concerning International Trade Law*[4] and the *Yearbook*.[5] The Register of Texts is a unique and valuable collection of most relevant documents used in the export trade.

UNCITRAL has so far[6] prepared the following texts:

The *Convention on the Limitation Period in the International Sale of Goods*, adopted by the United Nations in 1974.[7]

The *UNCITRAL Arbitration Rules*, approved by the United Nations in 1976. They provide a framework for international commercial arbitration and are applied where parties have agreed in writing that disputes shall be settled under them.[8]

The *Convention on the Carriage of Goods by Sea*, adopted by a United Nations conference at Hamburg in March 1978. The so-called Hamburg Rules adopted by that Convention were prepared by UNCITRAL and UNCTAD jointly. They are intended to replace the Hague Rules and the Hague–Visby Rules relating to Bills of Lading.[9] The Hamburg Rules have not yet been given effect in the United Kingdom.

A *Draft Convention on Contracts for the International Sale of Goods* was approved by UNCITRAL in March 1979. It combines the two Uniform Laws on International Sales approved by the Hague Conference in 1964.[10] The Draft Convention will be submitted to a United Nations Conference in 1980.

A *Draft Convention on International Bills of Exchange and International Promissory Notes* is likewise promoted.

Incoterms and other ICC publications

Incoterms, which have the sub-title *International Rules for the Interpretation of Trade Terms*, were published by the International Chamber of Commerce and have been amended from time to time.[11] Exporters and importers who wish to use them for an individual contract specify that the contract is governed by the provision of "*Incoterms*." Sometimes exporters, notably on the continent of Europe, provide in their general terms of

[4] So far Volumes I and II of the Register of Texts have been published. They can be obtained from the Sales Section of the United Nations in New York or Geneva or from the distributors of United Nations Publications throughout the world. The sales numbers are: Vol. I: E.71.V.3; Vol. II: E.73.V.3.

[5] Obtainable from the same suppliers as stated in the previous footnote.

[6] Position: June 1, 1978.

[7] See p. 148, *post*.

[8] See p. 420, *post*.

[9] See p. 347, *post*.

[10] See p. 140, *post*.

[11] See p. 8, n. 5, *ante*. Incoterms can be obtained from the British National Committee of the International Chamber of Commerce, 6–14 Dean Farrar Street, London SW1H 0DT (Tel: 01-222 3755/7).

business that all their contracts shall be governed by *Incoterms*, unless otherwise agreed in a particular instance.[12] In some countries *Incoterms* have been given statutory effect, *viz.* in Spain for import transactions[13] and in Iraq for all foreign trade transactions.[14]

The International Chamber of Commerce, which has consultative status under the Charter of the United Nations, has contributed other valuable publications which ease the flow of international trade and are from time to time referred to in this work. It is convenient to list them here:

The Uniform Customs and Practice for Documentary Credits (*1974 Revision*)[15] are widely adopted throughout the world; the list of countries in which the Uniform Customs have either been adopted by banking associations or by individual banks includes 175 countries,[16] amongst them the United Kingdom, the United States of America and the Soviet Union. The Uniform Customs are supplemented by the *Standard Forms for the Opening of Documentary Credits* (1971), the *Uniform Rules for Collections* (1978), and *Simplification of International Payment Orders* (1959).

The Problem of Clean Bills of Lading which contains a list of superimposed clauses declaring a defective condition of the goods or packaging put by carriers on bills of lading for reference and optional use.[17]

The Tables of Practical Equivalents in Marine Insurance in which the similarities and differences in marine insurance terms and covers in a number of important centres of the world are compared.

The Rules of Conciliation and Arbitration (1975), being the rules of the Court of International Arbitration of the International Chamber of Commerce.[18]

Commercial Agency, A Guide for the Drawing Up of Contracts between Parties residing in Different Countries (1960). This publication deals with the problems which have to be considered when agency agreements in the strict legal sense are drawn up.[19]

Company Formation, an international guide (1970). The aim of this guide is to operate as a check list indicating to businessmen the most important problems which arise if they intend to form companies abroad as a base of their industrial or commercial transactions.

Uniform Rules for a Combined Transport Document (1975).[20] This publication proposes the adoption of a single combined transport document for the transportation of goods in containers by means of two or more

---

[12] See, *e.g. The Albazero* [1975] 3 W.L.R. 491, 498.

[13] ICC Information, November 1969, p. 3.

[14] ICC Information, December 1971, p. 3.

[15] See p. 246, *post.*

[16] The list of countries is obtainable from the National Committees of the ICC or its headquarters in Paris.

[17] On clean bills of lading, see p. 352, *post.*

[18] See pp. 423 *et seq.*, *post.*

[19] See p. 162, *post.*

[20] Brochure No. 298.

modes (so-called "multi-modal") transport. The issue of such a document would avoid the need to issue a series of separate transport documents for each stage of the transport.[21]

Extortion and Bribery in Business Transactions (1977).[22] This brochure contains, first, recommendations to governments, to be adopted nationally and internationally to promote the elimination of bribery and extortion in business transactions, and secondly, rules of conduct for voluntary application by enterprises.

Uniform Rules for Contract Guarantees (1978)[23] deal with the issue of performance and bank guarantees supporting obligations arising in international contracts.

Uniform Laws on International Sales

In 1964 a diplomatic conference at The Hague approved two Uniform Laws, one on the International Sale of Goods and the other on the Formation of Contracts for the International Sale of Goods. These Uniform Laws have been introduced into the law of the United Kingdom by the *Uniform Laws on International Sales Act 1967*. This Act was put into operation on August 18, 1972 and is considered in a later chapter.[24] The Hague Conventions have also been introduced into the law of Belgium, W. Germany, Israel, Italy, the Netherlands, Gambia and San Marino.[25] Other countries, notably those of the European Community which have not done so already, are contemplating their adoption.

UNCITRAL, as we have seen,[26] is at present engaged in a revision of The Hague Conventions with a view to making them acceptable globally.

Revised American Foreign Trade Definitions 1941

These Definitions were adopted in 1941 by a joint committee representing the Chamber of Commerce of the United States of America, the National Council of American Importers, Inc., and the National Foreign Trade Council, Inc.

The Definitions do not have the status of law but sellers and buyers may adopt them as part of their contracts of sale.

American Uniform Commercial Code

Most commercial transactions in the United States of America are governed by local state laws, and not by federal law. Considering that the United States consists today of 50 states and jurisdictions, the inconvenience of this regulation is obvious. It is not surprising that since 1890 attempts have been made to have enacted by all states a uniform law for the most common commercial transactions.

---

[21] On container transport, see p. 377, *post*.
[22] Brochure No. 315.
[23] Brochure No. 325.
[24] See p. 140, *post*.
[25] Position as at June 1, 1978.
[26] See p. 46, *ante*.

This movement led to the publication of the *Uniform Commercial Code* which was prepared jointly by the American Law Institute and the National Conference of Commissioners on Uniform State Laws; its latest version is the "1972 Official Text with comments." This highly successful code has been adopted by all American states and jurisdictions except Louisiana which, however, has adopted the section dealing with Sales, including international sales.[27] Thus a uniform American commercial law has been created.

The Code deals, *inter alia*, with sales (including the terms of export sales discussed in the preceding chapter),[27] commercial paper (bills and notes),[28] collections and documentary letters of credit,[29] bills of lading and other documents of title.[30]

General Conditions of the Council for Mutual Economic Assistance

The member countries of the Council for Mutual Economic Assistance,[31] the regional trade organisation of Eastern European and other socialist countries, have adopted a series of General Conditions. They have the nature of inter-governmental agreements which are given effect in all member states of CMEA.[32] The General Conditions are widely used by the foreign trade corporations[33] of the Eastern European countries and normally govern the individual export transactions between those corporations.

The most important of these General Conditions are:

the General Conditions of Delivery of Goods 1968–1975;[34]

the General Conditions of Assembly and Provision of other Technical Services in connection with Reciprocal Deliveries of Machinery and Equipment (1973) (General Conditions of Assembly);

the General Conditions for the Technical Servicing of Machinery, Equipment and other Items (1973) (General Conditions of Technical Servicing).

The member countries of CMEA have also adopted a Convention on the Settlement by Arbitration of Civil Law Disputes between economic

---

[27] Article 2 of the Uniform Commercial Code.

[28] Article 3.

[29] Articles 4 and 5.

[30] Article 7.

[31] The member countries of the Council for Mutual Economic Aid are at present Bulgaria, Cuba, Czechoslovakia, the German Democratic Republic, Hungary, Mongolia, Poland, Romania, The USSR and Vietnam.

[32] Trajan Ionasco and Ion Nestor, "The Limits of Party Autonomy," in *The Sources of the Law of International Trade* (ed. Schmitthoff), London, 1964, p. 177.

[33] On Foreign Trade Corporation in the countries of planned economy, see Viktor Knapp, "The Function, Organisation and Activities of Foreign Trade Corporations in the European Socialist Countries," in *The Sources of the Law of International Trade* (ed. Schmitthoff), London, 1964, p. 52.

[34] See Iván Szász, "A Uniform Law on International Sale of Goods", (Akadémiai Kiadó, Budapest, 1976) (this work contains an English translation of the General Conditions of Delivery of Goods); Jerzy Rajski, "Le rapproducement et l'unification du droit delas le cadre du Conseil d'Aid Economique Mutuelle" (1976), *Revue internationale de droit comparé*, Paris, 30; Jyula Eörsi, "The 1968 General Conditions of Delivery," in [1970] J.B.L. 99. The CMEA Conditions 1968 were preceded by those of 1958.

organisations of the Member States; this convention was signed in Moscow on May 2, 1976. Uniform rules for arbitration tribunals of the CMEA countries were adopted by the Member States of CMEA in 1975.

Further, upon the recommendation of CMEA in 1966, the member states of CMEA and Yugoslavia have adopted General Principles concerning Supply of Spare Parts in their mutual trade.

Codifications of international trade law in the socialist countries

Czechoslovak International Trade Code

This enactment which came into force on April 1, 1964, has been described as "a municipal regulation which forms part of the Czechoslovak legal order but at the same time governs exclusively international trade relations between parties to international commercial contracts."[35]

The Code shall be applied by courts or arbitration tribunals in or outside Czechoslovakia, if

1. the issue is a matter of international trade, as defined by the Code, and
2. subject to a few exceptions, the parties are resident in different countries, and
3. the contract in question is governed by Czechoslovak law.[36]

The East German Law on International Economic Contracts

The German Democratic Republic adopted this Law on February 5, 1976.[37] The Law regulates international contracts in general and deals, more specifically, with contracts of sale, services, construction, agency, forwarding, warehousing, credit, insurance, leasing, licensing, guarantees and securities. The Law is intended to apply if the parties have adopted the law of the German Democratic Republic or if that law applies according to the rules of the conflict of laws.[38] But international arrangements are not affected; consequently in dealings between East German state enterprises and those of the other Member States of CMEA the General Conditions of CMEA,[39] and not the East German International trade code, apply.

Yugoslav General Usages of Trade 1954[40]

These are the uniform practices of international trade as applied in Yugoslavia. The General Usages are a well-drafted[41] code of the law of

---

[35] Pavel Kalensky, "The New Czechoslovak International Trade Code," in [1966] J.B.L. 179, 181.

[36] I owe this wording of the application of the Czechoslovak Code to Dr. Boris Illner, Prague.

[37] *Gesetz über internationale Wirtschaftsverträge* (GIV), in *Gesetzblatt*, 1976, Pt. I, 61.

[38] See p. 125, *post*.

[39] See p. 49, *ante*.

[40] Obtainable in English from the Federal Chamber of Foreign Trade, P.O. Box 47, Belgrade, Yugoslavia.

[41] They were the work of Professor A. Goldštajn, one of the outstanding modern authorities on the law of international trade.

international trade; they are founded on the universally accepted rules of the export trade.

The General Usages apply to foreign trade transactions between a Yugoslav and another party if the proper law of the contract is that of Yugoslavia or the parties have agreed on arbitration by the Yugoslav Foreign Trade Arbitration unless the parties have excluded the application of the General Usages in whole or in part.

Model Contract Forms applying to Specified International Transactions

The international trade in many commodities and capital goods is conducted on the basis of standard contract forms. Some of them are issued by international trade associations of which those of the United Kingdom have worldwide reputation. Others are drafted by the United Nations Economic Commission for Europe. Others again are used in construction contracts for works and installations abroad.

Both types of standard contracts have in common that they apply only if the parties to a contract of sale adopt them and that they normally can be varied by agreement of the contracting parties.

Standard conditions issued by trade associations

The most important standard commodity contracts are the various forms provided by the following trade associations[41a]:

the British Wool Confederation;
the Cocoa Association of London Ltd.;
the Federation of Oil, Seed and Fats Associations (FOSFA);
the Grain and Feed Trade Association (GAFTA);
the International Wool Textile Organisation;
the Liverpool Cotton Association;
the General Produce Broker's Association of London;
the London Jute Association;
the London Metal Exchange;
the London Rubber Trade Association;
the Refined Sugar Association;
the Timber Trade Federation of the United Kingdom.

Many of these, and some other trade associations, were formed into the British Federation of Commodity Associations.

[41a] A list of these markets and trade associations is provided in the Arbitration (Commodity Contracts) Order 1979 (S.I. 1979 No. 754).

Model contracts sponsored by the United Nations Economic Commission for Europe

Various sets of general conditions of sale and standard forms of contract have been drafted by working parties convened by the United Nations Economic Commission for Europe.[42]

Notable amongst them are:

Form 188 —For the Supply of Plant and Machinery for Export;
,, 574 —For the Supply of Plant and Machinery for Export;
,, 188A—For the Supply and Erection of Plant and Machinery for Import and Export;
,, 574A—For the Supply and Erection of Machinery for Import and Export;
,, 188B—Listing Additional Clauses for Supervision of Erection of Engineering Plant and Machinery abroad;
,, 574B—Listing Additional Clauses for Supervision of Erection of Engineering Plant and Machinery abroad;
,, 188D—Listing Additional Clauses for Complete Erection of Engineering Plant and Machinery abroad;
,, 730 —For the Export of Durable Consumer Goods and Engineering Articles.

Form 188 and its variations are used betwen enterprises of free market economy, and Form 574 and its variations are for use between enterprises of state-planned economy and for the East-West trade, while Form 730 can be used for international trade between any enterprises.[43]

In addition to these sets of model contracts, the Economic Commission for Europe has sponsored model contracts for the sale of cereals, citrus fruit, sawn softwood, solid fuels, potatoes and steel products.

Model contract forms used in construction contracts

The most frequently used model contract forms dealing with the erection of works and installations abroad are:

Conditions of Contract (International) for Works of Civil Engineering Construction (3rd ed., March 1977). These Conditions are sponsored by the *Fédération Internationale des Ingénieurs-Conseils (FIDIC).*[44]

General Conditions of Contract.
These Conditions are recommended by the Institution of Mechanical Engineers, the Institution of Electrical Engineers and the Association of Consulting Engineers.[45]

---

[42] The UN ECE forms can be obtained from H.M.S.O. On the preparation and aim of these contract conditions and forms: see Peter Benjamin, "The General Conditions of Sale and Standard Forms of Contract drawn up by the United Nations Economic Commission for Europe," in [1961] J.B.L. 113; André Tunc, "L'élaboration de conditions générales de vente sous les auspices de la Commission Economique pour l'Europe," in (1960) 12 *Revue Internationale de Droit Comparé* 108; Clive M. Schmitthoff, "The Unification or Harmonisation of Law by Means of Standard Contracts and General Conditions" (1968) 17 I.C.L.Q. 551; Henry Cornil, "The ECE General Conditions of Sale" in 3 *Journ. of World Trade Law* (1969) 390.

[43] On the difference between these forms, see [1965] J.B.L. 100 and [1966] J.B.L. 71. Of further importance is the "Preface to the General Conditions of Sale, Standard Forms of Contract and Commercial Arbitration Instruments prepared under the auspices of the United Nations Economic Commission of Europe."

[44] Obtainable from The Federation of Civil Engineering Contractors, Romney House, Tufton Street, Westminster, London SW1.

[45] Obtainable from the Institution of Electrical Engineers, Savoy Place, London WC2R 0BL.

Form B1 — Export Contracts with Delivery f.o.b.,c.i.f. or f.o.r. (4th ed., 1973);
Form B2 — Export Contracts, delivery f.o.b.,c.i.f. or f.o.r., with supervision of erection (4th ed., 1972);
Form B3 — Export Contracts (including delivery to and erection on site) (2nd ed., 1971).

Guidelines for Procurement under World Bank Loans and IDA Credits, August 1975.[46]

General Conditions for Public Works and Supply Contracts financed by the European Development Fund, applied to contracts financed in the Associated Overseas Countries and Territories, February 14, 1974.[47]

The model contract forms sponsored by the United Nations Economic Commission for Europe, which are listed in the preceding paragraph, are likewise used in international construction work. The model forms used in construction contracts will be considered in a later Part of this work.[48]

GENERAL TERMS OF BUSINESS ADOPTED BY INDIVIDUAL EXPORTERS

The importance, for international sales, of well-drafted general terms of business can hardly be exaggerated. They are particularly important where neither uniform conditions of export sales nor model contract forms are available. Litigation can often be avoided when the seller is able to refer the buyer to a clause in his printed terms of business which was embodied in the quotation or acceptance, and the fact that these terms apply to all transactions concluded by the seller adds persuasive force to his argument.

Some important clauses

The most important clauses which the exporter should embody in his general terms of business are:

1. *General clause.* Every contract of sale is subject to the seller's conditions of sale;
2. *Reservation of property clause.* The seller retains the legal property in the goods until he receives the purchase price in cash and is entitled to the proceeds if the buyer disposes of the seller's property, the buyer holding those proceeds as an agent and trustee for the seller[49];
3. *Price escalation clause.* Unless firm prices and charges are agreed upon, the seller shall be entitled to increase the agreed prices and charges by the same amount by which the prices or charges of the goods or their components including costs of labour to be paid or borne by the seller have been increased between the date of the quotation and the date of the delivery[50];
4. *Force majeure clause.* (An illustration of this clause is given later on);
5. *Choice of law and arbitration clause.* The validity, construction and performance of this contract shall be governed by the law of England and any dispute that may arise out

---

[46] Obtainable from the World Bank Headquarters, 1818 H Street, N.W., Washington, D.C., 20433, U.S.A., or the European Office of the World Bank at 66, avenue d'Jéna, 75116 Paris, France.

[47] Obtainable from the European Commission, 200 rue de la loi, Brussels, Belgium.

[48] See p. 443, *post.*

[49] This clause is founded on the famous *Romalpa* clause; see *Aluminium Industrie Vaassen B.V.* v. *Romalpa Aluminium Ltd.* [1976] 1 W.L.R. 676, and [1976] J.B.L. 209. In that case the reservation of property clause was much more detailed and comprehensive. See p. 79, *post.*

[50] Several variants of the price escalation or "rise and fall" clause are in use. Sometimes a "rise" clause is inserted into a c.i.f. contract; the clause provides for an increase of the purchase price if the freight and insurance charges are raised. See also Lars Gorton, "Escalation and Currency Clauses in Shipping Contracts" [12] *Journal of World Trade Law* (1978), p. 319.

of or in connection with this contract, including its validity, construction and performance, shall be determined by arbitration under the rules of the London Court of Arbitration at the date hereof which rules, with respect to matters not regulated by them, incorporate the UNCITRAL Arbitration Rules.[51]

The parties agree that service of any notices in reference to such arbitration at their addresses as given in this contract (or as subsequently varied in writing by them) shall be valid and sufficient.[52]

These essential clauses are indicated here only in general terms. The particular requirements of the exporter's business may demand a fuller treatment or the insertion of additional clauses in the general terms of business. The exporter is well advised to ask his solicitor to frame general terms of business appropriate to his activities and to revise them from time to time.

The buyer's agreement

The general terms of business should be printed on price lists, catalogues, estimates, offers, and all contract documents emanating from the seller, such as acceptances in a clear, legible and conspicuous manner. They should be embodied in the context of the seller's offer or acceptance but, where that is not feasible, the context should at least contain a clear and conspicuous reference to the fact that conditions of sale are printed on the reverse or on an attached sheet. It is also necessary to obtain the agreement of the buyer to the general terms of business of the seller. It is desirable that the buyer should agree in writing and later, when the offer and acceptance are discussed, the question will be examined how to obtain the buyer's written consent.[53] The Court of the European Communities has held[54] that a clause in the seller's conditions conferring exclusive jurisdiction on a national court—in that case the court in Hamburg—was not binding on the buyer because he had not assented thereto in writing, as required by article 17 of the EEC Convention of September 27, 1968 on Jurisdiction and the Enforcement of Judgments in Civil and Commercial Matters. However, the court pointed out that no written consent by the buyer was required if the parties were in a "continuing trading relationship" which had been conducted on the basis of the seller's general conditions. Although at present[55] the United Kingdom has not acceded yet to the Convention, the point is of importance in litigation between enterprises resident in the six original Member States of the EEC as all of them have accepted the Convention.

---

[51] p. 420, *post*.

[52] This is the arbitration clause suggested by the London Court of Arbitration; see p. 422, *post*. The clause should be adapted to the special requirements of the exporter, by omitting reference to arbitration if no arbitration is desired, or by substituting the arbitration tribunal customary in his trade for the one suggested above, or by providing as the law governing the contract, another legal system, if desired.

[53] See p. 61, *post*; see, in particular "Special Problems relating to General Coalitions," on p. 63, *post*.

[54] In *Galeries Segoura S.p.r.l.* v. *Firma Rahim Bonakdarian* [1977] 1 C.M.L.R. 361.

[55] Position: September 1, 1979.

In certain foreign countries, the courts will not admit general terms of business which are not embodied in the contract. In English common law it is immaterial that the buyer, in a particular case, did not read the conditions or had to refer to other documents in order to ascertain them; but it is necessary that the fact should be clearly brought to his notice that such conditions exist and that the contract is concluded subject to them.[56]

It may happen that the general terms of business of the two parties to the contract conflict. This is a problem pertaining to the law of offer and acceptance which will be treated later.[57]

Standard terms in home transactions

The Unfair Contract Terms Act 1977 provides[58] that where one of the contracting parties deals on the other's written standard terms of business, the party who inserted the standard terms cannot rely on them in order to exclude or restrict his liability, except if the standard term in question satisfies the test of reasonableness. The same rules apply if the party who inserted the standard terms wishes to rely on them in order to avoid performance of the contract.

These provisions will not, however, normally concern the exporter because they do not apply to international supply contracts, as defined in section 26 of the Act.[59]

SIMPLIFICATION OF EXPORT DOCUMENTS

The United Kingdom Simplification of International Trade Procedures Board (SITPRO)[60] has published a handbook entitled *Systematic Export Documentation*.[61] This work is the result of international co-operation carried out under the auspices of the United Nations Economic Commission of Europe.[62]

The object of *Systematic Export Documentation* is to save clerical labour by admitting the completion of export documents by the single-run process. A master stencil is prepared from which, after masking the parts not required, every document is run off. The documents which can be run off from the master include the bills of lading, certificates of insurance, certificates of origin, Customs and exchange documents, port forms and EEC movement certificates. If these documents are prepared in the form sug-

[56] *Phoenix Insurance Company of Hartford* v. *De Monchy* (1929) 45 T.L.R. 543. See further *MacLeod Ross & Co. Ltd.* v. *Compagnie d'Assurances Generales L'Helvetia of St. Gall* [1952] W.N. 56; [1952] T.L.R. 314; 96 S.J. 90; [1952] 1 All E.R. 331.

[57] See p. 64, *post*.

[58] In s. 3.

[59] See p. 65, *post*.

[60] Address; 11/12 Waterloo Place, London SW1Y 4AU.

[61] First edition published in October 1976.

[62] In the United Kingdom the work was first undertaken by the Department of Trade which in 1965 published a booklet entitled *Simpler Export Documents*. In 1971 SITPRO took over responsibility from the Department of Trade for maintaining, developing and promoting the British aligned series of export documents.

gested by the single-run process they are referred to as "the aligned series." The aligned series techniques have important advantages for undertakings in international trade and are widely used.

SITPRO co-operates closely with the COMPROs, the various National Facilitation Committees of the other Member States of the EEC. The EEC Commission itself has a document facilitation programme.

CHAPTER 4

MARKET INFORMATION FOR EXPORTERS

THE exporter who has decided on what terms to sell his goods is in a position to seek or accept orders from abroad.

They may be the result of his market research; he may have analysed the demand for his goods in various foreign countries, may have sought advice from the export section of his chamber of commerce or trade association, or from consultants or specialists, may have communicated with the export marketing adviser at the Export Services and Promotions Division of the Department of Industry[1] or at one of its regional offices. Or he may have visited overseas markets himself or have sent out or appointed representatives there; or inquiries may have been received from export merchants or commission houses in overseas territories, or perhaps from overseas customers directly who may have read his advertisements in the home or overseas press or obtained his address by other means.

GOVERNMENT SERVICES FOR EXPORTERS

The Department of Trade provides many valuable services for exporters; a summary of them is contained in the *Export Handbook, Services for British Exporters,*[2] published by the British Overseas Trade Board, which has overall control of the Department of Trade's export promotion work.

The *Export Handbook*, while not exhaustive, is a guide not only to the services available through Government offices but also to those afforded by trade associations, chambers of commerce and other non-official agencies with which the British Overseas Trade Board collaborates in the export promotion field. The *Handbook* is an index to services and facilities. But since the services offered by the Government mentioned in the *Handbook* change from time to time, the best way to find out about them is to contact the Export Services and Promotions Division or the regional offices which are located throughout the country.[3]

The *Export Handbook* can be obtained from the British Overseas Trade Board.[4]

The Export Intelligence Service

The computerised Export Intelligence Service is provided by the Export Data Branch of the Export Services and Promotions Division. It is tailored to the needs of the individual subscriber and designed to save him valuable

---

[1] The address of the Export Services and Promotions Division is: Export House, 50 Ludgate Hill, London EC4M 7HU.

[2] (8th ed., 1975).

[3] The addresses of the Regional Offices are contained in the *Export Handbook*.

[4] Address: 1 Victoria Street, London SW1H 0ET.

time. It supplies details of specific export opportunities and other important export intelligence matched to a subscriber's product or service, markets and intelligence required. The information reaches subscribers by first-class mail. Where exceptionally urgent it is sent by telephone or telex.

Subscribers can choose any of the following:

Specific export opportunities.
Short market pointers to new trade opportunities.
Market reports.
Overseas agents seeking British principals.
Calls for tender (including invitation to prequalify).
Successful bidders' awards of contracts and tender bidders.
Overseas visitors to the United Kingdom.
Opportunities for co-operation with overseas firms: manufacture under licence; licensing of "know-how," patents, designs, trade marks; joint ventures, sales of business; investment.
Inward opportunities for co-operation with overseas firms: manufacture under licence in the United Kingdom; offers to the United Kingdom of licences for "know-how," patents, designs and trade marks; joint ventures in the United Kingdom; inward investment.
Changes in overseas tariff and import regulations.
Aid and loan agreements (international and United Kindgom).
Trade agreements.
Notification of overseas trade fairs, exhibitions, missions (inward and outward), British Shopping Weeks, store promotions.
World economic comments.
National and other development plans and general economic reports.
General information of events and Government legislation (other than tariff and important regulations) affecting British exporters, ECGD lines of credit.

Trade promotion overseas

The Fairs and Promotions Branch of the Export Services and Promotions Division offers effective help for the arrangement of trade fairs, British weeks, British shopping weeks, store promotions and outward missions. The Division will advise about the prospects in the markets covered by these events. A comprehensive programme, looking ahead two years, of overseas trade promotions supported by the British Overseas Trade Board, together with lists of trade fairs throughout the world, is published in *Trade and Industry*, the journal of the Departments of Industry, Trade and Consumer Protection in January, April, July and October of each year.

The trade promotion schemes supported by the British Overseas Trade Board cover a great variety of possiblities. They are listed in the *Export Handbook*.

Notable is the *joint venture scheme* at specialised trade fairs or in specialised sections at general fairs. Under that scheme the British Overseas

Trade Board provides space and a shell stand for each firm taking part in a group display sponsored by a trade association or other non-profit-making body at an overseas trade fair. The primary purpose of the scheme is to encourage firms to use overseas trade fairs as a means of exploring, establishing and sustaining themselves in export markets.

The British Overseas Trade Board further organises British pavillions at international trade fairs, information stands, all-British exhibitions, technical symposia and seminars, British shopping weeks, store promotion, outward missions and group export educational visits for small firms. It also maintains a British Export Marketing Centre in Tokyo.

The British Overseas Trade Board

This Board,[5] which controls the whole of the export promotion work of the Departments of Trade and of Industry, consists of businessmen and a representative each from the Departments, the Foreign and Commonwealth Office, and the Export Credits Guarantee Department. The Board's main task is to ensure that the official export promotion activities are conducted with due regard to the needs of industry and commerce and to utilise the available Government resources to the best advantage.

The function of the Board is to give direction to the official export promotion services. The day-to-day work, which is of primary interest to the exporter, is handled by the Export Services and Promotion Division of the Department of Industry and the other Government offices concerned.

Export Publications

Many excellent trade publications exist which keep the exporter informed of the constantly changing market conditions in the overseas markets and the legal and consular requirements abroad. It is perhaps invidious to specify some of these publications but it is believed that the following are particularly useful for the exporter.[6]

Trade and Industry

This journal is published weekly by the Department of Trade and contains official announcements, reports on home and overseas trading conditions, tariff changes and reviews of economic conditions overseas.

Export Data; Exporter's Year Book

This useful work is published annually by Benn Brothers Ltd., London. It is not only concerned with export documentation although that is the primary interest, but contains also a wealth of commercial information on

---

[5] The British Overseas Trade Board was constituted on May 11, 1971, under the name of British Export Board. Its name was changed to the present name on March 1, 1972.

[6] Other useful publications are Croner's *Reference Book for Exporters* and Croner's *Export Digest* (monthly).

Great Britain, the countries of the Commonwealth and foreign sovereign states.

The information in *Export Data*, which is in loose leaf form, is kept up to date by the monthly Group publication *Export Notes*, likewise a Benn publication.

Commerce International

This journal, published by the London Chamber of Commerce, records alterations in the export and import regulations of many countries and contains much valuable information for the exporter. The same is true of journals published by other chambers of commerce. Many trade journals likewise publish export information.

Hints to Exporters

Hints to Exporters is a series of small booklets published by the Department of Trade and containing useful hints for the business traveller, and sources of fuller information. Each of the booklets covers a particular country. The booklets give details of United Kingdom official representation in the country, travel and hotel facilities, cost of living, local business methods and other topics, and contain appendices summarising the extent and nature of imports and exports. They were formerly called *Hints to Business Men*.

Publications dealing with particular export markets

These publications, usually contained in brochures, are so numerous that it is impossible to list them here. They are published by the Department of Trade, the various chambers of commerce,[7] banks and other bodies. A useful though incomplete bibliography will be found in the *Export Handbook*.[8]

In technical matters the exporter will further be able to obtain useful information from the *Technical Help to Exporters* (*THE*) *Section of the British Standards Institution*.[9]

---

[7] A list of London Chamber publications can be obtained from the Publications Department of the London Chamber of Commerce, 69 Cannon Street, London EC4N 5AB.

[8] See p. 57, *ante*.

[9] Maylands Avenue, Hemel Hempstead, Herts.

CHAPTER 5

OFFER AND ACCEPTANCE

THE OFFER

THE order of the overseas buyer normally represents an offer to conclude a contract of sale unless it is made as an unconditional acceptance of the seller's quotation. In the normal case, the seller should make certain that the essential elements of the offer are clearly stated in the communication received by the buyer. These elements are:

1. the goods ordered which should be described without ambiguity;
2. the purchase price and the terms of payment; and
3. the terms of delivery, including instructions for packing and invoicing, and shipping and insurance.

THE ACCEPTANCE

The buyer's offer, when addressed to export merchants or commission houses, is often accepted on a printed form, the counterfoil.

The acceptance must be unqualified and unconditional. If it is otherwise, it constitutes a rejection of the original offer, combined with a counteroffer. It follows that, if the original offeror receives a qualified acceptance and does not express agreement, there is no contract, although complete silence, after receipt of a modified acceptance, would hardly constitute good business practice. Thus, in *Northland Airliners Ltd.* v. *Dennis Ferranti Meters Ltd.*[1] the sellers, a company in North Wales, negotiated with the buyers, a Canadian company, for the sale of an amphibian aircraft. The sellers sent the following telegram: "Confirming sale to you Grummond Mallard aircraft . . , Please remit £5,000." The buyers replied: "This is to confirm your cable and my purchase Grummond Mallard aircraft terms set out your cable . . . £5,000 sterling forwarded your bank to be held in trust for your account pending delivery . . . Please confirm delivery to be made thirty days within this date." The sellers did not reply but sold the aircraft to a third person at a higher price. The Court of Appeal held that there was no contract. The buyers' reply introduced two new terms, one as to payment and the other as to delivery, and the sellers were not bound to reply to this counter-offer.

If the offer is made in an international sale to which the Uniform Law on the Formation of Contracts applies,[2] an acceptance which contains additional or different terms that do not materially alter the offer constitutes

[1] (1970) 114 S.J. 845; *The Times*, October 23, 1970.
[2] See pp. 140 and 147, *post*.

a valid acceptance with the proposed modifications, unless promptly objected to by the original offeror.[3]

The acceptance should invariably embody the seller's general conditions of business and here the earlier observations on General Terms of Business adopted by Individual Exporters[4] should be carefully kept in mind. When previous export transactions have taken place between the parties and their contracts are governed by the same conditions of sale, the buyer can be presumed to have placed his orders subject to those conditions,[5] and the unqualified acceptance by the seller will clinch the bargain. In most cases, however, the seller's conditions of sale will be unknown to the buyer when making his offer, and the acceptance by the seller "subject to our conditions of sale" represents in law a rejection of the buyer's offer combined with a counter-offer by the seller. In these cases the seller who wishes to be on safe ground should obtain the buyer's unqualified confirmation before carrying out the contract, particularly when the negotiations were conducted by correspondence. If litigation ensues, the whole correspondence is placed before the court and time will be saved and complications avoided when the agreement between the parties can be proved by reference to a few unambiguous and self-contained letters. In practice, the strict requirements of the law are sometimes disregarded; this is understandable, but may lead to unfortunate consequences.[6] The reasonable exporter should at least insist on strict observance of the legal requirements in the case of orders that are not routine transactions. Where the goods ordered represent a considerable value or have to be built to the buyer's specifications, a formal contract embodying all terms of the agreement should be prepared in duplicate; each copy should be signed by both parties, and each party should retain a copy of the contract.

A contract made verbally, by telephone or by telex[7] is concluded when the acceptance is notified to the offeror. A contract made by post is likewise concluded when the acceptance is notified to the offeror unless it is clear from the offer that posting shall be sufficient.[8] To exclude ambiguity, the

---

[3] Uniform Laws on International Sales Act 1967, Sched. 2, art. 7 (2). A similar rule applies under the American Uniform Commercial Code, s. 2–207(2) between merchants.

[4] See pp. 53–54, *ante*.

[5] See *The Kite* [1933] P. 154, 164; *Hardwick Game Farm* v. *Suffolk Agricultural Poultry Producers' Association* [1969] 2 A.C. 31.

[6] For instance, the court may hold, as in *J. Milhem & Sons* v. *Fuerst Brothers & Co. Ltd.* [1954] 2 Lloyd's Rep. 559, that the parties were never *ad idem*. See also *Northland Airliners Ltd.* v. *Dennis Ferranti Meters Ltd.*, above. Even where the court eventually holds that there was a valid contract between the parties as in *Macpherson Train & Co. Ltd.* v. *J. Milhem & Sons* [1955] 2 Lloyd's Rep. 396 and *Brown & Gracie Ltd.* v. *F. W. Green & Co. Pty. Ltd.* [1960] 1 Lloyd's Rep. 289, costly and protracted litigation might results from the disregard of the simple rules on offer and acceptance or from ambiguity.

[7] *Entores Ltd.* v. *Miles Far East Corpn.* [1955] 2 Q.B. 327. An allegedly false or negligent misrepresentation requires publication and, if made by a person abroad to a person in England by telephone or telex, the place where the tort is committed is the place where the communication is received, *i.e.* England: *Diamond* v. *Bank of London and Montreal Ltd.*, *The Times*, November 10, 1978.

[8] *Holwell Securities Ltd.* v. *Hughes* [1974] 1 W.L.R. 155.

offer should state that the offeror will only be bound if he actually receives the acceptance.

The Confirmation Slip

Where a contract is negotiated verbally or by correspondence and later one party sends the other an order or acceptance on a printed form with an attached confirmation slip, which has to be returned duly signed by the other party, it is always a matter of construction, which in some cases is not easy to resolve, whether the parties have agreed to the terms of the contract with sufficient precision and what those terms are. Even though the confirmation slip is not returned there may be a binding contract between the parties.[9] "The court will always lean towards giving legal effect to documents which the parties themselves regard as constituting a binding contract in law."[10]

Special Problems Relating to General Conditions

A verbal contractual promise may override general conditions

It is a general principle of law that where the parties have embodied the terms of their contract in a written document—and printed general conditions are a written document—verbal evidence is not admissible to vary or qualify the written agreement. However, this principle is subject to a number of exceptions. In particular, where a party has given another a verbal promise not to rely on a term in the general conditions and that promise has been accepted by the other party, he cannot rely on that term if it would make the verbal contractual promise wholly illusory. In one case[11] English importers of an Italian injection moulding machine in negotiations with their freight forwarders insisted that, if the machine was to be shipped in a container, the latter should be carried below deck because they feared that the machine might get rusty. The manager of the forwarders assured the importers orally that "if we use containers, they will not be carried on deck." When the machine was shipped from Rotterdam to Tilbury, the Dutch associated company of the forwarders failed to ensure that the container in which the machine was carried was shipped below deck. The ship met with a slight swell and the container which contained the machine and was shipped on deck fell off and became a total loss. In an action for damages by the importers, the forwarders sought to rely on their printed general conditions which gave them complete freedom as to the method of transportation. The Court of Appeal held that the verbal promise of the forwarders not to ship the goods on deck constituted an

---

[9] *Compagnie de Commerce et Commission S.A.R.L.* v. *Parkinson Stove Co. Ltd.* [1953] 1 Lloyd's Rep. 532.

[10] *Ibid.* p. 542, *per* Pilcher J.

[11] *J. Evans & Son (Portsmouth) Ltd.* v. *Andrea Merzario Ltd.* [1976] 1 W.L.R. 1078. See also *The Ardennes* [1851] 1 K.B. 55, p. 335, *post.*

enforceable contractual promise which overrode the relevant term in the printed general conditions. The court gave judgment for the importers.

Incorporation of current edition of general conditions

General conditions are revised from time to time in the light of experience. They should provide that the edition current at the date of the conclusion of the contract shall apply. But even where such a clause is not included, one would, in the absence of indications of another intention of the parties arrive at the same result. Where the contract provided that it was subject to general conditions "available on request," it was held[12] that that was a reference to the current edition. "It is common experience that the general conditions of various undertakers are revised from time to time, and anyone requesting a copy of such conditions would reasonably expect to receive the current up-to-date edition."[13]

Conflicting general conditions of contracting parties

It sometimes happens that one party sends the other an offer on his general conditions of business and the other accepts subject to his own general conditions. The two sets of conditions will normally not agree and the question may arise whether the parties are in contract and, if so, whose general conditions apply. This situation is sometimes referred to as *the battle of conditions*.

No battle of conditions will arise if one party has taken the precaution of obtaining the other party's consent to his own conditions by a suitably worded confirmation slip or a signed acceptance, as recommended earlier. Thus, in one case[14] the sellers quoted for a machine. Their general conditions which were printed on the reverse of the quotation contained a price escalation clause. The buyers ordered the machine on their general conditions which did not admit a price escalation clause. On the foot of the buyers' order was a tear-off slip stating that the order was accepted by the sellers "on the terms and conditions stated therein." The sellers signed the slip and returned it to the buyers. The Court of Appeal held that the contract was concluded on the buyers' terms and that the sellers were not entitled to increase the price by virtue of the escalation clause.

A real difficulty arises if the operation of the general conditions of one of the parties is not placed beyond doubt by a signed confirmation or acceptance of the other party. Here one would only with reluctance arrive at the result that there is no contract, as the strict application of the offer-acceptance-counteroffer analysis may demand, because that is not what the parties intended. One would have to analyse the other terms of the contract and the subsequent conduct of the parties in order to ascertain

[12] *Smith* v. *South Wales Switchgear Co. Ltd.* [1978] 1 W.L.R. 165.

[13] *Ibid. per* Lord Keith of Kinkel, 177.

[14] *Butler Machine Tools Co. Ltd.* v. *Ex-Cell-O Corporation* (*England*) *Ltd.* [1979] 1 W.L.R. 401; see [1978] J.B.L. 8.

whether the conditions of the man "who fired the last shot" or those of the man "who got in the first blow"[15] were intended to apply.

INTERNATIONAL SUPPLY CONTRACTS

In order to protect contracting parties of relatively weaker bargaining power and, in particular, the consumer, the Supply of Goods (Implied Terms) Act 1973 and the Unfair Contract Terms Act 1977 prohibit or restrict certain contract terms, such as clauses exempting a party from his liability under the general law. Normally the exporter will not be concerned with the provisions of these enactments[16] because the contracts which he concludes with his overseas customers will qualify as international supply contracts and, as such, are exempted from the protective provisions of those statutes.[17] Exceptionally, however, as we have seen,[18] an export contract may not qualify as an international supply contract.

An international supply contract is defined by the Unfair Contract Terms Act 1977, s. 26(3) and (4), as having the following characteristics:

"(*a*) either it is a contract of sale of goods or it is one under or in pursuance of which the possession or ownership of goods passes; and
(*b*) it is made by parties whose places of business (or, if they have none, habitual residences) are in the territories of different States (the Channel Islands and the Isle of Man being treated for this purpose as different states from the United Kingdom)."

In addition, the contract must satisfy the following requirements:

"(*a*) the goods in question are, at the time of the conclusion of the contract, in the course of carriage, or will be carried, from the territory of one State to the territory of another; or
(*b*) the acts constituting the offer and acceptance have been done in the territories of different States; or
(*c*) the contract provides for the goods to be delivered to the territory of a State other than that within whose territory those acts were done."

---

15 Lord Denning M.R. in the case quoted in the preceding note.
16 See p. 55, *ante*. On the definition of an international contract in American and French law, see G. R. Delaume, "What is an International Contract? An American and a Gallic Dilemma" (1979) 28 I.C.L.Q. 258.
17 Unfair Contract Terms Act, s. 26(1) and (2).
18 See p. 10, *ante*.

CHAPTER 6

INVOICES AND PACKING

INVOICES

CORRECT invoicing is a matter of great importance in the export trade. The smooth performance of the contract of sale will often depend on it. The seller may sometimes regard the buyer's instructions on this point as too exacting, but he should not forget that the buyer requires these details in order to comply with the regulations in force in his own country applying to such topics as import licences, customs duties and exchange restrictions. This explains why the buyer in certain circumstances will ask for a pro forma invoice in advance or for the invoice to be dated a month, or some other fixed time, later than the date of the last invoice. *All invoices must be correct and true.* If the exporter is asked by the buyer to insert in the invoice inaccurate particulars, he should decline to accommodate him[1] even where the inaccuracies refer to apparent trivialities. The seller's statement that such dealings are contrary to his practice will usually be accepted by the buyer, and the seller will have avoided a potential source of subsequent embarrassment for himself. The invoice is usually made out in triplicate or quadruplicate.

The commercial invoice

The trading invoice should state the names and addresses of the seller and buyer, the date and reference number of the buyer's order, a description of the goods sold, details of package (including the weight of every bale or case), exact marks and numbers appearing on the package, the terms of sale and the details of shipping (including the name of the steamer and the route). It is not unusual for the invoice to contain the note "*e. and o.e.*" (errors and omissions excepted). A typical reference to the shipping details would be—

INVOICE of 4 Cases Worsted Tweeds supplied by Messrs. Bubble and Squeak, of Liverpool, to Messrs. Bow and Line, of Sydney, Australia, to be shipped per *SS. Aurora* from Liverpool. Order Number XYZ/1345.

The invoice price has to be stated in accordance with the agreed terms of the contract as explained earlier; it may be the ex works price, or the f.o.b. price, or the c.i.f. price and so on. In the case of a c.i.f. contract, the price calculation in the invoice has to comply, in the absence of an agreement of the parties to the contrary, with the principles explained earlier.[2] The buyer will often ask that a detailed statement of the elements of the price

[1] See *Fielding & Platt Ltd.* v. *Najjar* [1969] 1 W.L.R. 357.
[2] On p. 31, *ante.* Blackburn J. in *Ireland* v. *Livingston* (1872) L.R. 5 H.L. 395, 406.

be shown on the invoice, setting out the actual net price at the factory and the further charges separately, because these details are required for submission to his own authorities. An f.o.b. seller is sometimes requested by his buyer to arrange freight and insurance for the consignment. As this goes beyond the normal duty of the f.o.b. seller and represents a separate arrangement, the buyer should not be debited for these items on the goods invoice but on a separate invoice which would cover the prepaid freight, the insurance premium and the incidental commissions and charges.[3]

Where commercial invoices have to be presented under a bankers' commercial credit and the *Uniform Customs and Practice for Documentary Credits* (1974 *Revision*) are applicable—as is almost invariably the case—Article 32 of that text applies which provides:

(a) Unless otherwise specified in the credit, commercial invoices must be made out in the name of the applicant for the credit.

(b) Unless otherwise specified in the credit, banks may refuse invoices issued for amounts in excess of the amounts permitted by the credit.

(c) The description of the goods in the commercial invoice must correspond with the description in the credit. In the remaining documents the goods may be described in general terms not inconsistent with the description of the goods in the credit.[4]

Invoices on official forms

Some countries prescribe the use of official forms for invoices and in these and other cases invoices have often to embody, or to be combined with, certificates of value and of origin. Sometimes a special invoice has to be certified by the consul appointed by the country of destination for the distict where the exporter resides; the consular invoice has to be attached, usually in several copies, to the trading invoice. The name of the country of origin of the merchandise must be indicated in all copies of special customs invoices; special declarations are required on the invoices for many specified articles; some overseas customs regulations relating to invoices are complex and the exporter has to comply with them strictly.

The requirements of foreign laws in respect of invoices vary greatly and are altered from time to time. The exporter who does not employ the services of a shipping agent should keep himself informed of these changes and make certain that he dispatches the goods in accordance with the latest invoice requirements in force in the country of destination. The alterations are recorded in *Commerce International*, the journal of the London Chamber of Commerce, and in the trade publications mentioned earlier.[5] In case of doubt the exporter can obtain the desired information from the consulate of the country of destination, his chamber of commerce or the Export Services and Promotions Division of the Department of Industry.

[3] See p. 20, *ante*.
[4] See p. 252, *post*.
[5] See pp. 59–60, *ante*.

Packing

The exporter has to give considerable attention to the packing of the goods to be shipped abroad; irrespective of the conditions of sale, it is his duty to pack the goods in a manner which assures their safe arrival and facilitates their handling in transit and at the place of destination.[6] Neglect in this respect will invariably result in delay in the delivery of the goods and might entitle the overseas customer to reject the goods or to claim damages. The legal position is aptly described in the General Conditions of Delivery of Goods 1968 of CMEA[7] in a provision which, it is believed, has general application[8]:

> If there are no special directions in the contract concerning packing, the seller shall ship the goods in packing used for export goods in the seller's country, which would assure safety of the goods during transportation, taking into account possible transhipment, under proper and usual handling of the goods. In appropriate cases the duration and methods of carriage shall also be taken into account.

In law, the problem of packing is relevant in three respects. First of all, the buyer is in certain circumstances entitled to refuse the acceptance of the goods if they are not packed in accordance with his instructions or with the custom of the trade. Where a particular package has been stipulated, the packing of the goods often forms part of the description of the goods within the meaning of section 13 of the Sale of Goods Act 1893. It may be essential for the overseas buyer that the goods should be supplied in the stipulated packings; if he has ordered jam in one and two pound jars, the contract is broken if the jam is supplied in 10 pound tins. According to section 13(1) of the Act it is an implied condition, where goods are sold by description, that the goods shall correspond with the description. That, however, has to be read in the light of the modern doctrine of the innominate term,[9] according to which it depends on the nature and gravity of the breach whether it entitles the buyer to rescind the contract or whether the contract still subsists and he is only entitled to damages.[10] If the deficiency in the packing affects the "substantial identity" of the goods, it will be treated as a breach of the condition implied by section 13(1). In that case the buyer is entitled to reject the goods, and where goods, which are

---

[6] The International Cargo Handling Co-ordination Association (ICHCA) have published a booklet, *Recommendations on the Marking of General Cargo*, which is designed to facilitate sorting and tallying at ports throughout the world. The recommendations, which are printed in English, French, Spanish and German, have received a wide measure of international acceptance and reprints in a number of other languages have been made by underwriting associations, etc. Some national standards have been formulated based on the recommendations. An up-dated edition is being prepared to include the *Dangerous Goods Labels* agreed upon by the International Maritime Congresses Organisation (IMCO). The United Kingdom National Committee of ICHCA (Abford House, Wilton Road, London, S.W.1) have also published a pamphlet detailing the advantages of pallet standardisation.

[7] See p. 49, *ante*.

[8] General Conditions of Delivery of Goods 1968, para. 20(1).

[9] See p. 91, *post*.

[10] Lord Wilberforce in *Reardon Smith Line Ltd.* v. *Yngvar Hansen-Tangen* [1976] 1 W.L.R. 989, 998.

packed in the stipulated manner, are mixed with other goods, the buyer may reject the whole consignment or, if he prefers, only that part of it that is packed contrary to the agreement (Sale of Goods Act 1893, s. 30(3)).[10a]

These rules have been repeatedly applied by the courts; in one case, where the description qualified as a condition, the buyer of Australian canned fruit was held to be entitled to reject the whole consignment because the cases did not all contain 30 tins each, as agreed upon, but there were included in the consignment smaller cases containing 24 tins each, and this, although an umpire had declared that there was no difference in the market value of the goods whether packed 24 or 30 tins in a case.[11] This is a remarkable extension of the rule: in an earlier case, where Siam rice had been rejected because it had been supplied in single bags instead of double bags (*i.e.* gunny bags) as stipulated, the buyer was required to prove that the rice was more easily saleable in double bags,[12] and today this kind of evidence or other evidence as to the gravity of the breach is necessary to establish that the breach had to be qualified as breach of a condition. When goods are sold on f.o.b. or c.i.f. terms, the price quotation includes packing charges unless it is stated expressly that an extra charge will be made for package. The British exporter, who wishes to make an extra charge for package, should state so clearly when sending out the quotation or confirmation.

Secondly, the package is relevant for the calculation of the freight. Freight is paid on the weight or measurement or value of the cargo and the shipowner is entitled to demand the calculation of the freight at the highest rate.[13] The seller should consult his shipping agent in order to ascertain the mode of packing which is required to secure a favourable rate of freight, but he should not place this consideration higher than the safety of the consignment and the convenience of the customer whose agents have to handle the packages on arrival. Where stowage on deck (*cargaison de tillac*) is agreed upon, the buyer presumably will have to provide stronger package than where the goods are stowed in the holds unless the goods are stowed in containers. The master of the ship will refuse to sign a clean bill of lading if the package is defective, and the seller, who under his contract with the buyer may be obliged to tender him a clean bill, will be unable to do so. The pieces should be marked and branded in strict compliance with the directions of the buyer who is entitled to refuse the acceptance of a bill of lading which refers to goods that are marked and branded differently. Further, under Article IV of the Schedule to the Carriage of Goods by Sea Act 1971, the liability of the carrier for

[10a] Cl. 30(4) of the Sale of Goods Bill 1979; see p. 7, *ante*.

[11] *Re an Arbitration between Moore & Co. Ltd. and Landaver & Co.* [1921] 2 K.B. 519. It is doubtful if this case would be decided in the same manner today; it is possible that the term in question may be classified as an innominate term. See also *Manbre Saccharine Co.* v. *Corn Products Co.* [1919] 1 K.B. 198, 207.

[12] *Makin* v. *London Rice Mills Co.* (1869) 20 L.T. 705.

[13] See p. 336, *post*.

loss or damage to the goods in transit is limited in amount; unless the nature and value of the goods have been declared before shipment and inserted in the bill of lading, the liability does not exceed at present £447.81 per package or unit or £1.34 per kilo of gross weight of the goods lost or damaged, whichever is higher.[14] In the case of transportation by air, the limitation of liability is calculated by weight and not by the number of packages (Carriage by Air Act 1961, Sched. I, Article 22(2)).

Thirdly, the package should conform with the legislation in force in the country of destination. In some cases certain types of packing are prohibited or restricted: *e.g.* the import regulations of New Zealand provide that, where hay, straw, chaff or flax rug is used as packing material, a certificate has to be added on the official invoice form that the packing material has been disinfected prior to the use in a manner approved by the New Zealand Government; this precaution is due to the experience that undisinfected packing material of this kind may be a carrier of foot and mouth disease. Australia requires that all shipments from the United Kingdom packed in straw or other unprocessed vegetable packing must be covered by a special declaration of the exporter before a magistrate that the packing material is the produce of the country from which it is exported, and such declaration must be endorsed by a Government veterinary surgeon stating that there has been no foot and mouth disease in that country three months before shipment.[15] In some foreign countries, import duties are levied on a particular kind of packing material, *e.g.* glass containers or metal sheeting. Many countries have nowadays strict regulations about the marking and branding of packages. The seller, if in doubt, should obtain full instructions from his buyer or, if it is more convenient, consult the trade publications or inquire of the institutions referred to earlier.[16]

---

[14] See p. 373, *post.*
[15] Reg. 69 of the Australian Quarantine Regulations.
[16] See p. 57, *ante.*

CHAPTER 7

MODES OF PAYMENT

THIS topic will be considered fully when the various methods of financing exports are analysed.[1]

It will be seen that mercantile custom has developed certain standardised methods of payment for exports, that extensive use is made in this connection of the bill of exchange as an instrument of payment,[2] and that the goods themselves, as represented by the bill of lading, can be used as a security for financing exports by arranging payment under a bankers' documentary credit.[3] If payment is not made under a documentary credit, particular caution is called for in two cases: if credit is allowed,[4] or if the purchase price is paid in advance[5]; in the latter case, if the seller becomes insolvent, the buyer might find that he has no title to the goods and that his claim for recovery of the price is practically worthless.

Exchange control legislation

By virtue of the exchange control legislation the parties may not be free to stipulate payment in the manner and currency which they wish to arrange.[6] That legislation is still in operation although in consequence of the liberalisation of international trade the transactions to which it applies have happily been reduced in number.

The scheduled territories

For exchange control purposes the world is divided into two areas: the scheduled territories and the countries outside the scheduled territories.

The scheduled territories, also called the sterling area, comprise:[7]

1. The United Kingdom,
2. The Channel Islands,
3. The Isle of Man,
4. The Republic of Ireland,
5. Gibraltar.

---

[1] See p. 233, *post.*
[2] See p. 234, *post.*
[3] See p. 244, *post.*
[4] See p. 103, *post.*
[5] See p. 77, *post.*
[6] See further Bank of England, Exchange Control, *Notice to Exporters*, dated October 28, 1975; and Notice EC45 to Banks and Bankers, entitled *Exports from the United Kingdom*, dated September 8, 1970 and amended October 28, 1975. See also Anthony Parker, *Exchange Control* (3rd ed., 1978).
[7] Exchange Control Act 1947, s. 1(3)(*b*) and Sched. I; Exchange Control (Scheduled Territories) (No. 2) Order 1972 (S.I. 1972 No. 930, amended by S.I. 1972 No. 2040).

The Treasury has power at any time to add territories to the list of scheduled territories or exclude them therefrom (s. 1(3)(*b*)). All countries which are not scheduled are outside the sterling area.

For administrative purposes the countries outside the scheduled territories are divided as follows:

(*a*) those countries which at present comprise the European Economic Community, namely Belgium, Denmark, France, West Germany, Italy, Luxembourg and the Netherlands (Ireland and the United Kingdom are scheduled territories).
(*b*) The overseas sterling area, *i.e.* those countries which, as on June 22, 1972, were treated as scheduled territories.
(*c*) The rest of the non-scheduled territories.

Special rules apply to certain transactions involving residents of the latter two areas; these rules can be ascertained from the Bank of England. Inquiries should normally be made through the exporter's own bank.

Surrender of specified currencies

Residents of the United Kingdom and overseas subsidiaries of enterprises resident in the United Kingdom have to surrender certain currencies, known as specified currencies, to authorised dealers.[8] Specified currencies are at present[9] all foreign currencies, including the Rhodesian pound. Exceptionally—but only by authority of the Bank of England itself—may the exporter retain specified currency in a "retained foreign currency account."

Protection as regards contracts expressed in foreign currency

Subject to certain exchange control regulations, the exporter's bank will purchase for forward delivery the sale proceeds of firm export contracts made in foreign currency. In addition, where the exporter is tendering for overseas contracts the Bank of England is prepared to consider applications from the exporter's bank to provide forward exchange cover in respect of a tender guarantee expressed and payable in a foreign currency, or for foreign components to be paid for in foreign exchange in contracts where the tender price is denominated and payable in sterling.

Exchange control rules relating to the payment of the price

The limits which the Exchange Control Act 1947, s. 23, and statutory instruments made thereunder impose on the liberty of parties exporting goods to an ultimate destination[10] outside the scheduled territories are that payment has, in principle, to be made:

1. to a person resident in the United Kingdom;

---

[8] Exchange Control (Specified Currency and Prescribed Securities) Order 1967 (S.I. 1967 No. 556), amended by S.I. 1968 No. 1233.

[9] Position: September 1, 1979.

[10] See s. 23(4). "Ultimate destination" means the final destination genuinely contemplated by the exporter: *Superheater Co. Ltd.* v. *Commissioners of Customs and Excise* [1969] 1 W.L.R. 858.

2. in such a manner as is prescribed in relation to goods of that description exported to a specified destination;
3. not later than six months after the date of exportation, or such longer time as the Treasury may direct[11]; and further,
4. the amount of payment has to be such as to represent a return for the goods which is in all the circumstances satisfactory in the national interest.

As regards No. 3, above, the Treasury has given a general permission for the arrangement of payment later than six months if:

(*a*) the goods are exported under a contract covered by Export Credits Guarantee Department insurance, and
(*b*) the period of credit has been approved by that Department.[12]

In other cases, where it is intended to extend the time for payment beyond six months, permission under the Exchange Control Act is required, and where payment was originally arranged within this period, any delay beyond six months in the receipt of the proceeds of sale must be reported to the Controller, Exchange Control (Exports), Customs and Excise,[13] together with the reasons for the delay. Special provisions apply to exports to Rhodesia.

Implied condition of compliance with exchange control regulations

The Exchange Control Act 1947 further provides in section 33(1) that a condition shall be implied in every contract that if permission of the Treasury is required under the Act for the performance of any term of the contract, that term shall not be performed except in so far as the permission is given or not required. The purpose of this provision is to make it clear that the contract is not normally frustrated on the ground that the permission of the Treasury required under the Act cannot be obtained.[14] The Act does not, however, allow the debtor a moratorium; on the contrary, it provides[15] that, in spite of the absence of Treasury permission, the creditor may sue the debtor at once "in a prescribed court"[16] for payment into court, and that the creditor's claim is admitted to proof in the bankruptcy of the debtor or, if the debtor is a company, in its winding up.[17]

The benevolent interpretation of section 33(1) which preserves the validity of the contract and merely controls the immediate destination of the debtor's payments does not apply if it is inconsistent with the intention of

---

[11] The direction may relate to specified goods, and the time limit may be dispensed with completely by the Treasury (s. 23(1), proviso); see next paragraph.

[12] General Permission of the Treasury, dated September 8, 1970 (Position: July 1, 1978).

[13] Vintry House, Queen Street Place, London EC4R 1BQ.

[14] *Contract and Trading (Southern) Ltd.* v. *Barbey* [1960] A.C. 244; *Cummings* v. *London Bullion Co. Ltd.* [1952] 1 K.B. 327, 337.

[15] In the fourth Sched., para. 4(1).

[16] Prescribed by the Exchange Control (Prescribed Courts) Order 1947 (S.R. & O. 1947 No. 2046) and the Exchange Control (Prescribed Courts) (Scotland, Northern Ireland and Isle of Man) Order 1948 (S.I. 1948 No. 709). "Prescribed courts" in England are the Supreme Court of Judicature and the county courts.

[17] Fourth Sched., paras. 5 and 6. A bill of exchange which is exported contrary to the provisions of the Exchange Control Act 1947, s. 22(1)(*e*)(iii) is enforceable: *Credit Lyonnais* v. *P. T. Barnard & Associates Ltd.* [1976] 1 Lloyd's Rep. 557, 562.

the parties (proviso to s. 33(1)), either because they intend the contract itself to be conditional upon the grant of the Treasury permission or because they intend to contravene the Act and to commit an act of illegality.[18]

Exchange contracts under the Bretton Woods Agreement

The Bretton Woods Agreement of 1944, to which effect was given in the United Kingdom by the Bretton Woods Agreements Acts 1945,[19] provides in article VIII, section 2(*b*):—

> "Exchange contracts which involve the currency of any member and which are contrary to the exchange control regulations of that member maintained or imposed consistently with this agreement shall be unenforceable in the territories of any other member. . . ."

An "exchange contract" within the meaning of this provision is only a monetary deal in currencies[20] but does not comprise a genuine commercial contract for the sale and purchase of merchandise or commodities, although the price is expressed in a foreign currency. Thus, a contract whereby Italian buyers purchased metal from English dealers but which had not been authorised by the Italian authorities did not qualify as an "exchange contract" and was enforceable against the buyers.[21]

English judgments and arbitration awards in a foreign currency

Where the currency of the contract is expressed in the money of a foreign country or damages have been suffered substantially in such country, the English courts and arbitration tribunals are prepared to express their decisions in the foreign currency in question. This subject will be treated later on.[22]

---

[18] *Bigos* v. *Bousted* [1951] 1 All E.R. 92; *Marcus* v. *Director of Public Prosecutions* [1950] W.N. 279; *Shaw* v. *Shaw* [1965] 1 W.L.R. 537. See also *Swiss Bank Corporation* v. *Lloyds Bank* [1979] 3 W.L.R. 201.

[19] And the Bretton Woods Agreements Order in Council (S.R. & O. 1946 No. 36).

[20] *Sing Batra* v. *Ebrahim, The Times,* May 3, 1977.

[21] *Wilson, Smithett & Cope Ltd.* v. *Terruzzi* [1976] Q.B. 683.

[22] As regards arbitration, p. 437, *post*; as regards judgments, p. 133, *post*.

CHAPTER 8

PERFORMANCE OF THE CONTRACT

THE disposal of the goods by the seller in performance of the contract of sale has to pass through three phases, namely, the delivery of the goods, the passing of the property in the goods and the passing of the risk. In the normal cases of overseas sales, in particular on f.o.b. and c.i.f. terms, these three phases do not coincide and should be clearly distinguished.

ENGLISH AND FOREIGN SALES LAW

The first question which has to be examined when a dispute arises between the parties about the delivery of the goods, the passing of the property or of the risk, is whether the matter is to be considered from the point of view of English law or of the foreign law prevailing in the country of the buyer. This question pertains to the branch of law known as the conflict of laws which will be discussed later.[1] The answer which the rules on the conflict of laws may provide is evidently that the issue is decided either by English law, in which case the provisions of the Sale of Goods Act 1893, as amended,[2] apply, or by the foreign law in question. If the latter conclusion is reached, the English courts may still have jurisdiction to hear the case; the questions of the law applicable to the contract and of the jurisdiction of the court are distinct and should not be confused; the only inference which has to be drawn from the application of foreign law to a particular contract is that the rules of foreign law might displace the provisions of the Sale of Goods Act 1893, as amended[2], and that foreign law might be relied upon in the English courts if its rules can be proved by expert witnesses or in another admissible manner.[2a] A third possibility is that the parties agree in their contract to apply the Uniform Laws on International Sales[3]; in this case the provisions of the Uniform Laws on International Sales Act 1967 apply.

If the contract of sale is governed by foreign law, it should be borne in mind that the rules of foreign law may be different from those of English law; for instance, in some Continental countries, such as France, Italy, Germany and Greece, if the seller delays the delivery of the goods and no time is fixed for the delivery, the buyer must normally demand delivery and allow the seller a reasonable time for performance (*délai de grâce*; *Nachfrist*) before he can treat the contract as repudiated[4]; this requirement

[1] See p. 125, *post*.
[2] See p. 7, *ante*.
[2a] See no 125, *post*.
[3] See p. 140, *post*.
[4] The requirements of the various laws as regards *délai de grâce* vary.

of *interpellation* is unknown in Anglo-American law which is much stricter in this respect and would treat the contract as automatically repudiated when a reasonable time for delivery has expired, provided that time is of the essence of the contract. While in English law a buyer who wishes to reject goods which are not in accordance with the contract has to inform the seller of this intention within "a reasonable time,"[5] in Swiss and Scandinavian law the defects have to be notified to the seller "at once" (*sofort*); in German law, if the parties are businessmen "without delay" (*unverzüglich*); in Italian law, on principle, within eight days; in Spanish law, as regards packed goods, within four days and as regards hidden defects (*vicios internos* or *occultos*) within 30 days[6]; and in French law the buyer has to start proceedings "within a short time" (*dans un bref délai*).[7] According to the Convention on the Limitation Period in the International Sale of Goods sponsored by UNCITRAL and signed in 1974,[8] the limitation period in respect of a claim arising from a defect or lack of conformity of goods in an international sale shall, on principle, be four years.

Further, under the laws of England, the United States of America, France, Belgium, Italy and Portugal the property in the goods sold passes when the parties intend it to pass, whether the delivery of the goods did or did not take place; the position is different under the laws of the Netherlands, Spain, Germany, the Argentine, Brazil, Chile and Columbia where the property passes, as a rule, only if the intention of the parties that it should pass is supported by the actual delivery of the goods. These very considerable differences in the national sales laws are not helpful to international trade and are hardly in keeping with the spirit of the second half of the twentieth century. The general adoption of the Uniform Laws on International Sales, possibly as amended by UNCITRAL, would, as already observed,[9] be of great benefit to the international trading community.

Let us assume that the United Kingdom exporter has avoided the pitfalls of foreign law—which, incidentally, sometimes operate in his favour—by the simple device of having embodied in his contract an express stipulation to the effect that the contract shall be governed, in all respects, by English law. In this case, the Sale of Goods Act[9a] applies, which contains a definition of the term "delivery" and a number of rules on the passing of the property and the risk.

Delivery of the Goods

According to section 62 of the 1893 Act[9b] "delivery" means the "voluntary

---

[5] See p. 95, *post*.
[6] In some South American laws the periods are shorter than in Spanish law.
[7] Sometimes trade usages applying to certain commodities provide for another regulation as regards the notification of defects.
[8] See p. 148, *post*.
[9] See p. 48, *ante*; p. 140, *post*.
[9a] See p. 7, *ante*.
[9b] Cl. 61 of the Sale of Goods Bill 1979.

transfer of possession from one person to another." The goods are normally delivered to the buyer when he, or his agent, acquires custody of the goods or is enabled to exercise control over them.[10] In cases in which no bill of lading is issued, delivery to the carrier for the purposes of transmission to the buyer, is prima facie deemed to be delivery to the buyer.[11]

The place and time of delivery are, in export sales, usually defined by the special trade clauses which have been considered earlier; these special arrangements displace the provisions of the Sale of Goods Acts 1893 on delivery which are mainly found in sections 27 to 37[11a]. In particular, where the seller has obtained a bill of lading, as is the case in f.o.b. contracts with additional services, or in c.i.f. or c. and f. contracts, the goods are deemed to be delivered when the bill of lading is delivered to the buyer.[12]

Passing of the Property

The rules of the Act on the passing of the property in the goods sold are likewise often modified by special arrangements made between the parties to an export sale. The Act provides here two fundamental rules, namely that, where the contract is for the sale of unascertained goods, the property does not pass to the buyer unless and until the goods are ascertained (s. 16) and, where the contract is for the sale of specific or ascertained goods, the property passes at such time as the parties intend it to pass (s. 17(1)).

These rules have caused difficulty and, on occasion, proved to be a trap for the unwary buyer where the purchase price was paid in advance. In one case[13] which concerned an import transaction a British merchant bought 1,000 tons of wheat on c.i.f. terms from American suppliers and resold a parcel of 500 tons to another British firm which paid the purchase price in spot cash; the wheat then was shipped in bulk to the merchant who went bankrupt before the ship arrived. The trustee in bankruptcy successfully resisted the sub-purchaser's claim for delivery of 500 tons of the bulk cargo; the court held that his parcel consisted of unascertained goods and the property in them had not passed to the sub-purchaser as there had never been an appropriation or identification of the 500 tons of wheat which represented the sub-purchaser's goods. In another case[14] which concerned an export transaction a Costa Rican company bought from an English company 85 bicycles f.o.b. British port and paid the price for them in advance. The bicycles were packed into cases, marked with the buyers' name and registered for shipment in a named ship which was to load at Liverpool but they had not yet been sent to that port and were

---

[10] See *E. Reynolds & Sons (Chingford) Ltd.* v. *Hendry Bros. Ltd.* [1955] 1 Lloyd's Rep. 258, 259; *Commercial Fibres (Ireland) Ltd.* v. *Zabaida* [1975] 1 Lloyd's Rep. 27 (delivery ex warehouse or ex dock of place of shipment).

[11] s. 32(1). The same applies where the goods are shipped not to the buyer but to a bank to which they are pledged by way of security (*Kum* v. *Wah Tat Bank Ltd.* [1971] 1 Lloyd's Rep. 439).

[11a] The provisions of clauses 27 to 37 of the Sale of Goods Bill 1979 are slightly different.

[12] *Biddell Bros.* v. *E. Clemens Horst Co.* [1912] A.C. 18, 22.

[13] *Re Wait* [1927] 1 Ch. 606.

[14] *Carlos Federspiel & Co. S.A.* v. *Charles Twigg & Co. Ltd.* [1957] 1 Lloyd's Rep. 240.

not yet shipped. A receiver and manager appointed by the debenture holders of the sellers claimed that the bicycles, like the other assets of the sellers, were charged in favour of the debenture holders. Pearson J. held that that contention was correct because the property in the bicycles had not yet passed; in the view of the learned judge the common intention of the parties was that the property should pass on shipment, or possibly later.

In the case of specific or ascertained goods the task is to ascertain the intention of the parties, who are at liberty to fix the time when the property passes. This is not an easy task, since the clues which the Act furnishes in section 17(2) for ascertaining that intention are couched in vague and general terms, and the five specific presumptions which are laid down in section 18 are not appropriate to the particular circumstances of an export sale. Two possibilities exist here which require separate consideration: the seller may reserve the property in the goods (or, as businessmen sometimes call it, the right of disposal of the goods) until certain conditions have been fulfilled, or he may not have made the transfer of the property conditional.

In the first contingency, the property does not pass to the buyer until the conditions imposed by the seller are satisfied, and that will even be the case where the goods have been delivered to the buyer, his agent, or a carrier for transmission to the buyer (s. 19(1)). Such a condition may be imposed by the seller inserting into the contract of sale a reservation of property clause, *i.e.* a clause making the passing of the property conditional on the receipt of the purchase price in cash.[15] The law provides two rebuttable presumptions in favour of a conditional transfer of the property: first, where goods are shipped and by the bill of lading the goods are deliverable to the order of the seller or his agent, it is presumed that the seller reserves the property in the goods until he or his agent delivers the bill to the buyer or his agent (s. 19(2))[16]; and secondly, where the seller has drawn on the buyer for the purchase price and transmits the bill of exchange and the bill of lading together to the buyer to secure acceptance or payment of the bill of exchange, the property does not pass to the buyer, if he does not honour the bill, and in that case he would have to return the bill of lading (s. 19(3)). These provisions apply to f.o.b. and c.i.f. contracts alike.

The second contingency arises where the seller has failed to make the passing of the property conditional and where neither of the legal presumptions provided by subsection (2) or (3) of section 19 can be invoked to remedy that failure. Where, *e.g.* the seller has taken out a bill of lading to the order of the buyer or his agent, all depends on whether the seller delivers the bill to the buyer; it has been held[17] that taking out a bill of lading in the name of the buyer does not necessarily reveal the seller's

[15] See p. 53, *ante* and p. 79, *post*.
[16] Presumption rebutted between related companies: *The Albazero* [1975] 3 W.L.R. 491, 512, 513; reversed on other grounds by H. L. in [1977] A.C. 274.
[17] *The Kronprinsessan Margareta* [1921] 1 A.C. 486, 517; *The Glenrog* [1945] A.C. 124.

intention of passing the property to him. Where the bill is delivered to the buyer or his agent, the inference is almost[18] irresistible that the seller intended to transfer the property in the goods to the buyer.[19]

These rules apply to all contracts under which it is the seller's duty to deliver a bill of lading. In cases where that duty does not exist, *e.g.* in ex works, strict f.o.b. or free delivered contracts, the delivery of the goods to the buyer or to the carrier is presumably the act which passes the property to the buyer.

Where under a c.i.f. or c. and f. contract, or under an f.o.b. contract under which the seller has taken out the bill of lading, the bill is delivered to the buyer or his agent, the inference is that the property which is intended to pass to the buyer is only *conditional*, *viz.* that the property in the goods shall revert to the seller if upon examination they are found to be not in accordance with the contract.[20]

In exceptional cases the c.i.f. seller may release the goods to the buyer before handing over the bill of lading to him, by giving the buyer a delivery order on the ship. It depends here on the intention of the parties whether this procedure is adopted in performance of the c.i.f. contract or merely as "mechanics of delivery."[21] The deliberate retention of the bill of lading by the seller may indicate an intention of the parties that property shall not pass to the buyer on such an anticipated delivery.[22]

The reservation of property clause

It has already been stated[23] that English law admits a clause which provides that the seller retains the property in the goods sold until he receives the purchase price in cash and the insertion of this clause into the general conditions of business, together with a clause making the buyer an agent and trustee of the seller with respect to the proceeds of sale if the goods are sold, has been recommended to exporters. The clause makes the passing of property conditional on a specified event, *viz.* the receipt of the price by the seller. It is clear from section 19(1) of the Sale of Goods Act 1893, as amended, that the clause is effective and defeats the general presumption that the property passes when the bill of lading is transferred from the seller (or his agent) to the buyer (or his agent). The clause may, as indicated, be extended by making the buyer an agent and trustee for the seller and giving him the right to trace into the proceeds if the buyer

---

[18] Exceptionally the circumstances may support another inference, see the observation of Roskill L.J. in *The Albazero*, [1975] 3 W.L.R. 491, 523, reversed in [1977] A.C. 774 (H.L.).

[19] In *The Albazero* [1977] A.C. 774, Brandon J., the Court of Appeal and the House of Lords agreed that by virtue of the transfer of the bill of lading the property and possession had passed to the consignees. See also *The San Nicholas* [1976] 1 Lloyd's Rep. 8, 11, 13.

[20] *Kwei Tek Chao* v. *British Traders and Shippers Ltd.* [1954] 2 Q.B. 459, 487. Another case in which the property passed only defeasibly was *McDougall* v. *Aeromarine of Emsworth Ltd.* [1958] 1 W.L.R. 1126.

[21] McNair J. in *Ginzberg* v. *Barrow Haematite Steel Co.* [1966] 1 Lloyd's Rep. 343, 353.

[22] *Cheetham & Co Ltd.* v. *Thornham Spinning Co. Ltd.* [1964] 2 Lloyd's Rep. 17; *Ginzberg* v. *Barrow Haematite Steel Co. Ltd.* [1966] 1 Lloyd's Rep. 343.

[23] See p. 78, *ante*.

has disposed of the goods.[24] In Germany and the Netherlands these extended reservation of property clauses are common.[25] In the *Romalpa* case[26] such a clause was upheld by the English courts. Aluminium Industrie Vaassen BV (AIV), a Dutch private company, sold a quantity of aluminium foil to Romalpa, an English company. The terms of delivery were ex works AIV in Holland and the price was expressed in Dutch currency. The contract contained an extended property clause which was worded in great detail.[27] A receiver was appointed for Romalpa. Although the contract was closely connected with Dutch law, that law was not pleaded and the case was decided according to English law. The Court of Appeal held that AIV were entitled to the property in the goods supplied by them and still being in existence. As regards the goods resold by Romalpa, the court held that Romalpa had acted as agents for AIV and were, therefore, in a fiduciary relationship to them; that admitted the application of the equitable doctrine of tracing, as developed in *Re Hallett's Estate*.[28]

It was, however, held by Slade J. in *Re Bond Worth Ltd.*[28a] that, where the property in the goods was transferred unconditionally to the buyer and the latter was not constituted an agent for the seller, the reservation of property clause constituted a floating charge on the goods and on the money obtained on their resale and, as such, was registrable under the Companies Act 1948, s. 95. To avoid that result, the reservation of property clause has to be worded with great care.

Passing of the Risk

The risk of accidental loss of the goods sold passes prima facie when the property passes (s. 20).[28b] This is an antiquated rule of the Act of 1893. Modern texts, *e.g.* the Uniform Commercial Code (s. 2–509) and the Uniform Law on the International Sale of Goods (art. 97), provide that, as a rule, the risk shall pass on delivery of the goods.

In the law of international trade, contrary to the presumption of section 20 of the Sale of Goods Act, the two concepts of the passing of the risk and the transfer of property are regularly separated and the statutory presumption is displaced by agreement of the parties. Here again, special arrangements are admitted between the parties; in the absence of them[29] the risk will generally pass in a contract for the sale of goods abroad when the goods leave the custody of the seller. In ex works and f.o.t. contracts, the risk normally passes when the goods are delivered to the buyer or his agent, or the railway, as the case may be. In f.a.s. contracts the risk passes

[24] See R. M. Goode, "The Right to Trace and its Impact in Commercial Transactions," in (1976) 92 L.Q.R. 360. [25] [1977] J.B.L. 295.

[26] *Aluminium Industrie Vaassen BV* v. *Romalpa Aluminium Ltd.* [1976] 1 W.L.R. 676. Also *Borden (U.K.) Ltd.* v. *Scottish Timber Products Ltd.*, [1979] 2 Lloyd's Rep. 168.

[27] The clause is reproduced fully in [1976] J.B.L. 209–210. [28] (1880) 13 Ch.D. 696.

[28a] (1979) 129 New L.J. 220, and 248. See also [1979] J.B.L. 216, where the reservation of property clause in *Bond Worth* is reproduced in full.

[28b] See cl. 20(1) of the Sale of Goods Bill 1979.

[29] In *President of India* v. *Metcalfe Shipping Co.* [1969] 2 Q.B. 123; affirmed by C.A. in [1970] 1 Q.B. 289, passing of the risk (and of the property) under an f.o.b. contract was postponed until delivery of bills of lading.

when the goods are placed alongside the ship and in f.o.b. and c.i.f. contracts normally when they are delivered over the ship's rail. It will be recollected that the c.i.f. buyer has to accept the shipping documents and to pay the price although he knows that the goods have been lost in transit.[30] If the contract provides for delivery franco domicile of the buyer, the intention of the parties as regards the passing of the risk can often be gathered from the terms of payment and the insurance arrangement: if the price is prepaid and the buyer is responsible for insurance, there is hardly a doubt that the goods travel at his risk; the result would be reversed if the price were collected on delivery and the seller had to cover the insurance risk.

The risk, unlike the property, may pass to the buyer although the goods are unascertained goods which have not been appropriated.[31]

The risk of accidental loss should not be confused with the risk of deterioration of the goods in transit. In f.o.b. and c.i.f. contracts relating to perishable goods and containing an implied condition that the goods shall be of merchantable quality,[32] the seller undertakes, by further implication, that the goods shall be in a merchantable state not only when they are loaded but also upon arrival at destination and a reasonable time thereafter, allowing for their normal disposal,[33] but this does not apply where the transit or disposal is unduly delayed.[34] Diplock J. stated this rule thus:[35]

> It is the extraordinary deterioration of the goods due to abnormal conditions experienced during transit for which the buyer takes the risk. A necessary and inevitable deterioration during transit which will render them unmerchantable on arrival is normally one for which the seller is liable.

Contract Guarantees

The practice of the export trade has developed two types of undertaking designed to facilitate the smooth performance of the export transaction, *viz.* the performance guarantee and the bank guarantee.

---

30 See p. 37, *ante*: *Manbre Saccharine Co.* v. *Corn Products Co. Ltd.* [1919] 1 K.B. 198.

31 Croom-Johnson, J. in *Comptoir d'Achat* v. *Luis de Ridder* [1947] 2 All E.R. 443, 453. Where unascertained goods are in the possession of a third person, *e.g.* a warehouseman, the property and the risk in the sold part pass when the third person has separated that part from the bulk and acknowledges that he holds that part as the buyer's goods: *Wardar's (Import & Export) Co. Ltd.* v. *W. Norwood & Sons Ltd.* [1968] 2 Q.B. 663.

32 See ss. 14(2), 15(2)(*c*) and 62(1A) of the Sale of Goods Act 1893, as amended by the Supply of Goods (Implied Terms) Act 1973, s. 62(1A) contains the following definition of merchantable quality: "Goods of any kind are of merchantable quality within the meaning of this Act if they are as fit for the purpose or purposes for which goods of that kind are commonly bought as it is reasonable to expect having regard to any description applied to them, the price (if relevant) and all the other relevant circumstances." These provisions are arranged differently in the Sale of Goods Bill 1979. The definition of merchantable quality is contained in cl. 14(6).

33 *Mash & Murrell Ltd* v. *Joseph I. Emanuel Ltd.* [1961] 1 W.L.R. 862; reversed on appeal on the facts [1962] 1 W.L.R. 16.

34 *Broome* v. *Pardess Co-operative Society* [1939] 3 All E.R. 978, 985; *Ollett* v. *Jordan* [1918] 2 K.B. 41, 47.

35 *Marsh & Murrell Ltd.* v. *Joseph I. Emanuel Ltd.* [1961] 1 W.L.R. 862; reversed on appeal on the facts [1962] 1 W.L.R. 16.

The International Chamber of Commerce has published a brochure entitled *Uniform Rules for Contract Guarantees.*[36] The Uniform Rules deal only with guarantees, bonds, indemnities, sureties or similar undertakings ("guarantees") given on behalf of the seller or supplier but do not deal with those given on behalf of the buyer. They deal with three types of guarantees: the tender bond which in this work is treated later on in the chapter on the construction of works and installations abroad,[37] the performance guarantee and the repayment guarantee. The Uniform Rules are only intended to regulate the case of guarantees given by banks, insurance companies or other third parties. The Uniform Rules apply only if the guarantee states that "it is subject to the Uniform Rules for Tender, Performance and Repayment Guarantees ('Contract Guarantees') of the International Chamber of Commerce (Publication No. 325)." It remains to be seen whether the adoption of these Uniform Rules will recommend itself to the practice.

Performance guarantees

If the buyer is not certain that the seller will be able to supply the sold goods, he will ask him to give a performance guarantee or to procure such a guarantee from a third person, *e.g.* a bank. Similarly the seller will ask the buyer for a performance guarantee if he is uncertain that the buyer will accept the goods, pay the price and meet his other obligations under the contract of sale.

Performance guarantees are often used in contracts for the erection of plant and machinery. They are also used in so-called string contracts[38] where there are several middlemen between the original seller and the ultimate buyer. Scrutton L.J. referred[39] to string contracts as "cases where A sells to B, then B to C, and so on through the alphabet." Performance guarantees are further used in other cases.

The normal legal meaning of the term "guarantee" is that a third person who is not a party to the contract assumes liability in the case of one of the contracting parties defaulting on his obligations, but, as Somervell L.J. observed,[40] "the word 'guarantee' is often used in other than its legal sense"; in commerce it sometimes denotes simply "undertaking." That explains that in practice two types of performance guarantee are found: one given by a third person—which in law is a proper guarantee[41]—and another given by the performer himself.[42] Performance guarantees given

[36] ICC Brochure No. 325 (1978).
[37] See p. 450, *post.*
[38] Andrew J. Bateson, "String Contracts" in [1958] J.B.L. 173.
[39] In *James Finlay & Co.* v. *N.V. Kwik Hoo Tong H.M.* [1929] 1 K.B. 400, 411.
[40] In *Heisler* v. *Anglo-Dal Ltd.* [1954] 1 W.L.R. 1273, 1276.
[41] See *Sinason-Teicher Inter-American Grain Corporation* v. *Oilcakes and Oilseeds Trading Co. Ltd.* [1954] 1 W.L.R. 1394, where the intermediate buyer had to procure a performance guarantee by the ultimate buyers guaranteeing "the ordered liquidation of the . . . contract."
[42] See *Heisler* v. *Anglo-Dal Ltd.* [1954] 1 W.L.R. 1273; *Newman Industries* v. *Indo-British Industries* (*Govindram Bros., Third Parties*) [1957] 1 Lloyd's Rep. 211.

by banks are treated in the following section. As regards performance guarantees given by the party under obligation himself, although, as Devlin J. pointed out,[43] to a lawyer a guarantee "that I will perform my contract" is quite worthless, at least as a guarantee, to the commercial man it has some value "as underlining, as it were, the promise that has been undertaken." Moreover, if the performance guarantee of the second type takes the form of a promise to pay a fixed sum, *e.g.* 10 per cent. of the price, or the deposit of such sum, it might be a stipulation by the person giving it to pay or forfeit that sum by way of liquidated damages[44] in the case of non-performance and might, as such, have legal significance.

Bank guarantees

Bank guarantees may be procured by the buyer or by the seller. If they are procured by the buyer, their aim is to secure the payment of the price to the seller by substituting a "reliable paymaster"[45] for the buyer. If they are procured by the seller, their purpose is to secure the buyer if he has a claim for damages against the seller for non-delivery of the goods, their defective delivery or other cases of non-performance.

In both cases the bank guarantee is normally an absolute undertaking by the bank to pay if the conditions for payment are satisfied. In that respect it is similar to a banker's confirmed documentary credit and many considerations applying to the latter likewise apply to the bank guarantee.[46] Only in rare cases will the bank guarantee be a guarantee in the strictly legal sense, *i.e.* an undertaking to pay only if the bank's customer is in default.

Bank guarantees procured by the buyer

The bank which guarantees the payment of the price or of part of it is obliged to make payment to the seller if the conditions on which payment is made dependent are satisfied. But, as Devlin J. observed,[47] "the bank guarantee is not a general performance guarantee but only a guarantee of a limited performance," *i.e.* of the payment of the price.

Where the buyer is obliged to obtain a confirmed documentary credit and the correspondent bank, instead of confirming the credit, absolutely guarantees payment of the price on the same conditions as were stipulated for the confirmed credit, it is thought that the bank guarantee is an adequate substitute for the confirmed credit. As far as the time for opening a bank guarantee by the buyer is concerned, the rules relating to documentary credits apply analogously.[47]

---

[43] In *Heisler* v. *Anglo-Dal Ltd.* [1954] 1 W.L.R. 1273, 1277. [44] See p. 86, *post.*

[45] *Per* McNair J. in *Soprama S.p.A.* v. *Marine & Animal By-Products Corporation* [1966] 1 Lloyd's Rep. 367, 385.

[46] See p. 244, *post.*

[47] In *Sinason-Teicher Inter-American Grain Corporation* v. *Oilcakes and Oilseeds Trading Co. Ltd.*, [1954] 1 W.L.R. 935, 941; affirmed [1954] 1 W.L.R. 1394 (C.A.). A buyer's bank guarantees was also provided in *Dalmia Dairy Industries Ltd.* v. *National Bank of Pakistan,* [1978] 2 Lloyd's Rep. 223.

On demand bonds and other bank guarantees procured by the seller

These guarantees, sometimes also referred to as performance guarantees, are procured by the seller in order to protect the buyer against non-performance[48] or to secure a refund to the buyer in cases of non-performance if part or all of the purchase price has been paid in advance.[49]

The condition on which the bank is obliged to pay is usually a first demand by the buyer. Here again, the bank enters into an absolute undertaking, similar to the confirmation of a documentary credit, and must meet its obligations even if the seller objects and there are circumstances strongly supporting his contention that the buyer's demand is unjustified. But if it is clearly established to the satisfaction of the bank that the buyer's demand is fraudulent, the bank should not pay or at least it should interplead, *i.e.* apply to pay the money into court and leave it to the parties to litigate on who is entitled to it. On demand bonds are often requested by Middle Eastern and African purchasers. In one case[50] the sellers in the United Kingdom agreed to supply greenhouses to a state enterprise in Libya. The buyers undertook to open an irrevocable confirmed credit in favour of the sellers through Barclays International. The sellers had to provide an on demand bond of 10 per cent. of the purchase price. They instructed Barclays International to issue such bond to the Umma Bank in Libya which gave its own bond to the buyers. Barclays International's bond was payable "on demand without proof or conditions." The buyers failed to open a satisfactory credit, as stipulated in the contract, and the sellers refused to supply the greenhouses. The buyers claimed under the on demand bond from the Umma Bank and the latter claimed from Barclays International under their guarantee. The Court of Appeal refused an injunction by the sellers enjoining Barclays International to pay. The Court treated payment under an on demand guarantee as analogous to payment under a confirmed documentary credit. Lord Denning M.R. observed:[51]

> "All this leads to the conclusion that the performance guarantee stands on a similar footing to a letter of credit. A bank which gives a performance guarantee must honour that guarantee according to its terms. It is not concerned in the least with the relations between the supplier and the customer; nor with the question whether the supplier has performed his contracted obligation or not; nor with the question whether the supplier is in default or not. The bank must pay according to its guarantee, on demand, if so stipulated, without proof or conditions. The only exception is when there is a clear fraud of which the bank has notice."

The bank will issue an on demand bond normally only on the counter-indemnity of the seller. The bond will usually state the maximum liability of the bank and has an expiry date. The Export Credits Guarantee Depart-

---

[48] *R. D. Harbottle (Mercantile) Ltd.* v. *National Westminster Bank Ltd.* [1977] 3 W.L.R. 752; *Edward Owen Engineering Ltd.* v. *Barclays Bank International Ltd.* [1977] 3 W.L.R. 764.

[49] *Howe Richardson Scale Co. Ltd.* v. *Polimex Cekop and National Westminster Bank* (1977) B.L.T. No. 270.

[50] *Edward Owen Engineering Ltd.* v. *Barclays Bank International Ltd.* [1977] 3 W.L.R. 764.

[51] *Ibid.* 773.

ment provides ECGD guarantees for bond support subject to certain conditions; in particular, the contract must be valued at £250,000 or more if support is sought for an on demand bond.[51a]

It is possible to make a performance guarantee conditional on the establishment of an event other than the demand by the buyer, such as the production of a judgment or award in favour of the buyer or the certificate of a neutral person that the money should be paid to the buyer. Banks are disinclined to issue conditional bonds because they do not want to be involved in disputes between the seller and the buyer. But other financial institutions such as surety or insurance companies, are prepared to issue conditional guarantees.

The on demand bond involves the seller in a heavy risk. "Performance guarantees in such unqualified terms," said Kerr J.[52] "seem astonishing, but I am told that they are by no means unusual, particularly in transactions with customers in the Middle East." The seller will try to reduce the risk inherent in this type of transaction by keeping the amount of the bank guarantee as low as possible.

Certificates of Quality and of Inspection

Certificates of quality, which should not be confused with certificates of origin,[53] are used in the export trade from time to time. Parties may, *e.g.*, arrange that the seller should provide a certificate of quality "by experts,"[54] a government certificate that certain army surplus goods were "new,"[55] that the goods—fruit—should be covered by "phytopathological certificates of freedom from disease"[56] or by a certificate certifying that the goods were of the quality of a trade association's "standard sample,"[57] or that "certificates for maize in government elevators"[58] should be produced; the parties may also agree that a certificate as to composition or quality should be given by the seller himself.[59]

Certificates of quality are of two types: certificates of standard quality addressed to all the world (also known as certificates *in rem*) and certificates

---

[51a] See p. 285, *post*.

[52] In *R. D. Harbottle (Mercantile) Ltd.* v. *National Westminster Bank Ltd.* [1977] 3 W.L.R. 752, 756.

[53] On certificates of origin, see p. 67, *ante*.

[54] *Equitable Trust Company of New York* v. *Dawson Partners Ltd.* (1926) 27 Ll.L.R. 49; see p. 248, *post*.

[55] *Bank Melli Iran* v. *Barclays Bank (Dominion, Colonial and Overseas)* [1951] 2 Lloyd's Rep. 367.

[56] *Yelo* v. *S. M. Machado & Co. Ltd.* [1952] 1 Lloyd's Rep. 183; *Phoenix Distributors Ltd.* v. *L. B. Clarke (London)* [1966] 2 Lloyd's Rep. 285.

[57] *F. E. Hookway & Co.* v. *Alfred Isaacs & Sons* [1954] 1 Lloyd's Rep. 491.

[58] *South African Reserve Bank* v. *Samuel* (1931) 40 Ll.L.R. 291. See: *Re Reinhold & Co. and Hansloh* (1896) 12 T.L.R. 422; *Foreman & Ellams Ltd.* v. *Blackburn* [1928] 2 K.B. 60; *Panchaud Frères S.A.* v. *Etablissements General Grain Co.* [1969] 2 Lloyd's Rep. 109.

[59] *Groupement National d'Achat des Tourteaux* v. *Sociedad Industrial Financiera Argentina* [1962] 2 Lloyd's Rep. 192.

of contract requirements addressed to the parties to the contract (so-called certificates *in personam*).[59] What type of certificate is required depends on the intention of the contracting parties. Examples of certificates of standard quality are a certificate of a public analyst or of a recognised engineering, shipbuilding or surveying classification organisation,[60] *e.g.* a Lloyd's certificate.

Certificates of quality *in personam* state sometimes that they shall be "final as to quality." In this case the certificate is binding on the seller and buyer even though the certifier acted negligently; but it ceases to be binding if it is set aside by a court or arbitration tribunal or revoked by the certifier.[61] Further, the parties to a contract of sale may draw a distinction between the quality of the goods and their condition, when they are loaded, and in such a case the certificate is not final with respect to the condition of the goods.[62] If the parties have omitted to draw that distinction, then "quality of goods" includes their state or condition.[63]

A certificate of inspection is not identical with a certificate of quality. The minimum requirements for such a certificate are that the inspector has visually inspected the goods and found them to be in apparent good condition. If a particular method of inspection shall be adopted or particular information as the result of the inspection shall be recorded, such as the test results of electrical appliances, the buyer must expressly stipulate this.[64] The contract between the inspecting organisation and its client is known as the *contract of goods inspection*.[65] Of the numerous inspecting organisations dealing with general merchandise, three may be mentioned here, as they are represented in most ports and many commercial centres of the world: Cargo Superintendents Ltd., London; Société Générale de Surveillance, Geneva; and Superintendence Co. Inc., New York.

Liquidated Damages or Penalties

The parties are at liberty to provide in their contract that in the case of non-performance or delayed performance the party in default shall pay a fixed sum the amount of which may be calculated either as a lump sum or on a scale varying with the length of the default.[66]

In British contracts concerning the export of merchandise, clauses fixing the amount recoverable on breach are seldom met but they are common in international standard contract forms, such as those used in the commodity trade[67] or sponsored by the United Nations Economic Council for

---

[60] *Minster Trust Ltd.* v. *Traps Tractors Ltd.* [1954] 1 W.L.R. 963, 977–979.
[61] *Alfred C. Toepfer* v. *Continental Grain Co.* [1973] 1 Lloyd's Rep. 289.
[62] *Cremer* v. *General Carriers S.A.* [1974] 1 W.L.R. 341, 354.
[63] See Sale of Goods Act 1893, s. 62.
[64] *Commercial Banking Co. of Sydney Ltd.* v. *Jalsard Pty. Ltd.* [1973] A.C. 279.
[65] See A. Goldštajn, "The Contract of Goods Inspection" in (1965) 14 Am.J.Comp.Law 383. Also Uniform Commercial Code, s. 2–515.
[66] As, *e.g.* in case of demurrage.
[67] See p. 51, *ante*.

Europe,[68] or in the General Conditions of Delivery of Goods used in the countries of CMEA.[69]

In English law[70] a fixed sum payable on breach of contract may either be *liquidated damages* or a *penalty*. It is the former if the contract, upon its proper construction, reveals the intention of the parties genuinely to pre-estimate the damages suffered by the breach of contract; it is the latter if the intention of the parties is to secure the performance of the contract by the imposition of a fine or penalty; such intention is, in particular, evident if the fixed sum is disproportionate to the possible or probable amount of damages, *i.e.* if it is extravagant or unconscionable. The genuine intention of the parties has to be ascertained; the use of the terms "liquidated damages" or "penalties" in the clause, though indicative of the parties' intention, is not conclusive. If the sum fixed in the contract qualifies as liquidated damages, the court will award that sum and it is no obstacle to its recovery that the consequences of the breach are such as to make the pre-estimate of damages almost an impossibility; it is equally irrelevant that the loss actually suffered is lower or higher. If, on the other hand, the fixed sum qualifies as a penalty, it will be ignored by the court.[71] The differences between these two types of clauses are also important in the law of procedure: if the clause stipulates liquidated damages, the party who claims damages need not prove the amount of damages but if it is a penalty clause (which, as has been seen, is ignored) he has to prove the amount of damages which he wants to recover.

A liquidated damages clause makes it unnecessary for the parties to have damages fixed by the court. The quantification of damages is a matter of mathematical calculation. The clause offers advantages not only to the buyer but also to the supplier because it limits his liability, unless he is in fundamental breach and section 3 of the Unfair Contract Terms Act 1977 applies.

As regards the treatment of penal contract clauses in other legal systems, Mr. Peter Benjamin refers to[72]—

> the extreme complexity of French, German or Soviet law on the subject of penal clauses, for starting from the principle that penal clauses are or are not subject to modification, each system has grafted on the rule it has adopted a whole series of exceptions that give rise to considerable uncertainty in practice. . . .

These observations do not, however, apply to the common law countries, such as Australia, New Zealand or the United States of America, in which the English distinction between liquidated damages and penalties is accepted. On the whole, there is justification in Mr. Benjamin's conclusion

---

[68] See p. 52, *ante*. In the ECE contract forms the fixed sums are described as "allowances."

[69] See p. 49, *ante*. In the General Conditions for Delivery the fixed sums are described as "sanctions" and are payable in case of delayed performance.

[70] See *Dunlop Pneumatic Tyre Co. Ltd.* v. *New Garage and Motor Co. Ltd.* [1915] A.C. 70, 87; further, *Ford Motor Co.* v. *Armstrong* (1915) 31 T.L.R. 267; *Law* v. *Redditch Local Board* [1892] 1 Q.B. 127, 132.

[71] *Lamdon Trust Ltd.* v. *Hurrell* [1955] 1 W.L.R. 391.

[72] "Penal Clauses in Commercial Contracts" in (1960) 9 I.C.L.Q. 600, 627.

that in international commercial transactions "these clauses, which appear so attractive at first sight, are a deadly weapon, due to the confusion and uncertainty engendered thereby in commercial relations," and that it is doubtful whether their procedural advantage is "a sufficient counterbalance to their uncertainty from the point of view of substantive law."

CHAPTER 9

ACCEPTANCE AND REJECTION OF GOODS

IN the performance of a contract of international sale the rules relating to the examination, acceptance and rejection of the goods are of great practical importance: questions connected with them often give rise to disputes between the parties and it happens sometimes that a buyer who would be entitled to reject the goods as not conforming with the contract forfeits this right by acting without regard to the legal position.

If the contract is governed by English law,[1] these rules are founded on the Sale of Goods Act 1893, as amended by the Misrepresentation Act 1967, the Supply of Goods (Implied Terms) Act 1973 and the Unfair Contract Terms Act 1977.[1a] While the Act of 1893 does not, on principle, differentiate between home and international sales, the amending Acts of 1973 and 1977, when dealing with the exclusion of terms implied by statute, provide for a different treatment of consumer sales, other sales in the home market and international sales. The definition of an international supply contract has already been considered and it has been seen that the prohibitions and restrictions of the Acts of 1973 and 1977 do not apply to those contracts.[2] The parties to an international sale may also adopt the Uniform Laws on International Sales, appended to the Uniform Laws on International Sales Act 1967; they will be treated later.[3]

The general principle on which the regulation of the Sale of Goods Act rests is that if the buyer is deemed to have accepted the goods he loses his right to reject them. But he does not lose all rights with respect to them: although he is now bound to retain them he can still claim damages if the value of the goods which were actually delivered is less than the value of the goods which the seller promised to supply. This claim for damages is not lost as the result of legal rules peculiar to the sale of goods. It is governed by general legal principles; thus it is not lost by lapse of time until it becomes barred under the Limitation Act 1939; since most mercantile contracts are in the nature of simple contracts the seller is normally[4] entitled to plead the defence of limitation after the lapse of six years from the breach of contract. The tendency of English sales law is thus to discourage the rejection of goods by the buyer but to admit, without serious restriction or qualification, his claim for damages if he has overpaid their value, as expressed in the contract price.

[1] See p. 75, *ante*, and p. 125, *post*.
[1a] See p. 7, *ante*.
[2] See p. 65, *ante*.
[3] See p. 140, *post*.
[4] The period of limitation may be longer if there is a new accrual of the action as the result of an acknowledgment in writing or part payment, or in case of fraud or of similar circumstances.

Conditions, Warranties and Innominate Terms

According to the Sale of Goods Act, the terms of the contract of sale are either *conditions* or *warranties*. This simple classification has proved to be insufficient in modern commercial circumstances and the courts have supplemented it by recognising a third type of contractual term, the *innominate term*, also referred to as the intermediate term.

We shall first consider the distinction between conditions and warranties and then deal with the innominate term.

Conditions and warranties

The buyer is entitled to reject the goods if a condition relating to them is broken, *e.g.* if they are not in accordance with their description in the contract (s. 13),[5] if they are unsuitable for the particular purpose for which, with the knowledge of the seller, they are bought (s. 14(3)), if they do not correspond with the sample (s. 15),[6] or with sample and description (s. 13), or if they are not of merchantable quality, a condition normally implied into some of these contracts.[7] These defects have one feature in common: a *condition* of the contract of sale is broken. A condition is a term to which the parties, when making the contract, attribute such importance that it can truly be described as being of the essence of the contract. A condition has to be distinguished from a *warranty*, a contract term of less significance which relates to matters collateral to the main purpose of the contract (s. 62). In the case of breach of a warranty the buyer is not entitled to reject the goods. He has to retain them but may claim damages which, if the goods have an available market, are prima facie the difference between the value of the goods as delivered and the value they would have if they had answered to the warranty (s. 53(3)).[8] As a condition is of higher legal quality than a warranty, every condition includes a warranty—a statement which cannot be reversed. The buyer is, therefore, at liberty to treat a broken condition as a broken warranty and, instead of rejecting the goods, he may keep them and claim the difference between those two values by way of damages (s. 11(1)(*a*)). If the buyer is deemed by the law to have accepted the goods (s. 35) and if, consequently, he has lost his right to reject them, he is bound henceforth to treat what originally was a condition as a warranty and his only claim is for damages for breach of warranty (s. 11(1)(*c*)).

In the eyes of the law the breach of a condition operates as a repudiation of the contract by the party who broke the condition.[9] Consequently, a

---

[5] The references in this chapter are to the Sale of Goods Act 1893, as amended by the Supply of Goods (Implied Terms) Act 1973 and Unfair Contract Terms Act 1977. The wording of the Sale of Goods Bill 1979 differs in some provisions.

[6] Provided that the contract, by its terms, is by sample (s. 15(1)).

[7] See s. 14(2).

[8] If he has not yet paid the full price, he may set off his claim for damages against the price in diminution or extinction of the latter (s. 53(1)(*a*)).

[9] See s. 11(1)(*a*).

buyer who is entitled to reject the goods is in the same position as a buyer to whom the goods were not tendered at all unless the broken term has to be treated as an innominate term,[10] or the rule of insignificance[11] or special considerations, such as a trade custom or an agreement of the parties to the contrary,[12] apply. In the normal case the buyer is entitled to claim damages from the seller for the non-delivery of the goods (s. 51). If he has paid the purchase price in advance he can recover it by way of damages, and if he has suffered other reasonably foreseeable loss, he can recover damages likewise. These damages will often be considerably higher than damages for breach of warranty. The practical point in the distinction between the buyer's right to reject the goods on the ground that a condition of the contract is broken and his right to claim damages for breach of warranty is often that in the former instance the buyer can claim damages on a higher scale than in the latter.

The innominate term

This is a contractual term which is neither a condition nor a warranty. Its characteristic is that, if the contract is broken, the effect of the breach depends on its nature and gravity.[13] If the breach is grave, the innocent party can treat the contract as rescinded but if the breach is not serious the contract subsists and the innocent party can only claim damages for any loss which he may have suffered.

The concept of the innominate term was developed in shipping contracts with respect to the stipulation that the ship should be seaworthy.[14] Unseaworthiness could be of serious or trifling character and its effect on the contract varied according to the facts which made the ship unseaworthy. The concept of the innominate term is of growing importance and has been extended to other types of contract, notably to the contract of sale.[15] Lord Wilberforce referred to it as "the modern doctrine" when he said[16]:

> The general law of contract has developed along much more rational lines . . ., in attending to the nature and gravity of a breach or departure rather than in accepting rigid categories which do or do not automatically give a right to rescind, and if the choice were between extending cases under the Sale of Goods Act 1893 into other fields, or allowing more modern doctrine to infect those cases, my preference would be clear.

---

[10] See below in the text.

[11] *De minimis non curat lex*; see *Moralice (London) Ltd* v. *E. D. and F. Man* [1954] 2 Lloyd's Rep. 526; *Rapalli* v. *K. L. Take Ltd.* [1958] 2 Lloyd's Rep 469.

[12] The conditions of trade associations which, *e.g.* in the commodity trade are widely adopted, sometimes exclude the rejection of goods.

[13] *Hongkong Fir Shipping Co. Ltd.* v. *Kawasaki Kisen Kaisha Ltd.* [1962] 2 Q.B. 26; *United Dominions Trust (Commercial) Ltd.* v. *Eagle Aircraft Services Ltd.* [1968] 1 W.L.R. 74, 80, 82; *The Mihalis Angelos* [1971] 1 Q.B. 164; *Cehave N.V.* v. *Bremer Handelsgesellschaft mbH, The Hansa Nord* [1975] 3 W.L.R. 447, 455, 464, 476; *Reardon Smith Line Ltd.* v. *Yngvar Hansen-Tangen* [1976] 1 W.L.R. 989, 998.

[14] *Hongkong Fir Shipping Co. Ltd.* v. *Kawasaki Kisen Kaisha Ltd.* [1962] 2 Q.B. 26.

[15] *Cehave N.V.* v. *Bremer Handelsgesellschaft mbH, The Hansa Nord* [1975] 3 W.L.R. 447.

[16] In *Reardon Smith Line Ltd.* v. *Yngvar Hansen-Tangen* [1976] 1 W.L.R. 989, 998; see also Lord Wilberforce in *Bremer Handelsgesellschaft mbH* v. *Vanden Avenne Izegem PVBA* [1978] 2 Lloyd's Rep. 109, 113, and p. 123, *post*. See also *Krohn & Co.* v. *Mitsui and Co. Europe GmbH* [1978] 2 Lloyd's Rep. 419.

An illustration of the application of the innominate term in the law of international sales is provided by *Cehave N.V.* v. *Bremer Handelsgesellschaft mbH, The Hansa Nord.*[17] Bremer Handelsgesellschaft, a German company, sold a quantity of U.S. orange pellets c.i.f. Rotterdam to Cehave, a Dutch company. The pellets were to be used in the manufacture of cattle food. The contract was made on a form of the Cattle Food Trade Association which contained the term "Shipment to be made in good condition." The consignment in issue was about 3,400 metric tons and was carried in *The Hansa Nord*. The contract price, converted into pound sterling, was about £100,000 but the market price at the time of arrival of the ship had fallen considerably. On discharge from *The Hansa Nord* the cargo ex hold no. 1 (1,260 tons) was found to be damaged but the cargo ex hold no. 2 (2,053 tons) was in good condition. The buyers rejected the whole consignment. The Rotterdam court ordered its sale. It was purchased by a middleman for a sum which, after deduction of the expenses, amounted to an equivalent of £29,903. The middleman sold the pellets the same day for the same price to the original buyers who took them to their factory and used them for the manufacture of cattle food although they had to admix a smaller quantity of pellets than they would have done if part of the consignment had not been damaged. The total result of the transaction was that the Dutch buyers received goods which they had bought for £100,000 at the reduced price of about £30,000. The case went to arbitration and then to the courts. The Court of Appeal held that the contractual term "shipment to be made in good condition" was not a condition within the meaning of the Sale of Goods Act 1893 but was an innominate term. Lord Denning M.R. said[18]:

> If a small portion of the whole cargo was not in good condition and arrived a little unsound, it should be met by a price allowance. The buyers should not have the right to reject the whole cargo unless it was serious or substantial.

The court held that the buyers were not entitled to reject the whole consignment but were entitled to damages for the difference in value between the damaged and sound goods on arrival in Rotterdam. The case was remitted to the arbitrators for the determination of these damages.

Examination of Goods

When the seller tenders delivery of the goods, the buyer, unless otherwise agreed, is entitled to request that he be given a reasonable opportunity of examining the goods for the purpose of ascertaining whether they are in conformity with the contract (s. 34(2)). A buyer who has not previously examined the goods is not deemed to have accepted them and, consequently, has not lost his right to reject them unless and until he has had a reasonable opportunity of examining them (s. 34(1)).

---

[17] *Cehave N.V.* v. *Bremer Handelsgesellschaft mbH, The Hansa Nord* [1975] 3 W.L.R. 447.
[18] *Ibid.* 456.

There exists, thus, a prima facie presumption that the place and time of examination are the place and time of delivery of the goods. This presumption is, however, displaced where the arrangements of the parties, the circumstances of the sale or a trade custom point to a different intention of the parties. Bailhache J. observed in one case [19]:

> In order to postpone the place of inspection it is necessary that there should be two elements: the original vendor must know, either because he is told or by necessary inference, that the goods are going farther on, and the place at which he delivers must either be unsuitable in itself or the nature or packing of the goods must make inspection at that place unreasonable.

An illustration of exceptional circumstances in which the place and time of examination were postponed occurred in *B. & P. Wholesale Distributors* v. *Marko Ltd.*, [20] in which the sellers, importers of meat, sold one ton of fat salted backs with rind to the buyers who were wholesale purveyors of meat. The buyers had an opportunity of inspecting the meat cursorily at the docks in London when it arrived, but failed to avail themselves of it and had it taken to their depot in Chester. In the depot the buyers noticed that the meat was not in accordance with the contract: they rejected it and stopped the cheque for the price which they had given the sellers. The latter sued the buyers on the cheque and the buyers counterclaimed for damages for non-delivery of the goods. Pearson J. decided in favour of the buyers. The learned judge held that the place of delivery was the docks in London but that the place of examination was postponed to the buyers' depot in Chester. He observed that the true meaning of section 34 of the Sale of Goods Act 1893 was that it must be possible and practicable to make a proper examination of the goods, and until such opportunity was afforded to the buyers they were not deemed to have accepted the goods within the meaning of section 35. In further support of his judgment, the learned judge could now refer to the words added to section 35 by the Misrepresentation Act 1967 [21]; these words make it clear that the buyer's right to reject exists until he is given a genuine opportunity of examining the goods.

In export sales the place and time of examination are frequently not those of delivery but are postponed. In a contract of export sale the place and time of delivery is, as we have seen, [22] usually defined by the special trade clause which the parties have adopted. Where the seller is not obliged to tender a bill of lading to the buyer, as in sales ex works, f.o.r. or f.o.t., f.a.s., or in strict f.o.b. contracts, physical delivery of the goods takes place in this country, [23] and where bills of lading have to be tendered, as in f.o.b. contracts providing additional services, c.i.f. contracts, and c. and f. con-

---

[19] *Saunt* v. *Belcher and Gibbons* (1920) 26 Com.Cas. 115, 119; see also *Perkins* v. *Bell* [1893] 1 Q.B. 193.

[20] *The Times*, February 20, 1953.

[21] See p. 95, *post*. See also the wording of cl. 35(1) of the Sale of Goods Bill 1979.

[22] See p. 8, *ante*.

[23] Normally when the goods are delivered to the carrier for transmission to the buyer (s. 32).

tracts, the delivery of the goods is constructive and completely divorced from the actual situation of the goods. Whether in an export sale the delivery is physical or constructive, the two conditions postulated by Bailhache J. in the case referred to earlier[24] for the postponement of the place of examination are normally satisfied: the goods are usually ordered and packed for export, and these facts alone indicate to the seller that they are going farther on, and the locality at which the delivery takes place is usually unsuitable for the examination of the goods, so that it is unreasonable to expect the buyer to carry out the examination there. Consequently, in an export sale, unless the parties have otherwise agreed or there are strong indications to the contrary or a trade custom provides a different regulation, it has to be assumed that the parties intend that the examination of the goods shall be postponed until the goods have arrived at the place of their destination and that that place is the agreed place of examination.[25] Thus, in *Molling & Co.* v. *Dean & Son Ltd.*[26] the sellers, colour printers in Germany, sold the buyers 40,000 toy books which, as they knew, the buyer had resold to sub-purchasers in the United States of America. The books were packed specially for carriage to America and the buyers, without opening the cases, sent them on to their sub-purchasers who rejected them rightly as not being in conformity with their contract and reshipped them to the original buyers (their sellers). It was held that the place of examination was postponed to America and that the buyers were entitled to reject the books and to claim by way of damages the cost of sending them to America and from there back to England, as well as the duty paid on them in New York.

In international sales, where the wharf at which the goods are landed or the Customs house into which they are taken after landing is unsuitable for examination, the place of examination is the business premises of the buyer[27] (or his agent in performance of the contract[28]). Where the place of destination is situated inland and the goods, after having been landed, have to be taken to that locality, the intended place of examination will normally be the place of ultimate destination.

It should be noted that the Act does not make the examination of the goods a condition precedent of the acceptance. It merely requires that the buyer be given a *reasonable opportunity* of examining the goods and provides that he is not deemed to have accepted the goods until he is given

---

24 *Saunt* v. *Belcher and Gibbons, supra.*

25 *Molling* v. *Dean* (1902) 18 T.L.R. 217; *Boks* v. *Rayner* (1921) 37 T.L.R. 800; *Bragg* v. *Villanova* (1923) 40 T.L.R. 154; *Scarliaris* v. *Ofverberg & Co.* (1921) 37 T.L.R. 307 (C.A.); *Biddell Bros.* v. *E. Clemens Horst Co.* [1911] 1 K.B. 934, 960; *Kwei Tek Chao* v. *British Traders and Shippers Ltd.* [1954] 2 Q.B. 459.

26 (1902) 18 T.L.R. 217.

27 This follows from *B. & P. Wholesale Distributors* v. *Marko Ltd., The Times*, February 20, 1953; see p. 93, *ante*.

28 As contrasted with an agent for the purposes of transmission (whose authority is limited to that purpose), such as a carrier, forwarder or warehouseman. (Unless, exceptionally, a buyer has a reasonable opportunity of inspecting the goods in the possession of any of those persons.)

that opportunity (s. 34(1)). Whether the buyer avails himself of that opportunity or waives his right of examination is for him to decide. He waives that right, *e.g.* by refraining from inspecting the goods when given that opportunity. In such a case the buyer loses his right to reject the goods. Thus, a buyer who after arrival of the goods orders them to be taken to his warehouse without inspecting them cannot reject them when many months later he discovers that they are faulty, because the retention of goods after the lapse of a reasonable time[29] without intimation that the goods are rejected is deemed to be an acceptance of the goods (s. 35). It is always prudent to examine the goods as early as practicable after their arrival at the place of examination, whether that is the place of delivery, the place of final destination or another place.

Where the goods have hidden defects, "not discoverable by any reasonable exercise of care or skill on an inspection,"[30] the place of examination with respect to that defect is postponed to the place at which such examination can effectively be carried out.

ACCEPTANCE OF GOODS

The acceptance of the goods should not be confused with their receipt or with their approval. The test adopted by section 35 is whether the buyer is "*deemed* to have accepted" the goods. The receipt of the goods is less than acceptance and the section does not provide that the mere receipt of the goods shall be deemed to be acceptance. On the other hand, approval is not always required by the section: in two of the three cases postulated by section 35 less than approval satisfies the statutory test and a buyer is deemed to have accepted the goods though he may not have approved them.

The buyer is deemed to have accepted the goods (s. 35)—

1. Whe he intimates to the seller that he has accepted them;
2. Except where section 34 otherwise provides,[31] when the goods have been delivered to him, and he does any act in relation to them which is inconsistent with the ownership of the seller; or
3. When, after the lapse of a reasonable time, he retains the goods without intimating to the seller that he has rejected them.

The first of these three cases is obvious and does not call for comment. As regards the third one, it should be noted that indecision on the part of the buyer may lead to the loss of his right to reject the goods, namely, if he retains them unreasonably long without intimating that he has rejected them. The Act refrains from requiring a fixed period of time within which the buyer has to intimate his rejection. "Reasonable time" is a flexible requirement which varies according to the circumstances of the case; the

[29] Assuming that he kept the goods in his warehouse unexamined an unreasonably long time.

[30] *Per* Brett J. in *Heilbutt* v. *Hickson* (1872) L.R. 7 C.P. 438, 456.

[31] These words were added by the Misrepresentation Act 1967, s. 4(2). S. 34 provides that goods are not deemed to have been accepted until the buyer has had a reasonable opportunity of examining them. On s. 34, see p. 92, *ante*.

question of what is a reasonable time is always a question of facts (s. 56). The prudent buyer will, as observed earlier,[32] examine the goods as soon as they arrive at the place of examination and will then decide whether to reject them or to keep them.

Of particular importance is the second case. First, this contingency arises only after the buyer has been afforded a reasonable opportunity of examining the goods; the words added by the Misrepresentation Act 1967 make this clear. Secondly, "an act inconsistent with the ownership of the seller" is deemed to be an acceptance of the goods only after the goods have been delivered to the buyer, but the delivery need not be physical: a delivery to a carrier for transmission to the buyer, *e.g.* under an f.o.b. or c.i.f. contract, would be sufficient (s. 32).[33] An act inconsistent with the ownership of the seller is any act by which the buyer behaves as if he were the owner of the goods. Any disposal of the goods, *e.g.* a resale and dispatch or delivery of the goods to a sub-purchaser, or the pledging of them as a security, is an act inconsistent with the ownership of the seller, because thereby the buyer accepts the title to the goods although he might not have accepted their quality.[34] Assuming an exporter in London sells by sample twenty pieces of cotton goods to an importer in Sydney, Australia. He then buys the goods in the same manner from a manufacturer in Lancashire under a contract which provides for delivery (not packed for export) at his, the exporter's, premises in London. On arrival of the goods the exporter notices that they do not correspond with sample. Although, according to section 15(2)(*a*), entitled to reject the goods, he decides to ship them to Australia, hoping that his customer will accept them in performance of the contract. The Australian importer, however, rightly rejects the goods. By having dispatched the goods to Sydney, the exporter has done an act inconsistent with the ownership of the manufacturer and, by virtue of section 35, he is deemed to have accepted the goods. The exporter can still claim damages from the manufacturer for breach of warranty,[35] the measure of damages being the difference in the value of the goods as contracted for and the value of them as delivered to him. If after the export order was placed the market in cotton goods slumped in Australia but was maintained in London, the exporter can recover only the difference between the London value of the inferior goods and the value of the sound goods. The exporter may in that case suffer serious financial loss, and not merely inconvenience, as the result of losing his right to reject. He cannot avoid this result by protesting to the manufacturer or by intimating to him, before shipping the goods to Australia, that he rejects them if his customer in Australia rejects them to him. In this respect

---

[32] See p. 95, *ante*.

[33] *Kwei Tek Chao* v. *British Traders and Shippers* [1954] 2 Q.B. 459.

[34] But a mere resale of the goods (unaccompanied by a disposal or an attempted disposal of them, such as a dispatch to the sub-purchaser), or an inquiry whether the goods are saleable, is not an act inconsistent with the ownership of the seller.

[35] See p. 90, *ante*.

English law and the legal systems of Commonwealth countries which found their sales law on English law are more strict than other legal systems.[36] If the exporter, on discovering the defects of the goods, rejects them to the manufacturer at once and, *before* shipping them to Australia, obtains his agreement that the goods be shipped without prejudice to his, the exporter's, right to reject them in the case of the Australian customer rejecting them to him, he preserves his right. In short, a buyer who contemplates passing on the goods to his sub-purchaser or disposing of them otherwise cannot by a *unilateral* act preserve his right to reject the goods to his supplier but may do so *by a new agreement* made before the disposal of the goods.

In the illustration just discussed the place of examination of the goods was London. The position would be different if under the contract of sale between the exporter and the manufacturer the examination is postponed to Australia. It has been observed earlier[37] that that is the normal arrangement in international sales; it would, *e.g.* apply if the exporter sells the goods to his Australian customer f.o.b. English port and buys them from the manufacturer in this country f.o.b. Manchester, and the manufacturer, in accordance with instructions received by the exporter, has to deliver the goods, packed for export, to a forwarder in Manchester for transmission to Sydney. In this case the exporter to whom the customer in Australia has rejected is still entitled to reject the goods to his manufacturer.

If the contract is indivisible and the buyer has accepted part of the goods, he can no longer reject the other part of the goods (s. 11(1)(*c*)).[38] The position is different, however, if the seller tenders the wrong quantity of goods or tenders the contract goods mixed with others; in any of these cases the buyer is entitled to reject the whole consignment or to accept the contract goods and to reject the others, but if he accepts a smaller or larger quantity than he bought he has to pay for what he accepted (s. 30). Where the buyer has bought "assorted" goods but is tendered only one type of goods he is entitled to accept a reasonable percentage of the tendered goods and to reject the remainder.[39]

Rejection of Goods

A buyer who wishes to reject the goods has to intimate to the seller that he refuses to accept them (s. 36). This notice should be clear and definite and should not be contradicted by an act relating to the goods by which the buyer denies the title of the seller to the goods. No form is prescribed for the notice of rejection; it may be given verbally or in writing but the buyer should make certain that it reaches the seller, otherwise it is ineffective.

---

[36] As is demonstrated by *Benaim* v. *Debono* [1924] A.C. 514, which is discussed on p. 131, *post*.

[37] See p. 94, *ante*.

[38] *J. Rosenthal & Sons Ltd.* v. *Esmail* [1965] 1 W.L.R. 1117; see p. 99, *post*. Cl. 11(4) of the 1979 Bill corresponds to s. 11(1)(*c*) of the 1893 Act.

[39] *Ebrahim Dawood* v. *Heath (est. 1927)* [1961] 2 Lloyd's Rep. 512.

The buyer who rejects the goods is not bound to return them to the seller unless this is agreed (s. 36) but, being a bailee, he has to exercise reasonable care with respect to them. Subject to this obligation, the risk of loss of, or damage to, the goods is with the seller.

In appropriate cases the buyer may reject the goods even before having received them, namely, if he notices from a provisional invoice or advice note that the seller has dispatched goods which are not in accordance with the contract.[40] A seller, except in c.i.f. sales, who has tendered goods not in accordance with the contract may cancel the original tender and make another tender but only if he can make the other tender within the time stipulated in the contract.[41] Branson J. said in one case[42]

> It does not prevent the seller, if he has time within which to do so, from tendering another parcel of goods, which may be goods which accord with the contract, and which the buyer must, therefore, accept and pay for. . . . It cannot be predicated in any particular case that, if the first tender is not a proper tender, there may not yet be another tender which is a proper tender.

Right of rejection in c.i.f. contracts

Some observations have to be added on c.i.f. contracts. As has been explained earlier,[43] the characteristic feature of these contracts is the importance attributed to the shipping documents. It has been held, *obiter*, in *Kwei Tek Chao* v. *British Traders and Shippers Ltd.*[44] that a disposal of the bill of lading (which is part of the shipping documents) is not necessarily an act inconsistent with the seller's ownership of the goods and that, in principle, a c.i.f. buyer does not lose his right to reject the goods by dealings with forged documents, *e.g.* by pledging the bill of lading to a bank. In that case, the question whether by dealing with the documents the buyers had done an act inconsistent with the sellers' ownership in the goods did not arise, but in the interest of "those who may be concerned" Devlin J. observed that so long as a buyer was merely dealing with the documents, he did not commit an act inconsistent with the seller's ownership in the goods and retained the right of rejecting the goods if upon examination after their arrival they were found not to be in conformity with the contract. The formidable argument that the buyer, when reselling the bill of lading or pledging it to a bank, intended to give the sub-purchaser or pledgee a proprietary interest in the goods and passed title to him, was rejected by Devlin J. on the grounds that the buyer himself had only *conditional* property, *viz.* property conditional on the goods being in accordance with the contract and that therefore he could not deal with more than conditional property. Devlin J. said[45]:

---

[40] *E. E. & Brian Smith (1928) Ltd.* v. *Wheatsheaf Mills Ltd.* [1939] 2 K.B. 302.
[41] *Ibid.*; and *Borrowman* v. *Free* (1878) 4 Q.B.D. 500.
[42] *E. E. & Brian Smith (1928) Ltd.* v. *Wheatsheaf Mills Ltd.* [1939] 2 K.B. 302, 314.
[43] See p. 29, *ante*.
[44] [1954] 2 Q.B. 459; see also p. 33, *ante*.
[45] [1954] 2 Q.B. 459, 487.

I think that the true view is that what the buyer obtains when the title under the documents is given to him, is the property in the goods, subject to the condition that they revest if upon examination he finds them to be not in accordance with the contract. That means that he gets only conditional property in the goods, the condition being a condition subsequent. All his dealings with the documents are dealings only with that conditional property in the goods. It follows, therefore, that there can be no dealing which is inconsistent with the seller's ownership unless he deals with something more than the conditional property.

Rejection where each delivery to be treated as separate contract

The contract may provide that "each delivery is to be treated as a separate contract."[46] Unless delivery by instalments is arranged, this term gives the seller an option; he may deliver in one consignment, in which case there is one indivisible contract, or he may make several deliveries, in which case there are several separate contracts. The seller exercises this option by the mode of performance.[47] Where the contract is on c.i.f. terms, the fact that the seller has shipped under separate bills of lading in different vessels indicates clearly that he has exercised the option in favour of several contracts. Difficult is the position if he ships under separate bills of lading in the same vessel; here it is a question of intention of the parties, *i.e.* whether they intend that there should be one transaction or several contracts. In one case[47] a seller in Hongkong sold 140 bales of grey cotton poplin to cotton converters in Manchester. The contract was c.i.f. Liverpool and provided that each delivery was to be treated as a separate contract. The seller shipped the whole consignment in the same ship but for reasons connected with the quota regulation in Hongkong the goods were shipped under two bills of lading, each relating to half the consignment. The buyers accepted one bill of lading and rejected the other. The House of Lords held that in the special circumstances of this case—the buyers requiring the goods for their own use and not for resale—the parties, in spite of the shipment under two separate bills of lading, treated the transaction as one, and the buyers, having accepted part of the goods, could no longer reject the other part.[48] This case, however, was founded on special facts. Normally, when the contract contains a separation clause and the goods are shipped under separate bills of lading, it has to be inferred that the parties intend that there should be several contracts.[49]

---

[46] In *Cehave N.V.* v. *Bremer Handelsgesellschaft mbH, The Hansa Nord* [1975] 3 W.L.R. 447, 450 the contract provided: ". . . each shipment shall be considered a separate contract."

[47] *J. Rosenthal & Sons Ltd.* v. *Esmail* [1965] 1 W.L.R. 1117.

[48] See p. 97, *ante*.

[49] A different question is whether shipments under several bills of lading constitute "partial shipments" for the purposes of documentary credits, entitling the bank to reject such bills of lading in the absence of contrary instructions. Here the Uniform Customs and Practice for Documentary Credits 1974 (see p. 246, *post*) provide in art. 35(2) that "shipments made on the same ship and for the same voyage, even if the bills of lading evidencing shipment 'on board' bear different dates and/or indicate different ports of shipment, will not be regarded as partial shipments."

Property in rejected goods

The property in the rejected goods revests in the seller when he accepts the rejection.[50] When he does not accept the rejection, it is believed that, if it is later decided by the court or arbitration tribunal that the rejection was justified, the property likewise revests in the seller because, as Devlin J. observed in the *Kwei Tek Chao* case,[51] the property passes to the buyer subject to a condition subsequent, namely, that on examination the goods are found to be in accordance with the contract. A buyer who has paid the price in advance and then rejects the goods is not entitled to retain them by virtue of an "unpaid buyer's lien"[52] until the price is refunded. In the case of c.i.f. contracts, dealings with the documents do not affect the right of the buyer to reject the goods, which right normally arises only after the arrival of the goods when they can be examined.[53]

Rejection and estoppel

If the buyer has a valid ground for the rejection of the goods but so conducts himself as to lead the seller to believe that he is not relying on that ground, he is estopped—precluded—from setting up that ground of rejection when it would be unfair or unjust to allow him so to do.[54] On the other hand, if a buyer has rejected the goods on a ground which he has notified to the seller, he is not confined to that ground and can later rely on other grounds for the rejection.[55]

Rejection and frustration

If owing to a frustrating event the rejection of the goods becomes impossible, it would appear that the buyer has lost the right to reject the goods.[56]

Relaxation of Strict Performance of Contract[57]

It happens sometimes that a party to a contract of international sale does not insist on strict performance of the contract because the other party asks for indulgence. The buyer may ask the seller to defer the date of delivery of the goods or the date of payment of the price, or the seller may ask for extension of the shipping time. The party to whom such request is addressed may fully realise that, according to the terms of the contract, he is entitled to refuse it and, if the other party does not perform, he may

---

[50] *J. L. Lyons & Co.* v. *May & Baker* [1923] 1 K.B. 685, 688.
[51] [1954] 2 Q.B. 459; see p. 98, *ante*.
[52] An analogy to the unpaid seller's lien (see p. 104, *post*) is not admissible: *J. L. Lyons & Co.* v. *May & Baker* [1923] 1 K.B. 685.
[53] See p. 98, *ante*.
[54] *Panchaud Frères S.A.* v. *Etablissements General Grain Co.* [1970] 1 Lloyd's Rep. 53, 57.
[55] *Ibid.* p. 56.
[56] *Mackay* v. *Dick* (1881) 6 App.Cas. 251; *Colley* v. *Overseas Importers* [1921] 3 K.B. 302.
[57] This paragraph is founded on Clive M. Schmitthoff, *Legal Aspects of Export Sales*, published by the Institute of Export (3rd ed., 1978), pp. 14–16.

treat the contract as repudiated and claim damages. But he may not wish to stand on his rights, for reasons of business policy. From the legal point of view this reasonable attitude might cause considerable difficulty. If the party who has been asked to relax the terms of the contract asks for a consideration in return for the favour, there is a true contract to vary the terms of the original contract and the new agreement is binding on both parties; but if the favour is merely a voluntary forbearance to insist on strict performance, the position is different. In that case, if "one party has by its conduct led the other to alter his position"[58] it is probable that the former party cannot change his mind at once and insist again on his strict rights. For instance, an overseas buyer of cloth asks an export seller to defer shipment for one month, and the seller agrees. It is probable that the seller cannot arbitrarily set aside that arrangement; that view is founded on what has become known as the *doctrine of waiver* which was formulated by Denning L.J. in a commercial case[59] as follows:

> If one party, by his conduct, leads another to believe that the strict rights arising under the contract will not be insisted upon, intending that the other should act on that belief, and he does act on it, then the first party will not afterwards be allowed to insist on the strict rights when it would be inequitable for him to do so.

But that does not mean that the terms of the original contract are varied, and can no longer be relied upon. Goddard J. (as he then was) said in this connection[60]:

> If what happens is a mere voluntary forbearance to insist on delivery or acceptance according to the strict terms of the written contract, the original contract remains unaffected and the obligation to deliver and to accept the full contract quantity still continues.

And Lord Simonds observed[61]:

> I would not have it supposed, particularly in commercial transactions, that mere acts of indulgence are apt to create rights.

If, therefore, in the above example the buyer, after expiration of one month, is still unwilling to accept delivery of the goods, the seller would be entitled to revert to the original terms of the contract. Moreover, if no time limit is provided for the indulgence, the party who has agreed to relax the strict terms can likewise unilaterally notify the other party that the indulgence is over and that the strict terms of the contract shall apply

[58] *Per* Lord Simonds in *Tool Manufacturing Co. Ltd.* v. *Tungsten Electric Co. Ltd.* [1955] 1 W.L.R. 761, 764.

[59] *Plasticmoda S.p.A.* v. *Davidsons (Manchester) Ltd.* [1952] 1 Lloyd's Rep. 527; see further, *Central London Property Trust Ltd.* v. *High Trees House Ltd.* [1947] K.B. 130; *Charles Rickards Ltd.* v. *Oppenhaim* [1950] 1 K.B. 616; *Hartley* v. *Hymans* [1920] 3 K.B. 475; *Panoutsis* v. *Raymond Hadley Corpn. of New York* [1917] 2 K.B. 473; *S.C.C.M.O. (London) Ltd* v. *Société Générale de Compensation* [1956] 1 Lloyd's Rep. 290, 300; *Harlow and Jones Ltd.* v. *Panex (International) Ltd.* [1967] 2 Lloyd's Rep. 509. See also *Panchaud Frères S.A.* v. *Etablissements General Grain Co.* [1970] 1 Lloyd's Rep. 53; *Woodhouse A.C. Israel Cocoa Ltd. S.A.* v. *Nigerian Produce Marketing Co. Ltd.* [1972] A.C. 741.

[60] *Bessler Waechter Glover & Co.* v. *South Derwent Coal Co.* [1938] 1 K.B. 408, 416.

[61] *Per* Lord Simonds in *Tool Manufacturing Co Ltd.* v. *Tungsten Electric Co. Ltd.* [1955] 1 W.L.R. 761, 764.

again. Normally the party who has shown indulgence has to give the other party notice of reasonable length "for readjustment before he is allowed to enforce his strict rights"[62]; but such notice is not always essential: it is not required if it is clear from the circumstances that the period of suspension is over or that, even if notice had been given, the other party could not have complied with it. Thus, in one case[63] a French company bought goods from an English company under an f.o.b. contract which provided that the price should be paid in sterling under a banker's commercial credit to be opened in London "within a few weeks." The time for the opening of the credit expired, as the court found, on August 19; there were extensions, and on October 22 the sellers informed the buyers peremptorily that, having regard to the delay in the establishment of the credt, they considered the contract as cancelled. Devlin J. held that the peremptory notice of October 22 was sufficient and that the sellers were not obliged to give the buyers further time because even if they had given them, say, a fortnight's notice the buyers could not have complied with it as they could not obtain transferable sterling from their bank; the legal principle was expressed by the learned judge[64] as follows:

> The position of a party who has started out with a contract where time is of the essence and has allowed the time to go by is, I think, quite clearly laid down in the authorities. He has got to make time of the essence of the contract again in the normal case, and that means that he has to give notice giving the other side what is a reasonable time in all the circumstances to comply with their obligations. . . . But in my judgment, although that is the ordinary doctrine, the giving of a notice is not always essential.

These equitable principles are of great importance in international sales. They enable a seller who has voluntarily forborne to insist on the strict performance of the contract, to reintroduce those strict terms again if the necessity arises.

---

[62] Lord Tucker in *Tool Manufacturing Co. Ltd.* v. *Tungsten Electric Co. Ltd.* [1955] 1 W.L.R. 761, 785; *S.C.C.M.O.* (*London*) *Ltd.* v. *Société Générale de Compensation* [1956] 1 Lloyd's Rep. 290, 300.

[63] *Etablissements Chainbaux S.A.R.L.* v. *Harbormaster Ltd.* [1955] 1 Lloyd's Rep. 303.

[64] *Ibid.* at p. 312.

Chapter 10

THE RIGHTS OF THE UNPAID SELLER

In international sales transactions the seller normally parts with the possession of the goods before receiving the purchase price because he wants to dispatch the goods with due expedition. Even where the sale is on a cash basis, some time will elapse before the buyer's remittance reaches the seller; where the sale is a credit transaction more time will pass before the bill of exchange drawn by the seller on the buyer is settled. Much may happen during that time; the buyer may become insolvent, he may issue debentures taking priority over ordinary trading debts, he may amalgamate with a firm that is heavily indebted, or the buyer's country may prohibit payment in the stipulated currency, *e.g.* sterling. It is imperative that the seller should be properly protected here.

Where the Property has been Reserved: The Right of withholding Delivery

The law would fail in its task if it omitted to devise special rules for the protection of the seller during the vulnerable period which commences when he gives up possession of the goods and continues until he has received the price. However, here again, the best protection is the seller's forethought. The seller who parts with his goods before obtaining the price and leaves his protection to the care of the law, will find himself in a weaker position than his friend who was wise enough by express stipulation in the contract of sale to reserve the property in the goods sold until he received the purchase price. Such a clause was suggested earlier when the general conditions of sale were discussed,[1] and it has been seen[2] that the property is retained by the seller where such a stipulation is inserted in the contract or the law presumes such a stipulation, even when the seller has delivered the goods to the buyer or his agent, or to a carrier for transmission to the buyer; this far-reaching effect is recognised by section 19(1) of the Sale of Goods Act. Section 39(2) entitles the unpaid seller, who has reserved the property in the goods, to withhold their delivery, and provides that his rights against the goods shall be similar to and coextensive with the right of lien and stoppage in transitu which an unpaid seller can claim who has not reserved the property in the goods. According to some foreign laws, the United Kingdom exporter who reserves his property can claim the goods in the bankruptcy of the foreign buyer.[3] In English law he may

[1] See p. 53, *ante*.
[2] See p. 79, *ante*.
[3] In English law if the seller is a natural person and in bankruptcy the reservation of property clause may, in certain circumstances, be defeated by the role of reputed ownership; this role does not apply to companies in liquidation.

retain the goods when the buyer is in default or the buyer has become insolvent. If the buyer has become insolvent and the goods are still in transit, the seller is entitled to stop their delivery even where the bill of lading has been delivered to the buyer or his agent. By section 62(3) of the Act a person is deemed to be insolvent who either has ceased to pay his debts in the ordinary course of business or cannot pay his debts whether he has committed an act of bankruptcy or not. Since, in the cases under examination, the seller retains at all times the property in the goods, there is no objection to the seller reselling them when the buyer is in default, and the third party who buys them will obtain a good title to them.

Where the Property has not been Reserved

Where the seller has failed to reserve the property in the goods, the rights of the unpaid seller are defined in sections 38–48 of the Act. These rights, which can be claimed by implication of the law, are (s. 39(1))[4]:

1. A lien on the goods for the price while he is in possession of them.
2. In case of the insolvency of the buyer, a right of stopping the goods in transitu after he has parted with the possession of them.
3. A right of resale, as limited by the Act.

Before these rights are examined in detail, it is appropriate to state that the Act provides, in section 38, a definition of that unfortunate person, the unpaid seller, who becomes such:

1. When the whole of the price has not been paid or tendered, or
2. When a bill of exchange or other negotiable instrument has been received as conditional payment and the condition on which it was received has not been fulfilled by reason of the dishonour of the instrument or otherwise.

The rights of the unpaid seller may likewise be claimed by an agent of the seller to whom the bill of lading has been indorsed or by a consignor or confirming agent who has himself paid or is directly responsible for the price or who, for other reasons, is in the position of a seller.[5]

The unpaid seller's lien

The conditions on which the unpaid seller can exercise this right are different from those governing his right of stoppage in transitu. First, he can claim the lien only if he still has possession of the goods, whereas the right of stoppage in transitu arises, on the contrary, when he has parted with the possession of the goods. Where the seller has delivered the goods to a carrier for the purpose of transmission to the buyer, or to the buyer

---

[4] The terms of the section are very wide and appear to vest the same rights in the unpaid seller who has retained the property in the goods. This seems redundant because he can exercise these rights qua owner of the goods and, besides, nobody can have a lien on his own goods. This position is recognised by s. 39(2) whereby the unpaid owner of the goods is given a right of withholding delivery of the goods which is *similar* to the lien and the right of stoppage in transitu.

[5] See p. 105, *post*.

or his agent, the lien on the goods is lost (s. 43), but the seller is entitled to claim the right of stoppage in transitu so long as the goods are passing through the channels of communication and have not been delivered into the possession of the buyer or his agent appointed in this behalf. Secondly, whereas the right of stoppage in transitu can only be claimed when the buyer is insolvent,[6] the lien can be claimed when the buyer is in default (s. 41(1)), whether the default amounts to insolvency or not. In the case of an international sale, the seller's lien is of practical value only in exceptional and relatively unimportant cases, because he will not often have transferred the property in the goods to the buyer and, at the same time, have retained possession in them. This situation can arise only when he learns of the buyer's default while the export transaction is still in an inchoate and preliminary stage of execution. An example would be the case of goods which have been sold f.o.r., the property in which has been conveyed to the buyer's agents at the works of the seller, but which are still on the seller's private sidings; as long as the goods are on the private sidings, the seller has a lien on them, but as soon as they have been shunted to the Railway Authority's sidings and delivered into the custody of the Railway Authority, the seller loses his lien and is limited to his right of stoppage in transitu.

The seller's right of lien is merely a right to retain the possession of the goods until the purchase price is paid and is not a right to resell them. The unpaid seller has, however, in certain contingencies a right of resale under the Act[7]; sometimes such right is given by mercantile custom, *e.g.* in the tea trade. The lien cannot be claimed for storage charges incurred when the goods are stored during the buyer's default.[8]

In the case of a credit sale, the unpaid seller has no right of lien during the credit period unless, during that period, the buyer becomes insolvent (s. 41(1)(*c*)). After the expiration of the credit period he can exercise the lien in any event. The seller is entitled to the lien even if he is in possession of the goods as an agent for the buyer (s. 41(2)); a confirming house, which acts as agent for a principal abroad, may exercise the lien on goods bought on behalf of the principal if he fails to pay the commission or incidental charges.

Stoppage in transitu

This right is of much greater practical value for the exporter than the right of lien, particularly as it has always been interpreted favourably for the seller by the courts, but it should be noted that it can only be claimed if the buyer is insolvent.[9] Stoppage in transitu operates, as it were, as the outstretched arm of the seller which snatches back goods, over which the

[6] A definition of insolvency is given in s. 62(3) of the Sale of Goods Act 1893.
[7] See below in text.
[8] *Somes* v. *British Empire Shipping Co.* (1860) 30 L.J.Q.B. 229.
[9] See p. 104, *ante*.

seller has lost control, from the danger route leading to the bankruptcy of the insolvent buyer.

This right can only be exercised during the transit of the goods; that period begins when the goods have left the possession of the seller or his agent, and ends when the goods have reached the possession of the buyer or his agent who is authorised to take delivery of the goods on behalf of the buyer. The Act defines the duration of transit as the time when the goods "are delivered to a carrier by land or water, or other bailee . . . for the purpose of transmission to the buyer, until the buyer or his agent in that behalf takes delivery of them from such carrier or other bailee . . ."[10] It follows that the term "transit" has in law a technical meaning which is entirely different from its natural meaning. Goods may be "in transit" although not in motion, and goods which are in motion may never have been "in transit" in the eyes of the law. If, *e.g.* the seller under an ex works contract delivers the goods to the buyer's agent in this country, the goods pass from the possession of the seller directly to that of the buyer, and the seller cannot claim a right of stoppage while the goods are being shipped to the place of destination. Only where the goods, after having left the seller's possession, are in neutral hands, *e.g.* in the custody of a carrier, shipping agent or other independent intermediary, and only so long as they are in those hands for the purposes of transmission, can the right of stoppage be claimed. The right operates against the goods themselves; its aim is to revest possession of the goods in the seller as long as they are in the course of transit and to enable him to retain them and claim a lien on them until the purchase price is paid (s. 44). If the goods are damaged, the seller who exercises his right of stoppage has no claim in that respect, as was decided in a case concerning the importation of timber from Sweden.[11] The plaintiff, a timber merchant in Sweden, sold timber to a firm in London; the timber was duly shipped but damaged during the voyage. The buyers, who had the timber insured, stopped payment before the timber arrived in England. The seller gave notice of stoppage to the captain of the ship, and the question was whether he was entitled to the insurance money which had been paid for the damage to the timber. It was held that the claim was untenable; in the words of Lord Cairns L.C.:

> The right to stop in transitu is a right to stop the goods in whatever state they arrive. If they arrive injured or damaged in bulk or quality the right to stop in transitu is so far impaired; there is no contract or agreement which entitles the vendor to go beyond those goods in the state in which they arrive.

The right of stoppage in transitu is exercised by the seller giving notice of his claim to the carrier or the carrier's principal, or by the seller taking actual possession of the goods if he can do so without breach of the peace. The notice to the carrier's principal, *e.g.* the line in whose ships the goods

---

[10] s. 45.
[11] *Berndtson* v. *Strang* (1868) L.R. 3 Ch.App. 588.

are carried, is only effectual if given in such time and under such circumstances that the principal, by the exercise of reasonable diligence, can communicate it to his servant or agent in time to prevent a delivery to the buyer (s. 46(1)).

The right of stoppage in transitu, which originally arose by custom of the merchants, gave rise to much litigation before it was cast in its present form. It is outside the scope of this work to dwell on further details; three points, however, may shortly be indicated.

First, delivery of the goods to a carrier or agent, who takes his instructions from the buyer, does not necessarily lead to a loss of the right of stoppage; in connection with that right, section 32(1) of the Act, which has been discussed earlier,[12] does not apply. If the carrier or agent is merely the buyer's agent for the purposes of transmitting the goods, the right of stoppage in transitu can still be claimed, provided that the goods are still in the agent's possession; if, on the other hand, the agent is authorised to accept delivery of the goods in accordance with the terms of the contract and has to dispose of them in compliance with the instructions of the buyer, the right is lost. The courts will generally lean in favour of the view that the master of the ship obtains possession of the goods in his capacity as carrier and not as agent of the buyer to take delivery under the contract of sale, and this applies even where the goods are delivered on a vessel chartered by him. Thus, where the seller, under an ordinary f.o.b. contract, delivers the goods to the master of the ship, who makes out the bill of lading in the buyer's name, the goods are still "in transit," and the right of stoppage can be exercised by the seller. But where, in the course of the shipment[13] or after arrival of the goods at the place of destination, the carrier acknowledges—"attorns"—to the buyer or his agent that he holds the goods on his behalf, the transit has come to an end even if the buyer orders the transhipment of the goods to another place (s. 45(3)).

Secondly, the right of stoppage is not lost when the bill of lading is made out in the name of the buyer (or his agent), or, if originally made out in the seller's name, is delivered to the buyer. The latter act is, as has been seen,[14] decisive for the passing of the property unless the seller has reserved the right of disposal; but these acts are irrelevant for the exercise of the right of stoppage. In fact, that right acquires particular practical importance after the bill of lading has reached the buyer and he has, thus, obtained the right of disposal of the goods.

Thirdly, while normally the unpaid seller's lien or right of stoppage in transitu is not affected by a sale or other disposition which the buyer has made with respect to the goods without the seller's assent (s. 47),[15] the position is different in one case: if the bill of lading was delivered to the

---

[12] See p. 77, *ante*.

[13] *Reddall* v. *Union-Castle Mail Steamship Co. Ltd.* (1915) 84 L.J.K.B. 360.

[14] See p. 79, *ante*.

[15] A case in which the seller assented to the sale by the buyer and thereby lost his rights against the goods was *D. F. Mount* v. *Jay & Jay (Provisions) Co. Ltd.* [1960] 1 Q.B. 159.

buyer and he has indorsed it for valuable consideration to a third person who is acting in good faith, the unpaid seller's rights are defeated and the third party acquires a valid title to the goods.[16] This rule is now laid down in the proviso to section 47 of the Act; it was first established in 1794 in the celebrated case of *Lickbarrow* v. *Mason,*[17] after six years of litigation.

The right of resale

Our unpaid seller has been fortunate enough to assert his right of stoppage in transitu; the carrier has redelivered the goods to him and he has thus regained his lien on them.[18] The question is now: How to dispose of the goods? It should not be overlooked that, as has been seen earlier,[19] the lien is only a right to retain but not to dispose of the goods. The seller may have reserved the right of resale in the original contract of sale and, in this case, if the buyer makes default, the seller may exercise that right and resell the goods, with the result that the original contract of sale is rescinded, but he may still claim damages from the defaulting buyer (s. 48(4)). More frequent will be the cases where the seller did not reserve the right of resale. Here the Act gives the unpaid seller the right to resell the goods:

1. where they are of a perishable nature, without further notice to the buyer; or
2. where they are not perishable, after he—the unpaid seller—has given notice to the buyer of his intention to resell, and the buyer has not within a reasonable time paid or tendered the price.

By the exercise of the right of resale the unpaid seller has put it out of his power to perform the original contract which is rescinded.[20] The property in the goods has reverted to the seller who transfers it to the second buyer. The seller is entitled to retain the proceeds of the resale, whether they be greater or less than the original contract price.[20] If the seller makes a loss on the resale, the seller can recover damages from the defaulting buyer for breach of contract (48(1)). A third person who buys the goods on resale acquires a good title to them as against the original buyer (s. 48(2)).

[16] The same rule applies to other documents of title, *e.g.* a delivery order addressed to a wharfinger; but the third person who acquires the goods from the buyer is only protected if the buyer indorses to him the same delivery order which he himself received from the seller; the third person is not protected by the proviso to s. 47 if the buyer delivers to him a "back-to-back" delivery order, *i.e.* a new delivery order corresponding to that received by the buyer from the seller; in that case the third person may, however, claim the protection of s. 25(2) if the requirements of that section are satisfied: *D. F. Mount* v. *Jay & Jay* (*Provisions*) *Co. Ltd.* [1960] 1 Q.B. 159.

[17] (1794) 5 T.R. 683. A delivery order addressed to a warehouseman is either a promise by the seller that the goods be delivered to the buyer or a mere authority to the buyer entitling him to receive the goods; whether it is one or the other, depends on the intention of the parties: *Alicia Hosiery Ltd.* v. *Brown Shipley & Co. Ltd.* [1970] 1 Q.B. 195.

[18] An unpaid seller who has not exercised the right of lien or stoppage in transitu but is still in possession of the goods has likewise a right of resale: Diplock L.J. in *R. V. Ward Ltd.* v. *Bignall* [1967] 1 Q.B. 534, 545.

[19] See p. 105, *ante*.

[20] *R. V. Ward Ltd.* v. *Bignall* [1967] 1 Q.B. 534.

CHAPTER 11

COMMERCIAL FRUSTRATION

IT may happen that the commercial aims which the parties pursued when concluding the contract are defeated through no fault of their own but by force of supervening circumstances. The situation existing at the conclusion of the contract may subsequently have changed so completely that the parties, acting as reasonable men, would not have made the contract, or would have made it differently, had they known what was going to happen. Modern English law has developed the doctrine of commercial frustration to meet this contingency. By virtue of this doctrine the parties are free from liability for acts of performance not yet due when their contract is regarded by the law as frustrated. This doctrine is exceptional because "in the ordinary way . . . it does not matter whether the failure to fulfil a contract by the seller is because he is indifferent or wilfully negligent or just unfortunate. It does not matter what the reason is. What matters is the fact of performance. Has he performed or not?"[1]

The doctrine of commercial frustration is of great importance in international trade transactions because they imply a greater element of uncertainty than home transactions in consequence of the fact that they are subject to political and economic influences in foreign countries. It is no accident that the doctrine in its present form emerged from litigation which was primarily concerned with transactions of international trade. It is intended to deal first with the conditions upon which the doctrine of commercial frustration may be invoked, and then with the effect of its application.

LEGAL MEANING OF FRUSTRATION

Frustration occurs only where, subsequent to the conclusion of the contract, a fundamentally different situation has unexpectedly emerged. Not every turn of events which the parties did not expect satisfies this test; such uncontemplated development might make the performance of the contract more difficult, onerous or costly than was envisaged by the parties when entering into the contract; it may be due to a sudden, and even abnormal, rise or fall in prices or to the necessity of obtaining supplies from other, and dearer, sources of supply than those anticipated.[2] These events, as such, do not operate as frustrating a contract of export sale; only where they are of such magnitude as to create a fundamentally different situation

[1] Sellers J. in *Nicolene Ltd.* v. *Simmonds* [1953] 2 Lloyd's Rep. 419, 425.

[2] The doctrine of frustration can be applied to a c.i.f. contract relating to unascertained goods but, in view of the nature of such contract and the possibility of buying goods afloat, it is more difficult to find a frustrating event in this case than in others: *Lewis Emanuel & Son Ltd.* v. *Sammut* [1959] 2 Lloyd's Rep. 629.

do they result in the frustration of the contract. This is clearly stated by Lord Simon in a leading case[3] in the following passage:

> The parties to an executory contract are often faced, in the course of carrying it out, with a turn of events which they did not at all anticipate—a wholly abnormal rise or fall in prices, a sudden depreciation of currency, an unexpected obstacle to execution, or the like. Yet this does not in itself affect the bargain they have made. If, on the other hand, a consideration of the terms of the contract, in the light of the circumstances, existing when it was made, shows that they never agreed to be bound in a fundamentally different situation which has now unexpectedly emerged, the contract ceases to bind at that point—not because the court in its discretion thinks it just and reasonable to qualify the terms of the contract, but because on its true construction it does not apply in that situation.

It is evident from these observations that the modern international merchant is expected to have a considerable degree of foresight. He should therefore guard himself against an unexpected, but in the view of the law, foreseeable turn of events by ordinary commercial safeguards, such as an appropriate *force majeure* clause,[4] insurance or a hedging transaction. It is further evident that frustration in the legal sense occurs at some—often not easily predictable—stage in a sequence of events which are in gradual transition and that it is a matter of degree whether an uncontemplated event does, or does not, amount in law to frustration. Denning L.J. recognised this in one case[5] in which the Court of Appeal held that the sellers of Brazilian piassava under a c.i.f. contract containing the clause "subject to any Brazilian export licence" were not relieved from their obligation to obtain the licence by a rise in prices by 20 to 30 per cent. in excess of the prices agreed upon with their buyers. Denning L.J. said: "Was that [payment of the higher price] a step which they could reasonably be expected to take? This depends on how much was the price they had to pay to get the licence. If it was . . . 100 times as much as the contract price, that would be 'a fundamentally different situation' which had unexpectedly emerged, and they would not be bound to pay it."[6] Consequently, regarding in that case the scale of rising prices, somewhere between a rise of 30 per cent. and one of 10,000 per cent. frustration occurred.

A similar question of degree arises where it is alleged that a contract is frustrated as the result of a government prohibition of exportation or importation, or as the result of a strike. In those cases the contract might, at the beginning of the event in question, merely be suspended and might become frustrated only after the lapse of a reasonable time when it becomes clear that the delay caused by the prohibition or strike affects the foundation

---

[3] *British Movietonews Ltd.* v. *London and District Cinemas Ltd.* [1952] A.C. 166. See further, *Davis Contractors Ltd.* v. *Fareham U.D.C.* [1956] A.C. 696; *Condor* v. *The Barron Knights Ltd.* [1966] 1 W.L.R. 87.

[4] See p. 121, *post*.

[5] *Brauer & Co. (Great Britain) Ltd.* v. *James Clark (Brush Materials) Ltd.* [1952] 2 All E.R. 497, 501. See also *Hongkong Fir Shipping Co. Ltd.* v. *Kawasaki Kisen Kaisha Ltd., The Antrim* [1962] 2 Q.B. 26 (C.A.); *Exportelisa S.A.* v. *Rocco Guiseppe & Figli Soc. Coll.* [1978] 1 Lloyd's Rep. 433.

[6] See *British Movietonews Ltd.* v. *London and District Cinemas Ltd.* [1952] A.C. 166.

of the contract.[7] What is a reasonable time is again a question of degree.[8] In these cases it is not necessary to ascertain the exact date on which the contract was frustrated but it is sufficient to state that the contract was frustrated by not later than a certain date.[9]

Conditions upon which the Contract is Frustrated

It is obviously impossible to give a complete catalogue of frustrating events. The following are typical sets of circumstances in which it has been contended—often successfully—that the contract was frustrated.

Destruction of subject-matter

The simplest case of frustration occurs where the performance depends on the continued existence of a given person or thing and, after the conclusion of the contract, that person or thing has been physically destroyed. In these cases, "a condition is implied that the impossibility of performance arising from the perishing of the person or thing shall excuse the performance."[10] Where a ship was chartered but failed to load because it had been disabled by an explosion which was not due to the negligence of the shipowners and their servants, the commercial object of the contract of affreightment was held to be frustrated.[11] When the subject-matter of the contract is the sale of specific goods, as, *e.g.* is the case in the sale of secondhand machinery or antiques, this effect is expressly provided for by section 7 of the Sale of Goods Act, which lays down:

> Where there is an agreement to sell specific goods, and subsequently the goods, without any fault on the part of the seller or buyer, perish before the risk passes to the buyer, the agreement is thereby avoided.

Illegality

Outbreak of war

When, after the parties have entered into the contract, war breaks out, the question arises whether the performance of the contract is rendered illegal by that event, or is only indirectly affected by the outbreak of war.

If performance has become illegal because it would constitute an act of trading with the enemy, *e.g.* if one of the contracting parties has become

---

[7] *Reardon Smith Line Ltd.* v. *Ministry of Agriculture, Fisheries and Food* [1962] 1 Q.B. 42; reversed in part on different grounds [1963] A.C. 691.

[8] Andrew J. Bateson, "Time as an Element of Frustration" in [1954] *Business Law Review*, p. 173; see also the same, "Time in the Law of Contract" in [1957] J.B.L. 357.

[9] *Marshall* v. *Harland & Wolff Ltd.* [1972] 1 W.L.R. 899, 904.

[10] Blackburn J. in *Taylor* v. *Caldwell* (1863) 3 B. & S. 826, 839.

[11] *Joseph Constantine Steamship Line Ltd.* v. *Imperial Smelting Corporation Ltd.* [1942] A.C. 154. Frustration also takes place where parties enter into a joint venture agreement for the development of an oilfield in a foreign country and subsequently the foreign government expropriates the interests of the parties in the oilfield: *B.P. Exploration Co. (Libya) Ltd.* v. *Hunt (No. 2)* [1979] 1 W.L.R. 783.

an enemy or the place at which the contract has to be performed has passed under the control of the enemy, the contract is frustrated. Thus, in the *Fibrosa* case,[12] a Polish company had ordered certain flax-hackling machines from manufacturers in Leeds shortly before the outbreak of the Second World War. The machines had to be delivered c.i.f. Gdynia within a certain time and the contract provided that in case of war or other events beyond the control of the parties a reasonable extension of the time of delivery should be granted. After the outbreak of the war, Gdynia was occupied by the Germans. It was held by the House of Lords that the contract was frustrated owing to war and the British manufacturers were discharged from delivering the machines; even the clause allowing for extension of the time of delivery did not save the contract because it was intended to cover merely minor delay as distinguished from a prolonged and indefinite interruption of contractual performance.

If, on the other hand, outbreak of war affects the contract only indirectly, *e.g.* the contract is for the exportation of goods from Great Britain to Iran and war breaks out between one of these countries and a third country, the legality of performance is not affected by the war and the contract does not automatically become frustrated by that event. It is, of course, an entirely different question whether in those circumstances the contract might be frustrated for other reasons, in particular on the ground that its performance is prohibited by the government of Great Britain or Iran, or the foundation of the contract has gone owing to a vital change in circumstances. These questions will be examined later on[13]; it is sufficient here to observe that only in exceptional cases will the answer be in the affirmative.

Export and import prohibitions

Apart from the case of war, a contract may be frustrated because subsequent to its conclusion the government has prohibited its performance, *e.g.* by placing an embargo on the exportation or importation of the goods sold.

Here, however, great care should be applied: not every governmental prohibition has the effect of rendering the contract illegal. Sometimes the effect is merely to suspend and postpone the performance of the contract. It is always necessary to relate the prohibition to the terms of the contract, especially those governing the time of performance. The prohibition operates as a frustrating event only if it is final and extends to the whole time still available for the performance of the contract. If these conditions are not satisfied a party would be well advised to wait until the time of performance has expired before treating the contract as frustrated because

[12] *Fibrosa Spolka Akcyjna* v. *Fairbairn Lawson Combe Barbour Ltd.* [1943] A.C. 32. The effect of frustration on the *Fibrosa* case is discussed on pp. 119, 120.
[13] See *supra* and p. 114, *post*.

the prohibition may be removed in time to allow performance.[14] If the government prohibition extends beyond the stipulated time for performance it is normally safe to assume that the contract is frustrated because there is an implied condition in every contract that its performance shall be legal at the date when the contract is to be performed.[15]

The rule that a subsequent government prohibition operates as a frustrating event only if it covers the whole of the contract period applies likewise if the prohibition does not come into operation at once and exporters are allowed a time of grace during which they may perform existing contracts. In one case [16] the contract provided for the shipment of horse beans from a Sicilian port c.i.f. Glasgow during October and November 1951. By an Italian regulation dated October 20, 1951, the exportation was prohibited as and from November 1, 1951, except under special licence. The sellers failed to ship and the buyers claimed damages. Devlin J. held that they were entitled to succeed. The prohibition did not operate as a frustrating event; it merely reduced the time of shipment from two months to one month and after the issue of the Italian regulation the sellers had still ten days' grace within which they could have effected shipment. If the prohibition of export had been instantaneous it would have operated as a frustrating event, and the same would have been the case if the sellers could have proved that they had no shipping facilities during the remaining 10 days.

The question has arisen whether a State trading corporation of a country of planned economy can plead a government prohibition of exports as a frustrating event. Normally the State trading corporation which has separate legal personality will not be so closely connected with its own government as to be precluded from relying on the prohibition, but there might be exceptional cases in which it can be proved that the foreign government had taken action in order to extricate the State enterprise from its contractual obligations and in these cases the courts might arrive at a different conclusion. These rules can be inferred from a case[17] in which a Polish State trading corporation sold a quantity of sugar to English sugar merchants. The contracts, which were subject to the standard rules of the Refined Sugar Association (RSA), were made in May and July 1974 and provided for delivery in November/December of that year. The Polish State corporation had been authorised to enter into these contracts and the sugar which formed the subject matter of the contracts was intended

[14] *Andrew Millar & Co Ltd.* v. *Taylor & Co. Ltd.* [1916] 1 K.B. 402; *Austin, Baldwin & Co.* v. *Wilfred Turner & Co.* (1920) 36 T.L.R. 769; *Atlantic Maritime Co. Inc.* v. *Gibbon* [1954] 1 Q.B. 105, 114, 132; *Compagnie Algerienne de Meunerie* v. *Katana Societa di Navigatione Marittima S.p.A., The Nizetti* [1960] 2 Q.B. 115, 125–126.

[15] *Walton (Grain & Shipping Ltd.)* v. *British Italian Trading Co. Ltd.* [1959] 1 Lloyd's Rep. 223.

[16] *Ross T. Smyth & Co. Ltd. (Liverpool)* v. *W. N. Lindsay Ltd. (Leith)* [1953] 1 W.L.R. 1280; explaining *Re Anglo-Russian Merchant Traders Ltd., and John Batt & Co. (London)* [1917] 2 K.B. 679.

[17] *C. Czarnikow Ltd.* v. *Rolimpex* [1978] 3 W.L.R. 474.

to be Polish beet sugar. The force majeure clause of the RSA provided, *inter alia*, that if "government intervention" occurred, there should be an extension and ultimately a cancellation of the contracts. Owing to heavy rains in August, the sugar crop failed in Poland and on November 5 the Polish Minister of Foreign Trade signed a decree making the export of sugar illegal by Polish law. This export ban remained in force until July 1975. The State corporation failed to deliver the sugar and pleaded force majeure. The House of Lords held that that claim was justified. The State trading corporation was independent of the government and the evidence showed that the export ban was imposed in order to avoid serious domestic, social and political unrest; that was "government intervention" within the meaning of the force majeure clause in the rules of RSA.

Where, subsequent to the conclusion of the contract, the exportation or importation of goods is prohibited except by government licence, a condition is often implied into the contract obliging the parties to collaborate in all reasonable endeavours to obtain the licence. This condition will be discussed later on[18] when licensing and quota regulations and the effect of their change subsequent to the conclusion of the contract will be examined.

Fundamental change in circumstances

A contract is further frustrated if, after it was made, such a radical change of circumstances has occurred that the foundation of the contract has gone and the contract, if kept alive, would amount to a new and different contract from that originally concluded by the parties. To hold the parties to their original bargain after the original common design is gone would mean that a different contract was substituted for their original contract.

While it is usually relatively easy to ascertain whether a contract is frustrated by impossibility, physical (destruction of the subject-matter) or legal (illegality), it is often extremely difficult to decide whether in cases in which performance would still be possible a fundamentally different situation has unexpectedly arisen in which the contract ceases to bind.[19] The English decisions show that the courts consider the principle of sanctity of contracts as of infinitely higher importance than the requirements of commercial convenience and that they will not lightly assume that a contract which is still capable of performance is frustrated. Only if the change in circumstances is so profound that the parties would have replied to another person—"the officious bystander"—when the contract was made: "of

[18] See p. 117, *post*.

[19] See Lord Simon in *British Movietonews Ltd.* v. *London and District Cinemas Ltd.* [1952] A.C. 166, and Lord Radcliffe in *Davis Contractors Ltd.* v. *Fareham U.D.C.* [1956] A.C. 696, 729.

course, if that event happens, the contract is off," is the contract regarded as frustrated.[20]

If, *e.g.* the performance of a contract for the supply of goods is delayed inordinately for reasons beyond the control of the parties and consequently the prices which were fixed in relation to the then existing conditions of labour and costs of raw material are entirely outdated, it may well be argued that the foundation of the contract has gone.[21] Into this category fall further cases in which the contract aimed at the execution of a particular object which has been defeated by supervening events. Normally an event which was within the contemplation of the parties when they entered into the contract does not operate as a frustrating event even though they did not expect or consider it probable that it would happen[22]; but in exceptional cases the doctrine has been applied where the parties were aware of the possibility that the frustrating event might occur but omitted to provide for that eventuality.[23]

How difficult it is to contend successfully that a change in circumstances is so fundamental that it results in frustration, may be seen from the cases[24] which arose in connection with the closure of the Suez Canal on November 2, 1956, as the result of military operations. In these cases exporters in East Africa had sold certain goods for shipment c.i.f. specified European destinations; the contracts were made before the date of the closure of the Canal but had to be performed after that date. On the date of performance the Canal was no longer open for shipment but it was still possible to ship the goods to their destination via the Cape of Good Hope. That route was very much longer than the voyage via the Canal and caused considerable additional expense. It was clear that the additional expense was not of such magnitude as to support the view that the contracts were frustrated on that account. More difficult was the question whether the necessity to ship by the alternative route round the Cape constituted a radical difference in the character of the seller's obligation. The House of Lords[25] answered that question in the negative; the court held that the sellers were under a duty, when the usual route—via the Canal—was no longer available to send the goods by a reasonable and practicable route; such a route was in the present case still available in the route around the Cape. In the Court of

---

[20] McNair J. in *Carapanayoti & Co. Ltd.* v. *E. T. Green Ltd.* [1959] 1 Q.B. 131, 148; Pearson J. in *Lewis Emanuel & Son Ltd.* v. *Sammut* [1959] 2 Lloyd's Rep. 629.

[21] *Metropolitan Water Board* v. *Dick, Kerr & Co.* [1918] A.C. 119, 139.

[22] *Davis Contractors Ltd.* v. *Fareham U.D.C.* [1956] A.C. 696.

[23] *W. J. Tatem Ltd.* v. *Gamboa* [1939] 1 K.B. 132.

[24] *Tsakiroglou & Co. Ltd.* v. *Noblee Thorl GmbH* [1962] A.C. 93 (H.L.); *Gaon (Albert D.) & Co.* v. *Société Interprofessionelle des Oléagineux Fluides Alimentaires*; *Tsakiroglou & Co. Ltd.* v. *Noblee Thorl GmbH* [1960] 2 Q.B. 318 (C.A.); *Carapanayoti & Co. Ltd.* v. *E. T. Green Ltd.* [1959] 1 Q.B. 131 (McNair J.); *The Eugenia* [1964] 2 Q.B. 226 (C.A.) and *The Captain George K.* [1970] 2 Lloyd's Rep. 21 (where contracts of a affreightment were in issue).

[25] In the *Tsakiroglou* case, *supra*. In the court of first instance there was a considerable difference of opinion. McNair J. in *Carapanayoti's* case decided in favour, and Diplock J. in *Tsakiroglou's* and Ashworth J. in *Gaon's* case against frustration; see [1959] J.B.L. 366.

Appeal Harman L.J. stated the general attitude of the English courts to issues of frustration in the following terms[26]:

Frustration is a doctrine only too often invoked by a party to a contract who finds performance difficult or unprofitable, but it is very rarely relied upon with success. It is, in fact, a kind of last ditch, and, as Lord Radcliffe says in his speech in the most recent case,[27] it is a conclusion which should be reached rarely and with reluctance.

Export and import licences and quotas

Considerable difficulty is often caused by the imposition or strengthening of restrictive government regulations affecting the exportation and importation of goods, such as licences and quotas. Where a contract cannot be performed because the licence is not granted or the quota is too small, it is often contended that the contract is frustrated.[28] Here the following propositions should be borne in mind:

(1) *Where the contract of sale does not contain the terms "subject to licence," "subject to quota" or a similar term making it conditional*, the question arises whether the party on whom the duty falls to obtain the licence or quota[29] intended to be bound absolutely by his undertaking or whether he merely intended to use all due diligence and to take all reasonable steps to obtain the licence or quota.[30] The legal position is different in both cases. Where a party has absolutely undertaken to perform, he has warranted to obtain the licence or quota and if he fails to do so he is in breach, but where he has merely undertaken to take all reasonable steps the contract is frustrated if he can prove that he has discharged that duty but failed. The question is one of construction of his contractual undertakings.

If a party has failed to make the nature of his obligation explicit in the contract by using such a phrase as "subject to"—"a piece of phraseology," as Devlin J. observed,[31] "with which all commercial men must be very familiar"—it is very doubtful and depends entirely on the circumstances of the case what interpretation the courts will place on this undertaking. Devlin J. once said[32] that "when nothing is said in the contract it is usually, indeed I think it is probably fair to say almost invariably, the latter class of warranty that is implied," *i.e.* the warranty to use all due diligence, but

---

[26] [1960] 2 Q.B. 318, 370.

[27] In *Davis Contractors* v. *Fareham U.D.C.* [1956] A.C. 696, 727.

[28] On government prohibitions rendering performance illegal, see p. 112, *ante*.

[29] On the duty to procure an export licence under an f.o.b. contract, see p. 23, *ante* (where *A. V. Pound & Co. Ltd.* v. *M. W. Hardy & Co. Inc.* [1956] A.C. 588, is treated). On the question whether in a c.i.f. contract the seller is bound to procure goods afloat if he cannot ship from the port of shipment, see p. 36, *ante*.

[30] *Re Anglo-Russian Merchant Traders Ltd., and John Batt & Co. (London) Ltd.* [1917] 2 K.B. 679, 685, 689; *Diamond Cutting Works Federation Ltd.* v. *Triefus & Co. Ltd.* [1956] 1 Lloyd's Rep. 216, 224.

[31] In *Peter Cassidy Seed Co. Ltd.* v. *Osuustukkukauppa I.L.* [1957] 1 W.L.R. 273, 279. It should not be thought that the phrase "subject to" is a general escape clause enabling the party in whose favour it is directed to withdraw from the contract in any circumstances; see *Hong Guan & Co. Ltd.* v. *R. Jumabhoy & Sons Ltd.* [1960] A.C. 684; p. 117, *post*.

[32] [1957] 1 W.L.R. 273 at p. 277; see also the cases quoted in note 30 above.

there are also strong dicta of other judges[33] to the contrary, and, in view of the widespread use of the phrase "subject to" by exporters there is always considerable risk that, in the absence of such a phrase, the court may hold the undertaking to be absolute.

Two illustrations of absolute undertakings by the seller may be added. In one case[34] Indian sellers of jute who had sold the goods under c.i.f. contracts not containing the clause "subject to quota" found themselves unable to supply the whole quantity of goods because the quota allotted to them was too small; when the contracts were made the exportation of jute from India was prohibited except under licence and a quota system was already in force; the sellers contended that an implied term should be read into the contracts that they were subject to the necessary licences and quotas being obtainable. The House of Lords rejected that view and held that the obligation of the sellers to deliver the goods was absolute. In another case[35] sellers in Finland sold to an English company a quantity of ant eggs f.o.b. Helsinki, "delivery: prompt, as soon as export licence granted." The sellers were unable to obtain the export licence and to ship, although they used all due diligence, because they were not members of the Finnish Ant Egg Exporters' Association. Devlin J. held that "as soon as" was not the same as "subject to" and that the sellers had undertaken absolutely to obtain the licence earlier or later; the learned judge upheld an award holding the sellers liable to pay damages to the buyers.

(2) *Where the contract of sale contains the term "subject to licence," "subject to quota" or a similar term making it conditional*, this clause gives the seller some, but not complete, protection: the seller is free from his obligation to deliver the goods but only if he can show that although he used *due diligence and took all reasonable steps* he was unable to obtain the licence or to comply with the government regulation, or that he could do so only on prohibitive terms which he could not reasonably be expected to accept. If he remains inactive and makes no attempt to obtain the licence because, as he alleges, such an attempt would have been useless, the burden that the attempt would have failed rests on him and, in the words of Devlin J., it "is always a difficult burden for a party to assume."[36] If the seller is ignorant of a local requirement of an export licence and therefore has failed to obtain such licence when, in all probability, he

[33] See Jenkins L.J. (approved by the House of Lords) in *Partabmull Rameshwar* v. *K. C. Sethia (1944) Ltd.* [1951] 2 Lloyd's Rep. 89, 97–98; Denning L.J. in *Brauer & Co. (Great Britain) Ltd.* v. *James Clark (Brush Materials) Ltd.* [1952] 2 All E.R. 497, 501.

[34] *Partabmull Rameshwar* v. *K. C. Sethia (1944) Ltd.* [1951] 2 Lloyd's Rep. 89, 97–98.

[35] *Peter Cassidy Seed Co. Ltd.* v. *Osuustukkukauppa I.L.* [1957] 1 W.L.R. 273.

[36] Devlin J. in *Charles H. Windschuegl Ltd.* v. *Pickering & Co. Ltd.* (1950) 84 Lloyd's Rep. 89, 93; Sellers J. in *Société D'Avances Commerciales (London) Ltd.* v. *A. Besse & Co. (London) Ltd.* [1952] 1 T.L.R. 644, 646; Denning L.J. in *Brauer & Co. (Great Britain) Ltd.* v. *James Clark (Brush Materials) Ltd.* [1952] 2 All E.R. 497, 501; *Joseph Pike & Sons (Liverpool) Ltd.* v. *Richard Cornelius & Co.* [1955] 2 Lloyd's Rep. 747, 750; *Aaronson Bros. Ltd.* v. *Maderera del Tropico S.A.* [1967] 2 Lloyd's Rep. 159, 160; *Smallman* v. *Smallman* [1971] 3 W.L.R. 588, 593.

might have been granted it, he has not used his best endeavours to obtain the licence.[37]

The duty to co-operate in order to comply with government requirements regulating the exportation or importation of goods arises from a general condition implied into every contract that the parties shall reasonably co-operate to ensure the performance of their bargain.[38] This duty rests on the seller and buyer alike. In one case[39] buyers of cotton seed which was to be shipped from Syria failed to send the seller a certificate stating that they did not intend to re-export the goods to Israel (against which Syria maintained an embargo) and consequently the seller was unable to obtain a Syrian export licence and to ship the goods. The court dismissed the action by the buyers against the seller for damages for non-performance because the buyers themselves had failed to co-operate by sending the seller the necessary information to obtain the export licence which, as both parties knew, was required.

While, as has already been observed,[40] it is always wise to stipulate expressly "subject to licence or quota," it is possible in appropriate cases to imply such term into the contract by way of necessary implication in order to give it business efficacy.[41] In this case the obligations of the parties are the same as if the term had been expressly adopted.

Partial frustration

Where a contract gives a party the right of electing one of several modes of performance and one mode has become frustrated, the contract is not completely destroyed but has to be performed in one of the remaining modes.[42] Thus, under a contract concluded shortly before the Second World War goods were to be shipped from Calcutta to Hamburg, Antwerp, Rotterdam or Bremen and the buyers had to declare the port of destination; the outbreak of the war did not frustrate the contract as delivery in Antwerp and Rotterdam (which at that time were not occupied by Germany) was still legal.[43]

If in a c.i.f. contract shipment at the contemplated port of shipment has become frustrated, the seller might often not be obliged to acquire the goods afloat and to tender bills of lading relating to them to the buyer.[44]

---

[37] *Malik Co.* v. *Central European Trading Agency Ltd.* [1974] 2 Lloyd's Rep. 279, 283.
[38] See Andrew J. Bateson, "The Duty to Co-operate" in [1960] J.B.L. 187.
[39] *Kyprianou* v. *Cyprus Textiles Ltd.* [1958] 2 Lloyd's Rep. 60.
[40] See p. 116, *ante*.
[41] *Re Anglo-Russian Merchant Traders Ltd., and John Batt & Co.* (*London*) *Ltd.* [1917] 2 K.B. 679, 685, 689; *Diamond Cutting Works Federation Ltd.* v. *Triefus & Co. Ltd.* [1956] 1 Lloyd's Rep. 216, 225; *Peter Cassidy Seed Co. Ltd.* v. *Osuustukkukauppa I.L.* [1957] 1 W.L.R. 273.
[42] *Waugh* v. *Morris* (1873) L.R. 8 Q.B. 202; *Reardon Smith Line Ltd.* v. *Ministry of Agriculture, Fisheries and Food* [1963] A.C. 691; see the notes of Raoul P. Colinvaux on this case [1960] J.B.L. 236 and [1961] J.B.L. 407.
[43] *Hindley & Co. Ltd.* v. *General Fibre Co. Ltd.* [1940] 2 K.B. 517; see also *Ross T. Smyth & Co. Ltd.* (*Liverpool*) v. *W. N. Lindsay Ltd.* (*Leith*) [1953] 1 W.L.R. 1280; p. 113, *ante*.
[44] See p. 36, *ante*.

No frustration where impossibility due to default of a party

This qualification of the doctrine of frustration has been stressed repeatedly in the preceding paragraphs. It may now be illustrated by reference to a Canadian case[45] where a party could not perform his contract because the performance required a government licence which was refused because the party had exhausted his quota by voluntarily electing to carry out certain other engagements. The Privy Council expressed the opinion that the contract was not frustrated because it was due to the election of the party in question, and consequently to his own default, that the licence was not granted for the contract between the parties. This result is plainly unsatisfactory. A better solution is provided by the American Uniform Code[46]:

> Where the causes mentioned in paragraph (a) affect only a part of the seller's capacity to perform, he must allocate production and deliveries among his customers but may at his option include regular customers not then under contract as well as his own requirements for further manufacture. He may so allocate in any manner which is fair and reasonable.

Effect of Frustration

In general

The consequences of frustration have been stated by Lord Simon L.C.[47] with admirable brevity: "When frustration in the legal sense occurs, it does not merely provide one party with a defence in an action brought by the other. It kills the contract itself and discharges both parties automatically." The contract is consequently avoided as from the date when the frustration occurs: the liability of those parties in respect of the future performance of the contract is discharged, and ali that remains to be done is to provide for an adjustment of their mutual rights and liabilities which arose under the contract prior to the time of discharge. This adjustment may involve difficult problems; thus, in the *Fibrosa* case[48] the Polish buyers had paid £1,000 on account of the purchase price of £4,800 when the frustrating event took place, and the British manufacturers had incurred considerable expense in building the machines, which were of an unusual type, to the specification of the buyers. In such a case, can the buyer recover the advance paid on the purchase price? Is the seller entitled to retain his expenses, and, if so, how have they to be calculated? These and similar problems arise when the adjustment is made between the parties.

The Law Reform (Frustrated Contracts) Act 1943

The adjustment of the contractual rights of the parties that arose before the time of the discharge of the contract has to be carried out in most

[45] *Maritime National Fish Ltd.* v. *Ocean Trawlers Ltd.* [1953] A.C. 524; *The Eugenia* [1964] 2 Q.B. 226.

[46] American Uniform Code, s. 2–615(b).

[47] *Joseph Constantine Steamship Line Ltd.* v. *Imperial Smelting Corporation Ltd.* [1942] A.C. 154, 163.

[48] See p. 112, *ante*.

cases[49] in compliance with the provisions of the Law Reform (Frustrated Contracts) Act 1943; this Act was passed following the *Fibrosa* litigation with the aim of enabling the courts to adjust these differences on the basis of equity and justice.[50] Under section 1(2) of the Act, all advances paid before the time of discharge can be recovered by the party that paid them, but the recipient of the money is entitled to retain such expenses incurred before that time in or for the purpose of the performance of the contract as the court may consider just. Where no advance was paid and consequently expenses cannot be retained, the court may allow a claim for payment of just expenses against the party who, at the time of the discharge of the contract, had obtained a valuable benefit at the cost of the claimant (s. 1(3)). The Act provides expressly that overhead expenses and personal labour may be included in the claim for retention or recovery of expenses (s. 1(4)) and that, when the adjustment is made, the court shall not take into account the fact that a party may have insured voluntarily against the frustrating event and obtained the insurance money, but, if the insurance was effected in consequence of an express term of the frustrated contract or under an enactment, *e.g.* if it was a c.i.f. contract, the insurance money has to be taken into account when the adjustment is made (s. 1(5)). The Act aims at the prevention of unjust enrichment of either party at the expense of the other.[50a]

The Act does not apply in the following exceptional cases:

(1) Where the contract is not governed by English law (s. 1(1)). This provision lacks precision because it does not state what is to happen when different aspects of the contract are governed by different laws.[51] Where, *e.g.*, a contract is concluded in England but is to be performed in Brazil, the essential validity of the contract is likely to be governed by English law, but the incidents of performance by the law of Brazil. It is believed that such a contract, if frustrated, cannot be adjusted under the provisions of the Act, but that those provisions apply only where English law governs the performance of the contract.

(2) Where section 7 of the Sale of Goods Act applies (s. 2(5) of the Law Reform (Frustrated Contracts) Act 1943). Section 7 provides for the avoidance of a contract for the sale of specific goods which have perished before the risk passed to the buyer.[52] In this case, advances paid on the purchase price can be recovered by the buyer, but the seller is not entitled to retain or recover just expenses.

(3) Certain contracts of insurance; certain charterparties and other contracts of carriage by sea (s. 2(5)). The contracts dealing with these topics normally contain special provisions for the adjustment of the rights of the parties when frustration occurs.

(4) When the contract contains provisions which are intended to have effect in the event of commercial frustration; in this case the court has to give effect to the contractual provisions and to apply the provisions of the Act only to such extent as appears to be consistent with the contractual provisions (s. 2(3)).

The Act provides especially (s. 3(2)) that it shall likewise apply when the dispute is to be determined by an arbitrator. An arbitration clause is normally not invalidated when a party maintains that the contract is frus-

---

[49] For exceptions, see *infra*.

[50] In the *Fibrosa* case it was held that the Polish buyers could recover the deposit of £1,000 on the ground that there was total failure of consideration. This rigid rule was abrogated by the Act of 1943.

[50a] *B.P. Exploration Co. (Libya) Ltd.* v. *Hunt* (*No. 2*) [1979] 1 W.L.R. 783, 799.

[51] See p. 127, *post*. [52] See p. 111, *ante*.

trated; and the arbitrator has to decide a dispute between the parties on the question whether the contract has been frustrated or not.[53]

FORCE MAJEURE CLAUSES

The attentive reader will conclude that it is not always easy to say whether, in an individual case, the contract has, or has not, been frustrated. He will reflect that it may be wiser for the parties to introduce a clause in their agreement defining in advance their mutual rights and duties if certain events beyond their control occur, whether or not such events result, in the eyes of the law, in the frustration of the contract or not.[54] Such clauses are, in fact, frequently employed in practice; they are known as force majeure clauses and vary considerably in ambit and effect.[55]

Different kinds of force majeure clauses

As regards the ambit of the clause, *i.e.* the events covered by the clause, it is sufficient to state simply that it shall apply in case of force majeure. This term has a clear meaning in law[56]; it includes every event beyond the control of the parties. Sometimes, however, the parties modify the normal meaning of the clause and it is, therefore, necessary to construe the clause in each case "with a close attention to the words which precede or follow it, and with a due regard to the nature and general terms of the contract. The effect of the clause may vary with each instrument."[57] Sometimes the parties define the ambit of the clause in considerable detail, as may be illustrated by the following clause[58]:

> Strikes, lockouts, labour disturbances, anomalous working conditions, accident to machinery, delays en route, policies or restrictions of governments, including restrictions of export and other licences, or any other contingency whatsoever beyond seller's control, including war, to be sufficient excuse for any delay or non-fulfilment traceable to any of these causes.

As regards the effect of the force majeure clause, sometimes these clauses provide for the extension of the time of performance, or the automatic suspension or cancellation of the contract in case of the occur-

---

[53] *Heyman* v. *Darwins Ltd.* [1942] A.C. 356; see further, p. 418, *post*.

[54] Lord Tucker in *Fairclough Dodd & Jones Ltd.* v. *J. H. Vantol Ltd.* [1957] 1 W.L.R. 136, 143. See also Bernard J. Cartoon, "Drafting an Acceptable Force Majeure Clause," in [1978] J.B.L. 230.

[55] A force majeure clause differs from an exception clause in that the latter is intended to protect a party who is in breach, whereas the former applies when a certain event happens, whether or not, in consequence of that event, the party would be in breach; see Lord Tucker, *ibid.*

[56] Although Donaldson J. said in *Thomas Borthwick (Glasgow) Ltd.* v. *Faure Fairclough Ltd.* [1968] 1 Lloyd's Rep. 16, 28 that "the precise meaning of this term, if it has one, has eluded the lawyers for years."

[57] McCardie J. in *Lebeaupin* v. *Crispin* [1920] 2 K.B. 714, 720. The protection of the clause "subject to force majeure and shipment" is not available to a seller who has, in fact, received a shipment of the goods sold from his supplier but uses it for the performance of other commitments: *Hong Guan & Co. Ltd.* v. *R. Jumabhoy & Sons Ltd.* [1960] A.C. 684.

[58] Taken from *Baltimex Ltd.* v. *Metallo Chemical Refining Co. Ltd.* [1955] 2 Lloyd's Rep. 438, 446, except that the words "labour disturbances, anomalous working conditions" are substituted for "differences with workmen."

rence of the disturbing element; sometimes they give each party or one party only an option of suspending or cancelling the contract in that event. Expressions such as "force majeure excepted" or "subject to force majeure" mean that in the event of force majeure the parties shall be excused from further performing the contract, subject to their obligation to co-operate reasonably to ensure the performance of their bargain.[59]

The two-stage force majeure clause

The form of force majeure clause which in modern international trade is increasingly used satisfies two requirements. First, it lists a catalogue of events which are considered as constituting force majeure and it then adds a general clause, such as "any other event beyond the control of the parties." Secondly, it provides for two stages with respect to the effect of force majeure. In the first stage the time for the performance of the contract is extended for a specified period, *e.g.* 28 days. If the event which constitutes force majeure continues after the expiration of that period, each party is entitled to cancel the contract.

Sometimes it is provided that the party claiming extension of the time for performance shall give the other party notice or even several notices, such as a warning notice and a final notice. These provisions, as those relating to the exercise of the option to cancel the contract, have to be complied with carefully.[60]

Force majeure clauses in standard contracts used in the commodity trade

Sometimes contracts, particularly standard contracts in the commodity trade, contain a more elaborate regulation. Thus, a contract[61] on a form of the London Oil and Tallow Trades Association provided for the shipment of Egyptian cottonseed oil from Alexandria to Rotterdam during December and January. The contract contained two force majeure clauses, one to the effect that in case of war or other specified events *preventing* shipment the contract should be cancelled, and the other providing that if another event *delayed* shipment, the period of shipment should be extended by two months. The Egyptian Government prohibited the exportation of the goods from December 12 to January 3 (during which period the sellers, in fact, intended to ship) but shipment was possible on January 31 when the shipment period expired. The sellers did not ship within the original shipment period, and the buyers claimed damages. The defence of the sellers was that, by virtue of the second clause, the performance of the contract was extended by two months. The House of Lords held, on the construction of the force majeure clause, that that contention was correct

---

[59] See p. 118, *ante*.

[60] *Bremer Handelsgessellschaft mbH* v. *Vanden Avenne Izegem PVBA* [1978] 2 Lloyd's Rep. 109. In *Tradax Export S.A.* v. *Andre & Cie S.A.* [1976] 1 Lloyd's Rep. 416 the Court of Appeal held that a "rolled up" notice, *i.e.* a notice combining several required notices, was sufficient, as long as it contained all the required information.

[61] In *Fairclough Dodd & Jones Ltd.* v. *J. H. Vantol Ltd.* [1957] 1 W.L.R. 136.

and that the clause became operative through the intermittent delay although the delay was no longer in existence at the end of the shipment period.

Elaborate force majeure and cancellation clauses were in issue in the so-called Mississippi flooding cases, which concerned the interpretation of standard contract forms of the Grain and Feed Trade Association (GAFTA).[62] In the *Vanden Avenne*[63] case Bremer Handelsgesellschaft, of Hamburg, sold a quantity of soya bean meal of American origin to Vanden Avenne, of Antwerp. The contracts, which were dated April 5, 1973 and provided for monthly instalment deliveries c.i.f. Rotterdam, were made on GAFTA form no. 100 which in clauses 21 and 22 contained detailed cancellation and force majeure clauses. Owing to the flooding of the Mississippi in the spring of 1973 the export of soya bean meal by American shippers was greatly impeded and the shortage caused the market price to rise sharply. On June 27, 1973 the United States Government imposed an embargo on the export of soya bean meal but after a few days, on July 2, it allowed exporters a quota by which they could export 40 per cent. of their contracted obligations. The sellers claimed that by virtue of the cancellation and force majeure clauses in GAFTA form no. 100 they were relieved from their obligation to ship the prohibited portion of the June 1973 instalment and the House of Lords, interpreting clauses 21 and 22, upheld that contention. One of the arguments of the buyers was that clause 21 (which provided for notices) was a condition precedent, the onus of satisfying it was on the sellers and, since the findings of fact by the arbitrators did not deal with that point, the case had to be remitted to them. The House of Lords rejected this argument. Lord Wilberforce said that clause 21 was an innominate term[63] and not a condition precedent and that no such finding was necessary. The court further held that there was no obligation on the sellers to purchase the goods afloat.[64]

Another illustration of a detailed force majeure clause in a commodity contract is provided by the Polish sugar beet case[65] where the contract was subject to the standard rules of the Refined Sugar Association.

Force majeure clauses which are too vague

While, as has been seen, the meaning of the phrase "force majeure" is clear in law and its use does not render the agreement of the parties invalid on the ground of uncertainty, the position is different where the contract contains an unspecified reference to the "usual" force majeure clause and

[62] *Bremer Handelsgesellschaft mbH* v. *Vanden Avenne Izegem PVBA* [1978] 2 Lloyd's Rep. 109; *Alfred C. Toepfer* v. *Peter Cremer* [1975] 2 Lloyd's Rep. 118; *Tradex Export S.A.* v. *Andre & Cie S.A.* [1976] 1 Lloyd's Rep. 416; *Toepfer* v. *Schwarze* [1977] 2 Lloyd's Rep. 380; *Bunge S.A.* v. *Schleswig-Holsteinische Landwirtschaftliche Hauptgenossenschaft Eingetr. GmbH* [1978] 1 Lloyd's Rep. 480; *Bunge GmbH* v. *Alfred C. Toepfer* [1978] 1 Lloyd's Rep. 506.

[63] See p. 91, *ante*.

[64] See p. 36, *ante*.

[65] *C. Czarnikov Ltd.* v. *Rolimpex,* [1978] 3 W.L.R. 274, see p. 113, *ante*.

it is impossible to state with certainty which of the numerous force majeure clauses used in practice the parties had in mind. In these cases the courts have held that the clause is too vague; if it is of the essence, it makes the whole contract in which it occurs invalid,[66] but if the meaningless clause is severable from the other terms of the contract it is ignored and leaves the other obligations unaffected and enforceable.[67] The position is different if the phrase "'usual' force majeure clause," by necessary implication, has a definite meaning, *e.g.* if it clearly refers to a clause usual in a particular trade; in that case it has full legal effect.

Further, it would be unwise for the parties to adopt words which have no clear legal connotation. Thus, in one case[68] a learned judge had to decide whether a contract embodying the clause "u.c.e." (unforeseen circumstances excepted) was discharged when unforeseen circumstances prevented the seller from obtaining the goods, which he had sold to the buyer, from the source of supply contemplated by him; his lordship observed:

> It is a pity that merchants will continue to use shorthand expressions of this kind, if I may so term them, without a definition of them in the contract, and thus leave them to be interpreted by the court,

and held that the clause did not mean that the seller should be free if the goods could not be obtained from that particular source of supply but were still obtainable elsewhere.

Force majeure clauses defeated by events

Exceptionally a force majeure clause may be defeated by events. The courts have disregarded such clauses where the supervening event rendered the performance of the contract illegal or was of such an unforeseeable magnitude that the contract, if upheld, would have constituted a new and different contract from the original one.

A force majeure clause does not protect a seller who claims that he is not bound to deliver the goods for the reason that he cannot obtain an export licence unless he pays a price 20 to 30 per cent. higher than the contract price; this is not a case of force majeure, there is no physical or legal prevention of the exportation, such as a prohibition or an embargo.[69]

---

[66] *British Electrical and Associated Industries (Cardiff) Ltd.* v. *Patley Pressings Ltd.* [1953] 1 W.L.R. 280, 285.

[67] *Nicolene Ltd.* v. *Simmonds* [1953] 1 Q.B. 543.

[68] Greer J. in *George Wills & Sons Ltd.* v. *R. S. Cunningham, Son & Co. Ltd.* [1924] 2 K.B. 220, 221.

[69] *Brauer & Co. (Great Britain) Ltd.* v. *James Clark (Brush Materials) Ltd.* [1952] 2 All E.R. 497, 499; see p. 110. *ante*.

CHAPTER 12

ENGLISH LAW AND FOREIGN LAW

THE exportation of goods from this country embodies, by necessity, a foreign element and falls, in so far, within the province of English law known as private international law or the conflict of laws. This branch of law applies to transactions extending over several legal units and determines in an individual case the law applicable to the dispute between the parties and the jurisdiction of the courts which have to adjudicate upon the issue. The two questions do not coincide; it is conceivable that according to the rules of the conflict of laws the dispute has to be heard by the English courts but that these courts are to apply a foreign system of law. In the eyes of the English lawyer and the English courts, every system of law applied in another country is considered to be foreign law, and no difference is made in this respect between the laws prevailing in the countries which have founded their law on English law, the Member States of the European Community, and other countries. "In the English courts, English law is the municipal system of law while the laws of Scotland, New Zealand or China are alike foreign laws."[1]

It is of great importance for the parties to know whether their contract is governed by English law or the foreign system of law prevailing at the place where the buyer resides or to which the goods have ultimately to be shipped. In fact, from the legal point of view, this is the central problem arising in an export transaction. It has been pointed out before that the rules of English and foreign law are often at variance; the expression f.o.b. has a different meaning in English and American law[2]; the Sale of Goods Act applies when the international contract is governed by English law but does not apply when it is governed by foreign law[3]; a contract may be regarded as frustrated by English law but as valid by foreign law; the provisions of the Law Reform (Frustrated Contracts) Act 1943 apply only to contracts governed by English law[4]; and so forth. The problem in these and similar cases is to ascertain the national law, also called municipal law, governing the contract of the parties.

Proof of foreign law

However, even if it is clear that the contract is governed by a foreign system of law, that does not mean that the judge or arbitrator has to ascertain the rules of that legal system *ex officio*. English judges and

---

[1] Clive M. Schmitthoff, *The English Conflict of Laws* (3rd ed., 1954), p. 5.
[2] See p. 11, *ante*.
[3] See p. 75, *ante*.
[4] See p. 120, *ante*.

arbitrators regard foreign law as a question of fact which has to be proved to their satisfaction by expert witnesses or other admissible evidence.[5] If a party fails to adduce such evidence, English law will be applied. Consequently a party in English proceedings will plead foreign law only if that is to his advantage; otherwise it is cheaper for him to have the issue decided in accordance with English law. Thus, in the *Romalpa* case[6] it was probable that the contract was governed by Dutch law but as neither party pleaded Dutch law, the case was decided according to English law. In many continental countries, judges and arbitrators have to ascertain the foreign law, which in their view applies, *ex officio*.

Methods of Conflict Avoidance

Repeated attempts have been made to avoid a conflict of laws in this sphere by the preparation of uniform laws on international sales, the creation of general conditions of sales or the adoption of model contract forms. These attempts, which have been discussed earlier,[7] have led to a considerable measure of success.

In particular, the two Uniform Laws on International Sales appended to the Uniform Laws on International Sales Act 1967 represent progress in the direction of conflict avoidance. The Act was brought into operation in the United Kingdom on August 18, 1972,[8] and the Uniform Laws have likewise been introduced into the law of Belgium, Western Germany, Italy, the Netherlands and San Marino, while Israel has given effect to the Uniform Law on the International Sale of Goods but not to that on the Formation of Contracts for the International Sale of Goods. Other Member States of the European Community intend to give effect to the Uniform Laws which may soon become the law governing international sales in the Community. The Uniform Law on the International Sale of Goods aims at excluding a conflict of laws; it states in article 2:

> Rules of private international law shall be excluded for the purposes of the application of the present Law, subject to the contrary in the said Law.

The Uniform Laws form the foundation of the Draft Convention of UNCITRAL on Contracts for the International Sale of Goods. This Draft Convention is intended to supersede the Uniform Laws. If it is universally accepted by the trading nations of the world, the danger of a conflict of laws in this area would be greatly reduced. That, however, will take a long

---

[5] The House of Lords, however, in an English or Northern Irish appeal, takes judicial notice of Scots law and vice versa. Moreover, by the Civil Evidence Act 1972, s. 4(2), where any question of foreign law has been determined by a specified higher court in England or by the Privy Council, then any finding or decision on that question is admissible in evidence in subsequent proceedings and the foreign law shall be taken to be in accordance with that finding unless the contrary is proved, provided that the finding or decision is reported or recorded in citable form, *i.e.* in a form in which it can be cited as an authority in an English court.

[6] *Aluminium Industrie Vaassen BV* v. *Romalpa Aluminium Ltd.* [1976] 1 W.L.R. 676; see p. 80, *ante*.

[7] See p. 45, *ante*.

[8] By the Uniform Laws on International Sales Order 1972 (S.I. 1972 No. 973).

time. Until then that danger will persist in international sales transactions.

In this situation it would be of great help if countries agreed on a uniform method to decide which national law should apply to international sales transactions in cases in which a dispute arose between the parties. With this end in view, the Hague Convention of June 15, 1955,[9] on the Law applicable to International Sales of Goods contains the following simple rule[10]:

1. A contract for the sale of goods is regulated by the domestic law designated by the parties;
2. Failing such designation, the domestic law of the country in which the seller has his habitual residence applies;
3. The preceding rule is subject to two exceptions:
   (*a*) where the order is received by a branch office of the seller, the contract is regulated by the domestic law of the country in which such branch is situated;
   (*b*) where the order is received by the seller or his agent in the buyer's country, the domestic law of the country in which the buyer has his habitual residence applies.

The Convention has been given effect[11] by Belgium, Denmark, Finland, France, Italy, Norway, and Sweden, but not by Great Britain. The principle that, unless otherwise agreed, the seller's law shall apply is likewise accepted by the CMEA General Conditions of Delivery of Goods 1968–1975 which apply to the trade between the Comecon countries.[12]

A committee of experts sponsored by the EEC adopted in June 1979 a *Draft Convention on Choice of Law in Contracts*, known as the P.I.L. Contracts Convention.[12a] It has not been approved by the Member States yet.

In the absence of a universally binding international arrangement, we have to turn to English private international law for an answer.

The Law Governing the Contract

According to English law, a contract is governed by the law which the parties intend to apply to their agreement or, if they have not formed such an intention, the law with which the contract is most closely connected. This law is, for brevity's sake, called the proper law of the contract. Lord Simonds[13] stated these rules in the following words:

> The proper law of the contract [is] the system of law by reference to which the contract was made or that with which the transaction had its closest and most real connection.

Although it is usual to talk of the proper law of the *contract* or to state that a contract is an English contract or a French contract or that a bill of exchange is an English or a French bill, it may happen that a particular aspect of the contract is governed by one legal system and the other aspects

---

[9] This Convention was adopted by the 7th Session of the Hague Conference on Private International Law in 1951. This Conference must not be confused with the Hague Conference of 1964 which adopted the Uniform Laws on International Sales; p. 140, *post*.

[10] Dr. G. C. Cheshire, "International Contracts for the Sale of Goods," [1960] J.B.L. 282.

[11] Position as on September 1, 1979.

[12] CMEA General Conditions of Delivery of Goods, para. 110.

[12a] See [1979] 2 C.M.L.R. 776.

[13] *Bonython* v. *Commonwealth of Australia* [1951] A.C. 201, 219. See also *Whitworth Street Estates (Manchester) Ltd.* v. *James Miller & Partners Ltd.* [1970] A.C. 583.

are governed by another law. It is conceivable that a manufacturer in Birmingham, through an agent in Melbourne, sells machine tools to an Australian buyer f.o.b. London. The parties may well have intended that the form and essential validity of the contract shall be governed by the law of the state of Victoria (Australia) in the territory of which Melbourne is situate, while the performance of the contract shall be governed by English law because the contract has to be performed in London. In short, "in English law a transaction may be regulated in general by the law of one country although as to parts of that transaction which are to be performed in another country, the law of that other country may be the law admissible."[14]

Thus, in *A. V. Pound & Co. Ltd.* v. *M. W. Hardy Inc.*,[15] although the proper law of contract for the sale of goods f.a.s. Lisbon was held to be English law, its performance was held to be regulated by the law of Portugal, and according to that law, only the Portuguese supplier could obtain the export licence.

But the courts will not subject different incidents of the contract to different laws readily or without good reason.[16]

The Law Intended by the Parties

The parties to a contract for the sale of goods abroad are well advised to provide expressly which legal system they desire to be applied to their contract. Difficulties will be avoided subsequently if attention is given to this point in time, and with this aim in view it has been suggested that the British exporter should, in his general terms of sale, make express provision for the application of English (or Scottish) law to the contract in question, in short he should embody a *choice of law clause* into his contract. Due attention should be given to the wording of that clause. Sometimes a short clause is chosen to the effect that the contract shall be governed by English law and sometimes the words "in all respects" are added to this clause; this form, without such an addition, is, in fact, adopted by section 1(1) of the Law Reform (Frustrated Contracts) Act 1943. This terminology is not commendable because it can be argued that the clause is intended to cover the formation of the contract only, and not its performance; if a contract whereby a British exporter sells goods to a French importer on free delivery terms contains a clause providing that the contract shall be governed by English law, the English courts might hold that the buyer's right of inspection and rejection of the goods is governed by French law because the express agreement of the parties covered the formation but not the performance of the contract. This unsatisfactory result is avoided if the parties

---

[14] *Per* Lord Roche in *R.* v. *International Trustee* [1937] A.C. 500, 574.
[15] [1956] A.C. 588; see p. 23, *ante*.
[16] Lord MacDermott in *Kahler* v. *Midland Bank* [1950] A.C. 24, 42.

state that both the conclusion and the performance of the contract shall be governed by English law.[17]

The parties may submit their contract to any legal system which they like to elect[18] and, in particular, they are not limited to a legal system with which the circumstances surrounding their contract have an actual connection. In one case[19] goods were shipped from a port in Newfoundland to New York in a vessel owned by a Nova Scotian (Canadian) company and the bill of lading embodied a clause providing that the contract should be governed by English law. The shippers brought an action against the shipowners in respect of damage to the goods, and the shipowners pleaded certain exceptions under the contract which they could only have claimed if the bill of lading was to have been construed by English law. It was contended on behalf of the shippers that the choice of English law failed as there was nothing to connect the contract in any way with English law. The Judicial Committee of the Privy Council, which heard the case on appeal from the Supreme Court in Nova Scotia, rejected this argument in no uncertain terms[20]:

> Connection with English law is not as a matter of principle essential. The provision in a contract (*e.g.* of sale) for English arbitration imports English law as the law governing the transaction, and those familiar with international business are aware how frequent such a provision is, even where the parties are not English and the transactions are carried out completely outside England.

The discretion of the parties to elect the law applicable to the contract is, however, not entirely unlimited: the parties must exercise this discretion bona fide and for a legal purpose. They cannot adopt a particular legal system, *e.g.* Americna law, for the majority of their stipulations and submit one provision, *e.g.* a restraint of trade, to another law, *e.g.* English law; in this case the choice of English law would not be exercised bona fide and for a legal purpose and the arrangement would fail if it would be evident that it was adopted with the aim of evading the American Anti-Trust Acts.

Where the parties have not expressly stated which law shall govern their contract, it may still be possible to gather their intention from other contract clauses. Thus, in one case[21] concerning the insurance of ships 30 per cent. of the cover was placed in London, 39 per cent. in the United States, and the balance in other countries. The insurance was effected in the United States, in particular by brokers in San Francisco. The policies contained a "follow London" clause which began: "Assurers herein shall follow Lloyd's underwriters and/or British insurance companies in regard to amounts, terms, conditions, alterations, additions, extensions, endorsements, cancellations, surveys and settlements of claims hereunder. . . ."

---

[17] See p. 53, *ante*.

[18] But submission to the law of a particular country does not necessarily mean that there is a submission to the jurisdiction of the courts of that country. If that is intended it should be expressly stated: *Dundee Ltd.* v. *Gilman & Co.* (*Australia*) *Pty. Ltd.* [1968] 2 Lloyd's Rep. 394 (Sup.Ct. of N.S. Wales).

[19] *Vita Food Products Inc.* v. *Unus Shipping Co.* [1939] A.C. 277.

[20] *Ibid.* at p. 290.

[21] *Armadora Occidental S.A.* v. *Horace Mann Insurance Co.* [1977] 2 Lloyd's Rep. 406.

But it contained also a "New York suable clause" which enabled the assured to sue at their option in New York or any other American State. The assured—the shipowners—were keen to bring proceedings in the English courts and applied for leave to serve proceedings out of the jurisdiction. The English courts would assume jurisdiction only if the assured could bring their case under the Rules of the Supreme Court 1965, Ord. 11, r. 1(1)(*f*) which provides that the contract "by its terms or by implication [is] governed by English law."[22] The Court of Appeal held that the "follow London" clause revealed such intention. Lord Denning said[23]: ". . . the New York suable clause does not alter in any way the effect of the 'follow London' clause. The judge said, and I would entirely agree with him, that the clause is of paramount importance. It shows that the contract is to be construed, interpreted and applied according to English law."

The Law with which the Contract is most Closely Connected

If the parties have omitted to state the law which is to govern their contract and if their intention cannot be gathered from the terms of the contract, it is the task of the courts to ascertain the legal system with which the contract is most closely connected.[24] All the circumstances surrounding the contract have to be examined to ascertain that law.

The single facts to which the courts have attached importance are manifold. Amongst them are: the place where the contract has been concluded, the place where the contract has to be performed, the language and terminology employed by the parties, the form of the documents made with respect to the transaction, the personality of the parties, the subject-matter of the contract, a submission to arbitration, the situation of the funds which are liable for the discharge, or security of the obligation, a connection with a preceding transaction, the effect attributed to the transaction by a particular legal system.[25]

In three sets of circumstances the courts have established rebuttable presumptions for the ascertainment of the proper law of contract.

Presumption in favour of the law of the place where the contract was concluded

Where a contract is to be performed in the same country in which it has been concluded, the form, construction and essential validity of the contract are presumed to be governed by the law of that country. This presumption is easily displaced by evidence showing that the parties are more likely to have intended the application of another legal system to their agreement.[26]

[22] See p. 434, *post*.
[23] [1977] 2 Lloyd's Rep. 406, 412.
[24] *Re United Railways of Havana and Regla Warehouse Ltd.* [1961] A.C. 1007 (overruled on another point by *Miliangos* v. *George Frank Textiles Ltd.* [1976] A.C. 443); also *Bonython* v. *Commonwealth of Australia* [1951] A.C. 201; *Offshore International S.A.* v. *Banco Central S.A.* [1976] 2 Lloyd's Rep. 402, 404.
[25] Clive M. Schmitthoff, *The English Conflict of Laws* (3rd ed., 1954), pp. 110, 111.
[26] *N.V. Handel My. J. Smits Import-Export* v. *English Exporters Ltd.* [1955] 2 Lloyd's Rep. 317, 323.

When, as frequently is the case in export sales, the contract is concluded between persons who are not present in the same locality, the contract is deemed to be concluded at the place where its definite and unequivocal acceptance is effected because this act transforms the arrangement from mere negotiations to an enforceable legal obligation.[27] Thus if a merchant in London receives a shipment order from a buyer in India on terms c.i.f. Calcutta and accepts this order, the courts are likely to hold that the contract is governed by English law, for it is concluded in this country and to be performed here by delivery of the goods on board a ship sailing for the agreed port of destination.[28]

Presumption in favour of the law of the place where the contract is to be performed

In many cases the place of performance of the contract is not identical with that of its conclusion. Here a strong presumption exists that the contract, or at least the part relating to its performance, is governed by the law prevailing at the place of performance. This presumption, like all other presumptions designed to assist in the ascertainment of the proper law, is rebutted by circumstances revealing that the contract, or at least the incidents of performance, are most closely connected with the law of another country. These rules were applied in a case[29] where a merchant residing in Malta bought goods from merchants carrying on business in Gibraltar; the contract, which provided for delivery f.o.b. Gibraltar, was concluded in Malta. The Maltese buyer rejected the goods on the ground of their inferior quality but he had, before rejecting them, tendered them to his sub-purchasers, who refused to accept them. According to the law of Gibraltar (which in this respect was identical with the English Sale of Goods Act s. 35), the buyer had lost the right of rescission because by tendering the goods to his sub-purchasers he had done an act inconsistent with the ownership of the seller in the goods; by the law of Malta (which is the civil law) the buyer was still entitled to rescind. The Privy Council which heard the case on appeal from Malta, concluded that under the f.o.b. clause the contract "was to be performed by the delivery of the goods on board a ship at Gibraltar selected by the buyer," and that the buyer's right or rescission was consequently to be determined by the law of Gibraltar.

Where an irrevocable and unconfirmed credit[30] is issued, the law of the place where the correspondent bank carries on business is, as regards the relationship between that bank and the seller (the beneficiary under the credit) the law of the closest and most real connection.[31] Otherwise "the

---

[27] See p. 62, *ante*.
[28] *Johnson* v. *Taylor Bros. & Co. Ltd.* [1920] A.C. 144.
[29] *Benaim & Co.* v. *Debono* [1924] A.C. 514; *Compagnie Tunisienne de Navigation S.A.* v. *Compagnie d'Armement Maritime S.A.* [1971] A.C. 572 (H.L.).
[30] See p. 260, *post*. The same principle applies, *a fortiori*, to a confirmed credit.
[31] *Offshore International S.A.* v. *Banco Central S.A.* [1976] 2 Lloyd's Rep. 402.

advising bank would have constantly to be seeking to apply a whole variety of foreign laws."[32] But the law governing the relationship between the buyer and the seller, or between the buyer and the issuing bank, or between the issuing and correspondent bank may well be another system of law.[33]

Presumption in favour of the law of the place where an arbitration is to be held

An export sale often embodies a clause providing for an arbitration to be held by a particular arbitrator or at a particular place. The contract may, *e.g.* provide that any difference or dispute shall be referred to the arbitration by the London Court of Arbitration.[34] The English courts have evolved the rule that such an arbitration clause normally admits the inference that the parties intended to submit their contract of sale to the law under which the aribitration proceedings were to be held, because it can be assumed that the arbitrator shall apply the law with which he is best acquainted.[35] In one case,[36] the arbitration clause contained the usual reference to the English Arbitration Acts[37]; it was ruled that that reference supported the inference that the arbitration proceedings were to be conducted according to English law and that, consequently, the contract itself was to be governed by English law. The presumption has likewise been applied where the parties agreed on neutral arbitration in a country providing a well-developed legal system for the solution of disputes of the type likely to arise, *e.g.* Swedish sellers of a ship agreed with the Greek buyer that disputes should be settled by arbitration in the City of London.[38]

It has never been decided that this presumption applies where the contract provides that a dispute shall be referred to arbitration by the Court of Arbitration of the International Chamber of Commerce[39] or to another arbitration tribunal convened, for reasons of convenience only, in a country other than the countries in which the parties to the dispute are resident. In these cases the place of the arbitration is purely coincidental and does not support the inference that the parties intended the law of the place of arbitration to govern their contract. It may well be that in these or similar circumstances the English courts may hold that the presumption

---

32 *Per* Ackner J., *ibid.* 404.

33 This topic is treated more fully on p. 255, *post.*

34 See p. 422, *post.*

35 *Maritime Insurance Co. Ltd.* v. *Assecuranz Union von 1865* (1935) 52 Ll.L.R. 16; *Hamlyn & Co.* v. *Talisker Distillery* [1894] A.C. 202. See further, *Kianta Osakeyhtio* v. *Britain & Overseas Trading Co. Ltd.* [1954] 1 Lloyd's Rep. 247; *Tzortzis* v. *Monark Line A/B* [1968] 1 W.L.R. 406 (C.A.).

36 *Spurrier* v. *La Cloche* [1902] A.C. 446.

37 See p. 413, *post.*

38 *Tzortzis* v. *Monark Line A/B* [1968] 1 W.L.R. 406, 414.

39 See p. 423, *post.*

under review is displaced and that one of the presumptions which have been discussed earlier has to be applied.[40]

The law applicable to the arbitration procedure may be different from the substantive law governing the contract.[41]

Money of Account and of Payment; Recovery in Foreign Currency

The parties may agree that a monetary obligation, *e.g.* the purchase price, shall be expressed in one currency but the debtor shall be at liberty to discharge this obligation in another. The currency in which the debtor's liability is measured is the *currency of account*, and the currency in which he may pay is the *currency of payment.* The effect of this distinction is that, if at the date of discharge the rate of exchange of the currency of payment has fallen against the currency of account, the buyer must acquire more currency of payment in order to satisfy his obligation. Thus, in one case[42] the Nigerian Produce Marketing Board sold Woodhouse a quantity of cocoa under contracts providing for delivery c.i.f. Liverpool. The purchase price was expressed in Nigerian currency, at that time the Nigerian pound,[43] which was equivalent to the pound sterling. In response to the request of the buyers, the sellers agreed that the buyers may pay the price in pounds sterling. Before payment was made, the pound sterling was devalued but the Nigerian pound retained its value. The House of Lords held that the money of account was still the Nigerian currency, nonwithstanding the sellers' agreement to accept pound sterling in discharge of the buyers' liability.

The distinction between the money of account and the money of payment has lost some of its importance because it is now possible to obtain judgments in foreign currency in the English courts if the contractual obligation is expressed in that currency; the conversion into pounds sterling then takes place at the date when enforcement of the foreign currency judgment is sought.[44] Arbitration awards can likewise be obtained in foreign currency in appropriate cases.[45] Further, judgment on a bill of exchange expressed in a foreign currency but payable in England may be obtained

---

[40] Thus, in *Compagnie Tunisienne de Navigation S.A.* v. *Compagnie d'Armement Maritime S.A.* [1971] A.C. 572 the presumption in favour of the place of arbitration (England) was displaced by the law with which the contract was most closely connected (France).

[41] *Whitworth Street Estates (Manchester) Ltd.* v. *James Miller & Partners Ltd.* [1970] A.C. 583.

[42] *Woodhouse A.C. Israel Cocoa S.A.* v. *Nigerian Produce Marketing Co.* [1972] A.C. 741; see also *Barclays Bank International Ltd.* v. *Levin Brothers (Bradford) Ltd.* [1977] Q.B. 270.

[43] It is now called Naira.

[44] *Miliangos* v. *George Frank Textiles Ltd.* [1976] A.C. 443; *Schorsch Meier GmbH* v. *Hennin* [1975] Q.B. 416.

[45] *Jugoslavenska Oceanska Plovidba* v. *Castle Investment Co. Inc.* [1974] Q.B. 292.

in the foreign currency.[46] It is also possible to recover damages in contract or tort in foreign currency if the loss was sustained in that currency.[47] The *Practice Direction* (*Judgment: Foreign Currency*)[48] states, *inter alia*:

The writ or statement of claim in which a claim is made for payment of a debt or liquidated demand in foreign currency must contain the following statements, namely: (i) that the contract under which the debt is claimed in the foreign currency is governed by the law of some country outside the United Kingdom; and (ii) that under *that* contract the money of account in which the debt was payable was the currency of that country or of some other foreign country.

Foreign State Immunity

When an enterprise contracts with a foreign State or a foreign State corporation and disputes occur, the question arises whether, if proceedings are commenced, the foreign State or State corporation can plead sovereign immunity and thereby evade its commercial obligations. Here two theories are advanced. Under the doctrine of *absolute immunity* the foreign State or State corporation can always plead immunity. Under the doctrine of *restrictive immunity* a distinction is drawn between acts in the exercise of sovereign authority (*acta jure imperii*) and ordinary commercial transactions (*acta jure gestionis*). Immunity is accorded to the former but refused to the latter.

This topic is now regulated by the State Immunity Act 1978[49] which is clearly founded on the doctrine of restrictive immunity.[50] Section 3 of the Act provides:

(1) A State is not immune as respects proceedings relating to—
(*a*) a commercial transaction entered into by the State; or
(*b*) an obligation of the State which by virtue of a contract (whether a commercial transaction or not) falls to be performed wholly or partly in the United Kingdom.

(2) This section does not apply if the parties to the dispute are States or have otherwise agreed in writing; and subsection (1)(*b*) above does not apply if the contract (not being a

[46] *Barclays Bank International Ltd.* v. *Levin Brothers* (*Bradford*) *Ltd.* [1977] Q.B. 270. That is so notwithstanding that according to the Bills of Exchange Act 1882, s. 74(4), such a bill shall be payable at the "rate of exchange for sight drafts at the place of payment on the day the bill is payable."

[47] *Jean Kraut A.C.* v. *Albany Fabrics* [1977] Q.B. 182; *The Despina R.* [1978] 3 W.L.R. 804. *Services Europe Atlantique Sud* v. *Stockholm Rederiaktiebolag Svea, The Folias* [1978] 2 W.L.R. 887. *George Vellings Rederi A/S* v. *President of India; The Bellami* [1978] 1 W.L.R. 982; *B.P. Exploration Co.* (*Libya*) *Ltd.* v. *Hunt* (*No. 2*) [1979] 1 W.L.R. 783, 837.

[48] Issued December 18, 1975; see [1976] 1 W.L.R. 83.

[49] Which came into operation on November 22, 1978 (The State Immunity Act 1978 (Commencement) Order 1978 (S.I. 1978/1572 (C.44)). See Gillian White, "The State Immunity Act 1978," in [1979] J.B.L. 105.

[50] Before the coming into operation of the State Immunity Act 1978 the position was as follows: The House of Lords in *Compania Naviera Vascongado* v. *S.S. Cristina; The Cristina* [1938] A.C. 485 had adopted the absolute theory but more modern decisions of other courts had expressed themselves in favour of the restrictive theory, *viz.* The Privy Council in *The Philippine Admiral* [1977] A.C. 373 and the Court of Appeal, obiter, in *Trendtex Trading Corporation* v. *Central Bank of Nigeria* [1977] 2 W.L.R. 356. In *I Congreso del Partido* [1977] 3 W.L.R. 778 Robert Goff J. likewise adopted the restrictive theory but held, on the facts, that the ordinary commercial transaction, in which the foreign State had engaged, as the result of subsequent events had become an act of state and entitled the foreign sovereign to immunity. However, in *Uganda Co.* (*Holdings*) *Ltd.* v. *The Government of Uganda* [1979] 1 Lloyd's Rep. 481, Donaldson J. still applied the absolute doctrine.

commercial transaction) was made in the territory of the State concerned and the obligation in question is governed by its administrative law.

(3) In this section "commercial transaction" means—

(*a*) any contract for the supply of goods or services;

(*b*) any loan or other transaction for the provision of finance and any guarantee or indemnity in respect of any such transaction or any other financial obligation; and

(*c*) any other transaction or activity (whether of a commercial, industrial, financial, professional or other similar character) into which a State enters or in which it engages otherwise than in the exercise of sovereign authority;

but neither paragraph of subsection (1) above applies to a contract of employment between a State and an individual.

It should be noted that in the cases mentioned in section 3(3)(*a*) and (*b*) the purpose of the transaction is irrelevant. Thus a foreign State cannot claim immunity if it has purchased equipment for its army. But in the case of section 3(3)(*c*) transactions *jure imperii* are excluded and the State can rely on its immunity in such transactions.

The Act further deals with State corporations which enjoy separate legal personality.[51] Such a separate entity does not enjoy immunity, except if:

(*a*) the proceedings relate to anything done by it in the exercise of sovereign authority; and

(*b*) the circumstances are such that a State (or in the case of proceedings to which section 10 above applies, a State which is not a party to the Brussels Convention) would have been immune.

The central bank or other monetary authority of a foreign State is not regarded a separate entity within the meaning of these provisions, even if under its own law it has that character, and its property is immune.[52] Where a State has agreed in writing to arbitration, it is not immune as respects proceedings in the courts of the United Kingdom which relate to arbitration; that may be done even before a dispute has arisen.[53]

It is possible to execute a judgment or arbitration award in respect of State property which is for the time being in use or intended for use for commercial purposes[54] and such property is likewise subject to execution if it is intended to enforce a foreign judgment or arbitration award in the United Kingdom, provided that the conditions for such enforcement are satisfied. It is not, however, possible to obtain an injunction against a foreign State even in commercial matters[55]—a decided shortcoming of the Act. It is, however, thought that one can obtain an injunction against a third party, *e.g.* a bank, which holds commercial property of the State because that possibility is not expressly barred by the Act.

---

[51] In s. 14(2).
[52] s. 14(4).
[53] s. 9.
[54] s. 13(4).
[55] s. 13(2)(*a*).

In the United States the restrictive theory is likewise adopted[56] and forms the basis of the Foreign Sovereign Immunities Act 1976.[57]

FOREIGN ILLEGALITY

Civil consequences

The English courts will not enforce "a contract where performance of that contract is forbidden by the law of the place where it is to be performed."[58] Thus, if the parties to a contract of export sale knowingly and deliberately agree to break the laws of a friendly country, *i.e.* a country with which Her Majesty is not at war and the Government of which is recognised by the Government of this country,[59] the English courts will not enforce such contract at the suit of one of the parties because to do so would disregard the rules of international comity. This applies even if the laws which the parties intended to infringe were the revenue laws[60] of another country, *i.e.* laws relating to customs duties and quotas, import or export prohibitions, exchange control regulations or taxation.

In *Regazzoni* v. *K. C. Sethia (1944) Ltd.*[61] the Government of India prohibited the direct or indirect exportation of specified goods, including jute bags, to the Union of South Africa because differences had arisen between the Governments of the two countries with respect to the treatment of Indian nationals in South Africa. Regazzoni, a Swiss merchant, bought from the defendants, a company incorporated in England and having Indian connections, a large quantity of jute bags c.i.f. Genoa; thence the goods were, as both parties knew, to be transhipped to South Africa. Both parties intended, as the court found, to infringe the prohibition of Indian law. The contract which was governed by English law was not carried out because the Indian Government did not sanction the exportation of the goods to Genoa, and the action by the buyer against the sellers for damages for non-delivery of the goods was dismissed by the English courts on the ground that it was against English public policy to enforce a contract intended by the parties to involve the breach of the laws of India.

The rule of which the *Regazzoni* case is an illustration is subject to certain qualifications and exceptions. Thus, the English courts will not enforce foreign revenue or penal laws at the suit of a foreign sovereign[62];

[56] In the U.S. the changeover from the absolute to the restrictive doctrine was accelerated by the so-called Tate letter of May 19, 1952, addressed by Mr. J. B. Tate, acting legal adviser to the State Department, to the then acting Attorney-General. The restrictive theory was applied by the Supreme Court in *Alfred Dunhill of London Inc.* v. *Republic of Cuba* (1976) 96 S.C. 1854.

[57] See Kazimierz Grzybowski, "The United States Foreign Sovereign Immunities Act 1976" in [1978] J.B.L. 111.

[58] Lord Wright M.R. in *International Trustee* v. *R.* [1936] 3 All E.R. 407, 428; see Clive M. Schmitthoff, *The English Conflict of Laws* (3rd ed.), p. 131.

[59] *Carl Zeiss Stiftung* v. *Rayner & Keeler Ltd.* (*No. 2*) [1967] 1 A.C. 853.

[60] But the English courts will not enforce revenue laws at the suit of an overseas government or government department; see below in the text.

[61] [1958] A.C. 301; see also *Foster* v. *Driscoll* [1929] 1 K.B. 470.

[62] *Indian Government* v. *Taylor* [1955] A.C. 491, and Schmitthoff, *op. cit.* p. 57.

a government of another country, even if within the Commonwealth or the European Community, cannot successfully claim in the English courts taxes or import duties from a person who is liable to pay them. Further the validity of the contract is not affected where only one party, but not the other, is aware of the illegality.[63] Thirdly, where the transaction in issue is completed and the illegality arises thereafter, or the illegality precedes the transaction and is exhausted before the parties contract, their bargain is unaffected by the illegality[64]; an ordinary sale, in England, of goods which, as the seller known or suspects, will be smuggled by the buyer into another country is likely to be valid. Fourthly, foreign illegality affects only the contract in which it arises but not supporting contracts; thus, the fact that export invoices were falsified in order to deceive the Customs authorities of the importer's country did not prevent the exporter from recovering damages in this country from carriers, when the exporter's goods were stolen from their lorry in transit to the docks of London.[65]

Criminal consequences[66]

Different from the civil consequences of foreign illegality is the question whether a British exporter who has committed a criminal offence under the laws of another country or has conspired to commit such offence can be convicted of it and punished in England.[67] Here the position is this:

1. The courts of this country do not enforce the criminal law of another country at the suit of that country, either directly or indirectly[68];
2. As a rule, an act committed abroad is not punishable in England. Speaking generally, the criminal law of this country is concerned with the "preservation of the Queen's peace and the maintenance of law and order within the realm,"[69] and the commission of criminal acts abroad is not its concern;
3. Exceptionally, however, certain acts committed abroad are made offences by the common law of England or United Kingdom statutes and are punishable in the English courts;
4. Where an offence falls within the list of extradition crimes, and the United Kingdom has reciprocal arrangements for extradition with a foreign country, a person accused or convicted of such crime may be extradited to the country in question. Extradition to most foreign countries is regulated by the *Extradition Acts 1870 to 1932*, and the

---

[63] *Archbolds (Freightage) Ltd.* v. *S. Spanglett Ltd.* [1961] 1 Q.B. 374; *Fielding & Platt Ltd.* v. *Najjar* [1969] 1 W.L.R. 357.

[64] *Regazzoni* v. *K. C. Sethia (1944) Ltd.* [1958] A.C. 301; also *Mackender, Hill and White* v. *Feldia A.G.* [1966] 2 Lloyd's Rep. 449.

[65] *Pye Ltd.* v. *B.G. Transport Service Ltd.* [1966] 2 Lloyd's Rep. 300.

[66] On the exporter's criminal liability for offences relating to customs, p. 479 *et seq., post.*

[67] See Schmitthoff, "Criminal Offences in Export Trade Law" in [1957] J.B.L. 146.

[68] Denning L.J. in *Regazzoni* v. *K. C. Sethia (1944) Ltd.* [1956] 2 Q.B. 490, 515; affd. [1958] A.C. 301, 318.

[69] *Per* Lord Tucker in *Board of Trade* v. *Owen* [1957] A.C. 602, 625; *R.* v. *Peter Stanley Cox* [1968] 1 W.L.R. 88.

Orders in Council made thereunder, and to British Commonwealth countries or to those foreign countries to which the Acts are made applicable by the *Fugitive Offenders Act 1967*. Both these Acts are amended by the *Suppression of Terrorism Act 1978*.

The third of these rules, *viz.* that an act committed abroad may be punishable in England by virtue of English law, was at least indirectly involved in *R.* v. *Reiss and John M. Potter Ltd.*, decided by Barry J. at Leeds Assizes on December 10, 1956.[70] The accused had exported wool tops from Uruguay directly to Italy and Greece under certificates of origin obtained from the Bradford Chamber of Commerce and certifying falsely that the wool tops were of United Kingdom manufacture. The certificates of origin were obtained in this manner: the accused submitted the usual application forms to the Chamber of Commerce which, in perfect good faith and not suspecting that they contained false details, verified them. The legislation then in force[71] stated that it was an offence for any person who, being within the United Kingdom, aided and abetted, "*without the United Kingdom,*" any act which, if committed in the United Kingdom, would be a misdemeanour. The accused were prosecuted and fined £5,000. The Trade Descriptions Act 1968, which has taken the place of that legislation, does not have extra-territorial effect and even provides that there shall be no prosecution in the United Kingdom if a false description is attached to goods intended for dispatch to a destination outside the United Kingdom.[72]

A person dispatching from England a forged end-user certificate purporting to be issued by a foreign authority can be convicted for uttering a forged document in England, contrary to the Forgery Act 1913, s. 6(2), if he knows that the document is a forgery.[73] A conspiracy to commit an export offence abroad is only punishable as such if it constitutes, at the same time, a conspiracy to commit a crime in England, *e.g.*, the crime of obtaining a pecuniary advantage by deception in England.[74] Conversely, a conspiracy entered into abroad to commit a crime in England, continues in existence so long as there are two or more parties to it intending to carry out its design; if the conspirators, having still that intention, come to England, the English courts have jurisdiction to try them for conspiracy.[75] In exceptional cases a dishonest or improper deal abroad by a person resident in England may be punishable in England as conspiracy to commit a public mischief to the prejudice of honest British traders but the courts

---

[70] The case is discussed in [1957] J.B.L. 147.

[71] s. 11 of the Merchandise Marks Acts 1887 and 1953. These enactments were repealed by the Trade Descriptions Act 1968.

[72] Trade Descriptions Act 1968, s. 32 (other particulars may be dispensed with by the Board of Trade).

[73] *Board of Trade* v. *Owen* [1957] A.C. 602.

[74] *R.* v. *Peter Stanley Cox* [1968] 1 W.L.R. 88; *R.* v. *Governor of Brixton Prison, ex p. Rush* [1969] 1 W.L.R. 165.

[75] *R.* v. *Doot* [1973] A.C. 807.

approach this crime with caution and circumstances must be very strong to pursuade them that it has been committed.[76]

EEC LAW

The Commission of the EEC published in 1972 a Preliminary Draft Convention on the Law applicable to Contractual and Non-contractual Obligations.[77] The aim of this convention is to unify the private international law of the Member States, as far as relating to the contract, torts and other non-contractual obligations. This measure is still under consideration and the convention envisaged has not been signed yet.[78]

---

[76] See *R.* v. *Newland* [1954] 1 Q.B. 158; *Board of Trade* v. *Owen* [1957] A.C. 602.
[77] XIV/398/72–E; Rev. 1.
[78] Position: September 1, 1979.

CHAPTER 13

THE UNIFORM LAWS ON INTERNATIONAL SALES

IT has already been pointed out[1] that it would be of great value to the international business community if the law relating to international sales were unified and no longer determined by different national legal systems which provide different answers to questions such as when an offer or acceptance becomes effective, when possession, property or risk in the goods sold passes, what the rights of a party are when goods not conforming to the contract are tendered, and similar questions. A unification of the law of international sales would avoid a conflict of laws in a particularly sensitive area of international business relations. Aware of the value of a unified sales law for the international business community, the International Institute for the Unification of Private Law in Rome, on the suggestion of the great German comparatist Ernst Rabel, drafted two Uniform Laws on International Sales and after 30 years' preparation these Laws were adopted by a conference at The Hague on April 25, 1964.[2]

The two Uniform Laws are *The Uniform Law on International Sale of Goods* (Uniform Law on Sales) and *The Uniform Law on the Formation of Contracts for the International Sale of Goods* (Uniform Law on Formation).[3] The former aims at the unification of the substantive law of international sales; apart from its general provisions, it is divided into four major parts, *viz.* the obligations of the buyer, the obligations of the seller, provisions common to the obligations of the seller and the buyer, and the passing of the risk. The latter is complementary to the former; it attempts to reconcile the considerable differences of the common law and European continental law on offer and acceptance leading to the conclusion of an international contract of sale. The provisions of the Uniform Laws differ in many important aspects from English law but represent, as such, an acceptable and logical code of the law of international sales.[4]

The two Conventions of 1964 have been ratified by the United Kingdom, Belgium, Western German, Italy, the Netherlands, Gambia, San Marino,

---

[1] See p. 126, *ante*.

[2] See pp. 48 and 126, *ante*. The two Uniform Laws are embodied in two Conventions, referred to here as the First Convention and the Second Convention; see further, Schmitthoff's *Sale of Goods*, (2nd ed.), pp. 36 and 321.

[3] Both appended as Schedules 1 and 2 to the Uniform Laws on International Sales Act 1967. The two Uniform Laws are reproduced in Schmitthoff's *Sale of Goods*, (2nd ed.), p. 321 *et seq.* The treatment of the Laws in this chapter is in part founded on the introductory note to the Uniform Laws in that work.

[4] A. Szakats, "The Influence of Common Law Principles on the Uniform Law on the International Sale of Goods" in (1966) 15 I.C.L.Q. 749; the same author, "The Sale of Goods Act 1893 and the Uniform Law on the International Sale of Goods" [1968] J.B.L. 235; and the note by J. D. Feltham in (1967) 30 M.L.R. 670; R. H. Graveson, E. J. Cohn and D. Graveson, *The Uniform Laws of International Sales Act 1967*, 1968.

and the first—but not the second—Convention has been ratified by Israel. The dates at which the Conventions become effective in the United Kingdom are stated in the next section.

The number of countries which so far have ratified the Hague Conventions of 1964 is disappointingly small. Neither the United States nor the Soviet Union or any other country of state-planned economy have ratified them, nor have the countries in the course of development in Africa, Asia and Latin America introduced them. UNCITRAL has therefore made the unification of the law relating to the international sale of goods one of its priority subjects and in March 1979 has produced a *Draft Convention on Contracts for the International Sale of Goods*. The Draft Convention is founded on the two Uniform Laws approved by the Hague Conference in 1964. The Draft Convention will be submitted to a United Nations Conference in 1980. It is to be hoped that, if it is accepted by the conference, it will be adopted more widely than the 1964 Hague Conventions.

THE UNIFORM LAWS IN THE UNITED KINGDOM

The Uniform Laws on International Sales Act 1967

This enactment introduces the two Uniform Laws adopted by the Hague Conference of 1964 into the law of the United Kingdom. The two Uniform Laws are appended to the Act as Schedules 1 and 2. By Order in Council[5] the Act of 1967 was activated and the two Uniform Laws came into operation in the United Kingdom on August 18, 1972.

Contracting States for the purposes of the Uniform Law on the International Sale of Goods (the First Convention) are:

Contracting state	*Effective date of ratification*
Belgium	August 18, 1972
Israel	August 18, 1972
Italy	August 23, 1972
Netherlands	August 18, 1972
San Marino	August 18, 1972
United Kingdom	August 18, 1972

Application of Uniform Laws only if adopted by parties

The Order in Council which gives effect to the two Uniform Laws provides that the Uniform Law on Sales shall only apply if it has been chosen by the parties to the contract[6]; the Uniform Law on Formation has only ancillary character and applies only to contracts to which the Uniform Law on Sales applied.[7]

While such a restriction considerably reduces the usefulness of the Uniform Laws and will, it is hoped, only be temporary, it might lead to

[5] The Uniform Laws on International Sales Order 1972 (S.I. 1972 No. 973).

[6] 1967 Act, s. 1(3). The United Kingdom was entitled to restrict the scope of the Uniform Law on Sales in this manner by virtue of art. V of the First Convention.

[7] 1967 Act, Sched. 2, art. 1.

a difficulty if one party to the contract is resident in the United Kingdom and the other in a country in which the Uniform Laws apply automatically (unless excluded by the parties). This raises a problem of private international law, *viz.* it has to be determined whether the proper law of the contract is English or foreign law.[8] In the latter case the Uniform Laws apply to an English party who has not adopted them in the contract but in the former case they apply only if adopted by the parties.

Mandatory provisions of proper law cannot be contracted out

When the parties adopt the Uniform Laws—and they may adopt them even if the conditions for the application of the Uniform Laws are not satisfied—the parties cannot, by so doing, contract out of the mandatory provisions of the law which would have been applicable if they had not chosen the Uniform Laws.[9] As far as the law of the United Kingdom is concerned, the only provisions which are mandatory by statute[10] are those aiming at the protection of the consumer in the domestic sale of goods, namely those contained in the Unfair Contract Terms Act 1977, ss. 2 to 7. These provisions apply, as already stated, only to domestic sales. They do not apply to international supply contracts.[11] As regards the latter type of contract, exemption clauses, if freely negotiated, are perfectly valid. The definition of international supply contracts was given earlier.[12]

Further, by adopting the Uniform Laws, the parties cannot contract out of provisions directly founded on public policy, *e.g.* those regulating exchange control.

General Limitations of Uniform Laws

Two of these general limitations have already been considered in the preceding paragraphs. They are the restriction of these Laws to cases in which the parties have chosen them as the proper law of contract[13] and the rule that the parties cannot exclude the mandatory provisions of the proper law by their adoption of the Uniform Laws.[14] There are, however, further limitations which may be introduced by States when ratifying the Conventions to which the Uniform Laws are appended.

Restriction to contracts between parties in Convention states

The Uniform Laws, as drafted, apply to all cases in which the parties to the contract have their places of business in the territories of different states or, if they have no place of business, are habitually resident in

---

[8] See p. 125, *ante*.
[9] Uniform Laws on International Sales Act 1967, s. 1(4); Uniform Laws of Sales, art. 4.
[10] Supply of Goods (Implied Terms) Act 1973, s. 5(2), as amended by the Unfair Contract Terms Act 1977.
[11] Unfair Contract Terms Act 1977, s. 26.
[12] See p. 65, *ante*.
[13] Uniform Law on Sales, art. 4.
[14] Art. II of both Conventions.

different states.[15] The Laws do not require that the places of business or habitual residence should be in the territories of contracting States; in brief, they do not require reciprocity in that respect. However, a State, when ratifying the Conventions embodying the Uniform Laws, may stipulate that it will apply them only if each of the parties to the contract has his place of business or habitual residence in the territory of a different State which likewise has ratified the Conventions.[16] For that reason it was necessary to state earlier[17] which States have become "contracting States" for the purposes of the Uniform Laws on International Sales.

A State which adopts this qualification introduces into its law an unfortunate complication. It has two legal régimes applying to contracts of international sale of goods, one in respect of residents in Convention States and the other in respect of residents in other foreign countries.

Restriction to proper law under P.I.L. Convention

A difficulty arises for the countries which have adopted the Hague Convention of June 15, 1955, on the Law applicable to International Sale of Goods (the P.I.L. Convention).[18] It will be recalled that this Convention provides, in essence, that, failing an agreement by the parties, the seller's law shall be the proper law of the contract. The difficulty is here to align the Uniform Laws with the P.I.L. Convention. This has been done by provided that a State which previously has adopted the P.I.L. Convention may declare, on ratification of the Conventions embodying the Uniform Laws, that these Laws shall only apply if the P.I.L. Convention requires their application.[19] If a State adopts this qualification, the application of the Uniform Laws will be restricted to contracts in which they are automatically the seller's law under the legal regulation applicable in the seller's country or to contracts in which they are chosen as the proper law of contract by the parties. In all other cases the Uniform Laws are inapplicable. By such a declaration the—older—P.I.L. Convention is given precedence over the Uniform Laws and the field of application of the latter is severely restricted. In the domain in which the two Uniform Laws apply, however, the rules of private international law are excluded.[20]

The United Kingdom, it will be recalled, has not adopted the P.I.L. Convention.

Effect of limitations

Even if a great number of States has given effect to the Uniform Laws, the unification achieved will be partial only and not complete. The United Kingdom exporter will be faced with a situation in which some of his

[15] Uniform Law on Sales, art 1(1) and (2).
[16] Both Conventions, art. III.
[17] See p. 141, *ante*.
[18] See p. 127, *ante*.
[19] Both Conventions, art. IV.
[20] Uniform Law on International Sales, art. 2.

contracts may be governed by the Uniform Laws and others not, and even more complicated will be the situation with regard to international sales contracts concluded by his foreign subsidiaries. Even if it appears that the Uniform Laws apply, the further question has to be examined whether they apply subject to a particular qualification.

It follows that even after the coming into operation of the Uniform Laws on International Sales Act 1967 the United Kingdom exporter should, at least for the time being, aim first at the adoption of English law as the law governing the transaction and only in the second place agree with the overseas importer on the adoption of the Uniform Laws.

Contracts of International Sale

The Uniform Laws apply only to contracts for the international sale of goods. They do not apply to home transactions.[21]

A contract of international sale, within the meaning of the Uniform Laws, is defined[22] as a contract of sale of goods entered into by parties whose places of business are in the territories of "different states,"[23] in each of the following cases:

(*a*) where the contract involves the sale of goods which are at the time of the conclusion of the contract in the course of carriage or will be carried from the territory of one State to the territory of another;
(*b*) where the acts constituting the offer and the acceptance have been effected in the territories of different States;
(*c*) where delivery of the goods is to be made in the territory of a State other than that within whose territory the acts constituting the offer and the acceptance have been effected.

Where a party to the contract does not have a place of business, the habitual residence of the party shall determine his situs. The nationality of the parties is irrelevant for the determination of the international character of the contract.[24] Further, the Uniform Laws apply to contracts of sale regardless of the commercial or private character of the parties.[25]

---

[21] Unless a state introduces legislation applying them to home transactions or the parties to a home transaction adopt them.

[22] Uniform Law on Sales, art 1. This definition should be compared with that of the international supply contract in section 26 of the Unfair Contract Terms Act 1977; see p. 65, *ante*.

[23] Two or more states may declare that they do not consider themselves as "different states" for the purposes of the Uniform Laws because their law of sale and their law on the formation of the contract of sale are substantially the same; see the two Conventions, art. II, and the two Uniform Laws art. 1(5). Such a declaration of conformity can, *e.g.* be made between the United Kingdom, on the one hand, and Australia, New Zealand and Canada (with the exception of Quebec) on the other hand, if the latter states decide to adopt the Uniform Laws.

[24] Uniform Law on Sales, art. 1(3).

[25] *Ibid.* art. 7.

THE UNIFORM LAW ON INTERNATIONAL SALES

The Uniform Law on Sales does not define the trade terms customary in international trade[26] but provides[27]:

1. The parties shall be bound by any usage which they have expressly or impliedly made applicable to their contract and by any practices which have been established between themselves.
2. They shall also be bound by usages which reasonable persons in the same situation as the parties usually consider to be applicable to their contract. In the event of conflict with the present Law, the usages shall prevail unless agreed by the parties.
3. Where expressions, provisions or forms of contract commonly used in commercial practice are employed, they shall be interpreted according to the meaning usually given to them in the trade concerned.

Consequently, where the parties have agreed on a trade term, such as f.o.b. or c.i.f., the regulation intended by that term takes precedence over the provisions of the Law. Further, the Law does not prevent the parties from agreeing on a uniform interpretation of these trade terms, *e.g.* by embodying into their contract Incoterms or a similar text.

The Uniform Law does not use the distinction between conditions and warranties which, as we have seen,[28] the Sale of Goods Act, adopts. It distinguishes, however, between two types of breach of contract, *viz.* a fundamental and a non-fundamental breach. A fundamental breach occurs[29]—

> wherever the party in breach knew, or ought to have known, at the time of the conclusion of the contract, that a reasonable person in the same situation as the other party would not have entered into the contract if he had foreseen the breach and its effects.

The principle of the Law is that where a breach is of fundamental nature, the person who suffers it may declare the contract as avoided but if the breach is not fundamental the contract continues to be in existence, subject to the right of the wronged party to claim damages. This is similar in effect to the modern English concepts of the innominate term, discussed earlier.[30] These rules may be illustrated by reference to the case of a seller who has failed to deliver the goods timely, *i.e.* at the date agreed in the contract. It depends here on the importance which the parties have attached to timely delivery. If the failure to deliver timely constitutes a fundamental breach, the buyer has the choice between requiring performance of the contract or declaring the contract avoided; if he does not exercise this choice within a reasonable time, the contract is automatically avoided.[31] On the other hand, if the failure to deliver timely does not amount to a

---

[26] See p. 8, *ante*.

[27] In art. 9 of the Uniform Law on Sales. [All references to articles in this section are to the Uniform Law on Sales (1967 Act, Sched. 1), unless stated otherwise.]

[28] See p. 90, *ante*.

[29] Art. 10.

[30] See p. 91, *ante*.

[31] See art. 26(1). This rule is subject to exceptions, see art. 26(2) and (3). "Avoidance of the contract" does not mean that the contract is null and void from the beginning, it merely releases both parties from their obligations thereunder (art. 78). In the case of avoidance of the contract the buyer may be entitled to damages (art. 84).

fundamental breach, the buyer may grant the seller an additional period of reasonable length, and failure to deliver within this period would turn the non-fundamental breach into a fundamental breach.[32]

Of further interest are the provisions of the Uniform Law on the rights of the buyer if the seller tenders or delivers "non-conforming goods," *i.e.* goods which fail to conform with their description in the contract or with the stipulated quantity or quality. Such a failure will normally constitute a fundamental breach of the seller's obligation to deliver the goods contracted for.[33] In these cases the buyer loses his right to rely on lack of conformity—

1. if he fails to notify the seller promptly[34] after he has discovered that lack or ought to have discovered it, but in no circumstances, not even in the case of hidden defects, can notice of lack of conformity be given after two years from the date when the goods were handed over, unless a longer guarantee was stipulated in the contract.[35] The notice of lack of conformity must specify the nature of the defects[36]; or
2. if he fails to take the matter to the court, by action or defence, within one year after having given notice of lack of conformity, except if he has been prevented from relying on lack of conformity by fraud on the part of the seller or if he claims reduction of the price in an action for payment of the price by the seller.[37]

If the buyer has given due notice of lack of conformity, he is entitled—

1. to demand performance of the contract by the seller.[38] But where the court would not order specific performance in respect of similar contracts not governed by the Law—as is the case in England—it is not compelled by the Law to order specific performance of an international contract[39]; or
2. to declare the contract as avoided, but only if the lack of conformity constitutes a fundamental breach[40]; or
3. to reduce the price[41]; and
4. in addition, to claim damages.[42]

If the lack of conformity does not constitute a fundamental breach, the seller is entitled, even after the date fixed for the delivery of the goods, to make a second tender of conforming goods or to remedy the defect, "provided that the exercise of this right does not cause the buyer either

---

[32] See art. 27. The requirement of an additional period follows the German requirement of a *Nachfrist*.
[33] Art. 33.
[34] *i.e.* "within as short a period as possible" (art. 11).
[35] Art. 39(1).
[36] Art. 39(2).
[37] Art. 49.
[38] Art. 41(1)(*a*).
[39] First Convention, art. VII.
[40] Art. 41(1)(*b*).
[41] Art. 41(1)(*c*).
[42] Art. 41(2).

unreasonable inconvenience or unreasonable expense."[43] Here again, however, the buyer can turn the non-fundamental breach into a fundamental one by fixing an additional period for further delivery or for remedying the defect.[44]

The Uniform Law on Formation

This Law, as adopted by the U.K. Uniform Laws on International Sales Act 1967, is ancillary to the Uniform Law on Sales, *i.e.* it applies only to contracts of international sale "which, if they were concluded, would be governed by the Uniform Law on the International Sale of Goods."[45] This curious provision postulates a retrospective consideration: one has first to assume that the contract was validly concluded, then to satisfy oneself that it falls within the ambit of the Uniform Law on Sales, and if that condition is satisfied, one has to revert to the primary assumption and to examine whether the contract was really validly concluded.

Three provisions of the Law on Formation deserve special mention. First, the Law attempts to reconcile the different attitude of English and European continental law to the problem of the firm offer. In English law an offer can, on principle, always be revoked until it is accepted; in short, unless the offer is by deed, rendered irrevocable by statute,[46] or supported by consideration, the concept of a binding offer is not admitted in English law.[47] In most European continental laws, on the other hand, an offeror is bound by his offer unless he has excluded its binding character. The compromise adopted by the Uniform Law on Formation is that on principle an offer can be revoked but such a revocation is excluded—

1. if the offer states a fixed time for acceptance or otherwise indicates that it is firm or irrevocable; or
2. if the revocation is not made in good faith or in conformity with fair dealing.[48]

Secondly, the Uniform Law on Formation attempts to solve the problem of an acceptance containing additional stipulations. In English law, if such stipulations are contained in the acceptance, the offer is normally regarded as rejected and the acceptance constitutes a counter-offer which may or may not be accepted by the original offeror. Logical as this rule is, it is iniquitous if the additional terms are only immaterial or trifling.[49] The Uniform Law provides that on principle an acceptance containing additions, limitations or other modifications shall be a rejection of the offer and a

[43] Art. 44(1).
[44] Art. 44(2).
[45] Uniform Law on Formation, art. 1. [All references to articles in this section are to the Uniform Law on Formation (1967 Act, Sched. 2), unless stated otherwise.]
[46] See Companies Act 1948, s. 50(5).
[47] American law differs in this respect from English law; the Uniform Commercial Code (1962 Revision), s. 2–205, admits in certain circumstances firm offers.
[48] Art. 5(2) and (3).
[49] Here again, modern American law adopts a different solution in the Uniform Commercial Code (1962 Revision), s. 2–207.

counter-offer, but if these additional or different terms do not alter the terms of the offer materially, the reply including these additions or modifications shall constitute the acceptance unless the offeror promptly objects to the discrepancy.[50]

Thirdly, the Uniform Law deals with the case of the late acceptance. Here it is provided that such an acceptance may be treated by the offeror as having arrived in due time if he promptly so informs the acceptor.[51] Further, if the delay in the receipt of the acceptance is due to unusual circumstances and the communication of the acceptance would have arrived in time if the transmission had been normal, the acceptance is deemed to have been communicated in due time, unless the offeror has promptly informed the acceptor that he considers his offer as lapsed.[52]

Limitation in the International Sale of Goods

On June 14, 1974, a *Convention on the Limitation Period in the International Sale of Goods* was signed at the headquarters of the United Nations in New York. It was the first proposal of UNCITRAL[53] which has reached fruition. Although the Convention has not been given effect in the United Kingdom yet, it deserves attention.

The Convention is intended to replace a variety of conflicting national laws which provide limitation periods ranging from six months to 30 years. The basic aim of the Convention is to establish a uniform time limit that prevents the pressing of claims at such a late date that evidence has become unreliable.

The Convention limits to four years the period within which a buyer or seller may press claims based on a contract for the international sale of goods.[54] The buyer and seller must have their places of business in different States for the Convention to apply.

Certain sales and types of goods are excluded from the reach of the Convention: consumer sales, sales by auction, sales on execution or otherwise by authority of law, sales of securities or money, sales of ships or aircraft and sales of electricity. Also excluded are claims based on death or personal injury, nuclear damage, a lien or other security interest in property, a judgment or award made in legal proceedings, a document on which direct enforcement or execution can be obtained, and bills of exchange or promissory notes. Nor does the Convention apply to contracts mainly concerned with the supply of services rather than goods.

The limitation period, during its running, can only be modified by the debtor by declaration in writing. When the person against whom a claim is brought performs his obligation under the contract after the limitation period has ceased to run, he is not entitled to recover or claim restitution

[50] Art. 7. This provision is referred to in *Butler Machine Tool Co. Ltd* v. *Ex-Cell-O Corporation (England) Ltd.* [1979] 1 W.L.R. 401, 406; see p. 64, *ante*.
[51] Art. 9(1).
[52] Art. 9(2).
[53] On UNCITRAL, see p. 45, *ante*.
[54] Art. 8 of the Convention.

even if he does not know at the time that the period had expired. If a limitation period expires with regard to a debt between buyer and seller, it also expires with regard to any interest outstanding on that debt.

The Convention contains provisions specifying exactly when the limitation period begins to run, which is usually the case when the claim becomes due. It also states when the limitation period ceases to run, under what circumstances it can be extended, how it can be modified by the parties and how it is calculated. In the case of a breach of contract, the limitation period begins on the date of the breach. When the buyer finds a defect in the goods supplied or discovers that they do not otherwise conform to the terms of the contract the limitation period starts from the date when the goods were handed over to him or its delivery is refused by him. The limitation period for claims based on fraud begins on the date on which the fraud is discovered or reasonably could be discovered.

The limitation period ceases to run when one party begins judicial or arbitral proceedings against the other. In the case of other proceedings, including those in which a party presses a claim upon the death or bankruptcy of the other party, the period ceases to run once the claim is asserted. When a party making a claim is prevented by circumstances beyond his control from starting legal proceedings, he may have a one-year extension from the time when those circumstances cease to exist. The overall limit for extensions of the limitation period is 10 years from the date when the period began to run. A circumstance occurring in another contracting State that affects the cessation or extension of the limitation period, shall be taken into account, provided that the creditor has taken steps to inform the debtor of it as soon as possible.

PART TWO

REPRESENTATIVES ABROAD

CHAPTER 14

SOLE DISTRIBUTION AGREEMENTS

THE exporter who has successfully carried out a number of individual sales may wish to secure a steady flow of export orders. Intensive exports can, as a rule, only be achieved if a permanent sales organisation is established overseas whose duty it is to create and maintain a demand for the goods in question and to convey first-hand intelligence to its United Kingdom principals on the special requirements of the market and the operation of the competition. The establishment of a permanent sales organisation is strongly favoured in modern export trade, and the exporter who wishes to put his export trade on a permanent basis has to examine the five possibilities which exist in this respect:

1. The exporter may conclude a *sole distribution agreement* with an importer abroad, or
2. He may entrust his representation to an *exclusive agent* abroad or ask his overseas customers to use the services of a *confirming house* in this country, or
3. He may establish his own *branch offices* and employ his own sales organisation abroad, or
4. He may act through a *subsidiary company* there which is created under the laws of the foreign country in question, or
5. He may combine with other traders in a *joint export organisation* which may take the form of a joint selling organisation, a consortium, a joint venture or a similar scheme.

It is intended to deal here with the first type of export organisation and to examine the other types in the following chapters of this Part. Since the choice of the export organisation most appropriate to the circumstances is greatly influenced by United Kingdom law relating to restrictive trade practices and the law of the European Communities on competition, chapters dealing with these topics are included in this Part.

NATURE OF SOLE DISTRIBUTION AGREEMENTS

Sole distribution agreements distinguished from contracts of sale and from agency agreements

Sole distribution agreements,[1] as customary in the export trade, provide, in essence, that the seller, a United Kingdom manufacturer or merchant, grants the buyer, an overseas merchant, sole trading rights within a par-

[1] See also Rudolf Graupner, "Sole Distributorship Agreements—a Comparative View" (1969) 18 I.C.L.Q. 879. On exclusive sales agreements in French law and on the law of the EEC, see R. Plaisant, *Les contrats d'exclusivité* in (1964) 17 *Rev.Trim. de Droit Commercial* 1; Thomas E. Carbonneau, "Exclusive Distributorship Agreements in French Law," (1979) 28 I.C.L.Q. 91.

ticular territory with respect to goods of a specified kind while the buyer undertakes to rely upon the seller as the sole source of supply whenever desirous of buying goods of the specified kind in Great Britain. Where such a contract is concluded between a manufacturer of typewriters in Great Britain and an Indian importer, the former is not entitled to sell his typewriters to other firms operating in India, nor, if that is the intention of the parties, is the latter at liberty to buy competitive makes of typewriters in this country. The sole distribution agreement is not a contract of sale of specific goods, it merely lays down the general terms on which individual contracts of sale will be concluded. Sometimes the sole distribution agreement contains the stipulation by the buyer to buy a quantity of specified goods which have to be delivered by instalments or on call. Even where such a stipulation is not agreed upon, the sole distribution agreement is not merely a contract to conclude a contract, but an agreement which is presently effective. Although its mandatory clauses are dependent on the conclusion of individual contracts of sale in the future, its restrictive clauses are immediately effective and remain in force for the duration of the agreement even when individual sales are never concluded. Where the exclusive buyer resides in a country which has strict laws safeguarding competition, such as another Member State of the European Community or the United States, great care has to be taken that the proposed agreement does not infringe these laws.[2]

The sole distribution agreement has some affinity with a contract granting exclusive agency rights; in both contracts an area or territory is defined where the exclusive trading rights are to be operative, but the sole distribution agreement differs from the exclusive agency agreement in a material aspect, *viz.* the contracts which are concluded within its framework are proper contracts of sale by which the foreign merchant—the distributor—buys in his own name and when he resells the goods in his territory no contractual bond is established between the third party and the British exporter. The sole distribution agreement has thus a distinct advantage over the exclusive agency agreement: the British exporter is not concerned with the credit of a multitude of buyers in the foreign territory, but he sells to one person only whose credit and commercial standing is well known to him or is at least relatively easily ascertainable.

Export distribution agreements

A sole distribution agreement might further be concluded between an exporter in this country and a manufacturer or wholesaler here. In this case the exporter, who is sometimes referred to as "export distributor," is granted the exclusive right of distributing the manufacturer's goods abroad, either anywhere or in a specified market. Two types of export distribution agreements are in use and the contract should make it clear in unambiguous terms which type is intended: under some export distri-

[2] See p. 218, *post*.

bution agreements the distributor undertakes to place annually orders of a fixed amount with the manufacturer, and under other agreements he merely undertakes to place such orders if and when he receives them from his customers abroad; although in the latter case—as in the former—the export distributor undertakes to place the order in his own name (and not as agent of the overseas customer) and to hold himself personally liable for the price, the nature of his obligation differs; in the latter case the distributor is only liable if he fails diligently to pass on to the manufacturer such customers' orders as are received by him while in the former case he is liable to order goods of the stipulated value whether he receives such orders or not. The importance of this distinction became evident in the following case[3]: The defendants, a confirming house, undertook to act as exclusive export distributors of the plaintiffs, manufacturers of water taps and other sanitary fittings, for certain foreign countries. The agreement was for 15 years but could be cancelled at the end of 10 years by giving six months' notice. Under clause 2(*k*) of the agreement the export distributors undertook to "pass on to the manufacturers customers' orders for the goods amounting to not less in volume than the volume of goods which at present price would amount to the value of £80,000." The agreement continued in operation for about 15 months when the amount of orders had fallen short of the stipulated value, mainly because in some foreign countries the issue of import licences for the goods in question was suspended. A dispute arose between the parties on the exact meaning of clause 2(*k*). The manufacturers maintained that the distributors were bound to place annually £80,000 worth of orders while the latter contended that they were only obliged to give them whatever orders they received from their customers. The manufacturers contended that the distributors had repudiated the agreement and claimed damages resulting, first, from the breach of clause 2(*k*) during the currency of the agreement and, secondly, from the repudiation of the entire contract. The Court of Appeal held that clause 2(*k*) obliged the export distributors to place annually £80,000 worth of orders with the manufacturers whether they received such orders from their customers or did not receive them, but that the construction which the distributors put on the clause, though being erroneous, was adopted in good faith and did not evince an intention to repudiate the entire contract. The court awarded the plaintiffs damages for non-performance of the distributors' undertakings during the 15 months during which the contract was in operation, but dismissed the claim for damages resulting from the repudiation of the contract which, in view of the long currency of the contract, would have been heavy.

When interpreting the clauses of a sole distribution agreement, it must be borne in mind that the parties intend to build up an enduring relationship. Minor deviations from the terms of the contract cannot be used as an

[3] *James Shaffler Ltd.* v. *Findlay Durham & Brodie* [1953] 1 W.L.R. 106. See also the Canadian case of *Wingold* v. *Wm. Looser & Co.* [1951] 1 D.L.R. 429.

excuse to treat the whole contract as repudiated although they may give rise to a claim for damages. This is particularly true if, without obligation on his part, the sole distributor has incurred considerable expense in order to promote the sales of the producer's goods. Thus in *Decro-Wall S.A.* v. *Marketing Ltd.*[4] Decro-Wall gave the sole distributing rights of their goods—decorative tiles—in the United Kingdom to Marketing, a small but reputable company. The sole distribution agreement was of indefinite duration and thus determinable by reasonable notice. Marketing was highly successful in building up a market in the United Kingdom. Two years after the conclusion of the agreement there were already 780 points of sale of Decro-Wall products in the United Kingdom. Marketing spent some £30,000 on advertising Decro-Wall products and had engaged at least six extra salesmen. There were, however, some minor differences between the parties due to slow payment by Marketing, although in the end it always paid fully; Marketing also alleged delayed deliveries by Decro-Wall. The managing director of Marketing thereupon submitted a new plan for smaller but more regular deliveries but that plan was rejected by Decro-Wall. Decro-Wall had already negotiated with another company in the United Kingdom and then arranged to appoint that other company its sole concessionaire. Decro-Wall alleged that its contract with Marketing had been repudiated by the latter by its failure to pay the bills punctually and purported to accept that repudiation. Decro-Wall sued Marketing in the English courts for the outstanding bills and also for a declaration that Marketing had ceased to be its sole concessionaire in the United Kingdom. Marketing, by its counterclaim, asked for a declaration that it was still the sole concessionaire of Decro-Wall in the United Kingdom. The Court of Appeal held that Marketing had not repudiated the agreement by its failure to pay outstanding bills punctually, as time was not of the essence of the payments, that the agreement between the parties still subsisted and could only be terminated by reasonable notice and that, in the circumstances, the length of such notice was twelve months.

Clauses in sole distribution agreements

Sole distribution agreements require careful drafting. An infinite variety of arrangements is possible here. The parties have complete liberty of contracting and should use that discretion for the purpose of creating, by their contract, a charter of trading which is fair and equitable to both of them, and closely adapted to the particular requirements of their trade and can be relied upon whether the market is a seller's or a buyer's market. In view of the variety of forms admitted by the law, it is impossible to give an exhaustive catalogue of the clauses embodied in these agreements; it

[4] [1971] 1 W.L.R. 361; see also *Evans Marshall & Co. Ltd.* v. *Bertola S.A.* [1975] 2 Lloyd's Rep. 373 (the contract of sole distributorship contains an implied term according to which the supplier must not charge the distributor prices which would prevent him from making a reasonable commercial profit).

is believed that the main points to be considered are indicated under the following heads which are illustrated by contract clauses when necessary.

Definition of the Territory

The following points have to be considered by the parties:

(1) The geographical definition of the territory which may consist of several political units, *e.g.* the Scandinavian countries, or of one political unit, *e.g.* Sweden, or of part of a political unit, *e.g.* the city of Stockholm.

(2) The extension of the territory at a future date. Sometimes such extension is merely expressed as a moral claim, sometimes the buyer is given a legal right to claim the extension on the happening of certain events, *e.g.* when the sales in his own territory have reached a certain amount over a fixed period.

(3) The seller's obligation not to sell directly to customers in the territory. In earlier agreements it was usual to provide that the seller should insert a clause into his contracts with his home buyers and overseas buyers (other than the contracting party) prohibiting the direct or indirect sale of the goods in the territory of the exclusive dealer. In modern practice such an undertaking is normally omitted, as far as the Member States of the EEC are concerned, because such restrictions are likely to infringe the provisions of the EEC Treaty against distortion of competition.[5]

(4) The seller's obligation to refer direct inquiries from consumers in the territory to the buyer.

(5) The buyer's obligation not to resell outside his territory.

(6) The territory in which the buyer is bound to buy exclusively from the seller. Here again, the former practice of providing that the buyer shall not buy any goods of the specified description from another source of supply than the buyer is now often abandoned in the EEC because of the danger that such restrictions may contravene the provisions of the EEC Treaty or of national legislations.

Definition of the Goods

(1) The contract may only refer to some lines produced or traded by the seller and not to his whole range of production or trade.

(2) A good method of defining the articles in question is to append to the contract a schedule of goods identified by the seller's catalogue number.

(3) Sometimes goods are described generally as "all kinds and types of goods, machinery and equipment designed for use in the . . . industry."

(4) The contract should cease to apply with respect to goods which the seller discontinues to manufacture or trade.

(5) The contract should allow for an extension to new lines manufactured or traded by the seller where the new lines are used in the same trade as the goods covered by the agreement.

[5] See p. 224, *post*.

SOLE BUYING AND SELLING RIGHTS

(1) A contract need not provide for sole buying and selling rights as concurrent terms but is valid if only establishing sole selling rights or sole buying rights. In practice, reciprocal agreements provide mutual satisfaction and are preferable to agreements whereby only one party is granted sole trading rights; but all depends here on the requirements of the particular trade.

(2) The contract should put it beyond doubt that the overseas importer acts as buyer and not as agent of the seller. The following draft clause illustrates this point:

> It is agreed and understood that the buyer is not the agent or representative of the seller for any purpose whatever, and that the buyer has no authority or power to bind the seller, or to contract in the name of, and to create a liability against, the seller in any way or for any purpose, but on the other hand it is understood that the buyer stands in the relation of an independent contractor with the exclusive rights to buy the seller's . . . machinery, and to resell, handle and deal in the same on his own account and responsibility in the said territory as hereinbefore set forth.

(3) The seller may ask for a clause obliging the buyer to offer the seller's goods in the market. The following clause is here sometimes found:

> During the life of this contract the buyer agrees vigorously, diligently, and in good efficient salesmanlike manner, to solicit orders for and to bring to the attention of buyers or potential buyers within the territory, the seller's entire line of . . . machinery and equipment, all to the end that as large a volume of sales of the seller's said machinery and equipment can and will be made to the ultimate users thereof in the territory as the circumstances of competition and general business from time to time permit.

(4) The seller asks sometimes that orders representing a minimum value shall be ordered within a fixed time; sometimes the agreement gives the seller an option of giving notice of determination when the orders placed by the buyer do not represent a minimum value for a fixed period.

ADVERTISING, MARKET INFORMATION, PROTECTION OF PATENTS AND TRADE MARKS

(1) The seller is normally not interested in the proceeds of the sale of goods in the territory, as his overseas contractor stands in the position of a buyer and not of an agent. The seller is, however, interested in seeing a demand created in the foreign market for his goods and having his trade mark advertised if the goods are distributed under that mark. The buyer is, therefore, sometimes asked to undertake certain minimum obligations with respect to the advertising of the goods. The following clause illustrates this point:

> All exhibiting, soliciting of orders, and advertising either by circulars or by paid advertisements in journals or magazines circulating in the territory, of the . . . machines and equipment of the seller shall be under the exclusive control and at the expense of the buyer, but the buyer agrees during the life of this contract to provide and pay for not less than 12 full-page advertisements per annum, appearing at regular monthly intervals in the national journals or magazines of the . . . industry circulating generally throughout the territory, and the buyer at his own expense will at the time of issue dispatch to the seller a copy of each

such monthly journal or magazine in which such advertisements of the seller's machinery or equipment appears.

(2) It is sometimes provided that the distributor shall visit certain prospective customers at regular intervals.[6]

(3) The buyer is often asked to provide the seller with market information which is accessible to him, *e.g.*:

The buyer agrees to the best of his ability to provide to the seller at intervals or at such reasonable times as the seller may request information concerning any developments in the territory relating to the demand, the reactions of the ultimate users, the activities of the competitors, or other matters of circumstances relating to this contract as far as such information is reasonably accessible to the buyer, and the latter agrees to do all such acts and things as may be necessary or helpful to extend and improve the sale of the seller's . . . machinery and equipment in the territory, and to extend and maintain the public goodwill towards the seller's said machinery and equipment.

(4) Due protection should be provided for the seller's patents and trade marks,[7] and the seller sometimes asks generally for an undertaking on the part of the buyer not to make, imitate or copy the goods.

Other Clauses

(1) The contract should embody the appropriate provisions of the seller's general conditions of sale which have been discussed earlier.[8]

(2) The contract is usually concluded for an indefinite time, and either party is given the right of determining the agreement upon a fixed date, *e.g.* the end of every calendar year, on having given notice a fixed number of days or months prior to that date. Sometimes the seller's right to determine the agreement depends on the purchases by the buyer falling below a certain minimum value over a fixed period.

Where the contract contains no provision for its determination, a party is entitled to give the other party notice of reasonable length.[9] In agreements in the commercial field, such as exclusive sales agreements, there is no presumption in favour of permanance.[10]

Laws Relating to Restrictive Practices

The sole distribution agreement must further conform with the laws relating to restrictive trade practices and restraints of trade, as in force in the United Kingdom and in the countries in which the agreement is intended to operate.

---

[6] In *L. Schuler A.G.* v. *Wickman Machine Tool Sales Ltd.* [1974] A.C. 235 the sole distributor agreement concerned panel presses and the sole distributor undertook to visit the six largest United Kingdom motor manufacturers at least once every week. Failure to comply with this clause was held not to be a breach of a condition although the clause was described in the contract as a condition.

[7] See p. 397, *post.*

[8] See p. 53, *ante.*

[9] See *Decro-Wall S.A.* v. *Marketing Ltd.* [1971] 1 W.L.R. 361, discussed on p. 156, *ante.*

[10] *Martin-Baker Aircraft Co. Ltd.* v. *Canadian Flight Equipment Ltd.* [1955] 2 Q.B. 556, 577.

In the United Kingdom, the Restrictive Trade Practices Act 1976[11] exempts from its operation sole distribution agreements and exclusive agency agreements unless a trade association is a party to such agreement. The general effect of the restrictive trade practices legislation on export transactions will be discussed later.[12] In common law a clause in restraint of trade is invalid unless it can be justified as reasonable in the circumstances of the case. Thus, a clause restraining a person, after the termination of his contract, from dealing in goods of a specified kind in the territory for a number of years is invalid if, *e.g.* covering an unreasonably large area or intended to last an unreasonably long time. Restraints of trade which can be shown to be reasonable will be enforced by the English courts.

An exclusive sales agreement may contravene the prohibitions of Articles 85(1) and 86 of the EEC Treaty. Great care has to be taken when it is drafted to avoid this danger. The regulation of European Community law, as far as affecting exclusive sales and agency agreements, will be examined later on.[13] In the United States of America "restraint of trade," "tying requirements" and "exclusive dealings" have, in individual cases, been declared invalid as representing unfair practices and may also infringe the various Anti-Trust Acts[14] in force.

---

[11] s. 28 and Sched. 3, para. 2.

[12] See p. 210, *post*.

[13] See p. 218, *post*.

[14] On the extra territorial effect of the American anti-trust legislation, see p. 228, *post*, and W. Friedmann, "Foreign Investment and Restrictive Trade Practices" [1960] J.B.L. 144.

CHAPTER 15

AGENCY ARRANGEMENTS

SELF-EMPLOYED AGENTS ABROAD

THE peculiar feature of this form of exporting is that the exporter enters into direct relations with the customer abroad, by means of a contract procured or concluded on behalf of the exporter, by a representative who resides abroad and is not his employee.[1] The remuneration of the self-employed agent is usually based upon a commission on the price of the goods sold by him, while the remuneration of the employee normally is a fixed salary sometimes enlarged by bonuses or commissions.

Great care should be taken by an exporter who wishes to market his goods in a foreign country through the instrumentality of a self-employed agent. A contract of agency is a confidential relationship, and the agent has, in certain conditions, implied authority to dispose of the principal's goods, to allow a customer credit terms or to receive the purchase price from him. The exporter should make searching inquiries about the personal reputation and financial standing of the agent before reposing his trust in him. These inquiries are often made through the exporter's bank or through his forwarder. When they result in a satisfactory reply, two further points should be observed. First, a precautionary measure is usually included in the contract, *e.g.* a short probationary period precedes the long-term commitment, or a minimum turnover is stipulated for a certain period, or the termination of the contract is admitted upon short notice but here the minimum periods of notice prescribed by some foreign laws[2] will have to be allowed. Secondly, personal contact should be established and maintained between the principal and agent; no agency agreement of consequence should be concluded before the principal has met the agent in person; and regular visits of the principal to the agent, or vice versa, should maintain the high standard of mutual confidence which is an essential element in every successful agency agreement. It may be worth while to recall the observations of a past Chairman of the Institute of Export[3]:

---

[1] But the United Kingdom exporter does not enter into relations with the overseas customer if his representative abroad is a *commissionaire*. Most European continental laws admit the concept of the *commissionaire*. He is a person who acts in his own name but for the account of his principal (see French *côde de commerce*, art. 94; German *Handelsgesetzbuch*, s. 383). English law does not know an exact equivalent to the *commissionaire* but his functions are, in part, performed by the confirming agent (p. 173, *post*), the agent acting for an undisclosed principal (p. 163, *post*), and the mercantile agent (p. 171, *post*). See further, Clive M. Schmitthoff, "Agency in International Trade, A Study in Comparative Law," 129 *Recueil des Cours*, Academy of International Law (Vol. 1, 1970), 107. D. J. Hill, "Some Problems of the Undisclosed Principal" [1967] J.B.L. 122.

[2] See pp. 181–182, *post*.

[3] G. T. MacEwan, *Overseas Trade and Export Practice*, London, p. 166.

The four points on which the manufacturer must be absolutely assured before entering into agreements of this kind, are—

(*a*) that he will be duly paid for his shipments;
(*b*) that the importers have all the organisation necessary to achieve the highest possible volume of sales;
(*c*) that they are of such standing in their own markets as to command the respect and goodwill of the local buyers and consumers; and
(*d*) that they are unconnected with other business interests likely to hinder them from doing justice to his own products.

The Export Services and Promotions Division Branch and the regional offices of the Department of Trade are prepared to assist exporters in finding the most suitable agents by local inquiry through their overseas officials and by other appropriate means.[4]

The Contract of Agency

The rights and duties of the exporter and his self-employed agent abroad are governed by the contract of agency which arises when a person (the principal) authorises another person (the agent) to procure or conclude contracts with third parties on his behalf.[5] In law, the term "agent" has a different meaning from that attributed to it in commercial parlance: it is wider in so far as it covers employees who conclude contracts with third parties on behalf of their employers,[6] and it is narrower in so far as it does not include representatives who buy and sell in their own name.[7] Scrutton L.J. in one case[8] referred to the well-known fact "that in certain trades the word 'agent' is often used without any reference to the law of principal and agent" and added that many difficulties have arisen from the habit of describing a purchaser as an agent. In particular, sole distribution agreements are not agency agreements,[8] and although they embody certain features similar to agency agreements, they differ from the latter in one important aspect, *viz.* the exporter is not in direct contractual relations with the customers abroad but his contracting party is the overseas importer who resells the goods to the customers in his own name.[9]

An agent who discloses his representative capacity to the customer to whom he sells the goods acts merely as the mouthpiece or conduit pipe of

---

[4] The address of the Export Services and Promotions Division is Export House, 50 Ludgate Hill, London EC4M 7HU. On Government services in general, see p. 57, *ante*.

[5] For a case of a procurement agency where the agent had only authority to introduce customers to his principal but not, without his prior consent, to accept orders, see *Vogel* v. *R. and A. Kohnstamm Ltd.* [1973] Q.B. 133.

[6] On Branch Offices Abroad, see p. 183, *post*.

[7] On Sole Distributor Agreements, see p. 153, *ante*.

[8] *W. T. Lamb & Sons* v. *Goring Brick Co.* [1932] 1 K.B. 710, 717; *The Regenstein* [1970] 2 Lloyd's Rep. 1, 5.

[9] The International Chamber of Commerce has published a guide for the drawing up of agency contracts between parties residing in different countries; the title of the guide is: *Commercial Agency*, 1961.

the principal, provided that he has acted within the scope of his actual or ostensible authority.[10] The contract of sale is concluded between the latter and the customer, and the agent disappears completely from the picture.[11] Every agency agreement creates three relationships:

1. That existing between the principal and the agent.
2. That existing between the principal and the third party, and
3. That existing between the agent and the third party.

The first is the internal arrangement between the principal and the agent, the contract of agency proper; it settles the rights and duties of these two parties, the scope of authority granted to the agent and the remuneration due to him. The second is a normal contract of sale, but superadded thereto are certain features which are due to the fact that the seller concluded the contract through an agent. The third relationship comes into play only in exceptional circumstances.

The agent is not obliged to disclose his representative capacity to the third party. From the viewpoint of the third party, *viz.* the customer abroad, the following possibilities exist here:

1. The agent does not disclose the existence of his principal and concludes the contract in his own name. Here he acts for an *undisclosed* principal, or
2. The agent discloses his principal's existence but not his name, *e.g.* by signing a contract "on behalf of our principals." In this case he acts for an *unnamed* principal, or
3. The agent discloses both the existence and the name of his principal. Here he acts for a *named* principal.

In the first of these three cases the customer, when discovering the true facts, may elect to sue the principal or the agent. This election must be unequivocal. If the customer commences proceedings against either of these persons, this is strong evidence that he has elected to hold him alone liable but this evidence may be rebutted, *e.g.* if the customer was not in possession of all relevant facts, and the customer can then still bring an action against the other.[12] If, however, the customer proceeds to judgment against either person that would terminate his right to elect and an action against the other would then be barred. Correspondingly, the undisclosed

[10] On the actual and ostensible authority, see Diplock L.J. in *Freeman & Lockyer* v. *Buckhurst Park Properties (Mangal) Ltd.* [1964] 2 Q.B. 480, 502, 503, and Lord Denning M.R. and Lord Pearson in *Hely-Hutchinson* v. *Brayhead Ltd.* [1968] 1 Q.B. 549, 583, 592; *Panorama Developments (Guildford) Ltd.* v. *Fidelis Furnishing Fabrics Ltd.* [1971] 2 Q.B. 711.

[11] Except if the agent undertakes personal liability to the third party, see, *e.g.* the liability of the confirming agent to the supplier in the U.K., p. 173, *post*. If the agent signs a deed he is personally liable even if he signs as "agent": *Plant Engineers (Sales) Ltd.* v. *Davies, The Times*, May 10, 1969.

[12] *Clarkson-Booker Ltd.* v. *Andjel* [1964] 2 Q.B. 775. See also D. J. Hill, "Some Problems of the Undisclosed Principal" in [1967] J.B.L. 122.

principal has the right to intervene and to make a direct claim against the customer. The customer's right of election and the principal's right of intervention thus enable these parties even in the case of undisclosed agency to constitute a direct bond between them.[13]

In the other two cases the customer can only sue the principal; he can sue the agent only if the law in force in the territory in question provides a different regulation or the agent has undertaken personal liability to the third party or is liable by custom of the trade. The agent who does not disclose the *existence* of his principal does not normally escape liability by merely adding to his firm style a descriptive term such as "export and import agencies."[14] If, however, he signs the contract with the customer "as agent," or addresses letters to him "on behalf of our principals," or "on account of our principals," no personal liability attaches to him, even if he does not disclose the *name* of the principal.[15] Sometimes it is clear from the circumstances that the person who acted did so as an agent although he did not indicate that he acted in that capacity, *e.g.* if the third party knew that he was merely a broker; in that case only the principal, but not the agent, is liable.[16]

The principal is in all three cases entitled to sue the third party in his own name. He has, according to English law, this right even where the agent concluded the contract without disclosing the existence of the principal, provided that the agent was duly authorised to act on his behalf.[17] Thus, an English confirming house or other agent can act for a foreign undisclosed principal who, if the goods do not conform with the contract, has a direct claim against the supplier in this country.[18] Some foreign laws differ in this respect from English law and provide that when the contract is concluded by the agent in his own name, only he and not the undisclosed principal can sue on it. In view of this divergency, the exporter who wishes to reserve the right to sue the customer abroad for the purchase price should expressly provide in the contract which he concludes with the agent that the agent should disclose his representative capacity when selling to the customers, or should, at least, ask the agent for an undertaking to assign to him any claims against customers if so required by him.

---

[13] See Clive M. Schmitthoff, "Agency in International Trade," quoted in n. 1, *ante*, 141–143.

[14] *The Swan* [1968] 1 Lloyd's Rep. 5, 13.

[15] Halsbury, *Laws of England* (3rd ed.), Vol. 1, p. 229. An agent who sells goods in his own name which involve a breach of the law relating to weights and measures is liable criminally even if he is not guilty of negligence. But he is not liable if he sells them as agent for a named principal: *Lester* v. *Balfour Williamson Merchant Shippers Ltd.* [1953] 2 Q.B. 168.

[16] *N. & J. Vlassopulos Ltd.* v. *Ney Shipping Ltd.; The Santa Carina* [1977] 1 Lloyd's Rep. 478.

[17] Although normally "ratification relates back and is deemed equivalent to an antecedent authority" (*per* Jenkins, L.J. in *Danish Mercantile Co. Ltd.* v. *Beaumont* [1951] Ch. 680, 686), it has been decided that if the *undisclosed* "agent" exceeds his authority or otherwise concludes a contract without authority, the "principal" cannot ratify the "agent's" act and sue the third party directly: *Keighley Maxted & Co.* v. *Durant* [1901] A.C. 240.

[18] *Teheran-Europe Co. Ltd.* v. *S. T. Belton* (*Tractors*) *Ltd.* [1968] 2 Q.B. 545 (C.A.).

Duties of the agent

The following are the principal duties of the agent, as far as relevant here:

(i) *To use reasonable diligence.* The agent has to carry out the duties, which he has undertaken, with customary and reasonable care, skill and diligence, and is responsible to the principal for any loss caused by a failure to observe these standards. A selling agent has no authority to give the buyer a warranty with respect to the goods sold unless such authority is given him expressly or impliedly or arises from a trade custom.[19]

(ii) *To disclose all material facts.* The agent is obliged to disclose all facts to his principal which are likely to influence the latter when deciding whether to accept the customer's order or not. If, *e.g.* the principal has instructed the agent not to sell to X, and Y, a subsidiary company of X, ordered the goods from the agent, the latter, when forwarding the order to the principal, would have to point out that Y is known as being controlled by X. In particular, the agent is obliged to disclose to the principal any personal interest which he might have in the transaction. He must not buy the principal's goods without having first obtained the consent of the principal, nor must he act as agent for the buyer and receive double commission on the transaction without prior disclosure to the principal.[20] A contract in which the agent has an undisclosed personal interest is voidable at the option of the principal.

(iii) *Not to accept bribes or to make secret profits.* The agent must not accept a bribe nor in other respects make a secret profit out of his representative position. Where a bribe has been promised, the principal can claim it from the third party or, if it has been paid over, from the agent[21]; further, he is entitled to dismiss the agent without notice, or to avoid the contract with the third party, or to refuse to pay commission on the tainted transaction, or to claim damages for any loss which he has sustained through entering into the contract; and the bribe which the principal has recovered is not taken into account when the damages are assessed. These consequences ensue even when the bribe or secret profit has been accepted by the agent with the definite intention not to be influenced by it in his judgment, or when it can be proved that the interests of the principal have not been injured.[22] It is a matter of business morality as well as of the law that the standards of honesty required from the agent should be exacting;

[19] *Benmag* v. *Barda* [1955] 2 Lloyd's Rep. 354 where McNair J. found on the facts that the seller had authorised his agent to warrant to the buyer that a consignment of goat hair was of the same quality as an earlier consignment.

[20] *Anglo-African Merchants Ltd.* v. *Bayley* [1970] 1 Q.B. 311 (insurance broker).

[21] *Reading* v. *Att.-Gen.* [1951] A.C. 507; *Grinstead* v. *Hadrill* [1953] 1 W.L.R. 696; *T. Mahesan S/O Thambia* v. *Malaysia Government Officers' Co-operative Housing Society Ltd.* [1978] 2 W.L.R. 444.

[22] In certain circumstances criminal proceedings may be instituted against the agent under the Prevention of Corruption Act 1906 and here again, "if a person does what is called a double-cross, and does not do what he was bribed to do, that is no reason why he should be acquitted of taking a bribe"; *R.* v. *Carr* [1957] 1 W.L.R. 165, 166.

they are relaxed only if the principal knows that the agent receives a remuneration from the third party and does not object.

(iv) *Not to divulge confidential information*. The agent must not divulge confidential information or material, which he has obtained in the course of his employment, to third parties during the existence or after termination of the agency agreement, nor must he use such information himself unfairly in order to compete with the principal. He cannot, on the other hand, be restrained from using the skill and experience, which he gained when acting for the principal, after termination of the agency agreement, unless the parties agreed upon a reasonable restraint of trade. Further, the agent may divulge confidential information concerning the principal to the police, a public authority or, it would appear, even the press if the facts in question constitute a crime or fraud committed by the principal, or a serious matter contravening the public interest.[23]

In one case[24] an international trade directory was published by a British publisher who employed agents in certain districts of the European Continent allotted to them exclusively. They were remunerated by a commission on the amounts received for advertisements; apparently it was their habit to take down, in their own notebooks, the material relating to the advertisers in their district which later was produced in the directory. On determining the agency agreement, the publisher successfully applied for an injunction to restrain the agents from using the material collected in their notebooks in their own interest or that of a rival publisher. It was argued on behalf of the agents that the advertisements after publication in the directory could be reprinted by anybody unless they were protected by copyright, but Kay L.J. dealt with this argument as follows:

> The jurisdiction against these defendants is because these materials which they want to use were obtained by them when they were in the position of agents for the plaintiff, and, although the plaintiff might not be able to prevent anybody else in the world from publishing or using such materials as he is trying to prevent these defendants from using, that would be no answer, because these defendants, from the position in which they were in, are put under a duty towards the plaintiff not to make this use of the material.

In very exceptional circumstances, where the principal has an overwhelming prima facie case, where actual or potential damage to him would be serious and there is clear evidence that the agent possesses vital confidential material which he might destroy or dispose of, the court has inherent jurisdiction to make an order to permit the principal's representatives to enter the agent's premises to inspect and remove the confidential material; in these exceptional cases such an order may be made even on an *ex parte* application of the principal.[25]

---

[23] *Initial Services Ltd.* v. *Putterill* [1968] 1 Q.B. 396.

[24] *Lamb* v. *Evans* [1893] 1 Ch. 218. See also *Nordisk Insulinlaboratorium* v. *C. L. Bencard* [1934] Ch. 430; *British Syphon Co. Ltd.* v. *Homewood* [1956] 1 W.L.R. 1190; *L. S. Harris Trustees Ltd.* (*Trading as L. S. Harris & Co.*) v. *Power Packing Services* (*Hermit Road*) *Ltd.* [1970] 2 Lloyd's Rep. 65; *Baker* v. *Gibbons* [1972] 1 W.L.R. 693.

[25] *Anton Piller KG* v. *Manufacturing Processes Ltd.* [1976] 2 W.L.R. 162; *Vapormatic Co. Ltd.* v. *Sparex Ltd.* [1976] 1 W.L.R. 939.

(v) *To account to the principal.* An agent is obliged to keep proper accounts of all agency transactions and to produce them to the principal in accordance with the terms of the agency agreement or upon request by the principal. The agent has to keep the customary office records and should keep the money and property of the principal apart from his own. He has to pay over to the principal all moneys actually received on behalf of the latter but, in the absence of contrary provisions in the agency agreement, is, in appropriate cases, entitled to a set-off or a lien on the principal's goods or money. These rights of the agent can be exercised where money is owing from the principal but the agent cannot claim these rights to retain arbitrarily expenses which have not been agreed upon.

Duties of the principal

The following are the main duties of the principal as far as relevant here:

(i) *To pay commission.* The principal has to pay the agent the agreed remuneration which customarily, but not by force of law, is a commission payable on the purchase price of the goods actually sold by the agent. This method of remuneration is intended to operate as an incentive for the agent, but it sometimes tempts an unscrupulous agent to pay greater attention to the volume of effected sales than the financial soundness of the customers whose orders he solicits. The principal who wishes to protect himself against this contingency has several possibilities. The most effective is to lay down in the contract of agency that the commission shall be earned when the purchase price is received by the principal in cash; a frequent provision of this type is that

> commission shall be paid at a rate of . . . per cent. on all moneys received by the principal as purchase price for goods sold by the agent.

Another possibility is to arrange *del credere* terms[26] whereby the agent, usually on payment of an additional commission, undertakes to indemnify the principal for any loss sustained through an insolvency of customers introduced by him.

It is advisable to state expressly when the commission is earned; if the contract is silent on this point the agent can claim the commission when the contract of sale is concluded, *e.g.* when the principal accepts the customer's order. It is customary to distinguish the date when the commission is payable from that when it is earned, and to provide that the commission shall be payable some time later than it was earned or at certain fixed dates; if the contract does not deal with this matter and no contrary trade usages exist, the agent can claim commission immediately it is earned. Advances on unearned commission must normally be repaid on termination of the agency agreement.[27]

---

[26] See p. 170, *post*.
[27] *Bronester Ltd.* v. *Priddle* [1961] 1 W.L.R. 1294.

An agent is only entitled to commission if he introduces a ready, willing and able purchaser[28]; if the buyer has no money to pay the price, he is not an able purchaser, and if after the termination of the agency the principal and the buyer enter into new negotiations and the former enables the latter by financial assistance to conclude the contract of sale, the effective cause of the sale is not the introduction by the agent, although to some degree it remained, but the provision of finance, and the agent is not entitled to commission.[29]

Three points require particular attention when the agent's commission is discussed by the parties: the reimbursement of the agent for expenses, the payment of commission on orders emanating from the agent's territory but received directly by the principal, and commission due on repeat orders. These matters should be dealt with in the contract in precise terms. The law does not provide detailed rules on these topics; it is based on the arrangement reached by the parties and, if the negotiating parties have expressed themselves thereon merely in general assertions of mutual good will, the court has the difficult task of inferring their presumed intention from the surrounding circumstances—a laborious process which sometimes leads to unsatisfactory results.

It happens sometimes—though more often in the home trade than in the export trade—that the principal agrees to pay the agent a fixed sum at monthly or other intervals "on account of the commission which will accrue to him"; such an arrangement would make the agent a servant of the principal rather than constitute him an independent contractor. If, in such a case, on the termination of the agency the payments by the principal exceed the commission earned by the agent, the agent has to repay the principal the excess unless the agency agreement contains an express or implied provision to the contrary.[30] As this point often gives rise to disputes, it is advisable to cover it in advance by an express term in the agency agreement.

Where, under the terms of the contrast of agency, the agent's commission has to be paid to countries outside the scheduled territories[31] by remittance from this country or retention, by the agent, of part of the proceeds of sale, the exchange control regulations have to be observed.

(ii) *Agent's expenses and indemnity*. The self-employed sales agent abroad who solicits orders for an exporter cannot claim his trading expenses from the principal unless this is expressly agreed upon in the contract of agency. If the agent, with the approval of the principal, incurs liabilities in the course of his duties, *e.g.* if he sues a defaulting customer in the courts of

---

[28] *Luxor (Eastbourne) Ltd.* v. *Cooper* [1941] A.C. 108; *Christie Owen & Davies* v. *Rapacioli* [1974] 2 W.L.R. 723.

[29] *Jack Windle Ltd.* v. *Brierley* [1951] 2 All E.R. 398.

[30] *Rivoli Hats Ltd.* v. *Gooch* [1953] 1 W.L.R. 1190; *Clayton Newbury Ltd.* v. *Findlay* [1953] 1 W.L.R. 1194.

[31] See p. 71, *ante*.

the country where the customer resides, he is entitled to be indemnified for any losses sustained or liabilities incurred by him.

(iii) *Orders emanating from agent's territory but not procured by him.* On principle, the agent is entitled to commission if the transaction for which commission is claimed is the direct result of his efforts. The agent can therefore claim commission if the customer with whom he has negotiated eventually orders goods directly from the principal, or if the customer whom he introduces offers a lower price than the list price and the principal decides to accept the offer at the lower price. He cannot claim commission if the customer places an unsolicited order with the principal, or if the order has been obtained by the principal himself or other agents. These rules of law are frequently modified by agreement of the parties or custom of the trade, and it may be provided that the agent shall be entitled to commission on all transactions emanating from his territory. These arrangements are particularly frequent when an agent is appointed sole agent for a defined district.

(iv) *Repeat orders.* It depends on the terms of the agency agreement whether the agent is entitled to commission on repeat orders. Normally the parties arrange for commission in these cases, sometimes by providing expressly that the agent shall be entitled to commission on "repeats on any accounts introduced by" him,[32] sometimes by stating generally that commission shall be due "on all orders from customers introduced by him."[33] Legal difficulties have arisen with respect to commission claims on repeat orders in the following circumstances: is such a claim justified when repeat orders have been accepted by the principal subsequent to the termination of the agency agreement by notice, mutual agreement or death of the agent? Here the fruits of the agent's work might well accrue to the principal after the agent ceased working for him. The numerous decisions on this point reveal the following principles: where the agency agreement is not for a limited period, the principal must pay commission on repeat orders received after termination of the agency agreement[34] and where the agency agreement was concluded for a limited time, no commission can be claimed on repeat orders.[35] But in the cases in which according to these principles the agent is entitled to commission, his claim is only for monetary compensation for loss of commission on the repeat orders; he

---

[32] *Levy* v. *Goldhill* [1917] 2 Ch. 297.

[33] *Salomon* v. *Brownfield* (1896) 12 T.L.R. 239; *Bilbee* v. *Hasse & Co.* (1889) 5 T.L.R. 677; *Wilson* v. *Harper, Son & Co.* [1908] 2 Ch. 370; *Roberts* v. *Elwells Engineers Ltd.* [1972] 2 Q.B. 586.

[34] *Levy* v. *Goldhill* [1917] 2 Ch. 297; *Bilbee* v. *Hasse & Co.* (1889) 5 T.L.R. 677; *Salomon* v. *Brownfield* (1896) 12 T.L.R. 239; *Wilson* v. *Harper, Son & Co.* [1908] 2 Ch. 370; *British Bank Ltd.* v. *Novimex Ltd.* [1949] 1 K.B. 623; *Sellers* v. *London Counties Newspapers* [1951] 1 K.B. 784. It should, however, be noted that the question is always one of construction of the relevant documents or terms and the decided cases afford little more than general guidance only: *Crocker Horlock Ltd.* v. *B. Lang & Co. Ltd.* [1949] W.N. 97.

[35] *Weare* v. *Brimsdown Lead Co.* (1910) 103 L.T.R. 429.

cannot claim a declaration and an account for the future because that would amount to an annuity "to the crack of doom."[36]

(v) *Principal's discretion to accept orders.* When the agent introduces a customer to the principal the latter has full discretion to accept or reject the customer's order, and the agent cannot claim commission on orders which the principal elects to refuse, unless the parties have agreed on special terms, *e.g.* that commission shall be paid on the introduction of or inquiries from potential customers, or established trade usages can be proved allowing commission on a reduced scale. The principal must not prevent the agent by a wrongful act or omission from earning his commission, and the agent can recover damages (though not commission) for the actual loss sustained if the principal contravenes this rule of law. Where the agency agreement provides that commission is to be paid on the purchase price received by the principal, and the customer does not pay because the principal refuses to supply him after having accepted the order, the agent can recover reasonable trading expenses spent when procuring the order; where the contract of agency provides that the commission has to be paid when the order has been accepted, the agent can, in these circumstances, claim his commission and not merely reasonable trading expenses.[37]

Where commission is to be paid on the purchase price received by the principal, and the customer repudiates the contract before paying the price, the principal is not bound to sue the customer in order to enable the agent to earn his commission, but if he receives some compensation from the customer the agent would appear to be entitled to a reasonable remuneration which may be a good deal less than full commission.[38]

Special Types of Agents

Commercial practice has evolved certain types of agency agreements which play an important role in the export trade.

The del credere agent

A *del credere* agent is an agent who undertakes to indemnify the principal for any loss which the latter may sustain owing to the failure of a customer, introduced by the agent, to pay the purchase price. The advantages of the *del credere* arrangement are evident: the principal is not sufficiently in touch with the foreign market in which the agent operates to judge the financial soundness of the customer who orders goods; credit terms cannot always be avoided if it is desired to market the goods on a competitive basis, and even where no credit terms are granted the exporter might find himself entangled in complicated and costly bankruptcy proceedings if the

[36] *Roberts* v. *Elwells Engineers Ltd.* [1972] 2 Q.B. 586.
[37] *Bentall, Horsley & Baldry* v. *Vicary* [1931] 1 K.B. 253; *Milsom* v. *Bechstein* (1898) 14 T.L.R. 159.
[38] *Boots* v. *E. Christopher & Co.* [1951] 2 All E.R. 1045.

customer fails. These pitfalls are avoided by the agent agreeing to accept the *del credere* for the customers introduced by him and, incidentally, the principal can be assured that the agent will not place considerations of turnover higher than the solvency of the customers whose orders he solicits. It is usual to pay an additional commission, called the *del credere* commission, to the agent who accepts a *del credere* responsibility. The *del credere* agreement need not be evidenced in writing; it is a contract of indemnity and not a contract of guarantee.[39] The *del credere* agent undertakes merely to indemnify the principal if the latter, owing to the insolvency of the buyer or some analogous cause, is unable to recover the purchase price, but the agent is not responsible if a perfectly solvent buyer refuses to pay the price on the ground that the principal has not duly performed the contract.[40] Lord Ellenborough expressed this rule in 1817 as follows[41]: "The (*del credere*) commission imports that if the vendee does not pay, the factor will; it is a guarantee from the factor to the principal against any mischief to arise from the vendee's insolvency. But it varies not an iota the rights subsisting between vendor and vendee."

By an announcement of December 24, 1962, the EEC Commission has indicated that it does not consider a *del credere* agency agreement as falling within the prohibition of Article 85(1) of the EEC Treaty, provided that the agent does not assume a financial risk other than that implied in the usual *del credere* obligation.

The agent carrying stock

Agents resident abroad have either authority to procure or accept orders and pass them on to the principal who then dispatches the goods to the customer directly, or they are entrusted with a store or consignment of stock lines, spare parts, etc. and have authority to supply customers directly from their store. Agents of the latter type are factors within the meaning of the Factors Act 1889 which defines a factor as a mercantile agent who in the customary course of his business has authority to sell goods, or to consign goods for sale, or to buy goods or to raise money on the security of goods.[42] The problem that arises with respect to consignment agents is that they may dispose of their principal's goods contrary to his instructions and without due authority; great uncertainty would be imported into business transactions if the deals of consignment agents in goods entrusted to them were invalid for lack of authority, particularly as these agents often do not disclose their representative capacity and the third party has no means of ascertaining the internal arrangement between the principal and agent. The Factors Act 1889 aims at the protection of third parties dealing

---

[39] Consequently, s. 4 of the Statute of Frauds 1677, which provides, *inter alia*, that a contract of guarantee, to be enforceable, must be evidenced in writing, does not apply. (This provision of s. 4 is not repealed by the Law Reform (Enforcement of Contracts) Act 1954.)

[40] *Gabriel & Sons* v. *Churchill & Sim* [1914] 3 K.B. 1272.

[41] In *Hornsby* v. *Lacy* (1817) 6 M. & S. 166, 171.

[42] s 1(1).

in good faith with the consignment agent and provides in particular that, where the factor, in his capacity of mercantile agent,[43] with the consent of the principal is in possession of goods or documents of title to the goods, any sale or other disposition transacted by him in the ordinary course of business in respect of these goods is as valid as if it were expressly authorised by the principal, provided the third party did not know of the lack of the factor's authority.[44] The Act cannot be invoked often in export transactions because the contract between the agent residing abroad and the customer there is normally governed by the law of the foreign country where the contract is concluded or to be performed,[45] but the laws of many foreign countries embody rules corresponding to the provisions of the Factors Act 1889. On the other hand, the Act provides a valuable protection in import transactions, as shown in the following case[46]: importers obtained an advance from Lloyds Bank on the security of bills of lading in respect of certain merchandise and the bank returned the bills of lading to the importers in order to enable them to sell the goods; on receipt of the bills of lading, the importers gave the bank a trust receipt wherein they acknowledged their holding of the documents under lien of the bank and agreed to clear the goods as trustees of the bank; the importers who were in financial difficulties pledged the bills of lading, in breach of trust, with the Bank of America which was unaware of the true position. The court decided that the importers received the documents of title as factors of Lloyds Bank and that the pledging of the documents with the Bank of America was valid as against Lloyds Bank.

Exclusive trading rights

The agency agreement may provide that the self-employed agent shall have sole and exclusive trading rights with respect to the principal's goods in a particular territory. The character of the agency here is territorial and not personal. The agent is paid commission on all sales emanating from his territory whether procured by his own efforts or those of other persons, and he usually undertakes to promote systematically in the territory reserved to him the distribution of the principal's goods by an organisation of subagents, advertisements or other means. Exclusive agency agreements are of great importance in the export trade though they are less frequently met than sole distribution agreements which have been considered in detail earlier.[47] The decisive difference between both types of exporting is that the exclusive agent concludes contracts with customers on behalf of his

[43] *Astley Industrial Trust* v. *Miller* [1968] 2 All E.R. 36. (It is doubtful whether this case was correctly decided and whether it was really necessary that the consent of the owner to the factor's possession must extend to such possession *qua* factor; see *Worcester Works Finance Ltd.* v. *Cooden Engineering Co. Ltd.* [1972] 1 Q.B. 210.)

[44] s. 2(1).

[45] See pp. 130–131, *ante*.

[46] *Lloyds Bank* v. *Bank of America National Trust and Savings Association* [1937] 2 K.B. 631; [1938] 2 K.B. 147.

[47] See p. 153, *ante*.

United Kingdom principal who then enters into a direct relationship with the third party,[48] while the sole distributor buys and resells the goods in his own name and no direct bond is established between the United Kingdom exporter and the customer abroad. Apart therefrom, the observations made earlier[49] on sole distribution agreements apply to exclusive agency contracts *mutatis mutandis*. In particular, the contract of agency should state expressly that the agent has to sell in the principal's name. In one case,[50] the terms of an exclusive agency contract were summed up by Lord Simon L.C. as follows:

> By a written contract dated February 19, 1938, the respondents, manufacturers of steel in Sheffield, as principals appointed the appellants, whose business address was in New York, to be sole selling agents of their tool steels in a wide area of territories including the western hemisphere (excluding U.S.A. and Argentine), Australia, New Zealand and India. The appellants were to sell in the name of the respondents, the respondents fixing f.o.b. prices and the appellants charging the purchaser with such excess price over f.o.b. prices as they could obtain. Any excess price over the f.o.b. price was for the credit of the appellants and the respondents were to account to the appellants in respect of such excess price after the respondents had received payment in full from the purchaser. The duration of the agreement was to be for three years from April 1, 1938, as a minimum. The agreement contained an arbitration clause.

An exclusive agency agreement, as such, is not prohibited by Article 85(1) of the EEC Treaty but may contravene it if it contains clauses which have as their object or effect the distortion of competition in the Common Market. However, the EEC Commission has granted important exemptions *en bloc* from the general prohibition of Article 85(1). The regulation of European Community Law, as far as affecting exclusive distribution and agency agreements will be considered later on.[51]

The confirming house

It happens often in the export trade that an overseas importer buys in the United Kingdom through a confirming house resident in the United Kingdom.[52] In modern practice these confirming houses are called *export houses*.[53]

Nature of the confirming house

The term "confirming house" has no definite meaning in law or in

---

[48] Unless the exclusive agent is a *commissionaire*, see p. 161, *ante*.
[49] See p. 157, *ante*.
[50] *Heyman* v. *Darwins Ltd.* [1942] A.C. 356, 357.
[51] See p. 222, *post*.
[52] The following observations are founded on my *Legal Aspects of Export Sales* (3rd ed. 1978), pp. 8–10.
[53] Their trade organisation is the British Export Houses Association, 69 Cannon Street, London, E.C.4. This Association has published a brochure describing the services of the export houses.

commercial practice. A confirming house enters usually into two legal relationships, namely, to its overseas customer who asks it to procure certain goods for him, and to the seller in the home market with whom it places the order or indent. The relationship to the overseas customer is normally that between principal and agent whereas the relationship to the seller in the home market depends on the nature of the contract which the confirming house concludes with him. Three possibilities exist in that respect: *first*, when placing the order with the seller, the confirming house may buy from the seller; in that case it enters into a direct contract of sale and is liable for the price and for the acceptance of the goods as a buyer; the fact that the seller knowns that the goods are destined for export and even knows the name of the overseas buyer is not relevant. The *second* possibility is that the confirming house places the order with the seller "as agents on behalf of our principals," either naming them or not; in that case the contract of sale is made directly between the seller and the overseas buyer and the confirming house does not intend to make itself liable for the price. The first and the second possibility are diametrically opposed: in the first case the confirming house places its client's order as a principal and in the second it does so as an agent. A *third* arrangement is possible and, indeed, this is the typical confirming arrangement: the confirming house may place the client's order as agent of the overseas importer but may indicate at the same time that it intends to hold itself personally responsible for the price; this type of confirmation is described by McNair J.[54] as follows:

> The critical question is: What is the meaning of "confirming order" or what is the meaning of "confirming house"? . . . It seems to me, using the word in its ordinary sense, "to confirm" means that the party confirming guarantees that the order will be carried out by the purchaser. In that sense he adds confirmation or assurance to the bargain which has been made by the primary contractor, just as a bank which confirms that a credit has been opened by the buyers in favour of the seller guarantees that payment will be made against the credit if the proper documents are tendered.

This third arrangement produces, as far as the liability for the price is concerned, the same effect as the first one; it is the normal and typical confirmation transaction into which the confirming house enters.

In practice, confirming houses when carrying out orders received from their customers abroad use two types of forms, one in which they order the goods from the supplier in the home market under their own liability, and another in which they merely pass on the order of the overseas importer as his agent; they use whatever form is appropriate in the case in question.

It should be noted that in the first of these cases the confirming house acts as agent and buyer at the same time. It is clearly established that a

---

[54] In *Sobell Industries Ltd.* v. *Cory Bros. & Co. Ltd.* [1955] 2 Lloyd's Rep. 82, 89; Donaldson J. in *Teheran-Europe Co. Ltd.* v. *S. T. Belton (Tractors) Ltd.* [1968] 2 Q.B. 53 (this part of the judgment was affirmed by the Court of Appeal in [1968] 2 Q.B. 545). See also *International Ry.* v. *Niagara Park Commission* [1941] A.C. 328, 342; and the American case of *Schoenthal* v. *Bernstein*, 93 N.L.S. 2d 187, 190 (1949).

person may combine these two qualities in the same transaction. Thus, Roche J. said[55]:

> Between a commission agent . . . and the foreign principal there is no relation except that of agency; but as between the British seller and the commission agent . . . as buyer there is no party to the contract except the commission agent . . . on that side.

Further, the Sale of Goods Act makes express provision for the protection of an agent, such as the confirming agent, who has himself paid, or is directly responsible for, the price: section 38(2) of that Act provides that he shall have the same rights against the goods as an unpaid seller: namely, the rights of lien, of stoppage *in transitu*, and resale.[56]

Obligations of confirming house

The confirming house which has made itself liable to the supplier, either by placing a buying order with him or by confirming its customer's order, is under a personal obligation to the supplier to pay the price for the goods. If before the execution of the transaction the customer cancels the order without valid reason, the confirming house is still bound to pay the price to the supplier; its position is similar in this respect to that of the confirming bank under a bankers' documentary credit.[57] If the confirming house has performed this obligation, it is entitled to be indemnified by the customer for what it has paid to the supplier and, in appropriate cases, can recover damages.[58]

As regards the client, the confirming house undertakes to give the supplier proper shipping instructions but—and this has to be emphasised—it does not undertake liability for the conformity of the goods with the contract, and in particular for their quality and quantity.[59] If a dispute of this character arises, the customer must make a direct claim against the supplier; in this respect the confirming house, if it has merely confirmed the customer's order, has acted for an undisclosed principal.[60] In order to have certainty about the confirming house's position in this type of case, it is advisable for confirming houses, which intend to hold themselves personally responsible to the supplier, to use the third form of transaction—the actual confirmation—rather than the first form under which they are buyers from the supplier.[61]

---

[55] In *R. & J. Bow Ltd.* v. *Hill* (1930) 37 Ll.L.R. 46 (the learned judge referred in this case to the famous case of *Ireland* v. *Livingstone* (1872) L.R. 5 H.L. 395); see further *Basma* v. *Weekes* [1950] A.C. 441, 454; *Brown & Gracie Ltd.* v. *F. W. Green & Co. Pty. Ltd.* [1960] 1 Lloyd's Rep. 289, 303; *Format International Security Printers Ltd.* v. *Mosden*, [1975] 1 Lloyd's Rep. 37.

[56] This interest can be covered by the confirming house by insurance, p. 306, *post*.

[57] *Hamzeh Malas & Sons* v. *British Imex Industries Ltd.* [1958] 2 Q.B. 127; see p. 259, *post*.

[58] *Anglo-African Shipping Co. of New York Inc.* v. *J. Mortner Ltd.* [1962] 1 Lloyd's Rep. 610 (C.A.).

[59] Provided that it has passed on the instructions of the customer correctly to the supplier.

[60] *Teheran-Europe Co. Ltd.* v. *S. T. Belton (Tractors) Ltd.* [1968] 2 Q.B. 545 (C.A.).

[61] See p. 174, *ante*.

Confirming houses often insert express clauses in their contracts with the customer and the supplier, to make this position clear. A typical clause is this:

> By confirming the order, we undertake full responsibility to pay the supplier for all goods delivered in accordance with our confirmation, but it expressly agreed that we are to incur no other liability whatsoever in respect of the said contract and are not to be made parties to any litigation or arbitration relating thereto.

The confirming house has a special lien on the goods and the bills of lading *vis-à-vis* the customer and is, in this respect, in the same position as an unpaid seller.[62] But where the confirming house has allowed the customer credit, it does not have a general lien entitling it to retain goods or bills of lading for an indebtedness of the customer resulting from earlier transactions, unless such a general lien is contractually granted to the confirming house; the confirming house is not in the position of a factor who, by custom of the trade, has a general lien.[63]

The contracts into which an English confirming house enters provide often that they shall be governed by English law and that the parties submit to the jurisdiction of the English courts.

Insolvency of the confirming house

If the confirming house becomes insolvent, the question arises whether the seller can still claim the price from the overseas buyer. If the confirming house has re-ordered the goods from the seller, the answer is clear: the seller can claim the price from the buyer on the contract of purchase originally placed by the buyer. If the confirming house has confirmed the buyer's order, the position is more difficult. If the intention of the parties was that the obligation of the confirming house shall be the sole obligation to the seller, there would be no claim against the overseas buyer. That conclusion would, however, be exceptional. Normally the confirmation by the confirming house, like the confirmation of the correspondent bank under a documentary credit, provides only conditional discharge and the seller has still his claim against the overseas buyer.[63a]

Illustrations

Two illustrations of transactions in which the confirming agent was held to be personally liable to the supplier may be added. In *Rusholme's* case[64] the plaintiffs, manufacturers in England, received in May 1951, through their Australian agents, orders for shirting material from an Australian importer; the orders provided "terms—confirmation and payment by" the defendants, a confirming house in London. The confirming house then ordered the shirting material from the manufacturers. The order stated

---

[62] Sale of Goods Act, s. 38(2).

[63] *Tellrite Ltd.* v. *London Confirmers Ltd.* [1968] 1 Lloyd's Rep. 236.

[63a] *Cf.* p. 268, *post*.

[64] *Rusholme & Bolton & Roberts Hadfield Ltd.* v. *S. G. Read & Co.* (*London*) *Ltd.* [1955] 1 W.L.R. 146.

"Purchased by [the confirming house], holders of Purchase Tax No. Central 2/3793 of goods as stock intended for export." There was nothing on the order to show that it had reference to another transaction except the words: "In confirmation of your agents' Indent No. 14." The order was accepted by the manufacturers by a letter of June 7 in these words: "We thank you for the above order for [name of the Australian importer] and have pleasure in confirming same herewith": then the terms of the contract were set out. Owing to an Australian trade recession before the delivery date the Australian importer cancelled the orders and the confirming house refused to accept delivery. Pearce J. found that the manufacturers would not have accepted the orders without the interposition of an English confirming house and held that the orders by the confirming house to the manufacturers constituted the true contracts between the parties and that the confirming house was liable to pay damages for non-acceptance of the goods. The learned judge said with respect to that order form:

> The document means what it says, namely, that the defendants are assuming liability as between themselves and the plaintiffs. It would have been easy for the defendants to put a different wording in the document had the intention been otherwise. The defendants at first claimed that their wording "Purchased by S. G. Read & Co. (London) Ltd." was inserted on the compulsion of the Board of Trade as a condition of the defendants holding a purchase tax certificate; but in cross-examination Mr. Read had to admit that this was not so. He could have set out in terms that they were purchasing only as agents.

In *Sobell Industries Ltd.* v. *Cory Bros. & Co. Ltd.*,[65] Sobell obtained a considerable order for radio sets from a firm in Istanbul and insisted on confirmation by Cory who, in addition to other activities, carried on the business of export merchants and shippers. Cory thereupon placed an order for the same goods in their own name with Sobell. The Turkish buyers accepted only part of the goods and the confirming house—Cory—likewise refused to accept the balance of the goods. The sellers successfully sued the confirmers for damages for non-acceptance of the goods. McNair J. founded his judgment on a very short point; he held that the contract was contained in the order by the confirming house to the sellers and that it was clear from that order that the confirming house acted as principal.

Whether an English confirming house is personally liable to a supplier in this country depends entirely on the terms of the contract between him and the confirming house. If the contract discloses an intention to constitute privity of contract between these two parties, the confirming house is liable but if the contract shows that privity of contract shall only be constituted between the customer and the supplier, the confirming house acting merely as agent of the customer, there is no liability on the part of the confirming house.

No presumption of liability of English agent acting for foreign principal

In older decisions the courts held that an English agent who acted for a foreign principal was presumed to constitute privity of contract between

---

[65] [1955] 2 Lloyd's Rep. 82.

himself and the English supplier. In modern practice such a presumption no longer exists.[66] "The most that can now be said is that in deciding whether privity of contract exists between an English supplier and the foreign principal of an English agent, [is that] the fact that the principal is foreign is a factor to be taken into account although its weight may be minimal."[67] These principles likewise apply where the foreign principal is unnamed (*e.g.* the English agent has acted "for our clients") or, it is thought, even where he is undisclosed.[68]

Confirmation by confirming house and by bank

It should not be thought that the confirmation by a confirming house has the same effect as that by a bank in all circumstances. Where the confirming house merely adds its own confirmation to that of the customer,[69] that is true to a certain extent, although the confirming house gives shipping instructions to the supplier and the bank does not do so. But where the confirming house itself places the order with the United Kingdom supplier,[69] the position is fundamentally different. In this case the confirming house, in the words of McNair J.,[70] confirms "the contract as a whole." The confirmed credit has, thus, the merit of safety, in view of the financial status of the confirmer, but the acceptance of personal liability of the confirming house by way of a purchasing order has the merit of giving the seller protection in contingencies which are not purely financial.

The freight forwarder

The services of freight forwarders, as forwarding agents are called now, are of great value to those engaged in the export trade, and particularly to small firms which do not possess their own export organisations and shipping department.[71] Forwarders have a specialised knowledge of the intricacies of carriage by sea, air and land[72] and are, in particular, acquainted with the constantly changing customs formalities at home and abroad, the rates and rebates of freight, the practices of maritime and air ports, the groupage of sea or air cargoes for container transport[73] and the package and handling of export goods. They also undertake on occasion the inspection of goods[74] and the collection of debts from customers abroad.

---

[66] *Teheran-Europe Co. Ltd.* v. *S. T. Belton (Tractors) Ltd.* [1968] 2 Q.B. 53; affirmed on this point by C.A. in [1968] 2 Q.B. 545.

[67] *Per* Donaldson J., *ibid.*, at p. 62.

[68] *Teheran-Europe Co. Ltd.* v. *S. T. Belton (Tractors) Ltd.* [1968] 2 Q.B. 53; affirmed on this point by C.A. in [1968] 2 Q.B. 545.

[69] See p. 174, *ante.*

[70] In *Sobell Industries Ltd.* v. *Cory Bros. & Co.* [1955] 2 Lloyd's Rep. 82, 89.

[71] See D. J. Hill, *Freight Forwarders,* Stevens, London, 1972.

[72] The activities of forwarding agents in connection with the reservation of freight space for cargoes are described on p. 330, *post.*

[73] On container transport, see p. 377, *post*; on groupage bills of lading, see p. 357, *post.*

[74] *P.S.A. Transport* v. *Newton, Lansdowne & Co.* [1956] 1 Lloyd's Rep. 121 (port dues and wharfage charges payable before release of the goods for inspection not included in agents' agreed charges and agents entitled to be reimbursed).

Most forwarders in the United Kingdom embody the *Standard Trading Conditions* sponsored by the Institute of Freight Forwarders Ltd. into the contracts with their customers[75] although they do not apply automatically by usage of the trade.[76] The *Conditions* give the forwarder a particular and a general lien; he may therefore retain the customer's goods until all debts due from the customer are paid.[77] They authorise the forwarder to retain and be paid all brokerages, commissions, allowances and other remunerations customarily retained or paid to shipping and forwarding agents or insurance brokers, *e.g.* rebates under shipping conference arrangements entered into by the forwarding agent and not by the customer, or commissions on insurance. Further, according to the *Conditions* "no insurance will be effected [by the forwarder] except upon express instructions given in writing by the customer"; in this connection is should be mentioned that insurance brokers instructed to effect marine insurance are normally not obliged, in the absence of express instructions, to insure the goods in the hands of forwarders or packers and are not liable if they fail to do so.[78] If, however, the forwarder has undertaken to insure the goods during storage by him, he must store them in such a manner that they are covered by his insurance policy; otherwise he is liable in damages.[79]

Further, where shipping agents were employed by importers for the clearance of imports through Customs but, in the course of dealing with their customers, did not make Customs entries without specific instructions from their customers, they were held not to be liable for failing to make such Customs entries before the date when the import duty for the goods went up.[80] Where a freight charge quoted by a forwarder to his customers

---

[75] The current issue of the *Standard Trading Conditions* is reproduced in Appendix 4, p. 494, *post*. These conditions are revised by the Institute of Freight Forwarders Ltd. from time to time. See *E. W. Taylor & Co. (Forwarding) Ltd.* v. *Bell* [1968] 2 Lloyd's Rep. 63.

[76] *Salsi* v. *Jetspeed Air Services Ltd.* [1977] 2 Lloyd's Rep. 57, 60.

[77] Clause 21; see *J. O. Lund Ltd.* v. *Anglo-Overseas Transport Co. Ltd.* [1955] 1 Lloyd's Rep. 142. The forwarder has no general lien by custom of the trade; if he wants to claim a general lien, he must provide for it in his contract with the customer, *e.g.* by incorporating the *Conditions*: *Langley, Beldon & Gaunt Ltd.* v. *Morley* [1965] 1 Lloyd's Rep. 297. Where the customer is a company and a receiver is appointed, the general lien is operative on goods reaching the forwarder's possession after the appointment of the receiver, provided that the contract under which the general lien arises was made before that event: *George Barker (Transport) Ltd.* v. *Eynon* [1974] 1 W.L.R. 462. Where a forwarder promised the customer that his goods, though shipped in containers, would be shipped under deck, he was held to be liable when they were shipped on deck and part of them fell overboard owing to a swell at sea: *J. Evans & Son (Portsmouth) Ltd.* v. *Andrea Merzario Ltd.* [1976] 1 W.L.R. 1078. Where forwarders deposited goods into a warehouse for consolidation in containers, the contractual general lien of the warehousemen did not operate against the owners of the goods (who did not know that the consolidation was carried out by the warehousemen); the warehousemen did not have a general lien: *K. Chellaram & Sons Ltd.* v. *Butlers Warehousing and Distribution Ltd.* [1978] 2 Lloyd's Rep. 412 (C.A.).

[78] *United Mills Agencies Ltd.* v. *R. E. Harvey, Bray & Co.* [1952] 1 T.L.R. 149. But insurance brokers are under a duty to use reasonable care to the customer; if the latter thinks that he is insured but the insurance has been cancelled, they are bound to advise him at once: *London Borough of Bromley* v. *Ellis* [1971] 1 Lloyd's Rep. 97.

[79] *Firmin & Collins Ltd.* v. *Allied Shippers Ltd.* [1967] 1 Lloyd's Rep. 633, 639.

[80] *World Transport Agency* v. *Royte* [1957] 1 Lloyd's Rep. 381.

is based on the weight and measurement of the goods, the customers are liable to make additional payment to the forwarder if he has to pay higher freight on the ground that the measurements of the goods are greater than originally stated.[81]

According to the custom of the London freight market, forwarders, who by request of their customers book freight space on board a ship, are personally liable for dead freight to the carrier if the customers fail to load the goods and the ship sails with the space unfilled; in that case the forwarders are entitled to be indemnified by their customers.[82]

Forwarder acting as forwarding agent or as carrier

A forwarder is not normally a carrier.[83] Exceptionally, however, he may act as such; in that case the *Conditions* provide[84] that he shall not be a commmon carrier, he is, therefore, not liable absolutely for loss of, or damage to, the goods in his possession.[85] It is, however, sometimes not easy to determine whether the forwarder has acted as a forwarding agent, *i.e.* whether his duty was only to procure the carriage, or whether he has acted as a carrier.[86] It is also possible for a forwarder to act in a "hybrid" character,[87] *e.g.* by acting as carrier for the land segments of the journey and as forwarder for the sea leg.[87]

The agent of necessity

Where an agent is in possession of his principal's goods and has a limited authority only, *e.g.* not to sell from his stock unless expressly authorised

[81] *Brushfield Sargent & Co. Ltd.* v. *Holmwright Engineering Co. Ltd.* [1968] 1 Lloyd's Rep. 439. But the forwarder cannot claim additional freight when he has given a firm quotation without finding out whether the goods which he has undertaken to transport have any peculiar characteristics: *S. Zimmermann & Son Ltd.* v. *Baxter, Hoare & Co. Ltd.* [1965] 1 Lloyd's Rep. 88.

[82] *Anglo-Overseas Transport Co. Ltd.* v. *Titan Industrial Corporation* (*United Kingdom*) *Ltd.* [1959] 2 Lloyd's Rep. 152. Similarly, air agents who undertake personal liability are entitled to be indemnified by the customer, if the latter ought to have known that the air agents rendered themselves personally liable: *Perishable Transport Co. Ltd.* v. *Spyropoulos* (*London*) *Ltd.* [1964] 2 Lloyd's Rep. 379.

[83] Rowlatt J. in *Jones* v. *European & General Express Co. Ltd.* (1920) 90 L.J.K.B. 159, 160; *Marston Excelsior Ltd.* v. *Arbuckle, Smith & Co. Ltd.* [1971] 2 Lloyd's Rep. 306 (arrangement made by English forwarders for carriage of a cold box weighing 65 tons from Tilbury to Austria).

[84] In Clause 2. On the liability of the forwarder for lost or stolen goods, see D. J. Hill, "Loss in Transit" [1969] J.B.L. 100.

[85] An inland carrier who has contracted under the Road Haulage Association Ltd.'s Conditions of Carriage is normally authorised to sub-contract unless the nature of the load or the surrounding circumstances exclude such authority: *John Carter* (*Fine Worsteds*) *Ltd.* v. *Hanson Haulage* (*Leeds*) *Ltd.* [1965] 1 Lloyd's Rep. 49, 60; *Garnham, Harris & Elton Ltd.* v. *Alfred W. Ellis Ltd.* [1967] 2 Lloyd's Rep. 22–27.

[86] See, *e.g. Chas. Davis* (*Metal Brokers*) *Ltd.* v. *Gilyott & Scott Ltd.* [1975] 2 Lloyd's Rep. 422. Under the CMR Convention (p. 392, *post*), where there are successive road carriers, the person who contracted to carry as well as the person actually carrying may be the "carrier" within the meaning of the Convention: *Ulster-Swift Ltd.* v. *Taunton Meat Haulage Ltd.* [1977] 1 Lloyd's Rep. 346.

[87] *Per* Beattie J. in *The Maheno* [1977] 1 Lloyd's Rep. 81, 86, 88 (N.Z.).

by the principal, or to return the consignment to the principal or, perhaps, to dispatch to him goods bought on his behalf, circumstances of such urgent necessity might occur as to justify the use of exceptional measures for the protection of the principal's property. Mercantile law has evolved the doctrine of agency of necessity under which an agent is allowed—but not obliged—to exceed his authority in an emergency and to do what is required for safeguarding his principal's property, including the sale of it where there is danger of deterioration or loss. But the conditions upon which an agency of necessity can be exercised are difficult to establish, and the courts are not prepared to extend them unduly.[88] These conditions are, first, that the excess of authority is required by an actual and definite commercial necessity,[89] and secondly that the agent cannot communicate with the principal and obtain his instructions before disposing of the goods. In 1920[90] London export merchants sent a parcel of goods to Batum through British carriers, who had establishments in London, Batum and Constantinople, with instructions to deliver the goods to a local merchant. When the goods arrived, Batum was on the verge of serious disturbances; British residents had to evacuate the town and a clash between Soviet and White Russian forces seemed imminent. The carriers thereupon removed the goods to Constantinople when evacuating Batum and did not deliver them to the local merchant. The court ruled that they acted as agents of necessity and were not liable for any loss suffered by the exporters owing to the removal of the goods to Constantinople. Bailhache J. expressed the decisive test as follows[91]:

> I have come to the conclusion that under all circumstances there never was a point of time that I can put my finger on and say "here the defendants ought to have communicated with this country and if they had done so at that particular date there was a reasonable chance of getting a reply."

It is extremely difficult to establish agency of necessity where there is no pre-existing agency relationship.[92]

Foreign Agency Laws

In English law the enactments securing the position of employees[93] do not apply to independent agents and there are no special legal rules protecting their position.[94]

---

[88] *John Koch Ltd.* v. *C. & H. Products Ltd.* [1956] 2 Lloyd's Rep. 59, 65–66 (*per* Singleton L.J.).

[89] *Sachs* v. *Miklos* [1948] 2 K.B. 23; *Munro* v. *Willmott* [1949] 1 K.B. 295.

[90] *Tetley & Co.* v. *British Trade Corporation* (1922) 10 Ll.L.R. 678.

[91] At p. 681.

[92] *Re Banque de Moscou, Royal Exchange Assurance* v. *The Liquidator* [1952] 1 All E.R. 1269, 1278.

[93] These enactments are mainly the Employment Protection (Consolidation) Act 1978.

[94] On their right to commission for orders placed after the termination of the agency contract, see p. 169, *ante*.

Some foreign laws,[95] however, provide far-reaching protection for the independent agent in a manner which cannot be contracted out. In particular, they entitle the agent after termination of the agency to claim compensation from the principal for the goodwill which he has created and which continues to accrue to the principal, but the conditions for claiming compensation differ in the various countries.[96] A claim for compensation (*Ausgleichsanspruch, indemnité de cliènte, indemnitá*) is admitted in Germany,[97] Switzerland,[98] France, Italy and Austria.[99]

A difficult question is whether the United Kingdom exporter can avoid the overseas agent's claim for compensation by providing that the agency agreement shall be governed by English law. As far as German law is concerned, such a clause is effective and, consequently, bars the agent's claim,[1] but in other legal systems it is uncertain whether the agent's claim for compensation, which is mandatory, can be excluded by submitting the contract of agency to English law. If the agency contract does not provide which law shall apply, many laws assume that that shall be the law of the place where the agent carries on his business; this is the view of the courts in France, Germany, Denmark, Holland and Switzerland, and presumably Belgium, Sweden and Norway.[2] In Italy the Civil Code states that the contract shall be governed by the law of the place where it was concluded.[3] In England, the proper law of the contract between the principal and the agent has to be ascertained in the manner discussed earlier[4]; this may be the law of the agent or the principal.[5]

---

[95] See Clive M. Schmitthoff, "Agency in International Trade," 129 *Recueil des Cours*, Academy of International Law (Vol. 1, 1970), 107, 165; Ole Lando, "The Commercial Agent in European Law" in [1965] J.B.L. 179, 374 and [1966] J.B.L. 82.

[96] [1966] J.B.L. 84.

[97] H.G.B., s. 89b (introduced by an Act of August 6, 1953).

[98] OR, s. 418u (as revised in 1953).

[99] Lando, *loc. cit.*, p. 85.

[1] German Federal Supreme Court, judgment of January 30, 1961.

[2] Schmitthoff, *loc. cit.*, p. 170; Lando, *loc. cit.*, p. 89.

[3] CC, *disp. prel.*, art. 25.

[4] See p. 127, *ante*.

[5] Dicey and Morris, *Conflict of Laws* (9th ed.), Rule 168, pp. 871–877. The contract between the principal (acting through the agent) and the third party is, it is thought, governed by its own proper law which may be entirely different from the law applicable to the contract between the principal and agent, *i.e.* the agency contract proper; see Dicey and Morris, *Conflict of Laws*, pp. 872–873.

CHAPTER 16

BRANCH OFFICES ABROAD

IN some instances exporters establish branch offices abroad which are staffed with resident employees working under the direct control of the exporter and, in this respect, do not differ from their colleagues employed at home. This organisation of export sales, where economically justified, offers distinct advantages over the methods of exporting to sole distributors or through self-employed agents abroad. It enables the exporter to build up his sales abroad systematically, to retain undivided the profits derived from export transactions and to impart his energy and enterprise to his collaborators abroad. Some markets, however, are too limited or too competitive to favour the establishment by an exporter of his own sales organisation, and other methods of exporting appear more appropriate there. The exporter will find valuable advice on the most suitable type of sales organisation in a particular market in the booklets on *Hints to Exporters*,[1] published by the Department of Trade. Each of these booklets deals with a particular country including the various overseas countries of the British Commonwealth. The Department has, further, prepared special publications dealing respectively with the United States of America, with Canada and with the Caribbean; they summarise the special features of these markets and the business practices and Government regulations affecting the British exporter in the countries in question.[1]

The Export Services and Promotions Division of the Department of Trade and the Regional Offices[2] are prepared to advise representatives of United Kingdom firms travelling overseas on export business, and to arrange for a local representative of the Department to meet those representatives on arrival who will then advise them on local conditions, furnish them with introductions and assist them generally.

A branch office abroad is normally staffed by two types of employees who work in co-operation, namely, United Kingdom personnel which the exporter has sent abroad and local personnel. From the legal point of view, this distinction is important. The contracts of employment with the former type of employees have to satisfy the requirements of the English law of employment as well as of the law of the country in which the branch office is situate, but the contracts with the latter type of employees have only to comply with the local foreign law, unless the parties have agreed that they

[1] See p. 60, *ante*.
[2] For address of the Division, see p. 57, *ante*.

shall be governed by English law in which case only the mandatory provisions of foreign law apply.[3]

It is intended first to consider the contract of employment which the exporter concludes with a United Kingdom employee whom he wishes to send abroad, and then to indicate some problems which might be raised by the foreign law in force in the country where the branch office is situate.

The Contract of Employment Abroad

Arrangements between exporters and employees at overseas branch offices[4] vary widely according to the nature of the goods intended to be exported and the circumstances existing in the country where the branch office is situate. Sometimes the United Kingdom executive has merely to supervise the staff of local sales agents, to assist them with his technical knowledge and to attend to the correspondence with the main office, sometimes he has to sell directly, but other arrangements are possible and customary. Where the branch office employee is not authorised to sell or conclude contracts with third parties on behalf of the exporter, his agreement with the latter is an ordinary contract of service. Where he is granted that authority his contract is a contract of agency which differs from the agreement with a self-employed agent[5] only in so far as the agent is employed and consequently the internal arrangement between the principal and agent is closer. Externally the employee who sells goods or concludes other contracts on behalf of the exporter acts as agent of the latter,[6] but internally the employee is obliged to act on the instructions of the principal and has not the same discretion of judgment which a self-employed agent normally possesses.

Salary and commission

The contract between the exporter and the United Kingdom employee serving abroad exhibits a number of special features which require consideration.

It is usual, in this case, to fix the employee's remuneration on a salary basis, sometimes augmented by an overseas allowance for himself and his family and often increased by a bonus on all sales effected in his territory or on a turnover exceeding a fixed minimum turnover. Formerly the employee in charge of a branch office abroad was often authorised to sell the principal's goods at prices exceeding stated minimum prices and to retain to his own credit any higher price which he might obtain, but this practice appears to have become obsolete. The employee is usually entitled to claim reimbursement for business expenses; he is sometimes provided

---

[3] *Cf. Sayers* v. *International Drilling Co. N.V.* [1971] 1 W.L.R. 1176 (Dutch company recruiting European personnel to work on oil rig; contract between Dutch employers and English employee governed by Dutch law).

[4] See William Hedley, "Sales Representatives Abroad" in [1958] J.B.L. 347.

[5] See p. 161, *ante*.

[6] The contract of agency is treated on pp. 162 *et seq.*, *ante*.

with a motor-car by his employer[7] and is often authorised to collect and accept the purchase price on behalf of his principal and to deduct and retain his remuneration from the incoming moneys.[8]

Accommodation abroad, payment of overseas passage

The principal sometimes undertakes to provide, at his own cost, suitable accommodation or board, lodging and service for the agent and his family residing at the place where the branch office is situate.

Contracts of overseas employment normally provide that the principal has to pay the forward and return passage of the employee and his family if they are to accompany him. It likewise is sometimes stated in these agreements that the furniture and household goods which it is reasonable for the employee to take to the country in question or to bring back again shall be conveyed at the expense of the employer.

In appropriate cases arrangements are made for the resident employee, at his option, to accumulate holidays and spend them in the home country.

Reports to the head office

Great attention has to be given to the liaison between the various branch offices and the exporter's head office. It is usual to request the branch offices to report at regular intervals on all important events in their area and on effected and prospective sales, sometimes on questionnaires or forms issued by the head office. The head office often sends confidential circulars and memoranda to the branch offices, informing them of the production progress at home and interesting dates and occurrences relating to the various branch offices. To this exchange of intelligence should be added, from time to time, personal visits of the United Kingdom export manager to the more important branch offices, or meetings at the head office of the heads of the branch offices and of the main executives of the export house.

Bonds and fidelity guarantees

An employee entrused with an executive position at a branch office abroad is sometimes asked to provide security by giving a bond in his own name or procuring a fidelity guarantee from an insurance company or third parties.

Termination of contract; security of employment

The clause dealing with the termination of the contract of employment should be drafted as precisely as possible. Often the contract is concluded for a fixed number of years, but sometimes either party is given the right to determine it upon serving notice on the other party a fixed number of months prior to the date of termination.

---

[7] On the problems arising in this case, see Hedley, *loc. cit.*, p. 351.

[8] On payment abroad of the agent's commission and salary, see p. 168, *ante*.

Modern laws of employment often contain provisions protecting the employee in case of termination of employment. When a person is normally employed in Britain and only sent on service abroad, it is necessary to take into account the relevant British and foreign legislation, but when a local employee is employed in an overseas country it is sufficient to comply solely with the law of that country. As far as British law is concerned, the provisions of the Employment Protection (Consolidation) Act 1978 have to be borne in mind.[9] The Act constitutes a comprehensive code containing provisions for the protection of employees ordinarily working in Great Britain. It demands the delivery, to the employee, of written particulars of the terms of employment, prescribes minimum periods of notice for the termination of the contract of employment (varying between one week and 12 weeks, depending on the length of employment), contains provisions on unfair dismissal, redundancy payment, maternity pay and the right to return to work, and deals with other rights arising in the course of employment, such as, *e.g.* the right to have time off for trade union activities; it also secures to some extent the position of the employee in the insolvency of the employer.

These protective provisions apply to employees ordinarily working in Great Britain. The Act provides[10] that the following shall not apply "to employment where under his contract of employment the employee ordinarily works outside Great Britain": maternity benefits, unfair dismissal, time off for trade union activities and other rights arising in the course of employment, and protection on insolvency of the employer. As regards redundancy payment, the Act provides[11]:

> An employee shall not be entitled to a redundancy payment if on the relevant date he is outside Great Britain, unless under his contract of employment he ordinarily worked in Great Britain.

As regards the calculation of the period of notice, it is stated[12] that the periods during which the employee is engaged in work wholly or mainly outside Great Britain shall not be included into the calculation "unless the employee ordinarily works in Great Britain and the work outside Great Britain is for the same employer."

Persons partly employed in Great Britain and partly outside

Where the employee, by the terms of his contract of employment, is wholly employed at the overseas branch of a United Kingdom enterprise, it is clear that the provisions of the Employment Protection (Consolidation) Act 1978 do not apply.

---

[9] On the application of the Act to Northern Ireland and the Isle of Man, see ss. 157 and 158.
[10] s 141(2).
[11] s. 141(3).
[12] s. 141(1).

A difficulty arises, however, where an employee is partly employed in Great Britain and partly outside. Here the courts apply the so-called base test.[13] Megaw L.J. expressed this test as follows[14]:

> . . . the correct approach is to look at the terms of the contract, express and implied . . . in order to ascertain where, looking at the whole period contemplated by the contract, the employee's base is to be. It is, in the absence of special factors leading to a contrary conclusion, the country where his base is to be which is likely to be the place where he is to be treated as ordinarily working under his contract of employment. Where his base, under the contract, is to be will depend on the examination of all relevant contractual terms. These will be likely to include any such terms as expressly define his headquarters, or which indicate where the travels involved in his employment begin and end; where his private residence—his home—is, or is expected to be; where, and perhaps in what currency, he is to be paid; whether he is to be subject to pay national insurance contributions in Great Britain. These are merely examples of factors which, among many others that may be found to exist in individual cases, may be relevant in deciding where the employee's base is for the purpose of his work, looking to the whole normal, anticipated, duration of the employment.

Restraint of trade clauses

A stipulation restraining the employee from trading after the termination of the contract is invalid in English law if the stipulation is unreasonably wide in the area of application or in point of time, or covers more goods or kinds of transactions than is reasonable.[15]

FOREIGN LEGISLATION

The exporter who wishes to maintain a branch office abroad has to comply with the legislation of the country where the branch office is situate. It is advisable to obtain expert advice on all aspects of the legislation in force in the country in question before establishing a branch office there.

Foreign aliens legislation

Where it is intended to employ United Kingdom personnel in an overseas branch office of a British enterprise, the first question is whether that branch is established in another Member State of the European Community or in a country which is not a member of the Community.

In the former case, the EEC Treaty and the secondary legislation made thereunder applies. The Treaty provides valuable privileges for workers of the Member States of the Community.[16] It is laid down that progressively the free movement of persons shall be secured within the Community and discrimination based on nationality shall be abolished between workers of the Member States as regards employment, remuneration and other conditions of work and employment.[17] Furthermore, by progressive stages the

[13] *Wilson* v. *Maynard Shipbuilding Consultants A.B.* [1978] 2 W.L.R. 466; *Todd* v. *British Midland Airways Ltd., The Times*, July 22, 1978.

[14] *Wilson* v. *Maynard Shipbuilding Consultants A.B.* [1978] 2 W.L.R. 466, 474.

[15] See p. 160, *ante*.

[16] The Treaty draws a distinction between persons in salaried or wage-earning employment who are described as workers, and self-employed persons. Articles 48–51 apply to the former, and Articles 52–58 to the latter.

[17] EEC Treaty, Art. 48.

restrictions on the freedom of establishment of nationals of a Member State in the territory of another Member State shall be abolished and it is provided[18]:—

> Such progressive abolition shall also apply to restrictions on the setting up of agencies, branches or subsidiaries by nationals of any Member State established in the territory of any other Member State.

It follows that no discriminatory requirements can be imposed in any of the other Member States of the Community against the employment of United Kingdom personnel in branches of British enterprises, except if limitations are justified on grounds of public policy, public security or public health[19]. Fortunately much progress has been made towards the realisation of these principles; thus, in France the requirement that a foreign business man must hold a *carte de commerçant étranger* is dispensed with for nationals of the other Member States of the Community.[20]

In the countries which are not Member States of the European Community, the business activities of United Kingdom citizens are governed by the aliens legislation. The permission to enter the country does not, as a matter of course, imply the right to engage in business there. Aliens legislation varies greatly in different countries; the alien is usually required to obtain a permission from a government department before allowed to commence business.

Attention should, further, be paid to the foreign tax legislation. In the United States British exporters conducting business through established branch offices or resident employees are subject to federal income tax while they are not liable to tax when conducting business through independent commission agents who keep no stocks in the United States and are merely authorised to solicit but not to accept orders on behalf of the principal; here the definition of a "permanent establishment" in the Double Taxation Relief Convention with the United States applies.[21]

Foreign labour legislation

The exporter who wishes to establish a branch office abroad is obliged to comply with the labour legislation in force in the particular country. He may have to arrange the terms of service with his employees there in compliance with the requirements of a collective labour agreement.[22] In some countries, particularly in Latin America, Egypt and other Arab

---

[18] *Ibid.*, Art. 52. See *Reyners* v. *Belgian State* [1974] 2 C.M.L.R. 305; *van Duyn* v. *Home Office* [1975] 1 C.M.L.R.I.; *van Binsbergen* v. *Bestuer van de Bedrysvereriging voor de Metaalnijverheid* [1975] 1 C.M.L.R. 298; *Thieffry* v. *Conseil de l'Ordre des Avocats à la Cour de Paris* [1977] 2 C.M.L.R. 373; *Patrick* v. *Ministre des Affaires Culturelles* [1977] 2 C.M.L.R. 523.

[19] Art. 48(3); see *van Duyn* v. *Home Office* [1975] 1 C.M.L.R.I.; *Roland Rutili* v. *French Minister of the Interior* [1976] 1 C.M.L.R. 140.

[20] Ordinance of August 28, 1969; see B. Goldman, *European Commercial Law* (Stevens, 1973) 131, para. 287.

[21] See Schmitthoff and Hall, "The Taxation of Exports" in [1969] J.B.L. 276.

[22] See W. G. Friedmann and R. C. Pugh, *Legal Aspects of Foreign Investment*, 1959, p. 744 *et seq.*

countries, the labour legislation goes further and requires the exporter to employ a proportionate number of indigenous employees. These ultra-nationalistic tendencies are reflected in the Brazilian Labour Code of 1943 which provides that, where an undertaking employs more than three employees, the proportion of Brazilians to be employed shall be two-thirds of the total number of employees and that the same proportion shall apply with respect to the total amount paid by way of salaries and wages.[23]

Foreign legislation protecting security of employment

It has already been noted[24] that in many countries, including Great Britain,[24] legislation exists aimed at the protection of the employee in the event of the termination of his service agreement, by providing that he shall be entitled to notice of a specified length or to compensation, but the qualifying conditions, the periods of notice and the amounts of compensation frequently differ from those applicable in Britain.

The exporter is well advised, before entering into a service agreement with an employee in an overseas country, to ascertain whether such legislation is in operation in that country. Thus, according to William Hedley,[25]

> in Switzerland, notice under these contracts (*contrats de travail*) is subject to specific statutory regulations: if the contract has not been in existence one year then either party can terminate it by giving at least one month's notice, though if the agreement has lasted more than 12 months the period of notice is to be at least two months.

Further, Hedley states that in Norway in agreements of this nature a period of not less than three months would be customary and in some instances, again depending on the facts, even up to six months.

Of particular importance in this connection are the various national provisions dealing with unfair dismissal.[26] The regulation of English law has already been discussed.[27] This branch of law is highly developed in the United States and is also known in France where the principle of *abus de droit* is applied, in Germany which knows protection against dismissal which is *sozial ungerechtfertigt*, and in Italy where dismissal without *giustificato motivo* has legal consequences.

The question whether the foreign legislation protecting security of employment can be contracted out by providing that the contract of employment shall be governed by English law is difficult to answer; it depends in every case on whether the foreign legislation in question is mandatory in character.[28]

---

[23] International Labour Office, Legislative Series, 1943, p. 71.
[24] See p. 186, *ante*.
[25] "Sales Representatives Abroad" [1958] J.B.L. 347, 350.
[26] See G. de N. Clark, "Remedies for Unfair Dismissal: A European Comparison," (1971) 20 I.C.L.Q., 397.
[27] See pp. 185–187, *ante*.
[28] On the discussion of this question in relation to the contract of agency, see p. 182, *ante*.

Travelling Representatives Abroad

The practice of sending travelling representatives overseas is in many instances not as satisfactory as that of establishing permanent branch offices there. The former practice is still in use where orders are solicited on the strength of samples shown to prospective customers by the travellers; sometimes these samples are exhibited at local showrooms. The customer, who wishes to place a repeat order, normally sends it direct to the principal's head office. Travelling representatives often visit their customers at regular intervals in order to show them a new range of samples.

Commercial travellers and their luggage are subject to the laws of the foreign countries which they visit, and these laws vary greatly. It is advisable to obtain the latest information from the Export Services and Promotions Division of the Department of Trade, a chamber of commerce or similar institution before sending a traveller to an overseas country. Three points have to be borne in mind here: does the traveller require a licence when soliciting or accepting orders, are taxes payable by the principal in respect of the traveller's activities, and is Customs duty payable on the samples which he carries?

In most countries a commercial traveller representing a principal resident abroad does not require a Government licence when pursuing his activities. That is certainly true with respect to the Member States of the European Community which are visited by the travelling representative of a principal resident in another Member State, but it also applies in the case of United Kingdom commercial travellers visiting countries outside the European Community, such as Australia, New Zealand, Canada, the United States, Brazil and Peru. Only in some African and South American countries does such a travelling representative have to obtain a licence before engaging in business.

In some countries transient traders' taxes are levied on principals represented by commercial travellers. Sometimes these taxes are State and sometimes municipal revenues. They provide a serious obstacle to the free movement of international trade. The conventions on relief from double taxation, which the United Kingdom Government has concluded with various overseas governments, aim at the exemption of United Kingdom firms from this form of taxation.

The Customs regulations of most countries provide special facilities for the importation of bona fide trade samples by travelling representatives. In some countries samples which are of no commercial value are admitted free of duty. Generally, however, trade samples are liable to Customs duties but it is often sufficient for a deposit to be paid to the Customs authorities; in other cases where the duty has to be paid, a refund or drawback is allowed when the samples are exported within a stated time, *e.g.* six or 12 months.

ATA and ECS Carnets

The importation of commercial samples and other goods temporarily required for exhibitions, scientific, professional and other purposes is regulated by a number of international conventions sponsored by the Customs Co-operation Council which has its seat in Brussels but is not connected with the European Community.[29]

Two of these conventions are of particular interest, namely that dealing with the issue of ECS carnets of March 1, 1956, and that dealing with the issue of ATA carnets for the temporary admission of goods of December 6, 1961.[30] All Member States of the European Community, including the United Kingdom, and many other countries have given effect to these conventions. The types of cases in which ECS or ATA carnets may be used are explained in Customs Notice No. 104.[31]

The carnets facilitate Customs clearance of certain classes of temporary importations and exportations by replacing:

(*a*) normal Customs documentation in the country of temporary exportation, and
(*b*) normal Customs documentation and security (*e.g.* by bond or deposit) in the country of temporary importation.

An ECS carnet may be used only to cover the movement of commercial samples. ECS carnets have now been largely superseded by ATA carnets but there are a few countries which have not yet accepted the Customs Convention on ATA carnets. ATA carnets may be used for the temporary exportation from the United Kingdom of:

(i) commercial samples;
(ii) professional effects;
(iii) exhibition goods; and
(iv) such other goods as the country of importation may allow.

They may also be used for the temporary importation into the United Kingdom of goods eligible for relief under the provisions of:

(i) The Commercial Samples (Temporary Importation) Regulations 1955 (see Customs Notice No. 105),
(ii) The Temporary Importation (Professional Effects) Regulations 1963 (see Customs Notice No. 46),
(iii) The Temporary Importation (Goods for Exhibition) Regulations 1963 (see Customs Notice No. 213).

Carnets are issued by chambers of commerce or similar organisations approved by the Customs authorities of the country in which they operate. The decision whether to issue a carnet is entirely a matter for the association concerned. Inquiries about the issue of carnets to cover goods to be sent abroad should be made to the London Chamber of Commerce[32] or to

[29] See Claude Jacquemart, *La Nouvelle Douane Européenne,* Collection "Exporter," Editions Jupiter, 1971, paras. 277–281.
[30] The letters ECS stand for *Echantillons Commerciaux—Commercial Samples* and ATA for *Admission Temporaire—Temporary Admission.*
[31] Of June 1971.
[32] Address: 69 Cannon Street, London EC4N 5AB.

certain chambers of commerce in the larger provincial cities. These associations will also give the names of associations abroad which will issue carnets for the temporary importation of goods into the United Kingdom. Carnets may not be used for goods sent to or from the United Kingdom by post.

The two carnets are substantially similar documents. Essentially each consists of a booklet which includes a list of the goods covered and a number of vouchers and corresponding counterfoils that have to be completed when goods leave and enter a country. The Customs of the country concerned detach and retain the appropriate voucher, and check that a temporary importation voucher is later discharged by a corresponding re-exportation voucher. The ATA carnet contains, in addition, transit vouchers. The importance of these carnets may be gathered from the fact that in 1978, the 33 participating countries issued 161,993 ATA carnets. (*I.C.I. Information*, 3/1979).

CHAPTER 17

SUBSIDIARY COMPANIES ABROAD

THE favoured form of modern export trading is the establishment of a subsidiary company in the country into which exports are directed.

The overseas subsidiary

The overseas subsidiary is incorporated under the law of that country; it possesses independent and separate legal personality and enjoys in the country of its incorporation the same status as an indigenous trading corporation. The control of the overseas subsidiary is vested in the parent firm which, *e.g.* is resident in the United Kingdom; it is exercised by various means, such as holding a majority of shares in, or a majority of the voting power of, the subsidiary company, or by reservation of the right to appoint its directors or managers, but these examples are illustrative only and not exhaustive.[1] In Nigeria a foreign company can only carry on business through the incorporation of a domestic company.[2]

The *overseas subsidiary* should be distinguished from another form of export trading: sometimes manufacturers or other trading concerns in the United Kingdom find it convenient to separate their export business from their other activities and form *a United Kingdom subsidiary* the objects of which are to promote exports generally or to a particular country. The International Chamber of Commerce has published an *International Guide to Company Formation*.[3] The object of the *Guide* is to draw attention to the most important questions to be considered when it is intended to form an overseas subsidiary.

The overseas subsidiary is capable of entering into the same contractual relations with the parent firm as can be entered into by a natural person resident in the overseas country. The relations between these two enterprises may be ordinary contracts of sale concluded on f.o.b. terms, c.i.f. terms or other trade terms; or the parent firm may arrange a sole distribution agreement with the subsidiary or employ it as its commission agent or resident representative or branch office; the observations made earlier in regard to these different forms of exporting apply here, *mutatis mutandis*. The form of a subsidiary company is particularly well suited when several United Kingdom exporters combine in export trading or when a United Kingdom exporter associates with an overseas concern in the production or distribution of certain goods. The overseas subsidiary is, thus, the ideal trading instrument for joint ventures; in view of the wide discretionary powers admitted by the company laws of most countries, it is not difficult

[1] *British American Tobacco Co. Ltd.* v. *Inland Revenue Commissioners* [1943] A.C. 335.
[2] Nigerian Decree No. 51 of 1968.
[3] ICC Brochure No. 263 (September 1970).

to arrange the distribution of power in the subsidiary and the participation in its profits and losses in harmony with the agreement between its constituent members.

The multinational enterprise

By establishing one or several subsidiaries overseas, the British parent company becomes a multinational or, as it is sometimes called, transnational enterprise. Such an enterprise has been defined "as a combination of companies of different nationality, connected by means of shareholdings, managerial control, or contract and constituting an economic unit."[4]

Two legal problems arise with respect to multinational enterprises. First, the interests of the host country in which the subsidiary is formed may conflict with those of the home country in which the controlling company has its seat. If a subsidiary is involved in such a conflict, the public policy of the host country must, in principle, prevail over that of the home country.[5] Secondly, in some circumstances the veil of separate legal status of the various constituent companies of the multinational enterprise is lifted and the multinational is treated as a legal unit. Thus, in the competition law[6] of the European Community the European Court, on occasion, has lifted the veil of corporateness and treated the multinational as a legal unit. The Court has, in particular, assumed jurisdiction[7] over a parent company incorporated in a non-Member State and having a subsidiary in a Member State if that subsidiary "does not determine its behaviour on the market in an autonomous manner but essentially carries out the instructions of the parent company."[8]

At present a proposal is being considered by the EEC authorities to create a new form of company, namely that of the European Company (*société Européenne, societas Europea, S.E.*).[9] The European Company will be registered with the European Court in Luxembourg and shall be treated in all Member States as a company of the public type incorporated under national law. Even when the project of the European company is eventually realised, the normal form of establishing an export organisation in the Common Market will be for a United Kingdom company to establish

---

[4] Clive M. Schmitthoff, in *Nationalism and Multinational Enterprise*, edited by H. R. Hahlo, J. Graham South and Richard W. Wright, Sijthoff, Leiden, 1973, 24; *Legal Problems of Multinational Corporations* (ed. K. R. Simmonds), (British Institute of International and Comparative Law, London, 1977).

[5] See Clive M. Schmitthoff, "Multinationals in Court," [1972] J.B.L. 103, 104; *affaire Fruehauf, ibid.*; *Decro-Wall S.A.* v. *Marketing Ltd.* [1971] 1 W.L.R. 361; *Acrow (Automation) Ltd.* v. *Rex Chainbelt Inc.* [1971] 1 W.L.R. 1676.

[6] Articles 85–90 of the EEC Treaty; see pp. 218, 221, *post*.

[7] In *I.C.I. Ltd. and Others* v. *E.C. Commission* (48–57/69) [1972] C.M.L.R. 557; and *Europemballage Corporation and Continental Can Company Inc.* v. *E.C. Commission* (6/72) [1973] C.M.L.R. 199; *Commercial Solvents Corporation* v. *Commission* [1973] C.M.L.R. 309; The Commission has done the same: *The Community* v. *Hoffmann-La Roche* [1976] 2 C.M.L.R.D. 25.

[8] In the *I.C.I.* case, on p. 629.

[9] *Proposal for a Council Regulation on the Statute for European Companies*, May 13, 1975, *Bulletin of the European Communities*, Supplement 4/75.

subsidiary companies in the other Member States of the Community. The overseas subsidiary is likewise the favoured form of export organisation in countries which are not Member States of the European Community.

In Company Law

It has been observed earlier[10] that, on principle, British company law requires a company or a group of companies to disclose in the directors' report its export turnover if the business of the company consists in, or includes, the supply of goods and the total turnover of the enterprise exceeds £250,000.[11] These requirements, which are founded on the Companies Act 1967,[11] are motivated by the national interest. They are of general character and apply to all companies or groups of companies which satisfy the conditions of the Act of 1967.

In this chapter the provisions of company law have to be considered which apply to overseas subsidiaries[12] of a United Kingdom company.[13] The statutes regulating the company law of Great Britain are the Companies Acts 1948 to 1976. According to these enactments an overseas subsidiary of a British company is, in principle, treated in the same manner as if the subsidiary was incorporated in the United Kingdom.

The Companies Act 1948 provides, in section 154(1), that a company shall be deemed the subsidiary of another (the holding) company if—

1. The holding company either
   (*a*) is a member of it and controls the composition of its board of directors, or
   (*b*) holds more than half in nominal value of its equity share capital, or
2. The company is a sub-subsidiary of the holding company.

The composition of a company's board of directors is deemed to be controlled by the holding company if the latter has power, without consent of any other person, to appoint or remove all or a majority of the directors (s. 154(2)). The equity share capital is defined in section 154(5) as the issued share capital excluding any part thereof which, neither as respects dividends nor as respects capital, carries any right to participate beyond a specified amount in a distribution: consequently, non-participating preference shares do not form part of the equity share capital.

The 1948 Act further provides for an extension of publicity of the company's affairs and lays down in particular that, as a matter of principle, group accounts shall be presented by the holding company (s. 150(1) as amended by the Companies Act 1976, s. 8). Group accounts[14] have to consist of—

---

[10] See p. 5, *ante*.
[11] Companies Act 1967, s. 20; Companies (Accounts) Regulations 1971 (No. 2044).
[12] Overseas subsidiaries are sometimes promoted as partnerships, and not as companies.
[13] A detailed treatment of this subject will be found in Palmer's *Company Law* (22nd ed.), Chap. 67, paras. 67–01 *et seq*.
[14] Detailed provisions on accounts where the company is a holding or subsidiary company are contained in Sched. 8, Pt. II of the 1948 Act, in the amended form of Sched. 2 of the Companies Act 1967.

Page 5 ✓ NB

(1) a consolidated balance sheet dealing with the state of affairs of the company and all the subsidiaries to be dealt with in group accounts;
(2) a consolidated profit and loss account dealing with the profit or loss of the company and those subsidiaries (s. 151(1), as amended by the 1976 Act).

If the directors of the holding company are of opinion that the information, if presented in the form prescribed by section 151(1), might not be readily appreciable by the shareholders, the group accounts may be prepared in another form,

and in particular may consist of more than one set of consolidated accounts dealing respectively with the company and one group of subsidiaries and with other groups of subsidiaries, or of separate accounts dealing with each of the subsidiaries, or of statements expanding the information about the subsidiaries in the company's own accounts, or any combination of these forms (s. 151(2)).

The obligation to lay group accounts before the general meeting of the holding company is subject to the following qualifications:

(1) group accounts are not required

where the company is at the end of its financial year the wholly owned subsidiary of another body corporate incorporated in Great Britain (s. 150(2)(*a*));

(2) group accounts need not deal with a subsidiary of the company if, in the opinion of the directors,

(*a*) it is impracticable, or would be of no real value to members of the company, in view of the insignificant amounts involved, or would involve expense or delay out of proportion to the value to members of the company; or
(*b*) the result would be misleading, or harmful to the business of the company or any of its subsidiaries; or
(*c*) the business of the holding company and that of the subsidiary are so different that they cannot reasonably be treated as a single undertaking (s. 150(2)(*b*));

but the directors require the approval of the Department of Trade if they do not wish to deal in group accounts with a subsidiary—

(*a*) on the ground that the result would be harmful, or
(*b*) on the ground of the difference between the business of the holding company and that of the subsidiary (s. 150(2), proviso).

Subsidiary companies incorporated in a foreign country which are subsidiaries of a United Kingdom holding company may find it difficult to arrange their financial year in such a manner that it coincides with that of the United Kingdom holding company because some foreign company laws lay down obligatory requirements about the commencing and terminal dates of the financial year. The Companies Acts 1948 to 1976 make allowance for this situation: the Act of 1948 obliges, in section 153(1), the directors of the holding company to secure that, except where in their opinion there are good reasons against it, the financial year of each of its subsidiaries shall coincide with the holding company's financial year, but provides, in section 152(2), that where the financial year of a subsidiary company does not so coincide, the group accounts shall deal with the subsidiary's state of affairs as at the end of its financial year ending with or last before that of the holding company and with the subsidiary's profit and loss for that year. If, in the circumstances of the case, this solution is impracticable an application may be made by the holding company's directors to the Department of Trade which is authorised to approve another arrangement (s. 152(2)).

Under the Exchange Control Act 1947

This enactment, which regulates the collection of payments due for United Kingdom exports, operates mainly on a territorial basis and applies to all persons and companies resident in the United Kingdom. The Act contains, however, certain provisions extending its application to overseas subsidiaries of United Kingdom enterprises. First, it is provided, in section 30(1), that "a foreign company," as an overseas subsidiary is termed in this enactment, may be required by a notice (which is to be served on behalf of the Treasury on the person resident in the United Kingdom and controlling the foreign company) to—

(i) furnish to the Treasury such particulars as to its assets and business as may be mentioned in the notice;
(ii) sell or procure the sale to an authorised dealer of any gold or specified currency mentioned in the notice, being gold or specified currency which it is entitled to sell or of which it is entitled to procure the sale;
(iii) declare and pay such dividend as may be mentioned in the notice;
(iv) realise any of its assets mentioned in the notice in such manner as may be so mentioned;
(v) refrain from selling, transferring, or doing anything which affects its rights or powers in relation to any such Treasury bills or securities as may be mentioned in the notice.

Further, a person resident in the United Kingdom and controlling a "foreign company" is not allowed to part with that control, except by permission of the Treasury (s. 30(2)). A resident in the United Kingdom is not allowed, except by permission of the Treasury, to lend money or securities to a corporation resident in the United Kingdom or any other part of the scheduled territories[15] if the corporation is controlled directly or indirectly by persons resident outside the sterling area (s. 30(3)). The provisions of section 30 apply even where the persons holding the controlling interest are associated with persons resident outside the area concerned if they together can override the influence of those other persons. If, *e.g.* three United Kingdom exporters, A, B and C, associate with two Dutch businessmen, X and Y, in the formation of a Dutch company, that company is subject to British exchange control if the combined interests of A, B and C can override those of X and Y.

Where a "foreign company" is ordered to sell gold or foreign currency through an authorised dealer in the United Kingdom, the Treasury may direct that the price (which is expressed in sterling currency) should be paid or credited to a blocked account of the company (s. 32). The treatment of the overseas subsidiary is, consequently, governed by considerations of fiscal convenience rather than equitable rules: the overseas subsidiary may be treated as resident in the United Kingdom so far as Treasury control

---

[15] See p. 71, *ante*.

is concerned (s. 30) and as resident overseas so far as the disposal of its funds in this country is at issue (s. 32). The following definition of "foreign companies" is provided in the Second Schedule to the Exchange Control Act 1947:

FOREIGN COMPANIES

1. The bodies corporate in question are bodies corporate not incorporated under the law of any part of the United Kingdom in the case of which any of the following conditions is fulfilled—

(*a*) that the body corporate is by any means controlled (whether directly or indirectly) by persons resident in the United Kingdom;

(*b*) that more than one-half of the sums which, on a liquidation thereof, would be receivable by holders of share or loan capital would be receivable directly or indirectly by or for the benefit of persons resident in the United Kingdom;

(*c*) that more than one-half of the assets which, on a liquidation thereof, would be available for distribution after the payment of creditors would be receivable directly or indirectly by or for the benefit of persons resident in the United Kingdom; or

(*d*) that more than one-half—

(i) of the interest payable on its loans and loan capital, if any; or

(ii) of the dividends payable on its preference share capital, if any; or

(iii) of the dividends payable on its share capital, if any, not being preference share capital.

is receivable, directly or indirectly, by or for the benefit of persons resident in the United Kingdom.

The Treasury has powers, by section 39, to direct that for certain specified purposes any transaction with or by a branch of any business, whether carried on by a body corporate or otherwise, shall be treated as if the branch were an incorporated subsidiary resident where the branch is situate, and a book entry debiting a branch in favour of another branch may be treated as a payment to that other branch. Under this power the Treasury can extend its control to unincorporated overseas branches of United Kingdom enterprises by declaring these overseas branches as "foreign companies."

FOREIGN LAW AFFECTING OVERSEAS SUBSIDIARIES

When it is intended to establish a subsidiary in an overseas country, the legal position in that country is an important factor to be considered, in addition to extra-legal factors, such as the political and economic stability of the country, the cost of labour, raw material and transport, the size of the market and the membership of the country in a regional trade group. The legal position will, in particular, determine whether it is more advisable to establish a subsidiary in that country or to trade through a branch. Two American authors[16] write:

The provisions of the local private law relating to business organisations become particularly important when the investor faces the problem of what type of commercial organisation to adopt for the investment. The two broad alternative methods of direct investment are: operation through a branch qualified to do business in the foreign country and the creation of a subsidiary company organised under the laws of the foreign country either with or without participation of local capital. Where the latter alternative is chosen, the capital

[16] W. G. Friedmann and R. C. Pugh, *Legal Aspects of Foreign Investment*, 1959, p. 735.

contribution of the foreign investor may take the form of cash, machinery, or, where permitted by local law, intangible assets such as patents, goodwill, or know-how. . . .

Often the investing [company] will find it advantageous not to establish a foreign branch or own shares of a foreign subsidiary directly but rather to establish an intermediate base company in a country where there is free convertibility and where the taxes on corporate income derived in other countries are low or non-existent—the familiar profit sanctuary.

Broadly speaking, there are four branches of foreign law to which the United Kingdom exporter must give attention when deciding whether the formation of an overseas subsidiary is the best form of export organisation in the country into which he wishes to direct his exports; *viz.* the law relating to companies, labour relations, taxation and foreign investment.

Foreign company laws

The principle of free registration of a company under the general laws of the country, without the requirement of a special Government licence, is recognised in many overseas countries, including the countries of the British Commonwealth, the United States, France, Spain and West Germany. In another group of countries a Government permission has to be obtained for the formation of the company but can be refused only for specified reasons; hereunder fall the laws of the Netherlands and Finland although such a permission is in most instances a mere formality. In a third group of countries, a Government licence is required which may be refused on grounds of administrative expediency and discretion; this is the position in Turkey, Indonesia, Argentina, Bolivia, Chile, Guatemala, Haiti and Honduras.

Not many laws adopt such a liberal attitude to the foreign investor as the law of the United Kingdom in which discrimination against non-resident or foreign shareholders or directors is entirely unknown. Generally speaking, apart from a few specified activities, the laws of the Member States of the EEC, of the Commonwealth, and of Austria and Israel do not restrict the participation of aliens. In other countries, however, whether industrially highly developed or not, legal restrictions exist.

According to a number of national laws, the majority of shares must be held by nationals of the country in question. In Spain, apart from exceptional cases, three-fourths of the capital, and in Mexico and the United Arab Republic, as a rule, 51 per cent. of the share capital, must be owned by nationals. In Sweden and Finland the articles must require that at least four-fifths of the capital are owned by nationals and cannot be transferred to aliens; if the articles do not so provide, restrictions are imposed on the company's right to own land.[17] Restrictions on ownership of land and mineral rights in the case of foreign participation are also found in other laws, notably those of Canada, Mexico and the Philippines. In Sweden all the founders of the company must be resident Swedish subjects. Similar provisions requiring the majority of promoters to be American citizens

[17] That makes it impossible to use bearer shares without permission of the Government. As regards Finland, see Dr. V. Reinikainen in "Aspects of the Right of Establishment by Aliens in Finland" in *Economic Review* (Helsinki), 1964, No. 3, pp. 119–139.

exist in some of the United States, notably in the states of New York and Pennsylvania. Often these restrictions can be lawfully avoided by the use of nominees or "dummies."

In several countries special qualifications are required as regards the nationality or residence of the directors and managers of a domestic company. Thus, in Sweden, Norway, Finland and Switzerland all or the majority of the members of the board of directors must be resident nationals of the respective country, but in some cases the Government may dispense with this requirement. In Iraq [18] companies are obliged to employ national lawyers as secretaries or legal advisers respectively.

Foreign labour laws

The laws of foreign countries often contain legislation protecting indigenous labour. Such legislation applies to a subsidiary incorporated in the country in question and controlled by aliens in the same manner as to individual alien employers. The general trend of that protectionist legislation has already been indicated.[19]

Foreign tax laws

The provisions of foreign tax law applying to overseas subsidiaries of British concerns vary considerably in the various countries. It is obvious that the incidence of taxation is one of the major considerations when a decision is taken whether to set up a subsidiary in a particular country. It is perhaps less obvious that what matters is not merely the legal regulation but the realities of the tax position, and, in particular, the administrative discretion vested in the revenue authorities which in overseas countries are not normally supervised by the courts. In some countries the revenue authorities have little discretion in the assessment and collection of taxes; in others foreign enterprise is treated apparently or actually preferentially because it is the policy of the country to attract foreign capital, and in one or two instances, notably in Liechtenstein, the rates of taxation can be settled by negotiation before the foreign subsidiary is formed. In other countries, on the other hand, while the rates of taxation for foreign and domestic enterprises are the same and the law does not admit open discrimination, the practical effect of taxation is such that its impact is stronger on foreign than on domestic enterprises and, from the practical point of view, considerable discrimination exists. The importance of bearing in mind the realities of the tax position is stressed by Friedmann and Pugh in the following passage[20]:

> While overt discrimination in tax rates between foreign and domestic enterprises is very rare, covert discrimination of a highly effective kind may occasionally be encountered. For example, in a capital-importing country in which the bulk of major enterprises are foreign-

[18] [1961] J.B.L. 211.
[19] On p. 189, *ante*.
[20] *Legal Aspects of Foreign Investment*, 1959, p. 741.

owned and foreign-controlled, high progressive tax rates may have an impact on the foreign firms that domestic enterprises escape because of their smaller size. Also, there is considerable room for administrative discrimination with regard to such matters as the fixing of depreciation rates and the allowance of business deductions.

Sometimes the operations of an overseas subsidiary attract taxation both in this country and in the country in which it is constituted; in these cases the question arises whether the exporter qualifies for double taxation relief in this country.

Foreign investment laws

National investment legislation

Many overseas countries which wish to develop their own industry with the help of foreign private investors having the necessary knowledge and capital have enacted legislation granting special privileges to foreign interests prepared to build up an industry in the country in question, either on their own or in collaboration with local industrialists. Amongst these countries are Egypt, Ghana, Greece, India, Iran, Israel, Italy, Nigeria, Pakistan, Portugal, Thailand and Turkey. The privileges provided by national investment laws are invariably only available if the enterprise is approved by the competent Government authority and are often reserved to particular industries, *e.g.* so-called pioneer industries in Ghana.[21] In some instances the privileges are limited in time, *e.g.* in Italy they applied, as a rule, only to companies incorporated before June 30, 1965[22]; and in some cases the investment must take a specified form, *e.g.* according to Portuguese law the form of a company incorporated under Portuguese law must be used.[23]

The investment privileges which national legislations normally provide, subject to many conditions and often not as generous as they appear at the first glance, relate to—

1. *Exchange control regulations.* The investor is allowed to transfer home profits and to repatriate his invested capital and any capital gain;
2. *Customs regulations.* Free entry or entry at a reduced rate is allowed for machinery required to set up or expand the new industry and sometimes also for the goods produced;
3. *Relief from taxation.* Hereunder fall relief from, or preferential rates of, national or municipal taxation, stamp duties and similar imposts; and
4. *Public credit facilities.* Thus in Italy financial grants or loans can be obtained from the *Cassa del Mezzogiorno*,[24] particularly if the location of foreign industry is in specified areas of Southern Italy.

International protection of foreign investments

The industrial development of the developing countries, particularly in Asia and Africa, which provide great potential markets for industrial goods,

---

[21] [1960] J.B.L. 379.

[22] Mario Fiore, "The Italian Location of British Industry in the Common Market" in [1960] J.B.L. 299, 303.

[23] Friedmann and Pugh, *loc. cit.*, p. 460.

[24] Mario Fiore, *loc. cit.*, p. 305.

is only possible if private investors in the developed countries are prepared to risk their capital and—more important than finance—to apply their knowledge and experience to the development of industries in those parts of the world. Here the danger exists that the exporter, possibly after having been invited into the capital-importing country by favourable investments legislation and having sunk considerable capital into his subsidiary in that country, is threatened by "creeping" or overt expropriation and thereby deprived of the fruits of his investment.[25]

Various measures have been adopted to alleviate that fear. In Greece, *e.g.* legislation expressly provides that the assets of enterprises established or substantially expanded through foreign capital shall be exempt from expropriation.[26] The United States have tried to protect American investors risking their funds and energies elsewhere against losses resulting from expropriation, inconvertibility of currency and war damages by inserting appropriate clauses into bilateral treaties of friendship, navigation and commerce and into so-called investment guarantee agreements which they have concluded with other countries.[27] In some cases Governments have undertaken in concession agreements or other contracts with foreign private investors not to expropriate their assets except in the case of overriding public interest and in that event to pay just and fair compensation without delay. However, these arrangements do not provide effective protection to the foreign investor. If they are broken by the Government which made them or—more likely—by its successor, the private investor is often helpless.

The general rules of international law afford at present little protection to the private investor. In the absence of an undertaking to the contrary, international law considers a sovereign state to be at liberty to carry out non-discriminatory measures of any kind in its own territory, including measures amounting to the expropriation of property of aliens, but in the modern view the expropriating state must pay the alien full, fair and speedy compensation. The English courts consider as effective[28] an expropriation decree of a foreign country the Government of which is recognised by the Crown unless—

1. the decree or order attempts to attach property situate outside the territory of the expropriating state;

[25] E. I. Nwogugu, *The Legal Problems of Foreign Investments in the Developing Countries*, Manchester, 1964; C. M. Schmitthoff, "The Law of International Trade and Investments" in (1967) 6 *Il Diritto negli scambi internazionali* 169; the same author, "British Aid to the Developing Countries" (1967) 1 *Journal of World Trade Law* 564; Karl E. Lachmann, "The Role of International Business in the Transfer of Technology to Developing Countries" in [1967] J.B.L. 346; G. Schwarzenberger, *Foreign Investments and International Law*, 1969; P. Kahn, "The Law applicable to Foreign Investments" in (1968) 49 Indiana L.J. 1; G. R. Delaume, "Public Debt and Sovereign Immunity" [1974] J.B.L. 175.

[26] Friedmann and Pugh, *loc. cit.*, p. 246.

[27] "The Role of Private Enterprise in Investment and Promotion of Exports in Developing Countries," 1968, United Nations Publications, Sales No. E.68 II D9; and the article by G. R. Delaume quoted in n. 25, *ante*

[28] Dicey and Morris, *The Conflict of Laws* (9th ed.), Rule 87, pp. 558–565.

2. the decree is of penal or purely discriminatory character, directed against a particular person or several of them; or
3. the decree constitutes a breach of international law, *e.g.* a breach of an undertaking or obligation of that state.

Attempts have been made to extend the protection which international law provides for the private investor by creating an *international investments code*, a multilateral convention, the signatories of which would undertake definite obligations protecting foreign private investment in their countries. Projects of such a code have been advanced by the Prime Minister of Malaya, the Council of Europe, the ICC, the OECD and various other organisations which sponsored drafts prepared by Lord Shawcross, the German banker Abs and others. So far these plans have not yet led to an international convention.

In view of this lack of international protection, manufacturers are often reluctant to invest capital in the building of factories in a less developed country unless their own Government guarantees to pay any losses caused by Government interference in the overseas country. In the United Kingdom such guarantee might be provided by the Export Credits Guarantee Department.[29] Another method favoured by United Kingdom manufacturers in appropriate cases is to sell the "know-how" of their manufacture to foreign interests, an arrangement which has distinct tax advantages because the consideration for such sale might be received for a capital asset and, if that is the case, might not be subject to income tax.[30]

The Arbitration (International Investment Disputes) Act 1966

An attempt has been made to approach the protection of foreign investors from the procedural angle, by providing machinery for the settlement of international investment disputes. This approach has been successful. In 1965 a *Convention on the Settlement of Investment Disputes between States and Nationals of Other States* was concluded in Washington.[31] This Convention has become effective. On October 23, 1978, it had been ratified by 72 countries, among them the United States, the United Kingdom, France and West Germany. The United Kingdom gave effect to it by the *Arbitration (International Investment Disputes) Act 1966*,[32] as amended.[33]

The Convention, which was sponsored by the International Bank for Reconstruction and Development, provides for the formation of an International Centre for Settlement of Investment Disputes at the principal

[29] See p. 274, *post*.

[30] *Moriarty* v. *Evans Medical Supplies Ltd.* [1958] 1 W.L.R. 66; *Jeffery* v. *Rolls-Royce Ltd.* [1961] 1 W.L.R. 897.

[31] The Convention entered into force on October 14, 1966. David M. Sassoon, "Convention on the Settlement of Investment Disputes" in [1965] J.B.L. 334; Joy Cherian, *Investment Contracts and Arbitration*, The World Bank Convention on the Settlement of Investment Disputes, Sijthoff, 1975.

[32] The Convention entered in force for the U.K. on January 18, 1967 (Treaty Series No. 25/1967); Cmnd. 3255. The Convention has been extended to various colonies, etc.; see S.I.s 1967 Nos. 159, 249, 585.

[33] By the Evidence (Proceedings in Other Jurisdictions) Act 1975, s. 8(2) and Sched. 2.

office of the Bank at Washington. The Centre makes available facilities to which contracting States and foreign investors who are nationals of other contracting States have access on a voluntary basis for the settlement of investment disputes between them in accordance with rules laid down in the Convention. The method of settlement might be conciliation or arbitration, or conciliation followed by arbitration in case the conciliation effort fails. The initiative for such proceedings might come from a State as well as from an investor. The Centre itself does not act as conciliator or arbitrator but maintains panels of specially qualified persons from which conciliators or arbitrators can be selected by the parties, and provides the necessary facilities for the conduct of the proceedings. Once a State and a foreign investor have agreed to use the facilities of the Centre, they are required to carry out their agreement, to give due consideration to the recommendations of a conciliator and to comply with an arbitral award. In addition, all contracting States, whether parties to the dispute or not, are required to recognise arbitral awards rendered in accordance with the Convention as binding and to enforce the pecuniary obligations imposed thereby.

The United Kingdom Arbitration (International Investment Disputes) Act 1966, as amended,[34] sets out the Convention in a schedule. The Act itself provides that a person seeking recognition or enforcement of an award made under the Convention is entitled to have it registered in the High Court.[35] If the award is in a foreign currency, the currency is converted on the basis of the rate of exchange prevailing at the date when the award was rendered.[36] The Act came into force on January 18, 1967.[37]

In 1978 the International Centre for Settlement of Investment Disputes in Washington extended its jurisdiction by adopting so-called *Additional Facilities* aimed at covering cases to which the 1965 Convention did not apply. There are four sets of Additional Facilities: the Administrative and Financial Rules, the Conciliation Rules, the Arbitration Rules, and, the Fact-Finding Rules.

Conclusions

It is evident from the preceding observations that the requirements of foreign law are so varied and in some respects so unexpectedly different from those of English law that the United Kingdom exporter should invariably obtain expert advice before deciding whether to establish a subsidiary company in an overseas country or not.

---

[34] By the Evidence (Proceeding in Other Jurisdictions) Act, s. 8(2) and Sched. 2.
[35] Act of 1966, s. 1(2).
[36] *Ibid.* s. 1(3).
[37] *Ibid.* s. 9(2).

CHAPTER 18

JOINT EXPORT ORGANISATIONS

IN modern export trade, increasing attention is paid to the various forms of combined exporting. The characteristics of this method of exporting are that a number of economically independent manufacturers or merchants, on their own accord or under guidance of the Government, voluntarily set up a joint organisation for the purpose of co-ordinating their exports but retain their liberty of action in other respects. The co-operation agreed upon between the members of the joint organisation may be close or relatively loose. The three most important types of this form of exporting are joint selling organisations, consortia and joint ventures.

JOINT SELLING ORGANISATIONS

The various forms of joint selling organisations intended to have permanent character are as follows[1]:

1. A group of manufacturers sharing the cost of maintaining an exclusive resident agent in an overseas market, who devotes all his time to marketing the products of the group.
2. A marketing company formed by a group of manufacturers to operate a particular overseas territory, the expense being shared between the members in agreed proportions.
3. An independent company with overseas branches which acts as the selling organisation for a limited number of manufacturers, who contribute to the overhead expenses on a turnover basis, and are charged individually with any costs incurred specially for their benefit.
4. An association of manufacturers in a particular industry, having a central sales organisation responsible for working overseas markets, and dividing the orders received amongst the associated firms, in agreed proportions.

From the legal point of view, the ideal forms are types (2) and (3), or sometimes a combination of both, namely an independent export company in the United Kingdom which distributes incoming export orders to the various manufacturers who are members of the selling organisation, and a number of overseas marketing companies acting as exclusive buyers or agents of the former company. The choice of form for the joint selling organisation depends on the nature and relationship of the member enterprises, the conditions of the overseas markets and, to no small extent, the personal susceptibilities of the manufacturers who agree to co-operate in the field of exports while remaining competitors in other respects. The form of the limited liability company provides the most adaptable instrument that the law can contribute when the co-ordination of conflicting economic interests is attempted. The provisions of the United Kingdom

[1] The classification in the text is founded on G. T. MacEwan, *Overseas Trade and Export Practice* (Macdonald and Evans, London, 1938), p. 171.

legislation relating to restrictive practices and, if the arrangement affects the Common Market, the regulation of competition by the European Community have to be observed. These topics are treated in the following two chapters.[2]

Two useful forms of modern co-operative selling abroad are the formation in the United Kingdom of—

(*a*) *A group sales company*. This company is incorporated as a company limited by shares by manufacturers whose products do not compete but which, when taken together, cover the whole range of products in a particular industry, *e.g.* machine tools: or

(*b*) *A wholly-owned subsidiary export company*. This type of organisation is used by large manufacturing concerns consisting of interconnected companies under the same financial control. The export company is charged with the duty of handling all the exports of the group.

In both cases it is necessary to have a representative or equivalent selling organisation in each of the overseas territories to which the group's exports are shipped. This may be a sales representative on the staff of the United Kingdom organisation who visits certain markets on specific selling assignments, it may be an associate selling company of the United Kingdom organisation which is set up in the overseas territory, or it may be an importer in the territory who is appointed an agent for the products of the United Kingdom organisation. Obviously the more important the territory the more likely it is that the United Kingdom export organisation will have its own associated company or representative selling on its behalf in the territory.

Consortia

A consortium, according to A. H. Boulton,[3] is "an organisation which is created when two or more companies co-operate so as to act as a single entity for a specific and limited purpose." Consortia have been formed by British companies to build abroad nuclear power stations, steel works, tyre factories, blast furnaces and rolling mills, foundries, paper mills, oil refineries and general large-scale engineering projects. Similar organisations exist in France, Holland, Germany and Switzerland. Sometimes international consortia are formed by companies incorporated in different countries; they are particularly useful to carry out international development schemes sponsored by the International Bank for Reconstruction and Development or similar international bodies.

Most British consortia are formed as companies incorporated under the Companies Acts 1948 to 1976, but sometimes a looser form of organisation bearing the characteristics of partnership is used. Particular attention has to be given to the financial structure, the profit distribution and the so-called superimposed obligation of the consortium.[4] The latter term denotes

[2] See pp. 210 and 218 respectively.

[3] A. H. Boulton, "Construction Consortia—Their Formation and Management" [1959] J.B.L. 234. See further A. H. Boulton, *Business Consortia* (Sweet & Maxwell, 1961).

[4] A. H. Boulton, "Finance in the 'Single Project' Consortium" [1961] J.B.L. 368.

the responsibilities of the consortium as a whole to the overseas Government or other contracting party; here the question is how the liability amongst the members of the consortium shall be distributed if the common venture encounters difficulties due to the fault of one of the members; *e.g.* a complete electric power station has to be built but additional expense is incurred owing to the faulty design of machinery supplied by one of the members. The mutual rights and duties of the members have to be agreed beforehand and to be clearly defined in the documents constituting the consortium. The choice of an "independent chairman . . . of suitable stature and acceptability"[5] will greatly facilitate the settlement of internal differences in the consortium.

JOINT VENTURES

Where a British company wishes to co-operate with an enterprise in the country to which its exports are directed, it will often form a joint venture with that enterprise.[6]

As in the case of the consortium, one has to distinguish between the contract whereby the parties agree to constitute a joint venture (the co-operation agreement) and the legal form of the joint venture itself.

The co-operation agreement has to be drafted with great care. It should define the form which the joint venture is to take, the contributions of the parties, their participation in the profits and losses, the management structure of the joint venture, its termination and the disposal of its assets after dissolution. It should also contain a choice of law clause and provide for arbitration if disputes arise between the parties. If in a joint venture the two co-operating parties hold equal portions of the venture's capital (50/50), a deadlock in the management may ensue if they disagree on management policy. The International Chamber of Commerce has devised the *ICC Rules for the Regulation of Contractual Relations* (*1979*) which provide for the prompt designation of a third party to resolve the deadlock and define the conditions under which he may perform his task.[6a]

The form of the joint venture should be as flexible as possible. Often the parties will choose the form of a private limited company but other possibilities exist. Thus in France the *Groupement d'Intérêt Économique* (GIE) offers distinct advantages. That form was introduced into French law by ordinance of September 23, 1967. The GIE has a separate legal personality but no corporation tax is paid by it on its profits. It must have a name and is registered under it in the commercial register; it has to show the letters GIE on all documents addressed to third parties. It is represented

---

[5] A. H. Boulton [1959] J.B.L. 240.

[6] Clive M. Schmitthoff, "Joint Ventures in Europe" in *Commercial Operations in Europe* (ed. R. M. Goode and K. R. Simmonds), Sijthoff, 1978), p. 327; George A. Zaphiriou, "Methods of Co-operation between Independent Enterprises (Joint Ventures)" 26 Am J. Comp. L. 245 (1978); Michael W. Gordon, "Joint Ventures in Eastern Europe," 9 Texas International L.J. 281 (1974).

[6a] ICC Brochure No. 326 (1979) on *Adaptation of Contracts,* see p. 456, *post.*

by one or several directors (*administrateurs*). It need not have a capital and passes its profits on to its members who are liable for its obligations without limitation.

In Germany the form of GmbH & Co. or GmbH & Co. KG[7] is frequently used. These are partnerships consisting of several limited companies as partners. Such partnerships have no separate legal personality and are not subject to corporation tax.

The parties who wish to co-operate in a joint venture have to comply strictly with the relevant law relating to restrictive trade practices, and in particular with the competition law of the European Community[8] and American anti-trust law. The joint venture is no magic wand by which the dangers of contravention of the restrictive practices legislation can be dispelled. In the United States the Supreme Court held[9] that there was no "reason or authority for the proposition that agreements between legally separate persons and companies to suppress competition amongst themselves and others can be justified by labelling the project a joint venture."[10]

The joint venture is of particular importance in East-West trade[11] and in the trade with the developing countries. In some Eastern European countries, notably Yugoslavia, Romania, Hungary and Poland, joint venture legislation admits profit-sharing for a number of years and thereafter the State-owned enterprise assume the sole control of the joint business and receives all the profits; "fade-out" provisions, whereby the property in the plant and machinery passes to the State-owned party in these Eastern European countries at the end of the joint venture period are hardly necessary because under the laws of those countries nearly all means of production and distribution are in the hands of the State or local citizens.[12]

The European Co-operation Grouping

The European Community intends to permit the creation of a new legal form, the European Co-operation Grouping (ECG). An amended Draft Regulation proposing this measure was presented by the Commission to the Council in April 1978.[13] The ECG is a projection to the European level of the *Groupement d'Intérêt Économique* which was introduced in France in 1967 and has met with a fair measure of success.[14]

The ECG will be a legal entity but it will not be a company limited by

---

[7] KG stands for *Kommandit-Gesellschaft* which is a limited partnership.

[8] See p. 218, *post*.

[9] In *Timken Roller Bearing Co.* v. *United States*, 341 U.S. 593, 598 (1951).

[10] In the U.S.A. the Webb-Pomerene Act of 1918 exempts from the prohibitions of the Sherman Act and of the Clayton Act, s. 7, associations entered for the sole purpose of engaging in export trade and not affecting prices within the U.S.; see George A. Zaphiriou, *op. cit.* in n. 6, 257.

[11] Michael W. Gordon, *op. cit.* in n. 6.

[12] *Ibid.* 303.

[13] 21 O.J. (1978) No. C103/4. The Regulation, if accepted by the Council, will be founded on Art. 253 of the EEC Treaty; see [1974] J.B.L. 83.

[14] See p. 207, *ante*; and Burchard Bott and Wolfgang Rosener, "The Groupement d'Intérêt Économique" in [1970] J.B.L. 313.

shares. It will be formed by contract and becomes a legal person when registered in the Member State in which its head office is situate. It can be formed by companies, firms and individuals residing in different Members States of the Community. An ECG may not have more than 500 employees.

The ECG need not have an initial capital, like a company, and cannot obtain capital from the investing public by issue of debentures or other means. The contract by which the ECG is formed may, however, require the members to make contributions in cash, kind or services. The members cannot limit their liability to third parties and are liable to them without limitation. The primary aim of the ECG is not to make profits but if profits are made they are distributed to the members and taxed in their hands. The activities of the ECG shall be limited to:

(*a*) the provision of services exclusively for its members;
(*b*) the production, processing or packaging of goods exclusively for the purposes of its members.

The ECG will be managed by one or more individuals who will be appointed by contract or by the general meeting.

The form of the ECG may, for instance, be used for the following activities:

Joint buying office. The ECG would collect the various orders of its members for the same product or similar products and on the strength of the combined orders seek to secure a better price from the suppliers;

Joint sales office. Manufacturers of the same product or similar products would combine to study their market and, if necessary, adopt a joint trade mark which the ECG would undertake to market by means of an advertising campaign and by seeking buyers on behalf of the members. It would collect orders and allocate them among the members in accordance with arrangements laid down by themselves;

Administration of specialised services. Members wishing to make economies in certain operations essential to each of them would entrust the ECG with administering these functions on their behalf. In this way the ECG could take over the management of the pay section for the employees of its members or supervise the installation of a mechanised accounting system;

Representation of the members in individual transactions. Members interested in a contract whose scope exceeded the capacity of any of them to handle, would establish an ECG to compete for the contract on their behalf and, if the contract has been awarded to them, allocate tasks and co-ordinate and supervise their execution.[15]

Co-ordination of certain technical activities of the members. The members would decide to entrust the ECG with the co-ordination of their research activities relating to a new product, the prototype of a machine, etc.

---

[15] An ECG formed for these purposes pursues aims similar to those of a consortium but the legal form is different, see p. 206, *ante*.

Chapter 19

RESTRICTIVE TRADE PRACTICES IN THE UNITED KINGDOM

Most countries of market economy have enacted legislation directed against trade practices restricting the free play of competition. The exporter who wishes to place his exports on a permanent basis has to ask himself whether the form of organisation which he wishes to adopt is in harmony with the anti-monopoly legislation of the United Kingdom and the country into which his exports are directed; if the latter country is a Member State of the European Community or the proposed arrangement affects competition in the Common Market, he has also to take care that the proposed arrangement does not infringe the competition law of the Community. Even ordinary export agreements, such as contracts granting exclusive selling, distributive or agency rights have, by virtue of the exclusive rights which they confer on the representative or agent, an element of trade restriction. Other instances of agreements containing such element are agreements or understandings by which exporters or manufacturers fix the prices or conditions on which they will sell their goods abroad or divide overseas markets into mutually exclusive spheres of interest. Sometimes overseas tenders of capital goods are made the subject of joint consultation of manufacturers or merchants in this country, and even the various forms of joint export selling may fall within the purview of the anti-monopolies legislation.

It is proposed in this chapter to deal with the restrictive trade practices legislation of the United Kingdom and in the next chapter to consider the competition law of the European Community, as far as is relevant here.

Restrictive trade practices legislation

The legislation relating to restrictive trade practices in the United Kingdom is mainly contained in the Restrictive Trade Practices Acts 1976 and 1977 and the Restrictive Practices Court Act 1976; the Resale Prices Act 1976 likewise requires attention in this connection. Monopolies are mainly regulated by the Fair Trading Act 1973.

As far as exports are concerned, the legislation just mentioned attempts to protect the legitimate interests of the trade but in some instances the exporter who wishes to escape from the otherwise stringent regulation has to comply with certain statutory requirements. Four aspects of this legislation affect the exporter directly and call for consideration here, *viz.* the duty to notify restrictive trade agreements, monopoly situations in relation to exports, collective price maintenance agreements intended to operate abroad, and in proceedings before the Restrictive Practices Court the justification of a restrictive agreement intended to operate in the home market on the ground that its removal would cause a substantial reduction of exports.

Duty to notify restrictive agreements

The Act of 1976, as amended, provides[1] that any agreement made between two or more persons carrying on business within the United Kingdom in the production or supply of goods or in the application to goods of any process of manufacture must be notified by any of them to the Director General of Fair Trading if restrictions are accepted by two or more parties in respect of the following matters:

(*a*) the prices to be charged, quoted or paid for goods supplied, offered or acquired, or for the application of any process of manufacture to goods;
(*b*) the prices to be recommended or suggested as the prices to be charged or quoted in respect of the resale of goods supplied;
(*c*) the terms or conditions on or subject to which goods are to be supplied or acquired or any such process is to be applied to goods;
(*d*) the quantities or descriptions of goods to be produced, supplied or acquired;
(*e*) the processes of manufacture to be applied to any goods, or the quantities or descriptions of goods to which any such process is to be applied; or
(*f*) the persons or classes of persons to, for or from whom, or the areas or places in or from which, goods are to be supplied or acquired, or any such process applied.[2]

The Act of 1976 extends to information agreements if they relate to the prices charged or quoted for selling or processing goods, or to the terms or conditions on which goods are supplied,[3] but agreements to inform each other or a third party only about the charges made for goods exported from the United Kingdom are exempted and need not be registered.[4] Further, the provisions of the 1976 Act have been extended to agreements relating to services,[5] and to information agreements relating to services.[6]

The Restrictive Practices Court, which was established by the Restrictive Trade Practices Act 1956 and now operates under the Restrictive Practices Court Act 1976, has jurisdiction to declare any registered agreement as contrary to the public interest, with the effect that the agreement is void (s. 1(3) and s. 2(1)).[7] In proceedings before the court it is presumed that a registered agreement is contrary to the public interest but the presumption is rebutted if certain specified sets of circumstances, the so-called gateways, are present (ss. 10(1), 19(1)).

As regards export agreements, three cases have to be distinguished: in some cases, agreements are not registrable at all and thus *completely*

[1] In s. 6(1).
[2] It should be noted that the Act does not apply to restrictions relating to employees and the conditions of employment (s. 9(6)); Restrictive Trade Practices (Information Agreements) Order 1969 (S.I. 1969/1842).
[3] s. 7.
[4] Restrictive Trade Practices Act 1976, Sched. 3, para. 6.
[5] s. 11; see Restrictive Trade Practices (Services) Order 1976 (S.I. 1976 No. 98). See Restrictive Trade Practices Act 1977, s. 1(3).
[6] *Ibid.* s. 12.
[7] All references in this chapter are to the Restrictive Trade Practices Act 1976 unless stated otherwise.

excepted from the operation of the Act; in other cases, *viz.* where a restrictive agreement is not exempt but contains *exclusively restrictions applying to the export trade*, particulars of it have to be furnished to the Director General of Fair Trading but it does not have to be registered by him, and in a third category of cases in which the agreement contains *mixed restrictions*, *i.e.* restrictions applying to the home as well as to the export trade, it has to be registered by the Director.

Excepted agreements

Agreements providing only exclusive selling, distributing or agency rights, whether in the export or home market or both, are completely excepted from the operation of the Restrictive Trade Practices Acts, provided that no trade association[8] is a party to the agreement and the agreement is made by not more than *two* persons or companies, interconnected companies[9] being counted as one (Sched. 3, para. 2). Thus the most frequently met forms of export agreements, *viz.* exclusive selling or agency arrangements between United Kingdom manufacturers or merchants and their overseas representatives, are completely unaffected by, and outside, the United Kingdom restrictive trading legislation. This exception is not available if the restriction applies to topics other than the supply of goods of the *same* description; in that case the export agreement might fall into the category of exclusive or mixed export agreements which are treated later. To give an example: a British manufacturer of rainwear appoints X his exclusive agent for raincoats in Canada; the contract provides that X shall not sell or distribute raincoats other than those manufactured by his principal; this would be an excepted agreement. If, however, the agreement provides that X shall not sell or distribute any textile goods of whatever material except his principal's raincoats, that agreement would not be covered by the exception of Schedule 3, paragraphs 3–5.

Further, contracts relating only to the grant of licences of patents[10] or registered designs, the exchange of information on manufacturing processes ("know-how"), or the use of trade marks[11] are excepted from the operation of the Restrictive Trade Practices Acts (Sched. 3, paragraphs 3–5).

Exclusive export agreements

Agreements (other than excepted agreements) which would be registrable if relating to the home trade are exempt from registration by the Director General of Fair Trading if their restrictions relate *exclusively*—

(*a*) to the supply of goods by export from the United Kingdom;
(*b*) to the production of goods, or the application of any process of manufacture to goods, outside the United Kingdom;

---

[8] As defined in s. 43(1).
[9] Defined in Sched. 3(6).
[10] Patent or design pooling agreements are, however, in principle, not excluded (Sched. 3, para. 5(4),(5)).
[11] Including certification trade marks, Sched. 3, para. 4.

(*c*) to the acquisition of goods to be delivered outside the United Kingdom and not imported into the United Kingdom for entry for home use; or

(*d*) to the supply of goods to be delivered outside the United Kingdom otherwise than by export from the United Kingdom,

but particulars of agreements mentioned under (*a*) have to be furnished to the Director.[12]

Considerable advantages are derived from this concession. An agreement, particulars of which have merely to be filed with the Director, is not open to public inspection but agreements which have formally to be notified and are registered by the Director can be freely inspected by members of the public, including competitors or representatives of overseas government departments. Further an export agreement, particulars of which have merely to be furnished to the Director, cannot be challenged by him before the Restrictive Practices Court as being void on the ground that it is contrary to the public interest. On the other hand, the furnishing of particulars of an export agreement to the Director does not preclude a reference to the Monopolies and Mergers Commission, and the same is true of export agreements with respect to which no particulars have to be furnished.

It obviously is advantageous for manufacturers or distributors who wish to provide for restrictions applying to the supply of goods for the home and the export market to do so in two separate agreements, one applying to the home market and the other to the export market. The former would have to be registered, and as regards the latter, particulars have to be furnished.

Mixed agreements

If an agreement containing restrictions which would make it registrable by virtue of section 6(1)[13] is intended to apply both to the home and the export market, it has to be notified to the Director General of Fair Trading; the mere furnishing of particulars would be insufficient.

Monopoly situations in relation to exports

The Director General of Fair Trading, as well as a minister, may make a reference to the Monopolies and Mergers Commission where it appears to him that a *monopoly situation* exists or may exist.[14] The Fair Trading Act 1973 sets out several types of monopoly situations, and one of them relates to exports. It arises if one-quarter or more of goods of a particular description and destined for export are produced in the United Kingdom by the same producer or his group, or is subject to agreements distorting

[12] s. 25. See also the Registration Trading Agreements (EEC Documents) Regulations 1973 (S.I. 1973 No. 950) which requires parties to inform the United Kingdom Director General when notifying an agreement to the EEC Commission, or when seeking negative clearance, or when proceedings are begun.

[13] See p. 211, *ante*.

[14] Fair Trading Act 1973, ss. 50 and 51.

competition. This monopoly situation is set forth in section 8 of the 1973 Act which runs as follows:

(1) For the purposes of this Act a monopoly situation shall be taken to exist in relation to exports of goods of any description from the United Kingdom in the following cases, that is to say, if—

(*a*) at least one-quarter of all the goods of that description which are produced in the United Kingdom are produced by one and the same person, or

(*b*) at least one-quarter of all the goods of that description which are produced in the United Kingdom are produced by members of one and the same group of interconnected bodies corporate;

and in those cases a monopoly situation shall for the purposes of this Act be taken to exist both in relation to exports of goods of that description from the United Kingdom generally and in relation to exports of goods of that description from the United Kingdom to each market taken separately.

(2) In relation to exports of goods of any description from the United Kingdom generally, a monopoly situation shall for the purposes of this Act be taken to exist if—

(*a*) one or more agreements are in operation which in any way prevent or restrict, or prevent, restrict or distort competition in relation to, the export of goods of that description from the United Kingdom, and

(*b*) that agreement is or (as the case may be) those agreements collectively are operative with respect to at least one-quarter of all the goods of that description which are produced in the United Kingdom.

(3) In relation to exports of goods of any description from the United Kingdom to any particular market, a monopoly situation shall for the purposes of this Act be taken to exist if—

(*a*) one or more agreements are in operation which in any way prevent or restrict, or prevent, restrict or distort competition in relation to, the supply of goods of that description (whether from the United Kingdom or not) to that market, and

(*b*) that agreement is or (as the case may be) those agreements collectively are operative with respect to at least one-quarter of all the goods of that description which are produced in the United Kingdom.

Where the conditions of section 8(2) or (3) are satisfied, that is where two or more persons and their groups are involved, a *complex monopoly situation*[15] exists, which likewise may give rise to a reference to the Monopolies and Mergers Commission, "although as previously no account can be taken of a provision that renders an agreement registrable under the Restrictive Trade Practices Acts."[16] A reference may further be made where a monopoly situation is limited to a part of the United Kingdom.[17]

The reference results in a report of the Monopolies and Mergers Commission, which is made to the minister.[18] The minister may make such orders on the report as appear to be appropriate to him for the purpose of remedying or preventing the adverse effect of the monopoly.[19]

Collective price maintenance agreements

Individual resale price maintenance is, on principle, unlawful in the United Kingdom; any term or condition of a contract between a supplier and a dealer obliging the latter to charge minimum prices for the goods

---

[15] *Ibid.* s. 11.

[16] Valentine Korah, "The Fair Trading Act 1973 and the Functions of the Director General" in [1973] J.B.L. 305, 306.

[17] Fair Trading Act 1973, s. 9.

[18] *Ibid.* s. 54.

[19] *Ibid.* s. 56.

on resale is illegal and avoided by the Resale Prices Act 1976, s. 9, unless the Restrictive Practices Court has ordered that the goods shall be exempt from this prohibition (s. 14). Contravention of the provisions of the Act is not a criminal offence but a person affected by it can claim damages for breach of statutory duty (s. 25). The Resale Prices Act 1976 applies, however, only to goods supplied for resale in the United Kingdom; it does not restrict the liberty of export suppliers to establish minimum prices for the resale of goods outside the United Kingdom.

The Resale Prices Act 1976 further makes, on principle, unlawful collective price maintenance agreements, including agreements whereby the enforcement of minimum prices is entrusted to a trade association (s. 1). This general prohibition of collective price maintenance agreements does not apply to agreements which deal only with the supply of goods abroad, nor does it affect persons carrying on business abroad, but particulars of such agreements would have to be furnished to the Director General of Fair Trading as exclusive export agreements under sections 24 and 25.

If, *e.g.* the sales distributors of British biscuits in an overseas market agree on certain minimum prices for their products, their agreement is not prohibited by English law but may infringe the provisions of the anti-trust laws in the overseas countries in which it is to operate, or, if those countries are members of the European Community, the competition law of the latter. As far as English law is concerned, the distributors may even set up a trade association with powers to supervise the price maintenance agreement abroad, to place offending retailers abroad on a stop list, to fine them or to apply other discriminatory devices against them.

On the other hand, overseas suppliers operating in the United Kingdom and, in particular, their resident sales representatives, have to comply with United Kingdom legislation; resale price maintenance conditions infringing the Resale Prices Act 1976 would be void.

Reduction of exports as defence in proceedings before the Restrictive Practices Court

It has already been observed that every registrable agreement is, on principle, capable of being challenged in the Restrictive Practices Court and that in proceedings before the court it is presumed that the agreement is contrary to the public interest, so that the burden of justifying it falls on the respondent, *i.e.* the party who wishes to uphold it.

A respondent who wishes to justify a restrictive agreement has to satisfy the court—

1. that one of the eight sets of circumstances listed in section 10(1) or 19(1) is present; and
2. that on balance the restriction is not unreasonable.[20]

[20] s. 10(1) refers to goods and s. 19(1) to services; the two sections have a similar wording, *mutatis mutandis*.

One of the eight sets of circumstances listed in that provision is the likelihood that the removal of the restriction would cause a substantial reduction in the value or earnings of the export business. Section 10(1)(*f*) expresses this requirement as follows:

that, having regard to the conditions actually obtaining or reasonably foreseen at the time of the application, the removal of the restriction or information provision would be likely to cause a reduction in the volume or earnings of the export business which is substantial either in relation to the whole export business of the United Kingdom or in relation to the whole business (including export business) of the said trade or industry.

The meaning of this complicated provision was considered by the Restrictive Practices Court in *Re Water-Tube Boilermakers' Agreement.*[21] The boilermakers who made or designed water boilers for use by power stations or factories had formed a trade association; their agreement provided that if a member received an inquiry a consultation had to be held between the members, the transaction would be allocated to one, or sometimes two, of them, and the price at which the order was to be carried out would be fixed. About 40 per cent. of the members' activities consisted of exports, and some members maintained offices and staffs abroad. The operations of the members had been highly successful in the past in securing orders against foreign competition. The association's attempt to justify its agreement under what is now section 10(1)(*f*) was successful. The court held that if the restriction on competition which the agreement imposed was removed a substantial reduction of export business of the trade was likely to result and that, on balance, the preservation of the capacity of this industry, engaged as it was in the manufacture of heavy capital goods, was in the national interest.

Further, section 10(1)(*f*) might protect an exporting association or a company which wishes to preserve for itself a share in the international market against stronger competitors, as, *e.g.* in the trade in tyres.[22]

Relationship between United Kingdom regulation and the competition law of the European Community and the Free Trade Agreements

Many agreements registrable by virtue of the Restrictive Trade Practices Acts 1976 and 1977 are unlikely to infringe the competition law of the European Community.[23] In some circumstances, however, an agreement may be registrable under United Kingdom law and, at the same time, contravene the competition provisions of Community law. Here the *doctrine of the double barrier* applies.[24] According to that doctrine the agreement must satisfy both the requirements of national and Community law. The European Court held in *Wilhelm* v. *Bundeskartellamt*[25] that the same agreement might be subject to two sets of proceedings, namely before the

---

[21] [1959] 1 W.L.R. 1118; L.R. 1 R.P. 285; [1959] J.B.L. 380.

[22] See *Pneumatic Tyres Report* (1955), p. 84, para. 1465.

[23] On the competition law of the European Community, see p. 218, *post*.

[24] Adrienne M. Page, "The Double Barrier" [1973] J.B.L. 332.

[25] [1969] C.M.L.R. 100; *Boehringer Mannheim GmbH* v. *Commission* [1973] C.M.L.R. 864.

Community authorities under Article 85 of the EEC Treaty and also before the national authorities in application of national law but if a conflict occurred between the two regulations, the Community regulation must take precedence. The Restrictive Trade Practices Act 1976, s. 5(1), provides that it shall apply to an agreement notwithstanding that it is or may be void by reason of any directly applicable Community provision, or is expressly authorised by such a provision, but the Restrictive Practices Court may decline or postpone the exercise of its jurisdiction if it appears to the court right, having regard to a Community provision, and the Director General of Fair Trading may refrain from taking proceedings in court. This provision is designed to avoid a conflict between the United Kingdom and Community law. United Kingdom parties are required[26] to inform the Director General of Fair Trading when notifying an agreement to the Commission or seeking negative clearance therefor and when proceedings are instituted and decisions given in respect of an agreement.

Before joining the European Community, the United Kingdom was a party to two free trade agreements, the EFTA Convention[27] and the Anglo-Irish Agreement.[28] Both agreements contained provisions relating to restrictive business practices. When the United Kingdom joined the European Community, the EFTA Convention ceased to have effect. As regards the countries which, with the United Kingdom, joined the Community (Denmark and the Irish Republic), the Community regulation applies. As regards the countries which did not join the Community (Austria, Finland, Iceland, Norway, Portugal, Sweden and Switzerland), the enlarged European Community entered into free trade agreements (FTAs) with them which include virtually all the goods that were eligible for duty-free treatment under EFTA. The FTAs, which are bilateral agreements between the Community and the country in question, contain also provisions relating to restrictive trade practices.[29] Section 12(1) of the Restrictive Trade Practices Act 1968 has not been repealed[30] but has not been extended to the FTAs; it is thought that the section has spent its effect.

---

[26] By the Registration of Restrictive Trading Agreements (EEC Documents) Regulations 1973 (S.I. 1973 No. 950).

[27] Convention of 1959 establishing the European Free Trade Association.

[28] Agreement of 1965 between the Governments of the U.K. and the Republic of Ireland establishing a Free Trade Area between the two countries.

[29] See p. 227, *post*.

[30] See Restrictive Trade Practices Act 1976, Sched. 6.

Chapter 20

THE COMPETITION LAW OF THE EUROPEAN COMMUNITY

It is the aim of the EEC Treaty to constitute a single—Common—Market from the territories of the Member States. With this aim in view, the Treaty contains rules regulating the competition in the Common Market. The British exporter cannot ignore them if he wishes to direct exports to the other member countries of the Community. The purpose of those rules is to prevent restrictive trade practices or monopolies which are likely to interfere with the trade between the Member States or to lead to a distortion of competition in the Common Market. They are directed against the division of the Common Market into separate national markets and a perpetuation of the national trade barriers within the Community.

The Basic Provisions

The basic provisions on competition are contained in Articles 85 and 86 of the EEC Treaty.[1] The former prohibits as incompatible with the Common Market certain restrictive trade practices which may affect trade between the Member States and have as their object or effect the prevention, restriction or distortion of competition in the Common Market. Agreements that fall within the prohibition and do not merit exemption are void and cannot be enforced in the courts of the Member States.[2] Article 86 contains a prohibition of the abuse of a dominant position within the Common Market, as far as it may affect trade between Member States. The following is the wording of these two articles:

Article 85

1. The following shall be prohibited as incompatible with the common market: all agreements between undertakings, decisions by associations of undertakings and concerted practices which may affect trade between Member States and which have as their object or effect the prevention, restriction or distortion of competition within the common market, and in particular those which:

(*a*) directly or indirectly fix purchase or selling prices or any other trading conditions;
(*b*) limit or control production, markets, technical development, or investment;
(*c*) share markets or sources of supply;
(*d*) apply dissimilar conditions to equivalent transactions with other trading parties, thereby placing them at a competitive disadvantage;
(*e*) make the conclusion of contracts subject to acceptance by the other parties of supplementary obligations which, by their nature or according to commercial usage, have no connection with the subject of such contracts.

2. Any agreements or decisions prohibited pursuant to this Article shall be automatically void.

---

[1] The whole chapter of the EEC Treaty on the Rules on Competition comprises Articles 85 to 90. For further reading: C. W. Bellamy and Graham D. Child, *Common Market Law of Competition* (2nd ed., 1978); Valentine Korah, *An Introductory Guide to EEC Competition Law and Practice* (1978).

[2] *Brasserie de Haecht* v. *Wilkin* (*No. 2*) [1973] C.M.L.R. 287.

3. The provisions of paragraph 1 may, however, be declared inapplicable in the case of:
—any agreement or category of agreements between undertakings;
—any decision or category of decisions by associations of undertakings;
—any concerted practice or category of concerted practices;
which contributes to improving the production or distribution of goods or to promoting technical or economic progress, while allowing consumers a fair share of the resulting benefit, and which does not:

(*a*) impose on the undertakings concerned restrictions which are not indispensable to the attainment of these objectives;
(*b*) afford such undertakings the possibility of eliminating competition in respect of a substantial part of the products in question.

ARTICLE 86

Any abuse by one or more undertakings of a dominant position within the common market or in a substantial part of it shall be prohibited as incompatible with the common market in so far as it may affect trade between Member States. Such abuse may, in particular, consist in:

(*a*) directly or indirectly imposing unfair purchase or selling prices or other unfair trading conditions;
(*b*) limiting production, markets or technical development to the prejudice of consumers;
(*c*) applying dissimilar conditions to equivalent transactions with other trading parties, thereby placing them at a competitive disadvantage;
(*d*) making the conclusion of contracts subject to acceptance by the other parties of supplementary obligations which, by their nature or according to commercial usage, have no connection with the subject of such contracts.

These articles are amplified by secondary legislation[3] and other measures of the Community. They are interpreted by numerous decisions of the Commission and the European Court of Justice. In the result a pattern of European competition law has emerged which, while admitting broad exceptions, is strict and effective and may expose an offender to heavy fines.[4]

The ambit of the Community regulation on competition is wide. It may affect horizontal as well as vertical arrangements,[5] market-sharing agreements, price-fixing agreements, agreements with exclusive dealers, forms of co-operation, joint ventures, and patent,[6] trade mark,[7] or copyright[8] licensing agreements.[9] The Community regulation applies to the supply of services as well as goods. Even inventors exploiting their inventions under a patent licence are "undertakings" within the competition rules.[10] Agreements with indirect effect on competition are also caught, such as agreements to exchange detailed information about price, customers, turnover, capacity available, etc.[11]

---

[3] Mainly founded on Art. 87(1) of the EEC Treaty.

[4] Arts. 15 and 16 of Reg. 17/62; see *I.C.I. and Others* v. *Commission* [1972] C.M.L.R. 557; *Commercial Solvents* v. *Commission* [1974] 1 C.M.L.R. 309.

[5] *De Geus* v. *Bosch* [1962] C.M.L.R. 1; *Consten and Grundig* v. *Commission* [1966] C.M.L.R. 418; *Italy* v. *Council and Commission* [1969] C.M.L.R. 39.

[6] *Re Davidson Rubber Co.* [1972] C.M.L.R. D52.

[7] *Sirena S.R.L.* v. *Eda S.R.L.* [1971] C.M.L.R. 260; *Van Zuylen Frères* v. *Hag A.G.* [1974] 2 C.M.L.R. 127.

[8] See *Deutsche Grammophon GmbH* v. *Metro-SB-Grossmärkte GmbH & Co. K.G.* [1971] C.M.L.R. 631.

[9] Alan Dashwood, "Exclusive Licences in the Common Market" [1973] J.B.L. 205.

[10] *A.O.I.P.* v. *Beyrard* [1976] 1 C.M.L.R. D14.

[11] *Re Cobelyn* [1977] 2 C.M.L.R. D28.

On principle the prohibitions of Articles 85 and 86 apply only to arrangements which may affect trade between the Member States. This requirement appears to exclude from the application of Community law arrangements confined in their effect to the trade in one Member State or being operative only outside the Community.[12] However, in *Vereeniging van Cementhandelaren* v. *Commission*[13] the European Court held that a cartel which was limited to the territory of one Member State, hindered the economic interpenetration to which the Treaty was directed and ensured protection for the national production. Consequently, an arrangement operative only within one Member State is subject to Community law if it obstructs the importation of the goods in question into that country from the other Member States or otherwise affects imports and exports between the Member States. Further, as we shall see,[14] in certain circumstances the competition law of the Community claims to have extra-territorial effect.

Procedure

The procedure for the application of Articles 85 and 86 is set out in Council Regulation 17 of 1962, as amended.[15] Agreements, decisions and concerted practices of the kind described in Article 85(1) must be *notified* to the Commission[16] and failure to notify intentionally or negligently may expose the offender to heavy fines.[17] There are the following exceptions from the duty to notify but in the excepted cases the arrangement may be notified in the discretion of the parties[18]:

1. The only parties thereto are undertakings from one Member State and the agreements, decisions or practices do not relate either to imports or to exports between Member States;
2. not more than two undertakings are party thereto, and the agreements only:
(*a*) restrict the freedom of one party to the contract in determining the prices for or conditions of business on which the goods which he has obtained from the other party to the contract may be resold; or
(*b*) impose restrictions on the exercise of the rights of the assignee (or user) of industrial property rights—in particular patents, utility models, designs or trade marks—or of the person entitled under the contract to the assignment, or grant, of the right to use a method of manufacture or knowledge relating to the use and to the application of industrial processes;
3. they have as their sole object:
(*a*) the development or uniform application of standards or types; or
(*b*) joint research for improvement of techniques, provided the results are accessible to all parties thereto and may be used by each of them.

The duty to notify falls on each party to the arrangement, and for the purposes of Articles 85 and 86, an undertaking which is resident in a non-Member State but has in a Member State a subsidiary which must act

---

[12] *Rieckermann/AEG-Elotherm* [1968] C.M.L.R. D78.
[13] [1973] C.M.L.R. 7.
[14] See p. 221, *post*.
[15] Reg. 17/62 was supplemented by numerous amendments, of which the most important are: Regs. 27/62, 99/63, 118/63, 1133/68, 2822/71; see also the draft amendment published in the *Official Journal* of February 7, 1978 (No. (34/4)).
[16] Reg. 17/62, Arts. 4 and 5.
[17] *Ibid.* Art. 15(2).
[18] *Ibid.* Art. 4(2).

according to its instructions, is regarded as being resident in the Common Market because it forms an economic units with the subsidiary.[19] Conversely, a wholly owned subsidiary is regarded as being part of the same economic unit as its parent company and agreements between those two companies do not fall within the ambit of Article 85(1).[20] Furthermore, an undertaking established in a non-Member State which is a party to an agreement that may have *effect* in the Common Market is subject to the jurisdiction of the Community authorities.[21] In these respects the Community authorities claim extra-territorial jurisdiction.

If a party thinks that the arrangement to which he is a party is outside the prohibition of Article 85(1) and wishes to obtain official confirmation of that view, he can apply to the Commission for *negative clearance* which, however, is only granted "on the basis of the facts in its possession."[22] If the agreement falls within Article 85(1) but the conditions of Article 85(3) are satisfied, the Commission, on the application of a party, can grant a *declaration of inapplicability* of Article 85(1). These applications can only be made when the arrangement is duly notified.

The notification of an arrangement and applications for negative clearance or inapplicability of Article 85(1) are made on combined form A/B.[23]

The Commission also has wide powers to obtain information. It may request an undertaking to give it information necessary to the performance of its functions in enforcing the competition rules, and may send an inspector to the premises of an undertaking to examine documents, ask oral questions, and so on.[24]

Measures providing exemption en bloc

Between 1962 and 1971 the Commission received some 37,000 notifications[25] and about 1,800 further notifications were submitted after the accession of the United Kingdom, the Irish Republic and Denmark. In order to eliminate the obviously innocuous arrangements, the Community made use of its powers under Article 85(3) to declare inapplicable the prohibition of Article 85(1) to certain categories of arrangements, in brief, to grant them *block exemptions*. It also published notices declaring its policy to exempt *en bloc* certain arrangements. The most important of these block exemptions and notices relate to exclusive agency contracts, exclusive dealing agreements, co-operation arrangements, and agreements

---

[19] *I.C.I. and Others* v. *Commission* [1972] C.M.L.R. 557; *Commercial Solvents Corpn.* v. *Commission* [1974] 1 C.M.L.R. 309 (the *Zoja* case); *Liptons Cash Register & Business Equipment Ltd.* v. *Hugin Kass-Register AB* [1978] 1 C.M.L.R. D19, D33; [1979] 2 C.M.L.R.

[20] *Re Christiani and Nielsen* [1970] C.M.L.R. D19.

[21] *Béguelin Import* v. *SAGL Import-Export S.A.* [1972] C.M.L.R. 81; *Re Pittsburgh Corning Europe-Formica-Belgium-Hertel* [1973] C.M.L.R. D2.

[22] Reg. 17/62, Art. 2.

[23] The most recent version of the form is founded on Reg. 1133/68.

[24] Reg. 17/62, Arts. 11 and 14.

[25] B. A. Wortley, "Competition," in *The Law of the Common Market*, Manchester, 1974, 88.

of minor importance. The last-mentioned notice will be treated here. The other three measures require separate consideration later.

Agreements of minor importance

The Commission had already stated in 1964[26] that an agreement did not infringe the prohibition of Article 85 if it did not distort the Common Market to an "appreciable" extent. By a *Notice of December* 29, 1977, *concerning Minor Agreements*[27] the Commission seeks to attach a concrete meaning to the term "appreciable." In the Notice it reasserts[28] its desire "to facilitate co-operation between small and medium-sized enterprises." The Notice then provides that an agreement is not regarded as infringing Article 85(1) if it satisfies two cumulative tests, namely a market test and a turnover test. These tests are satisfied if—

—the products which are the subject of the agreement and other products of the participating undertakings considered by consumers to be similar by reason of their characteristics, price or use do not represent in a substantial part of the Common Market more than 5 per cent. of the total market for such products, and
—the aggregate annual turnover of the participating undertakings does not exceed 50 million units of account.

An excess by less than 10 per cent. of each of these tests in the course of two consecutive years is admitted as being innocuous.

An agreement which satisfies these two tests need not be notified. A great number of agreements between small and medium-sized enterprises is thus completely exempted from the operation of the competition law of the European Community.

Exclusive Agency Contracts

By an *Announcement of December* 24, 1962, the Commission has granted block exemption to *Exclusive Agency Contracts made with Commercial Agents.*[29] This exemption covers only dependent agents who accept no financial risk, do not act as independent dealers for other suppliers, and who are prepared to take detailed instructions from their principals.[30] Such an agent may be treated as an auxiliary organ, forming an integral part of the principal's business.[31] The definition of an agent by the Commission

[26] In *Grossfillex-Fillistorf* [1964] C.M.L.R. 237. In *Völk* v. *Etablissements Vervaecke S.P.R.L.* [1969] C.M.L.R. 273 the European Court held that an agreement may escape the prohibition of Article 85(1) if the position of the parties was too weak to influence trade between the Member States.

[27] O.J. C 313/3. This Notice supersedes the Notice of May 27, 1970. A Notice of the Commission is a declaration of policy on the part of the Commission; it does not prevent the European Court from interpreting Article 85 differently.

[28] It had done so before in the notice of July 29, 1968, concerning co-operation agreements, J.O. C 75 of July 29, 1968.

[29] The Announcement, together with a further Announcement on Patent Licence Agreements, is published in J.O. of December 24, 1962.

[30] *Pittsburgh Corning* (*Europe*) [1973] C.M.L.R. D2 and D7–8; *Suiker Unie* [1975] E.C.R. 1663.

[31] See Bellamy and Child, *Common Market Law of Competition* (2nd ed.), 207–211.

is closer to that used in the common law than to that in the European continental countries. The Commission understands by an agent a person who has acted on behalf of a principal and regards it as irrelevant whether he has acted in the name of the principal or in his own name, provided that he does not accept the financial risk for the transaction.[32] The Announcement states:

> The Commission regards as the decisive criterion, which distinguishes the commercial agent from the independent trader, the agreement—express or implied—which deals with responsibility for the financial risks bound up with the sale or with the performance of the contract. Thus the Commission's assessment is not governed by the way the "representative" is described. Except for the usual *del credere* guarantee, a commercial agent must not, by the nature of his functions, assume any risk resulting from the transaction. If he does assume such risks his function becomes economically akin to that of an independent trader and he must therefore be treated as such for the purposes of the rules of competition.

An intermediary is regarded as an independent dealer, and not an agent within the meaning of the Announcement, if he—

—is required to keep or does in fact keep, as his own property, a considerable stock of the products covered by the contract, or

—is required to organise, maintain or ensure at his own expense a substantial service to customers free of charge, or does in fact organise, maintain or ensure such a service, or

—can determine or does in fact determine prices or terms of business.

Exclusive Dealing Agreements

The block exemption

A further block exemption, Regulation 67/67 of the Commission,[33] exempts certain *exclusive dealing agreements* from the prohibition of Article 85(1). This regulation is limited in time; the exemption is granted only until December 31, 1982[34] and the Commission has published the draft of an amending Regulation which will limit the scope of its application.[35]

A fundamental condition for the application of this exemption is that not more than two parties are concerned in the arrangement in question. The Regulation exempts the following agreements from the prohibition of Article 85(1)[36]:

(*a*) one party agrees with the other to supply only to that other certain goods for resale within a defined area of the Common Market; or

(*b*) one party agrees with the other to purchase only from that other certain goods for resale; or

(*c*) the two undertakings have entered into obligations, as in (*a*) and (*b*) above, with each other in respect of exclusive supply and purchase for resale.

---

[32] The only financial risk which he may assume is the *del credere* risk; on *del credere* agents, see p. 170, *ante*.

[33] Dated March 22, 1967 (J.O. No. 57/849 of March 25, 1967), Bellamy and Child, (2nd ed.), 424.

[34] Originally this exemption was granted only until December 31, 1972 (Art. 1 of Reg. 67/67) but it has been extended for 10 years by Reg. 2591/72.

[35] O.J. of February 2, 1978, No. C31/3. The reasons for the changes are described in the recitals.

[36] Reg. 67/67, Art. 1.

Certain additional clauses may be included in the exempt agreement. The most important of them are specified as follows[37]:

(*a*) the obligation not to manufacture or distribute, during the duration of the contract or until one year after its expiration, goods which compete with the goods to which the contract relates;
(*b*) the obligation to refrain, outside the territory covered by the contract, from seeking customers for the goods to which the contract relates, from establishing any branch, or from maintaining any distribution depot;
(*c*) to take measures for the promotion of sales, in particular . . .

On the other hand, an exclusive dealing agreement is not exempt in the following cases[38]:

(*a*) manufacturers of competing goods entrust each other with exclusive dealing in those goods. (According to the draft Regulation, this limitation will also apply if one manufacturer entrusts the other with exclusive dealing in competing or potentially competing goods. This limitation is also to be extended to cases where one of the parties hinders parallel imports or exports);
(*b*) the contracting parties make it difficult for intermediaries or consumers to obtain the goods to which the contract relates from other dealers within the Common Market, in particular where the contracting parties:
(i) exercise industrial property rights to prevent dealers or consumers from obtaining from other parts of the Common Market or from selling in the territory covered by the contract, goods to which the contract relates which are properly marked or otherwise properly placed on the market;
(ii) exercise other rights or take other measures to prevent dealers or consumers from obtaining from elsewhere goods to which the contract relates or from selling them in the territory covered by the contract.

Two new limitations are to be added by the draft Regulation. The exemption will not apply where:

(*c*) the population of the territory covered by the contract exceeds 100 million, unless intermediaries or consumers are able to obtain the goods to which the contract relates, not only from the exclusive dealer but also from at least two more undertakings established in different Member States at the same stage of distribution as that of the exclusive dealer;
(*d*) the goods represent, in a substantial part of the Common Market, more than 15 per cent. of such or similar goods.

Agreements prohibiting parallel exports or imports

Prohibited by Article 85(1) is, on principle, a clause whereby a supplier imposes an obligation on an exclusive dealer not to sell the goods to which the agreement relates outside the assigned territory to another part of the Common Market or not to import into his territory the goods in question from another source in the Common Market. Thus, in *Consten and Grundig* v. *Commission*[39] the German company Grundig appointed the French company Consten its sole dealer for France, the Saar and Corsica with respect to Grundig products. The agreement contained a clause according to which Consten undertook not to sell articles liable to compete with

---

[37] *Ibid.* Art. 2.

[38] *Ibid.* Art. 3.

[39] [1966] C.M.L.R. 418. Further, *Technique Minière* v. *Maschinenbau Ulm GmbH* [1966] C.M.L.R. 357; *Béguelin Import Co.* v. *SAGL Import-Export S.A.* [1972] C.M.L.R. 81. *Procureur du Roi* v. *Dassonville* [1974] 2 C.M.L.R. 436 (*Scotch Whisky* case; British Customs Certificate of Origin as measure equivalent to a quantitative restriction within Art. 30 of the Treaty); *Centrafarm BV* v. *Sterling Drug Inc.* [1974] 2 C.M.L.R. 480.

Grundig products and, not to export the goods to which the contract related directly or indirectly to other countries. Grundig had imposed similar restrictions on the sole concessionaires in other countries, including Germany. Consten was permitted to register and use in France the trade mark GINT which was carried by all goods manufactured by Grundig. Another French company, UNEF, bought Grundig products from German dealers and sold them in France more cheaply than the goods marketed by Consten. Consten commenced proceedings against UNEF in the French courts and the matter was referred to the European Court. The European Court held that the restrictions on exports and imports imposed on Consten and the other sole concessionaires of Grundig infringed Article 85(1). The same decision was given with respect to the exercise and use of the trade mark GINT in France because that industrial property right was, in effect, used to create an artificial national division of the Common Market.

The Commission thus relies on the possibility of parallel imports to reduce national price differences. It hopes that where price differences are great it will pay someone to buy in the low priced market and sell in the higher. Restraints on exports or imports are so inimical to the Common Market that few have been exempted under Article 85(3). In *A. Bulloch & Co.* v. *The Distillers Co. Ltd.*[40] the Distillers' conditions of sale for United Kingdom trade customers prohibited these customers to sell outside the United Kingdom whisky and other liquor produced by the Distillers. The effect of this prohibition was that the Distillers could operate a double pricing policy, enabling them to charge less for the same brand of liquor in the United Kingdom than in the other EEC countries. The Commission held that the Distillers' conditions of sale for United Kingdom trade customers infringed article 85(1) and refused to declare the provision inapplicable under subsection (3) of that article.

In the case of standard conditions agreed upon by a manufacturer with exclusive dealers who have special technical qualifications, the Commission may insist that clauses prohibiting the import and export to another Member State must be removed but will then approve the conditions.[41]

Co-operation Agreements

A further exemption *en bloc* is granted in order to enable enterprises, in particular of small and medium size, to co-operate with a view to enabling them to compete with stronger undertakings. This exemption is contained in a *Notice of the Commission of July* 29, 1968, *concerning Agreements, Decisions and Concerted Practices in the Field of Co-operation between Enterprises.*[42]

---

[40] [1978] 1 C.M.L.R. 400 (the *Distillers' Case*); *Re the Agreement between Kurt Eisele and Inra* [1978] 3 C.M.L.R. 434.

[41] *Re Kodak* [1970] C.M.L.R. D19; *Re Omega* [1970] C.M.L.R. D49.

[42] J.O. C 75 of July 29, 1968; Bellamy and Child, (2nd ed.), 467.

This exemption applies to agreements having as their sole object an exchange of opinion or experience (provided that it has no bearing on the restraint of competition), joint market research, the joint carrying out of comparative studies, the joint preparation of statistics and calculation models, co-operation in accounting matters, joint provision of credit guarantees, joint debt-collecting associations and joint business or tax consultancy agencies.

Agreements Relating to Standardisation, Research and Development, and Specialisation

In 1971 the Council of the EEC gave the Commission authority to grant block exemptions with respect to agreements relating to standardisation, research and development, and specialisation.[43] By Regulation 2779/72[44] the Commission availed itself of this power with respect to a limited range of specialisation agreements but so far has not made use of its powers with respect to other agreements. The operation of Regulation 2779/72 ceased on December 31, 1977, but has been extended until December 31, 1982, subject to a number of amendments.[45]

A specialisation agreement to which Regulation 2779/72 applies is defined as an agreement "whereby, with the object of specialisation, undertakings mutually bind themselves for the duration of the [agreement] not to manufacture certain products or cause them to be manufactured by other undertakings, and to leave it to the other contracting parties to manufacture such products or cause them to be manufactured by other undertakings."[46] The Regulation contains further detailed requirements which must be satisfied if it is claimed that an agreement falls under this block exemption.

To encourage co-operation between small and medium-sized undertakings, the limit on market share has been raised to 15 per cent. in a substantial part of the common market and the limit on aggregate turnover to 300 million units of account.

Abuse of Dominant Position

The European Court has given Article 86 of the EEC Treaty a wide interpretation. The "dominant position" referred to in that article relates to a position of economic strength which enables an enterprise to prevent effective competition being maintained on the relevant market by giving it the power to behave to an appreciable extent independently of its competitors, customers and ultimately the consumers.[47] An abuse of a dominant position may already exist where an undertaking of considerable

---

[43] Reg. 2821/71 concerning the application of Art. 85(3) of the Treaty to Categories of Agreements, Decisions and Concerted Practices (J.O. 1971 L285/46).

[44] Reg. 2779/72 on the application of Art. 85(3) of the Treaty to Categories of Specialisation Agreements (J.O. 1972 L292/23).

[45] Reg. 2903/77/[1977] O.J.L. 338/14 (December 28, 1977; [1978] 1 C.M.L.R. D9).

[46] Art. 1 or Reg. 2779/72.

[47] *United Brands Co.* v. *Commission* [1978] 1 C.M.L.R. 429, 486–487.

strength in the market attempts further to increase its share in a particular market by taking over a rival enterprise.[48]

It is also an abuse of a dominant position if an undertaking which is in control of certain raw material cuts off the supply of that material to a customer who needs it for the production of goods which are in competition with goods produced by the enterprise that has a monopoly with respect to the raw material.[49] In this case a dominant position is abused although the measure objected to applies to different stages of the production. In circumstances like these it is not easy to determine what is a relevant market in which an undertaking has a dominant position.[49] The "relevant market" is determined by two criteria: the particular features of the product in question and the geographical area in which it is marketed. The court held in *United Brands Co.* v. *Commission*[50] that bananas constituted a market which was sufficiently distinct from that of other fresh fruit to form a separate relevant market for the purposes of Article 86.[50] Even a relatively small company may enjoy a dominant position with respect to some of its products; thus in one case[51] a Swedish enterprise supplied only 12 or 13 per cent. of cash registers in the common market countries and was found not to have a dominant position with respect to cash registers, but the parts of the cash registers marketed by that company were not interchangeable with those of other registers, so that the users of its cash registers were utterly dependent on the Swedish company with respect to the supply of spare parts; the Commission ruled that the Swedish company had a dominant position with respect to the spare parts of its cash registers, but the EEC Court quashed this decision on the ground that trade between Member States was not affected.[51a]

THE COMPETITION LAW OF THE FREE TRADE AGREEMENTS

The EEC has entered into bilateral Free Trade Agreements (FTAs)[52] with the member states of EFTA[53] which did not join the Community, namely with Austria,[54] Finland,[55] Iceland,[56] Norway,[57] Portugal,[58] Sweden,[59] and Switzerland.[60] All the FTAs contain provisions relating to competition. Typical is Article 23 of the FTA with Sweden:

---

[48] *Europemballage Corpn. and Continental Can Co. Inc.* v. *Commission* [1972] C.M.L.R. 690.

[49] *Commercial Solvents Corpn.* v. *Commission* [1974] 1 C.M.L.R. 309; see the excellent note on this case, which is also known as the *Zoja* case, by Dr. Valentine Korah in [1974] J.B.L. 253.

[50] [1978] 1 C.M.L.R. 429, 483–484.

[51] *Liptons Cash Registers & Business Equipment Ltd.* v. *Hugin Kassa-Register AB* [1978] 1 C.M.L.R. D19. [51a] [1979] C.M.L.R.

[52] See p. 217, *ante*.

[53] European Free Trade Association.

[54] Austria: Cmnd. 5159 (January 1, 1973).

[55] Finland: O.J. 1973, L 328/1 (October 5, 1973).

[56] Iceland: Cmnd. 5182 (April 1, 1973).

[57] Norway: O.J. 1973, L 171/1 (May 14, 1973).

[58] Portugal: Cmnd. 5164 (January 1, 1973).

[59] Sweden: Cmnd. 5180 (January 1, 1973).

[60] Switzerland: Cmnd. 5181 (January 1, 1973).

"The following are incompatible with the proper functioning of the Agreement in so far as they may affect trade between the Community and Sweden:

(i) all agreements between undertakings, decisions by associations of undertakings and concerted practices between undertakings which have as their object or effect the prevention, restriction or distortion of competition as regards the production of or trade in goods;

(ii) abuse by one or more undertakings of a dominant position in the territories of the Contracting Parties as a whole or in a substantial part thereof;

(iii) any public aid which distorts or threatens to distort competition by favouring certain undertakings or the production of certain goods."[61]

If a practice is regarded to be incompatible with these provisions, a Contracting Party to the Agreement may complain to the Joint Committee constituted under the FTA and, if necessary, take unilateral measures designed to safeguard its position.[62]

The principles regulating competition in the European Community and the provisions of the block exemptions apply to the competition rules of the FTAs *mutatis mutandis*.

Foreign National Competition Legislation

It would not be profitable here to review the foreign national legislation aiming at the protection of free and fair competition. Too many differences exist and no general pattern of legal rules emerges; moreover, in some countries the legislative effort is in marked contrast to economic experience and the prohibitions can easily—and lawfully—be avoided. The only practical conclusion which can safely be drawn is that an exporter who, on the broadest possible view, fears that the expansion of his exports might come into conflict with the restrictive practices legislation of a particular country should at once seek expert advice.

Of the countries of the European Community, the most elaborate law relating to cartels and monopolies is that of West Germany.[63] Further, it should be noted that the anti-trust legislation of the United States has

---

[61] The Association Agreement between the EEC and Greece of July 9, 1961 (operative from November 1, 1962) contains in Art. 51 the following provision: "Les Parties contractantes reconnaissent que les principes éconcés dans les articles 85, 86, 90 et 92 du traité instituant la Communauté devront être rendus applicable dans leur rapports d'association."

[62] On the question of direct enforceability of Art. 23 see Neville March Hunnings, "Enforceability of the EEC–EFTA Free Trade Agreements" in (1977) 2 E.L.R. 163; M. Waelbroeck in (1978) 3 E.L.R. 27; and Neville March Hunnings in (1978) 3 E.L.R. 278.

[63] On the competition law of the Member States of the European Community, see Lipstein, *The Law of the European Community*, 1974, 188 *et seq*. For the German cartel law, and described more shortly, that of the other member states, see A. H. Bermann and Colin Jones, *Fair Trading in Europe* (1977). The OECD publish an accurate description of the way the Restrictive Practices laws of member states operate, but it is usually very out of date. The legislation of France, Germany and the United Kingdom is kept up to date in *Competition Law in Western Europe and the USA* (eds. Gijlstra and Murphy), a loose-leaf book. The law of other member states is to be added, and detailed commentaries on the legislation and experience under it are beginning to appear.

extra-territorial effect.[64] Consequently a United Kingdom company which combines with an American corporation in a consortium or joint venture for the purpose of making or distributing goods in a third country, *e.g.* India, has to make certain that the agreement to which it is a party satisfies not only the laws of India and the United Kingdom but also does not infringe the anti-trust legislation of the United States.

[64] *British Nylon Spinners Ltd.* v. *Imperial Chemical Industries Ltd.* [1953] Ch. 19; see C. M. Schmitthoff, *The English Conflict of Laws* (3rd ed.), p. 13; see further *U.S.* v. *Aluminium Co. of America*, 148 F. 2d 416 (1945); *U.S.* v. *Watchmakers of Switzerland Information Center*, 133 F.Supp. 40 (1955); and W. Friedmann, "Foreign Investment and Restrictive Trade Practices" [1960] J.B.L. 144.

PART THREE

MATTERS INCIDENTAL TO EXPORTING

CHAPTER 21

THE FINANCE OF EXPORT

IN every contract for the sale of goods abroad, the clause dealing with the payment of the purchase price embodies four elements: time, mode, place and currency of payment. The various methods of financing exports represent, in law, variations and permutations of these four elements. The liberty of the parties to the contract to make their own arrangements as regards the payment of the price is, to some extent, qualified by the provisions of the Exchange Control Act 1947 and the observations in this chapter should be read in conjunction with the treatment of the provisions of that Act in an earlier chapter.[1]

The custom of the merchants has developed typical payment clauses whereby it is attempted to reconcile the conflicting economic interests involved in the export transaction. The interest of the exporter is to obtain the purchase price as soon as possible, but not to part with the documents of title to the goods—notably the bills of lading—before having received payment or, at least, being certain that his draft has been accepted, while the buyer wishes to postpone payment of the price until he has had an opportunity of reselling the goods. The most important of these payment clauses arise under collection arrangements and bankers' documentary credits. These methods of payment are characterised by the interposition between the exporter and buyer of a bank. In a collection arrangement the bank acts as the agent of the seller and receives its instructions from him; the exchange of the documents of title representing the goods and the payment of the price is effected at the place at which the buyer carries on business. In the case of a documentary credit, conversely, the instructions to the bank emanate from the buyer and the bank acts as agent of the buyer; the exchange of the documents and the price is effected at the seller's place. A considerable amount of business is transacted under documentary credits under which the banker, on the instructions of the buyer, promises to accept, honour or negotiate bills of exchange drawn by the seller. Both these methods, the collection arrangement and the documentary credit, have normally in common not only that a bank is interposed between the seller and the buyer but also that the bank uses the documents of title as a collateral security.

Before these two methods of payment in the export trade are discussed, it is expedient to consider arrangements which provide for direct payment by the buyer without such an interposition of a bank.

---

[1] See p. 71, *ante*.

ARRANGEMENTS FOR DIRECT PAYMENT BY THE BUYER

Payment on open account

In the simplest case, the parties agree on "cash with order" terms. An exporter, who is able to sell on these terms, reduces the financial risk of the export transaction to a minimum.

Sometimes the parties agree on "sight payment" either in sterling or in a foreign currency. Here the buyer has to remit the purchase price when presented with the documents of title to the goods sold.

Sight payment is arranged when the exporter is acquainted with the financial status of the buyer and entertains no doubt about his solvency. The exporter sends the documents to the buyer who remits the agreed price by telegraphic transfer (T/T) or mail (M/T). These remittances are usually carried out through the buyer's bank. Sight payment is further sometimes arranged when the exporter sells goods to his own overseas branch or subsidiary. Here "the seller ships to his branch and settlement is usually a matter of periodical remittance. There may even be a two way trading, as where raw materials are drawn from the territory where the products are finally marketed, in which case settlement between parent and offspring is a matter of running accounts and periodical remittances of balances due."[2]

If the exporter is not acquainted with the financial status of the buyer or other circumstances demand it, he arranges that the purchase price shall be paid "cash against documents" or "cash on delivery." These clauses are particularly suitable when delivery of the goods sold is to take place ex works or f.o.r. In f.o.b. or c.i.f. contracts direct payment by the buyer is not the normal method of payment; usually payment is effected through a bank, either under a collection arrangement at the buyer's place[3] or under a bankers' documentary credit at the seller's place.[4]

Bills of exchange

Normally the buyer does not remit the purchase price on open account, but allows the exporter to draw a bill of exchange[5] on him.[6] This arrangement offers obvious advantages to both parties; the exporter obtains a negotiable instrument which he can negotiate at once, and the buyer is allowed a definite time of credit for settlement unless the bill is payable at sight.[7] If the parties fail to make express arrangements, the custom

---

[2] W. W. Syrett, "Finance of Exports," in *Talks about Exports*, published by the Institute of Export, Pitman, p. 44.

[3] See p. 242, *post*.

[4] See p. 244, *post*.

[5] The expressions "bill of exchange" and "draft" have the same meaning.

[6] For an example of such a transaction, see *Credito Italiano* v. *M. Birnhak & Sons Ltd.* [1967] 1 Lloyd's Rep. 314, 320.

[7] A bill which is payable at sight is sometimes referred to as payable without usance, while a bill which allows the drawee time to pay is known as a time bill or a draft with usance.

prevailing in the particular trade determines whether the price is to be paid on open account or by bill, and on which terms the latter has to be drawn.

In cases governed by the exchange control regulations, payment by draft is admitted in sterling or in foreign currency. In the case of conventional export transactions from the scheduled territories (except Rhodesia), *i.e.* transactions which have no unusual features as regards their terms, the destination of the goods or in other respects, banks need not refer the application to the Bank of England but can approve it themselves, but if the export transaction is unconventional they have to submit the application to the Bank of England for authorisation and registration.[8] The exporter and the overseas buyer are not concerned with the completion of this Form which is only used by banks in their dealings with the Bank of England.

Nature of the bill of exchange

The law governing bills of exchange is codified in the Bills of Exchange Act 1882. This Act, which has been referred to by an eminent commercial judge[9] as "the best drafted Act of Parliament ever passed," should be carefully studied by everybody who has to deal with bills of exchange. The Act defines in section 3 a bill of exchange as

> an unconditional order in writing, addressed by one person to another, signed by the person giving it, requiring the person to whom it is addressed to pay on demand or at a fixed or determinable future time a sum certain in money to or to the order of a specified person, or to bearer.

This definition can be expressed in graphical form as follows:

London, January 10, 19...

£500

*On demand** pay *Britannia Bank Limited or Order*** the sum of Five Hundred pounds for value received.

Exports Limited

To
Imports Inc.,
Boston,
U.S.A.

* or—*On March* 10, 19...
or—*Ninety days after sight.*

** or—*Bearer*

There are three original parties to a bill of exchange—the drawer, the drawee and the payee. They are, in the preceding example: Exports Ltd. (the drawer), Imports Inc. (the drawee), and Britannia Bank Ltd. (the payee). The drawer and the payee, or the drawee and the payee may be the same persons, but where the drawer and the drawee are the same persons the bill may be treated, at the option of the holder of the bill, as a promissory note or a bill of exchange (s. 5).[10]

The characteristics of a bill of exchange are—

(1) Every obligation arising under the bill must be expressed in writing on the bill and signed by the party liable (s. 23).

---

[8] See Bank of England Notice E.C. 67, fourth issue (October 11, 1968), as amended.
[9] MacKinnon L.J. in *Bank Polski* v. *K. J. Mulder & Co.* [1942] 1 K.B. 497, 500.
[10] References here and on the following pages are to the Bills of Exchange Act 1882.

(2) The obligations stipulated in the bill can be transferred easily by "negotiation" of the bill. This is done, in case of a bill to bearer, by mere delivery of the bill, and, in case of a bill to order, both by delivery of the bill and by indorsement (s. 31).

(3) Performance of the obligations stipulated in the bill can only be claimed by a person holding the document. This person is called the holder of the bill and is defined, in section 2, as the payee or indorsee or bearer of the bill, who is in possession of the bill.

(4) The person to whom a bill is negotiated may acquire a better right under it than his predecessors possess. This is a remarkable exception to the common law principle that no transferee can acquire a better title than his transferor. The object of this rule is to facilitate the negotiation of bills.

Section 38(2) expresses the rule as follows:

> where he [*i.e.* the holder of a bill] is a "holder in due course," he holds the bill free from any defect of title of prior parties, as well as from mere personal defences available to prior parties amongst themselves, and may enforce payment against all parties liable on the bill.

A holder in due course is a holder who took a bill, which is complete and regular on the face of it, in good faith and for value and without notice of any defect in the title of the person negotiating it to him, and before it was overdue and without notice that it was dishonoured (s. 29(1)). A holder who derives his title through a holder in due course and who is not himself a party to any fraud or illegality affecting the bill, has all the rights of that holder in due course as regards the acceptor and all parties to the bill prior to that holder (s. 29(3)). Consequently, where a bill is negotiated to a holder in due course but later on dishonour is returned into the possession of the drawer, the latter, by virtue of section 29(3), has all the rights of that holder in due course.[11]

It should be noted that a bill of exchange does not represent an individual obligation but a number of obligations which, while being independent in many respects, are in others closely interconnected for the reason that they are embodied in the same document. All three original parties normally are liable to honour the bill; the drawer by drawing it (s. 55); the drawee by writing his acceptance on, or usually across, the bill whereby he becomes the acceptor (s. 17); and the payee by indorsing the bill when negotiating it whereby he becomes the indorser (s. 52(2)(*a*)).

A bill is irregular on the face of it if, *e.g.* it bears an irregular indorsement. "When is an indorsement irregular? The answer is, I think, that it is irregular whenever it is such as to give rise to doubt whether it is the

[11] *Jade International Steel Stahl und Eisen GmbH & Co. KG* v. *Robert Nicholas* (*Steels*) *Ltd.* [1978] 3 W.L.R. 39.

indorsement of the named payee. A bill of exchange is like currency. It should be above suspicion."[12]

On principle every person signing a bill of exchange, even the mere "backer" of the bill (s. 56), incurs liability, but the drawer or the indorsers can negative their liability by adding the words "without recourse" (*sans recours*) to their signature.

Further, a person signing a bill as drawer, indorser or acceptor can negative his liability by adding words to his signature indicating that he signs for or on behalf of a principal or in a representative capacity[12a]; but the addition of descriptive words, such as "commission agent" or "company director," is not sufficient to exempt him from personal liability (s. 26(1)).

The primary liability to pay the bill rests upon the drawee; the drawer and indorsers are only liable if the drawee dishonours the bill and they have received notice of dishonour by the holder or a subsequent indorser. Return of the dishonoured bill is a sufficient notice of dishonour (s. 49(6)).

A bill is dishonoured if it is not accepted by the drawee when presented to him for acceptance (unless presentment is excused) or if not paid by him. Presentment for acceptance is required where the bill is payable a certain time after sight in order to fix the maturity of the bill (s. 39(1)).

The drawer or any indorser may insert in the bill the name of a person to whom the holder may resort if the bill is dishonoured by non-acceptance or non-payment (s. 15). Such person is called "the referee in case of need." The bill must be protested or noted[13] before it can be presented to the referee (s. 67). In the United Kingdom presentment in case of need is optional, but in many overseas countries such presentment is obligatory.

The time of payment is normally inserted in the bill when it is drawn. The bill is either a sight bill or a time bill. A sight bill is defined in section 10(1) of the Act, as a bill

(*a*) which is expressed to be payable on demand, or at sight, or on presentation, or
(*b*) in which no time for payment is expressed.

A time bill is payable at a fixed future time or a determinable future time (ss. 10, 11). In the latter case it is usually payable a fixed period after date or sight, *e.g.* "ninety days after sight." A bill payable at an uncertain date or on a contingency is not a bill of exchange in the meaning of the law; consequently, a bill would be bad if payable "on or before" a certain date,[14] "after sight," or "on arrival of steamer. . . ."[14a]

The place of payment is specified in the bill by the drawer or, if the drawer fails to do so, by the acceptor when accepting the bill. Usually a bill is made payable at a banker's office, but this is not a requirement of

---

[12] *Per* Denning L.J. in *Arab Bank Ltd.* v. *Ross* [1952] 2 Q.B. 216, 227.

[12a] But where the bill is accepted by a company and indorsed by a director "for and on behalf of the company" the director was held to be personally liable because his intention was to bind himself (s. 26(2)): *Rolfe Lubbell & Co.* v. *Keith and Greenwood* [1979] 2 Lloyd's Rep. 75.

[13] See pp. 238 and 244, *post*.

[14] *Williamson* v. *Rider* [1963] 1 Q.B. 89.

[14a] It was held in *Korea Exchange Bank* v. *Debenhams (Central Buying) Ltd.* [1979] 1 Lloyd's Rep. 548, 551 (C.A.) that the words "At 90 days documents against acceptance . . . pay" were "gibberish" and the instrument was not payable at a fixed or determinable future time.

the law. Where a particular place is specified as the place of payment, that place is not regarded as the exclusive place of payment (s. 19(2)(*c*)), and the acceptor can be sued for payment at another place. But where it is expressly stated that the bill shall be paid at the particular place only and not elsewhere, the acceptor can only be sued at that place; where the acceptor adds an exclusive place of payment to his acceptance, the holder of the bill is entitled to treat the acceptance as qualified and the bill as dishonoured (s. 44), but he cannot claim this right if the place of payment is not made exclusive. In one case[15] a Polish firm drew a bill on "X Y, Plantation House, Mincing Lane, London, payable in Amsterdam at the A B Bank"; the bill was drawn on May 1, 1939, and payable in Dutch florins on November 1, 1939. It was duly accepted by X Y, but could not be presented in Amsterdam owing to the outbreak of the Second World War. Although the place of payment was in Holland and the stipulated currency Dutch florins, the court held that the plaintiff was entitled to recover from X Y in London because Amsterdam was not stipulated as the only place of payment.

Foreign bills

The Bills of Exchange Act 1882 contains important provisions dealing with foreign bills.[16] A foreign bill is a bill which

(*a*) either is drawn by a person who is not resident in the British Islands,[17]

(*b*) or is drawn by a person resident in the British Islands on a person resident abroad *and* is payable abroad.

All other bills are inland bills (s. 4). It should be noted that a bill is not necessarily a foreign bill if it is payable abroad or if the drawee resides abroad; only if these two elements are combined is the bill a foreign bill, while it is always a foreign bill if the drawer resides abroad. If it is uncertain whether a bill is an inland bill or a foreign bill, it is treated as an inland bill (s. 4(2)). The main difference between inland bills and foreign bills is that the latter, as a rule, must be formally protested upon dishonour by non-acceptance or by non-payment (s. 51), while no protest is required for inland bills. In this respect English law differs from many foreign laws which likewise prescribe a protest for inland bills. In view of these and other differences between English and foreign law, it is often important to know whether the obligation of a person who signed a bill is to be judged by English law or a particular system of foreign law. The Act contains, in section 72, detailed rules on the conflict of laws, so far as relating to bills of exchange.[18]

---

[15] *Bank Polski* v. *K. J. Mulder & Co.* [1942] 1 K.B. 497.

[16] Cheshire's *Private International Law* (9th ed., 1974), pp. 551 *et seq.*

[17] The term "British Islands" includes any part of the United Kingdom of Great Britain and Ireland, the Islands of Man, Guernsey, Jersey, Alderney and Sark, and the islands adjacent to any of them being part of the dominions of the Crown.

[18] s. 72(1) and (2) are reproduced in Cheshire's *Private International Law* (9th ed., 1974), p. 55.

Where the bill is expressed in foreign currency, but is payable in England, judgment can be obtained in the English courts in foreign currency.[19]

International bills

The law of bills of exchange in the world is divided into two legal families. The Geneva system, founded on the Geneva Conventions,[20] is accepted by 19 countries of the European continent, including the U.S.S.R.,[21] and also by Brazil and Japan. The Anglo-American system applies in the United Kingdom, most parts of the Commonwealth, the United States and the other countries which found their law on the common law.

In order to reconcile these two systems, UNCITRAL is preparing a draft convention on international bills of exchange and promissory notes.[21a] The aim of the convention is to create a special instrument which persons engaged in international trade might use in place of the existing instruments to make payment or to give credit.

The claused bill

The draft customary in the export trade is not normally in the simple form set out on p. 235, *ante*, but contains a number of additional clauses. The following is an example of a draft as used in export transactions:

No. 1285

Liverpool, February 15, 19...

£500

Sixty days after sight of this our First of Exchange (Second and Third of the same date and tenor unpaid) pay Britannia Bank Limited or Order the sum of five hundred Pounds Sterling, payable at the collecting Bank's selling rate for sight drafts on London, with interest at six per cent. per annum added thereto from date hereof to due date of arrival of remittance in London, value received.

Exports Limited.

To
Imports Inc.,
Boston,
U.S.A.

Particular regard should be had to the clauses providing for payment at a specific rate of exchange or adding, to the sum payable, interest or specified charges. Thus payment is stipulated "at the collecting bank's selling rate for sight drafts on London" and it is provided that "interest at six per cent. per annum . . . from date hereof to due date of arrival of remittance in London" shall be added to the stipulated sum. Such clauses are very common, particularly when the bill is made payable in foreign currency because various rates of exchange normally exist for the currencies in force

[19] *Barclays Bank International Ltd.* v. *Levin Brothers (Bradford) Ltd.* [1977] Q.B. 270.

[20] There are three Geneva Conventions on the Unification of the Law relating to Bills of Exchange of June 7, 1930, and three further Conventions signed at Geneva on the Unification of the Law relating to Cheques of March 19, 1931.

[21] The U.S.S.R., Austria and Belgium have accepted the Geneva Conventions on Bills of Exchange, but not those on Cheques.

[21a] See p. 46, *ante*.

at the buyer's and seller's residence, and it is unavoidable, when the bill is negotiated, that incidental expenses, such as bankers' charges or foreign stamp duties, are incurred. Even where payment has to be made by sterling draft it is advisable to insert exchange and charges clauses in the bill in order to define with certainty the financial obligations of the parties in the case of any unforeseen fluctuations in the rate of exchange.

The following exchange clauses are found in drafts used in export transactions:

payable at the bank's drawing rate for demand drafts on London,
payable at collecting bank's selling rate for Telegraphic Transfer,
payable at collecting bank's selling rate for sight drafts on London,
payable at collecting bank's selling rate for ninety days after sight drafts on London,
payable by approved bank's draft on London, exchange per indorsement.

Some of these clauses are customary in the trade with particular overseas countries and others are used where the buyer intends to obtain finance in a particular manner; thus, "exchange as per indorsement" clauses are mainly used where the seller wishes to discount the bill to a bank; the bank then includes its discount in the sum payable when converting the stipulated currency into the local currency of the drawee.[22]

The following clauses relating to charges and interest are found, sometimes combined with one another and added to an exchange clause:

payable with interest at . . . per cent. per annum from date hereof to due date of arrival of remittance in London,
payable with exchange,
payable without loss in exchange,
payable with stamps,
payable with bankers' charges,
payable with collecting bank's charges,
payable with negotiating bank's charges.

If the bill does not provide for payment of interest from the date of the bill, interest can only be demanded from the time of maturity of the bill (s. 57(1)(*b*)). If the bill does not provide that the incidental charges should be borne by the drawee, they fall upon the drawer.

From the legal point of view, no objection exists to inserting in the bill clauses regulating the rate of exchange or the payment of interest or charges. The Bills of Exchange Act 1882 provides that the sum payable by the bill has to be "a sum certain in money,"[23] but adds, in section 9(1) that

the sum payable by a bill is a sum certain within the meaning of this Act, although it is required to be paid—
(*a*) with interest,
(*d*) according to an indicated rate of exchange or according to a rate of exchange to be ascertained as directed by the bill.

---

[22] In view of the possibility of currency devaluations, it is advisable to specify the exchange calculation expressly in the indorsement and not to rely on the details of the front of the bill: *Tropic Plastic and Packaging Industry* v. *Standard Bank of South Africa Ltd.*, 1969 (4) S.A. 108; see the note in [1970] J.B.L. 121–122.

[23] See p. 235, *ante*.

The clause "payable with interest at . . . per cent. per annum from date hereof to due date of arrival of remittance in London" is of doubtful legal validity. It was held by the highest court in Australia[24] that the clause was invalid on the ground of uncertainty, mainly because the terminal date of interest could not be ascertained from anything appearing on the face of the bill. It is submitted, with great respect, that this view is incorrect. That the requirement of payment of interest does not invalidate the bill is expressly provided by section 9(1)(*a*) of the Act of 1882. The payment of interest is merely ancillary to the payment of the main sum, and it is thought that the requirement of certainty does not extend to ancillary sums, such as interest and exchange, with the same rigour as to the main sum. But the rate of interest must be specified in the bill.[25] However, banks in the City of London sometimes consider the clause under examination as unacceptable on the ground of uncertainty, but the English courts have not yet been called upon to give their ruling on the clause.

The clause "payable without loss in exchange" is designed to protect the drawer against loss caused by an adverse alteration of the rate of exchange, particularly during the time which might elapse between the deposit of the price by the buyer in local currency with his bank and the release of the currency of exchange by the latter—or the foreign central bank—to the seller after compliance with the foreign exchange control regulations.

A draft expressed in foreign currency need not contain an exchange clause, the provisions of section 9(1)(*d*) of the Act are purely permissive[26]; if no exchange clause is inserted and the rate of exchange cannot be ascertained by reference to the custom of the trade, it is calculated according to the rate for sight drafts at the place of payment on the day the bill is payable (s. 72), but instead of claiming that rate of exchange, judgment may be obtained in the foreign currency in which the draft is expressed and the date of conversion into sterling is then the date on which enforcement of the judgment is sought, *i.e.* virtually the date of payment.[27]

The documentary bill

The seller often attaches to a bill of exchange which he has drawn on the buyer the bill of lading relating to the goods sold. Such a bill of exchange is known as a "documentary bill." The purpose of issuing a documentary bill is mainly to ensure that the buyer shall not receive the bill of lading and, therewith, the right of disposal of the goods, unless he has first accepted or paid the attached bill of exchange according to the arrangement between the parties. If the buyer fails to honour the bill of

---

[24] *Commonwealth Bank of Australia* v. *Rosenhair & Co.* [1922] Vic.L.R. 787 (High Court of Australia).

[25] The American Uniform Commercial Code, s. 3–106(1)(*b*), even admits different specified rates before and after default.

[26] *Cohn* v. *Boulken* (1920) 36 T.L.R. 767.

[27] *Barclays Bank International Ltd.* v. *Levin Brothers (Bradford) Ltd.* [1977] Q.B. 270.

exchange, he has to return the bill of lading, and, if he wrongfully retains the latter, the law presumes that the property in the goods sold has not passed to him.[28]

Occasionally the tenor of the documentary bill contains a clear reference to the export transaction to which the bill relates. Such statements do not render the bill of exchange void though they are, of course, superfluous (s. 3(4)(*b*)). The practice of inserting them is convenient, and facilitates the careful checking of bills and documents which is a paramount responsibility of those dealing with the financial aspects of the export trade.

It has been seen earlier[29] that the seller usually presents the buyer with several sets of shipping documents. In this case, the seller does not draw the bill of exchange as a "sola" but as "parts of a set" and attaches a part of the bill to every set of shipping documents which he dispatches. The tenor of every part indicates that the bill represents a part in a set, and states the number of parts existing in all. In the example on p. 239, *ante*, the words "First of Exchange (Second and Third of the same date and tenor unpaid)" indicate that the bill is drawn in triplicate. The Bills of Exchange Act 1882 regulates this practice by providing, in section 71(1), that

> where a bill is drawn in a set, each part of the set being numbered, and containing a reference to the other parts, the whole of the parts constitute one bill.

The parts of the set may be indorsed to different persons, but only one part is accepted by the drawee. If he is so foolish as to write his acceptance on more than one part and the accepted parts reach different holders, he is liable on each part as if it were a separate bill. In the normal case, payment of the accepted part discharges the whole bill and the acceptor is entitled to claim delivery of the accepted part.

Collection Arrangements

Where the parties have not arranged for payment of the purchase price to take place in the exporter's country the following problem arises: who is to present the bill drawn by the seller on the buyer at his residence and, if it is a documentary bill, to deliver the shipping documents to him when he accepts or pays the draft? Normally, the exporter asks his bank to arrange for the acceptance or payment of the bill overseas, and the bank will carry out this task through its own branch office abroad or a correspondent bank. Sometimes the seller entrusts these duties to his representative or subsidiary company, if he is represented at the buyer's place of business, or to his shipping agent.

The seller's instructions to present for acceptance or for payment the bill drawn for the price pass through many hands and have to be carried

---

[28] Sale of Goods Act, s. 19(3); p. 78, *ante*.
[29] On p. 29, *ante*.

out abroad.[30] They have to be precise and complete and to deal with the various contingencies which may arise in the course of their execution. The banks ask their customers to issue instructions on a *documentary bill lodgment form* which is designed to obtain instructions for all eventualities. The form, which should be obtained from the exporter's bank, is completed in duplicate and the duplicate sheet is retained by the remitting bank branch and forms part of its bill register.

The banking practice relating to collection arrangements is standardised by the *Uniform Rules for Collections* (1978 Revision), sponsored by the International Chamber of Commerce.[31] The Uniform Rules apply only if embodied by the parties into their contract. This is widely done, particularly in the intercourse between the remitting bank, instructed by the seller, and the collecting bank, which presents the bill to the buyer at his place on the instructions of the remitting bank. The following definitions of the Uniform Rules are of interest[32]:

(i) "Collection" means the handling by banks, on instructions received, of documents as defined in (ii) below, in order to—
- (*a*) obtain acceptance and/or, as the case may be, payment, or
- (*b*) deliver the commercial documents against acceptance and/or, as the case may be, against payment, or
- (*c*) deliver documents on other terms and conditions.

(ii) "Documents" mean financial documents and/or commercial documents:—
- (*a*) "financial documents" mean bills of exchange, promissory notes, cheques, payment receipts or other similar instruments used for obtaining the payment of money;
- (*b*) "commercial documents" mean invoices, shipping documents, documents of title or other similar documents, or any other documents whatsoever, not being financial documents.

(iii) "Clean collection" means collection of financial documents not accompanied by commercial documents.

(iv) "Documentary collection" means collection of—
- (*a*) financial documents accompanied by commercial documents;
- (*b*) commercial documents not accompanied by financial documents.

The Uniform Rules thus distinguish two types of collection arrangements, clean collections and documentary collections. In the latter type of arrangement the commercial documents are presented by the collecting bank to the buyer, together with the financial documents; it is this type of collection arrangement which is of interest to the exporter.

The Uniform Rules provide that all remittances must be accompanied by a *collection order* to be sent by the remitting bank to the collecting bank. The collection order must give complete and precise instructions. The collecting bank is only permitted to act upon the instructions in the collection order; if it cannot do so, it must advise the remitting bank immediately.[33] The collecting bank must advise the remitting bank of the fate of the collection immediately; the advice has to be sent by the quickest

---

[30] On the liability of the bank and the buyer if the instructions of the seller are not complied with, see *Midland Bank Ltd.* v. *Eastcheap Dried Fruit Co.* [1961] 2 Lloyd's Rep. 251; [1962] 1 Lloyd's Rep. 359 (C.A.).

[31] ICC Brochure No. 322.

[32] Uniform Rules for Collection (1978 Revision), General Provisions and Definitions, B(1).

[33] Uniform Rules, General Provisions and Definitions, para. c.

mail but in case of urgency may be sent by the collecting bank by a quicker method at the expense of the customer, *i.e.* the exporter.[34] The Uniform Rules contain the following provision which, in its generality, is of doubtful validity in English law[35]:

> Banks concerned with a collection assume no liability or responsibility for the consequences arising out of delay and/or loss in transit of any messages, letters or documents, or for delay, mutilation or other errors in the transmission of cables, telegrams, telex, or communication by electronic systems, or for errors in translation or interpretation of technical terms.

The remitting bank and probably also the collecting bank act as agents of the seller.

In the case of a documentary collection, the exporter has to instruct the remitting bank on the lodgment form, and the latter the collecting bank in the collection order, whether the documents shall be delivered to the buyer on acceptance of the bill (D/A) or on actual payment (D/P); whether the documents shall be handed to a representative in case of need[36] and what the powers of the representative are; whether the buyer shall be allowed a rebate for payment before maturity; and, if the documents are not taken up, whether the goods are to be warehoused and what insurance is to be effected. Precise instructions must further be given relating to the noting or protest by a notary public at the payee's residence if the bill is dishonoured by non-acceptance or non-payment. Noting means obtaining a minute on the bill by the notary public at the time of refusal of acceptance or payment; the minute which is dated and initialled by the notary is, in practice, a sufficient assurance for all parties concerned that the bill has been dishonoured, and only in particular cases, *e.g.* when the matter leads to litigation, is the notary public required to procure a formal protest. According to English law, which, of course, applies only if proceedings against the defaulting payee can be taken in England,[37] where a bill has been noted on the day of dishonour or the next succeeding business day, the protest may be drawn up subsequently and dated back to the date of noting (Bills of Exchange Act 1882, ss. 51 and 93).

The instructions for collection may contain additional requests; the exporter may, *e.g.* require the collecting bank to "cable advice if not paid."

Bankers' Documentary Credits

We now turn to a consideration of the various types of bankers' documentary credits. The feature common to all of them is that the buyer arranges with a bank to provide finance for the exporter in the country of the latter on delivery of the shipping documents. On presentment of the shipping documents, the banker pays the purchase price, normally by accepting a sight draft or time bill drawn by the buyer (acceptance credit)

---

[34] *Ibid.* Art. 20(ii).

[35] *Ibid.* Art. 4.

[36] The Uniform Rules contain detailed provision on the representative in care of need and the protection of the goods (Arts. 18 and 19).

[37] See p. 434, *post*.

or by paying cash (cash credit). A documentary credit has been described in these terms[38]:

> The banker, . . . acting on behalf of the buyer and either directly or through the intervention of a banker in the country of the seller, assumes liability for payment of the price in consideration, perhaps, of the security afforded to him by a pledge of the documents of title to the goods or of his being placed in funds in advance or of an undertaking to reimburse, and of a commission.

This description reveals the essence of the transaction, *viz.* that the goods represented by the bill of lading as a document of title are used as a means of financing the transaction. Lord Wright[39] describes the function of the documentary credit as follows:

> The general course of international commerce involves the practice of raising money on the documents so as to bridge the period between the shipment and the time of obtaining payment against documents.

The documentary character of this type of bankers' credit, as used in international trade, cannot be over-emphasised: the bank is prepared to provide finance to the exporter because it holds the shipping documents as collateral security for the advance and, if necessary, can take recourse to the buyer as instructing customer and the exporter as drawer of the bill. The bank invariably asks for the delivery of a full set of original bills of lading; otherwise a fraudulent shipper would be able to obtain payment under the documentary credit on one of them and advances from other bankers on the security of the other originals constituting the set.

A comprehensive definition of the documentary credit[40] is to be found in the *Uniform Customs and Practice for Documentary Credits 1974*, sponsored by the International Chamber of Commerce,[41] where it is provided[42] that a commercial credit is:

> any arrangement, however named or described, whereby a bank (the issuing bank), acting at the request and in accordance with the instruction of a customer (the applicant for the credit),[43] (i) is to make payment to or to the order of a third party (the beneficiary)[44] or is to pay, accept or negotiate bills of exchange (drafts) drawn by the beneficiary, or (ii) authorises such payments to be made or such drafts to be paid, accepted or negotiated by another bank,[45] against stipulated documents, provided that the terms and conditions of the credit are complied with.

---

[38] H. C. Gutteridge and Maurice Megrah, *The Law of Bankers' Commercial Credits* (4th ed., 1968), p. 1. See further A. G. Davis, *The Law relating to Commercial Letters of Credit* (2nd ed., 1954); E. P. Ellinger, *Documentary Letters of Credit* (1970).

[39] In *T. D. Bailey, Son & Co.* v. *Ross T. Smyth & Co. Ltd.* (1940) 56 T.L.R. 825, 828.

[40] Documentary credits are often referred to as "letters of credit." The American Uniform Commercial Code uses that term; see s. 5–101.

[41] ICC Brochure 222. The *Uniform Customs and Practice for Documentary Credits 1974* (Brochure 222) must not be confused with the *Uniform Rules for the Collection of Commercial Paper 1978* (Brochure 322), discussed on p. 243, *ante*.

[42] In General Provisions and Definitions, para. (*b*).

[43] This is the buyer.

[44] This is the seller (exporter).

[45] This is the correspondent bank at the seller's place.

Uniform Customs and Practice for Documentary Credits 1974

The banking practice relating to documentary credit is standardised by the *Uniform Customs and Practice for Documentary Credits 1974*, sponsored by the International Chamber of Commerce.[46] This is the branch of the law of international trade in which the attempts at unifying the law have been most successful; the Uniform Customs have, indeed, global effect.[47] This success has been achieved after almost 40 years of effort.[48]

According to English law the Uniform Customs do not apply automatically but must be incorporated into the contract of the parties.[49] Today, British banks, when contracting with a United Kingdom party, an overseas merchant, or other banks, will normally insist on the express adoption of the Uniform Customs. In other countries the general standard conditions of the national banking associations[50] provide that the Uniform Customs shall apply to all documentary credits opened by member banks of those associations. Whether the Uniform Customs are adopted specifically or generally, their provisions can be contracted out by express agreement of the parties; the Uniform Customs provide[51]:

> These provisions and definitions and the following articles apply to all documentary credits and are binding upon all parties therefto unless otherwise expressly agreed.

The Uniform Customs further contain a definition of the documentary credit.[52] An attempt has been made by the International Chamber of Commerce to standardise the documentation relating to documentary credits; the ICC has published the *Standard Forms for issuing Documentary Credits*[53] which are based on the layout key proposed by the UN Economic Commission for Europe and this aligns with the other items of export documentation.[54]

The fundamental principle of the Uniform Customs is to provide for a strict separation of the documentary aspect of the export transaction from the goods aspect and to make it clear that the banks are only concerned with the former but not with the latter; the Uniform Customs state[55]:

> Credits, by their nature, are separate transactions from the sales or other contracts on which they may be based and banks are in no way concerned with or bound by such contracts.

---

[46] ICC Doc. No. 470/247. See B. S. Wheble, "Documentary Credits—Uniform Customs and Practice," in (1963) *Journal of the Institute of Bankers*, February 1.

[47] By March 31, 1974, they had been adopted by banks and banking associations in 175 countries and territories.

[48] The first issue of the Uniform Customs was published in 1933, the second in 1951, and the third in 1962. As from October 1, 1975, the 1974 Revision, which is the fourth issue, has been operative. All references in this section are to the 1974 Revision, unless stated otherwise.

[49] In the following English cases the Uniform Customs were adopted by the parties in their contract: *Soproma S.p.A.* v. *Marine & Animal By-Products Corporation* [1966] 1 Lloyd's Rep. 367 (1951 Revision); *Elder Dempster Lines Ltd.* v. *Ionic Shipping Agency Inc.* [1968] 1 Lloyd's Rep. 529 (1962 Revision).

[50] In the U.K. no general standard conditions for banks exist.

[51] Uniform Customs, General Provisions and Definitions, para. (*a*).

[52] This definition is quoted on p. 245, *ante*.

[53] ICC Brochure 323.

[54] See p. 55, *ante*.

[55] Uniform Customs, General Provisions and Definitions, para. (*c*); see also Art. 8.

The Uniform Customs further demand[56] that credit instructions and the credits themselves shall be complete and precise and that the issuing banks shall discourage any attempt on the part of the buyer to include excessive detail.

The stages of a documentary credit

Where payment under a documentary credit is arranged, four stages can normally be distinguished—

(i) The exporter and the overseas buyer agree in the contract of sale that payment shall be made under a documentary credit.

(ii) The overseas buyer instructs a bank at his place of residence (known as the "issuing bank") to open a documentary credit for the United Kingdom exporter on the terms specified by the buyer in his instructions to the issuing bank.

(iii) The issuing bank arranges with a bank at the residence of the exporter (known as the "correspondent bank"[57]) to negotiate, accept or pay the exporter's draft upon delivery of the shipping documents by the seller.

(iv) The correspondent bank advises the exporter that it will negotiate, accept or pay his draft upon delivery of the shipping documents. The correspondent bank may do so either *without its own engagement* or it may *confirm* the credit opened by the issuing bank.[58]

Sometimes, when the bank is represented at the overseas buyer's and the exporter's place, stages (iii) and (iv) are combined and the issuing bank advises the exporter of the credit opened in his favour, either directly or through a branch at the exporter's place.

Three points emerge from this analysis: as a matter of law, stages (i) and (iv) are of singular importance to the exporter, *viz.* the arrangement, in his contract of sale with the overseas buyer, of the most appropriate type of documentary credit, and the binding force of the undertaking by the correspondent bank to pay the purchase price on delivery of the shipping documents; and, as a matter of fact, meticulous care is required on the part of the exporter in respect of the completion of the shipping documents because the correspondent bank will rightly refuse to accept tendered documents which do not correspond literally with the instructions received from the issuing bank, and ultimately from the buyer. "There is no room for documents which are almost the same, or which will do just as well."[59]

---

[56] *Ibid.* para. (*d*).

[57] In the Uniform Customs, the correspondent bank is called "the advising bank"; see Art. 3.

[58] The correspondent bank will confirm the credit only if the issuing bank has made it irrevocable; see Uniform Customs, Art. 3(b). On confirmed and unconfirmed credits, p. 257, *post*.

[59] *Per* Lord Sumner in *Equitable Trust Co. of New York* v. *Dawson Partners* (1927) 27 Ll.L.R. 49, 52; Devlin J. in *Midland Bank Ltd.* v. *Seymour* [1955] 2 Lloyd's Rep. 147.

The doctrine of strict compliance

The legal principle that the bank is entitled to reject documents which do not strictly conform with the terms of the credit is conveniently referred to as the doctrine of strict compliance. The reason underlying this rule—which is not always appreciated by exporters—is that the correspondent bank is a special agent of the issuing bank and the latter is a special agent of the buyer; if such agent who has a limited authority acts outside his authority (in banking terminology: his mandate) the principal is entitled to disown the act of the agent, who cannot recover from him and has to bear the commercial risk of the transaction. In a falling market a buyer is easily tempted to reject documents which the bank accepted, on the ground that they do not strictly conform with the terms of the credit. Moreover, the bank deals in finance, not in goods[60]; it has normally no expert knowledge of the usages and practices of a particular trade. If the documents tendered are not strictly in conformity with the terms of the credit and the bank refuses to accept them, the exporter should at once contact his overseas buyer and request him to instruct the bank to accept the documents as tendered; the refusal of the bank to depart even in a small and apparently insignificant matter not sanctioned by the instructions or the Uniform Customs, where applicable, from its instructions will, in the overwhelming majority of cases, be upheld by the courts if litigation ensues.

The doctrine of strict compliance may be illustrated by the following examples.

In *Equitable Trust Company of New York* v. *Dawson Partners Ltd.*[61] the defendants bought vanilla beans from a seller in Batavia (now Jakarta). They instructed the plaintiff bank to open a confirmed commercial credit in favour of the seller and to make finance available thereunder on delivery of certain documents including a certificate of quality to be issued "*by experts*." Owing to an ambiguity in the cabled codeword, the correspondent bank in Batavia advised the seller that the credit was available on the tender of a certificate "*by expert*." The seller who was fraudulent shipped mainly rubbish and the expert failed to discover the fraud. The House of Lords held that the plaintiff bank was not entitled to be reimbursed by the buyers because, contrary to their instructions, it made available finance on the certificate of one expert only instead of at least two experts.

In *Soproma S.p.A.* v. *Marine & Animal By-Products Corporation*[62] the buyers, an Italian company, bought a quantity of Chilean fish full meal from a New York company. The contract, which was on a London Cattle Food Trade Association form, was c. and f. Savona and provided that the buyers should open a documentary credit with a New York bank. The documents to be presented by the sellers to that bank had to include bills

---

[60] See Uniform Customs, Art. 8.

[61] (1927) 27 Ll.L.R. 49. See also *Gian Singh & Co. Ltd.* v. *Banque de l'Indochine* [1974] 1 W.L.R. 1234.

[62] [1966] 1 Lloyd's Rep. 367.

of lading issued to order and marked "freight prepaid" and further an analysis certificate stating that the goods had a content of minimum 70 per cent. protein. The credit was subject to the Uniform Customs (1951 Revision). The sellers tendered to the correspondent bank in New York bills of lading which were not to order and consequently were not negotiable[63] and which did not bear the remark "freight prepaid" but, on the contrary, bore the remark "collect freight"; the analysis certificate showed only a protein content of 67 per cent. minimum; and the goods, although described in the invoice as "Fish Full Meal," were described in the bills of lading only as "Fishmeal." The buyers rejected the documents. Thereupon (the time of validity of the documentary credit having expired) the sellers made a second tender of documents to the buyers directly,[64] adding a freight receipt showing that they had paid the freight and an analysis certificate of minimum 70 per cent. protein. The buyers likewise rejected the second tender and, after arbitration in London, the dispute came before the English court. McNair J. decided that the buyers had rightly rejected the documents, for the following reasons:

1. the second—direct—tender of documents was irrelevant[65] and had to be disregarded completely;

2. the first tender, *i.e.* the tender to the correspondent bank in New York, was defective because—

(*a*) the bills of lading did not bear the remark "freight prepaid"[66] but were in fact marked "freight collect." Further, they were not negotiable as they were not to order and consequently were not proper bills which could be tendered under a c.i.f. or c. and f. contract;

(*b*) the analysis showed too low a minimum protein content;

(*c*) but the description of the goods in the bills of lading in general terms (as "Fishmeal") was sufficient, since the goods were correctly described in the commercial invoice; the learned judge referred here to the Uniform Customs, Art. 33,[67] where it is provided that a general description in the bills of lading is sufficient if the goods are correctly described in the commercial invoice.[68]

---

[63] See p. 352, *post*.

[64] Not to the correspondent bank in New York.

[65] For reasons discussed on p. 267, *post*.

[66] Nor was the freight deducted from the price or a freight receipt tendered with the bills.

[67] This provision of the 1951 edition is substantially the same as Art. 32(*c*) of the 1974 Revision.

[68] In cases to which the Uniform Customs apply, reliance can no longer be placed on *S. H. Rayner & Co.* v. *Hambros Bank Ltd.* [1943] 1 K.B. 37. In this case the correspondent bank advised the sellers that a documentary credit in their favour was available upon delivery of certain documents evidencing the shipment of "Coromandel groundnuts." The sellers tendered a bill of lading describing the goods as "machine shelled groundnut kernels" and having in its margin the letters "C.R.S." which were an abbreviation of "Coromandels," but in the invoice the goods were described correctly as "Coromandel groundnuts." The Court of Appeal held that the bank had rightly refused payment under the credit, in view of the doctrine of strict performance. McNair J. rightly distinguished the *Soproma* case from the *Rayner* case because the Uniform Customs applied to the former but not to the latter.

Where a bank pays under a confirmed documentary credit although the documents tendered are defective, the principal—the issuing bank or the buyer, as the case may be—forfeits his right to refuse reimbursement if he ratifies the unauthorised payment.[69] The intention to ratify may, in appropriate circumstances, even be inferred from prolonged inaction or silence.[70] The documents should be rejected by the principal on their face value; if *e.g.* the buyer who is aware of their irregularity remains inactive and attempts to reject them after the arrival and inspection of the goods at the port of destination, he is likely to be deemed to have ratified the payment by the bank. In *Bank Melli Iran* v. *Barclays Bank D.C.O.*[71] an Iranian buyer purchased American trucks from English sellers. On the instructions of the buyer Bank Melli Iran opened a credit for the sellers, Barclays acting as the correspondent bank. The instructions of the issuing bank to the correspondent bank stated that the credit was for the price of "100 new Chevrolet trucks" and required the presentation of a certificate of the United States Government to that effect. The documents tendered to Barclays were ambiguous and contradictory. The invoice stated that the trucks were "in a new condition," the Government certificate referred to them as "new, good," and the delivery order described them as "new-good" (*sic*!). Barclays paid against these documents and passed them on to Bank Melli Iran. The latter informed Barclays that they considered the documents faulty but did not reject them. Indeed, later on they authorised Barclays to increase the credit and the buyer surveyed the first consignment of the goods on arrival in Iran. After approximately six weeks Bank Melli rejected the documents. McNair J. held (1) that the documents were faulty and should have been rejected by Barclays, (2) but in the circumstances Bank Melli had ratified the transaction and lost its right of rejection.

The documents tendered to the bank

According to the doctrine of strict compliance[72] the bank is within its rights when refusing documents tendered by the seller which do not contain all the particulars mentioned in the credit. But beyond this the bank is not obliged to go and should not go. In particular, it need not concern itself with the legal significance and value of the documents which it is instructed to demand. Even if their legal value appears to be questionable the documents in the required form may have some commercial value for the buyer and, as Devlin J. said,[73] "it is not for the bank to reason why." An illustration is the requirement of a credit that the bill of lading shall contain a specific description of the goods; the value of such description is nugatory

[69] *Bank Melli Iran* v. *Barclays Bank* (*Dominion, Colonial and Overseas*) [1951] 2 Lloyd's Rep. 367. *Cf.* also *Panchaud Frères S.A.* v. *Établissements General Grain Company* [1970] 1 Lloyd's Rep. 53, 57 (in this case payment was not to be made under a documentary credit).

[70] *Bank Melli Iran* v. *Barclays D.C.O.*, *ibid.*

[71] [1951] 2 Lloyd's Rep. 367.

[72] See p. 248, *ante*.

[73] In *Midland Bank Ltd.* v. *Seymour* [1955] 2 Lloyd's Rep. 147, 151.

in view of the—usual—clause in the bill that "weight, measure, marks, numbers, quality, contents and value if mentioned in the bill of lading are to be considered unknown"; nevertheless, the bank must insist that the bill contains the specified description but, unless instructed otherwise, need not reject such bill on the ground that the "weight, etc., unknown" clause is not deleted.[73] Speaking generally, in the absence of instructions to the contrary, banks are not under a duty to concern themselves with the clauses—the "small print"—on a bill of lading but all they have to do, in the words of Salmon J.,[74] is "to satisfy themselves that the correct documents are presented to them, and that the bills of lading bear no indorsement or clausing by the shipowners or shippers which could reasonably mean that there was, or might be, some defect in the goods or their packing." Unless otherwise authorised, British banks will reject bills which they consider to be "stale"[75] or which are issued under charterparties and embody charterparty clauses.[76]

Provisions relating to documents in the Uniform Customs

When a question of sufficiency of documents under a documentary credit governed by the Uniform Customs arises and this question cannot be resolved by reference to the instructions to the bank, it is necessary to turn to the Uniform Customs which define the documents normally acceptable to the bank in considerable detail. Some of these provisions of the Uniform Customs may be given here; they indicate the degree of precision aimed at by the Uniform Customs:

Article 18

(*a*) A clean shipping document is one which bears no superimposed clause or notation which expressly declares a defective condition of the goods and/or the packaging.

(*b*) Banks will refuse shipping documents bearing such clauses or notations unless the credit expressly states clauses or notations which may be accepted.

Article 19

(*a*) Unless specifically authorised in the credit, bills of lading of the following nature will be rejected:

(i) Bills of lading issued by forwarding agents.

(ii) Bills of lading which are issued under and are subject to the conditions of a charterparty.

(iii) Bills of lading covering shipment by sailng vessels.

(*b*) However, subject to the above and unless otherwise specified in the credit, Bills of Lading of the following nature will be accepted:

(i) "Through" Bills of Lading issued by shipping companies or their agents even though they cover several modes of transport.

(ii) Short Form Bills of Lading (*i.e.* Bills of Lading issued by shipping companies or their agents which indicate some or all of the conditions of carriage by reference to a source or document other than the Bill of Lading).

(iii) Bills of Lading issued by shipping companies or their agents covering unitised cargoes, such as those on pallets or in containers.

---

[74] In *British Imex Industries Ltd.* v. *Midland Bank Ltd.* [1958] 1 Q.B. 542, 552.

[75] On stale bills, see p. 359, *post*.

[76] On charterparty bills, see p. 354, *post*.

Article 20

(*a*) Unless otherwise specified in the credit, bills of lading must show that the goods are loaded on board a named vessel or shipped on a named vessel.

(*b*) Loading on board a named vessel or shipment on a named vessel may be evidenced either by a Bill of Lading bearing wording indicating loading on board a named vessel or shipment on a named vessel, or by means of a notation to that effect on the bill of lading signed or initialled and dated by the carrier or his agent, and the date of this notation shall be regarded as the date of loading on board the named vessel or shipment on the named vessel.

Article 21

(*a*) Unless transhipment is prohibited by the terms of the credit, bills of lading will be accepted which indicate that the goods will be transhipped en route, provided the entire voyage is covered by one and the same bill of lading.

(*b*) Bills of lading incorporating printed clauses stating that the carriers have the right to tranship will be accepted notwithstanding the fact that the credit prohibits transhipment.

Article 22

(*a*) Banks will refuse a Bill of Lading stating that the goods are loaded on deck, unless specifically authorised in the credit.

(*b*) Banks will not refuse a Bill of Lading which contains a provision that the goods may be carried on deck, provided it does not specifically state that they are loaded on deck.

Article 23

(*a*) If the credit calls for a combined transport document, *i.e.* one which provides for a combined transport by at least two different modes of transport, from a place at which the goods are taken in charge to a place designated for delivery, or if the credit provides for a combined transport, but in either case does not specify the form of document required and/or the issuer of such document, banks will accept such documents as tendered.

(*b*) If the combined transport includes transport by sea the document will be accepted although it does not indicate that the goods are on board a named vessel, and although it contains a provision that the goods, if packed in a container, may be carried on deck, provided it does not specifically state that they are loaded on deck.

Several documents to be read together

The bank is usually instructed to make finance available on tender of several documents in a set, normally the bill of lading, invoice and insurance policy or certificate. In that case, in the absence of instructions to the contrary, it is sufficient if all the documents in the set, taken together, contain the particulars required by the bank's mandate and it is not necessary that every document in the set should contain them. This rule is now contained in Article 32(*c*) of the Uniform Customs[77] which mitigates, to some extent, the effect of the doctrine of strict compliance.

The rule in Article 32(*c*) of the Uniform Customs is founded on the English case of *Midland Bank Ltd.* v. *Seymour*[78] In this case a merchant in England bought a quantity of ducks' feathers from sellers in Hong Kong c. and f. Hamburg; the instructions to the bank were that the documents had to evidence "shipment from Hong Kong to Hamburg of the undermentioned goods," and then, under "Description, Quantity and Price" it was stated: "Hong Kong duck feathers—85 per cent. clean; 12 bales each

[77] This rule, in the version adopted by the 1951 edition, was applied in *Soproma S.p.A.* v. *Marine & Animal By-Products Corporation* [1966] 1 Lloyd's Rep. 367; see p. 249, *ante*.

[78] [1955] 2 Lloyd's Rep. 147; see also *Panchaud Frères S.A.* v. *Etablissements General Grain Co.* [1970] 1 Lloyd's Rep. 53 (C.A.) p. 32, *ante*.

weighing about 190 lb.; 5s. per lb." The bill of lading described the goods merely as "12 bales; Hong Kong duck feathers" but all the documents, namely the bills of lading, invoices, weight account and certificate of origin, when read together, contained a complete description of the goods. The seller shipped worthless goods and the buyer claimed that the bank was not entitled to debit him with the credit since the bill of lading did not contain a full description of the goods. Devlin J. rejected this contention and held that the bank had complied with its mandate.

Time of opening of credit

Often the contract of sale will make express provision as regards the date at which the credit has to be opened. Sometimes it is stated that the credit shall be opened by a certain date, sometimes it is provided that it shall be opened "immediately" which means that the credit has to be opened at once within such time as is required for a person of reasonable diligence to establish the credit,[79] or sometimes the opening of the credit is made dependent on an act by the seller relating to the delivery of the goods, *e.g.* the sending of a provisional invoice[80] or of an advice that the goods are, or will soon be, ready for shipment.[81]

Where the contract does not provide when the credit shall be opened, the parties are not normally entitled to assume that the existence of the contract of sale depends on the opening of the credit by the buyer. Although the parties are at liberty to agree that the contract shall be "subject to the opening of a credit" in which case the opening of the credit is a condition precedent to the *formation* of the contract and, in the words of Denning L.J., "if no credit is provided, there is no contract between the parties,"[82] such interpretation of the buyer's promise is only possible where the parties have expressly or impliedly agreed that this promise shall be subject to that condition. In the normal cases in which the contract is unqualified, the stipulation to open a documentary credit relates to the performance of the contract and is only a condition precedent to the *performance* of the contract; it is the mechanism agreed upon for the payment of the price.

Where the contract of sale is unconditional but does not provide a date on which the credit shall be opened, the credit has to be opened within "a reasonable time."[83] This means a reasonable time calculated back from the first date of the shipment, not calculated forward from the date of the

[79] *Garcia* v. *Page & Co.* (1936) 55 Ll.L.R. 391. The seller may waive the rights arising from the delay in the opening of the credit expressly or impliedly: *Baltimex, etc.* v. *Metallo Chemical Refinery Co. Ltd.* [1956] 1 Lloyd's Rep. 450.

[80] *Knotz* v. *Fairclough, Dodd & Jones Ltd.* [1952] 1 Lloyd's Rep. 226.

[81] *Plasticmoda S.p.A.* v. *Davidsons (Manchester)* [1952] 1 Lloyd's Rep. 527. See also *Etablissements Chainbaux S.A.R.L.* v. *Harbormaster Ltd.* [1955] 1 Lloyd's Rep. 303.

[82] *Trans Trust S.P.R.L.* v. *Danubian Trading Co. Ltd.* [1952] 2 Q.B. 297, 304; see also *United Dominions Trust (Commercial) Ltd.* v. *Eagle Aircraft Services Ltd.* [1968] 1 W.L.R. 74, 80, 82.

[83] This is an implied term of the contract: *Diamond Cutting Works Federation* v. *Triefus & Co. Ltd.* [1956] 1 Lloyd's Rep. 216, 225.

conclusion of the contract.[84] Taking the first date of shipment as the starting point, the buyer has, it is thought, to open the credit a sufficient time in advance of that event to enable the seller to know before he sends the goods to the docks that his payment will be secured by the credit for which it is stipulated. Where a certain period for shipment is stipulated in the contract, *e.g.* shipment in February, March or April, in the absence of a stipulation to the contrary, the buyer has to open the credit not when the seller is ready to ship but he has to give the seller the benefit of the whole shipment period; as Somervell L.J. observed in one case[85]:

> When a seller is given a right to ship over a period and there is machinery for payment, that machinery must be available over the whole of that period. If the buyer is anxious, as he might be if the period of shipment is a long one, not to have to put the credit machinery in motion until shortly before the seller is likely to want to ship, then he must insert some provision in the contract by which the credit shall be provided, *e.g.* fourteen days after a cable received from the seller.

These rules apply equally to c.i.f. contracts[86] and f.o.b. contracts in which the seller has to make arrangements for freight and marine insurance for the account of the buyer,[87] and there is at least a prima facie rule that they likewise apply to f.o.b. contracts of the strict type[88] although in that case the shipping period is arranged for the benefit of the buyer and not the seller, because only in that way, in the words of Diplock J.,[89] can one get "certainty into what is a very common commercial contract."

The expiry date of the credit

The documentary credit invariably stipulates a date when it will expire and after which the correspondent bank will refuse to accept the documents presented by the seller. The Uniform Customs provide in Article 37:

> All credits, whether revocable or irrevocable, must stipulate an expiry date for presentation of documents for payment, acceptance or negotiation, notwithstanding the stipulation of a latest date for shipment.

The Uniform Customs further contain detailed provisions for the ascertainment of the expiry date and its extension in case of interruption of the bank's business owing to events beyond their control.

---

[84] *Sinason-Teicher Inter-American Grain Corporation* v. *Oilcakes and Oilseeds Trading Co. Ltd.* [1954] 1 W.L.R. 935.

[85] *Pavia & Co. S.p.A.* v. *Thurmann-Nielsen* [1952] 2 Q.B. 84, 88; see also *Tsakiroglou & Co. Ltd.* v. *Transgrains S.A.* [1958] 1 Lloyd's Rep. 562 (shipping period and nomination of port of destination by buyers); *Margaronis Navigation Agency Ltd.* v. *H. W. Peabody & Co. of London Ltd.* [1964] 1 Lloyd's Rep. 173 (laydays under charterparty).

[86] *Pavia & Co. S.p.A.* v. *Thurmann-Nielsen* [1952] 2 Q.B. 84; *Sinason-Teicher Inter-American Grain Corporation* v. *Oilcakes and Oilseeds Trading Co. Ltd.* [1954] 1 W.L.R. 935.

[87] See p. 20, *ante*; *N.V. Handel My. J. Smits Import-Export* v. *English Exporters (London) Ltd.* [1957] 1 Lloyd's Rep. 517, 519.

[88] See p. 19, *ante*. Particularly when they are string contracts in which the credit of the ultimate buyer is of overriding character: *Ian Stach Ltd.* v. *Baker Bosley Ltd.* [1958] 2 Q.B. 130, 143.

[89] *Ibid.* at p. 144.

The expiry date of the credit should not be confused with the shipment date. The shipment date is the—earlier—date shown in the bill of lading as the date when the goods were loaded. The credit sometimes stipulates, in addition to its expiry date, that the bills presented to the bank shall indicate a certain shipment date. If the bills of lading presented by the seller to the bank show a later date or if the bills are stale,[90] the bank will refuse to accept the documents even if presented before the expiry date.

Exceptionally, in long-term transactions the credit may have to be kept open for a considerable time. Thus, in one case[91] the parties agreed that upon expiration of the period of three years the credit was considered automatically invalidated but in the event of the matter being submitted to arbitration it should be deemed automatically extended without amendment for one year from any expiry date.

The law applicable to the credit

It will rarely be necessary to ascertain the law governing a documentary credit because, as has been seen,[92] banks in most countries operate credits under the Uniform Customs and that uniformity excludes the possibility of a conflict of laws with respect to most legal problems.

However, if it is necessary to determine the law governing a documentary credit and the credit itself does not contain a choice of law clause, in accordance with general principle[93] it is incumbent on the lawyer to ascertain the system of law with which the credit has its closest and most real connection.[94] This question is, of course, entirely separate from the ascertainment of the law governing the relationship between the seller and the buyer, *i.e.* the contract of sale which underlies the credit. When attempting to ascertain the law governing the credit, it should be borne in mind that the credit involves several legal relationships.

1. As between the buyer and the issuing bank, the law of the closest connection is likely to be that of the country in which the bank carries on business and has issued the credit. That relationship is founded on the contract of agency and in such a contract there is always a—rebuttable—presumption in favour of the law of the agent.

2. Where the seller, *i.e.* the beneficiary under the credit, is involved, the law of the closest connection is likely to be that of the correspondent bank. That is true not only as between the seller and the correspondent bank but also as between him and the issuing bank. Here the observations of Ackner J.[95] are incontrovertible:

> The advising [*i.e.* correspondent] bank would have constantly to be seeking to apply a whole variety of foreign laws [*if a different view were adopted*].

---

[90] See p. 359, *post*.
[91] *Offshore International S.A.* v. *Banco Central S.A.* [1976] 2 Lloyd's Rep. 402.
[92] See p. 246, *ante*.
[93] See p. 130, *ante*.
[94] *Offshore International S.A.* v. *Banco Central S.A.* [1976] 2 Lloyd's Rep. 402, 403.
[95] *Ibid.* 404.

if a different view were adopted.

3. The relationship between the issuing and correspondent bank causes the greatest difficulty. In these inter-bank transactions general conditions of business or a course of dealing may admit some conclusions as to the law of the closest connection. Where these indications are absent, there exists, it is thought, a rebuttable presumption in favour of the law of the correspondent bank because, as that law is likely to apply to the relationship with the seller-beneficiary, the application of different laws to two facets of the same commercial transaction would be undesirable.

Damages for failure to open or pay a credit

Where the buyer fails to open a credit as stipulated, the seller is entitled to claim damages for breach of that stipulation. The amount of damages recoverable under this heading is sometimes higher than the amount which the seller can recover for breach of the buyer's obligation to accept delivery of the goods. In the latter case, if the goods have an available market, the presumption of section 50(3) of the Sale of Goods Act applies which provides that the measure of damages is prima facie the difference between the contract price and the market price at the date when the goods ought to have been accepted. In a rising market damages for non-acceptance of the goods are nominal but damages for failure to open a commercial credit are not subject to the restriction of section 50(3) and may, in appropriate cases, include the loss of profit which the seller would have made had the transaction been carried out.[96] Where the correspondent bank delays the payment of the credit without excuse, although the documents were presented timely, it may be liable to the seller in damages.[96a]

Kinds of documentary credits

Payment, acceptance and negotiation credits

It is of importance to the seller to know in what manner he will obtain the moneys due to him under the credit. There exist three possibilities: the correspondent bank may be authorised to pay these moneys, to accept a bill of exchange drawn on it by the seller with respect to them, or to negotiate a bill drawn by the seller on the buyer or the issuing bank. The credit itself should state which of these three methods has been chosen by the parties and this point should be settled beforehand in the contract under which the credit is opened.

1. If the parties have arranged a *payment credit*, the correspondent bank is instructed to pay the seller the moneys due on presentation of the documents. This is a case of payment against documents.

2. If the credit is an *acceptance credit*, the seller draws the bill of exchange on the correspondent bank in the specified manner. The bill will normally be a time draft. By accepting the bill, the bank signifies its commitment to pay the face value on maturity to the party presenting it.

---

[96] *Trans Trust S.P.R.L.* v. *Danubian Trading Co. Ltd.* [1952] 2 Q.B. 297, 305.

[96a] *Ozalid Group (Export) Ltd.* v. *African Continental Bank Ltd.* [1979] N.L.J. 295.

An acceptance credit provides the seller with a considerable degree of security. If he does not want to hold the bill until it matures, he may turn it into money by negotiating it, *e.g.* by discounting it or selling it to his own bank.[97] On negotiation he is unlikely to receive the full amount of money stated in the tenor of the bill because the negotiating bank will deduct a discount or interest and commission.

There is no recourse by the correspondent bank against the seller. If that bank dishonours the bill by non-payment, *e.g.* because it becomes insolvent, the seller has still his claim for the purchase price against the buyer because the acceptance credit is only a conditional performance of the buyer's obligation to pay.[98]

3. Under the *negotiation credit* the correspondent bank is only authorised to negotiate[99] a bill of exchange drawn by the seller on the buyer or the issuing bank. The correspondent bank will indorse the bill and negotiate it, subject to deduction of discount or interest and commission. The bill may be a sight draft or a time draft, according to the terms of the credit.

The negotiation credit is subject to recourse against the seller as drawer of the bill, unless the credit has been previously confirmed by the correspondent bank.[1]

Sometimes the bank is only authorised to make an advance on the security of the documentary bill.[2]

Confirmed and unconfirmed credits

The two main types of documentary credits are the confirmed and the unconfirmed credit. Before considering them in detail it is necessary to refer to a question which in the past has caused much discussion amongst lawyers and bankers, *viz.* whether the terms "confirmed" and "irrevocable credit" are synonymous and, on the other hand, whether the terms "unconfirmed" and "revocable credit" have the same meaning.[3] These terms are normally used in modern terminology as referring to different aspects of the transaction: "revocable" and "irrevocable" relate to the instructions received by the correspondent bank from the issuing bank, "unconfirmed"[4] and "confirmed" relate to the advice sent by the correspondent bank to the exporter. While the correspondent bank advises the exporter only of a confirmed credit if it has received irrevocable instructions from the issuing bank, cases occur, as will be seen, in which an irrevocable credit emanating from the issuing bank is not confirmed by the correspondent bank.

---

[97] See p. 270, *post.*

[98] See p. 268, *post.*

[99] See p. 270, *post.*

[1] The treatment of a time draft as sight draft does not automatically operate as confirmation and does not prevent recourse: *Maran Road* v. *Austin Taylors Co. Ltd.* [1975] 1 Lloyd's Rep. 156, 161.

[2] *Plein & Co. Ltd.* v. *Inland Revenue Commissioners* (1946) 175 L.T. 453.

[3] The question is discussed in detail in the 3rd ed. of this work, p. 189.

[4] The Uniform Customs use the term "without engagement" for "unconfirmed." Art. 3(*b*).

From the point of view of the exporter, a particularly important feature of the credit is whether it is confirmed or unconfirmed. The instructions which the overseas importer gives the issuing bank when opening a confirmed or unconfirmed credit and which are passed on by the issuing bank to the correspondent bank are of secondary interest to the exporter who is first and foremost interested in the letter of advice which he receives from the correspondent bank and which details the terms on which that bank is prepared to pay, accept or negotiate the credit.

(a) Revocable and unconfirmed credits. The instructions of the buyer to the issuing bank to open an unconfirmed credit normally contain an express provision authorising the bank to revoke the credit during the time of its currency; the following is an example of such clause:

> This letter of credit expires in . . . on the . . . but you may cancel the credit at any time to the extent it has not been utilised.

The revocable nature of the credit is reflected in the advice sent by the correspondent bank to the exporter which normally states expressly that the credit is not confirmed. The following clause in the advice note is typical:

> We have no authority from our clients to confirm this credit. The credit is therefore subject to cancellation or modification at any time without notice.

From the exporter's point of view, an unconfirmed credit is a very unsatisfactory method of finance, but unconfirmed credits are sometimes preferred to confirmed credits because they are cheaper than the latter. The precarious position in which an exporter selling under an unconfirmed credit might find himself is well illustrated by the facts in *Cape Asbestos Co.* v. *Lloyds Bank.*[5] Importers in Warsaw bought a consignment of asbestos sheets from the plaintiffs and opened an unconfirmed credit in favour of the latter with the defendants. The defendants duly advised the plaintiffs of the credit, adding the clause "this is merely an advice of opening of the above-mentioned credit and is not a confirmation of the same." The plaintiffs shipped part of the consignment and their draft on the bank was duly accepted. The plaintiffs then shipped the remainder, but, on presenting their draft to the bank, acceptance of the draft was refused. In the meantime the importers in Warsaw had cancelled the credit, but the defendant bank had failed to notify the plaintiffs of the cancellation. It was held that the bank was entitled to refuse the acceptance of the draft for the remainder and Bailhache J. said in the course of the judgment that "an unconfirmed credit is practically worthless."

This case was based on unusual facts because normally the bank will notify the creditor of the revocation of an unconfirmed credit. The exporter who sells under such a credit should at least ask the bank to insert a *notice*

---

[5] [1921] W.N. 274; see also Lord Denning M.R. in *W. J. Alan & Co. Ltd.* v. *El Nasr Export and Import Co.* [1972] 2 Q.B. 189, 207.

clause in the advice. Under this clause the bank is obliged to inform the exporter forthwith of the cancellation of the credit.

Where the bank omits to state in the letter of advice whether the credit is confirmed or unconfirmed, the exporter has to assume that the credit is unconfirmed. In cases governed by the Uniform Customs, article 1 of this text applies which provides:

(*a*) All credits . . . should clearly indicate whether they are revocable or irrevocable.
(*b*) In the absence of such indication the credit shall be deemed to be revocable, even though an expiry date is stipulated.

(b) Irrevocable and confirmed credits. This is the type of documentary credit most favourable to the exporter because the correspondent bank stipulates here in terms that it will honour the exporter's drafts provided they are drawn and presented in conformity with the terms of credit.[6]

The instructions given by the buyer to the issuing bank expressly state that the credit is irrevocable; it is, *e.g.*, provided that—

This credit is to remain irrevocably valid but expires in . . . on the . . .

The irrevocable nature of the credit is reflected in the letter of advice sent by the correspondent bank to the exporter, which states expressly the undertaking of the correspondent bank to honour the drafts of the exporter. The following clause in the advice note is typical:

We undertake to honour such drafts on presentation provided that they are drawn and presented in conformity with the terms of this credit.

The effect of a confirmed credit has been described by Diplock J.[7] as constituting "a direct undertaking by the banker that the seller, if he presents the documents as required in the required time, will receive payment." The bank cannot withdraw from its liability to the exporter even if instructed by the buyer to cancel the credit. This is illustrated by *Hamzeh Malas & Sons* v. *British Imex Industries Ltd.*[8] where the plaintiffs, a Jordanian firm, contracted to buy from the defendants, a British firm, a quantity of reinforced steel rods, to be delivered in two instalments. Payment was to be made under two confirmed credits, one for each instalment, to be opened with the Midland Bank, London. Both credits were duly opened and confirmed by the bank to the sellers and the first was realised on shipment of the first instalment but a dispute arose with respect to the second credit. The buyers complained that the first instalment was not of contract quality and applied to the court for an injunction restraining the sellers from drawing on the second credit or recovering any

[6] In the eyes of the law, the confirmation by the correspondent bank constitutes an offer to the seller which is accepted by being drawn upon; see Donaldson J. in *Elder Dempster Lines Ltd.* v. *Ionic Shipping Agency Inc.* [1968] 1 Lloyd's Rep. 529, 535.

[7] In *Ian Stach Ltd.* v. *Baker Bosley Ltd.* [1958] 2 Q.B. 130.

[8] [1958] 2 Q.B. 127; a sequel of this litigation was the case of *British Imex Industries Ltd.* v. *Midland Bank Ltd.* [1958] 1 Q.B. 542, discussed on p. 251, *ante*. See also *Urquhart Lindsay* v. *Eastern Bank* [1922] 1 K.B. 318; further, see *Stein* v. *Hambros Bank* (1921) 9 Ll.L.R. 507; *National Bank of South Africa* v. *Banca Italiana* (1922) 10 Ll.L.R. 531; *Discount Records Ltd.* v. *Barclays Bank Ltd.*, [1975] 1 W.L.R. 315.

money under it. Donovan J. and the Court of Appeal refused to grant the injunction, on the grounds stated by Jenkins L.J. in a lucid judgment:

> It seems to be plain enough that the opening of a confirmed letter of credit constitutes a bargain between the banker and the vendor of the goods, which imposes upon the banker an absolute obligation to pay, irrespective of any dispute there may be between the parties as to whether the goods are up to the contract or not. An elaborate commercial system has been built up on the footing that bankers' commercial credits are of that character, and, in my judgment, it would be wrong for this court in the present case to interfere with that established practice.
>
> There is this to be remembered, too. A vendor of goods selling against a confirmed letter of credit is selling under the assurance that nothing will prevent him from receiving the price. That is no mean advantage when goods manufactured in one country are being sold in another.

Under a confirmed credit the bank does not have a right of recourse against the seller, even if the credit is only a negotiation credit,[9] except if the bank has obtained an indemnity from the seller.[10]

Where the credit does not conform to the terms of the contract of sale, two courses are open to the seller. He may reject the non-conforming credit; thus, where under the terms of the contract of sale he is entitled to a confirmed credit but is only advised of the opening of an unconfirmed credit, he need not ship the goods.[11] Or he may accept the non-conforming credit, and if he does so without objection, he is treated as having waived irrevocably his right to a conforming credit.[12]

Confirmed credits are very popular in modern export trade because they reduce the credit risk of the exporter. They are in many trades the normal terms of settlement. The banks have made an invaluable contribution to the smooth discharge of export transactions by perfecting this type of commercial credit.[12a]

(c) Irrevocable and unconfirmed credits. Where this type of credit[13] is used, the issuing bank cannot revoke its undertaking to the exporter, but the correspondent bank is not obliged to make payment or otherwise to provide finance at the place of the seller. The advice of an irrevocable unconfirmed credit would state:

> This credit is irrevocable on the part of the above-mentioned issuing bank but we are not instructed to confirm it and therefore it does not involve any undertaking on our part.

These credits are sometimes issued by leading banks, particularly American and British banks, which consider a local confirmation as unnecessary.

---

[9] See p. 257, *ante*, and *Maran Road* v. *Austin Taylor & Co.* [1975] 1 Lloyd's Rep. 156, 161.

[10] See p. 266, *post*.

[11] *Panoutsos* v. *Raymond Hadley Corp.* [1917] 2 K.B. 473.

[12] *W. J. Alan & Co. Ltd.* v. *El Nasr Export and Import Co.* [1972] 2 Q.B. 189, 212 (*per* Lord Denning) (C.A.).

[12a] Where the credit had to be confirmed by a first-class West European or U.S. bank, the fact that the opening of the credit was illegal under Turkish law (the law of the buyers) was immaterial because the sellers were not concerned with the machinery of providing the credit: *Toprak Mahsulleri Ofisi* v. *Finagrain Cie. Commerciale* [1979] 2 Lloyd's Rep. 98. 114.

[13] For examples, see *Cie Continentale d'Importation* v. *Ispahani Ltd.* [1960] 1 Lloyd's Rep. 293, 301; *Maran Road* v. *Austin Taylor & Co. Ltd.* [1975] 1 Lloyd's Rep. 156; *Discount Records Ltd.* v. *Barclays Bank Ltd.* [1975] 1 W.L.R. 315; *Trendtex Trading Corporation* v. *Central Bank of Nigeria* [1977] 2 W.L.R. 356; *E. D. & F. Man Ltd.* v. *Nigerian Sweets & Confectionary Co. Ltd.* [1977] 1 Lloyd's Rep. 50.

An application form for the opening of a credit issued by one of the principal banks in England states that "the irrevocable credit of . . . Bank is in most cases acceptable but occasionally a beneficiary requires the credit also to be confirmed by a bank in his own country."

While these credits are somewhat cheaper than confirmed credits, they have the disadvantage that they do not localise the performance of the contract of sale in the seller's country; if the correspondent bank refuses to pay on tender of the documents, the seller might be compelled to institute proceedings overseas—a situation which largely defeats the main purpose of the commercial credit.[14]

Revolving credits

Where the export sale is not an isolated transaction but the overseas buyer is a regular customer of the exporter, the buyer will arrange a revolving credit in favour of the latter. The buyer gives the bank standing instructions to arrange for a credit in favour of the exporter which at no time shall exceed a fixed maximum. The advantage of this arrangement is that no renewal is required and clerical labour is saved; a revolving credit is, *e.g.* a corollary of a sole distribution agreement.[15] The joint general manager of Lloyds Bank, when called in one case[16] as an expert witness to explain the meaning of this term, gave the following definition:

> A revolving credit is one for a certain sum which is automatically renewed by putting on at the bottom that which is taken off at the top. If you have a revolving credit for £50,000 open for three months to be operated on by drafts at 30 days' sight, as drafts are drawn they temporarily reduce the amount of the credit below the £50,000. As these drafts run off and are presented and paid they are added again to the top of the credit and restore it again to the £50,000. That is what is known technically as a revolving credit, and it is automatic in its operation and does not need renewal.

Several varieties of revolving credit are in use.

Air waybill credits; packing credits; red clause credits

In an air waybill credit the parties have agreed that the correspondent bank shall pay, accept or negotiate[17] against the presentation of an air waybill, supported by other specified documents. The air waybill, unlike the bill of lading, is not a document of title. Neither the correspondent nor the issuing bank acquires under it the collateral security which it obtains if it receives a bill of lading. But the payment mechanism of the documentary credit can be made available even if the documents to be presented to the correspondent bank are of a character inferior to that of a document of title.

The packing credit, sometimes called anticipatory credit, is intended to assist the exporter in the production or procurement of the goods sold.

---

[14] Clive M. Schmitthoff, "Confirmation in Export Transactions" [1957] J.B.L. 17.
[15] See p. 153, *ante*.
[16] *Nordskog* v. *National Bank* (1922) 10 Ll.L.R. 652.
[17] See p. 256, *ante*.

Finance is here made available at a time prior to the shipment of the goods, and again against a document of lower order than the bill of lading. The bank is instructed to pay the purchase price, or part of it, on production of documents other than the shipping documents, *e.g.* on delivery of a warehouse receipt (evidencing that the goods are in existence), or a forwarding agent's receipt (acknowledging that the goods have been received into his custody), or a forwarder's certificate of receipt (FCR)[18] (affirming that the goods have been received for shipment or have been shipped), or an air dispatch registered post receipt.[19]

The packing credit is a convenient method of finance for the small exporter who is not conversant with shipping practice; if he, *e.g.* sells cloth ex London store and arranges that the purchase price shall be paid under a documentary credit against delivery of a forwarding agent's receipt, he is not concerned with the actual shipping arrangements which are made by the forwarding agent on instructions of the buyer. The buyer, on the other hand, is certain that the goods sold are no longer in the possession of the seller when receiving the purchase price. In more complicated transactions, which are nearer in nature to commercial credits proper, the bank when advising the exporter of the credit inserts the so-called *red clause*[20] into the letter of advice and is prepared to honour the exporter's sight drafts to a certain amount against production of the stipulated documents, *e.g.* the warehouse receipts; when the exporter ships the goods and delivers the shipping documents to the bank, he presents a draft for the purchase price less the amount received by way of advance.

Credits available on presentation of documents other than documents of title are arranged as unconfirmed, confirmed or revolving credits. In the case of a packing credit, the arrangement can be construed, in the eyes of the law, as an agreement that the payment of the purchase price and the delivery of the stipulated documents shall be concurrent conditions, or as an agreement that the buyer, through the bank, is to make an advance on the purchase price, the advance being payable on production of the stipulated documents but the purchase price being only payable on delivery of the proper shipping documents. These interpretations lead to different legal conclusions which, however, have not yet been considered by the courts.

Back-to-back and overriding credits

Back-to-back credits, also called countervailing credits, are mainly used in the *external trade* where a United Kingdom merchant buys goods in one overseas country and sells them in another, and in *string contracts*[21] where

[18] See p. 357, *post.*
[19] *Diamond Cutting Works Federation* v. *Triefus & Co. Ltd.* [1956] 1 Lloyd's Rep. 216.
[20] Gutteridge and Megrah, *loc. cit.*, p. 12. This clause is called the red clause because it was originally written in red ink.
[21] That type of trading is used particular often in the commodity trade but is also found in other trades, see Clive M. Schmitthoff, *The Sale of Goods* (2nd ed.), p. 181.

the same goods are sold or resold by several middlemen before being bought by the ultimate purchaser.

The characteristic feature of the back-to-back credit is that the confirmed credit opened by the ultimate purchaser in favour of his immediate seller is used by the latter as security for the credit which he has to open for his own supplier. If there are several middlemen, each will use the credit in his favour as security for the credit which he has to open for his predecessor in the chain of contracts until the first buyer in the chain opens a credit in favour of the original supplier. The terms of these credits are literally identical, except so far as relating to prices and invoices.

The easiest method of operating back-to-back credits is to have the various credits controlled by the same bank but they can also be operated when several banks are concerned. Back-to-back arrangements can also be operated by means of a transferable credit[22] or by combining a documentary credit with a collection arrangement.[23]

Of particular importance in these arrangements is the confirmed credit to be opened by the ultimate purchaser. That credit, known as the *overriding credit*, is, as the middlemen are usually aware, the foundation on which the whole financial structure of the arrangement rests. For that reason the courts pay special attention to the terms of that credit if issues involving the whole chain of contracts arise.[24]

Transferable and divisible credits

A more popular method of financing the supply transaction than the back-to-back credit is the growing practice of making a credit transferable and sometimes likewise divisible.[25] The Uniform Customs provide in Article 46(*e*) that a transferable credit is automatically divisible, provided that partial shipments are not prohibited.

A documentary credit is not in the nature of a negotiable instrument. The correspondent bank is not authorised, unless receiving instructions to the contrary, to make finance available under the credit to *any* person satisfying the conditions of the credit; indeed if it paid on tender of the stipulated documents by a person other than the named beneficiary (or his agent) it would contravene its mandate.

It if is intended to make the benefit of the credit available to a person other than the named beneficiary, two possibilities exist: the assignment of the benefit of the credit and the transfer of the credit as such with its attendant rights and duties. These two possibilities require separate consideration.

---

[22] See below in text.

[23] See p. 268, *post*.

[24] *Ian Stach Ltd.* v. *Baker Bosley Ltd.* [1958] 2 Q.B. 130, 138; *Baltimex etc.* v. *Metallo Chemical Refinery Co. Ltd.* [1956] 1 Lloyd's Rep. 450, 455.

[25] See *e.g. Ian Stach Ltd.* v. *Baker Bosley Ltd.* [1958] 2 Q.B. 130; *W. J. Alan & Co. Ltd.* v. *El Nasr Export and Import Co.* [1972] 2 Q.B. 189.

A documentary credit is a thing in action[26]; where it is a confirmed credit under which a banker promises the seller payment upon the delivery of specified documents it is a conditional debt of the banker, *viz.* a debt subject to the condition precedent that the seller tenders the stipulated documents. The seller can assign this conditional debt, *viz.* the benefit accruing to him under the credit, without authority of the buyer or the correspondent bank, even though the credit is not advised to be transferable or assignable, provided that he complies with the requirements laid down for the assignment of things in action in section 136 of the Law of Property Act 1925, which are that the assignment has to be absolute and not in part, that it has to be in writing under the hand of the assignor, and that notice in writing of the assignment must be given to the debtor, *viz.* the bank. The assigned debt continues to be conditional and the condition can only be discharged by the seller (or his agent) but not by the assignee. That condition constitutes a *liability* which, according to general principles of law, cannot be assigned without consent of the other party, *viz.* the bank which, in that respect, has to act on the instructions of its principal, the issuing bank or the buyer. The assignability of the benefit of a commercial credit can be excluded by a term to that effect in the credit. The usefulness of an assignment of the benefit of a credit is limited to the cases in which the seller himself intends to ship and to present the documents to the bank.

Other, less formal, methods of making the benefit of the commercial credit available to the supplier are likewise in use. In *Trans Trust S.P.R.L.* v. *Danubian Trading Co. Ltd.*[27] the position was this: A gave B an option to buy; B sold to C; C sold to D. In the contract of sale between B and C, the latter undertook to procure a credit to be opened by D in favour of A, and B undertook to refund to C the difference between C's buying price and selling price which was thus disclosed to B. When D failed to open the credit, C was held to be liable to B for loss of profit.

A mere undertaking by the seller that he will pay the supplier out of the proceeds of the credit to be opened by the buyer affords little security to the supplier. This may operate as an equitable assignment but even if the seller notifies the bank of it, his interest in the credit may be defeated by a subsequent fraudulent transfer of the credit (if it is transferable) or a legal assignment of the benefit under it. Mere instructions by the seller to the bank to pay over the credit (or part of it) to the supplier on presentation of the proper documents by the seller likewise do not protect the supplier because they can be countermanded by the seller.

The transfer of the credit as such is very different from the assignment of the benefit under it. It means that the seller transfers the rights and at least certain of the duties arising under the credit to another person, usually his supplier, in such a manner that that person steps into the credit and

---

[26] *Per* Denning L.J. in *Trans Trust S.P.R.L.* v. *Danubian Trading Co. Ltd.* [1952] 2 Q.B. 297, 305.

[27] [1952] 2 Q.B. 297.

in advance is assured payment out of funds made available by the ultimate buyer, provided that the conditions of the original credit are complied with. This is the type of arrangement which businessmen have in mind when they make a credit transferable. From the legal point of view, such an arrangement is in the nature of a novation. It requires the consent of the buyer (who is not obliged to provide a transferable credit unless he has agreed to do so) and of the issuing bank; the credit should be stated in terms to be transferable. Where a credit is made transferable, it can normally be transferred once only and, if it is issued under the Uniform Customs, to a person who resides in the same country as the original beneficiary or another country, unless the credit specifically states otherwise.[28]

A transferable credit to which the Uniform Customs apply is, as already observed,[29] automatically divisible, provided that partial shipments are not excluded.[30] A transferable credit governed by English law, which is not subject to this provision of the Uniform Customs, would not appear to be automatically divisible. If this effect is desired, the credit should, it is thought, expressly be made transferable and divisible.

The Uniform Customs provide in Article 46:

(*a*) A transferable credit is a credit under which the beneficiary has the right to give instructions to the bank called upon to effect payment or acceptance or to any bank entitled to effect negotiation to make the credit available in whole or in part to one or more third parties (second beneficiaries).

(*b*) The bank requested to effect the transfer, whether it has confirmed the credit or not, shall be under no obligation to make such transfer except to the extent and in the manner expressly consented to by such bank, and until such bank's charges for transfer are paid.

(*c*) Bank charges in respect of transfers are payable by the first beneficiary unless otherwise specified.

(*d*) A credit can be transferred only if it is expressly designated as "transferable" by the issuing bank. Terms such as "divisible," "fractionable," "assignable" and "transmissible" add nothing to the meaning of the term "transferable" and shall not be used.

(*e*) A transferable credit can be transferred once only. Fractions of a transferable credit (not exceeding in the aggregate the amount of the credit) can be transferred separately, provided partial shipments are not prohibited, and the aggregate of such transfers will be considered as constituting only one transfer of the credit. The credit can be transfereed only on the terms and conditions specified in the original credit, with the exception of the amount of the credit, of any unit price stated therein, and of the period of validity or period for shipment, any or all of which may be reduced or curtailed. Additionally, the name of the first beneficiary can be substituted for that of the applicant for the credit, but if the name of the applicant for the credit is specifically required by the original credit to appear in any document other than the invoice, such requirement must be fulfilled.

(*f*) The first beneficiary has the right to substitute his own invoices for those of the second beneficiary, for amounts not in excess of the original amount stipulated in the credit and for the original unit prices stipulated in the credit, and upon such substitution of invoices the first beneficiary can draw under the credit for the difference, if any, between his invoices and the second beneficiary's invoices. When a credit has been transferred and the first beneficiary is

---

[28] The 1962 Revision admitted only the transfer to a person in the same country, unless the credit stated otherwise.

[29] On p. 263, *ante*.

[30] Uniform Customs, Art. 46(*e*). On the continent of Europe some, but not all, authorities take the view that, apart from the Uniform Customs, "transferable" includes the right to divide the credit between several sub-beneficiaries: Fernand Lison, "Crédits documentaires transférables" in *Revue de la Banque* (Belgium), 1952, pp. 1, 28.

to supply his own invoices in exchange for the second beneficiary's invoices but fails to do so on first demand, the paying, accepting or negotiating bank has the right to deliver to the issuing bank the documents received under the credit, including the second beneficiary's invoices, without further responsibility to the first beneficiary.

(*g*) The first beneficiary of a transferable credit can transfer the credit to a second beneficiary in the same country or in another country unless the credit specifically states otherwise. The first beneficiary shall have the right to request that payment or negotiation be effected to the second beneficiary at the place to which the credit has been transferred, up to and including the expiry date of the original credit, and without prejudice to the first beneficiary's right subsequently to substitute his own invoices for those of the second beneficiary and to claim any difference due to him.

A transferable credit can be used in a back-to-back arrangement in the following manner. Company A in country (A) sells goods to company B in country (B) and B undertakes to pay by an irrevocable and confirmed credit. Company B then resells the goods to company C in country (C), and C undertakes to pay B by another irrevocable and confirmed credit, which is made transferable and divisible. B then transfers to A the part of the credit opened by C which corresponds to the purchase price due to A. In such a case it is of the utmost importance that the credit of C is expressed in the same currency as that opened by B because otherwise currency fluctuations may affect the arrangement. In one case[31] the credit opened by B was expressed in Kenyan shillings and that opened by C in United Kingdom shillings. At the time of the transfer the two currencies were equivalent and company A did not object when the credit in United Kingdom currency was transferred to it. Later the United Kingdom currency was devalued but the Kenyan currency remained at its original value. The Court of Appeal held that by accepting the credit in the United Kingdom currency, company A had lost its right to claim payment in the undevalued Kenyan currency although the latter was the currency of account of the transaction.

Documentary credits and bank indemnities

Where the seller tenders non-conforming documents, as unfortunately sometimes happens, the correspondent bank, instead of refusing to accept the documents, as it is entitled to do, will ask the exporter to supply an indemnity and, on the strength of such indemnity, will make the credit available. Sometimes, where the correspondent bank is not identical with the exporter's bank, the correspondent bank asks for an indemnity by the exporter's bank. This procedure is adopted where there are discrepancies in the documents presented by the exporter and the instructions received by the correspondent bank, or when documents are presented after the expiry date of the credit and no arrangements have been made for its extension. An indemnity which the seller gives the correspondent bank cannot be transferred or extended by that bank to the issuing bank without consent of the seller.

[31] *W. J. Alan & Co. Ltd.* v. *El Nasr Export and Import Co.* [1972] 2 Q.B. 189. See also *Ets Soules et Cie.* v. *International Trade Development Co. Ltd.* [1979] 2 Lloyd's Rep. 122, 132.

Normally the bank points out to the exporter the irregularities which occasion the indemnity, and these irregularities are specified in the letter of indemnity which is sent to the bank. In some instances, however, indemnities are demanded which do not state the alleged irregularities but generally claim that the documents are not in conformity with the terms of credit. These indemnities import an element of uncertainty into the transaction which is unsatisfactory both from the point of view of the exporter and the bank. Besides, this practice shifts the burden of examining the documents from the bank to the exporter and, if it were to spread, would lead to laxity in the examination of documents by bankers and unnecessary litigation.

The exporter, when giving an indemnity to obtain finance under a documentary credit, should be aware that the bank may have recourse against him and may hold him liable on the indemnity[32]; he should, therefore, endeavour to settle the point, which has given rise to the discrepancy, forthwith by agreement with the overseas buyer.

An alternative to giving the bank an indemnity is for the seller to ask the correspondent bank to forward the documents as *collection under protection of the credit.* In that case the correspondent bank will pay the seller when the buyer has taken up the documents. This substitute arrangement, while avoiding the hazards of an indemnity by the seller, defeats completely the purpose of the documentary credit which the buyer was obliged to open.

If the buyer's refusal to amend the instructions to the bank is so serious as to amount to a repudiation of the buyer's undertaking to open the credit in accordance with the terms of the contract of sale, the seller has the further alternative of claiming damages from the buyer for breach of contract.

Short-circuiting of documentary credit

On principle, no short-circuiting

On principle, where the parties to the contract of international sale have arranged for the payment mechanism of a documentary credit, they must abide by their agreement and cannot short-circuit the credit by making direct claims connected with the payment of the price against each other. The documentary credit, said McNair J. in the *Soproma* case[33]

> is of mutual advantage to both parties—of advantage to the seller in that by the terms of the contract he is given what has been called in the authorities a "reliable paymaster" generally in his own country whom he can sue, and of advantage to the buyer in that he can make arrangements with his bankers for the provision of the necessary funds. . . .

For this reason McNair J. in the *Soproma* case regarded the second tender of documents by the sellers to the buyers as ineffective.

---

[32] *Moralice (London) Ltd.* v. *E. D. & F. Man* [1954] 2 Lloyd's Rep. 526.

[33] *Soproma S.p.A.* v. *Marine & Animal By-Products Corporation* [1966] 1 Lloyd's Rep. 367, 385; see p. 248, *ante*.

The conditional character of the credit

Exceptionally, however, the short-circuiting of the documentary credit is admissible. In the ordinary way the credit operates as conditional payment of the price; it does not operate as absolute payment.[34] If, *e.g.* the bank whom the parties have interposed as intermediary becomes insolvent, the seller normally can claim the price from the buyer directly, making a direct tender of documents to the latter.[35] The implied condition is discharged by the insolvency of the intermediary.

Thus, in one case[36] Nigerian buyers bought a quantity of sugar from London sugar merchants. Payment was to be made under an irrevocable documentary credit to be opened with Merchants' Swiss Ltd., a merchant bank most shares in which were owned by the Nigerian buyers. The credit was an acceptance credit providing for 90 days' drafts on the bank. The sugar was supplied and the buyers transferred the purchase price to Merchants' Swiss Ltd. Before the bank paid over the price to the London sellers, it went into a creditors' voluntary winding up. The sellers claimed the price from the buyers in arbitration in London which eventually resulted in court proceedings. Ackner J. held that the sellers could claim the price from the buyers although they had already transferred the money to the bank. Ackner J. said[37]:

> It follows from the finding that [the documentary credits] were given only as a conditional payment, that if they were not honoured the respondents' debt has not been discharged. This is because the buyers promised *to pay* by [documentary credits] not to provide by a [documentary credit] the source of payment which did not pay. . . . The respondents' liability to the sellers was a primary liability. This liability was suspended during the period available to the issuing bank to honour the drafts and was activated when the issuing bank failed.[38]

Other instances of short-circuiting

Similar considerations were applied in *Sale Continuation Ltd.* v. *Austin Taylor & Co. Ltd.*[39] In this case N, a timber exporter in Malaysia, used the services of A, the defendant, as selling agent for the sale of timber. A sold N's timber to G, a Belgian timber importer. Payment was arranged by a back-to-back arrangement[40] which consisted of a combination of an irrevocable credit and a collection arrangement. A Belgian bank was instructed to collect the price from G against the documents, and A, through the plaintiffs, an English merchant bank which acted as issuing

---

[34] *W. J. Alan & Co. Ltd.* v. *El Nasr Export and Import Co.* [1972] 2 Q.B. 189 (C.A.). Also *Maran Road* v. *Austin Taylor & Co. Ltd.* [1975] 1 Lloyd's Rep. 156, 159; *E. D. & F. Man Ltd.* v. *Nigerian Sweets & Confectionary Co. Ltd.* [1977] 2 Lloyd's Rep. 50. The credit constitutes absolute payment only if the seller stipulates, expressly or impliedly, that it should be so.

[35] *Soproma S.p.A.* case [1966] 1 Lloyd's Rep. 367, 386.

[36] *E. D. & F. Man Ltd.* v. *Nigerian Sweets & Confectionery Co. Ltd.* [1977] 2 Lloyd's Rep. 50.

[37] *Ibid.* p. 56.

[38] The fact that the parties had agreed on a particular bank as issuing and correspondent bank, did not convert the conditional obligation into an absolute one.

[39] [1967] 2 Lloyd's Rep. 403.

[40] See p. 262, *ante*.

bank in this transaction, opened a credit in favour of N, the seller, who drew a bill of exchange on the plaintiffs; that bill was accepted by the latter. The plaintiffs then passed the documents to A under a trust receipt, and A handed them to G who paid the purchase price to A and received the timber. The plaintiffs then became insolvent and dishonoured the bill drawn by N on them. A thereupon transferred the purchase price received from G directly to N. The plaintiffs sued A, claiming that they were entitled to the price and that N had merely a claim in their insolvency. Paull J. rejected the plaintiffs' argument and held that the defendant A had rightly transferred the purchase price directly to N. Since the plaintiffs had evinced the intention not to honour the bill drawn by N on them A was free from his obligation to put the plaintiffs in funds to enable them to meet N's bill. As to the effect of the trust receipt, N was entitled to cancel the contract of pledge of the documents with the plaintiffs when the latter intimated that they would not honour his bill. No doubt, this decision of Paull J. is clear common sense.

Fraud affecting documentary credits

In the case of a confirmed documentary credit the confirmation by the bank constitutes an absolute undertaking to provide finance if the conditions of the credit are satisfied.[41] The bank is not concerned with disputes which have arisen between the buyer and the seller. The Uniform Customs state in General Provisions and Definitions, para. (*c*):

> Credits, by their nature, are separate transactions from the sales or other contracts on which they may be based and banks are in no way concerned with or bound by such contracts.

Difficulties arise, however, where fraud is alleged, *e.g.* the buyer alleges that the seller has shipped rubbish instead of conforming goods or has shipped no goods at all. Here the following distinction has to be drawn. Where there is only a unilateral allegation of fraud, the bank has to pay because, in the words of Megarry J.,[42] "I would be slow to interfere with bankers' irrevocable credits, and not least in the sphere of international banking, unless a sufficiently grave cause is shown." But if it is clearly established to the satisfaction of the bank that a fraud occurred, the bank should refuse to honour the credit because "fraud unravels all."[43] The bank is not obliged actively to ascertain whether the alleged fraud can be proved; it may adopt a passive attitude and evaluate the evidence tendered by the buyer.

The position of the bank with respect to the allegation of fraud is the same as has already been discussed in connection with on demand bonds.[44]

[41] *Hamzeh Malas & Sons* v. *British Imex Industries* [1958] 2 Q.B. 127; see p. 259, *ante*.
[42] In *Discount Records Ltd.* v. *Barclays Bank Ltd.* [1975] 1 W.L.R. 315, 320. See also *Etablissement Esefka International Anstatt* v. *Central Bank of Nigeria* [1979] 1 Lloyd's Rep. 445 and *The American Accord* [1979] 1 Lloyd's Rep. 267.
[43] *Szteijn* v. *J. Henry Schroder Banking Corporation* (1941) 31 N.Y.S. 2d, 631, 634.
[44] See p. 84, *ante*.

Negotiation of Bills by Exporters

It is vital for the exporter as for every other business man to turn over his capital as quickly as possible. The exporter therefore frequently asks his bank to make an advance on the security of a documentary bill handed to the bank for collection or to discount or purchase bills which he is entitled to draw on a correspondent bank under an acceptance credit opened by the buyer.

In the case of advances, specific advances against individual bills are distinguished from general overdrafts allowed on security of a steady flow of bills for collection held by the bank. These advances are in law in the nature of bankers' loans to customers[45]; in case of the exporter's failure, the bank would be in the position of a secured creditor in respect of the documentary bills held by it and the proceeds thereof.

Where the buyer has agreed to pay the purchase price under a documentary credit, the exporter who wishes to obtain finance before delivery of the shipping documents to the correspondent bank might negotiate the draft drawn on the buyer or the bank to another bank[46] for cash. Here bankers distinguish two transactions: bills are said to be discounted where the exporter (drawer) pays the bank's interest; and they are said to be purchased where the drawee pays the bank's interest and the exporter receives the nominal value of the bill. Whether a bill is purchasable or discountable depends on the clauses in a bill.[47] The rates of discount are here of great practical importance.

In law no difference is drawn between purchased and discounted bills. They are both negotiated to the bank by indorsement and delivery of the bill, and in both cases the bank is entitled to have recourse to the drawer. Where the circumstances under which a documentary credit has been opened allow the inference that the exporter may negotiate drafts, the purchaser of such drafts takes the drafts subject to the conditions of the credit and can claim acceptance from the correspondent bank only if the terms of the credit have been complied with. In particular, the purchaser of a bill drawn under an unconfirmed credit cannot sue the correspondent bank if, having been informed of the cancellation of the credit, it refuses to accept the bill. To hold otherwise would enable the exporter to convert an unconfirmed credit into a confirmed credit by negotiating the draft to a third person.

Merchant Finance for Exports

In addition to the financing methods described in the preceding sections, a variety of other financing procedures is used in modern export trade. They have in common that finance is made available by merchant banks

---

[45] *Plein & Co. Ltd.* v. *Inland Revenue Commissioners* (1946) 175 L.T.Rep. 453.

[46] On negotiation credits where the correspondent bank is authorised to negotiate the bill drawn by the seller, see p. 256, *ante*.

[47] See p. 239, *ante*.

or finance houses. Two of these additional financing methods call for treatment here, *viz.* non-recourse finance and factoring services.

Non-recourse finance

This type of finance occupies a half-way position between the facilities offered by the confirming house[48] and by the confirming bank under a documentary credit.[49] The typical transaction of this kind differs from the activities of a confirming house in so far as the finance house does not undertake to export the goods and does not concern itself with making arrangements for shipment, insurance or export documentation; and it differs from the position of the confirming bank in so far as the exporter is not required to undertake personal liability as the drawer of a bill of exchange, so that in case of dishonour of the bill by the overseas buyer the finance house has no recourse to the exporter.[50] Consequently, in this type of transaction the finance house accepts the financial risk of the transaction. This arrangement offers the exporter very real advantages.

The terms on which finance houses make non-recourse finance available differ considerably and the rights and obligations of the exporter depend largely on his arrangement with the finance house. In a typical non-recourse transaction—always bearing in mind that other arrangements are possible—the finance house enters into two contracts, one with the exporter and the other with the overseas buyer.

In the contract with the exporter the finance house undertakes to pay him at once the purchase price in full, less a deposit paid by the overseas buyer to the exporter,[51] such payment to be made on delivery of specified shipping documents to the finance house. Some finance houses, but not all, undertake this liability only after the name of the buyer is disclosed to them and they are satisfied as to his financial standing. Normally the finance house itself is covered by an Export Credit Guarantees policy[52] and further agrees in its contract with the exporter to relieve him of the credit and political risk attending the transaction, as far as it is itself covered by that policy.[53] The contract will then contain a clause making it clear that the finance house is not involved in the goods aspects of the transaction, *e.g.*—

> We shall not be responsible for any claim arising out of or in connection with your transactions with the buyer, on whatever legal ground such claim may be founded or whether it is for loss, damage or otherwise or made by you against the buyer or by the buyer against you.

---

[48] See p. 173, *ante*.
[49] See p. 257, *ante*.
[50] Under the terms of his contract with the finance house, the exporter will, however, be liable to the finance house if the buyer refuses to pay for reasons for which the exporter is responsible *e.g.* if he has supplied goods not conforming to the contract.
[51] The payment of such a deposit is normal in this type of transaction.
[52] See p. 282, *post*.
[53] The policy must not be disclosed to the buyer.

The contract also provides for a particular and a general lien in favour of the finance house, for the application of English law and for London arbitration.

The second contract relating to the same transaction is concluded between the finance house and the overseas buyer. This contract provides an obligation on the part of the buyer to pay to the finance house the purchase price and the charges of the finance house, less the deposit paid directly to the exporter; usually the buyer, on presentation of the shipping documents to him, has to accept drafts drawn on him by the finance house; this procedure enables the finance house to grant the buyer credit or to accept instalment payments from him. The contract does not, of course, refer to the ECGD policy of the finance house. Some finance houses request an indemnity from the buyer and ask for an affirmation that he has any necessary import licences and exchange control permissions for transfer of funds to the finance house. In other respects the contract with the buyer contains similar clauses to those with the exporter.

Factoring services

The essence of export factoring is that a finance house, called the factor, agrees to relieve the exporter from the financial burden of the export transaction, in particular the collection of the price due from overseas buyers, so that the exporter can concentrate on his real business, the selling and marketing of his products.[54] Unlike the facilities of non-recourse finance, the shipping documents are not passed from the exporter to the finance house but made available by him directly to the overseas buyer. There exist two types of export factoring, the open and the undisclosed factoring. In both cases the export factor is not a factor in the legal sense.[55]

The open factoring transaction[56] is carried out in this manner. The factor enters into a contract with the exporter whereby he agrees to purchase from him his short-term debts owed by the overseas buyers. When the exporter sells goods abroad, the claim for the price is assigned to the factor and the overseas buyer is asked to pay to him; the buyer is thus informed of the fact that the price shall not be paid to the exporter; thus so far the position is similar to that of non-recourse finance but the legal construction is different. The factor further takes over from the exporter the operations previously handled by the exporter's credit control, sales accounting and collection departments; in practice, the exporter passes duplicate invoices to the factor to enable him to carry out these activities. Internally, *i.e.* in the relationship between the factor and the exporter, several arrangements are possible. The exporter may wish to make use only of the price collection services, or he may also wish to obtain finance. In the former case the factor makes payment to the exporter on a calculated average settlement

[54] Mocatta J. in *Hamilton Finance Co.* v. *Coverley Westray and Another* [1969] 1 Lloyd's Rep. 53, 58, described the expression "factoring" as somewhat confusing.

[55] See p. 171, *ante*.

[56] T. G. Hutson, "Factoring," *Journal of the Institute of Bankers*, February 1965, p. 69.

date; the exporter thus receives a single assured payment regularly on a specified date, instead of a number of small payments spread over an indefinite period. Payment by the factor is on a non-recourse basis and, from the exporter's angle, bad debts are eliminated. If the exporter wants the factor to finance the transaction, in addition to providing collection services, the factor will make an immediate payment to the exporter, usually up to 90 per cent. of the book value of approved invoices, while extending his credit to the overseas buyer. Here again, the whole credit risk is assumed by the factor and the payment to the exporter is on a non-recourse basis. Since the leading factors have international correspondents, overseas buyers can make their payments to these correspondents in their own countries in their own currency. The factor selects the exporters whom he accepts as clients with great care. He claims a commission on the basis of the whole business transacted by him for the exporter, and if he provides immediate finance in addition to his collecting services a charge will be made which varies with the money rates and is usually 1½ to 2 per cent. per annum above the lending rate.[57]

In the case of undisclosed factoring, the exporter sells the goods to the factor for cash, and the factor, as undisclosed principal, resells them through the exporter as agent to the overseas customer on a credit basis. The latter, who is unaware of the factor, pays the price to the exporter, who, as agent, passes it on to the factor. Undisclosed factoring is normally more expensive for the exporter than open factoring.

Factoring should be of interest to exporters of merchandise which is sold on reasonably standard terms in fairly wide markets, such as textiles, electrical equipment, toys, hardware. It is generally not suitable for goods specially made or requiring intricate negotiations and extended credit terms. The business consideration which underlies factoring is that, from the viewpoint of the factor, it might be safer to extend credit to a multitude of small debtors spread over many countries than to a single exporter in his own country.

---

[57] In an open factoring transaction, if the contract between the factor and the exporting company provides that any payment made direct to the latter is to be held in trust for the factor, the director of the exporting company commits the tort of conversion and has to refund such payment to the factor if, on receipt of such payment, he puts it into the company's account: *International Factors Ltd.* v. *Rodriguez*, [1978] 3 W.L.R. 877.

Chapter 22

EXPORT CREDITS GUARANTEES

The Government provides insurance facilities covering risks which are peculiar to export transactions but are not normally covered by commercial insurance. The legislative basis for these so-called export credits guarantees [1] is the Export Guarantees and Overseas Investment Act 1978.

The Act authorises the Secretary of State, after consultation with the Advisory Council, to give *export guarantees* to an amount of 25,000 million pounds, and, in respect of foreign currency transactions, an amount of 10,000 million special drawing rights. Export guarantees are given for "the purpose of encouraging trade with other countries," [2] and this definition includes any transaction involving a consideration in money or money's worth accruing from a person trading outside the United Kingdom, the Isle of Man and the Channel Isles to a person trading in the United Kingdom, the Isle of Man or the Channel Isles,[3] whether the transaction concerns "visible" or "invisible" exports or the external trade. Guarantees are available to and for the benefit of persons carrying on business [4] in the United Kingdom "in connection with the export, manufacture, treatment or distribution of goods, the rendering of services or any other matter which appears to the Secretary of State conducive to the purpose of encouraging trade with other countries" [5] and to companies directly or indirectly controlled by any such person.[6]

The Secretary of State is further authorised by the same Act to give *guarantees in the national interest* for such purposes and "for the purpose of rendering economic assistance to countries outside the United Kingdom." [7] These guarantees are likewise available to, and for, persons carrying on business in the United Kingdom, the Isle of Man and the Channel Isles and their overseas and other subsidiaries.

The Secretary of State may also, with the consent of the Treasury, make arrangements for the purpose of insuring investment overseas against the risk of war, expropriation, restrictions on remittances and such other risks as appear to the Secretary of State not to be commercial risks.

The Export Credits Guarantee Department

The administration of the scheme of export credits guarantees is in the

[1] "Guarantee" includes any contract to indemnify: see s. 15(1) of the Act of 1978.
[2] s. 1(1).
[3] s. 15(5).
[4] "Business" includes a profession: s. 15(1).
[5] s. 1(2).
[6] s. 15(4).
[7] s. 2.

hands of the Export Credits Guarantee Department which is in law a separate government department under the Secretary of State for Trade.[8] The insurance facilities offered by the Department are extensive and enable the exporter to eliminate export risks which are not covered by the usual marine and war risk policies. The premium rates charged by the Department vary according to the risks involved and to the countries to which the export is intended. As the Department does not aim at making a commercial profit but merely at paying its way, actual premium rates are moderate. An exporter will find it easier to obtain advances from his bank for exports insured with the Department than if the transactions are not so covered. Where the Department issues one of its Bankers' Guarantees to a policy-holder's bank, the bank will provide finance at a lower interest rate than otherwise.

Exporters may approach the Export Credits Guarantee Department either directly through one of its branch offices or through insurance brokers. By completing the appropriate proposal form, the exporter can obtain a quotation for the premium rates applicable to his class of business, free of charge and without an obligation to conclude an insurance. The headquarters of the Export Credits Guarantee Department are at Aldermanbury House, Aldermanbury, London, EC2P 2EL, and the department has regional offices in the main industrial centres.

Insurance Facilities offered by the Export Credits Guarantee Department

It is not the function of the Department to compete with commercial insurers. Most policies issued by the Department provide that the Department shall not be liable for loss in respect of any risk which, at the date when the export contract is made, "can be insured with any other government department or is normally insured with commercial insurers."

Insurance facilities offered by the Department are available on a "declaration" basis where the overseas buyer is granted a short-term credit, normally not exceeding six months and this form of cover is extended by a supplemental guarantee for credit of up to 5 years, or in exceptional cases even longer, for engineering goods involving a recurring pattern of trade; for capital goods, constructional works or projects falling outside any regular pattern specific policies are available covering single contracts. In addition other types of direct guarantees are available to banks providing finance for exports.

Short-term credits

These credits are normally covered by a standard policy, the *Comprehensive Short Term Guarantee*: (*Comprehensive ST Guarantee*).

---

[8] s. 12(1).

This standard policy covers, in principle, the whole overseas trade of the exporter[9] on "cash" or short-term credit (*i.e.* up to six months' credit). It is continuous, remaining in force until either ECGD or the exporter decides to terminate it, which either may do annually. The Comprehensive Guarantee protects the exporter from the time the goods are shipped to the time of receipt of payment, but can include the "pre-credit" risk as an optional extra. The basic policy is suitable for exporters who can readily dispose of the goods sold in the home, or other overseas, markets in the event of the original overseas buyer becoming insolvent or the performance of the export contract being impossible.

Extended terms

Over the years changes in credit terms have carried large categories of engineering goods outside the field of six months' credit normally covered by the Comprehensive ST Guarantee although the types of these goods and the size of the individual contracts would not make them eligible for individual "Specific Guarantees."[10] A Comprehensive ST Guarantee can be supplemented to cover this type of intermediate business transaction on terms of payment of up to five years' credit or sometimes longer, by a supplemental Extended Terms Guarantee.

The Comprehensive Short Term Guarantee

Under the basic guarantee the following causes of loss are covered:

R.01 The insolvency of the buyer;

R.02 The failure of the buyer to pay to the insured within six months after the due date of payment the amount owing in connection with goods delivered to and accepted by the buyer;

R.03 The failure or refusal of the buyer to accept goods despatched, where such failure or refusal does not arise from any breach of contract on the part of the insured:

Provided that this cause of loss shall not apply unless the insurer has stated in writing that he is satisfied that no useful purpose would be served by the institution or continuation of legal proceedings against the buyer;

R.04 A general moratorium decreed by the government of the buyer's country or by that of a third country through which payment must be effected;

R.05 Any other measure or decision of the government of a foreign country which in whole or in part prevents performance of the contract;

R.06 Political events, or economic difficulties, arising outside the United Kingdom or legislative or administrative measures taken outside the United Kingdom, being events, difficulties or measures which prevent or delay the transfer of payments or deposits made in respect of the contract;

R.07 The operation of a law (including an order, decree or regulation having the force of law) in the buyer's country which has the effect of giving the buyer a valid discharge of the debt under the law (not being a valid discharge under the proper law of the contract) for payments made notwithstanding that, as a result of fluctuations in exchange rates, such payments, when converted into the currency of the contract, are less than the amount of the debt at the date of transfer;

R.08 The occurrence outside the United Kingdom of war (including civil war, hostilities, rebellion and insurrection), revolution or riot, cyclone, flood, earthquake, volcanic eruption or tidal wave which in whole or in part prevents performance of the contract:

---

[9] This policy applies equally to confirming houses.

[10] See p. 281, *post*.

Provided that no liability shall arise under this cause of loss in respect of any risk which is normally insured with commercial insurers;

R.09 (i) The cancellation or non-renewal of an export licence; or

(ii) the operation, after the date of contract, of any law in the United Kingdom which prohibits or restricts the export of the goods to the buyer's country, other than the refusal to grant an export licence in relation to goods which on the said date of contract were subject to licence; or

R.10 Where in respect of any contract the insurer has stated in writing that—

(i) the buyer under that contract is a public buyer, or

(ii) he is satisfied, in the case of a guarantee of payment and indemnity for breach of that contract, that the giver of the guarantee and indemnity is a national government authority,

and the insurer has confirmed that this cause shall apply (subject only to such conditions as the insurer may think fit), the failure or refusal on the part of the buyer to fulfil any of the terms of that contract.

The percentages of the amount of any losses which are covered are:

90 per cent. in respect of causes of loss R.01, R.02 and R.03;

90 per cent. in respect of all other causes of loss where loss is ascertained under the pre-credit risk section;

95 per cent. in all other cases.

It should be noted that the guarantee does not give cover for loss sustained:

(*a*) by reason of any failure by the insured or by any person acting on his behalf to fulfil any of the terms and conditions of the contract or to comply with the provisions of any law (including any order, decree or regulation having the force of law) in so far as that law affects performance of the contract;

(*b*) by reason of the failure to obtain any import licence or any other authorisation necessary for the performance of the contract under any law (including any order, decree or regulation having the force of law) in force at the date on which the insurer's liability in respect of the contract commences under this guarantee;

(*c*) which provides that payment is to be made in a currency other than sterling if, on the date on which the insurer's liability in respect of that contract commences under this guarantee, the use of such currency for that payment would contravene any exchange control regulations in force at that date in the United Kingdom, the buyer's country, the country in whose currency payment is to be made, or any country through which under the terms of the contract payment is to be made;

(*d*) unless the insured gives to the insurer notice in writing of the insured's intention to make a claim in respect of the contract and states all available particulars of such claim within two years of the date of the occurrence of the cause of loss.

The insurer shall not, unless he otherwise agrees in writing (whether or not in a relevant section), be under any liability:

(*a*) in respect of any contract which does not specify—

(i) the nature and quantity of the goods sold or agreed to be sold, and

(ii) the terms of payment, and

(iii) the currency in which payment is to be made, being

a. sterling, or

b. any currency which, at the date on which the liability of the insurer in respect of that contract commences under this guarantee is specified in the Appendix of Overseas Currencies annexed to schedule 2, or

c. such other currency as may be agreed in writing by the insurer; or

(*b*) if the pre-credit risk section is applied to this guarantee, in respect of any contract in connection with which any goods have not been despatched within 12 months from date of contract; or

(*c*) in respect of any contract if the insured consents to any extension of a due date of payment under that contract without the insurer's prior agreement in writing:

Provided that unless the insurer otherwise states in writing, the insured shall be entitled in the event of need arising at or shortly before the original due date of payment to extend that due date of payment for a period not exceeding 90 days, except—

(i) in the case of a cash against documents, documentary sight draft or documents against payment transaction, or

(ii) where the insured has either in the contract or otherwise agreed in advance to any such extension; or

(*d*) in respect of any contract in connection with which goods are to be despatched to any person in any country other than the buyer's country:

Provided that this paragraph d. shall not apply where—

(i) under the terms of the contract, payment by the buyer is not dependent upon the goods being despatched to or imported into such other country and the cause of loss is specified in the relevant section and is either—

(a) cause R.09; or

(b) not such as prevent such despatch or importation; and

(ii) on the date on which the insurer's liability in respect of such contract commences under this guarantee, this guarantee is not excluded by reason of any special condition contained in schedule 2 from applying to all contracts made with buyers in such other country; or

(*e*) in respect of any contract under which payment is to be made from a country other than the buyer's country; or

(*f*) in respect of any contract in relation to which the relevant authorisation to import goods and to pay for them is made subject to conditions as to the export of other goods from any country or subject to conditions as to the payment for such other goods when so exported.

The policy contains detailed provisions regarding the ascertainment, payment and amount of loss, the payment of claims and the subrogation, after payment, of the guarantors to the rights of the exporter.[11]

The Comprehensive ST Guarantee contains a credit limit in respect of overseas buyers which shall determine the maximum amount as defined at any one time outstanding to which the guarantee shall apply in respect of goods sold or agreed to be sold on credit terms, after they have been delivered to and accepted by the buyer; and in respect of goods sold or agreed to be sold on payment terms of cash against documents, documentary sight draft, or documents against payment, after they have been placed at the buyer's disposal.

The amount of the *credit limit* for any particular buyer shall be:

(*a*) where the insured has made a single contract of not more than £250 in value with a buyer with whom the insured has made no previous contract and at the date of contract the insured is not aware of any circumstances which would make it undesirable for him to enter into such a contract with that buyer, £250, or

(*b*) the amount on such terms and conditions, if any, which may be—

(i) recommended in writing, not more than six months before the date of contract, or where the pre-credit risk section is not applied to this guarantee, the date of despatch of the goods, by a bank or credit information agency operating in the buyer's country or in the United Kingdom; or

(ii) justified by information in writing about the buyer and his financial condition obtained from such a source not earlier than the said six months, subject in either case to a maximum of such amount as may be stated in schedule 1 as the maximum discretionary limit, or, where no amount is so stated, £5,000; or

(*c*) the amount approved in writing by the insurer for the insured; or

(*d*) 25 per cent. more than the highest amount which has at any one time been owed by the buyer and has been paid to the insured during the two years preceding the date of contract or, where the pre-credit risk section is not applied to this guarantee, the date of despatch of the goods, no part of which was paid later than 60 days from the original due date of payment of that part, subject to a maximum of the greater of—

---

[11] On the right of the department to subrogation, see *Re Miller, Gibb & Co. Ltd.* [1957] 1 W.L.R. 703; p. 325, *post*.

(i) £20,000; and

(ii) 25 per cent. more than the amount of the currently valid credit limit approved by the insurer;

Provided that if any amount so paid was secured by an irrevocable letter of credit, an independent guarantor or other surety, such amount may be used for the purpose of establishing a credit limit under this paragraph (*d*), but only if the credit limit is subject to the same terms of security.

It follows that the exporter may grant, under (*b*) above, a reasonable credit to the buyer up to a fixed maximum without further reference to the department and under (*d*) above he may grant credit 25 per cent. over and above the highest amount he had had outstanding against the particular buyer previously, provided that such earlier debt has been paid satisfactorily.

Under the guarantee the exporter agrees to declare to the guarantors all contracts and exports made by him to which the provisions of the guarantee are, or may be, applicable including any insurance, freight and other charges paid by the exporter on the buyer's behalf; and all amounts which at the end of the previous month remained wholly or partly unpaid for more than three months from the original due date of payment in respect of exports previously declared.

The declarations are made on special forms which are simply constructed so that clerical labour is kept down to a minimum. An *Operational Guide*–form ECG 3001–is provided to each holder of an ECGD Comprehensive ST Guarantee.

The premium is payable on demand on each £100 of the face value of the contract or, as the case may be, on the gross invoice value of the exports to which the guarantee applies.

An invoice is sent to the exporter following each monthly declaration of contracts and exports.

A minimum premium of a stated sum is payable annually in respect of the guarantee; it is not returnable. This premium is determined by reference to the exporter's annual turnover and the use made by him of ECGD's credit limit services, but is not less than £50. The policy also contains in article 24 provisions relating to recoveries made by or on behalf of the insured. In one case[12] the Department covered by its policy an export to the United Arab Republic; the purchase price was payable in United States dollars. The policy provided that "any sums recovered in respect of a loss to which this guarantee applies," were to be divided between the Department and the insured in the proportion of 90 to 10.[13] The Government of the United Arab Republic imposed exchange control restrictions and the Department paid the insured 90 per cent. of the total price due to him. Later the currency restrictions were lifted and as in the meanwhile the

[12] *L. Lucas Ltd.* v. *Export Credits Guarantee Department* [1974] 1 W.L.R. 909.

[13] The policy in issue was an earlier version of the Department's Guarantee. The recovery clause in the current version is worded differently but the expression "loss" which was interpreted by the House of Lords in that case is retained.

pound sterling had been devalued, the exporter received a much higher amount in pounds sterling than the original purchase price of the goods. He paid back to the Department the sterling amount received from it but the Department claimed to be entitled to participate in the surplus (which remained after a deduction of 10 per cent. for the exporter) to the amount of 90 per cent. The House of Lords, interpreting the expression "loss" in the recovery clause, held that that expression denoted the sum of money which the exporter did not receive at the time when he should have received it, and decided that the exporter was entitled to retain the whole surplus.

Before the Department issues a guarantee the exporter must complete a proposal form stating details of his export transactions, in particular the various countries where his exports are directed, the value of exports and bad debt experience. He must also give the approximate number of overseas accounts and the credit limits of such accounts. The proposal forms part of the guarantee. Every guarantee issued states the maximum total liability which the department undertakes to guarantee.

Re-exports

Normally re-exports can be covered by indorsement under a Comprehensive ST Guarantee provided that the goods concerned do not compete with similar goods of United Kingdom origin.

Stocks held overseas

The Comprehensive ST Guarantee and the "pre-credit" variant may, by supplemental guarantee, also cover stocks of the exporter's goods held overseas by agents in readiness for quicker delivery to buyers. The cover provides against loss by confiscation of the goods held in stock, loss through civil disturbance or war or a ban on the re-export of the goods.

External trade

Where there is no conflict with British trade, a Comprehensive External Trade Guarantee covering external trade may be given by the Department. This usually applies to the merchanting trade of primary produce from one overseas country going direct to another (where the goods are not brought into the United Kingdom).

This guarantee provides cover from the date the goods are shipped from the country of origin, or can be extended to include the pre-credit risk.

Constructional and Engineering Works and Service Policies

As well as providing insurance against certain risks incurred in the sale of goods (visible exports) to overseas buyers, ECGD offers cover against the non-payment of earnings from the rendering of services to overseas principals. The classes of "invisible" exports coming under this heading are varied but include, for instance, constructional work on the building of bridges, dams, airfields, etc.; services of engineering and other consultants, etc., refits, conversions, overhauls and repairs; processing; hiring; sale or lease of "know-how," etc.

The services policy does not give cover for any loss due to the failure of the insured or the overseas principal to comply with any law of the United Kingdom or the principal's country relating to the performance of the service or making of payment in respect of it, and further does not give cover in cases where authorities have to be obtained and can be and are not obtained before the service is rendered, for the performance of the service and/or the making of payment in respect of it.

Services policies can be used to apply to individual transactions or a series of transactions under one or a number of contracts, depending upon the nature of the services involved.

The Constructional Works policies relate to contracts which provide for both the supply of goods and the performance of services. These policies have been drafted to provide for business done under the standard Conditions of Contract (International) recognised by the Export Group for the Constructional Industries, although they may be modified to other contracts. Cover is given on a "Specific" basis.

Medium and long-term credits

To cover against loss in the "capital goods field" the Department provides the *Specific Guarantee*: the terms of payment involved are unusually long. Terms of payment under the Specific Guarantee may extend to 10 years from completion, or 15 years from date of contract but five years from completion is more normal. The insurance can run from the date the export contract is completed until the date of final payment or alternatively (and at cheaper rates of premium) from the time the goods are shipped overseas until the time of receipt of final payment. Unlike the guarantees for short-term credit (where the exporter must insure the whole of his export trade or a good selection of it) the Specific Guarantee is given for an individual contract.

Where the buyer is an overseas government, the guarantee can be extended to cover the buyer's failure or refusal to fulfil the terms of the contract provided such action does not arise from any breach of contract on the part of the exporter.

Alternatively, long-term credit for capital goods may often be covered by a Buyer Credit Guarantee securing a loan direct to the buyer (p. 283, *post*).

ECGD and the provision of finance

The Department does not itself provide finance for exports, but it does assist an exporter to obtain the finance he requires in the following ways:

Hypothecation of insurance sum

By operating a simple form of hypothecation, rights to the proceeds of a valid claim can be transferred from the exporter to the financing bank. There are four ways in which this can be done: the first—by form ECG 3051—applies to individual transactions where the exporter's authority is required for each transaction for which finance is provided; the second—by form ECG 3055—covers all transactions on one or more named markets; the third—by form ECG 3053—relates to all transactions covered under the exporter's policy; and the fourth—by form ECG 3057—relating to transactions with a specific buyer. The procedure is for the exporter to complete and send to the financing bank the relevant "Letter of Authority" authorising ECGD to pay direct to the financing bank any moneys which may become due to him under his policy; the bank countersigns the form and forwards it to ECGD; the Department then returns the duplicate copy to the bank acknowledging the arrangement.

Direct guarantees to banks

The completeness of the protection afforded to the bank by assignment of a policy in this way is dependent on the extent to which the bank can rely on the exporter to perform the contract and comply with the conditions of the policy. Where the credit period is two years or more and particularly where the exporter is seeking finance from a specialist bank, the bank is likely to look for the security afforded by an *ECGD Bank Guarantee.* Such a guarantee is an undertaking given direct by ECGD to the financing bank, promising to make good 100 per cent. of any payment under the contract in question which is more than three months overdue, irrespective of the cause of non-payment. Such Bank Guarantees are operative from date of acceptance of the goods or works by the buyer. ECGD retains the right, wherever such a payment made against a Bank Guarantee would not have been made under its normal insurance cover, to take recourse against the exporter for the recovery of such amount.

A similar facility is available for business on credit up to two years from date of exportation secured by buyers' bills of exchange or promissory notes and for business on cash against documents terms or short-term credit (180 days credit from receipt of goods) not secured by bills of exchange or promissory notes.

In either case the exporter must provide the bank with specified documents proving shipment, and a warranty that the transaction is covered by valid ECGD insurance. Where the business is on Open Account the exporter gives the bank his promissory note for repayment of the advance. Finance is available from approved banks in respect of ECGD insured business at favourable rates: 5⁄8 per cent. over base rate for terms of credit up to two years; a minimum of 7¼ per cent. for credit of two to five years; a minimum of 7½ per cent. for credit over five years determined case by case, and governed by international consensus guidelines on the category of the buyer's country as "relatively rich; intermediate; relatively poor." For trade with EEC countries on credit terms of two or more years the rate of interest is set by the financing bank.

Buyer Credit Guarantees

In many large contracts for which specific supplier credit insurance is available, exporters may prefer to negotiate on cash terms and arrange a loan to the buyer on repayment terms equivalent to the credit he might expect from the supplier. ECGD *Buyer Credit Guarantees* are available to banks making such loans in respect of contracts of £1 million or more. They are normally expressed in foreign currency usually in U.S. dollars.

Under a Buyer Credit Guarantee the overseas purchaser, out of his own resources, is normally required to pay direct to the supplier not less than 20 per cent. of the contract price, including an adequate down-payment on signature of the contract. The remainder is paid to the supplier direct from the loan made to the buyer or a bank in his country by a United Kingdom bank and guaranteed by ECGD, as to 100 per cent. of capital and interest, against non-payment for any reason. The contract may include some foreign goods and services, but the amount of the loan will normally be less than the British goods and services to be supplied.

The loan agreement covered by ECGD is separate from the contract of sale.

The contractual relationships involved are:

(i) a supply contract between the British supplier and the overseas buyer;
(ii) a loan agreement between a British lender and the overseas buyer or his bankers;
(iii) Buyer Credit Guarantee given by ECGD to the British lender, in consideration of
(iv) a premium agreement between the British supplier and ECGD.

The same favourable interest rates mentioned above apply to Buyer Credit Guarantees.

Foreign Currency Specific Bank Guarantee

This guarantee will enable export contracts concluded on a supplier credit basis—*i.e.* credit extended by the exporter to his overseas buyer—to be financed in foreign currency.

This guarantee is designed to help capital goods exporters who are recourse-worthy under supplier credit arrangements and who find supplier credit more appropriate to their business arrangements than buyer credit, or who are selling to those markets which prefer supplier credit. The guarantee is available for one-off United Kingdom export contracts with credit terms of two years or more in either US dollars or Deutsche marks. Contracts will normally be expected to be worth at least £1m.

Under the terms of the foreign currency specific bank guarantee ECGD undertake to continue funding a loan should the lending bank be unable to raise sufficient funds on the Euromarket. This funding agreement is in line with that given under foreign currency buyer credits.

Cover for lines of credit

Many governments, or government agencies contemplating, for example, an electrification scheme, farm mechanisation, or development of one or more industries prefer to arrange the credit facilities without at the same time committing themselves to any one supplier. To meet this need, and to promote openings for British goods generally, ECGD will in many cases guarantee a *line of credit* offered by a British bank to the government or agency, and in some cases to private sector institutions.

How these are arranged varies from case to case, but, typically, ECGD will give a Buyer Credit Guarantee to one British bank which will have secured the backing of other banks and will undertake to provide credit up to a specified amount in respect of contracts for British goods or services falling within the terms of the credit agreement. A terminal date is specified by which contracts must be placed to qualify for the credit, and the decision as to what contracts should be made use of the credit usually lies with the foreign government or agency.

In order that such agreements should not lead to any lengthening of credit terms they are usually limited to purchases of a capital nature and the lengths of credit for individual contracts are usually related to specified minimum contract values, sometimes down to £20,000. The amount to be paid on or before shipment and the extent to which local costs in the buyer's country may be financed are also specified.

Insurance for overseas investments

All companies carrying on business in the United Kingdom are in principle eligible for *cover for investment overseas*, but subsidiaries or branches of foreign companies are excluded. Investment is defined as a contribution of resources to an enterprise; this includes equity capital in the form of cash, plant or know-how, as well as loans to overseas enterprises and guarantees of such loans. To qualify for cover, the investment must be new and the investor must apply for cover before becoming irrevocably committed to it; existing investment does not qualify.

The United Kingdom investor is offered insurance against expropriation (including discrimination against the investor or the overseas enterprise), war damage (including damage from revolution or insurrection), and restrictions on remittances. No insurance is given in respect of the commercial risk of the investment. The standard commitment of ECGD is normally for 15 years for 90 per cent. of any loss arising in respect of the three risks covered. An overall maximum insured amount will be determined at the outset, within which the investor proposes a current insured amount at the beginning of each 12 months of the contract of insurance. The cover includes not only the initially invested contribution but also the earnings retained in the enterprise up to 100 per cent. of the initial contribution.

Cost-escalation cover

ECGD has the power to provide a measure of cover against United Kingdom cost increases on the eligible part of major capital goods contracts, or complete projects, worth at least £2 million, which have a manufacturing period of at least two years. Similar contracts for consultancy and other services may also be considered for this cover. Where a contract is for the supply of several similar units, in addition to meeting all the other access rules, each unit must be worth £500,000 or more. The scheme is not available for contracts with EEC countries.

To make it easier to establish how much of the basic United Kingdom costs are eligible for cover under the scheme, ECGD usually regards as eligible a standard proportion of these costs which it is intended should be incurred within the period of cover (excluding fixed price sub-contracts). For cash business this proportion is 75 per cent., for credit 70 per cent. ECGD and the exporter agree at the outset a threshold up to which increases in these eligible costs will be borne by the exporter or his buyer. ECGD then compensates for further increases in these eligible costs up to a maximum amount of annual increases—the ceiling on liability—which is also agreed at the outset. The band of cover above the threshold widens progressively as exporters choose higher thresholds; there is always a wider band of cover for cash than for credit business. Full details of the bands of cover, minimum acceptable threshold, etc., are available to exporters on request.

Performance bonds[14]

For contracts worth £250,000 or more on cash or near cash terms which are insured with ECGD against the normal credit risks, ECGD assists in suitable cases by providing support for the issue of performance bonds. ECGD does not provide the bonds, but gives support by means of an indemnity to a bank or surety company which is willing to issue the bond. Under its indemnity, ECGD is unconditionally liable to reimburse the bond giver in full for the amount of bond call.

Any payment by ECGD to the bond holder becomes the subject of a claim by ECGD against the contractor under a related recourse agreement. ECGD will refund the contractor if it is established that he is not in default under the terms of the contract, or that his failure to comply is due to specified causes outside his control.

ECGD can also give similar support for tender, advance payment, and progress payment bonds.

Cover against unfair calling of on demand bonds[15]

ECGD offers insurance to exporters against the unfair calling of on demand bonds raised without ECGD support. This cover is available for

[14] See p. 82, *ante*.
[15] See p. 84, *ante*.

any contract on cash or credit terms insured under a normal ECGD guarantee (except external trade and re-exports), provided the form of the bond is acceptable to ECGD and the buying country is considered suitable for this form of cover.

The insurance takes the form of an addendum to the basic guarantee. ECGD agrees to reimburse the exporter for 100 per cent. of any loss due to the calling of a bond if it is subsequently shown that the exporter was not in default in his performance of the contract, or if any failure on his part is due to specified events outside his control.

Project participants insolvency cover

British members of a consortium contracting overseas for a large project may be exposed to heavy losses which they are unable to bear arising from the insolvency of a member of a consortium.[16] ECGD can insure main contractors or consortium members participating in major export projects of £20 million or more for 90 per cent. of the loss arising from unavoidable costs, expenses or damages due to the insolvency of a sub-contractor or fellow consortium member. This facility is available to United Kingdom companies for joint venture or sub-contract relationships with either United Kingdom or non-United Kingdom companies in acceptable cases.

The main contractor or consortium member should nominate the amount and period for which cover is required. Since the liability of ECGD is related to the items for which the defaulting party is contractually liable, it is necessary for sub-contracts or joint venture agreements for which insurance is required to set out in detail all additional costs which would be faced by the contractor in completing an aborted contract.

Loss is ascertained on the basis of the expenditure incurred by the policyholder in continuing the sub-contract or work that would otherwise have been undertaken by the insolvent consortium member. Interim claims are accepted against an undertaking from the policyholder that amounts claimed are included in the ultimate claim lodged with the liquidator.

Joint and several cover

ECGD has also introduced a Joint and Several Facility, which is available selectively for such projects with a minimum contract value of £50 million, where they are judged to be of exceptional national interest. This will enable estimated sums in the tender price to cover such risks to be reduced to the level of the ECGD premiums, and thus make the bid more competitive.

The facility can be taken advantage of by main contractors in relation to United Kingdom sub-contracts amounting to 5 per cent. or more of the total project value, or it can be adapted to cover United Kingdom members

---

[16] See p. 206, *ante*.

of consortia or joint ventures. ECGD will indemnify the insured contractor against cost over-runs, which are judged by ECGD to be unavoidable and irrecoverable, incurred for reasons outside the insured's control in connection with sub-contracts. The causes of loss covered are:

default by an insured sub-contractor which necessitates termination of his sub-contract and completion of his work by a replacement sub-contractor at a total cost exceeding the original sub-contract price provided for in the tender price;

unavoidable additional cost incurred by the main contractor and attributable to an insured sub-contractor but not recoverable from him by reason of limitations imposed in his contract, other than that arising from an event occurring in the buyer's country.

The amount of ECGD's cover will be 80 per cent. of the admissible losses with a maximum liability of 20 per cent. of the total United Kingdom value of the project contract.

Unusually for ECGD, applications for this cover should be made to:

Overseas Project Group
Department of Trade,
1 Victoria Street, London SW1H 0ET

on an application form obtainable from that address.

This Group will select those projects suitable for this cover and pass them to ECGD for further consideration. A prerequisite of the issue of this facility is basic credit insurance cover with ECGD, which should be sought from ECGD in the normal way as early as possible in the negotiations.

CHAPTER 23

INSURANCE OF EXPORTS

IT is customary to insure goods sold for export against the perils of the journey. According to the method of transportation, a marine, aviation or overland insurance is effected.

The term "marine insurance" is somewhat misleading because the contract of marine insurance can, by agreement of the parties or custom of the trade, be extended so as to protect the assured against losses on inland waters or land which are incidental to the sea voyage.[1] In the export trade it is usual to arrange an extended marine insurance in order to cover the transportation of goods from the warehouse of the seller to the port of dispatch, and from the port of arrival to the warehouse of the overseas buyer.[2] Marine insurance is an institution of great antiquity; it was known in Lombardy in the fourteenth century, the first English statute dealing with it was passed in 1601, and Lloyd's Coffee House, the birthplace of Lloyd's London, is first mentioned in the records of 1688. The law relating to marine insurance is codified in the Marine Insurance Act 1906.[3] This enactment provides a standard policy, known as Lloyd's S.G. policy, which the parties may adopt if they so desire whether they insure the risk with underwriters at Lloyd's or elsewhere.

The International Chamber of Commerce has prepared a publication entitled *Tables of Practical Equivalents in Marine Insurance*, in which the similarities and differences existing in marine insurance terms, clauses and covers in 13 important centres of the world are analysed and compared from the marine insurance point of view.[4]

In the law relating to aviation or overland insurance no standard policy has been developed yet and Lloyd's S.G. policy is used with suitable alterations.

MARINE INSURANCE

Stipulations in the contract of sale

In an export transaction, the terms of the contract of sale provide normally whether the costs of marine insurance shall be borne by the seller or by the buyer. If the goods are sold on f.o.b. terms, these costs have to be paid by the buyer and that is even true if the f.o.b. seller, by request of the buyer, has taken out the policy.[5] If the goods are sold on c.i.f. terms,

---

[1] Marine Insurance Act 1906, s. 2(1), see p. 293, *post*.

[2] On the transit clause (incorporating warehouse to warehouse clause), see p. 310, *post*.

[3] References to sections on the following pages relate to this Act.

[4] The *Tables* are obtainable from the British National Committee, International Chamber of Commerce, 6–14 Dean Farrar Street, London SW1H 0DT.

[5] See p. 20, *ante*.

it is the duty of the seller to take out the policy and pay the costs of insurance.[6] In a c. and f. contract the seller need not insure, nor need the buyer (at whose risk the goods travel), but if the c. and f. contract contains a clause "insurance to be effected by the buyer" or a clause in similar terms, that will normally place the buyer under a contractual obligation to insure and has not merely declaratory effect, the obligation to insure is thereby "put into the reverse," and the buyer must take out the same policy which the seller would have been obliged to obtain if the contract had been a c.i.f. contract.[7]

The marine insurance policy forms part of the shipping documents.[8] Where goods are sold c.i.f. the seller is obliged to take out a marine insurance policy which provides cover against the risks customarily covered in the particular trade in respect of the cargo and voyage in question, but he is not required to do more.[9] He need not take out an all risks[10] policy unless the parties have agreed thereon or it is demanded by the custom of the trade.

The assured, the insurer and the broker

The parties to a contract of marine insurance are known as the assured and the insurer. Insurers are either underwriting members of Lloyd's or marine insurance companies. The "Society of Lloyd's" has underwriting and non-underwriting members. The former, known as the "names," form groups called "syndicates," which conduct the actual underwriting through an underwriting agent; every member of a syndicate is liable for a proportionate fraction of the risk, and thus the aim of all insurance is achieved, namely to spread the risk to many persons while, at the same time, providing indemnity for the assured if a loss occurs. The underwriting agent is usually, but not necessarily, a member of the syndicate or syndicates for which he acts. Insurance at Lloyd's is effected in "The Room," which is situate in London, and underwriting members accept only risks offered through Lloyd's brokers (who have access to The Room). A person who wishes to effect an insurance at Lloyd's has thus to employ the services of such a broker. The marine insurance companies have been early competitors of Lloyd's in the field of marine insurance, and can be approached directly or through an agent of the company (sometimes called an "underwriting agent" though his functions are different from those of an underwriting agent at Lloyd's), or through an insurance broker.

In the normal course of business the exporter, who wishes to have his goods insured, does not approach the insurer directly but instructs an

---

[6] See p. 28, *ante*.

[7] *Reinhart Co.* v. *Joshua Hoyle & Sons Ltd.* [1961] 1 Lloyd's Rep. 346.

[8] See p. 29, *ante*.

[9] In the cotton trade the ordinary insurance policy to be taken out under a c.i.f. contract includes "country damage," *i.e.* pre-shipment damage to the goods: *Reinhart Co.* v. *Joshua Hoyle & Sons Ltd.* [1961] 1 Lloyd's Rep. 346, 353.

[10] On the meaning of "all risks" insurance, see p. 316, *post*.

insurance broker to effect the insurance on his behalf. Where the exporter is the regular client of the insurance broker, he forwards his instructions on a form supplied by a broker and gives the required particulars on that form. The broker, who is usually authorised to place the insurance within certain limits as to the rates of premium, writes the essentials of the proposed insurance in customary abbreviation on a document called "the slip"[11] which he takes to Lloyd's or a marine insurance company. An insurer, who is prepared to accept part of the risk, writes on the slip the amount for which he is willing to insure and adds his initials; this is known as "writing a line." The broker then takes the slip to other insurers who successively likewise write lines until the whole risk is covered. It is important for the broker to secure a good "lead" because the second and following underwriters to whom the broker presents the slip are usually more ready to accept the risk if the lead is a well-known name.

When the risk is covered, the broker sends the assured a memorandum of the insurance effected which is conveniently executed on a duplicate form of the instructions. According to the nature of insurance which the broker was instructed to obtain, the memorandum assumes the form of a closed or open cover note.[12] A closed cover note is sent if the assured, in his instructions, has given full particulars as to cargo and shipment and the insurance has, thus, been made definite. An open cover note is sent if the instructions of the assured are so general and indefinite that further instructions are required from him to define the cargo, voyage or interest shipped under the insurance; this happens where the assured requires a "floating policy"[13] or an "open cover,"[14] or where he reserves the right to give "closing instructions."

The insurance broker should, as a matter of prudent business practice, notify the assured promptly of the terms of the insurance which he arranged for him and forward the cover note as soon as possible, but he is not under a legal duty to do so. In *United Mills Agencies Ltd.* v. *R. E. Harvey, Bray & Co.*,[15] the plaintiffs instructed the defendants, insurance brokers, to effect an open marine insurance on their goods, obtaining immediate cover. On April 2 the brokers reported that the cover was placed, and on April 4 they sent the assured the cover note which did not contain a clause covering the goods while at packers. In the night of April 4–5 goods of the value of £8,000 were destroyed by fire at a warehouse of packers. The action of the assured against the brokers for damages was dismissed. McNair J. held that the brokers had no knowledge that the goods in the hands of the packers were uninsured and that the brokers were not negligent by not insuring them in the hands of the packers or not informing the

[11] See p. 299, *post*.

[12] The open cover note should not be confused with the type of insurance known as the "open cover"; see p. 297, *post*.

[13] See p. 294, *post*.

[14] See p. 297, *post*.

[15] [1952] 1 T.L.R. 149.

assured that they had not so insured them.[16] The learned judge likewise rejected the contention of the assured that the brokers were under a duty to notify the assured at once of the terms of the insurance:

> It was, no doubt, prudent to do so, both to allay the client's anxiety and possibly to enable the client to check the terms of insurance, but that was very different from saying it was part of the broker's duty.

It may be added that at present no standard or approved clause has been devised to extend insurance cover while goods are in the hands of packers.

The position of the insurance broker is anomalous in two respects: he is normally the agent of the assured but is paid by the insurer.[17] Even more remarkable is the fact that he is personally and solely responsible to the insurer for payment of the premium[18] while, as between insurer and assured, by a legal fiction the premium is regarded as paid. The historical origin of the rule is that underwriting members of Lloyd's refused, at an early date, to deal with assured persons directly, and accepted insurances only from brokers whom they knew personally as financially trustworthy.[19] Today, the rule is laid down, in respect of marine insurance effected at Lloyd's or elsewhere, in the Marine Insurance Act 1906, ss. 53 and 54.

The anomalous position of the insurance broker, in the second respect mentioned above, has been repeatedly commented on by the Bench. Bayley J. said in an early case[20]:

> As between the assured and the underwriter the premiums are considered as paid. The underwriter, to whom, in most instances, the assured are unknown, looks to the broker for payment, and he to the assured. The latter pays the premium to the broker only, who is a middleman between the assured and the underwriter. But he is not merely an agent, he is a principal to receive the money from the assured, and to pay it to the underwriter.

The broker has a lien on the policy until the premium, commission and other charges due to him have been paid (s. 53(2)).

Kinds of marine insurance

(i) *Valued and unvalued policies*. The Marine Insurance Act 1906 distinguishes between valued and unvalued policies. A valued policy is a policy which specifies the agreed value of the subject-matter insured (s.

---

[16] If they had acted negligently, the result would have been different; see *Osman* v. *J. Ralph Moss Ltd.* [1970] 1 Lloyd's Rep. 313 where, in the case of motor insurance, it was held that the brokers were under a duty to advise and protect their clients; similarly *McNealy* v. *Pennine Insurance Co. Ltd.* [1978] R.T.R. 285 (C.A.); (likewise a case of motor insurance).

[17] On his duties as agent, see *Anglo-African Merchants* v. *Bayley* [1970] 1 Q.B. 311; *North and South Trust Co.* v. *Berkeley* [1971] 1 W.L.R. 470, 480. Exceptionally, he may be the agent of the insurer; see *Stockton* v. *Mason,* [1978] 2 Lloyd's Rep. 430 (which concerned a provisional motor insurance cover granted by the broker orally over the telephone).

[18] In *Wilson* v. *Avec Audio-Visual Equipment Ltd.* [1974] 1 Lloyd's Rep. 81, the insurance broker who had effected burglary and transit insurances was held to have no authority to pay the premium, but the case rests on its own very special facts; the assured had expressly revoked the authority to pay the premium to the insurers after they had become insolvent.

[19] See p. 289, *ante*.

[20] *Power* v. *Butcher* (1829) 10 B. & Cr. 329, 340.

27(2)); an unvalued policy[21] states merely the maximum limit of the sum insured and leaves the insurable value to be ascertained subsequently (s. 28).

The main difference between these two types of policy is that in the case of a valued policy the value fixed by the policy is, in the absence of fraud, conclusive of the insurable value of the subject insured (s. 27(3)), while in the case of an unvalued policy the value of the insured goods has to be proved by production of invoices, vouchers, estimates and other evidence. In the case of an unvalued policy, the insurable value of goods or merchandise is the prime cost of the goods, plus the expenses of and incidental to shipping and the charges of insurance upon the whole (s. 16(3)).

The difference between valued and unvalued policies is of great practical importance. In a valued policy, the buyer's anticipated profits are normally included in the value declared by adding a percentage, say, 10 or 15 per cent., to the invoice value and the incidental shipping and insurance charges of the goods. In an unvalued policy, the buyer's anticipated profits cannot be included in the insurable value.

In modern export practice, valued policies are the rule and unvalued policies are rarely used. This tendency goes so far that, in the case of floating policies and open covers where the assured cannot always declare the insurable value before arrival of the goods or notices of their loss, special provision is made for the valuation of such shipments.[22]

The difference between valued and unvalued policies is evident in various common Institute Clauses[23]; the exporter may, *e.g.* obtain cover under the

Institute Theft, Pilferage and Non-Delivery (Insured Value) Clause

or

Institute Theft, Pilferage and Non-Delivery (Shipping Value) Clause.

The "insured value" is the value specified in the policy; the "shipping value" is defined in identical terms with the definition of insurable value for unvalued policies, as set out in section 16(3).

If there is the possibility of rising market prices during the transit of the goods, the assured who has covered the goods under an ordinary policy can obtain a so-called "*increased value*" policy. Institute clauses in ordinary policies include often the following wording which takes this practice into account:

> In the event of any additional insurance being placed by the assured for the time being on the cargo herein insured, the value stated in this policy shall, in the event of loss or claim, be deemed to be increased to the total amount insured at the time of loss or accident. INCREASED VALUE POLICIES TO CONTAIN THE FOLLOWING CLAUSES: £ . . . being increased value of cargo to be deemed to be part of the total amount insured on the cargo valued at such total amount. . . .

---

[21] Unvalued policies are sometimes called open policies. This term should not be confused with the open cover; see p. 297, *post*.

[22] See p. 297, *post*.

[23] On Institute Clauses, see p. 308, *post*.

(ii) *Voyage, time and mixed policies*

Another classification of policies is into voyage, time and mixed policies (s. 25). Under a voyage policy the subject-matter is insured in transport from one point to another; under a time policy the subject-matter is insured for a fixed time. Under a mixed policy the subject-matter is insured both for a particular journey and a certain period of time.

In voyage policies great care should be taken to define exactly the moments when the risk commences and when it ceases. Where goods are insured "from the loading thereof," the risk does not attach until the goods are actually on board ship, and the insurer is not liable for them while they are in transit from the shore to the ship. This is expressly provided in rule 4 of the Rules of Construction of Policy in the First Schedule to the Marine Insurance Act 1906.[24] English law differs in this respect from that of almost all continental countries where the respective commercial codes lay down that the risk attaches at an earlier moment, sometimes when the goods leave shore, sometimes even when they are taken to the quay in order to be loaded.[25] The strictness of the English rule is mitigated by the general practice of inserting into the policy a clause covering the transit of the goods from the shore to the ship; the customary form of such clause is—

including risk of craft to and from the vessel.

The "transit" clause, by which marine insurance cover is extended to land risks incidental to the sea voyage and which is very common in export transactions,[26] naturally covers port risks and the risk of craft to and from the ship.

The rules defining the end of the risk are more favourable for the assured. The standard S.G. Policy provides that the goods shall be covered until "safely landed." This phrase is defined in rule 5 of the Rules for Construction of Policy as meaning that—

they must be landed in the customary manner and within a reasonable time after arrival at the port of discharge, and if they are not so landed the risk ceases.

According to Arnould[27]—

by "safely landed" is meant safely delivered on shore, at the ordinary wharves and quays or customary landing-places within the limits of the port of discharge. . . . It is frequently necessary to employ smaller craft such as lighters, shallops, etc., to carry the goods from the ship to the shore. Whenever it is established that such a usage exists by the general course of trade, the underwriters are liable for any loss or damage that may happen to the goods in the course of their being so carried; for they are being landed in the customary manner.

Here again, the "transit" clause provides protection; it covers the landing risks in the port of destination as part of the transit from the warehouse of the seller to that of the buyer.

---

[24] See Appendix 1, p. 484, *post*.
[25] Arnould, *The Law of Marine Insurance and Average* (British Shipping Laws, Vols. 9 and 10, 1961), para. 488, p. 462, n. (3).
[26] See p. 310, *post*.
[27] Arnould, *loc. cit.*, paras. 493 and 495.

Time policies[28] were rarely used in export transactions but are found more frequently in recent times. These policies may cover a period exceeding 12 months[29]; they often contain the "continuation" clause under which the parties agree that—

should the vessel at the expiration of this policy be at sea, or in distress, or at a port of refuge or of call, she shall, provided previous notice be given to the underwriters, be held covered at a *pro rata* monthly premium to her port of destination.[30]

Mixed policies are issued in the frequent instances where goods are insured under one of the Institute Cargo Clauses[31]; they include the transit clause which incorporates the warehouse to warehouse clause; this clause covers land risks incidental to the sea voyage.[32]

(iii) *Floating policies*

The floating policy lays down the general conditions of insurance, but not the particulars of the individual consignments intended to be covered. These particulars are usually unknown to the assured when effecting the insurance. Notwithstanding this element of uncertainty, the floating policy covers automatically all shipments made thereunder and the assured is obliged to "declare" the individual shipments to the insurer with due expedition. The floating policy might cover, say, shipments to stated destinations within 12 months to the aggregate amount of £50,000; when the assured ships and declares a shipment of £3,000, the available cover is reduced to £47,000, and when the policy is fully declared, it is written off.[33]

The use of the floating policy has diminished in recent years. Open covers have taken their place in many cases. Brokers have also effected time policies in their stead, and more recently the informal "slip" policy has taken the place of the floating policy in Lloyd's market.[34] A consideration of the floating policy is, however, still required because that type of policy forms the model on which the frequently used informal open cover is framed.

Under the floating policy it is usual to supply the assured with a book of declaration forms or certificates of insurance on which he declares the shipments as they go forward.

---

[28] For a discussion of the nature of a time policy, see *Compania Maritima San Basilio S.A.* v. *Oceanus Mutual Underwriting Association* (*Bermuda*) *Ltd.* [1977] Q.B. 49.

[29] s. 25(2) of the Marine Insurance Act 1906, which, on principle, prohibited time policies exceeding 12 months, was repealed by the Finance Act 1959, s. 30(5). S. 23(2) to (5) of the Marine Insurance Act 1906 was likewise repealed by s. 30(5) of the Finance Act 1959.

[30] Other forms of the continuation clause are in use; see Arnould, *loc. cit.*, para. 482. The continuation clause in the Institute Time Clauses makes the prolongation of the risk dependent on notice being given to the insurer.

[31] See p. 308, *post*.

[32] Stamp duties on insurance policies were abolished by the Finance Act 1970, Sched. 7, para. 1(2)(*b*) with effect from August 1, 1970.

[33] Arnould, para. 186.

[34] V. Dover, *A Handbook of Marine Insurance* (8th ed., London, H. F. and G. Witherby Ltd., 1975) p. 133.

The Marine Insurance Act 1906 contains, in section 29, the following provisions on floating policies:

1. A floating policy is a policy which describes the insurance in general terms, and leaves the name of the ship or ships and other particulars to be defined by subsequent declaration.
2. The subsequent declaration or declarations may be made by indorsement on the policy, or in other customary manner.
3. Unless the policy otherwise provides, the declarations must be made in the order of dispatch or shipment. They must, in the case of goods, comprise all consignments within the terms of the policy, and the value of the goods or other property must be honestly stated, but an omission or erroneous declaration may be rectified even after loss or arrival, provided the omission or declaration was made in good faith.
4. Unless the policy otherwise provides, where a declaration of value is not made until after notice of loss or arrival, the policy must be treated as an unvalued policy as regards the subject-matter of that declaration.

Unless the policy otherwise provides, the assured is bound to declare all cargoes within the terms of the policy. The insurer likewise cannot refuse an individual risk which falls within the terms of the policy though he is entitled to refuse a risk which the policy was not intended to cover, or a declaration which is made dishonestly. In the *Institute Standard Conditions for Floating Policies*[35] the mutual obligations of assured and insurer in respect of declarations are expressed in the following form:

It is a condition of this insurance that until completion of the contract the assured is bound to declare hereunder each and every shipment without exception whether arrived or not, underwriters being bound to accept same up to but not exceeding the amount specified therein.

By this precaution the insurer protects himself against the declaration of losses only. But the assured need not, and, in fact, sometimes cannot declare the shipment before the ship sails; as we have seen, the Act provides in section 29(3) that an omission or erroneous declaration may be rectified even after loss or arrival, provided the omission or declaration was made in good faith.

The floating policy often contains a clause obliging the assured to make declarations of shipment as early as possible. The following is a specimen of such a clause:

Declarations of interest to be made to insurer's agent at port of shipment where practicable or agent in London as soon as possible after sailing of vessel to which interest attaches.

It has been held[36] that an assured who, in breach of this undertaking, omitted to make a declaration at the earliest possible moment was not entitled to recover under the policy for loss suffered by him: the assured could not rely on section 29(3) because it was a case in which no declaration at all had been made within the express terms of the contract, and the insurer had, consequently, lost the opportunity of reinsuring the risk.

The floating policy is not a time policy but an aggregation of voyage policies. The asssured, who desires to avoid leaving some of his shipments

[35] On Institute Clauses, see p. 308, *post*.
[36] In *Union Insurance Society of Canton Ltd.* v. *George Wills & Co.* [1916] 1 A.C. 281.

unprotected, has to take out a further floating policy before the expiration of the current policy. This is a disadvantage of the floating policy because, if an assured forgets to take out a new policy the goods may travel uninsured. This disadvantage is avoided if an "always open" open cover is taken out. In the case of a floating policy, the new policy which follows the old one, contains the clause

to follow and succeed policy No. . . . dated . . . .

The meaning of this clause is, in the words of Lord Blackburn,[37] "there being consecutive policies any loss declared is to be borne first by the earlier policies, and that it is not till after the earlier policy is exhausted, either by losses or declared adventures which have come in safe, that the underwriters on the policy which follows are to bear the loss, if any."

The floating policy often contains a clause limiting the risk per vessel, *e.g.* a policy granting cover for a total of £50,000 may provide—

limit per bottom, £5,000.

The assured who wishes to ship in excess of the limit per vessel, should make arrangements for a separate additional cover prior to shipment.

The per bottom clause is regularly supplemented by a location clause by which the insurer restricts to a fixed maximum sum his liability for accumulation of covered risks in one locality. The location clause is invariably inserted by underwriters where insuring land risks incidental to sea transit. The following is an example of the location clause:

In the case of loss and/or damage before shipment to the insured interest in any one locality the underwriter, notwithstanding anything to the contrary contained in this contract, shall not be liable in respect of any one accident or series of accidents arising out of the same event for more than his proportion of an amount up to, but not exceeding, the sum of £ . . . . in all taken in conjunction with preceding and/or succeeding insurances. The conveyance of the insured interest upon interior waterways or by land transit shall not be deemed to be shipment within the meaning of this clause.

The individual location risk is often limited to the same amount as the per bottom risk. As a result of the location clause, if goods accumulated in one warehouse prior to shipment are destroyed by fire, the insurers are only liable to the sum stated in the location clause although the aggregate insurable value of the goods may far exceed that limit. Dover maintains[38] that the location clause limits only pre-shipment accumulations in one locality but not accumulations at the port of discharge or later; this view is supported by the present wording of the clause but the clause can, of course, be extended by agreement of the parties to limit the liability of the insurer for accumulations subsequent to the discharge from the overseas vessel.

---

[37] In *Inglis* v. *Stock* (1885) 10 App.Cas. 263, 269.
[38] V. Dover, *loc. cit.*, p. 294, *ante*.

The premium is often arranged at fixed rates for specified kinds of goods, *e.g.* textiles, hardware, motor-cars, etc. Sometimes a "held covered" clause[39] is added providing:

other interests held covered at rates to be arranged.

The floating policy is normally a valued policy. It often contains the following clause about the declaration of value which the assured has to make when declaring the particulars of shipment:

goods and/or merchandise and/or interest to be hereafter declared and valued at invoice price and charges plus 15 per cent.

The Act provides that, where a declaration of value is not made until after notice of loss or arrival, the policy must be treated as unvalued unless it contains special provisions for this contingency (s. 29(4)). This means that the consignment would have to be valued in accordance with section 16(3),[40] but it is nowadays usual for policies to contain special provisions for the valuation of the insured interest in case of belated declarations.

The assured should consider carefully whether, in the circumstances of the contemplated journey of the goods, special protection is required covering transhipment risk. In the absence of a special transhipment clause, the underwriters are exempted from liability where the goods are transhipped from one ship to another without their consent or without necessity because the risk has been changed. This rule applies even if the substituted ship is stronger or bigger than the former ship,[41] but transhipment does not determine the liability of the underwriters if it was necessitated by a peril insured against (s. 59).

(iv) *Open covers*

The open cover, combined with the issue of insurance certificates, has become the most common and most popular form of insurance used in the export trade. The open cover is another method of effecting a general insurance for recurring shipments, the details of which are unknown when the insurance is taken out. This method resembles, in many respects, the floating policy; in particular, the assured is likewise bound to declare all individual shipments effected thereunder unless the contract of insurance otherwise provides.

The open cover, like the slip,[42] is not an insurance policy but is a document by which the underwriter undertakes subsequently to issue duly executed floating or specific policies within the terms of the cover. Before the abolition of stamps on marine insurance policies with effect from August 1, 1970,[43] the open cover did not require stamping while a floating policy required a 6d. stamp. Open covers sometimes embody the *Institute*

[39] The "held covered" clause is discussed on p. 303, *post*.
[40] See p. 292, *ante*.
[41] Arnould, *loc. cit.*, paras. 247–249.
[42] See p. 299, *post*.
[43] See p. 294, n. (32), *ante*.

Standard Conditions for Open Covers[44] which are identical in wording with the Institute Standard Conditions for Floating Policies, except that they use the words "open cover" instead of "floating policies."

The open cover may be limited in time or may be permanent while the floating policy is normally limited to twelve months. Where the open cover is perpetual in character ("always open"), a clause is inserted enabling both parties to give notice of cancellation of the cover within a stated time, *e.g.* thirty days or three months.

The open cover normally contains a maximum limit of the insurer's liability per bottom and a location clause like the floating policy.[45]

Frequently special conditions are laid down in the open cover for the determination of the insurable value. It is sometimes provided that, if the value of a consignment is declared before the loss occurs, the declaration of value shall be binding, but, where the loss occurs before the declaration, the basis of valuation shall be the prime cost of the goods plus expenses, freight, insurance and a fixed percentage of profit, usually 15 per cent.; and sometimes it is stated that this amount is to be increased by the value of any duty payable or paid on the goods.

From the practical point of view, the difference between the floating policy and the open cover may be stated as follows: in the case of a floating policy the assured "buys" a fixed insurance cover which is written off as declarations are made. In case of an open cover the insurance does not run out but covers, within the time (and other) limits of the insurance, every shipment falling within the terms of the cover.

A recital of the main terms of the open cover is normally found on certificates of insurance issued under the cover in respect of individual shipments declared thereunder.[46]

If the open cover contains unusual conditions which an assignee of a certificate of insurance issued under it might not expect to be included in the contract of insurance, they should be printed specifically on the certificate; a mere reference to the open cover does not embody them, particularly if other conditions contained in the open cover are reproduced in the certificate. Thus, in one case[47] an open cover issued by a Swiss insurance company to a French firm of forwarding agents contained a provision that the insurers could only be sued in the commercial tribunals of the place where the contract was entered into, *i.e.* in the Swiss courts. Customers of the French forwarding agents sold a quantity of canned ham to an English company, and asked the French forwarding agents to insure it. The forwarding agents sent declarations of the consignment to the insurers, who issued certificates of insurance which, though referring to the open cover and reprinting some of its terms, did not state, or refer to,

---

[44] On Institute Clauses, see p. 308, *post*.

[45] See p. 296, *ante*.

[46] See below in the text.

[47] *MacLeod Ross & Co. Ltd.* v. *Compagnie d'Assurances Generales L'Helvetia of St. Gall* [1952] W.N. 56.

the provision giving exclusive jurisdiction to the Swiss courts. The documents, including the insurance certificates, were accepted by the buyers who claimed under the insurance for damage which, as they alleged, was covered by the contract of insurance. In an action commenced by the buyers against the insurers in the English courts, the latter asked for a stay of proceedings on the ground that the Swiss courts had exclusive jurisdiction. The English Court of Appeal refused the stay because, on construction of the documents, the open cover and the certificates were separate contracts and the buyers were not bound by the clause relating to the jurisdiction of the Swiss courts in the open cover. In support of this view the judges in the Court of Appeal referred to the rule in *Phoenix Insurance Co. of Hartford* v. *De Monchy*.[48]

(v) *Blanket policies*

In the case of floating policies and open covers the assured has normally to make declarations of the individual shipments falling under these insurances to the assured. This is inconvenient to the exporter and requires a considerable amount of labour and costs where the various consignments are of small value or the voyage is of short duration. In these cases the assured will take out a "blanket policy" which usually provides that he need not advise the insurer of the individual shipments and that a lump sum premium—instead of a premium at several rates—shall cover all shipments.

The contract of insurance

We have now to consider the rights and duties of the parties to the contract of insurance.

The slip and the policy

The contract of marine insurance is completed when the slip which the broker presents to the insurers is initialled by the last underwriter and thus the risk is fully covered; before the last underwriter has written his line, the previous underwriters retain the right to vary the terms on which they are prepared to grant cover; the contract of insurance is thus subject to identical terms for all underwriters.[49] Subject to these considerations, the insurer who initials the slip accepts the offer of a contract of insurance made on behalf of the assured, and it is immaterial whether an insurance policy is issued subsequently or not (section 21). The completely initialled slip is, in the words of Blackburn J.,[50] "the complete and final contract between the parties; neither party can, without the assent of the other,

[48] (1929) 45 T.L.R. 543; see p. 55, *ante*.

[49] *Jaglom* v. *Excess Insurance Co. Ltd.* [1972] 2 Q.B. 250, 257. The underwriters may also agree on "t.b.a. L/U" which means that they will be bound by "terms to be agreed with leading underwriters" without requiring further consultation: *American Airlines Inc.* v. *Hope* [1973] 1 Lloyd's Rep. 233, 245.

[50] In *Ionides* v. *Pacific Fire and Marine Insurance Co.* (1871) L.R. 6 Q.B. 674, 684; *Eagle Star Insurance Co.* v. *Spratt* [1971] 2 Lloyd's Rep. 116.

deviate from the terms thus agreed on without a breach of faith, for which he would suffer severely in his credit and future business."

When a policy has been obtained, the slip or covering note is admissible in evidence in legal proceedings (s. 89). If there is a discrepancy between the slip and the policy, the terms of the slip prevail; if insurers wish "to make their obligations as expressed in the policy differ from the obligation which they have undertaken in the slip, they must reserve in the slip power to make such alteration."[51]

Certificates of insurance; brokers' cover notes; letters of insurance

In modern export practice, much use is made of documents which though lacking the legal characteristics of an insurance policy and, therefore, being of a lower order than the latter, acknowledge that insurance cover has been obtained. The most important of these documents are certificates of insurance, but brokers' cover notes and letters of insurance issued by the seller of the insured goods are likewise occasionally used. The reasons for the popularity of these documents are explained by Bailhache J.[52] as follows:

> The preparation of a policy of insurance takes some little time, particularly if there are a number of underwriters or several insurance companies, and when documents require to be tendered with promptness on the arrival of a steamer in order that expense may not be incurred through delay in unloading, or through the buyer not being ready to take delivery, it is not always practicable to obtain actual policies of insurance. In order to facilitate business in circumstances such as these, buyers are accordingly in the habit of accepting brokers' cover notes and certificates of insurance instead of insisting on policies.

The certificate of insurance is particularly frequently used when an open cover has been obtained. It consists of two parts: the first part recites the main terms of the open cover under which the goods are insured[53]; the second part contains the declaration of the goods stating the value insured, the voyage and the marks, numbers and other particulars of the goods. The certificate is signed by the insurance broker who procured the open cover, or by the assured himself. A certificate issued by an insurance broker or assured had not to be stamped before August 1, 1970, when stamp duties on insurance policies were abolished because such a certificate was not issued by the insurer.

Since 1970 certificates of insurance which are issued by an insurance broker or assured entitle the holder to demand the issue of a policy in the terms of the certificate and to claim for losses. But the buyer under a c.i.f. contract is not obliged, in English law, to accept a certificate of insurance in the place of an insurance policy unless he has agreed to do so or there is an established custom of the trade to that effect[54]; having regard to the intention of the parties, it may not be difficult in modern law to establish an agreement to accept an insurance certificate in lieu of a policy. In the

[51] *Per* Scrutton L.J. in *Symington & Co.* v. *Union Insurance Society of Canton Ltd.* (*No.* 2) (1928) 34 Com.Cas. 233, 235.
[52] In *Wilson, Holgate & Co.* v. *Belgian Grain and Produce Co.* [1920] 2 K.B. 1, 8.
[53] See p. 298, *ante*.
[54] See p. 31, *ante*.

United States it is common practice to issue certificates of insurance and it appears that in some respect they are treated like policies, but it has been repeatedly decided by the English courts that the c.i.f. buyer need not even accept an American certificate of insurance unless it incorporates all the terms of the insurance policy and conforms, in all respects, with the requirements of a policy.[55]

Brokers' cover notes are merely advice notes sent by brokers to their clients and informing them that insurance cover has been obtained.[56] Their practical value is even smaller than that of certificates of insurance and, in the absence of stipulations to the contrary, the c.i.f. buyer need not accept a cover note in the place of a policy.

Letters of insurance, addressed by the seller (the assured) to the buyer, confirm that an insurance has been effected. Such an advice may or may not be correct; its value depends on the trust which the buyer reposes in the seller. Letters of insurance have no established status in law but are admissible in evidence against the seller (the assured) if litigation ensues between him and the buyer.

The duty to disclose

A contract of marine insurance, like every contract of insurance, is a contract based upon the utmost good faith (contract *uberrimae fidei*), and if the utmost good faith is not observed by either party the contract may be avoided by the other party (s. 17).[57] It follows from the confidential nature of the contract that the assured is bound to disclose to the insurer, before the contract is concluded, every material circumstance which is, or in the ordinary course of business ought to be, known to him (s. 18(1)). Every circumstance is regarded as material which would influence the judgment of a prudent insurer in fixing the premium or determining whether he will take the risk (s. 18(2)). Thus, in one case the goods were leather jerkins ex-government surplus and were manufactured at least 20 years earlier, but they were declared to the insurers simply as "new men's clothing in bales for export"; the court held that there was a failure to disclose material facts and the assured could not recover under the policy when the goods were stolen.[58]

---

[55] *Diamond Alkali Export Corporation* v. *Fl. Bourgeois* [1921] 3 K.B. 443; *Phoenix Insurance Co. of Hartford* v. *De Monchy* (1929) 45 T.L.R. 543.

[56] See p. 290, *ante*.

[57] It is not quite clear whether a party who has failed to disclose a material circumstance, contrary to ss. 17 and 18, is liable in damages by virtue of the Misrepresentation Act 1967, s. 2, unless he proves that he has not acted negligently. It is thought that there is no liability under the 1967 Act if what the assured has done consists merely of *silence*; if there is a positive act on his part, the Act of 1967 might well apply.

[58] *Anglo-African Merchants* v. *Bayley* [1970] 1 Q.B. 311, 319–320. In *Woolcott* v. *Sun Alliance and London Insurance Ltd.* [1978] 1 W.L.R. 493 it was held that the insurance company could avoid a fire insurance policy on the ground of material non-disclosure because the assured had failed to disclose that he had been convicted of robbery. See also *Lambert* v. *Co-operative Insurance Society Ltd.* [1975] 2 Lloyd's Rep. 485.

Where the contract is concluded through an insurance broker or other agent, the agent must disclose to the insurer every material circumstance which is known to himself or has been communicated to him, or ought to be known by him, in addition to material circumstances that should be disclosed by the assured (s. 19); but a policy effected by the agent in ignorance of a material fact known to the assured cannot be avoided if it has come too late to the knowledge of the assured to be communicated to the agent (s. 19(*b*)). In the absence of inquiry, the following circumstances need not be disclosed:

(*a*) Any circumstance which diminishes the risk.
(*b*) Any circumstance which is known or presumed to be known to the insurer. The insurer is presumed to know matters of common notoriety or knowledge, and matters which an insurer in the ordinary course of his business, as such, ought to know.
(*c*) Any circumstance as to which information is waived by the insurer.
(*d*) Any circumstance which it is superfluous to disclose by reason of any express or implied warranty.

The exporter who wishes to insure goods sold for export will ask himself whether he has to give the insurer detailed information of the nature of the cargo, and especially of an unusual and particularly dangerous propensity of the consignment. The following rules emerge from the decisions of the courts[59]:

(1) Where the goods are an ordinary species of lawful merchandise which may fairly be described as a parcel of ordinary cargo, the exporter need not, in strict law, disclose details of the insured risk to the insurer, but where there is the slightest doubt which a reasonable person can entertain, the exporter would be wise to disclose details.

(2) Where the goods are of an unusual and particularly dangerous kind, the duty of disclosure arises.[60]

(3) Where the cargo is tendered in such a manner—*e.g.* under a novel or unusual description—as to put an ordinary careful insurer on inquiry, and he fails to inquire, a waiver of information under section 18(3)(*c*) can be assumed.[61]

The Rules for Construction of Policy, which are appended to the Act,[62] provide, that the term "goods" means goods in the nature of merchandise but, in the absence of any usage to the contrary, deck cargo and living animals must be insured specifically, and not under the general denomination of goods (r. 17).

---

[59] *Greenhill* v. *Federal Insurance Co. Ltd.* [1927] 1 K.B. 65; see further *Mann, Macneal and Steeves* v. *Capital and Counties Insurance Co.* [1921] 2 K.B. 300. The old decisions of *Boyd* v. *Dubois* (1811) 3 Camp. 133 and *Carter* v. *Boehm* (1766) 3 Burr. 1905 have received a restricted interpretation in these modern cases.

[60] Arnould, *op. cit.*, para. 616.

[61] Sargant L.J. in *Greenhill* v. *Federal Insurance Co. Ltd.* [1927] 1 K.B. 65, 89.

[62] See Appendix 1, p. 485, *post*.

The "held covered" clause

In practice goods are normally specified in detail, and the assured has to take great care to describe the goods correctly. A material misdescription of the goods in the policy enables the insurer to avoid the contract on the ground of misrepresentation. This is even true where the erroneous description was due to the fact that the assured failed to realise the materiality of the description, or where he acted under an innocent mistake or where the misdescription was due to an accident. In view of these serious consequences the parties sometimes insert a "held covered" clause into the contract which covers, at any rate, innocent misdescription of the goods but obliges the assured to pay an additional premium if necessary. The clause "held covered at premium to be arranged" places the insurer on risk.[63] The following illustration of such a clause is taken from the Institute Cargo Clauses:

> Held covered at a premium to be arranged in case of change of voyage or of any omission or error in the description of the interest vessel or voyage.

The following Note is added at the end of these Clauses—

> NOTE—It is necessary for the Assured when they become aware of an event which is "held covered" under this insurance to give prompt notice to Underwriters and the right to such cover is dependent upon compliance with this obligation.

In one case,[64] the assured described a case of second-hand machinery simply as machinery, innocently believing that that description was sufficient, and the insurance policy contained a "held covered" clause. The machinery suffered breakage during the voyage, and it was held that, while the description of the subject-matter was a material misrepresentation which normally would entitle the insurer to rescind the contract, this defect was cured by the "held covered" clause and the insurers had to pay for the loss suffered by the assured but were entitled to an additional premium.

The exporter can obtain the protection of the "held covered" clause only if he has acted with the utmost good faith towards the insurer, this being an obligation which rests on him throughout the currency of the policy. In one case[65] the assured imported canned pork butts from France to the United Kingdom and effected an "all risks" policy[66] covering inherent vice and hidden defects and the condemnation of the goods by the authorities; the policy provided that the assured warranted that all tins were marked by the manufacturers with an indication of the date of manufacture and it contained a "held covered" clause. Some of the tins were not properly marked, and when part of the consignment was rejected by the sub-purchasers of the assured, the assured claimed that, despite the innaccurate markings, they were protected by the "held covered" clause.

---

[63] *American Airlines Inc.* v. *Hope* [1973] 1 Lloyd's Rep. 233, 241.

[64] In *Hewitt Brothers* v. *Wilson* [1915] 2 K.B. 739. Further, *Kirby* v. *Consindif Societa per Azioni* [1969] 1 Lloyd's Rep. 75.

[65] *Overseas Commodities Ltd.* v. *Style* [1958] 1 Lloyd's Rep. 553.

[66] The policy was actually an "all loss or damage" policy; see p. 317, *post*.

McNair J. rejected the contention and decided in favour of the insurers on the ground that the assured had not been frank with their insurers and that the "held covered" clause could not have been invoked if, "at the time when the assured seeks to invoke the clause, they have been and are unable to correct the misdescription."[67]

The insurable interest

It is a fundamental principle of insurance law that the assured must have an insurable interest in the subject-matter insured at the time of loss (s. 6). In relation to the insurance of goods, this rule means that the assured must have some kind of interest in the property of the goods or that the goods must, at least, be at his risk.[68]

The requirement of an insurable interest rarely causes difficulties in export transactions. The exporting vendor naturally obtains insurance cover only if the risk or the property has not passed to the overseas buyer. In c.i.f. or "free delivery" transactions, his insurable interest is obvious, and normally he obtains insurance cover in f.o.b. sales only if the overseas buyer asks him to effect an insurance on his account; in this case he acts as an (undisclosed) agent for the buyer and no doubt can arise in respect of the insurable interest of the principal. The Act provides expressly that the nature and extent of the insurable interest need not be disclosed (s. 26(2)).

In exceptional cases, however, difficulties might ensue. An f.o.b. seller might have sold on credit terms and might not have received payment of the purchase price. He has a vital economic interest in the goods and might become entitled to claim the right of stoppage *in transitu*.[69] While it is not doubtful that he has an insurable interest in the goods after he has properly exercised this right, it is not settled whether he has an insurable interest before having given notice of stoppage. It is believed that the unpaid seller has in these circumstances an insurable interest, but the opposite view is held by the weighty authority of Arnould.[70] The matter can only be settled conclusively by judicial authority. Similar difficulties arise when unascertained goods are sold on f.o.b. terms and the buyer wishes to take out an insurance, *e.g.* when part of a bulk cargo is sold or unspecified goods of the same description are shipped to several unconnected buyers at the same place; here the buyer does not acquire property in his portion of the goods before they are appropriated,[71] but normally the goods are carried at his risk and this is sufficient to give him an insurable interest.[72]

---

67 *Overseas Commodities Ltd.* v *Style* [1958] 1 Lloyd's Rep. 553,559.

68 *Cf.* McNair J. in *Gardano and Giampieri* v. *Greek Petroleum George Mamidakis & Co.* [1962] 1 W.L.R. 40, 54.

69 See p. 105, *ante*.

70 Arnould, *loc. cit.*, para. 343.

71 Sale of Goods Act, ss. 16, 18, r. 5(1).

72 Marine Insurance Act 1906, s. 8, declares that partial interest of any nature is insurable; *Inglis* v. *Stock* (1885) 10 App.Cas. 263.

In cases in which the f.o.b. or c. and f. seller retains an interest in the goods during the transit, *e.g.* because he has not received the price, but it is doubtful whether he retains an insurable interest in the goods after shipment, the seller may *insure* his interest *on a seller's interest contingency basis*. Such cover, if suitably worded, would, *e.g.* protect him if the buyer defaults in payment or refuses to accept the documents or goods, and the goods are lost or damaged. Insurance on a contingency basis is now generally recognised as a valid method of insurance, for the reasons explained above. This type of insurance is used nowadays by many exporters although it entails additional cost; it is obtainable from commercial insurers and is not covered by ECGD insurance. If the payment of freight is the buyer's liability, as is, *e.g.* the case under an f.o.b. contract, it is advisable to include in the valuation of the goods for the purposes of contingency insurance some provision for freight because not only is the value of the goods increased by the carriage to the port of destination but the seller might have to satisfy the carrier's lien for freight before being able to resume possession of the goods. The seller should make contingency insurance arrangements with his own insurers under his floating policy or open cover. Another—less satisfactory—method to protect the seller's interest is for the buyer to arrange expressly with his insurers that the seller shall receive the protection of the buyer's insurance, should the goods be rejected, stoppage *in transitu* be claimed or should they be at the seller's risk for other reasons.

A simple method of avoiding the difficulties which the requirement of an insurable interest on the part of the seller may create in cases in which the insurance of the goods is arranged by the buyer is a stipulation in the contract of sale that the seller reserves his property until he receives the price in cash; in this case his insurable interest in the goods is beyond doubt and will cease only when his financial interest in them ceases.

A person to whom a bill of lading is indorsed and delivered normally acquires an insurable interest in the goods to their full value because, unless the parties have a different intention, the property in the goods passes by the indorsement and delivery of the bill. Where the parties pursue, with the transfer of the bill, a limited object only, *e.g.* where they wish to enable the indorsee to obtain possession on behalf of the indorser, both the indorser and indorsee have an insurable interest in the goods.

Where goods are smuggled into this country, the assured who deliberately contravened the law has an insurable interest but cannot recover under the policy; the contract of insurance is unenforceable because otherwise the assured can claim to be indemnified for goods the importation of which was prohibited and that would be contrary to public policy. The assured can, however, recover if he is innocently in the possession of smuggled goods.[73]

---

[73] *Geismar* v. *Sun Alliance & London Insurance Ltd.* [1978] 2 W.L.R. 38.

An agent who is instructed by an overseas principal to buy goods may order these goods in the home market in his own name. This procedure is often adopted by confirming houses.[74] If in these cases the agent has already shipped the goods and the insurance covering the transit risks has been arranged by the principal, the agent may find himself under a liability to the seller in the home market which would be onerous if the principal became insolvent. The agent would in this case have the right of stoppage *in transitu* as if he were a seller,[75] but it is not always certain that the exercise of this right will lead to practical satisfaction. As a result of an agreement between the institute of London Underwriters and the British Export Houses Association insurance cover is available to protect the agent against these eventualities. The facilities under this protection are only available on prior request to the underwriters concerned. The Export Credits Guarantee Department is likewise prepared to cover agents against these risks.[76]

The premium

The premium is payable to the insurer when he issues the policy unless another arrangement is agreed upon by the parties or required by trade custom (s. 52). It has been explained earlier[77] that in normal cases the broker is responsible solely and directly to the insurer for payment of the premium.

A proportionate part of the premium can be reclaimed where the assured has over-insured under an unvalued policy (s. 84(2)(*e*)), but not where he has done so under a valued policy because here the agreed valuation is, as a rule, binding on both parties. Where an over-insurance has been effected by double insurance, the assured who is covered only to the value of the insured interest can reclaim a proportionate amount of the several premiums paid by him. In case of loss the assured can claim the whole payment due to him from any one of the several underwriters and leave it to them to adjust the loss amongst themselves rateably (s. 32). In a few exceptional cases the assured is barred from recovering the overpaid portions of the premium—

1. If the double insurance was effected by the assured knowingly, or
2. If a claim has been paid for the full sum insured, or
3. If the policies were effected at different times and an earlier policy bore, at any time, the entire risk (s. 84(3)(*f*), proviso).

Double insurance occurs only if the same insurable interest and the risk is insured twice or more frequently in excess of its value. It does not occur if two persons, *e.g.* the seller and the carrier, are interested in the same consignment and insure their (different) interests therein.[78]

[74] See p. 173, *ante*.
[75] Sale of Goods Act, s. 38(2); see pp. 104, 175, *ante*.
[76] See p. 276, *ante*.
[77] See p. 291, *ante*.
[78] See *A. Tomlinson (Hauliers) Ltd.* v. *Hepburn* [1966] A.C. 451.

The rates of premium require careful attention by the exporter who has to rely here on the expert advice of his broker. The rates quoted normally include the cover under the Institute Cargo Clauses.

According to United Kingdom exchange control regulations,[79] policies relating to exports from and imports to residents in the sterling area may be issued in sterling or any foreign currency; policies may be switched from one currency to another. Policies issued to non-residents may likewise be issued in sterling or any other currency and can be switched, but the premium should be received in sterling from an external account or in foreign currency.

In cases in which the policy has been taken out in sterling, the transfer of claim moneys abroad in sterling or foreign currency was authorised by the exchange control authorities, when exchange control was still in operation.

Assignment

When insured goods are sold or transferred, the insurance effected in respect of them does not pass automatically to the buyer; the assured, when conveying the property in the insured goods to the buyer does not automatically assign the "policy" (ss. 15, 51). Insurance is not, as Arnould puts it, an "incident of the property insured."[80]

Normally, however, a contract to sell insured goods contains an express or implied condition that the seller shall assign the insurance to the buyer. In modern practice, the assignment is carried out by indorsing the policy in blank and delivering it to the buyer. This procedure is in accordance with the law (s. 50(3)); the assignee of the policy is entitled to sue thereon in his own name (s. 50(2)). The consent of the underwriter is not necessary for an assignment. The policy can be assigned after a loss. An insurance policy is not a negotiable instrument.

When insured goods are sold and the policy is assigned to the buyer, the buyer is entitled, in case of loss, to claim the full value of the insurance even if the cargo was sold at a price lower than the value insured; the seller cannot claim the difference between the insurance money and the purchase price.[81] The buyer, on the other hand, cannot claim the benefit of an insurance on "increased value" which the seller concludes as his own speculation and which he would not be bound to transfer to the buyer under the contract of sale.[82]

---

[79] Bank of England Notice E.C. 74 (September 19, 1972), para. 3(*b*).

[80] Arnould, *loc. cit.*, para. 230.

[81] *Ralli* v. *Universal Marine Insurance Co.* (1862) 31 L.J.Ch. 207; *Landauer* v. *Asser* [1905] 2 K.B. 184.

[82] *Strass* v. *Spiller and Bakers* (1911) 16 Com.Cas. 166. In this case the insurers had paid the insurance sum to the sellers and had not raised the question of an insurable interest remaining in the sellers after the sale; the buyers then claimed the insurance money from the sellers, but their claim was dismissed.

Risks covered by marine insurance

"*Warranted*" *and* "*warranted free*." The word "warranty" is used, in marine insurance, in a contradictory and confusing manner. "First, it is used to denote a condition to be fulfilled by the assured. Secondly, it is used to denote a mere limitation on, or exception from, the general words of the policy."[83] The first type of warranty is known as *promissory warranty*. These warranties are promises by the assured that certain facts exist; they take the following form:

warranted professionally packed,

or

warranted no iron ore.

They are, in general legal terminology, conditions[84] which, if not exactly complied with, entitle the insurer to disclaim liability from the date of their breach (s. 33(3)). Entirely different is the second type of warranty, known as an *exceptive warranty*, by which the insurer obtains exemption from liability in the indicated circumstances. These warranties are expressed by the words "warranted free . . ."; that means that the risk is not covered; *e.g.* the clause—

warranted free of loss or damage caused by strikers, locked-out workmen or persons taking part in labour disturbances, riots or civil commotions

means that the insurer is not liable for any loss due to these causes.

The difference between "warranted" and "warranted free" is of fundamental importance for an exporter who wishes to obtain a clear idea of the protection which the policy provides for his shipments.

Policy clauses and Institute clauses

The risks against which the insurer undertakes to hold the assured covered are stated in standardised clauses, some to be found in the body of the policy itself, others, so-called Institute clauses, normally attached to the policy on separate slips of paper.

The form of policy in general use today is Lloyd's S.G. Policy[85]; it is appended as a model form to the Marine Insurance Act 1906.[86] It is used as the standard form by underwriting members of Lloyd's and marine insurance companies alike. The clauses relating to risks are expressed in old-fashioned terminology which is preserved for traditional reasons and, further, because most of the terms used have been judicially interpreted by litigation during the eighteenth and nineteenth centuries and have acquired a definite technical meaning. The result of this process of judicial

---

[83] Chalmers, *Marine Insurance* (8th ed., 1976), p. 51.

[84] Diplock J. in *Vaughan Motors & Sheldon Motor Services Ltd.* v. *Scottish General Insurance Co. Ltd.* [1960] 1 Lloyd's Rep. 479, 481. On conditions generally, see p. 90, *ante*. It should be noted that the term "warranty," as used in insurance law, has a different meaning from that term as used in the law of contract generally.

[85] "S.G." stands for ships and goods. There was formerly an S. Policy covering ships only and a G. Policy covering goods only, but they have fallen into disuse.

[86] See Appendix 1, p. 483, *post*.

construction is consolidated in the Rules for Construction of Policy[87] which likewise are appended to the Act and should be read in conjunction with the S.G. Policy.

The policy clauses are, in many respects, amended and qualified by the Institute clauses. They likewise are standardised clauses adopted and published by the Institute of London Underwriters which was founded in 1884 as an organisation of marine company underwriters. The Institute has a Technical and Clauses Committee on which Lloyd's underwriters are represented. The committee has drafted a great number of clauses, some of general character and others dealing with special commodities or particular voyages. The clauses are constantly revised, and are obtainable in book form[88] or as separate slips.[89]

The insurance of goods sold for export is normally effected under the *Institute Cargo Clauses* which are often in the f.p.a. (free from particular average), w.a. (with average) or all risks form[90]; the present version of the *Institute Cargo Clauses* which came into operation on January 1, 1963, embodies the following:

1. Transit Clause (incorporating Warehouse to Warehouse Clause);
2. Termination of Adventure Clause;
3. Craft, etc., Clause;
4. Change of Voyage Clause (this is the "held covered" clause, printed on p. 303, *ante*);
5. F.P.A., W.A. or All Risks Clause;
6. Constructive Total Loss Clause;
7. General Average Clause;
8. Seaworthiness Admitted Clause;
9. Bailee Clause;
10. Not to Inure Clause;
11. "Both to Blame Collision" Clause;
12. Free from Capture and Seizure Clause (if deleted the current Institute War Clauses to apply);
13. Free from Strikes, Riots and Civil Commotion Clause (if deleted the current Institute Strikes, Riots and Civil Commotion Clauses to apply);
14. Reasonable Despatch Clause.

These Clauses are followed by the Note relating to the "held covered" clause which is reproduced on p. 303, *ante*.

Added thereto are often clauses covering special risks, of which the *Institute Theft, Pilferage and Non-Delivery Clause*[91] is frequently adopted, either in the "insured value" or in the "shipping value" form.[92]

[87] See Appendix 1, p. 484, *post*.
[88] *Reference Book of Marine Insurance Clauses*, published annually by Witherby & Co., 5 Plantain Place, Crosby Row, London SE1 1YN. The same publishers issue a *Clause Revision Service*, enabling subscribers to keep the *Reference Book* up to date.
[89] Obtainable from Witherby & Co.
[90] See p. 313, *post*.
[91] "Theft" within the meaning of the Institute Theft, Pilferage and Non-Delivery Clause covers unlawful appropriation of the cargo by the master on behalf of the shipowners; consequently under this clause the assured is entitled to be indemnified for expenses incurred to recover property so stolen: *Nichina Trading Co. Ltd.* v. *Chiyoda Fire and Marine Insurance Co. Ltd.* [1968] 1 W.L.R. 1325.
[92] See p. 292, *ante*.

The strike clauses now in use are the *Institute Strikes, Riots and Civil Commotion Clauses*, but these clauses cover only physical loss and not consequential damage caused by loss of market.[93] Further, these clauses do not cover loss or damage caused by hostilities, civil war, or by revolution, rebellion, insurrection or civil strife arising therefrom.

If it is intended to cover breakage of machinery, the *Institute Replacement Clause* may be adopted under which the insurer undertakes to pay for the repair or replacement of any broken part; under this clause the liability of the insurer is limited to the cost of replacing, forwarding and refitting the lost or broken parts.

If the adoption of a war risk clause becomes necessary, special provision should be made for loss from the effects of atomic warfare. The English *Institute War Clauses*[94] do not contain such cover but the American war clause is worded as follows:

> This insurance is only against the risks of capture, seizure . . . weapons of war employing atomic fission or radioactive force.

A peculiar type of insurance cover is sometimes obtained by importers who buy goods on a c.i.f. basis. It may happen that the insurance cover which the seller obtains might conform with the requirements of the law and practice at the port of shipment but may be insufficient from the buyer's point of view. Thus, in the wine trade from the Continent, franchises as regards the shipped quantity are sometimes deductible.[95] The buyer has here two courses open: either he may stipulate in the contract of sale that the seller shall include in the shipping documents an insurance policy giving him the desired full cover, or he may take out an insurance on the "difference in conditions" between the two types of insurance cover.

The transit clause

By this clause, which incorporates the warehouse to warehouse clause, the liability of the insurer is extended to cover pre-shipment and post-shipment risks. The assured can, under this clause, *e.g.* insure a consignment of goods from Birmingham to Paris, provided these places are named in the policy as commencement and destination of the transit.[96] The clause is embodied in the Institute Cargo Clauses and, in its former wording, has been customary for cargo insurance for a long time. It was settled as early as 1900 that sellers who undertook to insure "on usual Lloyd's conditions" had not discharged their duty by obtaining a cover which was not as comprehensive as the customary warehouse to warehouse clause.[97]

---

[93] *Lewis Emanuel & Son Ltd.* v. *Hepburn* [1960] 1 Lloyd's Rep. 304.
[94] The latest version of that clause came into operation on July 1, 1976.
[95] On franchises, see p. 314, *post*.
[96] The clause does not cover damage to the goods before they reach the warehouse at the commencement of the transit: *Reinhart Co.* v. *Joshua Hoyle & Sons Ltd.* [1961] 1 Lloyd's Rep. 346, 354, 358.
[97] *Ide* v. *Chalmers* (1900) 5 Com.Cas. 212; see also *Marten* v. *The Nippon Sea and Land Insurance Co. Ltd.* (1898) 3 Com.Cas. 164. The warehouse to warehouse clause is in the nature of a mixed policy; see p. 293, *ante*.

In the present version of the Institute Cargo Clauses[98] the transit clause which includes the warehouse to warehouse clause is supplemented by the termination of adventure clause. These two clauses are worded as follows:

1. *Transit Clause* (*incorporating Warehouse to Warehouse Clause*). This insurance attaches from the time the goods leave the warehouse or place of storage at the place named in the policy for the commencement of the transit, continues during the ordinary course of transit and terminates either on delivery

(*a*) to the Consignees' or other final warehouse or place of storage at the destination named in the policy,

(*b*) to any other warehouse or place of storage, whether prior to or at the destination named in the policy, which the Assured elect to use either

(i) for storage other than in the ordinary course of transit

or

(ii) for allocation or distribution, or

(*c*) on the expiry of 60 days after completion of discharge overside of the goods hereby insured from the oversea vessel at the final port of discharge.

whichever shall first occur.

If, after discharge overside from the oversea vessel at the final port of discharge, but prior to termination of this insurance, the goods are to be forwarded to a destination other than that to which they are insured hereunder, this insurance whilst remaining subject to termination as provided for above, shall not extend beyond the commencement of transit to such other destination.

This insurance shall remain in force (subject to termination as provided for above and to the provisions of Clause 2 below) during delay beyond the control of the Assured, any deviation, forced discharge, reshipment or transhipment and during any variation of the adventure arising from the exercise of a liberty granted to shipowners or charterers under the contract of affreightment, *but shall in no case be deemed to extend to cover loss damage or expense proximately caused by delay or inherent vice or nature of the subject-matter insured.*[99]

2. *Termination of Adventure Clause.* If owing to circumstances beyond the control of the Assured either the contract of affreightment is terminated at a port or place other than the destination named therein or the adventure is otherwise terminated before delivery of the goods as provided for in Clause 1 above, then, subject to prompt notice being given to Underwriters and to an additional premium if required, this insurance shall remain in force until either

(i) the goods are sold and delivered at such port or place, or, unless otherwise specially agreed, until the expiry of 60 days after completion of discharge overside of the goods hereby insured from the overseas vessel at such port or place, whichever shall first occur, or

(ii) if the goods are forwarded within the said period of 60 days (or any agreed extension thereof) to the destination named in the policy or to any other destination, until terminated in accordance with the provisions of Clause 1 above.

It follows from these clauses that the Institute Cargo Clauses are in the nature of a mixed policy.[1] Under the transit clause, with its additional termination of adventure clause, the goods are covered from the time when they leave the warehouse at the place named in the policy for the commencement of the transit and continue to be covered until they are delivered to the final warehouse at the destination named in the policy or another warehouse, whether prior to or at the destination named in the policy, but

[98] This version came into operation on January 1, 1963. It replaced the 1958 version of the "warehouse to warehouse" clause. The redrafting was necessary in order to nullify the effect of *John Martin of London Ltd.* v. *Russell* [1960] 1 Lloyd's Rep. 554, where it was held that goods unloaded in a transit shed in the port of Liverpool were not at a "final warehouse" within the meaning of the old "warehouse to warehouse" clause.

[99] The words *in italics* are omitted in the Institute Cargo Clauses (All Risks).

[1] See p. 293, *ante*.

the policy provides an overriding time-limit of 60 days[2] after the completion of discharge overside the overseas vessel at the final port of discharge; on the expiration of that time-limit cover ceases to protect the goods even though they have not reached a warehouse. If before the expiration of the 60 days but after discharge overside from the overseas vessel at the final port of discharge the goods are forwarded to a destination other than that named in the insurance, the cover terminates when the transit begins. The 60 days' cover is very valuable for the assured if, for one reason or another, the goods cannot proceed to the warehouse, *e.g.* they are retained in the customs shed because the buyer has not paid the import duties, and the assured cannot dispose of them quickly. The principle underlying these provisions is that the assured shall be covered until he or a buyer from him can reasonably be expected to have made further insurance arrangements for the goods. The clauses under review further protect the goods during a variation of the contemplated transit, such as deviation, delay beyond the control of the assured, forced discharge, re-shipment, transhipment or the exercise of a liberty of the carrier under the contract of carriage by sea[3] but, except in the case of an "all loss or damage" policy,[4] do not protect the goods against loss caused by delay or inherent vice or nature of the goods; if under the contract of affreightment the goods are unloaded at a place other than the contemplated place of destination owing to circumstances beyond the control of the assured, as happened in the *Caspiana* case,[5] they continue to be insured, subject to the overriding time-limit of 60 days, until they are forwarded to the agreed or another destination and have arrived at the final warehouse, or until they are sold and delivered.

The word "warehouse" has to be given its ordinary and natural meaning.[6] The assured need only prove that the goods were lost in transit, *i.e.* when covered by the clause, but need not prove the cause of the loss.[7]

Of further importance is the *bailee clause* which is to be found in the Institute Cargo Clauses. It reads as follows:

> It is the duty of the assured and their agents, in all cases, to take such measures as may be reasonable for the purpose of averting or minimising a loss and to ensure that all rights against carriers, bailees or other third parties are properly preserved and exercised.

This clause is followed by the *Not to Inure clause* which is worded:

> This insurance shall inure to the benefit of the carrier or other bailee.

---

[2] There exists also a so-called South American 60-day clause which appears to be similar to the English clauses, except that it provides a 90 days' extension for shipments via the Magdalena River.

[3] On the contract of carriage by sea, see p. 334, *post*.

[4] See p. 317, *post*.

[5] *G. H. Renton & Co.* v. *Palmyra Trading Corporation of Panama, The Caspiana* [1957] A.C. 149.

[6] *Leo Rapp Ltd.* v. *McClure* [1955] 1 Lloyd's Rep. 292; *Reinhart Co.* v. *Joshua Hoyle & Sons Ltd.* [1961] 1 Lloyd's Rep. 346, 358.

[7] *Electro Motion Ltd.* v. *Maritime Insurance Co. Ltd. and Bonner* [1956] 1 Lloyd's Rep. 420.

In the case of bills of lading which are subject to the Hague–Visby or Hague Rules[8]—and most of them are—proceedings against the carrier must be commenced in good time,[9] otherwise the carrier and ship are discharged from all liability. The assured who wishes to avoid difficulties with his insurers on account of this clause should carefully follow the claims procedure laid down in the so-called red clause discussed later.[10]

Types of insurance cover used in cargo insurance

The exporter who ships goods to an overseas destination under a contract of export sale can arrange one of the following types of insurance cover for the goods:

(*a*) an f.p.a. policy;
(*b*) a w.a. policy;
(*c*) an "all risks" policy;
(*d*) an "all loss or damage" policy.

The first of these covers provides the least comprehensive cover, the following are more comprehensive in an ascending scale and the last of them is the best cover which the exporter can obtain. These policies are described in the following pages.

F.p.a. and w.a.

The distinction between the clauses f.p.a. (free from particular average) and w.a. (with average) is of considerable significance. Policies embodying a clause of the former type can be obtained at a cheaper rate of premium than those embodying a w.a. clause, but do not provide such comprehensive insurance cover as the latter, and the w.a. policy provides, in turn, less extensive cover than the more expensive "all risks" policy.

In modern practice, the choice of the exporter is often between the f.p.a. policy and the "all risks" policy; the w.a. policy is less frequently used. The exporter has to decide in each particular case whether f.p.a. terms are sufficient or whether he should exercise his discretion in favour of a more comprehensive insurance notwithstanding the higher rates of premium. Where fragile or delicate goods are shipped, *e.g.* machinery or textiles, an "all risks" policy is generally apposite even if the goods are expertly packed. When rough cargoes are shipped, *e.g.* sheet-iron or coal, an f.p.a. policy is sufficient.

Both clauses f.p.a. and w.a. deal with particular average, and particular average only. Particular average is damage caused to the insured subject-matter by a peril insured against, provided

(1) the loss or damage is partial (and not total) and
(2) it is not due to a general average act[11] (s. 64(1)).

---

[8] See p. 347, *post*.
[9] See p. 376, *post*.
[10] See p. 322, *post*.
[11] On general average, see p. 318, *post*.

A particular average loss occurs, *e.g.* if crated bicycles are corroded by seawater or if, owing to heating, a cargo of hay has to be sold at an intermediate port. No question of particular average arises when the goods are totally lost; here the assured can always hold the insurer liable whether the goods are insured f.p.a. or w.a. or though no express arrangement has been made with regard to average.

We shall first consider the provisions contained in the standard S.G. Policy in respect of particular average and shall then deal with the variation of this liability under specially arranged average clauses. If the parties to the contract of insurance have not made special arrangements, the liability of the insurers is regulated by the so-called Memorandum which is in the following terms:

N.B.—Corn, fish, salt, fruit, flour and seed are warranted free from average, unless general, or the ship be stranded, *sunk or burnt*; sugar, tobacco, hemp, flax, hides and skins are warranted free of average under five pounds per cent.; and all other goods, also the ship and freight, are warranted free from average under three pounds per cent. unless general, or the ship be stranded, *sunk or burnt.*[12]

In the light of the earlier observations about the meaning of the expression "warranted free,"[13] this obscure clause may be restated as follows:

(1) If the cargo consists of corn, fish, salt, fruit, flour or seed, the insurers are in no circumstances liable for a particular average loss, but they are fully liable therefor if the ship is stranded, sunk or burnt.

(2) If the cargo consists of sugar, tobacco, hemp, flax, hides or skins, the insurers are not liable for a particular average loss amounting to less than five pounds per cent. but if the amount of the particular average loss is five pounds per cent. or more they are liable fully, and not merely for the excess. The same applies if the ship is stranded, sunk or burnt.

(3) If the cargo consists of other goods, also in case of the ship and freight, the insurers are not liable for a particular average loss amounting to less than three pounds per cent. but if the amount of the particular average loss is three pounds per cent. or more they are liable fully, and not merely for the excess. The same applies if the ship is stranded, sunk or burnt.

The main purpose of the provisions in the Memorandum completely exempting the insurer (case (1)) is to protect him against claims for damage caused by seawater to particularly susceptible cargoes. The franchises, as the percentages limiting liability are called (cases (2) and (3)), are introduced to protect the insurer against petty and trivial claims.

The provisions of the Memorandum are materially qualified by the average clauses which the parties insert in their contract of insurance. It would, however, be an over-simplification to maintain that the f.p.a. clause reduces, and the w.a. clause extends, the standard cover of the Memorandum. The f.p.a. clause likewise extends the insurance cover in some respects while in others it improves the position of the insurer.

The f.p.a. clause in the Institute Cargo Clauses is worded as follows:

Warranted free from particular average unless the vessel or craft be stranded, sunk or burnt, but notwithstanding this warranty the underwriters are to pay the insured value of any

---

[12] The words in italics are not contained in the Memorandum on the S.G. Policy as appended to the Marine Insurance Act 1906, but are frequently added; as are also words extending the liability of the underwriter in case of collision.

[13] p. 308, *ante*.

package or packages which may be totally lost in loading, transhipment or discharge, also for any loss of or damage to the interest insured which may be reasonably attributed to fire, explosion, collision or contact of the vessel and/or craft and/or conveyance with any external substance (ice included) other than water, or to discharge of cargo at a port of distress, also to pay special charges for landing warehousing and forwarding if incurred at an intermediate port of call or refuge, for which underwriters would be liable under the standard form of English marine policy with the Institute Cargo Clauses (W.A.) attached.

This clause shall operate during the whole period covered by the policy.

This clause establishes the principle that the insurer is not liable for any particular average loss, but the strictness of this rule is mitigated by a number of exceptions. The most important of them is the insurer's undertaking to pay "the insured value of any package or packages which may be totally lost." In short, he stipulates to treat every package as separately insured. If, *e.g.* the goods are packed in 20 cases, 19 of which arrive sound and one is totally lost, the insurer will pay the total insured value of that one case. If, on the other hand, all 20 cases arrive partly damaged, the insurer is free, unless the ship is stranded, sunk or burnt. The usefulness of this arrangement for the assured depends on the nature of the shipped goods. Where f.p.a. insurance is taken out, it is advisable to value the several packages separately in the insurance policy, and the value insured should be the total of the values of the several packages. The weight attached by the courts to these and similar facts will be gathered from the following observations of Bailhache J. in a case[14] where two parcels of vanillin and one parcel of caffeine were sent under one f.p.a. policy from London to Switzerland and the parcels of vanillin were lost:

It seems to me to be clear that here the goods insured were of different species, and also that they were separately valued, and therefore there is a double reason for holding that the loss of the two packages of vanillin was not a particular average loss of the whole of the goods insured but was a total loss of these particular goods.

Where the assured wishes to obtain a somewhat fuller insurance cover than is available under the f.p.a. clause, he takes out an appropriate w.a. insurance. W.a. clauses vary considerably, according to the custom of the trade or special agreements. They can be divided into two types: clauses based on percentages (franchises)—these franchises are, of course, different from those laid down in the Memorandum—and clauses dispensing completely with franchises. As regards the former types, franchises are often standardised by an established custom of the trade, and, generally speaking, the more delicate the goods, the higher the franchise is likely to be. Here again, it is customary to treat portions of the consignment as separately insured, *e.g.* for cotton the customary series is "ten bales, running numbers," for silk "each package," and so on. The result of such arrangement if that the damaged parts of the cargo are collected in the tail series, and that, if the stipulated percentage is reached in the tail series, the insurer is liable for the full loss suffered in respect of that series although the loss would be below the franchise if calculated over the whole cargo. Where, on the other hand, the damage exceeds the stipulated franchise, it would

[14] *La Fabrique de Produits Chimiques* v. *Large* [1923] 1 K.B. 203, 209.

be more advantageous for the insured to disregard the series clause. As this clause is inserted in his interest, he is entitled to waive it and to calculate the damage over the whole shipment.[15] Franchise and series clauses are often so generally accepted in particular trades that it is sufficient to arrange for "average as customary."

The other type of w.a. clause is similar in effect to an all risks clause; it is sometimes expressed as

average payable irrespective of percentage.

Sometimes more elaborate forms are in use of which the following is an illustration:

This insurance is to cover all and every risk and all damage and all loss however caused irrespective of percentage from the commencement of the assured's risk by any conveyances by land or water until safely delivered into the warehouse of the final receivers, including war, riot, strike, civil commotion, and malicious damage.

Where a w.a. clause is arranged, the Institute Cargo Clauses (W.A.) have to be adopted; they contain the following average clause which supplements the special arrangement of the parties:

warranted free from average under the percentage specified in the policy, unless general, or the vessel or craft be stranded, sunk or burnt, but notwithstanding this warranty the underwriters are to pay the insured value of any package which may be totally lost in loading, transhipment or discharge, also for any loss of or damage to the interest insured which may reasonably be attributed to fire, explosion, collision, or contact of the vessel and/or craft and/or conveyance with any external substance (ice included) other than water, or to discharge of cargo at port of distress.

This clause shall operate during the whole period covered by the policy.

All Risks

The All Risks clause of the Institute Cargo Clauses[16] reads as follows:

This insurance is against all risks of loss of or damage to the subject-matter insured but shall in no case be deemed to extend to cover loss damage or expense proximately caused by delay or inherent vice or nature of the subject-matter insured. Claims recoverable hereunder shall be payable irrespective of percentage.

It should be noted that All Risks insurance does not indemnify the assured against all possible losses which he may suffer. The clause contains three important limitations:

(*a*) It insures against *risks*, *i.e.* against the happening of a fortuitous event, as Lord Sumner[17] pointed out in the following passage:

---

[15] Arnould, *loc. cit.*, para. 893.

[16] All risks policies are also used for purposes other than marine insurance. In *Australia & New Zealand Bank* v. *Colonial and Eagle Wharves Ltd., Boag* (*Third Party*) [1960] 2 Lloyd's Rep. 241, warehousemen were held to be covered by all risks policies for a liability resulting from the unauthorised delivery of warehoused goods which had been released by one of their employees who was guilty of dereliction of duty; see [1961] J.B.L. 295. For other illustrations of an all risk policy, see *Frewin* v. *Poland* [1968] 1 Lloyd's Rep. 100; *Anglo-African Merchants Ltd.* v. *Bayley* [1970] 1 Q.B. 311 and *Lambert* v. *Co-operative Insurance Society Ltd.* [1975] 2 Lloyd's Rep. 485.

[17] *British and Foreign Marine Insurance Co.* v. *Gaunt* [1921] 2 A.C. 41, 57.

> There are, of course, limits to "all risks." They are risks and risks insured against. Accordingly, the expression does not cover inherent vice or mere wear and tear or British capture. It covers a risk, not a certainty; it is something, which happens to the subject-matter from without, not the natural behaviour of that subject-matter, being what it is, in the circumstances under which it is carried. Nor is it a loss which the assured brings about by his own act, for then he has not merely exposed the goods to the chance of injury, he has injured himself.

A natural deterioration of the goods, *e.g.* of perishable goods, is not in the nature of a fortuitous event or a casualty. The assured must prove that the damage or loss is due to such event but he need not prove the nature of the accident or casualty which in fact occasioned the loss;

(*b*) delay is *not* covered. This is evidently a matter of great importance to the exporter who, in order to obtain cover for delay, would have to insure against this risk specifically at additional rates;

(*c*) loss or damage caused by inherent vice or nature of the subject-matter is *not* covered, for the reasons explained by Lord Sumner in the passage quoted earlier.

A difficulty arises where the loss or damage is caused not by the goods themselves but by insufficient packing. Sellers J. held in *F. L. Berk & Co. Ltd.* v. *Style*[18] that insufficiency of packing was an inherent vice of the goods—kieselguhr packed in bags—themselves, but the learned judge had found as a fact that the goods in no circumstances would have withstood the necessary handling and transport, and for that reason refused the assured's claim for the costs of re-bagging. Where, on the other hand, the packing would have been sufficient to withstand ordinary handling and transit but failed to protect the goods as the result of an extraneous event, that event—and not the insufficiency of packing—would be the effective cause of the damage or loss and the assured could, it is thought, recover under the All Risks policy.

"*All loss or damage*" *policies*

In some instances exporters try to obtain greater protection than is offered by the approved All Risks cover and insure against "All Loss or Damage." This type of cover is legally admissible[19] but not approved by the Institute of London Underwriters and there is a widespread opinion amongst insurers that no wider cover should be granted than that provided by the All Risks policy. However, some insurers underwrite "All Loss or Damage" policies, the effect of which is described by H. H. T. Hudson in *The Insurance of Cargo against All Risks and against All Loss or*

[18] [1956] 1 Q.B. 180. See also *Gee & Garnham* v. *Whittall* [1955] 2 Lloyd's Rep. 562, where aluminium kettles insured under an "all risks" policy arrived damaged; Sellers J. dismissed the claim of the assured, treating again insufficient packing as inherent vice of the goods.

[19] *Sassoon & Co. Ltd.* v. *Yorkshire Insurance Co.* (1923) 16 Ll.L.R. 129, 133; *Dodwell & Co. Ltd.* v. *British Dominions General Insurance Co. Ltd.*, Ll.L.Newsp., April 9, 1918; *London and Provincial Processes Ltd.* v. *Hudson* [1939] 2 K.B. 724.

Damage.[20] According to Hudson, the only limitations of a cover against "all loss and damage however arising" are—

(1) the loss must occur during the currency of the policy;

(2) there must be a loss to the assured. Where the contract of sale provides that the buyer has to pay on a "net delivered weight" basis, which allows for normal loss in transit, the assured cannot recover for such loss under the policy;

(3) loss or damage attributable to the wilful misconduct of the assured is not recoverable.

Sometimes insurers offer cover against "inherent vice from any cause whatever"; this cover does not go as far as "all loss or damage" and is likewise unusual.

General average[21]

The insurance policy gives the assured full cover for general average loss. The clauses dealing with this subject show little variety and, unlike the case of particular average, the assured need not concern himself with the selection of the appropriate clause.

The difficulty that arises here is of a different character. It is due to the fact that the law of general average pertains to general maritime law and affects two relationships in which the exporter stands, namely the contract of carriage by sea which he concludes with the carrier, and the contract of insurance which he concludes with the insurer.[22] The same general average act might affect both contracts, and the rights and duties of the exporter under the contract of carriage are different from those arising under the contract of insurance.

A general average act occurs in the following circumstances. During the sea voyage, three interests are at risk: the ship, the cargo and the freight. They form a common adventure and they are exposed to the same risks. When these interests encounter a common peril, it may become necessary voluntarily to make an extraordinary sacrifice or to incur an extraordinary expenditure in order to preserve the property imperilled in the common adventure (s. 66(2)). The ship may encounter heavy weather and it may be necessary to jettison part of the cargo or of the ship's equipment in order to lighten it; the sacrifice that is made here is made for the benefit of all concerned in the common adventure and it is only just and fair that the owners of all interests saved by a deliberate sacrifice of a co-adventurer's property should contribute proportionately to his loss. The situation which arises here is totally different from that arising in the case of a particular

[20] The Chartered Insurance Institute, 1952.

[21] See Lowndes and Rudolf's *Law of General Average* (British Shipping Laws, Vol. 7, 10th ed., 1975).

[22] The law of general average might even affect a third relationship, namely the right of a cargo owner to recover from another ship that negligently collided with the carrying ship, the general average contribution which the cargo owner paid to the carrying ship in consequence of the collision; *Morrison Steamship Co.* v. *Greystoke Castle* [1947] A.C. 265.

average loss, *e.g.* where the cargo deteriorates owing to sea water or the ship's rudder is lost. A particular average loss is a misfortune that befalls an individual interest and has to be borne by the owner of that interest alone. A general average loss is expenditure caused[23] or a sacrifice incurred as the result of a general average act (s. 66(1)); and a general average act has to satisfy the following requirements (s. 66(2)). It must be—

(1) an extraordinary sacrifice or expenditure,
(2) purposely resorted to,
(3) reasonably made or incurred,
(4) in time of peril,
(5) for the purpose of preserving the property imperilled in the common danger.

It must also appear

(6) that the sacrifice or the expenditure was judiciously incurred;
(7) that it is not included in those ordinary duties or expenses which are incidental to the navigation of the ship, and are paid out of the freight;
(8) that it was not due to any wrongful act, for which the claimant is responsible.

A general average loss may arise from a general average sacrifice, *e.g.* when cargo is jettisoned or, if the ship is in danger of foundering, where part of the cargo is loaded on boats and lost. Jettison of cargo does not constitute a general average act unless such cargo is carried in accordance with recognised customs of the trade.[24] A general average loss may also arise from general average expenditure, *i.e.* extraordinary expenditure incurred for the common benefit to secure the physical safety of ship and cargo, *e.g.* the expense of making and entering a port of refuge. It is disputed whether costs incurred at the port of refuge for repair of the ship, warehousing the cargo, etc., are general average expenditure, in view of the fact that these interests are no longer in physical jeopardy, but it is the general English practice to allow costs of warehousing of the cargo at the port of refuge as general average expenditure, provided the ship put into the port of refuge in consequence of damage which was itself the subject of general average.[25]

The laws of the maritime nations differ materially in their definition of general average. It has been said with justification that "no two of the leading maritime states of the world agree completely in their provisions regarding general average."[26] It is to the merit of the International Law Association to have secured some measure of uniformity in this confused situation. The association drafted standard rules dealing with the adjustment of general average which in their present form are known as the York-Antwerp Rules 1974; they came into force on July 1, 1974.[27] These

[23] An indemnity paid to tugowners whose tugs were called in to tow a ship to safety is a "direct consequence" of a general average act and recoverable as general average expenditure: *Australian Coastal Shipping Commission* v. *Green* [1971] 1 Q.B. 456; see York-Antwerp Rules 1974, Rule VI.

[24] See York-Antwerp Rules 1974, Rule I.

[25] Rules of Practice of the Association of Average Adjusters, Rule 17.

[26] Gow, *loc. cit.*, p. 311.

[27] The York-Antwerp Rules 1974 superseded the 1950 version, which in turn superseded the York-Antwerp Rules 1924.

rules, though not having the force of law, are in practice frequently adopted by the parties. Sometimes the parties make other arrangements, *e.g.* they may provide that "average, if any, shall be adjusted according to the British rule." Where the York-Antwerp Rules are not adopted and the parties have not made special arrangements, general average is adjusted in accordance with the law in force at the port of destination, and if the ship does not reach that port, at the port at which the journey is broken up.

It is now necessary to deal separately with the contracts of carriage by sea and insurance, so far as they are affected by the law of general average. In the law of maritime transport, where there is a general average loss, the party on whom it falls is entitled to a rateable contribution from the other parties interested in the venture (s. 66(3)). According to circumstances this contribution may be a right or a duty of the cargo owner. If he suffers a general average loss, he is entitled to claim contribution from the shipowner and the other cargo owners. If their interest is lost and his is saved by their sacrifice or expenditure, he is liable to make a contribution to them.[28] These rights and duties arise from the contract of carriage by sea. They have no immediate connection with insurance and exist whether the cargo owner is insured or not. The cargo owner is not liable to contribute to general average expenditure, if the York-Antwerp Rules were embodied in the bill of lading and ship and cargo were completely lost after the expenditure was incurred.[29] The shipowner has, at common law, a lien on the cargo for general average contributions as long as he continues to be in possession of the goods. He refuses sometimes to give up possession of the goods unless the persons entitled thereto have signed an *average bond, i.e.* a formal undertaking that they will pay their respective general average contributions after they have been ascertained, and have paid a deposit into a bank in the joint names of trustees nominated by the shipowner and the cargo owners. The cargo owner who has paid the deposit receives a general average deposit receipt which states the name of the adjuster and which he has to produce when the refund found to be due to him is paid out. The average bond is normally concluded between the shipowner on the one hand and all cargo owners on the other hand. If, in an individual case, a cargo owner wishes to act on his own and to obtain possession of his cargo independently, he offers the shipowner an indemnity or guarantee issued by a bank. The adjustment of general average loss, *i.e.* the calculation of the individual contributions, is a complicated and often lengthy operation

[28] Except where the claimant was at fault, *e.g.* the shipowner negligently failed to make the ship seaworthy; in that case the cargo owners do not lose their defences and counterclaims if they do not sue the shipowner within one year, as provided by the Hague Rules, Art. III, r. 6 (see p. 376, *post*): *Goulandris Brothers Ltd.* v. *B. Goldman & Sons Ltd.* [1958] 1 Q.B. 74 (interpreting the York-Antwerp Rules 1950, Rule D). Further, *The Aga* [1968] 1 Lloyd's Rep. 431.

[29] *Chellew* v. *Royal Commission on Sugar Supply* [1922] 1 K.B. 12.

which is carried out by average adjusters.[30] The shipowner is entitled to appoint the average adjuster.

The risks which may fall upon the cargo owner under the law of general average are normally fully covered by his marine insurance. They are twofold: either physical loss of, or damage to, his goods, or liability to pay a general average contribution. The Marine Insurance Act provides, in section 66(4) and (5):

(4) Subject to any express provision in the policy, where the assured has incurred a general average expenditure, he may recover from the insurer in respect of the proportion of the loss which falls upon him; and in the case of a general average sacrifice, he may recover from the insurer in respect of the whole loss without having enforced his right of contribution from the other parties liable to contribute.

(5) Subject to any express provision in the policy, where the assured has paid, or is liable to pay, a general average contribution in respect of the subject insured, he may recover therefor from the insurer.

The first of these provisions enables the cargo owner to claim, in respect of the loss suffered, payment of the insurance money from the insurer without becoming involved in the complications of the average adjustment. The underwriter, on payment of the insurance money, is subrogated to the rights of the assured under the contract of affreightment and is thus enabled to pursue the cargo owner's claim for contribution.[31] This is, of course, an eminently practical solution; provided that there was no underinsurance the exporter can recover his loss from the insurer forthwith and leave the technicalities of the general average adjustment to the latter. The exporter, when advised of such loss, should lose no time in notifying the insurer who is generally prepared to pay the deposit money and to sign the average bond or a similar undertaking. Where the exporter has already paid the deposit, the underwriter normally refunds it upon delivery of the general average deposit receipt, although in strict law he might not be bound to do so.[32]

The Institute Cargo Clauses contain a so-called foreign adjustment clause which is worded as follows:

general average and salvage charges payable according to foreign statement or to York-Antwerp Rules if in accordance with the contract of affreightment.

The object of this clause is to bring the liabilities of the underwriter into line with those of the assured if the contract of affreightment concluded by the latter embodies the York-Antwerp Rules[33] or general average has to be settled under foreign law[34]; by this clause the insurer is deprived of the defence that he is not liable for general average loss because the loss was not caused by a peril insured against, but general average due to a

[30] For the Rules of Practice of the Association of Average Adjusters, see Lowndes and Rudolf, *The Law of General Average* (British Shipping Laws, Vol. 7, 10th ed. 1975), paras. 1041 *et seq.*

[31] See p. 325, *post.*

[32] *Brandeis, Goldschmidt & Co.* v. *Economic Insurance Co. Ltd.* (1922) 38 T.L.R. 609.

[33] *Harris* v. *Scaramanga* (1872) L.R. 7 C.P. 481; *De Hart* v. *Compania Anonima de Seguros "Aurora"* [1903] 2 K.B. 503.

[34] See p. 320, *ante.*

peril specifically excluded by the policy[35] would not be recoverable from him.[36]

Claims

(i) *Preparation of claims.* If the assured learns, even unofficially, that the goods might possibly be lost or damaged in transit he should forthwith inform his insurance broker and act on his advice. It is customary to employ brokers not only for the conclusion of a contract of insurance but also for the settlement of claims. If the consignee is informed that the goods have arrived damaged, he should immediately notify Lloyd's local agent at the port of discharge who will survey the goods and issue a *survey report*, unless the claim is for less than £3; in this case no survey report is required. The assured should further try to ascertain whether the loss is due to particular average or general average. In the former case, if the loss is recoverable under the policy, the assured requires the following documents to support his claim: the policy, invoice, bill of lading and survey report.[37] Other documents have to be added if necessary in the circumstances, *e.g.* the weight notes on loading and discharge if the loss is due to short weight, an extract from this ship's log or the master's protest if the loss is due to the perils of the sea.[37] The *master's protest* is a formal statement made by the master, often supported by members of the crew, before a consul or notary public and explaining the cause of damage. In the case of general average loss, the procedure indicated earlier[38] should be followed. As has already been observed,[39] the assured need not prove the cause of loss but must prove that the goods were undamaged when the insurance began to cover them. The broker acting for the assured should not be employed by the insurer for the purpose of obtaining the report of a claims assessor.[40]

Cargo policies payable abroad frequently embody a special red clause, known as the "*Important*" *Clause* (because it is headed by that word), stating the requirements of the insurer as regards claims procedure. The provisions of this clause are as follows:

Liability of carriers, bailees or other third parties

It is the duty of the assured and their agents, in all cases, to take such measures as may be reasonable for the purpose of averting or minimising a loss and to ensure that all rights against carriers, bailees or other third parties are properly preserved and exercised. In particular, the assured or their agents are required:

1. To claim immediately on the carriers, port authorities or other bailees for any missing packages.

---

[35] *e.g.* war peril under a "free of capture and seizure" clause.

[36] Although claims for a general average contribution have their origin in the common law, if they relate to events during the operation of a charterparty, they are claims arising out of the charterparty and are subject to an arbitration clause in the charterparty: *Union of India* v. *E. B. Aaby's Rederi A/S* [1975] A.C. 797.

[37] Dover, *A Handbook of Marine Insurance* (8th ed., 1975), p. 618.

[38] See p. 320, *ante*.

[39] See p. 312, *ante*, where reference was made to *Electro Motion Ltd.* v. *Maritime Insurance Co. Ltd. and Bonner* [1956] 1 Lloyd's Rep. 420.

[40] *North and South Trust Co.* v. *Berkeley* [1971] 1 W.L.R. 470.

2. To apply immediately for survey by carriers' or other bailees' representatives if any loss or damage be apparent and claim on the carriers or other bailees for any actual loss or damage found at such survey.
3. In no circumstances, except under written protest, to give clean receipts where goods are in doubtful condition.
4. To give notice in writing to the carriers or other bailees within three days of delivery if the loss or damage was not apparent at the time of taking delivery.

NOTE.—The consignees or their agents are recommended to make themselves familiar with the regulations of the port authorities at the port of discharge.

Survey

In the event of loss or damage which may result in a claim under this insurance, immediate notice should be given to the Lloyd's agent at the port or place where the loss or damage is discovered in order that he may examine the goods and issue a survey report.

Documentation of claims

To enable claims to be dealt with promptly, the assured or their agents are advised to submit all available supporting documents without delay, including when applicable:

1. Original policy or certificate of insurance.
2. Original or copy shipping invoices, together with shipping specification and/or weight notes.
3. Original bill of lading and/or other contract of carriage.
4. Survey report or other documentary evidence to show the extent of the loss or damage.
5. Landing account and weight notes at final destination.
6. Correspondence exchanged with the carriers and other parties regarding their liability for the loss or damage.

The Corporation of Lloyd's has published *Lloyd's Survey Handbook* which, though primarily for the use of surveyors, contains valuable information for exporters and importers who wish to make a claim under cargo insurance policies.[41]

(ii) *Total and partial loss*

It will be recalled[42] that in respect of particular average loss a distinction is drawn between total loss and particular loss and that the insurer remains liable for total loss even though his liability for partial loss is qualified by the provisions of the Memorandum or an f.p.a. clause. The law attaches a special technical meaning to the term "total loss," and treats every loss that is not total as partial loss.

Total loss is either actual or constructive total loss. Actual total loss (sometimes called "absolute total loss") occurs:

(1) where the subject-matter insured is destroyed, or
(2) where the assured has been irretrievably deprived thereof, or
(3) where the subject-matter has been so damaged that it has lost its commercial identity (s. 57).

Constructive total loss, as far as goods are concerned, occurs:

where the costs of repairing the damage and forwarding the goods to their destination would exceed their value on arrival (s. 60(2)(III)).

The difference between actual and constructive total loss is that, in the former case, the subject-matter is so completely and irretrievably lost that

---

[41] Compiled and edited by the Controller of Agencies, Lloyd's, obtainable from Lloyd's.
[42] See pp. 313–314, *ante*.

the only course open to the assured is to recover the loss from the insurer, whereas, in the latter case, the damage is repairable, though at considerable cost, and the assured is put to his election either to treat the loss as partial loss or to abandon the subject-matter to the insurer and treat the loss as total loss (s. 61). Consequently, where the total loss is actual, the assured need not give the insurer notice of abandonment as this would be an empty form; but, where total loss is constructive, the assured has to give notice of abandonment in order to indicate which course he elects to take, and, if he fails to give notice with reasonable diligence the loss is treated as a partial loss only (s. 62). If a constructive total loss of goods is followed by a justifiable sale by the master, this is treated as an actual total loss and no notice of abandonment is required because the goods are in this case irretrievably lost and no benefit would accrue to the insurer if notice were given to him (s. 62(7)).[43]

It is not always easy to say whether a loss is an actual or constructive total loss. Numerous cases have been decided on this issue but have not yielded, so far, well-defined principles. The best illustration is still provided by an old case[43] where hides were insured from Valparaiso to Bordeaux f.p.a. unless the ships were stranded. During the voyage the ship was stranded, the hides were damaged by seawater and became so putrid that they would have been completely destroyed on arrival in Bordeaux, and the master sold them at one fourth their value at an intermediate port. The assured failed to give notice of abandonment to the insurers but the court held that no notice was necessary as the loss was an actual total loss.

(iii) *Measure of indemnity*

In case of a total loss, the assured is entitled, if the policy is a valued policy,[44] to recover the sum fixed in the policy, and, if the policy is an unvalued policy, to recover the insurable value of the goods, subject to the limit of the sum insured (s. 68). The assured who has insured the goods at their arrival value plus estimated sales profits of the buyer[45] receives in this case full indemnity.

In case of partial loss of the goods, the measure of damages is—

(1) where part of the goods insured by a valued policy is lost, such proportion of the fixed value as the lost part bears to the whole insurable value of the insured goods;

(2) where part of the goods insured by an unvalued policy is lost, the insurable value of the part lost;

(3) where the whole or part of the goods insured arrives damaged, such proportion of the fixed value in case of a valued policy, or insurable value in the case of an unvalued policy, as the difference between the gross sound and damaged values at the place of arrival bears to the gross sound value (s. 71).

In case of partial loss, where the goods are not lost but damaged, section 71 does not always give the assured full indemnity. As the percentage of the insurance sum which the insurer has to pay is calculated by comparison

[43] *Roux* v. *Salvador* (1836) 3 Bing.N.C. 266.
[44] See p. 291, *ante*.
[45] See p. 292, *ante*.

of the gross arrival value of the goods, if they had arrived sound, with the gross value of the damaged goods, the percentage remains constant and is independent of market fluctuations, while the result would be different if the calculation were based on net values (*i.e.* values after deduction of freight charges).[46] The result of maintaining a constant measure of indemnity is that the assured in making a claim has greater advantage in a falling market than in times of boom conditions. This effect of the calculation prescribed by section 71 will be seen from the following:

Illustration

Data

(1) Goods insured by valued policy at £600
(2) *Case I*: if arriving sound in gaining market, saleable at gross value of ... £800
(3) *Case II*: if arriving sound in losing market, saleable at gross value of £400
(4) In both cases, goods arrive damaged and are sold at gross price of 75 per cent. of their sound value

	Case I	*Case II*
(*a*) Sound gross value	£800	£400
(*b*) Damaged gross value	600	300
Difference	£200= 25 per cent.	£100= 25 per cent.

In each case, the insurers have to pay 25 per cent. of £600 = £150.

The measure of indemnity is not always ascertained so easily as in the preceding example. Where different species of property are insured under a single valuation and one species only is damaged, the value of the damaged goods must first be apportioned in the proportion which the damaged item bears to the different species before the ordinary rules of calculation can be applied (s. 72).

(iv) *The insurer's right of subrogation*

On payment of the insurance money the insurer is entitled to be subrogated to all rights and remedies of the assured in respect of the interest insured in so far as he has indemnified the assured (s. 79). The purpose of subrogation is to prevent the assured from recovering more than once for the same loss, *e.g.* where goods are lost owing to a collision, the assured cannot claim the insurance money from the insurer and then sue the owners of the ship that negligently caused the collision. Under the doctrine of subrogation the right to sue the owners of the negligent ship passes from the insured to the insurer on payment of the insurance money. The insurer is subrogated to all rights of the assured arising from tort or contract, *e.g.* the assured's rights against the carrier under the contract of affreightment. If the assured has already recovered damages from the third party, the insurer can claim from the assured the moneys received.[47]

The right of subrogation is subject to two qualifications—

---

[46] V. Dover, *loc. cit.*, p. 453.

[47] See *R. Miller, Gibb & Co. Ltd.* [1957] 1 W.L.R. 703 (subrogation to ECGD of right to the price, after having paid the seller); *H. Cousins Ltd.* v. *D. & C. Carriers Ltd.* [1971] 2 Q.B. 230 (subrogation of interest after insurer has paid assured).

(1) the insurer can only claim to stand in the shoes of the assured, he cannot acquire a better right than the latter possessed, and

(2) unless the parties have otherwise agreed by way of a contractual subrogation clause, the insurer can claim to be subrogated to the rights of the assured only in so far as he has indemnified him. If, *e.g.* an insurance policy covering six bales of textiles contained a clause providing for f.p.a. cover under 5 per cent., each bale deemed to be separately insured,[48] and one bale is damaged to 20 per cent. and the other five to 4 per cent., the insurer is subrogated to the claims in respect of one bale only, while the claims in respect of the other five bales might be pursued by the assured who, in respect of them, cannot recover from the insurer.

The insurer can claim to be subrogated to the rights and remedies of the assured in case both of total and partial loss, but, in case of total loss, he has an additional right, *viz.* he becomes the owner of whatever remains of the interest he paid for (even if the value of that interest on salvage is greater than the insurance money paid by him).[49] If the insurer pays for partial loss only, the title in the subject-matter insured remains vested in the assured and any benefits derived from salvage may be retained by him (s. 79).

In practice, the insurer invariably asks the assured, on payment of the insurance money, to sign a letter of subrogation and retains the documents, including the bill of lading, in order to prosecute the rights subrogated to him.

The right of subrogation should not be confused with the right of the insurer, on abandonment, to take over the subject-matter insured (s. 63). Abandonment has effect only where there is a constructive total loss,[50] whereas subrogation applies to all cases where loss is paid, whether the loss is total or partial. In case of abandonment, the property in the subject-matter passes but the claims for recovery of damages against third persons do not—as in the case of subrogation—pass. In case of subrogation, payment of the insurance money is a condition precedent to the passing of the assured's rights, but not so in the case of abandonment. This means in practice that, even in case of a constructive total loss, the insurer cannot pursue the assured's claims against third persons, *e.g.* negligent carriers, before he has paid the insurance money to the assured.

---

[48] See p. 315, *ante*.

[49] But if, owing to depreciation of currency, the assured recovers more from the person liable for the loss than the insurer paid, the assured is entitled to retain the excess: *Yorkshire Insurance Co. Ltd.* v. *Nisbet Shipping Co. Ltd.* [1962] 2 Q.B. 330; *L. Lucas Ltd.* v. *Export Credits Guarantee Department* [1974] 1 W.L.R. 909.

[50] See p. 323, *ante*.

(v) *Payment of insurance claims to overseas buyers*

The United Kingdom exporter naturally insures his exports with insurers in the United Kingdom and, as has been seen earlier,[51] can do so in sterling or any foreign currency according to his arrangements with the overseas buyer. Where the goods are lost or damaged and the insurance claim is paid, the United Kingdom exporter may hold the proceeds of such claim on account of the overseas buyer, *e.g.* where he sold c.i.f. or where, on selling f.o.b., he took out an insurance policy by request and on account of the buyer. In these cases the United Kingdom exchange control regulations apply but they permit the transfer of claims, even to an overseas buyer residing in a country outside the scheduled territories, without the slightest difficulty.

Aviation Insurance

Aviation insurance is taken out through marine insurance brokers; probably the greater part of air cargo insurance is underwritten in the marine market by both Lloyd's and the companies but a certain amount is written by specialised aviation insurance companies, such as the British Aviation Insurance Co. Ltd.

Similar to the case of marine insurance, the practice has evolved standard forms, *viz.* the *Institute Air Cargo Clauses* (*All Risks*), the *Institute War Clauses* (*Air*), and the *Institute War Clauses* (*including on-carriage by Air*); all three clauses exclude sendings by post.

It is a moot point whether the insurance of goods carried overseas by an air carrier is a contract of marine insurance or not. The perils which the goods encounter are, in many respects, similar to maritime perils as defined in the Marine Insurance Act 1906, s. 3(2). However, the point is not free from doubt and most policies issued by aviation insurers contain specific provisions denying that they are, or are to be construed as, policies of marine insurance. Nevertheless, it is likely that policies covering the carriage of goods by air will in many cases have to be construed by reference to the body of marine insurance law because there is no other precedent and because marine insurance law embodies, to a large extent, the general principles of common law so far as they relate to insurance.

The Institute Air Cargo Clauses (All Risks) (excluding sendings by post) referred to earlier contains a transit clause similar to but not identical with the transit clause usual in marine insurance.[52] It covers the goods when they leave the warehouse of the sender and may continue until the expiration of 30 (not 60) days after unloading. The following is the wording of the air transit clause:

1. This insurance attaches from the time the subject-matter insured leaves the warehouse, premises or place of storage at the place named in the policy for the commencement of the transit, continues during the ordinary course of transit and terminates either on delivery

---

[51] See p. 307, *ante*.
[52] See p. 310, *ante*.

(*a*) to the Consignees' or other final warehouse, premises or place of storage at the destination named in the policy,

or

(*b*) to any other warehouse, premises or place of storage, whether prior to or at the destination named in the policy, which the Assured elect to use either

(i) for storage other than in the ordinary course of transit

or

(ii) for allocation or distribution,

or

(*c*) on the expiry of 30 days after unloading the subject-matter insured from the aircraft at the final place of discharge,

whichever shall first occur.

This insurance shall remain in force (subject to termination as provided for above and to the provisions of Clause 2 below) during delay beyond the control of the Assured, any deviation, forced discharge, reshipment or transhipment and during any variation of the adventure arising from the exercise of a liberty granted to the air carriers under the contract of carriage.

CHAPTER 24

CARRIAGE OF EXPORTS BY SEA, AIR AND ROAD

EXPERT knowledge and experience are required to arrange efficiently the transportation of goods to the overseas port of destination. If the turnover of exports warrants it, the exporter has his own shipping department which is charged with the execution of export orders in general and with the arrangement of shipping in particular. If the turnover of exports is too small to allow the employment of a shipping manager or specialised shipping clerks, two courses are open to the exporter: he may employ the services of a freight forwarder, loading broker or forwarding department of a shipping company, or may sell only on terms which leave the actual shipping arrangements to be made by the buyer, *e.g.* ex warehouse, f.o.r., f.a.s., or free to docks.

CARRIAGE BY SEA

The general course of business

Let us assume that the United Kingdom exporter, under his contract of sale with the overseas buyer, is obliged to arrange for the carriage of goods by sea to the place of destination and wishes to carry out this arrangement himself. Evidently he has to conclude a contract of carriage with a shipowner whereby the latter undertakes to carry the goods in his ship from the United Kingdom port of dispatch to the overseas port of destination. This contract is known as the contract of carriage by sea (sometimes the old-fashioned expression "contract of affreightment" is still used); the remuneration to be paid to the shipowner is the freight, and the exporter, as a party to the contract of carriage by sea, is referred to as the shipper. The exporter has first to decide whether the quantity of goods to be exported warrants the hire of a complete ship; in this case he charters a ship and the terms of the contract of carriage are embodied in a document called the charterparty. In most cases, however, the goods form only part of the intended cargo of the ship; they are carried in the ship together with goods belonging to other shippers; here the terms of the contract of carriage are evidenced by a document called the bill of lading which, in effect, is a receipt by the shipowner acknowledging that goods have been delivered to him for the purpose of carriage [1] and reiterating the terms of the contract, but this document is issued after the contract of carriage is well on its way to performance. [2]

---

[1] *Scrutton on Charterparties and Bills of Lading* (18th ed., 1974), p. 2.
[2] See p. 335, *post*.

Usually the shipper instructs a forwarder to procure freight space for the cargo. The shipowner, on the other hand, likewise employs an agent, the loading broker, to obtain cargoes for his ships. Devlin J. described the duties of these agents as follows[3]:

> The forwarding agent's normal duties are to ascertain the date and place of sailing, obtain a space allocation if that is required, and prepare the bill of lading. The different shipping lines have their own forms of bill of lading which can be obtained from stationers in the City, and it is the duty of the forwarding agent to put in the necessary particulars and to send the draft . . . to the loading broker. His duties include also arranging for the goods to be brought alongside, making the customs entry and paying any dues on the cargo. After shipment he collects the completed bill of lading and sends it to the shipper. All the regular shipping lines operating from the United Kingdom appear to entrust the business of arranging for cargo to a loading broker. He advertises the date of sailings in shipping papers or elsewhere, and generally prepares and circulates to his customers a sailing card. It is his business to supervise the arrangements for loading, though the actual stowage is decided on by the cargo superintendent who is in the direct service of the shipowner. It is the broker's business also to sign the bill of lading, and issue it to the shipper or his agent in exchange for the freight. His remuneration is by way of commission on freight[4] and that is doubtless an inducement to him to carry out his primary function, at any rate when shipping is plentiful, of securing enough cargo to fill the ship . . .
>
> The loading broker and the forwarding agent thus appear to discharge well-defined and separate functions, but in practice the same firm is often both the loading broker and the forwarding agent, though the two sets of dealings may be kept in two separate compartments of the business. The firm generally acts as loading broker only for one line and does all the line's business, so that it is free in respect of other business to act as it will.

The shipowner, through his loading broker, advises the shipper or his agent in due course of the name of the ship that is to carry the consignment, of the locality where the goods should be sent for loading and of the time when the ship is ready to receive the goods. This is often done by a printed notice, called the sailing card, which contains a reference to the closing date, *i.e.* the last date when goods are received by the ship for loading. The closing date is usually a few days in advance of the actual sailing date in order to give the ship an opportunity to get ready for the voyage. The exporter should be careful to send the goods to the appointed locality in good time, for if they arrive after closing date, the shipowner is entitled to shut them out even if the ship has not sailed.

When the goods are sent to the docks, the shipper sends shipping instructions to the shipowner which state briefly the particulars of the intended shipment, and a shipping note to the superintendent of the dock advising him of the arrival of the goods and stating their particulars and the name of the ship for which they are intended.

The place and mode of delivery of the goods to the shipowner are subject to agreement of the parties or fixed by the custom of the port. The law provides that, in the absence of special agreement or custom, the shipper has, at his own expense, to deliver the goods alongside the ship or within reach of her tackle. When the goods are delivered to the shipowner, the shipper receives a document known as the mate's receipt unless there are

---

[3] In *Heskell* v. *Continental Express Ltd.* [1950] 1 All E.R. 1033, 1037.

[4] The commission of the loading broker is paid by the shipowner, while the commission of the forwarder is paid by the shipper.

special customs of the port to the contrary. In the Port of London, for instance, the shipper receives a mate's receipt only if waterborne goods are delivered alongside the ship. Where goods are sent to the docks by land, they are stored in a shed of the Port of London Authority which issues a wharfinger's note or dock receipt and later receives the mate's receipt when placing the goods on board ship. In some foreign ports, mate's receipts are issued for all cargo whether received by water or land.

Special considerations apply to the modern method of *container transport* the legal implications of which are considered later.[5] The essential feature of containerisation is that cargoes are carried by multimodal transport in one article of transport—the entire container—and are not handled separately for inland and sea transport. The course of business in container transport is that the exporter, having made arrangements with a forwarder or directly with the office of a container shipping line, sends goods to the nearest container loading depot of the forwarding agent or shipping line; these depots are situate in all major industrial centres inland or at the ports. If the cargo fills a full container load (FCL), the forwarding agent or shipping line is prepared to send the empty container to the exporter for loading. If the cargo is less than a full container load (LCL), it will be consolidated with others at the depot to fill a container. The container shipping line issues a container bill of lading[6] to the exporter with respect to his cargo. If the consolidation of the cargo is carried out by a forwarder, he issues, if required, a house bill of lading[7].

If no container is used but the goods are sent by the exporter directly to the docks, a *mate's receipt* is issued. The mate's receipt is a document of some importance. When the goods are loaded on board ship, they are inspected by tally clerks who take down a "record or tally of their date of loading, identification marks, individual package, numbers, their weight and/or measurement, and any defect or comment about the condition in which the goods are received."[8] The tally clerks note, in particular, any damage to packages, lack of protection, old cases, ambiguous markings, etc. When the loading is completed, the ship's officer in charge of loading operations signs the mate's receipt which is based on the notes of the tally clerks and embodies any comments and qualifications in respect of the condition of the goods received. If the mate's receipt is qualified, it is known as foul[9]; if it does not contain adverse observations, it is a clean receipt. The qualifications on the mate's receipt are later embodied in the bill of lading and make that document a clean or claused bill respectively. In law, the issue of the mate's receipt has two consequences:

---

[5] See p. 377, *post.*
[6] See p. 356, *post.*
[7] See p. 357, *post.*
[8] *Harris & Son Ltd.* v. *China Mutual Steam Navigation Co. Ltd.* [1959] 2 Lloyd's Rep. 500, 501.
[9] See *Cremer* v. *General Carriers S.A.* [1974] 1 W.L.R. 341. (In this case the qualifications on the mate's receipt were not transferred to the bill of lading which was issued clean.)

(1) The mate's receipt is an acknowledgement by the shipowner that he has received the goods in the condition stated therein, and that the goods are in his possession and at his risk. It sometimes contains a statement to the effect that

> these goods are received subject to the conditions contained in the bill of lading to be issued for the same,[10]

but it has been held[10] that, even where no such clause is expressly inserted, the goods are held by the shipowner subject to the conditions and exemptions of his usual bill of lading.

(2) The mate's receipt is prima facie evidence of ownership of the goods. The shipowner may safely assume, unless he has knowledge to the contrary, that the holder of the receipt or the person named therein[11] is the owner of the goods and the person entitled to receive the bill of lading in exchange for the mate's receipt. But the mate's receipt is not a document of title; its transfer does not pass possession of the goods and it is, in so far, of a lower order than the bill of lading.[12] Consequently, the shipowner is within his rights if he issues a bill of lading without insisting on the return of the mate's receipt.[13]

The records of loading which the tally clerks take during the loading operation are handed to the shipowner's port clerks who compare them with the draft bills of lading sent by the shipper to the shipowner's office. The shipping companies which run regular shipping services publish their printed forms of bills of lading which are revised from time to time and obtainable from stationers. The shipper or his agent completes usually a set of two or three original bills of lading in respect of the consignment,[14] and when the particulars on the bills agree with the tally notes taken during the loading, the bills are signed by the loading broker or another agent on behalf of the shipowner. But a bill is not always clean; if it is disputed complications might arise because, where payment is arranged under a commercial credit, the correspondent bank is likely to refuse the shipper finance when he presents a claused, instead of a clean, bill of lading. These complications, and the proper and improper means of resolving them, will be considered later.[15]

The particulars of all bills of lading are entered on the *ship's manifest*. "This manifest must contain full particulars of marks, numbers, quantity, contents, shipper, and consignee, with particulars required by the consular

[10] *De Clermont and Donner* v. *General Steam Navigation Co.* (1891) 7 T.L.R. 187.

[11] If a person is named; the majority of receipts do not name a person.

[12] Exceptionally, however, by local custom, the mate's receipt may be a document of title but the addition of the words "not negotiable" would destroy its character as a document of title: *Kum* v. *Wah Tat Bank Ltd.* [1971] 1 Lloyd's Rep. 439, 443.

[13] *Nippon Yusen Kaisha* v. *Ramjiban Serowgee* [1938] A.C. 420.

[14] In 1970 the OCL/ACT announced that they would no longer accept shipper-prepared container bills of lading but, for a small charge, would prepare the bills themselves; the reason given for this change was an endeavour to expedite the documentation.

[15] See p. 367, *post*.

authorities of the country to which the goods are being forwarded."[16] The ship's manifest is produced to naval, port, customs or consular authorities; it contains details of the complete cargo of the ship.

Bills of lading are usually issued in a set of two or more original parts, all of the same tenor and date. If one of them is "accomplished," *i.e.* the goods are delivered against it, the others stand void.

The various parts of the set are forwarded to the consignee by subsequent air mails, preferably registered, to secure their speedy and safe arrival. It is of great importance that at least one part of the set should be in the consignee's hands before or at the time of the arrival of the goods because the shipowner is not bound to hand over the goods unless a bill of lading is delivered to him. Sometimes one part of the bill, together with the other papers forming the shipping documents,[17] is dispatched by letter in the ship's bag of the ship carrying the goods. Control of the contents of ship's bags is exercised in the United Kingdom by the Senior Naval Officer at the port of departure or arrival. The exporter sends the documents in an unsealed envelope which is addressed to the overseas buyer or to his own representative or a referee in case of need.[18] Correspondence not relating to the cargo and remittances must not be included, and the dispatch is covered by a cover letter addressed to the master and asking him to deliver the dispatch to the addressee. On arrival, the master delivers the letter to the addressee who, if he has not received a part of the bill of lading before, delivers the bill of lading to the shipowner's representative or agent at the port of destination and receives from him a *delivery order* which he presents to the ship's officer in charge of unloading.

If the exporter sells under a documentary credit,[19] he normally hands all parts of the bill, together with the other shipping documents, to the correspondent bank, and that bank then forwards the documents by air mail to the issuing bank. Where various parts of a bill of lading are in the hands of different persons, the shipowner or the master (acting as the shipowner's agent) may hand over the cargo to the first person presenting a bill, "provided that he has no notice of any other claims to the goods, or knowledge of any other circumstances raising a reasonable suspicion that the claimant is not entitled to the goods. If he has any such notice or knowledge he must deliver at his peril to the rightful owner or must interplead. He is not entitled to deliver to the consignee named in the bill of lading without the production of the bill of lading, and does so at his risk if the consignee is not in fact entitled to the goods."[20]

On presentation of the delivery order, the goods are delivered from the ship to the person authorised by the order to take delivery. In the absence of agreement of the parties or a custom of the port of discharge to the

---

[16] E. F. Stevens, *Shipping Practice* (9th ed., 1970), p. 4.
[17] See p. 29, *ante*.
[18] See p. 244, *ante*.
[19] See p. 244, *ante*.
[20] Scrutton, *loc. cit.*, p. 298.

contrary, the shipowner or master is not bound to notify the consignee of the arrival of the ship or his readiness to unload; it is the duty of the consignee to ascertain these facts. Where nothing else is arranged or customary, delivery has to take place over the ship's rail, and the consignee has to pay for lighters and stevedores to take delivery. The shipowner's responsibility for the goods does not cease when the ship arrives at the port of destination but only after he has duly delivered the goods to the consignee in accordance with the provisions of the contract of carriage, as evidenced by the bill of lading or as stipulated by law, but delivery does not necessarily mean transfer of the goods into the physical custody of the consignee; often delivery to a dock company or appropriate warehousing of the goods is sufficient. Normally the bill of lading contains detailed provisions about the methods of delivery and the cessation of the shipowner's liability. Where goods are imported from overseas into the United Kingdom, sections 492–501 of the Merchant Shipping Acts 1894 to 1979 apply. They contain detailed provisions for the delivery of the goods and the continuation of the shipowner's lien for freight after the landing of the goods.[21]

The contract of carriage by sea

Carriage covered by bill of lading or charterparty

The two types of contract of carriage by sea, *viz.* contracts evidenced by bills of lading and contracts contained in charterparties, have few points in common.

Charterparties are mainly governed by the rules of common law. The principle of liberty of contracting applies to them and the shipowner may, by agreement with the charterer, modify his normal liability as a carrier without any limitations apart from those postulated by the general principles of common law. Contracts of carriage evidenced by bills of lading, on the other hand, are to a large measure regulated by statute law, in particular by the Carriage of Goods by Sea Act 1971[22] which qualifies the contractual liberty of the parties and restrains the shipowner from introducing exemptions from his liability beyond those admitted by the standard Rules relating to Bills of Lading—the Hague-Visby Rules—appended to the Act.

Charterparties are of little interest to the average exporter because only in exceptional cases is the quantity or bulk of his shipments such that the hire of a whole ship would be profitable for him; the exporter who has chartered a whole ship may issue bills of lading under the charterparty, but if payment is to be made under a banker's documentary credit, bills which contain a clause incorporating the terms of the charterparty will not normally be accepted by the bank unless it is authorised to accept charterparty bills of lading.[23]

---

[21] See p. 343, *post*.

[22] See p. 346, *post*.

[23] *Uniform Customs and Practice for Documentary Credits* (*1974 Revision*), Art. 19 para. (*a*)(ii). On the incorporation of charterparty clauses into bill of lading, see p. 354, *post*.

The following observations deal only with contracts of carriage covered by bills of lading.

Conclusion of the contract of carriage by sea

It has been seen earlier[24] that the contract of carriage by sea is concluded prior to the issue of the bill of lading, and that the latter merely evidences the terms of a contract which has already been partly performed. This position can hardly be illustrated better than by reference to *The Ardennes*.[25] In this case a shipper of mandarines in Spain verbally agreed with a carrier that the goods should be shipped directly to England so that they would reach this country before December 1, 1947, when the import duty on these goods was to be raised. The bill of lading covering the consignment contained the usual clause providing that the carrier was at liberty to proceed by any route and to carry the goods directly or indirectly to the port of destination. The ship proceeded first to Antwerp and then to London which it did not reach until December 4. Lord Goddard C.J. held that the contract of carriage was concluded before the issue of the bill of lading, that it was an express warranty in the contract of carriage that the carrier would not rely on a liberty which otherwise would have been open to him, and that that verbal warranty overrode the terms set out in the bill of lading, and awarded the consignor damages.

Shutting out goods

When the goods of a shipper are shut out by the shipowner for want of room, though the goods were sent to the appointed place of loading before the closing date, two cases have to be distinguished: if, in reliance on the statement in the sailing card, the shipper sends the goods to the docks without previous agreement with the shipowner, he cannot claim damages because no contract has been concluded. The notification on the sailing card is in the nature of an invitation to make an offer, the dispatch of the goods to the docks is the offer, and the shipowner is free to accept or refuse this offer. But the position is different if, as is the modern practice, the shipper has booked freight space in advance; here "the contract of affreightment is prima facie broken and an action will lie against the shipowner."[26] Even in this case, actions are rarely brought for damage caused by "shutting out." There are several reasons for this. First, shipowners' notifications of closing dates usually contain the reservation that

last day for goods is . . . unless the ship is previously full.

Secondly, in such a case, the shipowner normally refunds without dispute freight if already paid, and loss of profits on goods shut out cannot usually be recovered.[27]

---

[24] See p. 329, *ante*.
[25] [1951] 1 K.B. 55.
[26] Scrutton, *loc. cit.*, p. 118.
[27] Bigham J. in the unreported case of *Hecker* v. *Cunard S.S.*, July 1898 (referred to by Scrutton, *loc. cit.*, p. 118, n. (2)).

Freight

"Freight is the reward payable to the carrier for the safe carriage and delivery of the goods; it is payable only on the safe carriage and delivery; if the goods are lost on the voyage, nothing is payable."[28] This definition clearly indicates that, in law, the shipowner is not entitled to claim freight unless he is ready to deliver the cargo to the consignee at the port of destination, except if he is prevented by the cargo owner from so doing. Two rules are based on this proposition: first, the shipowner cannot claim freight if the cargo is lost. "If the goods are lost on the way, *no matter how*, no freight is earned. The excepted perils afford the shipowner a good excuse for non-delivery of the goods, but he cannot earn freight by virtue of one of them."[29] If the cargo arrives, though damaged, the shipowner is entitled to freight unless the damage is so serious that the goods have completely lost their merchantable character. Secondly, freight is not payable before the goods have arrived at the port of destination and the shipowner is ready to deliver them. In practice, both rules are invariably abrogated by the terms of the contract of carriage as evidenced in the bill of lading.

Calculation of freight

Freight payable under bills of lading is calculated by weight, measurement or on an *ad valorem* basis. The shipowner is entitled to elect the mode of calculation most favourable to him. However, the customary bases of freight calculation are at present in a state of transition, in view of the increased use of combined transport and containerisation.

Bills of lading sometimes provide that if the shipper fails to make a correct or sufficient declaration of the cargo the shipowner shall be entitled to charge double freight calculated according to the true contents, value or nature of the goods, such double freight being liquidated damages and not a penalty.

Freight rates

The standard freight rates for shipments under bills of lading are fixed by so-called shipping conferences. These are combinations or pools of shipowners maintaining regular liner services to particular parts of the world, *e.g.* ports of the River Plate, South Africa, or Australia. The rates which they offer are normally lower than those which non-conference shipowners are able to quote, but regular services can only be profitably maintained if supported by regular freight bookings. The members of the conference have, therefore, to guard against the defection of their regular clients who may transfer their custom occasionally to tramp steamers or other outsiders if offered freight space at cheaper rates than the conference rates.

---

[28] *Kirchner* v. *Venus* (1859) 12 Moore P.C. 361, 390.
[29] Payne's *Carriage of Goods by Sea* (9th ed., 1972), p. 190.

In modern practice shipping conferences have evolved two systems of granting their regular clients preferential rates: they may use the system of deferred rebates of varying amounts up to 10 per cent. on the total freight; these rebates are retained by the shipping company for three or six months when they are payable, provided that during that period the shipper has not sent goods to the area in question in non-conference ships; if he has used the services of a non-conference shipowner, the percentage, which is sometimes inaccurately described as primage,[30] is forfeited.

The other method which they may use is the so-called contract system under which a shipper signs a contract whereby he undertakes to ship only by conference lines; he is then entitled to receive an immediate—not a deferred—rebate on the freight or—what amounts to the same—to ship at lower tariff rates; the immediate rebate is usually lower than the deferred rebate, *e.g.* 9½ per cent. instead of 10 per cent. The contract normally provides that a shipper who breaks his undertaking has to pay an amount equivalent to the immediate rebate by way of liquidated damages. Sometimes a shipping conference offers shippers both systems of rebates according to their choice.

The rebate will be paid only to the shipper evidenced by the bill of lading. This is a point to which attention should be paid in the relationship between the exporter and his forwarding agent. If the intention is that the rebate shall be passed on to the exporter it is advisable that the bills of lading are taken out in his name, and not in that of the forwarding agent.

The validity, in common law, of a conference arrangement was upheld in the famous *Mogul* case,[31] where a non-conference shipowner sued members of the conference formed for the shipment of tea from China to Europe; it was held that the conference arrangement was not illegal as being a conspiracy because its members pursued the lawful object of protecting and extending their own trade and had not employed unlawful means to achieve this object.

The dual rate system used by conference lines whose ships called on American ports came into conflict with United States legislation, and notably the Bonner Act 1961, which admits this system only subject to stringent conditions.[32] The U.S.A. Federal Maritime Commission attempted to probe into contracts and arrangements made between shipowners in conferences governed by English law and even attempted to control contracts of carriage between British exporters and British shipowners. This attempt of the American authorities to arrogate extraterritorial jurisdiction led to the passing of the United Kingdom *Shipping Contracts and Commercial Documents Act* 1964.[33] Section 1 of this Act empowers the Minister of Transport in matters relating to shipping to

---

[30] See p. 342, *post*.
[31] *Mogul Steamship Co.* v. *McGregor, Gow & Co.* [1892] A.C. 25.
[32] John P. Gorman, "Shipping Conferences and the Bonner Act 1961" in [1962] J.B.L. 24.
[33] David A. Godwin Sarre, "The Shipping Contracts and Commercial Documents Act 1964" in [1964] J.B.L. 293.

prohibit a person from complying with foreign governmental measures. Section 2 deals generally with foreign demands for the disclosure of commercial documents and information and is not limited to shipping; under this section a Minister may prohibit the production of a document which is outside the territorial jurisdiction of the requesting sovereign, if the request constitutes, under international law, an infringement of the jurisdiction of the United Kingdom. The dispute about shipping conference contracts between the U.S.A. Federal Maritime Commission and the United Kingdom and other maritime nations was later amicably settled.[34]

By whom freight is payable

From the point of view of the exporter, the question to whom freight is payable normally causes little difficulty, while the question from whom the shipowner may demand payment of the freight is of great practical significance. This question cannot be answered by reference to the contract of sale under which the exporter sold and shipped the goods. That contract regulates the ultimate responsibility for freight between the two parties to the sale but is irrelevant as far as a liability for freight to the shipowner is concerned.

The liability for freight is often expressly regulated by the bill of lading. The following clause is typical:

> Freight for the said goods with primage, if any, shall be due and payable by the shipper on shipment at port of loading in cash, without deduction, and shall not be repayable, vessel or goods lost or not lost.

Where the bill does not contain express provisions, the following rules apply:

(1) The shipper is primarily liable for payment of the freight because he is the person with whom the shipowner concludes the contract of carriage. This liability is purely contractual; it is irrelevant, in this respect, whether the shipper was at the time of the shipment the owner of the goods or not, or whether under the bill of lading the goods were made deliverable to the shipper or his order, or to a third person. But the shipper is free from liability if, in the circumstances of the case, it was abundantly clear to the shipowner, at the time when the goods were shipped, that the shipper acted merely as agent for another person.[35] The burden of proof which rests upon the shipper is, in this respect, heavy.

(2) The consignee is in an entirely different position. He is not liable for freight under the contract of carriage because he is not a party thereto unless, of course, the shipper concluded the contract as his agent. Notwithstanding this fact, the shipowner may demand freight from him in either of the following cases:

---

[34] David A. Godwin Sarre, "Shipping Conferences and the Federal Maritime Commission" in [1965] J.B.L. 93.

[35] See p. 162, *ante*.

(*a*) where he is named in the bill of lading as consignee and the bill of lading is indorsed to him, *and* he has acquired the property in the goods. The liability which attaches only if these two conditions concur is of statutory character, being laid down by the Bills of Lading Act 1855, s. 1.[36] The consignee is not liable if he does not acquire the property in the goods.[37] For this reason, a banker who accepts the bill of lading as security for an advance, or an agent who accepts delivery of the goods for their owner, is normally not liable for freight; or

(*b*) where he undertakes even by implication, to pay the freight. Such undertaking is readily inferred from his course of dealing with the shipowner. If the agent of the owner of the goods persuades the master to deliver the goods to him and thereby to give up the shipowner's lien on the goods, the courts are likely to hold that he (being the consignee) concluded a new contract with the shipowner whereby he promised payment of the freight in consideration of delivery of the goods to him.

(3) An indorsee, who is liable for freight by virtue of the Bills of Lading Act 1855, s. 1 (above No. (2)(*a*)), ceases to be liable when reindorsing the bill *and* transferring the property in the goods to the person to whom he reindorses the bill, provided that the bill is reindorsed while the goods are in transit and before they are delivered. Here again, both conditions of reindorsement and transfer of property have to be satisfied; the indorsee, who became liable for freight by virtue of the Act, remains liable if he merely resells the goods but retains the bill of lading, or indorses the bill, *e.g.* as a security, but retains the goods.

(4) The seller, who exercises his right of stoppage *in transitu*,[38] is liable to pay the freight to the shipowner, even if not liable under Rule 1.

Prepaid freight

It has been seen[39] that, in law, the shipowner is not entitled to claim freight before the cargo arrives safely and he is ready to deliver it. The parties are at liberty to modify these rules by agreement, and their discretion is not qualified by the Carriage of Goods by Sea Act 1971.

In respect of freight payable under a bill of lading, the rules of law are, in practice, invariably abrogated by express agreement of the parties.

[36] The Act is treated in Appendix 1 to Clive M. Schmitthoff's *The Sale of Goods* (2nd ed.), pp. 255–229.

[37] *Gardano and Ciampieri* v. *Greek Petroleum George Mamidakis & Co.* [1962] 1 W.L.R. 40. The consignee will normally acquire property (and thus the right to sue) by indorsement and delivery of the bill of lading to him or his agent: *The San Nicholas* [1976] 1 Lloyd's Rep. 8, 11; on the right to sue, see p. 344, *post*.

[38] See p. 105, *ante*.

[39] See p. 336, *ante*.

Clauses in bills of lading stipulating prepayment of freight vary considerably; the clause referred to on p. 338, *ante*, is fairly typical.

Most freight clauses in bills of lading contain the words "ship lost or not lost," often supplemented by the words "freight deemed to have been earned on shipment." Where words to this effect are inserted in the bill of lading, the nature of prepaid freight is beyond dispute: it is, in legal terminology, advance freight. Such freight is due and earned when the stipulated event happens, *e.g.* on shipment of the goods, or on signing of the bill of lading. Apart from exceptional cases, the right of the shipowner to claim freight is not affected by the subsequent loss of the goods, and the shipowner is not only entitled to retain the full amount of prepaid freight but may even sue the shipper therefor if, for one reason or another, due prepaid freight has not been paid.[40] These rules are subject to three exceptions: the shipowner has to return advance freight:

(1) if "the ship never earned freight and never began to earn freight,"[41] *e.g.* because she did not sail, or
(2) if the goods are lost before advance freight becomes due, or
(3) if the goods are lost by an event other than an excepted peril.[42]

If the bill of lading omits to state when advance freight shall become payable, it appears to be payable on the final sailing of the ship. As the shipper bears the risk in respect of prepaid freight, he has an insurable interest therein which he may cover by marine insurance.[43]

In modern practice the wording of freight clauses in the bill of lading or charterparty puts it normally beyond doubt that prepaid freight is intended by the parties to be advance freight. In older days, it was sometimes doubtful whether prepaid freight was in the nature of advance freight or merely a loan by the shipper on account of freight payable in accordance with the general rules of the common law, namely, on safe arrival of the cargo. The difference in the interpretation of the prepayment clause is considerable: when the goods are lost in transit, the prepaid sum, if advance freight, cannot normally be recovered, but if paid as a loan can be recovered by the shipper. The interpretation of the clause depends entirely on the intention of the parties, which it is not always easy to ascertain; the courts have evolved the rule that, when freight has to be insured by the shipowner, the prepayment is likely to be a loan, but if it has to be insured by the shipper it is likely to be advance freight.

Freight prepaid and freight collect bills of lading

We have so far considered the obligations arising from the contract of carriage by sea, as far as they concern the questions who has to pay the freight and when freight is payable. Another problem arises between the

[40] *Oriental Steamship Co. Ltd.* v. *Tylor* [1893] 2 Q.B. 518.
[41] *Per* James L.J. in *Ex p. Nyholm, re Child* (1873) 43 L.J.Bk. 21, 24.
[42] *Dufourcet* v. *Bishop* (1886) 18 Q.B.D. 373; *Rodocanachi* v. *Milburn* (1886) 18 Q.B.D. 67.
[43] See p. 304, *ante*.

seller and the buyer under a c.i.f. contract. It is obvious that the c.i.f. price includes a freight element but the question is whether that freight element has to be paid to the shipowner by the seller by way of prepaid freight or by the buyer on arrival of the goods, in which case the seller has to give the buyer credit for the freight, by deducting the freight element from the invoice price. Whether the one or the other method is used, depends on the agreement of the parties. "When the first method is used the seller provides *freight prepaid bills of lading*. When the second method is used he provides what have been conveniently called *freight collect bills of lading*, that is to say, bills of lading under which freight is payable by the receiver (who may be the buyer himself or a sub-buyer from the buyer) to the ship at the port of discharge."[44]

The distinction is of considerable commercial importance. If freight collect bills are used, the buyer's obligation to pay freight to the shipowner is conditional on the arrival of the goods, but notwithstanding this condition, the contract is a true c.i.f. contract.[44]

Dead freight

Where the shipper fails to load the cargo or the full cargo after arranging with the shipowner for its carriage, he has broken the contract of carriage and is liable to pay the agreed freight as damages (dead freight). But the shipowner who uses the freight space which would have been taken up by the goods of the defaulting shipper and carries therein goods of other shippers has to deduct the earned freight when claiming damages. He may claim from the defaulting shipper the difference between the agreed and actually earned freight, *e.g.* if he had to accept cargo which earned a lower rate of freight.

Lump sum freight

While freight is normally arranged according to weight, measurement or value,[45] the shipper may agree to pay a lump sum as freight for the use of the entire ship or a portion thereof.[46] In this case, the amount of freight payable by the shipper is fixed and invariable and, if the shipowner is ready to perform his contract, is payable whether the shipper uses the hired space to full capacity, or loads below capacity or does not load at all. Moreover, in the absence of agreement to the contrary, the whole lump sum freight is payable if only part of the loaded cargo is delivered by the shipowner at the port of destination and the remainder is lost,[47] but the shipowner cannot claim lump sum freight if he is unable to deliver at least part of the cargo.

Lump sum freight is not customary in a contract of carriage evidenced by bills of lading, but is sometimes arranged under charterparties when

---

[44] *The Pantanassa* [1970] 1 Lloyd's Rep. 153, 163 *per* Brandon J. See also *Federal Commerce and Navigation Ltd.* v. *Molena Alpha Inc., The Nanfri* [1978] 3 W.L.R. 991 (H.L.).

[45] See p. 336, *ante*.

[46] Scrutton, *loc. cit.*, p. 338.

[47] *William Thomas & Sons* v. *Harrowing Steamship Co.* [1915] A.C. 58.

the shipper is uncertain of the quantity or species of the goods which he has to ship.

Back freight

The shipper is liable to pay back freight where the goods shipped are carried, on his instructions or in his interest, to a place other than the port of destination. Where the shipper, in his capacity of unpaid seller, exercises his right of stoppage *in transitu*[48] and instructs the shipowner to deliver the goods at a port other than the port of destination named in the bill of lading, the shipper is liable for any additional freight and, if he instructs the shipowner to deliver the goods short of the original port of destination, he has to pay the total original freight as damages because, by giving notice of stoppage, he broke the contract of carriage concluded with the shipowner and prevented the latter from earning the freight.[49] Where the master, in the interest of the shipper, considers it advisable to carry the goods to another place than the bill of lading destination, *e.g.* because that port is strikebound,[50] the shipper is liable to pay the additional freight as "back freight."

Pro rata freight

Pro rata freight is payable in exceptional circumstances only, namely, where the parties to the contract of carriage conclude a new contract[51] to the effect that the goods shall be delivered at an intermediate port, and not the port of destination named in the bill of lading. Such agreement unless concluded expressly is only inferred from the circumstances where the shipper has a genuine choice of having his goods carried to the destination originally agreed upon. The shipper is, therefore, not obliged to pay *pro rata* freight where the shipowner leaves the goods at an intermediate port and is unable or unwilling to carry them to the port of destination. The shipowner likewise is entitled to *pro rata* freight where he loads only part of the agreed cargo or delivers only part of the total loaded cargo, the delivery of the remainder having become impossible through excepted perils.[52]

Primage

Some bills of lading refer to the remuneration payable to the shipowner as

freight and primage (if any).

[48] See p. 105, *ante*.
[49] *Booth Steamship Co. Ltd.* v. *Cargo Fleet Iron Co. Ltd.* [1916] 2 K.B. 570.
[50] *G. H. Renton & Co. Ltd.* v. *Palmyra Trading Corporation of Panama; The Caspiana* [1957] A.C. 149.
[51] *St. Enoch Shipping Co. Ltd.* v. *Phosphate Mining Co.* [1916] 2 K.B. 624, 627.
[52] Scrutton, *loc. cit.*, p. 341; on excepted perils, see p. 371, *post*.

Primage was originally a small payment made by the shipper to the master in consideration of the care and attention which he was to give during the voyage to the shipper's cargo, but such payment is no longer customary.

In modern practice, primage is not normally charged. Where it is claimed, it means hardly more than a percentage added to the freight and payable to the shipowner. Where primage is charged, it is normally 10 per cent. of the net freight.

Sometimes the deferred rebate payable to the shipper under conference arrangements[53] is referred to as primage.

Shipowner's lien

The shipowner has a lien on the goods of the shipper which are in his possession. The shipowner's lien is derived from common law or based on express agreement.

At common law the shipowner has a lien:

(1) for freight which is payable on delivery of the goods, but not for advance freight,[54] dead freight,[55] or freight payable after delivery of the goods;

(2) for general average contributions. This lien has been considered earlier[56];

(3) for "expenses incurred by the shipowner or master in protecting and preserving the goods."[57]

The common law lien of the shipowner is a possessory lien; it can be exercised only as long as the goods are in the shipowner's possession on board ship or in a warehouse ashore. This shipowner's lien is lost when the goods are duly delivered or the shipowner agrees to accept freight subsequent to delivery. Where goods are imported into the United Kingdom from overseas, the shipowner's lien for freight and other charges is subject to the provisions of the Merchant Shipping Acts 1894 to 1979, Pt. VII, ss. 492 to 501. The Acts provide that the lien is maintained when the shipowner, on landing the goods and placing them into the custody of a warehouseman, gives the warehouseman notice in writing that the goods are to remain subject to the lien to an amount stated in the notice, but the owner of the goods is entitled to deposit with the warehouseman the claimed sum and thereupon to receive possession of the goods. The deposit takes the place of the goods and, if there is a dispute about the freight between the parties to the contract of carriage, the right to the deposit is ascertained by arbitration[58] or litigation.

Where the shipowner's lien is not discharged and no deposit is made, and the shipowner instructs the warehouseman to sell the goods by public

---

[53] See p. 337, *ante*.
[54] See p. 340, *ante*.
[55] See p. 341, *ante*.
[56] See p. 318, *ante*.
[57] Scrutton, *loc. cit.*, p. 380.
[58] See Arbitration Act 1950, s. 29.

auction, such auction may not take place until 90 days after the goods were placed in the warehouseman's custody: only if they are perishable may they be auctioned before that period. The provisions of the Merchant Shipping Acts 1894 to 1979 do not apply to the lien of the shipowner for outward voyages. At common law the shipowner's lien attaches to all goods carried to the same consignee on the same voyage under the same contract; and it is immaterial that several bills of lading have been issued in respect of them. If part of the goods is delivered without payment of freight the shipowner may still claim his lien on the remainder of the goods for the whole freight due to him. But the position is different where goods are shipped under different contracts of carriage. Where *e.g.* the shipowner carries goods under one contract of carriage and delivers them without insisting on payment of freight, and later ships goods of the same shipper to the same consignee under another contract of carriage, he cannot claim a lien on these goods for the unpaid freight due under the previous contract.

The lien of the shipowner is usually extended beyond the limits of the common law lien by agreement of the parties. Bills of lading normally contain special clauses dealing with the shipowner's lien. The following clause is typical:

> The carrier, his servants or agents shall have a lien on the goods and a right to sell the goods whether privately or by public auction for all freight (including additional freight payable as above stipulated) primage, dead freight, demurrage, detention charges, salvage, average of any kind whatsoever, and for all other charges and expenses whatsoever, which are for account of the goods or of the shipper, consignee or owner of the goods under this bill of lading, and for the costs and expenses of exercising such lien and of such sale and also for all previously unsatisfied debts whatsoever due to him by the shipper, consignee or owner of the goods. Nothing in this clause shall prevent the carrier from recovering from the shipper, consignee or owner of the goods the difference between the amount due from them or any of them to him and the amount realised by the exercise of the rights given to the carrier under this clause.

The shipowner's lien is often extended by these special clauses to cover dead freight,[59] advance freight,[60] freight payable after delivery of the goods, unsatisfied previous freight, inland or forwarding charges, porterage, fines, costs and other charges or amounts due from the shippers or consignees, to the shipowners or their agents.[61] The clauses dealing with the shipowner's lien usually authorise the shipowner to realise the lien by sale of the goods by public auction or otherwise.

The right to sue

The contract of carriage by sea is often concluded by the consignor, particularly where he has sold the goods on delivery terms such as c.i.f. or arrival. If it is necessary to bring an action against the carrier, the question arises who is entitled to sue, the consignor or the consignee.

---

59 See p. 341, *ante*.
60 See p. 340, *ante*.
61 *Whinney* v. *Moss Steamship Co. Ltd.* (1910) 15 Com.Cas. 114.

If the bill of lading has been transferred to the consignee or indorsee of the bill with the intention of passing property to him, by virtue of section 1 of the Bills of Lading Act 1855 such consignee or indorsee:

> shall have transferred to and vested in him all rights of suit, and be subject to the same liabilities in respect of such goods as if the contract contained in the bill of lading had been made with himself.

In other words, this provision operates as a statutory transfer of the right to sue and the consignee or indorsee is clearly entitled to bring an action against the carrier for damages for any loss of or damage to the cargo, as he has suffered these damages himself as the owner of the goods.[62]

The consignor, however, cannot normally sue the carrier for substantial damages suffered by the consignee or indorsee of the bill of lading because he has not suffered these damages himself and under section 1 of the Bills of Lading Act 1855, in the words of Lord Diplock[63]:

> the right of suit against the shipowner in respect of obligations arising under the contract of carriage passes to [the consignee or indorsee] from the consignor. Furthermore, a holder of a bill for valuable consideration in exercising his own right of suit has the benefit of an estoppel not available to the consignor that the bill of lading is conclusive evidence against the shipowner of the goods described in it.

Occasionally, however, in cases in which the Bills of Lading Act 1855 does not apply, the consignor may recover from the carrier substantial damages suffered by the consignee or indorsee to whom the property in the goods has passed, on the ground that privity of contract exists between him and the carrier.[64] He has, of course, to hand over the damages recovered to the person who suffered them (or his insurer). It may be added that a bailee of goods, such as a carrier or warehouseman, can recover substantial damages suffered by his bailor in respect of the goods of the latter, if the loss or damage was caused by negligence or another tort was committed by a third party,[65] or the bailor's proprietary interest in the goods was insured by the bailee.[66]

Carriage covered by bills of lading

Nature of the bill of lading. The principal purpose of the bill of lading is to enable the owner of the goods, to which it relates, to dispose of them rapidly although the goods are no longer in the hands of the owner but already in the custody of the shipowner. When goods belonging to a merchant in London are on the high seas in transit from London to Singapore, the bill of lading representing the goods enables their owner to pledge the goods with his bank in London or to sell them to a buyer in New York. The bill of lading is a creation of mercantile custom, a typical institution of international trade. It came into use in the sixteenth century.

---

[62] See *The San Nicholas* [1976] 1 Lloyd's Rep. 8.
[63] *Albacruz* (*Cargo Owners*) v. *Albazero* (*Owners*) [1977] A.C. 774, 847.
[64] *Dunlop* v. *Lambert* (1837) 6 Cl. & F. 600, as interpreted in *The Albazero.*
[65] *The Winkfield* [1902] P. 42.
[66] *A. Tomlinson* (*Hauliers*) *Ltd.* v. *Hepburn* [1966] A.C. 451.

A book on mercantile law, published in 1686, stated that "bills of lading are commonly to be had in print in all places and several languages."[67] The character of the bill of lading as a document of title was first recognised by the courts in 1794 in *Lickbarrow* v. *Mason*.[68]

From the legal point of view, a bill of lading[69] is—

(1) a formal receipt by the shipowner acknowledging that goods of the stated species, quantity and condition are shipped to a stated destination in a certain ship, or at least received in the custody of the shipowner for the purpose of shipment;

(2) a memorandum of the contract of carriage, repeating in detail the terms of the contract which was in fact concluded prior to the signing of the bill; and

(3) a document of title to the goods enabling the consignee to dispose of the goods by indorsement and delivery of the bill of lading.

The international Rules relating to bills of lading

Although the clauses contained in a duly tendered and signed bill of lading represent, in law, the terms of agreement between the shipper and the shipowner, the shipper has little discretion in the negotiation of these terms. The terms of the contract which he concludes, are fixed in advance,[70] and his position is not unlike that of a railway passenger who, when buying a ticket, concludes an elaborate standard contract with the railway authority for the carriage of his person from one locality to another. The shipper, like the railway passenger, is protected by Act of Parliament against abuse of the greater bargaining power of the other party. As far as the shipper is concerned, this protection is now contained in the *Carriage of Goods by Sea Act 1971*. The legislative intention is, in the words of Lord Sumner,[71] to "replace a conventional contract, in which it was constantly attempted, often with much success, to relieve the carrier from every kind of liability, by a legislative bargain, under which . . . his position was to be one of restricted exemption."

The Act of 1971 was preceded by the *Carriage of Goods by Sea Act 1924* which has an interesting history[72]: the clauses in bills of lading exempting the shipowner from liability had become so complex and diffuse that the

[67] Malynes, *Lex Mercatoria* (3rd ed., 1686), p. 97.

[68] (1794) 5 T.R. 683.

[69] The most frequently used format of the bill of lading is today that known as the "Model B" bill of lading. This format was first developed as the result of the international co-operation under the auspices of the UN Economic Commission for Europe (ECE), which devised the so-called ECE layout key. In this work the ECE was greatly assisted by the International Chamber of Shipping which acted in consultation with the International Chamber of Commerce. This form of bill of lading is used as a model in the Board of Trade aligned series, published in *Systematic Export Documentation* (see p. 55, *ante*).

[70] See p. 335, *ante*.

[71] In *Gosse Millard Ltd.* v. *Canadian Government Merchant Marine* [1929] A.C. 223, 236 (in respect of the Carriage of Goods by Sea Act 1924, which preceded the 1971 Act).

[72] See the excellent account in Chap. 1, "Historical Antecedents," of Raoul P. Colinvaux, *The Carriage of Goods by Sea Act 1924* (Stevens, 1954).

usefulness of bills of lading as "currency of trade"[73] was seriously threatened. This was particularly unsatisfactory to holders of bills of lading who were not the original parties to the contract of carriage and consequently had no influence on its formation, such as further purchasers of goods, bankers who accepted the bills as security for advances, or insurers who were subrogated to the rights of the shipper. On the initiative of the International Law Association the *Hague Rules* 1921 relating to Bills of Lading were formulated and diplomatic conferences held in Brussels in 1922, 1923 and 1924[74] recommended their international adoption. In the United Kingdom, effect was given to the Hague Rules by the Carriage of Goods by Sea Act 1924. The Hague Rules imposed on the carrier certain minimum responsibilities which he could not reduce, *e.g.* to exercise due diligence to provide a seaworthy ship, to load, handle, stow, carry, keep, care for and discharge the goods and to issue a bill of lading in a particular form, and put upon him the liability for the proper and careful conduct of these operations while giving him certain maximum exemptions which he could not increase.

The Hague Rules were revised by the Brussels Protocol of 1968. The revised Rules, known as the *Hague-Visby Rules*, are appended to the Carriage of Goods Act 1971 and form part of it. That Act came into operation on June 23, 1977. It has repealed the Carriage of Goods by Sea Act 1924[75] and is the enactment in force at present. The Hague-Visby Rules have been accepted by the following States which are "contracting States" within section 2(1)(*a*) of the Act[76]:

Belgium, Denmark, Ecuador, France, Lebanon, Norway, Singapore, Sweden, Switzerland, Syria, Tonga, United Kingdom (which has extended the application of the Hague-Visby Rules to the Isle of Man and Gibraltar), and the German Democratic Republic.

The Hague-Visby Rules were fundamentally revised by the United Nations Convention on the Carriage of Goods by Sea 1978, which accepted the so-called *Hamburg Rules.* They were prepared by UNCITRAL and adopted by a United Nations conference at Hamburg on March 30, 1978. They have been signed already by 27 States.[77] The major alterations proposed by the Hamburg Rules are: they shall apply to all contracts for the carriage of goods by sea between two different States, except charterparties, even if the carriage is not carried out under a bill of lading; the period of responsibility of the carrier is extended so as to cover the whole period during which the goods are in his charge; the exclusion of the carrier's liability in case of error in navigation is abolished; a distinction

---

[73] Scrutton, *loc. cit.*, p. 402.

[74] The final conference was in 1924, after the United Kingdom Act, which was based on an earlier draft, had been adopted.

[75] The Carriage of Goods by Sea Act 1971 (Commencement) Order 1977 (S.I. 1977 No. 98 (c.35)) contains transitional provisions with respect to bills of lading issued on or before December 23, 1977.

[76] The Carriage of Goods by Sea (Parties to Convention) Order 1978 (S.I. 1978 No. 1885). Position: April 30, 1979. More states may be added by Statutory Instrument.

[77] Position: April 30, 1979.

is drawn between the contractual carrier and actual carrier, the contractual carrier being liable for the actual carrier and, on principle, both being liable to the shipper jointly and severally; the maximum limits of the carrier's liability are greatly increased and fixed by reference to the special drawing rights of the International Monetary Fund; the Rules may apply to transport documents other than bills of lading.

The present position is this: The Hamburg Rules are not in force yet and may, therefore, be disregarded for the purposes of this treatise. The Hague-Visby Rules are law in the United Kingdom and the other contracting States referred to earlier. A considerable number of states have not adopted the Hague-Visby Rules yet but still adhere to the original Hague Rules, amongst them, in particular the United States of America.[78] The original unity of international regulation in the law relating to bills of lading is thus lost, at least temporarily, until all sea-going States will have adopted again uniform Rules. The following treatment is founded on the United Kingdom Carriage of Goods by Sea Act 1971 and the Hague-Visby Rules contained in the schedule to that Act and reproduced in Appendix 2, below.[79]

But it should be noted that the original Hague Rules may still be relevant in proceedings before arbitrators or in the courts in the United Kingdom, *e.g.* if a dispute concerns a homeward bill of lading relating to a shipment from a State which is not a contracting State under the Hague-Visby Rules but still adheres to the original Hague Rules; such a bill would not be governed by the 1971 Act.

Application of the Carriage of Goods by Sea Act 1971

DOCUMENTARY APPLICATION. The Act, including the Hague-Visby Rules, applies to all shipments where "the contract expressly or by implication provides for the issue of a bill of lading or any similar document of title."[80]

It also applies to a receipt which is a non-negotiable document, if it expressly states that the contract for the carriage of goods by sea contained in or evidenced by it shall be governed by the Hague-Visby Rules, as if the receipt were a bill of lading.[81] A liner waybill or a data freight receipt[82] can thus be subjected to the Rules if the parties so desire.

The Rules do not normally apply to deck cargo or live animals,[83] but if the bill of lading or other receipt refers to such cargo, it may state expressly that the Rules shall apply.[84]

TERRITORIAL APPLICATION. Article X of the Rules provides:

---

[78] See U.S. Carriage of Goods by Sea Act 1936. For a list of States which have adopted the original Hague Rules, see Schmitthoff's *Export Trade* (6th ed.), pp. 310–311.

[79] See pp. 486, *et seq.*

[80] s. 1(4).

[81] s. 1(6)(*b*).

[82] See p. 357, *post.*

[83] See the definition of "goods" in Art. I(*c*).

[84] s. 1(7).

The provisions of these Rules shall apply to every bill of lading relating to the carriage of goods between ports in two different States if:

(*a*) the bill of lading is issued in a contracting State; or

(*b*) the carriage is from a port in a contracting State; or

(*c*) the contract contained in or evidenced by the bill of lading provides that these Rules or legislation of any State giving effect to them are to govern the contract,

whatever may be the nationality of the ship, the carrier, the shipper, the consignee, or any other interested person.

The Rules thus apply by force of law to outward bills of lading relating to all goods exported from Great Britain and Northern Ireland and any other contracting State and also to bills issued in these countries, but they do not normally apply to the transportation of live animals,[85] and deck cargo which is carried on deck in pursuance of the contract of carriage.[86] But where cargo is carried on deck without specific agreement between the parties as to the carriage on deck, and no statement appears on the face of the bill of lading that goods carried on deck are in fact so carried, the carriage is subject to the Rules. Where the bill of lading contains the usual clause that the shipowner shall be at liberty to carry on deck, he is free to do so but is not relieved, by that clause, of his obligations under Article III, r. 2, *e.g.* to stow diligently.[87] The Hague-Visby Rules apply to coastal as well as to international voyages.[88]

Carriers cannot contract out of these rules.[89]

The clause paramount

The Carriage of Goods by Sea Act 1924 provided[90] that every bill of lading to which it applied must contain an express statement that it was to have effect subject to the provisions of the original Hague Rules. Such a statement was frequently referred to in bills of lading as the *clause paramount*. The 1971 Act has discontinued this requirement and consequently there is no longer a legal obligation to insert a clause paramount into the bill.

Nevertheless, in practice in many instances a clause paramount is inserted into the bill of lading. The following is an example of the clause:

All the terms, provisions and conditions of the Carriage of Goods by Sea Act 1971 and the Schedule thereto are to apply to the contract contained in this bill of lading, and the company are to be entitled to the benefit of all privileges, rights and immunities contained in such Act, and the Schedule thereto as if the same were herein specifically set out. If anything herein contained be inconsistent with the said provisions it shall, to the extent of such inconsistency and no further, be null and void.

---

[85] As the carriage of live animals is not subject to the Act, shipowners are entitled to insert the "mortality" clause in the bill of lading.

[86] Sched., Art. 1(*c*).

[87] *Svenska Traktor Akt.* v. *Maritime Agencies* (*Southampton*) *Ltd.* [1953] 2 Q.B. 295.

[88] The original Hague Rules did not apply to coastal transport (Carriage of Goods by Sea Act 1924, s. 4; see 1971 Act, s. 1(3)).

[89] Sched., Art. III, r. 8.

[90] s. 3.

Lord Denning M.R. described the effect of the clause paramount as follows[91]:

> When a paramount clause is incorporated into a contract, the purpose is to give the Hague Rules contractual force; so that, although the bill of lading may contain very wide exceptions, the Rules are paramount and make the shipowners liable for want of due diligence to make the ship seaworthy and so forth.

Sometimes bills of lading embodying the clause paramount are used for homeward shipping from States other than contracting States and the question arises whether the Act applies in that case to such a bill. The answer depends on the wording of the clause; the Act applies if the clause is intended to subject such bills to the Act,[92] and it does not apply if the clause is only intended to restate the position as existing under the Act.[93] Generally speaking, the Hague Rules have shown a remarkably expansive character and are often adopted by contract, *i.e.* by insertion of a clause paramount, to shipping to which they do not apply by statute.[94] The Rules are even adopted, as far as applicable, by charterparties.[95]

Where a dispute arises whether English or foreign law governs the contract of carriage, the law referred to in the clause paramount is presumed to be the proper law of the contract.[96]

In modern law, very little weight is attributed to the presumption that the contract of carriage by sea is governed by the law of the flag of nationality which the ship carries because, as Willmer J. said in *The Assunzione*,[97] "in modern times there are a number of ships sailing the seas wearing the flags of countries with which their owners have no association at all." That presumption is, as Hodson L.J. observed in the Court of Appeal, in the same case,[98] available "only as a last resort, when the evidence is so evenly balanced that the court cannot otherwise reach a fair and just conclusion." Sometimes a charterparty bill of lading[99] incorporates a choice of law clause; in that case that clause applies to the bill of lading issued under the charterparty and the contract represented by the bill.[1]

Kinds of bills of lading

(a) "Shipped" and "received" bills. At present, unless the goods are shipped in containers, most bills of lading are "shipped" bills but occa-

---

[91] *Adamastos Shipping Co. Ltd.* v. *Anglo-Saxon Petroleum Co. Ltd.* [1957] 2 Q.B. 233, 266; *Nea Agrex S.A.* v. *Baltic Shipping Co. Ltd.* [1976] Q.B. 933.

[92] *Golodetz* v. *Kersten, Hunik & Co.* (1926) 24 Ll.L.R. 374; *Silver* v. *Ocean Steamship Co.* [1930] 1 K.B. 416, 424.

[93] *Tudor Accumulator Co. Ltd.* v. *Ocean Steam Navigation Co. Ltd.* (1924) 41 T.L.R. 81.

[94] K. Grönfors, "The Mandatory and Contractual Regulation of Sea Transport" [1961] J.B.L. 46.

[95] *Adamastos Shipping Co. Ltd.* v. *Anglo-Saxon Petroleum Co. Ltd.* [1959] A.C. 133; *The Merak* [1964] 2 Lloyd's Rep. 527, 536.

[96] *Kadel Chajkin and Ce De Ltd.* v. *Mitchell Cotts & Co.* (*Middle East*) *Ltd.* [1948] L.J.R. 535; *Stafford Allen & Sons Ltd.* v. *Pacific Steam Navigation Co.* [1956] 1 W.L.R. 629, 637.

[97] [1953] 1 W.L.R. 929, 938.

[98] [1954] P. 150, 194.

[99] See p. 354, *post*.

[1] *The San Nicholas* [1976] Lloyd's Rep. 8, 12.

sionally "received for shipment" bills (also called "alongside" bills) are used.

The difference between these types of bills may be seen from the following examples:

Shipped in apparent good order and condition by . . . on board the steam or motor vessel . . .

and

Received in apparent good order and condition from . . . for shipment on board the ship . . . or other ship or ships either belonging to this line or to other persons.

A "shipped" bill is also called an "on board" bill, particularly in the United States. United Kingdom businessmen buying in the United States of America usually call for an "on board ocean" bill of lading if they wish to get a "shipped bill of lading," as understood in this country. The practical difference between the shipped and received form is considerable.

Where the shipowner issues a "shipped" bill, he acknowledges that the goods are loaded on board ship; where he issues a "received for shipment" bill, he confirms only that the goods are delivered into his custody; in that case the goods might be stored in a ship or warehouse under his control. The "received" bill is, thus, less valuable than the "shipped" bill because it does not confirm that the shipment has already begun. The buyer under a c.i.f. contract need not accept a "received for shipment" bill as part of the shipping documents but may insist on a "shipped" bill, unless the contrary is expressly agreed upon by the parties to the contract of sale or is customary in a particular trade.[2] Where payment is arranged under a documentary credit, the terms of the credit usually provide that the bills of lading to be tendered have to be

clean, on board, to order and blank indorsed.

A "received" bill does not satisfy these terms because it is not an "on board" bill.

In *Yelo* v. *S. M. Machado & Co. Ltd.*,[3] the terms of the credit provided for "shipped" bills; Sellers J. held that the tender of "received" bills (which were not indorsed with the date of shipment) was insufficient.

The shipper is entitled, in all cases to which the Carriage of Goods by Sea Act 1971 applies,[4] to demand from the shipowner—

(1) The issue of a bill of lading after the goods have been received into the charge of the shipowner (Sched., Art. III, Rule 3). At this stage the shipowner is only obliged to issue a "received" bill, but if the goods are actually loaded he will, of course, issue a "shipped" bill.

(2) The issue of a "shipped" bill, after the goods are loaded (Sched., Art. III, Rule 7). The Act provides that where formerly another

---

[2] See p. 29, *ante*, and *Diamond Alkali Export Corporation* v. *Fl. Bourgeois* [1921] 3 K.B. 443.

[3] [1952] 1 Lloyd's Rep. 183.

[4] See p. 348, *ante*.

document of title, *e.g.* a "received" bill, was issued relating to the same goods, the shipowner may note the document at the port of shipment with the name of the ship upon which the goods are shipped and the dates of shipment, and when so noted, the document shall have the same functions as a "shipped" bill. The noting of "received" bills is not a customary practice in the United Kingdom.

A container bill of lading issued at an inland loading depot of the container shipping line is invariably a "received" bill of lading.

(b) Freight prepaid and freight collect bills of lading. These two types of bills of lading have already been considered.[5]

(c) Clean and "claused" bills. The difference between these types of bills and the consequences attending the issue of a qualified or "claused" bill of lading are dealt with elsewhere.[6]

It may be added that a clause which does not refer to the state of the goods when loaded but refers to the subsequent fate of the goods and their state when discharged does not make a bill a claused bill. It was held in one case[7] that the clause on the bill "Cargo covered by this bill of lading has been discharged . . . damaged by fire and/or water used to extinguish fire for which general average declared" did not deprive the bill of its character of a clean bill. Sometimes a charterparty bill of lading (which refers to the terms of the charterparty) is described as a claused bill.[8]

(d) "Negotiable" and other bills. Bills of lading can perform their principal function of enabling a person to dispose of goods which are no longer in his possession only if they are, at least to some extent, negotiable. But mercantile custom has mobilised cargoes to a smaller extent than credit, and consequently the negotiability of bills of lading is less developed in law than that of bills of exchange.

Bills of lading, like bills of exchange, may be made out to bearer, or to a particular person or his order; if made out to bearer, they are transferred by delivery while, if made out to order, they are transferred by indorsement and delivery of the bill. In practice, bills of lading made out to bearer are rarely used, as the bill of lading is a document of title which is a symbol of the goods represented by the bill[9]; a transfer of the bill of lading passes such rights in the goods as the parties wish to pass, *e.g.* the property if the goods are sold and the parties intend to pass the property on delivery of the bill, or a charge if the goods are pledged. It is the quality of the bill of lading as a document of title which, though logically distinct from its mode of transfer,[10] confers great practical significance on the latter: by making the bill of lading "negotiable" the cargo is, in fact, made negotiable.

---

[5] See p. 340, *ante*.
[6] See pp. 331–332, *ante*, and p. 360, *post*.
[7] *Golodetz & Co. Inc.* v. *Czarnikow-Rionda Co. Inc., The Times,* November 22, 1978.
[8] *Federal Commerce and Navigation Ltd.* v. *Molena Alpha Inc.* [1978] 3 W.L.R. 991.
[9] See p. 364, *post*.
[10] *Cf. Wah Tat Bank Ltd.* v. *Kum* [1967] 2 Lloyd's Rep. 437; *sub. nom. Kum* v. *Wah Tat Bank Ltd.* [1971] 1 Lloyd's Rep. 439 (P.C.).

It follows that a buyer who in the contract of sale has stipulated for "negotiable" bills of lading is entitled to reject non-negotiable bills.[11]

In two aspects, the negotiability of bills of lading is less developed than that of bills of exchange. First, while a bill of exchange is negotiable *unless* its negotiability is expressly *excluded*, a bill of lading is only negotiable if *made* "negotiable" by the shipper. The shipper when making out the bill has the choice of creating an instrument that can generally be used by the consignee as a medium of transfer of the goods represented by the bill, or of merely obtaining from the shipowner a formal receipt stipulating delivery to a named person.

In the modern bill of lading a box on the left-hand corner of the bill usually provides:

Consignee (if "Order" state Notify Party).

If the shipper intends to make the bill "negotiable," he completes this box by inserting "order" and adding as "notify party" the name of the consignee.[12]

A shipper who wishes to make out a bill of lading which is not "negotiable" does not insert the word "order" in the appropriate box of the bill but inserts the name of the consignee in the following box.[13] The effect of this procedure is that the consignee cannot transfer the property in the goods in transit by transfer of the bill, nor can the shipper do so except that he may pass the property in the goods to the consignee by delivering the bill to him.

The second aspect in which the negotiability of bills of lading varies from that of bills of exchange is that a holder of a bill of lading, unlike the holder in due course of a bill of exchange, cannot acquire a better title than his predecessor possessed.[14] He does not take "free of equities." This is a significant difference; it means that, where a "negotiable" bill of lading is obtained by fraud and indorsed to a bona fide indorsee for value, the latter does not acquire a title to the goods represented by the bill, while, if the same happens in case of a bill of exchange which is not overdue or dishonoured, the indorsee is entitled to all rights arising under the bill of exchange. In view of this difference, some authorities deny the bill of lading the character of a negotiable instrument and classify it as "quasi-negotiable."

In two exceptional cases, however, statutory provisions enable the bona fide indorsee of a bill of lading to acquire, upon certain carefully defined

[11] *Soproma S.p.A.* v. *Marine & Animal By-Products Corporation* [1966] 1 Lloyd's Rep. 367, see p. 248, *ante*.
[12] The shipper may name himself as consignee.
[13] These bills are referred to in the American practice as *straight bills of lading*. The U.S. Bills of Lading Pomerene Act 1916 (which, unlike the U.S. Carriage of Goods by Sea Act 1936, applies only to outward bills of lading) appears in Art. 9 to authorise a carrier to deliver the cargo to a consignee named in a straight bill of lading, without requiring the return of a bill.
[14] See p. 236, *ante*.

conditions, a better title than his predecessor possessed: The Factors Act 1889, s. 2(1), protects an indorsee who takes a bill from a factor acting in excess of his authority,[15] and the Sale of Goods Act, s. 47, provides that the unpaid seller's right of stoppage *in transitu* is defeated by a previous transfer of a bill from the buyer to an indorsee who takes the bill in good faith and for valuable consideration.[16]

(e) Steamship and charterparty bills of lading. It is, as has been explained in the preceding section, an important feature of the bill of lading that it is "quasi-negotiable." That implies that the bill itself shall contain all essential terms of the contract of carriage and the assignee (or other holder of the bill) shall be able to gather them from the document itself. A steamship bill of lading, sometimes abbreviated as S.S. Co.'s bill of lading,[17] satisfies that requirement but a charterparty bill does not.

A charterparty bill of lading is a bill which incorporates, by reference, some of the terms of the charterparty, so that they will have effect against the assignee of the bill. That introduces an undesirable element of uncertainty because it is by no means settled which clauses of the charterparty operate against the assignee and which do not apply to him.[18]

It should be noted that not every bill issued under a charterparty is a charterparty bill in the technical sense. In *Enrico Furst & Co.* v. *W. E. Fischer Ltd.*[17] the buyers bought a quantity of cast iron piping f.o.b. London; they chartered a tramp ship which proceeded to London and issued bills in the form authorised by the London Short Sea Traders' Association; these bills did not contain any reference to the terms of the charterparty; Diplock J. held that they fulfilled the requirements of a documentary credit stipulating for the tender of either "bills of lading" or "S.S. Co.'s bills of lading."

The importance of the distinction between steamship and charterparty bills is that, according to universal banking practice, a bank, unless instructed to the contrary, will refuse to accept a charterparty bill of lading

---

[15] See pp. 171–172, *ante*.

[16] See pp. 107–108, *ante*.

[17] *Enrico Furst & Co.* v. *W. E. Fischer Ltd.* [1960] 2 Lloyd's Rep. 340.

[18] On charterparty bills of lading, see Scrutton, *loc. cit.*, p. 61 *et seq.*; and Carver, *loc. cit.*, para. 404 *et seq.* See also *President of India* v. *Metcalfe Shipping Co.*; *the Dunelmia* [1970] 1 Q.B. 289 (C.A.) (charterer being the holder of the bill of lading by assignment from the original shippers; arbitration clause in charterparty held to be applicable to contract between shipowners and charterers); *The Annefield* [1971] P. 168 (arbitration clause in charterparty held not to be applicable to contract evidenced by the bills of lading); *The San Nicholas* [1976] 1 Lloyd's Rep. 8 (choice of law clause in charterparty held to be incorporated into bill of lading referring to the charterparty); *Federal Commerce and Navigation Ltd.* v. *Molena Alpha Inc.; The Nanfri* [1978] 3 W.L.R. 991. (charterparty bill of lading defeating commercial purpose of time charter). The American law on incorporation of charterparty arbitration clauses into bills of lading appears to be less exacting than English law, see John P. McMahon, "The Hague Rules and Incorporation of Charterparty Arbitration Clauses into Bills of Lading" in 2 *Journ. Maritime Law and Commerce* (1970), 1.

as good tender under a commercial credit. The *Uniform Customs and Practice for Commercial Documentary Credits 1974* state in article 19, para. (a)(ii), that, unless specifically authorised in the credits, there will be rejected "bills of lading which are issued under and are subject to the conditions of a charterparty."

(f) Through bills of lading. Where the ocean shipment forms only part of the complete journey and, subsequent[19] thereto, the goods have to be carried by other land or sea carriers, it is more convenient for the shipper to take out a through bill of lading than to contract with the various carriers who have to carry the goods at the consecutive stages of the journey.[20] The through bill compares with the extended marine insurance policy as obtained under the transit clause which embodies the "warehouse to warehouse" clause.[21] The necessity for a through bill arises, *e.g.* where goods have to be carried from the United Kingdom to such places as Baghdad. Through bills of lading are increasingly used in modern transport.

The following clauses are usually found in through bills; they illustrate clearly the points arising here:

> The freight received is inclusive of the cost of forwarding to . . . which will be arranged through the present carrier acting as agent for the shipper and/or consignees of the goods without any liability whatsoever, the conditions of such forwarding to be covered by the current lawful forms of contract.
>
> To avoid the tendering of separate documents at each stage of the journey delivery at destination will be given only on due presentation of one of these sets of bills of lading unto . . . or to his or their assigns and notice to this effect shall be included in the oncarrier's bill of lading or other freight contracts.

The shipper, who takes out a through bill, has only to deal with the carrier who signs the through bill. This carrier undertakes to arrange the transhipment with the on-carriers. The carrier charges an inclusive freight,[22] which, if prepayable, is due on the stipulated event[23] and governed by the rules explained earlier in respect of prepaid freight.[24] The goods are only delivered by the last on-carrier upon delivery of one part of the through bill which has to be dispatched to the consignee.

The principal contract of sea carriage is superimposed upon the contracts with the on-carriers, and this fact is sometimes expressed by a clause in the through bill adopting

> "all conditions expressed in the regular forms of bills of lading in use by the steamship company" performing the ocean carriage.

Through bills invariably contain a clause exempting the carrier arranging

---

[19] Through bills are also used where the oncarriage occurs prior to shipment, *e.g.* if goods are shipped from Chicago to the U.K. The observations in the text apply to such bills *mutatis mutandis*.

[20] For a detailed treatment of the through bill of lading, see Dr. A. Heini, *Das Durchkonnossement* (Through Bills of Lading) (1957, Freiburg, Switzerland).

[21] See p. 311, *ante*.

[22] As freight is charged at a higher rate than in normal cases, through bills are sometimes printed in red.

[23] See p. 339, *ante*.

[24] See p. 340, *ante*.

on-carriage from all liability or stating that transhipment is at owner's risk, or that the responsibility of the shipowner shall cease on delivery of the goods to the on-carrier.

Where legal difficulties arise between the shipper and an on-carrier, it may become relevant to ascertain whether the on-carrier is a party to a contract with the shipper or not. The answer depends, in the first instance, on the construction of the terms of the through bill. If the shipper contracted exclusively with the carrier, and the on-carrier is merely the carrier's servant, the carrier alone can claim against the on-carrier, he alone is responsible to the shipper and the direction of the on-carriage rests solely with him. If, on the other hand, the carrier, when contracting with the shipper, acts as agent of the on-carrier, a direct contract of carriage has come into existence between the shipper and the on-carrier. The former alternative is the more common practice.

The Carriage of Goods by Sea Act 1971 and the Rules adopted by the Act apply to through bills issued in respect of goods dispatched from a port in the United Kingdom and Northern Ireland, or of any other contracting State or issued in those countries, even after the goods have been transhipped at a foreign port. If and when the Hamburg Rules become law, the relationship between the shipper and the contractual and actual carrier will be fundamentally altered.[25]

(g) Through bills of lading covering oncarriage by air. This type of through bill is used where the goods, after having been unloaded at the port of discharge, are carried to their ultimate inland destination by air; this method is used, *e.g.* in East and Central Africa where inordinate delay would occur if inland transport were used for the oncarriage.

There is no reason why a through bill should not cover oncarriage by air. The legal difficulty is that the bill of lading is a document of title[26] but the air consignment note is not.[27] It is thought that a combination of these two documents does not give the combined through bill the character of a document of title. While in practice the goods might sometimes not be delivered to the consignee at the final place of destination without surrender of the through bill of lading by him, no commercial custom exists to that effect; the exporter cannot rely on this practice and has no legal remedy if it is not observed.

(h) Container bills of lading. These bills are issued by container shipping lines to cover the multi-modal transport of goods in a container from an inland place of dispatch to the final place of arrival. Container bills have features not present in other bills; they are considered later in this work.[28]

---

[25] See pp. 347–348, *ante*.
[26] See p. 364, *post*.
[27] See p. 386, *post*.
[28] See p. 378, *post*.

(i) Liner waybills; data freight receipts. In modern times the use of non-negotiable receipts has become more frequent than it was before.[29] Indeed, these instruments are perfectly satisfactory if the only persons involved in the transaction are the shipper, the shipowner and the consignee. On the other hand, if the consignee intends to transfer the title in the goods to a repurchaser before taking physical delivery of the goods, or if it is intended to pledge the goods before their arrival as a security to a bank, a traditional bill of lading must be used because only that instrument has the character of a document of title which enables the assignee of the document to acquire the general or special property in the goods.

The non-negotiable receipt is called a *liner waybill*[30] or a *data freight receipt.*[31] These receipts are issued by shipowners. They are used in ordinary as well as in container transport and are usually issued in the "received for shipment" form. They have this in common that they embody the terms of the contract of carriage by sea only by reference to the bills of lading issued by the shipowners in question, but do not state these terms in detail on the reverse, as is customary in the case of bills of lading.

(j) House bills of lading; groupage bills of lading; delivery orders. House bills of lading[32] are issued by forwarding agents who consolidate several cargoes belonging to different owners or forming the subject-matter of different export transactions in one consignment shipped under a groupage bill of lading issued by the carrier to the forwarding agent. Such a consolidation of cargoes is particularly frequent in the case of shipment in mixed containers.[33] An example of such a document is the *FIATA Combined Transport Bill of Lading.*[34]

A house bill of lading is a misnomer because such a document is not a bill of lading in the technical legal sense. It is not a document of title giving the consignee or assignee a right to claim the goods from the carrier. The provisions of the Bills of Lading Act 1855[35] which make bills of lading quasi-negotiable do not apply to it. It follows that a house bill of lading cannot be tendered under a c.i.f. contract as a proper bill of lading and, if the contract allows such a tender, the contract cannot be regarded as a proper c.i.f. contract.[36] Further, if payment is arranged under a documentary credit, the bank will reject a house bill of lading, unless specifically authorised in the credit to accept it; the *Uniform Customs and Practice for Documentary Credits* (*1974 Revision*) provide in article 19:

---

[29] It may be recalled that the Carriage of Goods by Sea Act 1971 makes the Hague-Visby Rules applicable to non-negotiable receipts which expressly state that the Rules shall apply; see p. 348, *ante*.

[30] *e.g.* the standard non-negotiable liner waybill, sponsored by Sitpro, with the support of General Council of British Shipping. This form of liner waybill has a further advantage in that it can be used for all shipping lines supporting this scheme.

[31] *e.g.* the instrument issued by ACL or Intercargo.

[32] Sometimes called shipping certificates.

[33] See p. 379, *post*.

[34] FIATA stands for *Fédération Internationale des Associations de Transitaires et Assimilés.*

[35] See p. 345, *ante*.

[36] *Comptoir d'Achat* v. *Luis de Ridder* [1949] A.C. 293.

(*a*) Unless specifically authorised in the credit, bills of lading of the following nature will be rejected:
(*i*) bills of lading issued by forwarding agents.

The splitting up of a consignment shipped under one bill of lading into smaller parcels sold to different buyers can be achieved by the use of delivery orders relating to specified portions of the whole consignment. Such delivery orders may be of two kinds,[37] and from the legal point of view this distinction is important: they may either be directed to an agent of the seller or they may be directed to the carrier; the latter type are called "ship's delivery orders." "[Ship's delivery orders] must . . . be documents issued by or on behalf of shipowners while the goods are in their possession or at least under their control and containing some form of undertaking that they will be delivered to the buyers (or perhaps to the bearer) on presentation of the documents."[38] The issue of delivery orders directed to an agent of the seller is similar to the issue of house bills of lading. In this case the whole consignment is consigned to a forwarding agent or to another person acting as agent of the seller at the port of destination, and the order directs the agent to deliver the portion or quantity of the goods stated in it to the holder of the order.

An order such as the one issued in *Comptoir d'Achat* v. *Luis de Ridder*,[39] does not give the buyer a direct right against the carrier.[40] Where it is provided in a contract described by the parties as being on c.i.f. terms that the seller may tender such a delivery order instead of a bill of lading the contract is not a true c.i.f. contract but is an "ex ship" or "arrival" contract.[41]

Ship's delivery orders are addressed to the carrier and instruct him to deliver the goods specified in them to the holder. They are of a higher legal quality than delivery orders addressed to an agent of the seller in so far as they give the holder in certain circumstances a direct right of action against the carrier, and where it is stipulated in a c.i.f. contract of sale that the seller may tender them in the place of bills of lading, the contract is regarded in law as creating the typical effect attributed to a c.i.f. contract, *viz.* that in certain respects the tender of the shipping documents constitutes the performance of the contract.

---

[37] An excellent explanation of the various types of delivery orders is contained in the judgment of Kerr J. in *Cremer* v. *General Carriers S.A.* [1974] 1 W.L.R. 341, 349.

[38] Kerr J. in *Waren Import Gesellschaft Krohn & Co.* v. *Internationale Graanhandel Thegra N.V.* [1975] 1 Lloyd's Rep. 146, 155.

[39] [1949] A.C. 293; see p. 38, *ante*. Further, *Margarine Union GmbH* v. *Cambay Prince Steamship Co. Ltd.* [1969] 1 Q.B. 219.

[40] Nor does it render the buyer liable to the shipowner for discharging port demurrage: *Tradax Internacional S.A.* v. *R. Pagnan & Fratelli* [1968] 1 Lloyd's Rep. 244 (in this case, on the terms of the contract of sale, the buyers likewise were not liable to the sellers for the demurrage which the latter as charterers had to pay to the shipowners).

[41] See p. 42, *ante*.

But even a delivery order to the ship is not of the same order and quality as a bill of lading, as was pointed out by Denning L.J. in one case[42] in the following passage:

> A seller often only has one bill of lading for the whole consignment, and he cannot deliver that one bill of lading to each of the buyers because it contains more goods than the particular contract of sale, so in each of his contracts of sale the seller stipulates the right to give a ship's delivery order . . . The ship's delivery order is not as good a protection for the buyer as a separate bill of lading would be, because it gives no cause of action against the ship unless the master attorns to the buyer and then it gives a different cause of action which may not be as favourable as a bill of lading. To overcome these drawbacks so far as possible, the contract provides for the ship's delivery order "to be countersigned by a banker, shipbroker, captain, or mate, if so required."

(k) "Stale" bills of lading. The expression "stale bill of lading" is used in banking practice. A bank which is instructed by, or on behalf of, a buyer to make finance available under a documentary credit upon presentation, by the seller, of a bill of lading (and of other documents) might feel obliged, in order to safeguard the interest of its principal, to reject the bill as being "stale." By that is meant that the bill, though conforming in all respects with the requirements of the credit, is presented so late that, as the result of the delay in its presentation, the consignee might become involved in legal or practical complications or might have to pay additional costs, *e.g.* for the warehousing of goods.

The *Uniform Customs and Practice for Documentary Credits 1974* provide in article 41 that documents must be presented within a specified time after issuance and that, if no time is specified, banks may refuse documents if presented to them later than 21 days after issuance of the bill of lading or other shipping documents. In many instances the introduction of a definite time limit has reduced the uncertainty inherent in the concept of the stale bill.

Often the bank will accept a bill which it might regard as stale on an indemnity being given by the seller.

Description of goods

The bill of lading, being a receipt of the shipowner for the goods, contains in its free space, known as the margin, a description of the goods. This description is perhaps the most vital part of the whole bill because the intended indorsee of the bill, who wishes to buy the goods by having the bill indorsed to him, normally has no opportunity of verifying the representations of the buyer as to their quantity and quality by examining them, and parts with the purchase price in reliance upon the shipowner's description of the goods in the bill of lading. In numerous cases disappointed buyers have tried, often successfully, to hold the shipowner responsible for an inaccurate description of the goods in the bill and ingenious clauses have been devised by shipowners to restrict that liability.

---

[42] *Colin & Shields* v. *Weddel & Co. Ltd.* [1952] 2 All E.R. 337, 343.

By the provisions[43] of the Rules, the shipper is entitled to demand that the bill of lading which the owner is obliged to issue to him should contain the following leading marks and other particulars:

(*a*) The leading marks necessary for identification of the goods as the same are furnished in writing by the shipper before the loading of such goods starts, provided such marks are stamped or otherwise shown clearly upon the goods if uncovered, or on the cases or coverings in which such goods are contained, in such a manner as should ordinarily remain legible until the end of the voyage;
(*b*) Either the number of packages or pieces, or the quantity, or weight, as the case may be, as furnished in writing by the shipper;
(*c*) The apparent order and condition of the goods:

Provided that no carrier, master or agent of the carrier, shall be bound to state or show in the bill of lading any marks, number, quantity, or weight which he has reasonable ground for suspecting not accurately to represent the goods actually received, or which he has had no reasonable means of checking.

When the shipowner affirms that the goods received are in "apparent good order and condition," he issue a "clean" bill; when this statement is qualified the bill is "claused."[44] The following definition of a clean bill of lading is provided by the *Uniform Customs and Practice for Documentary Credits 1974*, Art. 18[45]:

A clean shipping document is one which bears no superimposed clause or notation which expressly declares a defective condition of the goods and/or the packaging.

The words "in apparent good order and condition" denote that "apparently, and so far as met the eye, and externally [the goods] were placed in good order on board this ship,"[46] but the statement does not extend to qualities of the goods "which were not apparent to reasonable inspection having regard to the circumstances of loading."[47] The statement does not constitute a promise or undertaking by the shipowner, but is merely a statement of fact, an affirmation that certain facts are correct.[48] The shipowner who gives a clean bill does not promise to deliver goods "in apparent good order and condition" to the consignee, and may prove that the goods were damaged subsequent to the issue of the bill by an excepted peril, but he is prevented ("estopped") from denying that he received the goods in apparent good order and condition and cannot escape liability by alleging that an excepted peril existed prior to the issue of the clean bill, *e.g.* insufficient packing.[49] This estoppel operates only in favour of a

---

[43] Art. III, r. 3.

[44] See p. 352, *ante*, and Salmon J. in *British Imex Industries Ltd.* v. *Midland Bank Ltd.* [1958] 2 Q.B. 542, 551.

[45] See also "The Problem of Clean Bills of Lading" ICC Brochure 223 (1963). This brochure gives a list of superimposed clauses in current use for reference and optional use.

[46] *Per* Sir R. Phillimore in *The Peter der Grosse* (1875) 1 P.D. 414, 420.

[47] *Per* Branson J. in *Re National Petroleum Co., The Athelviscount* (1934) 39 Com.Cas. 227, 236; *Harris & Son Ltd.* v. *China Mutual Steam Navigation Co. Ltd.* [1959] 2 Lloyd's Rep. 500, 501 (inherent defect); see also Art. IV, r. 2, of the Rules.

[48] Channel J. in *Compañia Naviera Vascongada* v. *Churchill & Sim* [1906] 1 K.B. 237, 247.

[49] *Silver* v. *Ocean Steamship Co.* [1930] 1 K.B. 416; *Cremer* v. *General Carriers S.A.* [1974] 1 W.L.R. 341, 500.

consignee who *relies* on the statement in the bill that goods were in apparent good order and condition, but, as was said by Scrutton L.J.,[50]

the mercantile importance of clean bills is so obvious and important that I think the fact that he (*i.e.* the consignee) took the bill of lading which in fact is clean, without objection, is quite sufficient evidence that he relied on it.

The shipowner, when asked to issue a clean bill contrary to the facts, is in an evident predicament. If he obliges, he may be liable to the consignee; if he refuses, he inconveniences his client, the shipper, who might have difficulties in negotiating the bill. This explains why sometimes a—dangerous—attempt is made to induce the shipowner upon receipt of an indemnity from the shipper or his bank to issue a clean bill contrary to facts.[51] It further explains the tendency of clausing the bill in an apparently innocent form which, while protecting the shipowner, does not frighten off the unwary consignee. This accounts for vague qualifying remarks such as "weight unknown," "quality unknown," or "condition unknown" which are occasionally found in the margin of the bill. Some forms of bills of lading have the following or similar words imprinted in their context:

Measurement, weight, quantity, brand, contents, condition, quality and value as declared by shipper but unknown to the carrier.

The protective value, from the point of view of the shipowner, of qualifying clauses is greatly diminished in the cases to which the Carriage of Goods by Sea Act 1971 applies because under this Act the shipper is entitled to demand a clear statement in the bill of lading as to some of the particulars in question.[52] Where the required particulars are stated they cannot be negatived or contradicted by a clause that they are "unknown" to the shipowner. Such a qualifying clause is ineffective in law.

It should, however, be noted that the shipowner is only obliged, by Art. III, (3)(*b*) of the Rules, to state in the bill *either* the number of packages or pieces, *or* the quantity *or* the weight, but not *all* these particulars.[53] Where he states the number of packages, and adds a qualifying clause in respect of other particulars, *e.g.* "weight and quality unknown," the qualifying clause affords him protection in respect of the latter particulars.[54] But the shipowner who admits having received the goods in apparent good order and condition cannot nullify this admission by adding "condition unknown," as was held in one case[55] where the cargo consisted of timber which was loaded in a deteriorated condition; the master recorded in his log that the timber was "very black, wet and partly musty" but issued a clean bill qualified only by the words "condition unknown." Langton J.

---

[50] *Loc. cit.*, p. 429.
[51] See p. 368, *post.*
[52] See p. 360, *ante.*
[53] As regards air transport under the Warsaw Convention 1929, compare *Corocraft Ltd. and Vendome Jewels Ltd.* v. *Pan American Airways Inc.* [1969] 1 Q.B. 616 (C.A.); see p. 387, n. 85.
[54] *Pendle & Rivet* v. *Ellerman Lines* (1927) 33 Com.Cas. 70, 77; *Re National Petroleum Co., The Athelviscount* (1934) 39 Com.Cas. 227.
[55] *The Skarp* [1935] P. 134.

held that the clause was insufficient to convey to the consignee that the timber was damaged. The learned judge said[56]:

> The straightforward thing to do was surely to put upon the bill of lading, in the ample margin which is apparently provided for that purpose, a clause which would clearly advertise to any buyer of a particular bill of lading that the goods he was going to receive were not in good order and condition. It would not have been beyond the master's power to take the entry from his own log and to put upon the bill of lading "very black, wet and partly musty." If he could see it for the purposes of his log, he could with the same eyes have seen it for the purposes of the bill of lading.

Another question is whether the shipowner can escape from the effect of the estoppel created by a clean bill of lading by pleading that under the terms of the contract of sale the consignee was bound to accept the defective goods in any event.[57] Kerr J.[58] rejected this contention because the consequences of the issue of a clean bill of lading arise from the contract of carriage, and a party thereto cannot avail himself of a defence which originates in quite a different contract, namely the contract of sale.[59]

The shipper is deemed to have guaranteed to the shipowner the accuracy of the marks, number, quantity and weight as furnished by him, and the shipper has to indemnify the shipowner against loss or damage arising from inaccuracies in such particulars; the right of the shipowner to be indemnified by the shipper in these circumstances cannot be pleaded by the shipowner in defence against a consignee who tries to hold the shipowner responsible.[60] Where a bill of lading is disputed and the shipowner is hesitant to issue a clean bill, the shipper sometimes gives him an express indemnity in order to induce him to issue a clean bill, but such indemnity might be illegal and in that case does not protect the shipowner.[61] Bills of lading often contain clauses providing that in case of incorrect or insufficient declaration of the cargo the shipper shall be obliged to pay double freight by way of liquidated damages.[62]

A bill of lading issued under the Carriage of Goods by Sea Act 1971 is *prima facie evidence* of the receipt of the goods by the carrier as described in accordance with Article III(3)(*a*)–(*c*); this provision[63] applies to "shipped" and "received" bills alike. The Hague-Visby Rules—different from the original Hague Rules—further provide[64] that the bill shall be *conclusive evidence* regarding those particulars in the hands of a third party acting in good faith; such a third party, it is thought, would be the consignee,

---

[56] *Ibid.* at p. 142.

[57] Essentially this is a question of reliance on the estoppel. In *The Skarp* [1935] P. 134 Langton J. held, on the facts of the case before him, that the consignee would have accepted the goods even in their defective condition.

[58] In *Cremer* v. *General Carriers S.A.* [1974] 1 W.L.R. 341, 353.

[59] This would be *res inter alios acta* (a transaction between other parties).

[60] Hague-Visby Rules, Art. III(5).

[61] See p. 367, *post*.

[62] See p. 86, *ante*.

[63] Rules, Art. III(4); *Att.-Gen. of Ceylon* v. *Scindia Steam Navigation Co. Ltd.* [1962] A.C. 60 (but the bill is not even prima facie evidence as to the weight or contents of the packages; see p. 361, *ante*).

[64] r. 4, second sentence.

to whom the bill is transferred, and an indorsee. As far as these persons are concerned, the Rule goes further than the Bills of Lading Act 1855, s. 3, which provides that a "shipped" bill of lading in the hands of a consignee or indorsee for valuable consideration is conclusive evidence of such shipment—*but not of the leading marks and other particulars of the goods as stated in the bill*—as against the master or other person signing the bill, even if the goods or part of them have not been shipped; but the person signing the bill is exonerated by showing that the consignee had actual notice of the true position, or that the misrepresentation was due to a fraud of the shipper, the consignee or a person under whom the consignee claims. The bill is only conclusive evidence of shipment against the person who actually signed it, *e.g.* the master of the ship, and not against the shipowner who did not sign it in person, but the shipowner cannot normally repudiate the signature of the master or another agent unless he can prove that the shipper was aware of the lack of the agent's authority. The master or other agent has no authority to sign a shipped bill of lading for goods which were never loaded, and consequently the shipowner is not liable on such a signature.[65] But the—unauthorised—agent himself may be liable for breach of an implied warranty of authority.[66]

Bills of lading sometimes contain a clause cautioning shippers against shipping dangerous or damaging goods[67]; *e.g.*:

> Shippers are cautioned against shipping goods of a dangerous or damaging nature as by so doing they may become responsible for all consequential damage and also render themselves liable to penalties imposed by statute.

The liability of the shipper for damage done by his goods to the ship or other cargoes arises from an implied warranty on his part that the goods are fit for carriage in the ordinary way.[68] The shipper warrants not only that the goods will not cause physical injury or damage but also that the goods can be discharged without delay due to import restrictions or prohibitions.[69] The shipper is not liable under the warranty if he duly informs the shipowner of the nature of the goods or if the shipowner knows, or ought to know, that they are dangerous or that delay in the discharge may be encountered. Under the Merchant Shipping Acts 1894 to 1979[70] a shipper is liable to fines for shipping in any vessel, British or foreign, explosives, petrol or other goods scheduled as "dangerous" without giving the shipowner due notice in writing and distinctly marking the nature of the goods on the outside of the packages, or for knowingly sending dangerous goods under false description of the goods or the sender. In addition, shippers are required to furnish, prior to shipment, a statement in writing

---

[65] *Grant* v. *Norway* (1851) 10 C.B. 665; *Heskell* v. *Continental Express* [1950] W.N. 210; *V/O Rasnoimport* v. *Guthrie & Co. Ltd.* [1966] 1 Lloyd's Rep. 1, 8.

[66] *V/O Rasnoimport* v. *Guthrie & Co. Ltd.* [1966] 1 Lloyd's Rep. 1, 8.

[67] The clauses are also found in charterparties: *Micada Confedria S.A.* v. *Texim* [1968] 2 Lloyd's Rep. 57.

[68] Art. IV, r. 6.

[69] *Mitchell, Cotts & Co.* v. *Steel Brothers & Co. Ltd.* [1916] 2 K.B. 610.

[70] ss. 446–450.

of the identity of the goods and nature of the danger to which the goods give rise and of other particulars.[71] Further, the nature of the danger and the identity of the goods has to be marked clearly with a distinctive label or stencil on the outside of each package of dangerous cargo. Failure to comply with these regulations will result in the cargo being refused for shipment and renders the sender liable to heavy penalties. Goods of inflammable, explosive or dangerous nature may be rendered innocuous by the shipowner or his agent without liability on his part; if they are carried without the shipowner's consent, this right can be exercised at any time; if they are carried with his consent, this right can only be exercised if the goods endanger the ship or cargo and subject to liability for general average, if any.[72]

The bill of lading as a document of title

It has been seen[73] that the principal purpose of the bill of lading is to enable the person entitled to the goods represented by the bill to dispose of the goods while they are in transit. By mercantile custom, possession of the bill is in many respects equivalent to possession of the goods and the transfer[74] of the bill of lading has normally the same effect as the delivery of the goods themselves. The bill of lading is, in so far, a symbol of the goods themselves. We have this function of the bill of lading in mind when referring to it as a document of title.

Two points should be noted in this connection: first, the transfer of the bill of lading is merely deemed to operate as a symbolical transfer of possession of the goods, but not necessarily as a transfer of the property in them. The transfer of the bill passes such rights in the goods as the parties intend to pass. Where the consignee or indorsee of the bill is the agent of the shipper at the port of destination, it is evident that the parties, by transferring the bill of lading, intend only to pass the right to claim delivery of the goods from the shipowner upon arrival of the goods, but not the property in them. Where the consignee or indorsee is a banker who advances money on the security of the goods represented by the bill, the parties are likely to intend, by the transfer of the bill, the creation of a charge or pledge on the goods in favour of the banker, but not the transfer of the property in them to him. Where the seller of goods transfers the bill of lading to the buyer, as he is bound to do in case of a c.i.f. sale and as he sometimes voluntarily undertakes in other cases, it depends again on the intention of the parties whether the property passes by transfer of the bill of lading or remains in the seller. As far as specific or ascertained goods are concerned, this is in accordance with the fundamental rule laid

[71] Merchant Shipping (Dangerous Goods) Rules 1965 (S.I. 1965 No. 1067; S.I. 1968 No. 332; S.I. 1972 No. 660). These Rules were made under the Merchant Shipping (Safety Convention) Act 1949, s. 23.

[72] Art. IV, r. 6.

[73] See p. 345, *ante*.

[74] On the transfer of the bill of lading, see p. 352, *ante*.

down in the Sale of Goods Act, s. 17(1),[75] which, it should be noted, applies irrespective of whether the goods sold are represented by a bill of lading or not. The provisions of the Act governing the passing of property in the goods sold have been reviewed earlier,[75] and it is only necessary here to recall that it has been decided that taking out a bill of lading in the name of the buyer does not necessarily reveal the seller's intention of passing the property to him.[76]

Secondly, only a person holding a bill of lading is entitled to claim delivery of the goods from the shipowner. The shipowner is protected if he delivers the goods to the holder of an original bill—though it is only one in a set[77]—and need not inquire into the title of the holder of the bill or the whereabouts of the other parts of the bill. The bill of lading retains its character of document of title until the contract of carriage by sea is discharged by delivery of the goods against the bill,[78] and the shipowner is not responsible for wrongful delivery of the goods against the bill unless he knows of the defect in the title of the holder. If the shipowner (or his agent) delivers the goods to a person who is not the holder of the bill of lading, he does so at his peril. If that person is not the true owner, the shipowner is liable to the latter for conversion of the goods. In practice, shipowners rigorously insist on the production of a bill of lading, but, where the bill is produced and the identity of the consignee is in doubt, they sometimes deliver the goods against letters of indemnity which, in some instances, have to be provided by a bank.

The difficulties which might arise when the shipowner releases the goods without insisting on the production of the bill of lading are demonstrated by *Sze Hai Tong Bank* v. *Rambler Cycle Co. Ltd.*[79] In that case an English company had sold bicycle parts to importers in Singapore; the goods were shipped in the *SS. Glengarry* which belonged to the Glen Line Ltd. The sellers instructed the Bank of China to collect the proceeds and release the bills of lading to the buyers on payment. The buyers, however, induced the carriers to deliver the goods to them without bills of lading, on an indemnity given by the buyers and their bank, the Sze Hai Tong Bank. When the sellers discovered what had happened they brought proceedings in the courts of Singapore against the carriers for damages for breach of contract and conversion, and the carriers brought in as third parties the Sze Hai Tong Bank against which the carriers claimed a declaration of indemnity. The High Court of Singapore held the carriers to be liable and held further than the bank was obliged to indemnify them. The bank

[75] See p. 77, *ante*.

[76] *The Kronprinsessan Margareta* [1921] 1 A.C. 486, 517. For the right of the consignor to sue when the bill of lading has been transferred to the consignee or an indorsee, see p. 344, *ante*.

[77] See p. 333, *ante*.

[78] *Barclays Bank Ltd.* v. *Commissioners of Customs and Excise* [1963] 1 Lloyd's Rep. 81 (the bill does not lose its character of document of title by "exhaustion," *i.e.* by non-presentation immediately on arrival of the ship).

[79] [1959] A.C. 576.

appealed without success to the Court of Appeal in Singapore and eventually to the Judicial Committee of the Privy Council. Lord Denning who gave the judgment of the court said[80]:

> It is perfectly clear that a shipowner who delivers without production of the bill of lading does so at his peril. The contract is to deliver, on production of the bill of lading, to the person entitled under the bill of lading. . . . The shipping company did not deliver the goods to any such person. They are therefore liable for breach of contract unless there is some term in the bill of lading protecting them. And they delivered the goods, without production of the bill of lading, to a person who was not entitled to receive them. They are, therefore, liable in conversion unless likewise protected.

The Judicial Committee rejected the argument that the carriers—and consequently the bank—were relieved from liability by a clause in the bill of lading that the responsibility of the carriers should cease absolutely after the goods were discharged from the ship, because that exemption clause was not intended to protect a carrier who deliberately disregarded his obligation and committed a fundamental breach of contract by releasing the goods without production of a bill of lading.

On the other hand, even the true owner of the goods cannot claim the goods if unable to produce a bill of lading. In one case[81] a Canadian company bought six trucks and certain spare parts from a seller in England. The seller shipped the goods from Southampton to Montreal and paid the freight but the carriers refused to deliver the bills of lading (which were duly drawn up and signed) to the seller until he paid them certain shipping charges incurred in respect of previous shipments. The carriers who alleged to have a general lien on the bills of lading forwarded them to their agents at Montreal with instructions to hold them until they sanctioned their release. The Canadian company claimed to be the owners of the goods and applied to the English court for an interim injunction ordering the carriers to deliver the goods to them without production of a bill of lading. The Court of Appeal refused to make such an order. Denning L.J. said[82]: "Whether the property has passed or not, in my opinion, they [the buyers] ought to produce the bills of lading duly endorsed in order to make a good title at this stage," and Lloyd-Jacob J. observed[83]: "A decision affirming title at this stage may create grave injustice to some person or persons acquiring a title through the bills of lading in ignorance of the circumstances with which this action is concerned."

In some foreign countries, notably Venezuela and other South American countries, a consignee may obtain delivery of the cargo without actual tender of the bill of lading.

---

[80] *Ibid.* at p. 586.
[81] *Trucks & Spares Ltd.* v. *Maritime Agencies* (*Southampton*) *Ltd.* [1951] W.N. 597.
[82] At p. 983.
[83] At p. 984.

Logically the function of the bill of lading as a document of title is distinct from its quality as a "negotiable" instrument.[84] Even a bill of lading which is not made "negotiable," operates as a document of title because the consignee named therein can only claim delivery of the goods from the shipowner if able to produce the bill of lading. But the great practical value of the bill of lading as a means of making goods in transit rapidly transferable is due to the customary combination of the two features of the bill, *viz.* its quasi-negotiability and its function as a document of title.

Indemnities and bills of lading

It has already been observed[85] that a difficult situation develops if the carrier feels compelled to refuse the issue of a clean bill of lading. Where payment is arranged under a documentary credit, the exporter will be unable to obtain finance from the bank if he presents a claused, instead of a clean, bill, and, on the other hand, the carrier who issues a clean bill although he knows that the goods are not in apparent good order and condition when shipped or received for shipment, is estopped from denying as against the bona fide consignee or assignee that he received the goods in such condition and might be liable to him.[86]

The obvious way out of this difficulty is for the exporter to offer the carrier an indemnity under which the exporter will recompense him for any loss sustained as the result of the issue of a clean bill of lading. Such indemnity, however, does not provide a solution in all circumstances. If both parties, the exporter and the carrier, know that the clean bill for which the indemnity is given, should never have been issued, in view of the condition of the cargo, they have conspired to defraud the bona fide consignee or assignee who will take up the bill and part with his money, thinking that the goods did not show any defect when shipped or received for shipment. Such fraud vitiates the indemnity and renders it illegal; the carrier cannot claim under it against the exporter and, from the carrier's point of view, such indemnity is completely worthless.

Not all indemnities given for clean bills of lading are illegal. Two cases have to be distinguished: the clausing of the bill may concern a technicality which, as the exporter well knows, does not entitle the buyer to reject the goods; in that case the tender of an indemnity is legitimate and convenient. Only if the clausing of the bill concerns a serious matter which would entitle the buyer to reject the goods, is the indemnity tainted by fraud[87] and invalid; the proper course for the exporter is here to inform the buyer

[84] See p. 352, *ante*. The quality of the bill of lading as a document of title originates in the custom of the merchants and was first recognised by the courts in *Lickbarrow* v. *Mason* (1794) 5 T.R. 683; the character of the bill of lading as a quasi-negotiable instrument was created by the Bills of Lading Act 1855.

[85] On pp. 360–362, *ante*.

[86] See p. 360, *ante*.

[87] A consignee or indorsee of a fraudulently issued clean bill of lading can sue for fraudulent misrepresentation: *Cordova Land Co. Ltd.* v. *Victor Brothers Inc.* [1966] 1 W.L.R. 793, 800.

at once of the true facts and to ask him to amend the credit and to authorise the bank to pay against the bills of lading as issued. These principles were stated in *Brown, Jenkinson & Co. Ltd.* v. *Percy Dalton* (*London*) *Ltd.*[88] where the majority of the Court of Appeal held that an indemnity was invalid which was given by the exporters [the defendants] to the plaintiffs who were loading brokers for the shipowners; the cargo consisted of 100 barrels of orange juice and the tally clerk had described the casks on his tally card as "old and frail" and recorded some leaking, but the plaintiffs, on the request of the defendants, had issued clean bills of lading against the defendant's indemnity. Pearce L.J. said[89]:

> Trust is the foundation of trade; and bills of lading are important documents. . . In trivial matters and in cases of bona fide dispute where the difficulty of ascertaining the correct state of affairs is out of proportion to its importance, no doubt the practice [of accepting indemnities] is useful. But here the plaintiffs went outside those reasonable limits . . . Recklessness is sufficient to make a man liable in damages for fraud. Here the plaintiffs intended their misrepresentation to deceive, although they did not intend that the party deceived should ultimately go without just compensation.

London banks have for some time past by mutual consent refused to issue and countersign indemnities required to obtain clean bills of lading.[90]

An indemnity given to the carrier in order to induce him to deliver the goods to the consignee without production of the bill of lading, although in some instances equally reprehensible, is valid and enforceable by the carrier, as has been seen from the discussion of *Sze Hai Tong Bank* v. *Rambler Cycle Co. Ltd.*[91]

The limitation period for an action for an indemnity is not one year from the date of the delivery of the goods but such action can be brought within the time allowed by the law of the court seized of the case.[92] In English law the limitation period for a claim founded on a simple contract is six years after the cause of action accrued.[93]

Liability of shipowner for loss of or damage to the goods

(a) General rules of liability. The liability of the shipowner for goods exported from the United Kingdom is governed by the Carriage of Goods by Sea Act 1971 which, it will be remembered,[94] applies to all outward shipments under bills of lading, from any port of the United Kingdom or a contracting state, except in a few relatively unimportant cases, and of which the parties cannot contract out.[95] The Rules relating to Bills of Lading, as appended to the Act, are further often adopted by the clause

---

[88] [1957] 2 Q.B. 621. Referred to with approval in the Indian case of *Ellerman & Bucknall Steamship Co.* v. *Sha Misrimal* [1966] All India Rep. 1892.
[89] [1957] 2 Q.B. 621, 639.
[90] [1957] J.B.L. 173.
[91] [1959] A.C. 576; see p. 365, *ante*.
[92] But the time must not be less than three months; Art. III(6 bis); see p. 376, *post*.
[93] Limitation Acts 1939 and 1975, s. 2(1).
[94] See p. 349, *ante*.
[95] Rules, Art. III(8).

paramount[96] for journeys not covered by the Act. Where the Rules do not apply by force of law or voluntary agreement, the liability of the shipowner is determined by the contract of the parties as evidenced in the bill of lading which, as a rule, will contain stipulations exempting the shipowner from liability in case of loss of or damage to the goods entrusted to his care. In the absence of contractual stipulations the rules of common law apply to contracts of carriage by sea not governed by the statutory Rules; according to common law, the shipowner impliedly undertakes the same liability as a common carrier, namely to carry the goods at his own absolute risk, except if the goods are lost or damaged by act of God, the Queen's enemies, inherent defect of the goods themselves or the shipper's default.[97] For practical purposes, it is sufficient to consider in the following paragraphs the shipowner's liability under the Carriage of Goods by Sea Act 1971.

The responsibilities of the shipowner in respect of the safety of the goods entrusted to his care are described in detail in the Rules,[98] Article III:

1. The carrier shall be bound, before and at the beginning of the voyage, to exercise due diligence to—
(*a*) Make the ship seaworthy.
(*b*) Properly man, equip and supply the ship.
(*c*) Make the holds, refrigerating and cool chambers, and all other parts of the ship in which goods are carried, fit and safe for their reception, carriage and preservation.
2. Subject to the provisions of Article IV,[98] the carrier shall properly and carefully load, handle, stow, carry, keep, care for and discharge the goods carried.

The principle underlying these provisions is that the shipowner is only liable if acting negligently. This is clearly expressed by the words, in paragraph 1, enjoining the shipowner "to exercise due diligence," and, in paragraph 2, postulating that he should act "properly and carefully." The responsibilities of the shipowner under the Act are thus lighter than they are at common law though this is compensated by the provision that he cannot contract out of the Act. In particular, at common law the shipowner is under an absolute obligation to provide a seaworthy ship, *i.e.* a ship that in all respects is fit to load, carry and discharge the cargo safely having regard to the ordinary perils encountered on the voyage. Under the Act, he is only responsible if he fails, upon reasonable inspection, to discover the lack of seaworthiness of his ship.[99] "Under the old rule, the only relevant question was whether the ship was seaworthy or unseaworthy. That rule was no doubt well adapted to more simple days when ships were not very complicated wooden structures . . . but in modern times, when ships are complicated steel structures full of complex machinery, the old unqualified rule imposed too serious an obligation on carriers by sea . . . he is to be liable for all such duties as appertain to a prudent and careful

[96] See p. 349, *ante*.
[97] Halsbury's *Laws of England* (3rd ed.), Vol. 35, "Shipping and Navigation," pp. 286–287.
[98] See App. 2, p. 486, *post*.
[99] Carriage of Goods by Sea Act 1971, s. 3.

carrier acting as such by the servants and agents in his employment."[1] The obligation of the shipowner to use due diligence in the cases stated in Article III(1) and (2) is not limited to his personal diligence; he is liable if servants and agents in his employment fail to act with due diligence[1] and he was even held to be liable for a reputable independent contractor whom he instructed to repair his ship and whose workman acted negligently although the shipowner himself, or his servants and agents, were not guilty of any negligence.[2] That under Article III(1) and (2) the shipowner is liable for the negligence of his servants and agents is an important extension of his liability and should be contrasted with Article IV(2)(*a*)[3] which provides that the shipowner is not liable for the neglect or the fault of his servants or agents in the navigation or management of the ship. On the other hand, a servant or agent of the carrier—but not an independent contractor—if sued, is entitled to the same defences and limits of liability which the carrier may invoke under the Rules.[4]

The liability of the shipowner for the negligent acts or omissions of his servants exists not only in the cases listed in Article III(1) but also in those mentioned in Article III(2). Thus, shipowners were held liable to owners of a cargo of maize for damage caused by bad stowage. Above the maize, which was carried mostly in bulk in a lower hold, a cargo of tallow in casks was carried. During the voyage some of the casks were broken and the tallow which became heated began to leak and penetrated to the hold in which the maize was stowed, causing it damage.[5] Shipowners were likewise held liable for damage caused during the loading operation by the negligence of their servants,[6] for the destruction, by negligently caused fire of the goods after they were loaded but before the ship sailed,[7] and for the loss of a tractor carried on deck without specific agreement with the shipper that it should be deck cargo, and washed overboard because it was not properly secured.[8] On the other hand, shipowners did not act negligently and were not held to be responsible when in an intermediate port, in spite of a careful watch, the cover plate of a storm valve in a hold was stolen by stevedores during unloading and loading and sea water damaged the

---

[1] *Per* Wright J. in *W. Angliss & Co. (Australia) Proprietary* v. *Peninsular and Oriental Steam Navigation Co.* [1927] 2 K.B. 456, 461; *Ministry of Food* v. *Lamport and Holt Line Ltd.* [1952] 2 Lloyd's Rep. 371; *International Packers London Ltd.* v. *Ocean S.S. Co. Ltd.* [1955] 2 Lloyd's Rep. 218, 236; *Riverstone Meat Co. Pty. Ltd.* v. *Lancashire Shipping Co. Ltd., The Muncaster Castle* [1961] A.C. 807; *Union of India* v. *N.V. Reederij Amsterdam, The Amstelslot* [1963] 2 Lloyd's Rep. 223; *Albacora S.R.L.* v. *Westcott & Laurance Line Ltd., The Maltasian* [1966] 2 Lloyd's Rep. 53; *The Flowergate* [1967] 1 Lloyd's Rep. 1, 7.

[2] *Riverstone Meat Co. Pty. Ltd.* v. *Lancashire Shipping Co. Ltd.*; *The Muncaster Castle* [1961] A.C. 807.

[3] See App. 2, p. 488, *post*.

[4] Art. IVbis; see p. 375, *post*.

[5] *Ministry of Food* v. *Lamport and Holt Line Ltd.* [1952] 2 Lloyd's Rep. 371.

[6] *Pyrene Co. Ltd.* v. *Scindia Navigation Co. Ltd.* [1954] 2 Q.B. 402; see p. 19, *ante*.

[7] *Maxine Footwear Co. Ltd.* v. *Canadian Government Merchant Marine Ltd.* [1959] A.C. 589.

[8] *Svenska Traktor Akt.* v. *Maritime Agencies (Southampton) Ltd.* [1953] 2 Q.B. 295.

cargo in the hold on the further voyage.[9] But if the master, when stowing the goods, follows strictly the instructions of the shipper's agent (who acts within his authority), the shipper may be estopped by conduct from asserting that the stowage was defective.[10]

The carrier is practically bound to play some part in the loading operation but the scope and area of the part which he has to play is determined by the contract of the parties, and may further depend upon the custom and practice of the port and the nature of the cargo. The phrase "shall properly and carefully load" in Article III(2) is not designed to define the scope and area of the carrier's part in the loading operation but defines the terms on which that service is to be performed.[11] Thus, where goods sold under an f.o.b. contract and loaded from the quay in the ship's tackle onto the ship were damaged by the negligence of the shipowner's servants before they crossed the ship's rail, *viz.* they were dropped on the quay, the shipowners were liable because *under the contract of carriage* in question they were responsible for the *whole* of the loading, and not only for the part following the crossing of the rail.[12]

The duty of the carrier properly and carefully to discharge the goods carried, which is stipulated in Article III(2), is normally ended when the goods are delivered from the ship's tackle to a person entitled to receive them[13] in the same apparent order and condition as on shipment,[14] but where they are discharged into a lighter, the shipowner continues to be liable if the goods loaded into the lighter are damaged by other cargoes stowed negligently on top of them[15] Since these words of Article III(2) likewise define the terms on which the contract of carriage is to be performed and have no geographical connotation, they do not invalidate a clause according to which the carrier is entitled, if the port of discharge is strikebound, to discharge the goods at any other safe and convenient port[16]; the costs of oncarriage to the agreed port of discharge have to be borne by the shipper.

(b) Excepted perils. The Rules contain, in Article IV, a "long list of matters in respect of loss or damage arising or resulting from which the carrier is not liable."[17] The catalogue of excepted perils is reproduced in

[9] *Leesh River Tea Co. Ltd.* v. *British India Steam Navigation Co. Ltd., The Chyebassa* [1966] 1 Lloyd's Rep. 450.

[10] *Ismael* v. *Polish Ocean Lines* [1976] Q.B. 893.

[11] *G. H. Renton & Co. Ltd.* v. *Palmyra Trading Corporation of Panama, The Caspiana* [1957] A.C. 149.

[12] *Pyrene Co. Ltd.* v. *Scindia Navigation Co. Ltd.* [1954] 2 Q.B. 402; see p. 19, *ante*.

[13] *Sze Hai Tong Bank Ltd.* v. *Rambler Cycle Co. Ltd.* [1959] 2 Lloyd's Rep. 114, 120.

[14] Wright J. in *Gosse Millard* v. *Canadian Government Merchant Marine*; *American Can Co.* v. *Same* [1927] 2 K.B. 432, 434.

[15] Roche J. in *Goodwin, Ferreira & Co. Ltd.* v. *Lamport and Holt Ltd.* (1920) 34 Ll.L.R. 192, 194; see also *East & West Steamship Co.* v. *Hossain Brothers* [1968] 2 Lloyd's Rep. 145, 149 (Pakistan Sup.Ct.).

[16] *G. H. Renton & Co. Ltd.* v. *Palmyra Trading Corporation of Panama, The Caspiana* [1957] A.C. 149.

[17] Wright J. in *Gosse Millard* v. *Canadian Government Merchant Marine* [1927] 2 K.B. 432, 434.

Appendix 2.[18] The burden of proof rests upon the shipowner who wishes to claim exemption from his liability on the ground that the damage or loss of the cargo is due to one of the excepted perils.[19] Among the grounds on which the shipowner will frequently try to rely, is inherent vice of the cargo (Art. IV(2)(m)).[20]

From the point of view of the shipper, the catalogue of exceptions is not so disconcerting as it would appear at the first glance. A comparison of the catalogue with the standard form of marine insurance policy, as appended to the Marine Insurance Act 1906,[21] shows that some exceptions, which are not based on the shipper's own fault or neglect (such as insufficient packing), are normally covered by marine insurance, in particular, acts of God, perils of the seas, restraint of princes and the King's enemies. Others can be covered by additional insurance which is often obtainable under Institute Clauses.[22]

It is of great practical importance for the shipper to make certain that the clauses of his contract of carriage and contract of marine insurance are duly co-ordinated. Risks which the shipper has to bear under the contract of carriage should be covered by his marine insurance policy.

Sometimes bills of lading contain a clause drawing the attention of the shipper to the necessity of obtaining adequate insurance cover; the following is an example of such a clause:

> Shippers are requested to note particularly the terms and conditions of this bill of lading with reference to the validity of their insurance upon their goods.

It can be seen from the catalogue of excepted perils that the shipowner is not responsible for loss or damage arising from strikes, lock-outs, riots or civil commotion. The shipper who wishes to be protected against these risks has to take out additional insurance covering these risks. Sometimes special transhipment or storage risks have to be covered by additional insurance, and the same applies to the risks of theft and pilferage. Where the bill of lading gives the master liberty to stow the goods as deck cargo, the shipper should arrange with the shipowner to be informed forthwith if the master exercises this discretion because deck cargo has to be insured specifically[23] and is sometimes subject to special rates of insurance. Where, as is normally the case, freight is payable in advance,[24] the shipper should

---

[18] See p. 488, *post*.

[19] *Per* Wright J. in *Gosse Millard* v. *Canadian Government Merchant Marine*; *American Can Co.* v. *Same* [1927] 2 K.B. 432, 435; *Svenska Traktor Akt.* v. *Maritime Agencies (Southampton) Ltd.* [1953] 2 Q.B. 295.

[20] *Albacora S.R.L.* v. *Westcott & Laurance Line Ltd., The Maltasian* [1966] 2 Lloyd's Rep. 53; *The Flowergate* [1967] 1 Lloyd's Rep. 1, 7; *Chris Foodstuffs (1963) Ltd.* v. *Nigerian National Shipping Line, The Amadu Bello* [1967] 1 Lloyd's Rep. 293 (concealed pre-shipment damage).

[21] See App. 1, p. 483, *post*.

[22] See p. 308, *ante*.

[23] See p. 301, *ante*.

[24] See p. 339, *ante*.

include the freight and incidental expenses in the value declared for insurance.[25]

If the exporter is in doubt whether, in view of the exceptions in the bill of lading or special circumstances connected with the shipment, his insurance cover is sufficient, he should seek the expert advice of his insurance broker or shipping agent.

(c) Maximum limits of shipowner's liabilities. The Hague-Visby Rules provide in Article IV(5) the following maximum limits for the shipowner's liability for damage to or loss of the goods shipped:

(*a*) Unless the nature and value of such goods have been declared by the shipper before shipment and inserted in the bill of lading, neither the carrier nor the ship shall in any event be or become liable for any loss or damage to or in connection with the goods in an amount exceeding the equivalent of 10,000 francs per package or unit or 30 francs per kilo of gross weight of the goods lost or damaged, whichever is the higher.

(*b*) The total amount recoverable shall be calculated by reference to the value of such goods at the place and time at which the goods are discharged from the ship in accordance with the contract or should have been so discharged.

The value of the goods shall be fixed according to the commodity exchange price, or, if there be no such price, according to the current market price, or, if there be no commodity exchange price or current market price, by reference to the normal value of goods of the same kind and quality.

(*c*) Where a container, pallet or similar article of transport is used to consolidate goods, the number of packages or units enumerated in the bill of lading as packed in such article of transport shall be deemed the number of packages or units for the purpose of this paragraph as far as these packages or units are concerned. Except as aforesaid such article of transport shall be considered the package or unit.

(*d*) A franc means a unit consisting of 65·5 milligrammes of gold of millesimal fineness 900. The date of conversion of the sum awarded into national currencies shall be governed by the law of the Court seized of the case.

(*e*) Neither the carrier nor the ship shall be entitled to the benefit of the limitation of liability provided for in this paragraph if it is proved that the damage resulted from an act or omission of the carrier done with intent to cause damage, or recklessly and with knowledge that damage would probably result.

(*f*) The declaration mentioned in sub-paragraph (*a*) of this paragraph, if embodied in the bill of lading, shall be prima facie evidence, but shall not be binding or conclusive on the carrier.

The sterling values of the gold franc mentioned in Article IV(5)(*a*) are at present[26] £447·81 per package or unit or £1·34 per kilo of gross weight of the goods lost or damaged, whichever is the higher. In cases to which the original Hague Rules apply, under the *British Maritime Law Association Agreement 1950*,[27] as amended in 1977, British shipowners and British insurers accept liability to the amount of £400 instead of £100 as stated in Article IV(5) of the original Rules. The Agreement is also accepted by a number of foreign insurance companies, the Crown Agents for the Colonies, and oil companies of the British Petroleum and Shell groups.

---

[25] See pp. 291–292, *ante*.

[26] Position: November 4, 1978.

[27] The Agreement is sometimes referred to as the Gold Clause Agreement. Before the amendment the maximum liability was £200.

The maximum limits provided by the Rules for the shipowner's liability are not of an absolute character. They may be increased by agreement of the parties or by adoption of the following procedures[28]:

(1) A declaration of the nature and value of the shipped goods by the shipper before shipment, *and*

(2) insertion of the declaration in the bill of lading.

Where the declared value of the goods is embodied in the bill, the shipper may, in case of damage or loss due to other than excepted perils, claim damages in excess of the maximum limits. The measure of damages is the loss actually suffered by the shipper, and it is open to the shipowner to prove that that loss is smaller than the value of the goods stated in the bill.

The shipper, who wishes to hold the shipowner liable in excess of the statutory maximum limit, should note that two conditions have to be satisfied, *viz.* the declaration of the nature and value of the goods, and the insertion of these particulars in the bill. In one case,[29] the shipper had satisfied the first condition, but the value of the goods was not embodied in the bill. MacKinnon J. said: "Though the plaintiffs did declare the value of the goods before shipment, that was not inserted in the bill of lading; and in those circumstances only one of the conditions on which the defendants could be liable for more than £100 was fulfilled," and ruled that the maximum limits applied. Where the parties arrange for the shipowner's liability in excess of the maximum limits, the freight rate is higher than in the case where the limits apply.

The shipowner can plead the maximum limits of liability not only against the party to the contract of carriage by sea and his assignee but, in the case of a strict f.o.b. contract,[30] also against the seller who loads the goods on board a ship contracted for and nominated by the buyer, if the goods are damaged by the negligence of the shipowner's servants before they cross the ship's rail.[31]

Where the maximum limits apply, the liability of the shipowner may be calculated per package or unit or per gross weight, whichever is higher. "'Package'," in the words of a former Lord Chief Justice,[32] "must indicate something packed"; therefore, a motor-car put on a ship without a box, crate or any form of covering is not a package.[32] The reference to "unit" is to freight units in use in various trades, *e.g.* in case of bulk shipment of grain. If the measure of damages is calculated on the number of packages or units, their weight is irrelevant.

(d) Protection of servants and agents, but not independent contractors. The question arises whether persons whom the carrier employs in the performance of his duties can, when sued by the cargo owner (*e.g.* for

---

[28] Art. IV(5)(*a*) and (*f*).

[29] *Pendle & Rivet Ltd.* v. *Ellerman Lines Ltd.* (1927) 33 Com.Cas. 70, 78.

[30] See p. 19, *ante*.

[31] *Pyrene Co. Ltd.* v. *Scindia Navigation Co. Ltd.* [1954] 2 Q.B. 402; see p. 19, *ante*.

[32] Goddard J. (as he was then) in *Studebaker Distributors Ltd.* v. *Charlton Steam Shipping Co. Ltd.* [1938] 1 K.B. 459, 467.

negligent damage to the cargo), plead the protection of the maximum limits of liability and other defences which the carrier could have pleaded under the Rules if he had been sued. The Hague-Visby Rules admit the extension of these protective provisions to servants and agents of the carrier but do not admit their extension to independent contractors.[33] The Rules provide in Article IVbis (2) to (4):

2. If such an action is brought against a servant or agent of the carrier (such servant or agent not being an independent contractor), such servant or agent shall be entitled to avail himself of the defences and limits of liability which the carrier is entitled to invoke under these Rules.

3. The aggregate of the amounts recoverable from the carrier, and such servants and agents, shall in no case exceed the limit provided for in these Rules.

4. Nevertheless, a servant or agent of the carrier shall not be entitled to avail himself of the provisions of this article, if it is proved that the damage resulted from an act or omission of the servant or agent done with intent to cause damage or recklessly and with knowledge that damage would probably result.

That independent contractors employed by the carrier are not protected by the Rules was decided in *Midland Silicones Ltd.* v. *Scruttons Ltd.*[34] In that case the House of Lords held that stevedores (employed by the carrier) who negligently damaged cargo when unloading it, in an action for negligence brought against them by the cargo owners, could not claim the maximum limitation of liability under the contract of carriage which embodied the Hague Rules[35] because there was no privity of contract between the stevedores and the cargo owners.

If it is intended, in addition to the carrier's servants and agents, to protect independent contractors employed by the carrier or, in the case of a bill of lading governed by the original Hague Rules, to provide protection to all three categories of auxiliary persons, it is necessary to insert into the bill of lading the so-called *Himalaya* clause[36] which provides that the *shipowner*, as agent of his own servants and agents (including independent contractors from time to time employed by the shipowners), contracts with the cargo owner that these servants, agents and independent contractors shall be protected by the limits of liability and other defences arising from the contract of carriage. A majority of the Privy Council in *New Zealand*

---

[33] The original Hague Rules did not even admit the extension to servants and agents and the only way to protect these auxiliary persons was to insert into the bill of lading the *Himalaya* clause described above in the text.

[34] *Scruttons Ltd.* v. *Midland Silicones Ltd. sub nom. Scruttons* v. *Midland Silicones Ltd.* [1962] A.C. 446. Stevedores and ship's agents may be liable to the owner for loss of goods on mere acceptance of the goods for bailment; no contract or attornment is necessary: *Gilchrist Watt and Sanderson Pty. Ltd.* v. *York Products Pty. Ltd.* [1970] 1 W.L.R. 1262.

[35] By virtue of the U.S. Carriage of Goods by Sea Act 1936.

[36] *Adler* v. *Dickson; The Himalaya* [1955] 1 Q.B. 158 where in a case concerning personal injury to a passenger it was held that an exclusion clause in favour of the carrier did not bar an action in negligence against the master of the ship. According to Pearce L.J. in the *Midland Silicones* case [1961] 1 Q.B. 106, 128 the principles governing the liability of shipowners under contracts of passage and of carriage of goods by sea are, in that respect, the same. The object of the *Himalaya* clause is to remedy the difficulties resulting from *Adler* v. *Dickson* for shipowner's servants, agents and independent contractors.

Shipping Co. Ltd. v. *A. M. Satterthwaite & Co. Ltd., The Eurymedon*[37] held that such a clause achieved the desired effect. The decision has been criticised ,[37a] but its fundamental approach is correct.[37b]

(e) Claims for loss of or damage to goods. The shipper or consignee, or their agents at the port of destination, have to act with expedition and circumspection if the condition of the goods on arrival is such that a claim against the shipowner has to be contemplated. The Rules provide in Article III(6) and (6bis) the following procedure for claims:

> 6. Unless notice of loss or damage and the general nature of such loss or damage be given in writing to the carrier or his agent at the port of discharge before or at the time of the removal of the goods into the custody of the person entitled to delivery thereof under the contract of carriage, or, if the loss or damage be not apparent, within three days, such removal shall be prima facie evidence of the delivery by the carrier of the goods as described in the bill of lading.
>
> The notice in writing need not be given if the state of the goods has at the time of their receipt been the subject of joint survey or inspection.
>
> Subject to paragraph 6*bis* the carrier and the ship shall in any event be discharged from all liability whatsoever in respect of the goods, unless suit[38] is brought within one year of their delivery or of the date when they should have been delivered. This period may, however, be extended if the parties so agree after the cause of action has arisen.
>
> In the case of any actual or apprehended loss or damage the carrier and the receiver shall give all reasonable facilities to each other for inspecting and tallying the goods.
>
> 6*bis*. An action for indemnity against a third person may be brought even after the expiration of the year provided for in the preceding paragraph if brought within the time allowed by the law of the Court seized of the case. However, the time allowed shall be not less than three months, commencing from the day when the person bringing such action for indemnity has settled the claim or has been served with process in the action against himself.

By the British Maritime Law Association Agreement 1950, as amended in 1977, the period of *one* year set forth in paragraph 3 of Article III(6) is extended, as between the British members and cargoes underwriters, parties to the Agreement, to *two* years, subject to the cargo owner giving the carrier notice and best particulars of his claim within the first year and having acted without delay,[39] and court proceedings in respect of such claims being brought only in the United Kingdom. These provisions are sometimes modified in slight but significant detail by clauses in the bill of lading. Thus, the bill of lading might provide:

> The ship's protest[40] relating facts and circumstances exempting carriers from liability duly

[37] [1975] A.C. 154; N. E. Palmer, "The Stevedore's Dilemma: Exemption Clauses and Third Parties" [1974] J.B.L. 101.

[37a] See *Salmand and Spraggen (Australia) Pty. Ltd.* v. *Port Jackson Stevedoring Pty. Ltd.; The New York Star* [1979] 1 Lloyd's Rep. 298 (High Ct. of Australia).

[37b] See P. J. Davies and N. E. Palmer, "The Eurymedon Five Years On" in [1979] J.B.L.

[38] "Suit" includes arbitration proceedings, *The Merak* [1965] P. 223; *Ch. E. Rolimpex Ltd.* v. *Aura Shipping Co. Ltd.*; *The Angeliki* [1973] 2 Lloyd's Rep. 226, 229; *Nea Agrex S.A.* v. *Baltic Shipping Co. Ltd.* [1976] Q.B. 933.

[39] For cases in which the period of limitation does not operate against the cargo owners, see *Goulandris Brothers* v. *B. Goldman & Sons Ltd.* [1958] 1 Q.B. 74; noted on p. 320, n. 28, *ante*, and *Rambler Cycle Co.* v. *P. & O. Steam Navigation Co.* [1968] 1 Lloyd's Rep. 42 (Malaysia Fed.C.(Appellate)). "Delivery" within Art. III(6) occurs when the goods are landed on the quay or at least placed at the consignee's disposal: *The Beltana* [1967] 1 Lloyd's Rep. 531 (Aust.).

[40] Also called the master's protest, see p. 322, *ante*.

sworn by the captain and/or one or more members of the crew will be deemed sufficient proof by parties to this bill of lading of such facts and circumstances.

The extension of time, as provided by the amended British Maritime Law Association agreement, applies to claims under the original Hague Rules as well as to claims under the Hague-Visby Rules.

Further, the time limit of one year and its extension, in appropriate cases, to two years under the British Maritime Law Association Agreement does not apply to actions by the carrier against a third party having given him an indemnity.[41] Here the time limits are those allowed by the law of the court seized of the case.[42] In English law the carrier can bring an action against the indemnor within six years after the cause of action accrued.[43]

Most bills of lading issued by shipping companies in England contain a clause providing that the contract of carriage evidenced by the bill of lading shall be governed by the law of England.

The protection of the limitation clause in paragraph 3 of Article III(6) is available to the carrier in respect of loss or damage arising by reason of the provisions of Article III; it is not available to him for a default to which the Hague Rules do not apply and to which they have not been extended by the terms of the contract of carriage, *e.g.* if *after* the discharge from the ship the carrier delivers the goods to a person not entitled to them.[44]

Container transport

The traditional international transport operation consists of three distinct parts: the on-carriage of the goods to the port of dispatch, the carriage by sea to the port of destination, and the off-carriage to the final place of arrival. Each of these stages is governed by different legal rules and, if the transportation in any stage is international, may be subject to different international conventions.[45]

Modern transport has developed new techniques for the multi-modal carriage of goods. They are known as container transport or combined transport operations.[46] Two types of container transport have to be distinguished, the door-to-door container and the mixed container, but sometimes a combined transport operation falls under both headings at the same time.

---

[41] Art. III(6bis). [42] But the time limit must not be less than three months.

[43] If the indemnity is given by simple contract. If it is given by deed, the time limit is 12 years: Limitation Acts 1939 and 1975, s. 2(1) and (3).

[44] *Rambler Cycle Co.* v. *P. & O. Steam Navigation Co., supra*; also *The New York Star, supra.*

[45] Thus, in European law the international carriage of goods by sea is widely governed by the Hague-Visby Rules relating to Bills of Lading (p. 347, *ante*); international carriage by rail by CIM (*Convention internationale concernant le transport des marchandises par chemins de fer*); see U.K. Cmnd. 2187 (1961); and international carriage by road by CMR (*Convention relative au contrat de transport international des marchandises par route*, appended to the U.K. Carriage of Goods by Road Act 1965). See p. 391, *post*, and F. G. Fitzpatrick, "Combined Transport and the CMR Convention" in [1969] J.B.L. 311.

[46] Lord Diplock "The Genoa Seminar on Combined Transport" [1972] J.B.L. 269.

The door-to-door container

The object of multi-modal transportation is to carry goods in the same article of transport from the inland place of dispatch to the final place of arrival. In practice the whole transport is treated as a single movement operation, albeit by different means of transport[47] and the former distinction into separate parts of transport, according to their nature as inland and sea transport, becomes of subordinate significance.[48]

Door-to-door container transportation raises a number of important legal problems: who is the "main" contractor, the carrier by sea or one of the inland carriers? Secondly, what is the measure of liability of the international container contractor; is it negligence, as under the Hague Rules, or strict liability with the exception of *force majeure*, as under CIM and CMR? Thirdly, which maximum limits of liability apply, those provided for by the Hague Rules or those laid down by CIM or CMR? Fourthly, is it possible to have one transport document for the whole door-to-door operation? And last but not least, what are the most appropriate insurance arrangements for door-to-door container transport?

The various attempts to solve these problems by international convention have not yet led to a result,[49] but the International Chamber of Commerce has sponsored *Uniform Rules for a Combined Transport Document*[50] which can be embodied into the contract of combined transport by agreement of the parties. A general acceptance of the Uniform Rules would greatly contribute to the simplification of a complex international situation, particularly as considerable time will elapse before the governments have agreed on a Combined Transport Convention and given effect to it in their national jurisidiction. In the meantime, the practice has evolved its own answer to some of these questions by providing container bills of lading. Several types of these bills are in use but no common form has yet emerged. All container bills are "received for shipment" bills[51] and not "shipped" bills, and most contain clauses defining the responsibility of the door-to-door carrier. The most elaborate of these clauses is found in the bill used by the Atlantic Container Line Ltd. (ACL)[52]; its relevant parts run as follows:

---

[47] Hence the expression "multi-modal."

[48] The progressive use of container transport means that the decisive points of departure and arrival are no longer sea ports but are transferred to inland locations. This might in course of time have some effect on the practical usefulness of customary trade terms, such as f.o.b. and c.i.f.

[49] See Jan Ramberg, "The Combined Transport Operator" in [1968] J.B.L. 132. There exists a Draft Convention on Combined Transport of 1972 which is being studied jointly by IMCO and ECE.

[50] ICC Brochure 298 (First published in November 1973). See F. J. J. Cadwallader, "Uniform Rules for Combined Transport" [1974] J.B.L. 193.

[51] Although the wording differs in the various forms.

[52] Which is an affiliate of Cie Générale Transatlantique, Cunard Steam-Ship Company Ltd., Holland-America Line, Swedish-American Line, Swedish Transatlantic Line, Wallenius Line.

When either the place of receipt or place of delivery set forth herein is an inland point in the U.S.A. or Europe, the responsibility of ACL with respect to the transportation to and from the sea terminal ports will be as follows:

(*a*) Between points in Europe, to transport the goods:

(1) if by road, in accordance with the Convention on the Contract for the International Carriage of Goods by Road, dated May 19, 1956 (CMR);

(2) if by rail, in accordance with the International Agreement on Railway Transports, dated February 25, 1961 (CIM);

(3) if by air, in accordance with the Convention for the Unification of certain Rules relating to International Carriage by Air, signed Warsaw, October 12, 1929, as amended by the Hague Protocol, dated September 28, 1955.

(*b*) Between points in the U.S.A., to procure transportation by carriers (one or more) authorised by competent authority to engage in transportation between such points and such transportation shall be subject to the inland carrier's contracts of carriage and tariffs. ACL guarantees the fulfilment of such inland carriers' obligations under their contracts and tariffs.[53]

. . .

When the goods have been damaged or lost during through-transportation and it cannot be established in whose custody the goods were when the damage or loss occurred, the damage or loss shall be deemed to have occurred during the sea voyage and the Hague Rules as defined above shall apply.

Most container bills include a clause according to which, if it cannot be established in whose custody the goods were when the damage or loss occurred, the Hague Rules shall apply. By virtue of the 1974 Revision of the Uniform Customs, and Practice for Documentary Credits, banks will accept container bills of lading.[54]

The mixed container

The groupage of cargoes shipped by several exporters in one container is carried out at the container loading depots of container shipping lines or of freight forwarders[55] in the major industrial centres inland or at the ports.[56] Mixed container shipment, like all container shipment, offers considerable advantages to the exporter: it means less handling and less likelihood of damage and the elimination of in-transit pilferage; it might also reduce the cost of export packing and freight. If the exporter can offer a full container load (FCL), the freight charges are lower than if he merely offers a less than full container load (LCL) and the container operator has to carry out the groupage of the exporter's goods with others into a full load.

Where a forwarder assembles cargoes in a mixed container, he issues, if required by the exporter, so-called house bills of lading. These documents

[53] It would appear that ACL are not allowed to carry out inland transport themselves in U.S.A.

[54] See p. 252, *ante*.

[55] See, *e.g.* the Container and Unit Load offered by Thomas Meadow & Co. Ltd. Many forwarders collect the cargo from their customers.

[56] If the cargoes are large or full loads, empty containers may be sent to the exporter's premises. There exists a trade usage in England according to which a customs clearance agent appointed by an importer is responsible to the forwarder for demurrage for retention of the forwarder's container if the return of the container is unreasonably delayed through the fault of the clearance agent: *Kuehne and Nagel Ltd.* v. *W. B. Woolley* (*Scotland*) *Ltd.* (unreported, Westminster County Court, August 15, 1973, Plaint No. 73 50487).

have been considered earlier[57]; it has been seen that they lack the qualities of bills of lading in the technical legal sense. Sometimes forwarders use for container transport the *FIATA Combined Transport Bill of Lading* which is sponsored by the International Federation of Forwarding Agents Association[58]; its legal nature is that of a house bill of lading.

Definition of "package or unit" in container transport

The mixed container itself, as distinguished from the individual cargoes contained therein, is normally shipped under an ordinary "shipped" bill of lading which is a groupage bill. As far as the transport by sea is concerned, it is important to ascertain whether the whole container or each of the individual cargoes contained therein constitutes a "package or unit" within the meaning of the Hague-Visby Rules, Art. IV, r. 5, which provides a maximum limit of liability in favour of the carrier in case of loss or damage to such a package or unit.[59] The Rules attempt to solve this problem by providing in Article IV(5)(*c*) a container clause which was already cited earlier.[60]

In other words, the wording of the bill of lading issued by the carrier by sea, prima facie, appears to be decisive. If the bill only refers to "one container said to contain general merchandise" then the container itself is the package or unit, but if it enumerates any cargoes included in the container separately, each of those cargoes constitutes a separate package or unit. If the bill mentions specifically one or two cargoes but not the other contents of the container, the separately mentioned items are separate packages for the purposes of maximum limitation of liability, and the rest of the container contents falls under the weight limitation. The English courts have not considered the interpretation of that clause yet.

The American courts held in *The Mormaclynx*[61] that bales of leather packed in a container were separate packages; the bill of lading referred to "1 container s.t.c. 99 bales of leather."[62] In *The Kulmerland,*[63] on the other hand, the American courts treated the container as the package or unit; in that case the bill of lading stated "1 container said to contain machinery," without "indication to the carrier of the number of cartons or the intention of the shipper to contract on that basis."[64] It thus appears that the American courts arrive at a result not dissimilar to the provisions

---

[57] See p. 357, *ante*.

[58] FIATA stands for *Féderation Internationale des Associations de Transitaires et Assimilés*, the French designation of the International Federation.

[59] See p. 373, *ante*.

[60] See p. 373, *ante*.

[61] *Leather's Best Inc.* v. *The Mormaclynx* [1970] 1 Lloyd's Rep. 527. This decision was followed in the Canadian case *The Tindefjell* [1973] 2 Lloyd's Rep. 253.

[62] The abbreviation "s.t.c." signifies "said to contain."

[63] *Royal Typewriter Co., Division Litton Business Systems Inc.* v. *M.V. Kulmerland and Hamburg-Amerika Linie* [1973] 2 Lloyd's Rep. 428.

[64] *Per* Collier J. in *The Tindefjell, supra*, p. 259.

of Article IV(5)(*c*) of the Hague-Visby Rules, although the amended rules do not form part of American law.[65]

Every container bill provides that the shipowner shall be entitled to carry the goods on deck in containers. In an American case[66] which was concerned with the shipment of books from New York to Yokohama the container in which the books were carried was stowed on deck but the bill of lading did not contain an indication on its face to that effect; the ship encountered heavy weather when crossing the Pacific and the books were damaged by sea water; the court held that the shipowner had forfeited the defence of pleading the limitation of liability under the Hague Rules by stowing the cargo on deck; one of the reasons which the court gave was that "no consignee or assignee could tell from the bill whether it was below deck or on deck cargo."[67] In an English case[68] a forwarder promised an importer orally to ship a container containing his goods below deck. Contrary to his promise he shipped them on deck and when the ship met a slight swell the container fell off and went to the bottom of the sea. The Court of Appeal held the forwarder liable for the loss.

General average claims and contributions

The law of general average, so far as it affects the rights and duties of the shipper under the contract of carriage by sea, has been discussed in the chapter on insurance,[69] as a necessary preliminary to an explanation of the rules of insurance law protecting the shipper in case of general average loss or expenditure.

Bills of lading regularly contain a clause providing that general average shall be adjusted in accordance with the York-Antwerp Rules 1974. Sometimes it is added that the practice of English Average Adjusters shall apply to all points on which the Rules do not contain provisions.

CARRIAGE BY AIR

The air law relating to the carriage of goods has reached a considerable measure of international uniformity.

---

[65] In *The Kulmerland* the American court did not consider the declaration of the goods in the bill of lading as the decisive criterion but attributed weight to the fact that the goods in the container were not packed for export ("the functional test") but Collier J. in *The Tindefjell* rightly referred to the vague declaration of the cargo in the bill issued by *The Kulmerland.* In another American case, *Insurance Company of North America* v. *S/S Brooklyn Maru, Japan Line Ltd.*; *The Brooklyn Maru* [1975] 2 Lloyd's Rep. 512, the court likewise applied the "functional economics" (*sic!*) test.

[66] *Encyclopaedia Britannica Inc.* v. *The Hong Kong Producer and Universal Marine Corpn.* [1969] 2 Lloyd's Rep. 536, 542.

[67] *Ibid.* p. 542.

[68] *J. Evans & Sons* (*Portsmouth*) *Ltd.* v. *Andrea Merzario Ltd.* [1976] 1 W.L.R. 1078; see p. 63, *ante*, where the case is treated fully.

[69] See p. 318, *ante*.

History of the Carriage by Air Acts 1932, 1961 and 1962

These three enactments, like the Carriage of Goods by Sea Acts 1924 and 1971, are the outcome of international negotiations. The Act of 1932 gave statutory effect, in the United Kingdom, to a Convention for the unification of certain rules relating to international air carriage which was signed in Warsaw in 1929.

Over the years it became evident that the Warsaw Convention required amendment. In particular, the limitation of liability in the event of death or injury of a passenger was found to be too low.[70] For that reason an amendment was agreed at The Hague on September 28, 1955; the amendment is known as the Hague Protocol. The "Warsaw Convention, as amended at the Hague, 1955" is scheduled to the Carriage by Air Act 1961 and came into force on June 1, 1967, in the United Kingdom, the Channel Isles, the Isle of Man and twenty British territories overseas.

The 1961 Act repeals the Carriage by Air Act 1932, but by means of an ingenious use of section 10 of the 1961 Act, provision is made to give effect to the unamended Convention in applicable cases.

The basic Convention regulates the legal liabilities and relationships between carriers by air on the one hand, and passengers as well as cargo consignors and consignees on the other. But neither the original nor the amended Warsaw Convention makes it clear whether the "carrier" referred to therein is the carrier in contractual relationship with the passenger or consignor, or whether it is the carrier who actually performs the carriage. It was therefore necessary to supplement the Warsaw Convention by a further Convention which was signed in 1961 at Guadalajara in Mexico. This supplementary Convention aims at the unification of certain rules relating to international carriage performed by a person other than the contracting carrier. The Guadalajara Convention is embodied in the Carriage by Air (Supplementary Provisions) Act 1962 which applies to carriage governed by the original and the amended Warsaw Convention.

Based on these international agreements, English statute law now provides a comprehensive but complex code of reasonable uniformity for the carriage of goods by air, so far as actions in the English courts are concerned, not only for so-called international carriage, which is the subject of the Conventions, but also for what will be referred to below as non-Convention carriage,[71] which includes carriage which in the ordinary sense of words is international but is not governed by the Conventions.

General introduction

The basic scheme of carrier's liability is uniform in all the three régimes recognised by English law which apply equally well to carriage for reward

---

[70] See Harold Caplan, "Ratification of Hague Protocol by United Kingdom" in [1961] J.B.L. 170.

[71] Often called "non-international carriage" because it is not "international" as defined in the Convention.

as to gratuitous carriage by an air transport undertaking: it is therefore convenient first to describe the basic system of liability and then to note the differences which exist in each of the three régimes, *viz.*—

1. carriage governed by the original Warsaw Convention;
2. carriage governed by the amended Convention;
3. non-Convention carriage.

Basic system of liability

The carrier of goods by air is automatically liable for destruction or loss of, or damage to or delay of cargo if it occurs during the carriage by air. The carrier has the right to use specified defences if he can, but he cannot contract out of liability or for a lower limit of liability. In return for this liability the carrier can rely on the benefit of maximum limits for his liability, and even that liability arises only if the claimant can prove damage to that extent. The maximum limits of the air carrier's liability are—

250 gold francs per kilogram; or
the value declared by the shipper for which any supplementary charge has been paid.

The franc, also known as the Poincaré gold franc, consists of 65½ milligrams of "gold of millesimal fineness nine hundred" and the current value of 250 francs is declared to be £10·25.[72]

The carrier loses the benefit of the limits in the event of certain kinds of misconduct.

The only persons who have rights of action are the consignor and the consignee.[73] In the absence of fraud by the carrier, these rights are only exercisable provided that written complaints are made to the carrier within specified time limits in cases of damage or delay. The right to damages is extinguished if an action is not brought within two years reckoned from the date of actual or expected arrival at destination, or the date on which carriage stopped. Receipt of cargo by the person entitled to delivery without complaint is prima facie evidence of delivery in good condition.

Damage during "carriage by air"

So far as the destruction, loss of or damage to cargo is concerned, "carriage by air" comprises the whole period during which the cargo is in the charge of the carrier, whether in an aerodrome or on board an aircraft, or in the case of landing outside an aerodrome in any place whatsoever. If surface carriage takes place outside an aerodrome for the purpose of loading, delivery or transhipment of air cargo, any damage is presumed to have taken place during the carriage by air, subject to contrary proof.

---

[72] The Carriage by Air (Sterling Equivalents) Order 1979 (S.I. 1979 No. 765). Provisions of the Carriage by Air and Road Act 1979 which are not in force yet (August 1, 1979) will substitute Special Drawing Rights (SDRs) for the Poincaré gold franc.

[73] The owner, for example, has no status and can only claim in his capacity of consignor or consignee.

Carrier's defences

The carrier is not liable if he proves that he and his servants or agents[74] have taken all necessary[75] measures to avoid the damage or that it was impossible for him or them to take such measures.

If the carrier proves that the damage was caused or contributed to by the negligence of the injured person the court may exonerate the carrier wholly or partly.

There is nothing to prevent a carrier from refusing to enter into a contract of carriage or from making rules which do not conflict with the applicable law.

Carriers who may be sued

(a) *a successive carrier.* He is deemed to be a party to the original contract of carriage so far as is relevant to the carriage performed under his supervision.

(b) *the contracting carrier.* He, as a principal, makes an agreement for carriage with the consignor or the consignor's agent. In many cases the contracting carrier will be the first or sometimes the only carrier by air, but the contracting carrier may also be one who merely issues a waybill, or an aircraft charterer, or a cargo consolidator or forwarder.

(c) *the actual carrier.* By virtue of authority from the contracting carrier, he performs the whole or part of the carriage and is neither a successive carrier nor a contracting carrier.

Who may sue

(a) The consignor has a right of action against the first carrier and the carrier who performed the carriage during which destruction, loss, damage or delay took place (the performing carrier) unless the first carrier has expressly assumed liability for the whole carriage.

(b) The consignee has a right of action against the last carrier and the performing carrier.

(c) The first carrier, the performing carrier and the last carrier are jointly and severally liable respectively to the consignor and the consignee.

(d) The contracting carrier is liable for the whole of the carriage.

(e) The actual carrier is only liable for the part performed by him.

(f) At the plaintiff's option, written complaints may be made and actions may be brought against either the actual carrier or the contracting carrier or against both together or separately.

---

[74] s. 29 of the Air Navigation Act 1936 substituted "servants and agents" for "agents" in the English text of the Warsaw Convention scheduled to the Carriage by Air Act 1932, thereby correcting an error in the translation of *préposés* which appeared in the authentic French text of the Convention. The correction has been continued in force by the Carriage by Air Act 1961 and Orders made thereunder.

[75] Interpreted as reasonably necessary by Greer L.J. in *Grein* v. *Imperial Airways Ltd.* [1937] 1 K.B. 50, 69–71.

Servants and agents of the carrier acting within the scope of their employment can claim the benefit of the limits of liability applicable to the carrier.[76] Acts and omissions of the actual carrier, including his servants and agents, are deemed to be those of the contracting carrier and vice versa, but the actual carrier's liability cannot be measured beyond 250 francs per kilogram by reason of—

(i) any act or omission of the contracting carrier;
(ii) any special agreement entered into by the contracting carrier; or
(iii) special declarations of value made to the contracting carrier,
unless in cases (ii) and (iii) the actual carrier has agreed to be bound.

When do the various régimes apply?

It is no longer a straightforward matter to determine when the various régimes apply, but the following may assist. Carriage of cargo for reward by aircraft or gratuitous air carriage by an air transport undertaking is governed by:

1. *The original Warsaw Convention*[77]

When, according to the contract between the parties, the places of departure and destination (regardless of breaks, miscarriage,[78] transhipment or numbers of consecutive contracts or successive carriers) are located—

either in the territories of two States parties to the original Convention;
or in the territory of a single such State with an agreed stopping place anywhere outside that State. However the original Convention does not apply to carriage "with a view to the establishment of a regular line of air navigation" or carriage "in extraordinary circumstances outside the normal scope of an air carrier's business."[79]

2. *The amended Convention*[80]

When, according to the agreement between the parties, the places of departure and destination (regardless of breaks, transhipment or numbers of consecutive contracts or successive carriers) are located—

either in the territories of two States both of which are parties to the amended Convention;
or in the territory of a single State party to the amended Convention with an agreed stopping place anywhere outside that state.

Difficulties can arise when, *e.g.* the place of departure is in the territory of a State party to the original Convention (*e.g.* U.S.A.) whilst the place of destination is in the territory of a State which is not only a party to the original Convention but has also become a party to the amended Conven-

[76] Internationally this is a feature of the amended Convention, but it was applied to actions arising in the English courts by s. 4 of the Carriage by Air (Supplementary Provisions) Act 1962, now continued for this purpose in art. 25A of Part B of Sched. 2 to the Carriage of Air Acts (Application of Provisions) Order 1967 (S.I. 1967 No. 480).
[77] Sched. 2 to the Carriage by Air Acts (Application of Provisions) Order 1967.
[78] See *Rotterdamsche Bank N.V.* v. *B.O.A.C.* [1953] 1 W.L.R. 493.
[79] There is no similar reservation of such a wide scope in the amended Convention.
[80] s. 1 and 1st Sched. to the Carriage by Air Act 1961.

tion (*e.g.* the U.K.). In such circumstances, the only obligations which bind both of the States concerned are those contained in the original Convention.

For the purposes of actions in the English courts, the Carriage by Air (Parties to Conventions) Orders[81] certify those States and their associated territories which are parties to either or both the original and the amended Conventions.[82]

3. *The non-Convention rules*

When the carriage of cargo is governed neither by the original nor by the amended Convention, *e.g.* if the place of destination is in Peru (party to neither Convention) and there is no agreed stopping place in another State then whatever the place of departure, no part of the carriage would, as a matter of law, be governed by either of the two Conventions, and in an action before the English courts the carriage would be governed by the non-Convention rules, even though the carriage is international in the ordinary meaning of that word but not within the technical meaning which governs the applicability of the two Conventions.

The non-Convention rules also govern:

(*a*) carriage when the points of departure and destruction are both within the territory of one State (including its overseas territories), unless there is an agreed stopping place in the territory of another State and regardless of whether that other State is a party to either of the Conventions.[83] Carriage from London to Jersey is therefore non-international, as is carriage from London to Hong Kong in the absence of an agreed stopping place in the territory of another State, and

(*b*) carriage of mail or postal packages[84] presumably of both a domestic and an international character.

Each régime contains variations on the basic system of liability as follows:

Carriage governed by the original Warsaw Convention

Document of carriage

The document of carriage is called the *air consignment note* (ACN). The carrier has the right to require the consignor to make out an air consignment note and to require a separate one for each package, and the carrier is required to accept it. Nevertheless, the absence, irregularity or loss of the document does not affect the validity of the contract or the operation of the Convention rules. The ACN is not a document of title.

Each air consignment note must be in three original parts and handed over with the goods. The First Part is marked "for the carrier" and signed by the consignor; the Second Part is marked "for the consignee," is signed

[81] The Carriage by Air (Parties to Convention) Order 1977 (S.I. 1977, No. 240); the Carriage by Air (Parties to Convention) (Supplementary) Order 1977 (S.I. 1977 No. 1631); and the Carriage by Air (Parties to Convention) (Supplementary) Order 1978 (S.I. 1978 No. 1058). These Orders are too lengthy to be reproduced here.

[82] *Phillipson* v. *Imperial Airways Ltd.* [1939] A.C. 332 has very little practical application today.

[83] Sched. 1 to the Carriage by Air Acts (Application of Provisions) Order 1967.

[84] Art. 4 of the Carriage by Air Acts (Application of Provisions) Order 1967.

by the consignor and accompanies the goods; the Third Part is signed by the carrier and handed to the consignor after the goods have been accepted for carriage. The consignor must furnish the additional information and documents necessary for customs and police purposes before the goods can be delivered to the consignee and the consignor is liable to the carrier for any damage arising out of the absence or irregularity of such information or documents. This obligation of the consignor extends also to particulars and statements inserted by him in the air consignment note, and if the carrier makes out the air consignment note at the request of the consignor he is deemed to have done so as the consignor's agent.

But if the carrier accepts goods without an air consignment note or if the air consignment note does not contain any of the following particulars, then he cannot take advantage of the provisions of the Convention which would otherwise exclude or limit the carrier's liability:

(*a*) place and date of execution of the air consignment note;
(*b*) places of departure and destination;
(*c*) agreed stopping places (which the carrier may alter in case of necessity);
(*d*) name and address of consignor;
(*e*) name and address of first carrier;
(*f*) name and address of consignee "if the case so requires" [*sic*];
(*g*) nature of the goods;
(*h*) number of packages, method of packing and the particular marks or numbers on them;
(*i*) either the weight, quantity, volume or dimensions of the goods.[85];
(*j*) a statement that the carriage is subject to the rules relating to liability established by the Convention.[86]

The air consignment note and the statements therein are prima facie evidence of the conclusion of the contract, receipt of the goods, the conditions of carriage, the weight, dimensions, packing and number of goods. Statements relating to quantity, volume or condition are not evidence against the carrier unless expressly stated on the air consignment note to have been either checked in the presence of the consignor or they relate to apparent condition.

Basic liability

In addition to the two basic defences, the carrier is not liable if he can prove that "the damage was occasioned by negligent pilotage or negligence in the handling of the aircraft or in navigation and that in all other respects he and his agents have taken all necessary measures to avoid the damage." This defence is never used because it is not available in case of injury or death of passengers, and to raise this defence for cargo might give rise to

[85] The Court of Appeal has decided to follow the original French text and the American translation and has concluded that only *one* of these particulars need be given: *Corocraft Ltd.* v. *Pan American World Airways Inc.* [1969] 1 Q.B. 616.

[86] The formula used in IATA tickets and waybills is "Carriage hereunder is subject to the rules relating to liability established by the Warsaw Convention unless such carriage is not 'international carriage' as defined by the Convention." This formula has been approved in an American case, *Seth* v. *B.O.A.C.* [1964] 1 Lloyd's Rep. 268, and an English case, *Samuel Montagu & Co. Ltd.* v. *Swissair* [1965] 2 Lloyd's Rep. 363.

unlimited liability for passengers if it amounted to wilful misconduct within the meaning of Article 25.

Special rights of consignor and consignee

Unless varied by express provision in the air consignment note, the consignor and the consignee have the following rights:

The consignor—

(*a*) has the right of disposal prior to delivery to the consignee, subject to the production of the consignor's copy of the air consignment note to the carrier and payment of all expenses involved; and

(*b*) may enforce rights in his own name even if acting in the interests of another, subject to fulfilment of all obligations of the consignor under the contract of carriage.

The consignee—

(*a*) has the right to require the carrier to hand over goods and the air consignment note on arrival at the destination on payment of proper charges and compliance with any other conditions set out in the air consignment note; and

(*b*) may enforce rights in his own name even if acting in the interests of another, subject to the fulfilment of all obligations of the consignee under the contract of carriage.

Complaints and actions

(*a*) Unless otherwise stated in the air consignment note the consignee can exercise his rights if the carrier admits loss of the goods or if they have not arrived seven days after they should have arrived.

(*b*) Complaints by the person entitled to delivery must be made in writing either upon the air consignment note or separately:

in cases of damage: forthwith after discovery, or at the latest within seven days of receipt[87];
in cases of delay: within 14 days from the date on which the goods were placed at his disposal.

Carriage governed by the amended Warsaw Convention

Document of carriage

The document of carriage is called an *air waybill* (AWB). All the provisions of the original Convention relating to the air consignment note apply to the air waybill under the amended Convention with the most important exception of the particulars to appear therein and the penalties for omission.

If, *with the consent of the carrier*, cargo is loaded on board[88] without an air waybill or if the air waybill does not contain a notice to the consignor "to the effect that, if the carriage involves an ultimate destination or stop in a country other than the country of departure, the Warsaw Convention may be applicable and that the Convention governs and in most cases limits the liability of carriers in respect of loss of or damage to cargo,"[89] then, in either of these circumstances, the carrier cannot take advantage of the

---

[87] "damage" does not include partial loss: *Fothergill* v. *Monarch Airlines Ltd.* [1977] 2 Lloyd's Rep. 184; affirmed by C.A. (unreported at the time of writing) but reversed by the Carriage by Air and Road Act 1979, s. 2, in relation to losses occurring on or after April 4, 1979.

[88] The original Convention, as scheduled to the Carriage by Air Act 1932, says "accepted."

[89] These words appear on the face and on the reverse side of the latest IATA air waybills.

limits of liability. The carrier will not suffer these consequences if the carriage is "performed in extraordinary circumstances outside the normal scope of an air carrier's business."

It is stated expressly in the amended Convention that nothing therein "prevents the issue of a negotiable air waybill," but equally well there was nothing in the original Convention to prevent the issue of a negotiable air consignment note. The fact is that the speed of air transport has largely eliminated the need for a negotiable document of carriage, and waybills in practice are printed "not negotiable."

Basic liability

There are no defences in addition to the basic two: the defence of negligent pilotage has been dropped.

Servants and agents of the carrier enjoy the benefit of the same limits of liability as the carrier if they have acted in the course of their employment. The aggregate liability of a carrier, his servants and agents cannot exceed the limit (if a limit applies).

When calculating the limits of liability, the weight to be used is the weight of the package or packages concerned, and not necessarily the weight of all packages recorded on the same air waybill, unless the loss, damage or delay of one package affects the value of others on the same air waybill.

The carrier may insert contractual provisions relieving him of liability or fixing a lower limit in respect of inherent defect, quality or vice of the cargo carried. Arbitration clauses are allowed if arbitration is to take place within one of the jurisdictions allowed by the Convention.

The nature of the misconduct which will disentitle the carrier from relying on the limits of liability has been re-defined.

Special rights of consignor and consignee

These have not been varied in the amended Convention.

Complaints and actions

The time limits for written complaint by the person entitled to delivery have been varied as follows:

in cases of damage: the maximum is increased from 7 to 14 days[90];
in cases of delay: the maximum is increased from 14 to 21 days.

Non-Convention carriage

The basic system of liability including limits and times within which written complaint must be made for non-Convention carriage[91] is exactly

[90] On partial loss, see *Fothergill* v. *Monarch Airlines Ltd.* [1977] 2 Lloyd's Rep. 184, see p. 388 No. 87, *ante*.

[91] The rules applicable here are contained in Sched. 1 to the Carriage by Air Acts (Application of Provisions) Order 1967.

the same as those in the amended Convention, but there are no provisions whatsoever relating to documents of carriage or what has been described above as Special Rights of Consignor and Consignee.

The non-Convention rules were also applied to the *carriage of mail or postal packages* because it became clear that at common law the sender of an airmail package had a right of direct action without any limitation of liability against the air carrier.[92]; the particular case involved carriage between London and Kuwait which would not have been governed by the original Warsaw Convention even if the package had been ordinary cargo instead of airmail because Kuwait was not then a party to the Convention. In any event, the original Convention "does not apply to carriage performed under the terms of any international postal Convention" and the amended Convention "shall not apply to carriage of mail and postal packages." The point has now been dealt with by section 29(3) of the Post Office Act 1969 which provides that the carrier of mail is to be liable only to the Post Office.

For non-convention carriage, Special Drawing Rights (SDR) are already substituted for gold francs.[92a]

IATA carriage

A further measure of uniformity in the rules relating to cargo is introduced by the practices of members of the International Air Transport Association (IATA) who have for over 40 years been using a common form of air waybill and associated conditions of contract which appear on the reverse of the three Original copies, all of which have been revised from time to time. The IATA style of waybill and conditions of contract are used by IATA members for interline and online carriage, and also by non-members who either participate in interline carriage involving IATA members or merely wish to adopt the international standards set by IATA members. As from January 1, 1969, a new format of IATA air waybill is in use, designed, amongst other things, to facilitate production of a copy air waybill which can easily be transmitted by electronic means but is not a document of significance for legal purposes.

IATA conditions of contract do not in any way derogate from the provisions of either the original or the amended Convention. Sample copies of the latest forms are freely made available to exporters on application to the leading IATA airlines.

Condition No. 4 of the IATA Conditions provides that in non-Convention situations, where the applicable law permits, the carrier is only liable on proof of negligence or wilful fault, and in the absence of any declared value, the carrier's liability is restricted to the Convention limits of 250

[92] *Moukataff* v. *B.O.A.C.* [1967] 1 Lloyd's Rep. 396, in which the senders of £20,000 in bank notes to Kuwait recovered the missing balance of over £17,000 from B.O.A.C. by reason of the theft of the money from a sealed mailbag by a B.O.A.C. employee who was convicted of the offence.

[92a] The Carriage by Air Acts (Application of Provisions) (Second Amendment) Order 1979 (S.I. 1979 No. 931).

gold francs per kilogram. Thus, for all practical purposes, the Convention limits prevail in all but the most rare of situations internationally and are applied by law and by contract to all actions in the English courts.

Extension to territories overseas

By means of a series of Orders in Council, the system of law for carriage by air described above for the United Kingdom has been extended to[93]—

the Channel Isles, the Isle of Man, Bermuda, British Antarctic Territory, Belize (British Honduras), British Indian Ocean Territory, British Virgin Islands, Cayman Islands, Central and Southern Line Islands, Cyprus (only in the sovereign base areas of Akrotiri and Dhekelia), Falkland Islands and dependencies, Gilbert and Ellice Islands Colony, Hong Kong, Montserrat, St. Helena and Ascension, Turks and Caicos Islands.

CARRIAGE BY ROAD

The international carriage of goods by road is of growing importance. The international convention applicable to it is the *Convention on the Contract for the International Carriage of Goods by Road*, signed at Geneva on May 19, 1956 and known as the CMR.[94] Effect was given to it in the United Kingdom by the *Carriage of Goods by Road Act 1965*, which came into operation on June 5, 1967. The application of the Act has been extended to Gibraltar, the Isle of Man and Guernsey.[95]

Scope of application

The CMR applies to every contract for the carriage of goods by road in vehicles[96] for reward, when the place of taking over the goods and the place designed for delivery, as specified in the contract, are situated in two different countries of which at least one is a contracting party,[97] *i.e.* a State which has accepted the Convention. Contracting parties are[98]:

Austria, Belgium, Denmark, France, West Germany, Gibraltar, Guernsey, Hungary, Italy, Luxembourg, Isle of Man, Netherlands, Norway, Poland, Portugal, Sweden, Switzerland, Yugoslavia, and the United Kingdom of Great Britian and Northern Ireland.

The Convention also applies where the carriage is carried out by States or by governmental institutions or organisations.[99] A contracting party is, for the purposes of any proceedings brought in a court in the United Kingdom under the Convention, be deemed to have submitted to the jurisdiction of the court,[1] and the same applies as regards submission to arbitration.[2] The Crown is bound by the Act.[3] The CMR does not apply to traffic between

---

[93] Position: October 25, 1978.

[94] CMR stands for *Convention relative au contrat de transport international de marchandises par route*. The international transportation of goods by rail is regulated by the CIM which stands for *Convention internationale concernant le transport des marchandises par chemin de fer* (1961). The CIM is not treated here. [95] By virtue of s. 9 of the Act.

[96] "Vehicles" includes articulated vehicles, trailers and semi-trailers; Art. 1(2).

[97] Art. 1(1).

[98] s. 2 of the Act and S.I.s 1967 No. 1683; 1969 No. 385; 1973 No. 596 (Position: November 13, 1978).

[99] Art. 1(3). [1] s. 6 of the Act. [2] s. 7 and Art. 33. [3] s. 13.

the United Kingdom and the Irish Republic.[4] Further, the CMR does not apply[5]:

(*a*) to carriage performed under an international postal convention;
(*b*) to funeral consignments; or
(*c*) to furniture removal.

The CMR further provides that, where the vehicle containing the goods is carried over part of the journey by sea, rail, inland waterways or air and, except in cases of emergency, the goods are not unloaded from the vehicle, the CMR shall apply to the whole of the carriage.[6] But if the loss, damage or delay has occurred during the carriage by the other means of transport and was not caused by an act or omission of the carrier by road, the liability of the carrier by road is determined not by the CMR but by the applicable international convention; if there is no such convention, the CMR applies.[6]

The CMR provides that if the carriage by road is governed by a single contract but performed by successive road carriers, each shall be responsible for the performance of the whole operation, the second and each successive carrier becoming a party to the contract of carriage, under the terms of the consignment note,[7] but, except in the case of a counterclaim or set-off, legal proceedings in respect of liability for loss, damage or delay may only be brought against the first carrier, the last carrier or the carrier who was in control of the goods when the event which caused the loss, damage or delay occurred, but several carriers may be sued at the same time.[8] In the case of successive carriers the one responsible for the loss or damage is, as between the carriers, solely liable for compensation but if it cannot be ascertained to which carrier liability is attributable, the compensation has to be borne by them proportionally.[9] If one of the carriers is insolvent, the share of compensation due from him has to be paid by the other carriers in proportion to the share of the payment for the carriage due to them.[10]

It is not always easy to decide whether the person with whom the owner of the goods contracts undertakes only to *procure* carriage, *i.e.* to act as a forwarder,[11] or whether he contracts to *carry*, *i.e.* to act as carrier, even if he sub-contracts the actual carriage to somebody else. In the former case the CMR does not apply to him but in the latter case it does. If a person has contracted to carry the goods to their destination by a single contract but does not take the goods into charge himself and arranges for them to be delivered directly to the actual carrier to whom he has sub-contracted the job, he is nevertheless the first carrier and the actual carrier is the

---

[4] Protocol of Signature, attached to the Act.
[5] Art. 1(4).
[6] Art. 2(1).
[7] Art. 34.
[8] Art. 36.
[9] Art. 37.
[10] Art. 38.
[11] Rowlatt J. in *Jones* v. *European and General Express Co. Ltd.* (1920) 25 Com.Cas. 296, 298; *Marston Excelsior Ltd.* v. *Arbuckle, Smith & Co. Ltd.* [1971] 2 Lloyd's Rep. 306, 309.

successive carrier within article 34 of the CMR. Apart from the contract of carriage with the first carrier, in the words of Megaw L.J.,[12] "the CMR Convention then sets out to create an artificial statutory contract between the actual carrier and the owner of the goods." The learned judge continued:

> Looking at article 1(1), I think that the CMR Convention must have contemplated that for this purpose the company, or individual, with whom the owner of the goods contracts is the first carrier, whether or not he himself takes possession of the goods, and that all subsequent carriers are the successive carriers within the meaning of these provisions.

On the other hand, if the owner of the goods himself contracts with several contractors, each for a part of the journey, there is no single contract of carriage with the first contractor and the rules of the CMR on successive contractors do not apply, although the Convention may apply to the individual carriers.

The consignment note

The CMR provides that the contract of carriage by road shall be confirmed by a consignment note but that the absence of, or any irregularity in, the note shall not affect the validity of the contract which will remain subject to the Convention.[13] The consignment note has to be made out in three original copies signed by the sender and the carrier. The first copy is handed to the sender, the second accompanies the goods, and the third is retained by the carrier. When goods are carried in different vehicles or are of a different kind or are divided into different lots the seller or the carrier is entitled to require a separate consignment note for each vehicle or each kind or lot of goods.[14] The consignment note is not a negotiable instrument, nor a document of title.

The consignment note is prima facie evidence of the making of the contract of carriage, the conditions of the contract and the receipt of the goods by the carrier.[15] If the consignment note does not contain a clausing, it is presumed—though not irrebuttably—that the goods and their packaging appeared to be in good order and condition and that, when the carrier took them over, their marks and numbers corresponded with the statements in the consignment note.[16]

For the purposes of the Customs or other formalities which have to be completed before delivery of the goods, the sender shall attach the necessary documents to the consignment note or place them at the disposal of the carrier and shall furnish him with all the information which he requires.[17]

The sender is entitled to dispose of the goods, in particular by asking the carrier to stop the goods in transit, to change the place at which delivery

[12] In *Ulster Swift Ltd.* v. *Taunton Meat Haulage Ltd.* [1977] 1 Lloyd's Rep. 346, 360–361.
[13] Art. 4.
[14] Art. 5.
[15] Art. 9(1).
[16] Art. 9(2).
[17] Art. 11.

is to take place, or to deliver the goods to a person other than the consignee designated in the consignment note,[18] but that right ceases when the second copy of the consignment note has been handed over to the designated consignee or that consignee has required the carrier, against his receipt, to deliver up to him the second copy of the consignment note and the goods.[19] Furthermore, the consignee is entitled to dispose of the goods already from the time when the consignment note is drawn up, if the sender has made an entry to that effect on the consignment note.[20] If the sender, in exercising his right of disposal, has ordered the delivery of the goods to another person, that person is not entitled to name another consignee.[21] The sender who wishes to exercise the right of disposal, has to produce the first copy of the consignment note to the carrier and the new instructions must be entered thereon; he must further give the carrier an indemnity and a division of the cargo on such a diversion is not permissible.[22] The right of the sender to stop the goods in transit given by these provisions should not be confused with the right of stoppage in transitu of the seller under the contract of sale.[23] The right under the CMR exists against the carrier and is not dependent on the insolvency of the buyer but the right under the Sale of Goods Act exists against the buyer and can be exercised only if the buyer has become insolvent.

When circumstances prevent delivery of the goods after their arrival at the place of destination, the carrier shall ask the sender for his instructions. If the consignee refuses the goods, the sender is entitled to dispose of them without being obliged to produce the first copy of the consignment note, but in spite of his refusal the consignee may still require delivery as long as the carrier has not received instructions to the contrary from the seller.[24]

Liability of the carrier

The carrier is liable for the total or partial loss of the goods and for damage thereto occurring between the time when he takes over the goods and the time of delivery, as well as for delay in the delivery.[25] But the carrier is relieved of liability if the loss, damage or delay was caused:

1. by the wrongful act or neglect of the claimant; or
2. by the instructions of the claimant given otherwise than as the result of a wrongful act or neglect on the part of the carrier; or
3. by inherent vice of the goods; or
4. through circumstances which the carrier could not avoid and the consequences of which he was unable to prevent.[26]

The CMR contains a catalogue of special risks which relieve the carrier from liability; among them are the use of open unsheeted vehicles when

---

[18] Art. 12(1).
[19] Art. 12(2) and Art. 13.
[20] Art. 12(3).
[21] Art. 12(4).
[22] Art. 12(5).
[23] See p. 105, *ante*.
[24] Art. 15.
[25] Art. 17(1).
[26] Art. 17(2).

their use has been expressly agreed and specified in the consignment note.[27] The burden of proving that loss, damage or delay was due to one of the exempting causes specified in article 17(2) rests on the carrier.[28] If the carriage is performed in vehicles specially equipped to protect the goods from the effects of heat, cold, variation in temperature or the humidity of the air, the carrier cannot claim the benefit of the special risks otherwise applicable unless he proves that all steps incumbent on him in the circumstances with respect to the choice, maintenance and use of such equipment were taken and he complied with any special instructions issued to him.[29]

The fact that the goods have not been delivered within 30 days following the expiry of the agreed time limit or, if no time limit has been agreed, within 60 days from the time when the carrier took over the goods, shall be conclusive evidence of the loss of the goods, and the person entitled to make a claim may thereupon treat them as lost.[30]

If the goods are sent on a "cash on delivery" charge and the carrier hands them over without insisting on payment in cash, he is liable for compensation not exceeding the amount of the charge without prejudice to his right of action against the consignee.[31]

The compensation which the carrier is liable to pay in respect of total or partial loss of the goods is subject to a maximum limitation of liability. That is 25 gold francs per kilogram of gross weight short.[32] Reference to the gold franc is here to the Latin Union gold franc. How this value has to be ascertained, is uncertain. In the British practice 25 gold francs are widely regarded as equivalent to £3·403 per kilo or £3403 per tonne.[32a]

In addition, the carrier has to refund in full the carriage charges incurred, customs duties and other charges incurred in respect of the carriage of the goods.[33] In *James Buchanan & Co. Ltd.* v. *Babco Forwarding and Shipping (U.K.) Ltd.*[34] a consignment of whisky for export from Glasgow to Iran was stolen from a lorry park in Woolwich. The export value of the whisky was some £7,000 but the Customs demanded from Buchanan excise duty to the value of about £30,000 and according to Customs law Buchanan had to pay that duty. Buchanan then tried to recover that amount from the carriers. The House of Lords considered that claim as justified. The court decided that the excise duty constituted "other charges incurred in respect of the carriage of goods" within Article 23(4) and held that the carriers were liable for the full £37,000 because there was no limit placed on the

---

[27] Art. 17(4).
[28] Art. 18(1).
[29] Art. 18(4) and *Ulster Swift Ltd.* v. *Taunton Meat Haulage Ltd.* [1977] 1 Lloyd's Rep. 346.
[30] Art. 20.
[31] Art. 21.
[32] Art. 23(3).
[32a] Provisions of the Carriage by Air and Road Act 1979 which are not in force yet (August 1, 1979) will substitute Special Drawing Rights (SDRs) for gold francs and will carry out other amendments.
[33] Art. 23(4).
[34] [1977] 3 W.L.R. 907.

items mentioned in paragraph 4 but, on the contrary, it was provided that the carrier had to pay them "in full."

In the case of delay, the measure of damages is limited to the carriage charges if the claimant can prove that he has suffered damage to that amount.[35]

The defences which exclude or limit the liability of the carrier are also available if the action is founded on tort and not on contract.[36] The agents and servants and any other persons of whose services the carrier makes use for the performance of the carriage may avail themselves of the same defences, if they have acted within the scope of their employment.[37]

Time limits

If the consignee takes delivery of the goods and does not within seven days of delivery send the carrier a notice of reservations, giving a general indication of the apparent loss or damage, the fact of taking delivery is prima facie evidence that he received the goods in the condition described in the consignment note.[38] No compensation is payable for delay in delivery unless a reservation has been sent in writing to the carrier within 21 days from the time that the goods were placed at the disposal of the consignee.[39]

The period of limitation for bringing an action arising out of the carriage under the CMR is one year. Nevertheless, in the case of wilful conduct or such default as in accordance with the law of the court or tribunal seized of the case is considered equivalent to wilful misconduct, the period of limitation is three years.[40] Time begins to run:

(*a*) in the case of partial loss, damage or delay in delivery from the date of delivery;
(*b*) in the case of total loss, from the 30th day after the expiry of the agreed time limit or, where no time limit is agreed, from the 60th day from the date when the goods were taken over by the carrier, or
(*c*) in all other cases on the expiry of three months after the making of the contract.

Nullity of stipulations contrary to the Convention

Apart from the internal arrangements between successive carriers,[41] any stipulation which would directly or indirectly derogate from the provisions of the CMR is null and void.[42] In particular, a benefit of insurance in favour of the carrier or any other similar clause or any clause shifting the burden of proof is null and void.[43]

---

[35] Art. 23(5).
[36] Art. 28.
[37] Art. 28(2).
[38] Art. 30(1).
[39] Art. 30(3).
[40] Art. 32(1).
[41] The exempted provisions of the Convention are Articles 37 and 38.
[42] Art. 41(1).
[43] Art. 41(2).

Chapter 25

PROTECTION OF PATENTS AND TRADE MARKS ABROAD

Patents and Designs

The regulation in the United Kingdom

In the United Kingdom the law relating to patents and registered designs is treated separately in the Patents Acts 1949–61 and 1977, the Registered Designs Acts 1949–61, and the Design Copyright Act 1968.[1]

A patent is intended to reward the disclosure of a novel invention by the grant of a 20-year monopoly. This empowers the patentee to prevent others from making, using, offering or putting on the market the invention or from supplying means "relating to an essential element of the invention" for putting the invention into effect when it is known to the supplier that the invention will be put into effect.[2] Most inventions within the fields of technology and agriculture fall within the scope of the system[3]; computer programs are, however, specifically excluded.[4] The present British system is in a state of transition. The Patents Act 1977 governs all patents granted on applications filed on or after June 1, 1978. Existing patents and patents granted on applications filed before June 1, 1978 are governed in part by the Patents Acts 1949–1961 and in part by the Patents Act 1977. The new Act modernises British patent law and provides for the assimilation of the European Patent Convention[5] into the British system. It also contains provisions whereby the Community Patent Convention[6] will take direct effect in the United Kingdom once it is in force.[7]

The registered design system is intended to foster the introduction of novel designs for industrially produced articles. The proprietor gains the right, for a maximum of fifteen years, to prevent others from marketing goods in Britain which bear his registered design. Designs are "features

---

[1] See generally, T. A. Blanco White, *Patents for Inventions and the Protection of Industrial Designs* (4th ed., 1974); P. Meinhardt, *Inventions, Patents and Trade Marks* (1971). Blanco White *et al.*, *Encyclopedia of United Kingdom and European Patent Law* (1977); Walton and Laddie, *Patent Law of Europe and the United Kingdom* (1978).

[2] s. 60, Patents Act 1977. Subs. (2) introduces so-called contributory infringement into British law for the first time.

[3] Specific exclusions from patentability are set out in s. 1(2), Patents Act 1977. This is a departure from the old law under which questions of patentability were answered by reference to case law and principle. Methods of human treatment are outside the scope of the patent system. The development of novel plant varieties and seeds is dealt with by separate legislation, the Plant Varieties and Seeds Act 1964.

[4] Patents Act 1977, s. 1(2).

[5] Text included in Blanco White *et al.*, *Encyclopedia,* and Walton & Laddie.

[6] *Ibid.*

[7] The early 1980s is the target date.

of shape, configuration, pattern or ornament applied to an article by an industrial process or means being features which in the finished article appeal to and are judged solely by the eye, but [not including] a method of principle of construction or features of shape or configuration which are dictated solely by the function which the article . . . has to perform."[8] Like the patentee, the design proprietor must obtain a grant from the Patent Office in order to gain protection. Since 1968, he may, in addition, obtain protection for any artistic copyright that is embodied in his industrial designs.[9] While he will have to establish that an infringer has copied his own design, no formal step is necessary in order to gain this protection. As a result the decline in popularity of the registered design system has accelerated in recent years. The Whitford Committee, which reported in 1977, was split three ways on the best method of protection for industrial designs and was unable to recommend any particular course of action.

Territorial scope of patents

A patent has effect only in the territory of the sovereign who has granted it. In the United Kingdom, letters patent are granted by the Crown through the Patent Office[10] for a period of 20 years,[11] and registered designs for a period of 15 years.[12] Such patents and designs have effect in the United Kingdom and the Isle of Man,[13] but not in any other part of the Commonwealth[14] or in foreign countries. Similarly, a patent granted or design registered under the laws of an overseas country has, as a matter of principle, no effect outside the country where it is granted.[15]

The requirements of the various territorial patent laws vary, and it is not uncommon for a patent for a particular invention to be granted in one country but refused in another. In a few countries, notably in West Germany, Japan, Poland, Spain and Brazil, petty patents or utility designs[16] are registrable for technical improvements which enhance the usefulness

[8] Registered Designs Act 1949, s. 1(3). See the House of Lords construction of this definition to exclude totally functional articles: *Amp* v. *Utilux Pty.* [1972] R.P.C. 103.

[9] The Design Copyright Act 1968 amended the Copyright Act 1956, s. 10, so as to permit this. At least, in the case of designs that are capable of being registered, copyright protection as regards industrial reproductions lasts for fifteen years from first marketing with the copyright owner's consent.

[10] Southampton Buildings, Chancery Lane, W.C.2.

[11] Patents Act 1977, s. 25(1), subject to the payment of renewal fees (s. 25(3)(4)). Existing patents with more than five years to run on June 1, 1978 are automatically extended to 20 years; those with less than five years to run have a period of 16 years subject to an extension of up to four years on the grounds of inadequate remuneration: Patents Act 1977, Sched. 1, paras. 3 and 4.

[12] Registered Designs Act 1949, s. 8(1). Renewal fees are payable after the fifth and tenth years.

[13] Patents Act 1977, s. 132; Registered Designs Act 1949, ss. 7(1), 47.

[14] The Channel Islands and certain Commonwealth countries, however, have a system of protection based simply upon the registration of British patents and designs.

[15] G. Vojáček. *A Survey of the Principal National Patent Systems* (New York, Prentice-Hall, Inc., 1936, with addenda (1956)), p. 181; J. W. Baxter, *World Patent Law and Practice* (2nd ed., 1973, with supplements, 1978).

[16] *Gebrauchsmuster, Modèles d'utilite.*

of an article without being sufficiently important to qualify as inventions. Utility designs enjoy a smaller degree of protection than ordinary patents.

"International patents," in the sense of patents providing protection in all or several patent territories, are as yet a novel concept. Patents granted under the Community Patent Convention will constitute the first supra-national patents of this kind. It is intended that the Community patent will be one product of the broader European system under which by a single application to the European Patent Office it will be possible to obtain patents, in common form, for numerous European countries. The Convention covering this European granting system was signed in Munich in 1973 and came into force in October 1977. The European Patent Office, situated in Munich, opened for the filing of patent applications on June 1, 1978. An *International Convention for the Protection of Industrial Property*[17] exists which will be more closely considered in the following section, but the regulation provided by the Convention is based on the unqualified recognition of the territorial effect of the patent grant. An inventor who obtains a patent in one member country has still to apply to the patent authorities of the other member countries if he desires to obtain protection there; he has to pay fees there and to comply, in all respects, with the patent laws of those countries, and, although his application may be granted in one member country, his further applications in other member countries may be refused.[18] The principal advantage which he secures by filing, in other Convention countries, a *Convention application* is that his application in those countries takes priority over subsequent competing applications provided he files his application in the respective countries within a year from the date of the basic application.

The question whether an inventor in the United Kingdom should seek protection of his invention abroad arises normally before he is in a position to export articles which embody it. This question arises when he applies for British letters patent or shortly afterwards. If he merely obtains a British patent and allows the priority year, during which he can obtain priority in the Convention countries, to pass, he is unlikely to secure a patent in the foreign countries to which his exports are directed because the publication of his patent specification in the United Kingdom is detrimental to the novelty of his invention which all countries regard as an essential requirement for a patentable invention. The stipulations of national patent laws as to the requirement of novelty vary; in some countries, like Australia, India, Pakistan, Switzerland and Greece, a prior application affects the novelty of an invention only if the publication has been made available in the country where the patent is applied for; in most other countries, including the United Kingdom, the United States and Canada, prior publication anywhere is detrimental and in many countries prior public use anywhere has the same effect. But in many countries there

[17] Blanco White *et al., Encyclopedia* gives the Stockholm revision of the text (1967).
[18] J. W. Baxter, *op. cit.* Chap. 10.

is not the same insistence as is found in the British system that there be no revelation of the invention prior to the inventor's application for a patent. Limited periods of grace are admitted.[19]

An inventor in the United Kingdom who intends to export the products of his invention and contemplates obtaining, in addition to his British patent, patents in overseas countries to which his exports are likely to be directed has two courses open: he may, simultaneously with his application in the United Kingdom, arrange for ordinary patent applications to be filed abroad or he may during the priority year make a Convention application in the overseas countries in question, provided they are members of the International Convention.[20] The inventor should consult his patent agent in the United Kingdom on the question of foreign filings. If it is decided to apply for a patent in an overseas country, he will instruct a patent agent resident in that country on behalf of the inventor.

The Patents Act 1977 provides that a compulsory licence of a British patent may be granted where, by reason of the refusal of the patentee to grant a licence, an export market of the patented article manufactured in the United Kingdom is not being supplied[21]; an application can only be made after the expiration of three years from the grant of the patent.

International Conventions

The International Convention for the Protection of Industrial Property was concluded in Paris in 1883 and has been repeatedly revised, in particular in London in 1934, in Lisbon in 1958 and in Stockholm in 1967. The Convention of 1883 has been ratified by approximately 80 states.

It deals with the protection of industrial property in the broadest sense, and is concerned with patents, utility models, industrial designs and models, trade marks, service marks, trade names and indications of source or appellations of origin and the repression of unfair competition. It applies not only to products of industry but also to agricultural products such as wines, tobacco, fruit, flowers, flour and to minerals, etc.

The Convention provides for the constitution of a Union for the Protection of Industrial Property. The administration of the Convention is entrusted to the World Intellectual Property Organisation (WIPO) in Geneva, which also administers the International Union under the Berne Copyright Convention.

The United Kingdom is a member of the International Convention. Apart from the International Convention, the United Kingdom has concluded bilateral conventions for the protection of industrial property with a number of countries which are not members of the International Con-

[19] *Ibid.* Chap. 4.
[20] *Ibid.* pp. 161–177.
[21] Patents Act 1977, s. 48(3)(*d*)(i). The Registered Designs Act 1949 does not provide for the grant of a compulsory licence on the ground that the export market is not supplied but authorises the grant of a compulsory licence on the ground that the design is not applied in the United Kingdom to a reasonable extent (s. 10(1)).

vention. The United Kingdom recognises the following countries as Convention countries[22]:

Algeria, Argentina, Australia, Austria, Bahamas, Bangladesh, Belgium, Benin, Brazil, Bulgaria, Burundi, Cameroons, Canada, Central African Republic, Chad, Cuba, Cyprus, Czechoslovakia, Denmark, Dominican Republic, Egypt, Finland, France, Gabon, German Democratic Republic, Federal Republic of Germany, Ghana, Greece, Haiti, Hong Kong, Hungary, Iceland, India, Indonesia, Iran, Iraq, Ireland (Republic), Israel, Italy, Ivory Coast, Japan, Jordan, Kenya, Korea (South), Lebanon, Libya, Liechtenstein, Luxembourg, Madagascar, Malawi, Malta, Mauritania, Mauritius, Mexico, Monaco, Morocco, Netherlands, New Zealand, Niger, Nigeria, Norway, Pakistan, Philippines, Poland, Portugal, Rhodesia, Romania, San Marino, Senegal, Singapore, South Africa, Spain, Sri Lanka, Surinam, Sweden, Switzerland, Syrian Arab Republic, Tanzania, Togo, Trinidad and Tobago, Tunisia, Turkey, Uganda, U.S.S.R., U.S.A., Upper Volta, Uruguary, Vatican City, Vietnam, Yugoslavia, Zaire, Zambia.[23]

The Crown has power to add further countries to the list of Convention countries and to make further inter-Commonwealth arrangements.[24]

The principal rights granted by the International Convention, as far as patents are concerned,[25] are:

(1) Persons within the jurisdiction of a Convention country, whether nationals or residents of that country or merely having an industrial or commercial establishment there, enjoy in all other Convention countries the same rights, protection, privileges and remedies as the national patent laws grant to the nationals of their countries. Discriminatory treatment of foreign inventors, so far as subject to the jurisdiction of a Convention country, is not admitted.

(2) A person who has duly deposited an application for a patent in one Convention country enjoys a right of priority for twelve months following that date in other Convention countries. If during the priority period he files an application in another Convention country, the date when the basic application was filed in his own country is regarded as the application date in the other country. The novelty of the invention is, in most patent systems, judged according to the position prevailing at that date.[26] This, as has been seen,[27] gives the inventor an opportunity of delaying foreign filings until he has gauged the commercial prospects of his invention.

(3) If renewal or other fees are not paid, a time of grace is allowed which is either not less than three months plus the right of restoration

---

[22] The recognition is subject to minor variations, due to the fact that some countries have adopted revisions of the Convention and others have not done so and to other circumstances. A list of Member States indicating the versions to which they adhere is given in *Industrial Property*, January 1978.

[23] In addition there exist bilateral conventions, similar in scope of protection to that given by the International Convention, between Great Britain and Burma (in relation only to patents), and Great Britain and Ecuador (in relation only to trade marks and registered designs).

[24] See note 22.

[25] As far as trade marks are concerned, the provisions of the Convention are considered on p. 404, *post*.

[26] Meinhardt, *loc. cit.*, p. 125.

[27] See p. 399, *ante*.

of a forfeited patent, or not less than six months without such additional right. Where payment is made during the time of grace a supplementary fee may be charged.

(4) The Convention countries temporarily protect patentable inventions in respect of goods exhibited at official or officially recognised international exhibitions held in the territory of one of them by providing that this exhibition does not amount to an anticipation destroying the novelty of the invention; but this protection does not prolong the priority period (see (2) above).[28]

The Convention provides that no compulsory licence may be granted in a Convention country within three years from the date of the grant of the patent on the ground of failure to work or insufficient working. Many countries provide for the grant of compulsory licences for other reasons than this abuse of monopoly power.

Proposed International Developments

The U.S.S.R. and most other countries in the Soviet bloc have severely limited the right of their nationals to apply for protection of their inventions in the form of patents and instead have encouraged applications for inventors' certificates. The purpose of such a certificate is to provide an adequate means of rewarding an inventor for his invention while allowing its exploitation by all government and co-operative agencies. The inventor becomes entitled to a remuneration based on the saving to enterprises which use it for a period which may run to five years from its first exploitation. A new provision in the Stockholm revision of the International Convention gives international status to the inventor's certificate by allowing an application to have convention priority as if it were an application for a patent.[29] A foreign inventor may apply for an inventor's certificate rather than a patent under the legislation of these socialist countries, and the financial advantages of doing so are currently causing an increasing number of foreigners to take this course.

The convention signed at Stockholm in 1967 and establishing the World Intellectual Property Organisation (WIPO)[30] draws together the secretariats administering the International Convention for the Protection of Industrial Property and the Berne Copyright Union. It was from this source that the Patent Co-operation Treaty of 1970 emanated.[31] This establishes

---

[28] For details of temporary protection, as far as the United Kingdom is concerned, see Patents Act 1977, ss. 2(4)(*c*), 130(1); Registered Designs Act 1949, s. 6.

[29] Art 41 (see Cmnd. 3474, 1967).

[30] Cmnd. 3442, 1967. Convention ratified by the U.K. on February 26, 1969. See S. P. Ladas, "The Convention establishing the World Intellectual Property Organisation," 2 *Journ. of World Trade Law* (1968) 684.

[31] In force October 24, 1977. The parties to the Treaty were by July 16, 1979, Austria, Brazil, Cameroon, Central African Empire, Chad, Congo, Denmark, France, Gabon, Germany (Federal Republic), Japan, Luxembourg, Madagascar, Malawi, Monaco, Netherlands, Romania, Senegal, Soviet Union, Sweden, Switzerland, Togo, U.K., U.S.A.. Chaps. I and II came into effect in 1978.

a system of international searching and (eventually) of examination of patent applications to be conducted by offices equipped to do so.

The European Patent Convention,[32] which came into force in October 1977, has similar aims to that of the Patent Co-operation Treaty and is intended to work in harmony with it. It became operative on June 1, 1978 and provides as an alternative to applications to national patent offices in the territories concerned, a system of application to, and search and examination by the European Patent Office established in Munich. If successful, the end product will be a bundle of national patents.[33] It is also intended, however, that there will be a single EEC patent covering the territories of the Common Market countries as an alternative to national patents. This alone will be available if the European application procedure is pursued. The Community Patent Convention establishing this supranational patent was signed in 1975 but has not yet come into force.

EEC LAW

Patents are national rights and are strictly territorial in effect; hence a patentee can use his patent to prevent imported goods entering the country. The European Court of Justice has made use of the doctrine of exhaustion of rights and of the principle of the free movement of goods set out in Articles 30 to 36 of the Treaty of Rome to hold that a patentee having patents in more than one Member State cannot use his national patent rights in one Member State to repel imports from another Member State where the goods have been put on the market either by the patentee himself or with his consent.[34] Where there is no patent protection in the country of export because, for example, the invention is not patentable there,[35] or where the goods originate outside the EEC altogether,[36] the patentee is free to use his national patent rights to repel the goods. Patent licence agreements fall prima facie within Article 85 and require notification to the Commission. Certain clauses, such as no-challenge clauses, improvement grant-backs and tie-ups after the patent has expired are not allowed.[37] Exclusive manufacturing and sales licences are scrutinised carefully by the Commission. A draft block exemption under Article 85(3) is under active consideration by the Commission.[38]

---

[32] The parties to the Convention are Belgium, France, Germany (Federal Republic), Luxembourg, Netherlands, Sweden, Switzerland and the U.K.

[33] The Patents Act 1977, s. 77 provides that a European patent designating the U.K. shall be treated as if it were a patent granted under the Act. In this way a European patent (U.K.) takes effect as a British patent.

[34] *Centrafarm* v. *Sterling Drug Co.* [1974] 2 C.M.L.R. 480; [1975] E.C.R. 1147.

[35] *Parke, Davis* v. *Probel* [1968] C.M.L.R. 47.

[36] *EMI* v. *CBS* [1976] 2 C.M.L.R. 235; *Re Tylosin* [1977] 1 C.M.L.R. 460.

[37] See for example, *AOIP-Beyrard Agreements* [1976] 1 C.M.L.R. D14.

[38] The texts of the first and second drafts are given in Blanco White *et al. Encyclopedia.*

TRADE MARKS

In export trade, the sale of goods under a trade mark is perhaps even more important than in home trade. The trade mark has rightly been described as the link between the proprietor of the mark and the consumer of the goods.[39] It is often the only means of building up lasting goodwill for the exporter's goods, and its importance is enhanced where the exporter sells in the overseas market by methods which do not give him direct control over the distributors, *viz.* by virtue of sole distribution agreements[40] or through self-employed agents.[41]

The registration and maintenance of a trade mark in the United Kingdom is easy and inexpensive, and protection abroad can, in most instances, be obtained at relatively small cost.

Registered and unregistered trade marks

The trade mark laws of the world have been classified into three systems[42]—

(1) The system of ownership based on priority of use;
(2) The system of ownership based on priority of registration;
(3) The system of ownership based on uncontested registration for a specified period.

Under the first system, the use of the trade mark in connection with the manufacturer's or trader's goods creates the proprietary right in the trade mark. A registration of the trade mark in a public register is merely "declaratory" and can be impeached at any time by the true owner of the trade mark. This antiquated system attributes little more than evidential value to the registration of a trade mark. From the point of view of the United Kingdom exporter, overseas trade mark laws based on this system are not detrimental because they enable the exporter to sell his goods in the country in question without first obtaining registration of his trade mark and to defend his trade mark against any person infringing it, whether that person obtained registration of the infringing mark or not.

Under the second system the position is very different. Here the right of the person first obtaining registration prevails over all other users of the trade mark, including those who used the trade mark before him. Registration is "attributive," not "declaratory." This system which can prove detrimental to the trade mark of unsuspecting exporters who fail to obtain registration *before* building up their export market in the countries in question, is substantially in force in

Bulgaria, Chile, China (People's Republic), Czechoslovakia, Denmark, Egypt, Finland, France, German Democratic Republic, German Federal Republic, Greece, Hungary, Iran,

---

[39] MacEwan, *Overseas Trade and Export Practice*, p. 340.
[40] See p. 153, *ante*.
[41] See p. 161, *ante*.
[42] Stephen P. Ladas, "The International Protection of Trade Marks by the American Republics," *Harvard Studies in International Law*, Vol. 1, 1929, p. 37.

Italy, Japan, Lebanon, Mexico, Norway, Peru, Portugal, Spain, Sweden, Turkey, U.S.S.R. and most South American countries.[43]

The third system, which is the most advanced and has been recommended as a model for a uniform trade mark law,[44] represents a compromise between the preceding two systems. Under this system, as under the first system, the use of an unregistered trade mark by one person is an obstacle to the registration of the same or a similar trade mark by another person, and, even if an unauthorised person obtains registration, the proprietor of the trade mark may take proceedings to have the registration declared invalid, but, if the right of the registered user has not been attacked for a time laid down by law, the ownership of the registered user becomes absolute and can only be impeached in exceptional circumstances. This is the arrangement which, in principle, the Trade Marks Act 1938 of the United Kingdom adopts in respect of registration in Part A of the Register and which likewise is adopted—

by the laws of many members of the Commonwealth including Australia, Bangladesh, Canada, India and New Zealand, and also by the law of the Benelux territories, Indonesia, Ireland, Israel, Pakistan, South Africa, Sri Lanka, Switzerland, Thailand and U.S.A.[45]

In the United States of America, the Federal Trade Mark Act 1946[46] abolished the "declaratory" system and introduced a regulation similar to that existing in the United Kingdom; the Act provides that the mark becomes incontestable after five years of registration on the principal register.

In the result, whatever system of trade mark regulation prevails in the countries into which the exporter intends to direct his exports, registration of his trade mark in those countries prior to the carrying out of export transactions is always advisable, and omission to do so in the countries which have adopted the attributive system of registration may lead to irretrievable loss.

Registration of trade marks in the United Kingdom

In the United Kingdom, the registration of a trade mark is effected in accordance with the provisions of the Trade Marks Act 1938.[47] The Act defines a trade mark as

a mark used or proposed to be used in relation to goods for the purpose of indicating, or so as to indicate, a connection in the course of trade between the goods and some person having the right either as proprietor or as a registered user to use the mark.[48]

Where a registered trade mark is infringed, the person entitled to the mark may claim damages and obtain an injunction to prevent further

---

[43] See for complete lists of countries falling within each category, White and Ravenscroft, *Trade Marks throughout the World* (2nd ed., 1930, with supplements (1978)).

[44] See Ladas, *op. cit.* p. 41.

[45] See for complete lists of countries falling within each category, White and Ravenscroft, *Trade Marks throughout the World* (2nd ed., 1930, with supplements (1978)).

[46] Pub. I, No. 489, 79th Cong. 2d sess.

[47] See D. M. Kerly, *Law of Trade Marks and Trade Names* (10th ed., 1972).

[48] s. 68(1).

infringements, but where the trade mark is not registered legal redress must be sought through the common law tort of "passing off."[49] This tort protects traders against the filching of their trade reputation by competing traders; it is committed when a person represents his goods as the goods of someone else, and it is not necessary to prove that the defendant acted fraudulently or that a member of the public was, in fact, deceived; it is sufficient to prove that deception was likely to ensue. A passing-off action requires the plaintiff to establish that he has a public reputation in the mark, and it was largely this difficulty which led to the introduction of the system of registered trade marks. It should be noted that some forms of business reputation, such as business names and service marks, cannot be registered as trade marks; these can only be protected by passing-off actions.

The Register of Trade Marks is kept by the Patent Office.[50] In addition to the Trade Marks Register, trade marks for textile goods are registered in the Manchester Record, and for metal goods in the Sheffield Register kept by the Cutlers' Company at Sheffield if the applicant carries on business in Hallamshire or within six miles thereof. The Trade Marks Register consists of 34 classes of goods. It is possible to register the same trade mark in different classes, but a separate application is required for each class.[51] A trade mark may be registered in Part A or Part B of the Trade Marks Register; the registration in Part A provides greater protection because it is stated in section 13 of the Act that

> in all legal proceedings relating to a trade mark registered in Part A of the register . . . the original registration in Part A of the register of the trade mark shall, after the expiration of seven years from the date of that registration, be taken to be valid in all respects, unless:
> (*a*) that registration was obtained by fraud, or
> (*b*) the trade mark offends the provisions of section 11 of this Act.[52]

A trade mark registered in Part B is not protected by the presumption of valid registration after seven years, but the requirements for registration in Part B are less stringent than those for registration in Part A.[53]

A person who intends to register a trade mark may ask the registrar for advice whether the trade mark appears prima facie to possess the legal requirements of inherent distinctiveness (s. 42). Where the registrar answers in the affirmative and the inquirer then applies for a trade mark within three months and the registrar, upon further consideration, holds that the trade mark does not possess these requirements, the inquirer is entitled

---

[49] s. 2.

[50] Communications in connection with trade marks should be addressed to: The Registrar, The Trade Marks Registry, The Patent Office, 25 Southampton Buildings, Chancery Lane, London, W.C.2.

[51] Trade Marks Rules 1938, r. 21.

[52] s. 11: "It shall not be lawful to register as a trade mark or part of a trade mark any matter the use of which would, by reason of its being likely to deceive or cause confusion or otherwise, be disentitled to protection in a court of justice, or would be contrary to law or morality, or any scandalous design." See generally *General Electric Co. of America* v. *General Electric Co. Ltd.* [1972] 1 W.L.R. 729; [1973] R.P.C. 297.

[53] See Trade Marks Act 1938, ss. 9, 10; Kerly, *op. cit.*, Chap. 8, ss. 2, 3.

to a repayment of the fees paid by him on the filing of his application,[54] but this right does not exist if the application is refused on other grounds.

The justification of the privilege obtained by registration of a trade mark is its use; without use it becomes an unjustifiable obstruction in the path of other traders who might wish to use it for their goods. The Act provides in section 26 that a trade mark may be removed from the register if registered without bona fide intention of using it, or if there has been no bona fide use of the mark for a continuous period of five years or longer[55]; that period must have continued to one month before the making of the application for removal. Use on goods exported from the United Kingdom constitutes use of the trade mark, as if the goods were sold or otherwise traded in within the United Kingdom.[56] The rule of section 26 is subject to certain exceptions; the most important of them is admitted in the case of a "defensive mark." A defensive mark may be registered if a trade mark consists of an invented word (*e.g.* the word Kodak) which has become so closely associated in the mind of the public with a particular product (*e.g.* photographic articles), that the word, if used for other goods (*e.g.* film projectors), might be taken to indicate that the other goods are connected with the manufacturer producing the first-mentioned goods. Such invented words may be registered, by way of defensive registration, for goods for which they are not intended to be used (s. 27).

A person other than the registered proprietor may be registered, upon application by the latter, as "registered user" of the trade mark, provided that an agreement exists between the proprietor and the user under which the former retains control over the permitted use; the registered user is, in certain circumstances, entitled to institute legal proceedings for infringement of the trade mark.[57] As far as United Kingdom legislation is concerned, a trade mark can be assigned or transmitted with or without goodwill of the business in which it is used.[58] But all dealings in trade marks that affect Common Market countries are subject to the interpretations placed upon the EEC Treaty by the European Court of Justice. Thus, it is no longer permissible to assign a trade mark for one EEC country to an exclusive dealer there in order to prevent the import into that territory of goods marketed in another of the countries and bearing the same trade mark with the assignor's consent.[59] The owner of the mark in all the Member States can, however, repel goods lawfully bearing the mark which originate outside the EEC even though the marks are of common origin.[60]

---

[54] Trade Marks Act 1938, s. 42.
[55] Kerly, *op. cit.*, pp. 210–216.
[56] Trade Marks Act 1938, s. 31.
[57] s. 28.
[58] s. 22.
[59] EEC Treaty, Arts. 30–36, 85; *Consten and Grundig* v. *Commission* [1966] C.M.L.R. 418; *Sirena S.R.L.* v. *Eda S.R.L.* [1971] C.M.L.R. 260; *Van Zuylen Frères* v. *Hag A.G.* [1974] 2 C.M.L.R. 127; see p. 225, *ante*.
[60] *EMI* v. *CBS* [1976] 2 C.M.L.R. 235.

The duration of a registered trade mark is not limited in time, provided the renewal fees are paid. Initial registration is for a period of seven years, thereafter registration is renewed for periods of 14 years, on payment of certain fees.

The registration of a trade mark under the Trade Marks Act 1938 has effect in the United Kingdom and the Isle of Man, but not elsewhere.

Registration of trade marks for exports only

A trade mark can be registered for use only on goods to be exported from the United Kingdom.[61] It is possible to obtain registration for exports generally, but, if the application is opposed, registration will be limited to those countries in respect of which the applicant can prove that the mark is distinctive of his goods.[62]

A trade mark, which cannot be used in this country because it contains features similar to those of a trade mark appropriated by another trader, may be registered for exports only,[63] unless the proprietor of the other trade mark uses it in the overseas market in question; but a trade mark which is inherently incapable of registration in this country, *e.g.* because it is in common use in the particular trade in this country, is not registrable for export only because such registration might unduly embarrass traders in this country, particularly if they are desirous of developing their export trade.[64]

Use of a trade mark on exported goods constitutes use in the same manner as if the mark were used in this country (s. 31).[65]

International protection of trade marks

Trade marks, like patents and other types of industrial property, are protected by the International Convention for the Protection of Industrial Property, originally concluded at Paris, to which the United Kingdom is a party.[66] Trade marks registered in the United Kingdom enjoy the advantages of the International Convention in countries tabulated on pp. 401 and 402 *ante*.

The International Convention provides for trade marks similar protection to that laid down for patents. Where a person is entitled to a trade mark registered in the United Kingdom, his principal rights in another Convention country are:

---

[61] s. 31. This is possible even where sale to the public in the United Kingdom might be deceptive; the Registrar, however, has a general discretion to refuse to register a mark where the use would be deceptive: ss. 17(2), 68(1).

[62] *Re Glenforres Glenlivet Distillery Co. Ltd.'s Application* (1934) 51 R.P.C. 325.

[63] Official Ruling (1931) 48 R.P.C., Appendix; *Re Evans, Sons, Lescher and Webb Ltd.'s Application* (1934) 51 R.P.C. 423.

[64] *George Banham & Co. Ltd.* v. *F. Reddaway & Co. Ltd.* [1927] A.C. 406, as interpreted in the Official Ruling.

[65] See p. 407, *ante*.

[66] See p. 400, *ante*.

(1) The right to enjoy in that country the same rights, protection, privileges and remedies as are granted by the trade mark law of that country to nationals of that country. The provisions of the Convention against discriminatory treatment are, in this respect, identical with those applying to patents.[67]

(2) The right of priority for six months following the date of application for the trade mark in the United Kingdom. If during that period the applicant files an application in another Convention country, the date when the original application is filed in his own country is regarded as the application date in the other country. The benefits of priority are accorded, although the registration in the country of origin may not be completed until after the expiration of the priority period.

(3) In principle, every trade mark duly registered in one Convention country is admitted for registration and protected in its original form in the other Convention countries.

(4) The proprietor of a trade mark registered in one Convention country may oppose the registration of a trade mark in another Convention country, or, if registered, claim its cancellation on the ground that that trade mark is a reproduction of, or imitation capable of creating confusion with, his own trade mark which is well known in his own country for the same or similar classes of goods. The submission of such claims is, in some countries, limited in time, but the time limit must not be less than three years, and no time limit exists if the infringing trade mark was registered in bad faith.

(5) Registration cannot be cancelled on the ground of non-use of the trade mark until a reasonable period has elapsed, and then only if the person interested cannot justify the cause of his inaction.

(6) Renewal of registration of a mark in the country of origin does not involve the obligation to renew the registration in other Convention countries where the mark is registered.

(7) A time of grace of not less than three months is allowed for the payment of renewal or other due fees.

(8) Temporary protection is granted for trade marks on goods shown at official or officially recognised exhibitions.

(9) The Convention countries have undertaken to prohibit the utilisation, without due authority, of armorial bearings, flags and other state emblems of the parties to the Convention as trade marks or parts of trade marks.

Apart from the General Union for the Protection of Industrial Property which was created by the Convention of Paris, there exists a Restricted Union which is based on the Madrid Agreement for International Registration of Trade Marks that was concluded in 1891 and has been repeatedly revised. The arrangement adopted by the Restricted Union represents a great improvement upon the provisions of the General Union because it

---

[67] See p. 401, *ante*.

allows for international registration of trade marks at the International Bureau at Berne. International registration is effective in every member country of the Restricted Union unless a member country vetoes the protection in its own territory; the veto can only be exercised within 12 months from the date of international registration. The United Kingdom, the other countries of the Commonwealth and the United States are not members of the Restricted Union.

CHAPTER 26

ARBITRATION AND LITIGATION

IT is almost a truism to state that arbitration is better than litigation, conciliation better than arbitration, and prevention of legal disputes better than conciliation. The reasonable exporter who, in spite of the care which he has taken in the preparation of the contract of sale, has to contemplate whether or not to commence legal proceedings against the buyer for a breach of contract might, in appropriate circumstances, prefer to cut his losses rather than to engage in costly and protracted litigation. There are, however, circumstances where this solution is out of the question. The subject-matter in issue might be too valuable to accept the loss, interests of third parties might be involved, the breach might appear too flagrant to allow it to pass unchallenged. Here the question is how to utilise the most convenient, speediest and cheapest machinery to settle the dispute and, if possible, to settle it in such a manner as to leave no sting to poison the business relations between the parties after the settlement of the dispute. With this object in view, the exporter should insist on the embodiment of an arbitration clause in the contract of sale and should obtain the formal acceptance of that clause by the buyer. It has been seen earlier that an arbitration clause is often embodied in the general conditions of sale on which the seller transacts his business. In these cases the seller should make certain that the conditions, including the arbitration clause, have come to the buyer's notice, and should obtain a formal letter of acceptance where there is an element of doubt on this point. It is the general experience that it is easier to obtain agreement on arbitration when the contract is concluded than when the dispute has arisen, and the aggrieved party has, in the latter case, no means of compelling the other party to accept arbitration.

ARBITRATION

The general opinion amongst businessmen and lawyers is that arbitration proceedings offer marked advantages over court proceedings. They are often cheaper, less dilatory and less formal, they take place in private, and in many instances no appeal and further appeal is possible. There are, however, some experienced businessmen who, for various reasons, are reluctant to submit to arbitration; their objection can usually be met by appropriate provisions in the arbitration clause about the person of the arbitrators and the place where the arbitration is to be held.

Where the dispute between the parties concerns only questions of fact, *e.g.* whether the goods are of the stipulated quality or description, or are in accordance with sample, arbitration offers overwhelming advantages over litigation. Most of these so-called *quality arbitrations*, particularly those arranged under the rules of the great trade associations,[1] are expeditiously and cheaply disposed of, and it happens rarely that a dispute arising from them is later taken to the court.

On the other hand, where the facts of the matter are not in dispute, *viz.* where the dispute concerns the construction of a document or a purely legal question, it is often cheaper and more expeditious[2] for the parties to submit their dispute to the court. In these so-called *technical arbitrations* it is often to the advantage of the parties to waive arbitration by mutual agreement and to go straight away to the Commercial Court. In one case[3] Singleton L.J. observed in respect of a contract embodying the arbitration clause of the London Jute Association:

> This dispute was referred to arbitration, and subsequently there was an appeal to the committee. Thereafter a special case was stated by the committee and came before Lord Goddard C.J. Most respectfully, I would point out that this procedure adds greatly to the cost and trouble which the parties have to encounter in a case of this kind. It would, I think, be better that a dispute such as this should go direct to the Commercial Court, and there be dealt with, as it would be a saving of costs for the parties.

Very frequently the dispute concerns both questions of fact and of law. In these *mixed arbitrations* the function of the arbitrator is mainly to find the facts; although he likewise pronounces on the law, his decision on legal questions may be examined by the court.[4] Devlin J. observed in one case[5]:

> Arbitration has great advantages and it also has some disadvantages. Splitting up questions of fact and of law may be one of the disadvantages . . . It is important that people who are going to argue points of law before the court should get facts found which they want found for the purposes of arguing the point of law which they want to submit to the court.

Since the division of functions between the arbitrator and the court can lead to delay and additional costs, the parties may, if they so desire, appoint a judge of the Commercial Court as sole arbitrator or as umpire[6]; such an appointment avoids the procedure by judicial review and the splitting up of questions of fact and of law. An appeal from the judicial arbitrator lies to the Court of Appeal.[7]

---

[1] See p. 51, *ante*.

[2] In *British Imex Industries Ltd.* v. *Midland Bank Ltd.* [1958] 1 Q.B. 542 (see p. 251, *ante*) the Commercial Court gave judgment eleven days after the issue of the writ.

[3] *K. C. Sethia (1944) Ltd.* v. *Partabmull Rameshwar* [1950] 1 All E.R. 51, 58; affd. [1951] 2 All E.R. 352; *Macpherson Train & Co. Ltd.* v. *J. Milhem & Sons* [1955] 2 Lloyd's Rep. 59, 64 (Singleton L.J.); *J. H. Vantol Ltd.* v. *Fairclough Dodd & Jones Ltd.* [1955] 1 W.L.R. 642, 648 (McNair J.), 1302 (C.A.); *Compagnie Tunisienne de Navigation S.A.* v. *Compagnie d'Armement Maritime S.A.* [1971] A.C. 572, 600 (Lord Wilberforce).

[4] See p. 416, *post*.

[5] *Sinason-Teicher Inter-American Grain Corporation* v. *Oilcakes and Oilseeds Trading Co. Ltd.* [1954] 1 W.L.R. 935, 942–943.

[6] Administration of Justice Act 1970, s. 4.

[7] *Ibid.* s. 4(5).

In export transactions an additional point requires attention. The parties to the contract are resident in different jurisdictions and the transaction extends over various countries. The arbitration clause has, therefore, to provide machinery appropriate to the international character of the transaction and, in particular, facilitating the execution of the award in the various jurisdictions concerned.

English arbitration

The arbitration agreement and the arbitrators

The English exporter naturally will suggest to his customer overseas that, in case of disputes, arbitration proceedings shall take place in this country and be governed by English law. This suggestion is often accepted without hesitation because the English institutions of arbitration are well developed and enjoy a general reputation of fairness, impartiality and reasonableness; in fact they are often invoked by overseas merchants in respect of transactions which are in no way connected with the English jurisdiction.[8] The English Arbitration Acts 1950 to 1979[9] define an arbitration agreement as "a written agreement to submit present or future differences to arbitration whether an arbitrator is named therein or not" (s. 32[9a]); written agreements within the meaning of the Acts need not be signed by the parties; it is sufficient that the clause is expressed in writing and the contract wherein the clause appears has been accepted or acted upon by the parties.[10] Oral arbitration agreements, which are rare in practice, are valid at common law, but not governed by the Arbitration Acts 1950 to 1979 and import, consequently, an element of uncertainty with respect to the implications and enforcement of the arbitration agreement. It is, therefore, desirable that the arbitration clause should be in writing. If there is an arbitration clause in a contract of sale or of partnership, it does not extend to the submission of claims under bills of exchange given by merchants in performance of those contracts unless there is a clear intention of both parties to that effect.[11]

The following are examples of arbitration clauses[12]:

---

[8] See p. 129, *ante*.

[9] The Arbitration Act 1975, which amended the Arbitration Act 1950, aims at giving effect in the U.K. to the New York Convention on the Recognition and Enforcement of Foreign Arbitral Awards of June 10, 1958; see p. 431, *post*. The Arbitration Act 1979, which came into operation on August 1, 1979, repealed, *inter alia*, the special case procedure; see p. 417, *post*.

[9a] All references are to the 1950 Act unless stated otherwise.

[10] Bankes L.J. in *Anglo-Newfoundland Development Co.* v. *R.* [1920] 2 K.B. 214, 223.

[11] *Nova (Jersey) Knit.* v. *Kammgarn Spinnerei GmbH* [1977] 1 Lloyd's Rep. 463, 467 (H.L.).

[12] A clause worded "suitable arbitration clause" in an English contract is not void on the ground of uncertainty because, if the parties fail to agree, the court will appoint an arbitrator under s. 6 of the Arbitration Act 1950: *Hobbs Padgett & Co. (Reinsurance) Ltd.* v. *J. C. Kirkland Ltd.* [1969] 2 Lloyd's Rep. 547.

EXAMPLE 1

If any dispute, difference or question shall at any time hereafter arise between the parties in respect of or in connection with the present contract,[13] the same shall be referred to the arbitration of a person to be agreed upon by the parties or, failing agreement, to be nominated by . . . (*e.g.* the London Court of Arbitration) . . . in accordance with and subject to the provisions of the Arbitration Acts 1950 to 1979 or any statutory modification thereof for the time being in force.

EXAMPLE 2

If any dispute, difference or question shall at any time hereafter arise between the parties in respect of or in connection with the present contract, the same shall be referred to the arbitration of two arbitrators, one to be appointed by each party. This arbitration agreement shall be deemed to be a submission to arbitration within the meaning of the Arbitration Acts 1950 to 1979 or any statutory modification thereof for the time being in force.

On comparing these two examples, it will be observed that in the first case the arbitration is to be held by a single arbitrator, while in the second case it is to be held by two arbitrators.[14] In the former case the arbitrator may be appointed by concurrence of the parties or by a neutral body or person, *e.g.* a chamber of commerce, a trade association, the chairman of the English Bar Council, or the president of the Law Society, London, but before entrusting the appointment to a neutral body or person it is advisable to ascertain that the appointee is prepared to make the appointment, if the necessity arises.[15] When the parties have to concur in the appointment of the arbitrator and fail to reach agreement, the court has power to appoint the arbitrator (s. 10). In the case illustrated by example 2, the usual arrangement is that each party is entitled to appoint one arbitrator; the two arbitrators may then appoint an umpire forthwith who has to decide alone when the arbitrators fail to agree (s. 8), but the two arbitrators are also entitled to appoint the umpire after they have conferred and disagreed.[16] If the arbitrators cannot agree on the person of the umpire, the court will appoint him (s. 10). It may happen that one party desires to go to arbitration and appoints his arbitrator while the other party is unwilling to do so. Here the former party may serve the defaulting party with notice to appoint the arbitrator, and, if the defaulting party has not done so within seven clear days after the notice was served, the party who appointed the arbitrator may direct him to act as sole arbitrator and his award is binding

---

[13] "Arising out of a contract" is much wider than "under a contract": *Heyman* v. *Darwins Ltd.* [1942] A.C. 356; *Government of Gibraltar* v. *Kenney* [1956] 2 Q.B. 410, 421. However, in *Union of India* v. *E. B. Aaby's Rederi A/S* [1974] 3 W.L.R. 269, 282 Lord Salmon expressed doubt that there is a difference between these two versions.

[14] On the appointment of a judge of the Commercial Court as arbitrator, see p. 412, *ante*.

[15] By virtue of the Arbitration Act 1950, s. 10(2), added by the 1979 Act, s. 6(4), the court may make the appointment if the neutral person fails to do so. *National Enterprises Ltd.* v. *Racal Communications Ltd.* [1975] Ch. 397 is overruled by this provision.

[16] Arbitration Act 1950, s. 8, as amended by the 1979 Act, s. 6(1).

on the parties (s. 7(*b*)).[17] The arbitrator must consent to act in this capacity before the appointment is effective.[18]

It is more convenient to arrange for arbitration by two arbitrators than by one arbitrator because if one party desires to proceed to arbitration and the other fails to co-operate, in the event of two arbitrators, the arbitrator appointed by the willing party may be directed by that party to act as sole arbitrator while, when arbitration by one arbitrator is arranged, the willing party would have to apply to the court for the appointment of the arbitrator (s. 10(*a*)). The two arbitrators in a commercial arbitration have often an unusual dual role in so far as they are judges and advocates in the same person, as may be seen from the following observations of Diplock J.[19]:

> once the arbitrators have disagreed and appointed an umpire they are *functus officio* as arbitrators. If they attend, as they do, the hearing before the umpire, it is as advocates for the parties who appointed them, for unless they attend in that capacity as representatives of the parties, they have no right to discuss the matter with the umpire at all.

In their capacity as advocates the arbitrators are authorised to waive minor irregularities of procedure in the hearing before the umpire.[20] It is, however, also possible to appoint the third arbitrator as *chairman*, and not as *umpire*; in that case the majority of arbitrators decide. The chairman procedure is presumed if the reference is to three arbitrators unless a contrary intention is expressed.[20a]

The following provisions are implied by the law in every written arbitration agreement unless a contrary intention is expressed therein:

(1) If no other mode of reference is provided, the reference shall be to a single arbitrator (s. 6).

(2) If the reference is to two arbitrators, the two arbitrators may appoint an umpire at any time after they are themselves appointed and shall do so forthwith if they cannot agree (s. 8(1)).

(3) If the arbitrators have delivered to any party to the submission or to the umpire a notice in writing, stating that they cannot agree, the umpire may forthwith enter on the reference in lieu of the arbitrators (s. 8(2)).

(4) The parties to the reference, and all persons claiming through them respectively, shall, subject to any legal objection, submit to be examined by the arbitrators or umpire, on oath or affirmation, in relation to the matters in dispute and shall, subject as aforesaid, produce before the arbitrators or umpire all books, deeds, papers, accounts, writings and documents within their possession or power respectively which may be required or called for, and do all other things which during the proceedings on the reference the arbitrators or umpire may require (s. 12(1)).

(5) The witnesses on the reference shall, at the discretion of the arbitrators or umpire, be examined on oath or affirmation (s. 12(2)).

---

[17] Many arbitration clauses contain a time limit for the appointment of arbitrators by the parties; in the event of non-compliance with such a time limit the court has a discretion to give relief if otherwise "undue hardship" is caused (s. 27); *Liberian Shipping Corporation* v. *A. King & Gough Ltd.* [1967] 1 Lloyd's Rep. 302. This discretion exists also if the time limit is imposed by statute, *e.g.* by the Hague Rules relating to bills of lading: *Nea Agrex S.A.* v. *Baltic Shipping Co. Ltd.* [1976] Q.B. 933. The discretion exists if the substantive law of arbitration clause is English law: *International Tank and Pipe* v. *Kuwait Aviation Fuelling Co.* [1974] 3 W.L.R. 721.

[18] *Tradax Export S.A.* v. *Volkswagenwerk A.G.* [1970] 1 Q.B. 537.

[19] *Wessanen's Koninklijke Fabrikien* v. *Isaac Modiano & Sons Ltd.* [1960] 1 W.L.R. 1243.

[20] *Wessanen's* case, *ibid.* Where the arbitration clause provides that the arbitrators and the umpire shall be "commercial men," a practising member of the Bar cannot be appointed umpire by the arbitrators who have no authority to waive these provisions of the arbitration clause: *Rahcassi Shipping Co. S.A.* v. *Blue Star Line Ltd.* [1969] 1 Q.B. 173. A professional maritime arbitrator is a "commercial man": *Pando Compania Naviera S.A.* v. *Filmo S.A.S.*, *The Times*, February 12, 1975.

[20a] Arbitration Act 1950, s. 9, as amended by the 1979 Act, s. 6(2).

(6) The award to be made by the arbitrators or umpire shall be final and binding on the parties and the persons claiming under them respectively (s. 16).
(7) The costs of the reference and award shall be in the discretion of the arbitrators or umpire who may direct to and by whom and in what manner those costs or any part thereof shall be paid, and may tax or settle the amount of costs to be paid or any part thereof, and may award costs to be paid as between solicitor and client (s. 18).
(8) The arbitrators or umpire shall have the same power as the court to order specific performance of any contract other than a contract relating to land or any interest in land (s. 15).
(9) The arbitrators or umpire may, if they think fit, make an interim award (s. 14).

Domestic and non-domestic arbitrations

The Arbitration Acts draw a distinction between domestic and non-domestic arbitrations.

A domestic arbitration agreement is an arbitration agreement:

which does not provide, expressly or by implication, for arbitration in a State other than the United Kingdom and to which neither—
(*a*) an individual who is a national of, or habitually resident in, any State other than the United Kingdom; nor
(*b*) a body corporate which is incorporated in, or whose central management and control is exercised in, any State other than the United Kingdom;
is a party at the time the arbitration agreement is entered into.[21]

All other arbitrations are non-domestic, *i.e.* international. The distinction is important in two respects, as we shall see presently, *viz.* with respect to the power of the court to break an arbitration clause[22] and as regards the right of the parties to exclude the judicial review of the arbitration award *before*[23] the commencement of the arbitration proceedings.[24]

The supervisory jurisdiction of the court

It is one of the features of English arbitration that it is strictly supervised by the court.[25] This supervision assumes three forms, the power of the court to remove an arbitrator who misconducts himself or fails to use due dispatch in conducting the arbitration and making the award (ss. 13(3), 23), the power to break an arbitration agreement (s. 4), and the judicial review of arbitration awards (Arbitration Act 1979, s. 1).

"Misconduct" on the part of the arbitrator means not only a deliberate or careless breach of duty but includes a purely technical error of law, *e.g.* if he receives inadmissible evidence which goes to the root of the case or makes an award on a point which was not in issue before him.[26] Under the

---

[21] Arbitration Act 1979, s. 3(7). In the Arbitration Act 1975, s. 1(4), the relevant time is "the time the proceedings are commenced."
[22] See p. 417, *post*.
[23] *After* the commencement of arbitration proceedings a judicial review can be excluded in domestic as well as non-domestic arbitrations; Arbitration Act 1979, s. 3(6).
[24] See p. 418, *post*.
[25] C. M. Schmitthoff, "The Supervisory Jurisdiction of the Courts" [1967] J.B.L. 318.
[26] *Société Franco-Tunisienne d'Armament-Tunis* v. *Government of Ceylon* [1959] 1 W.L.R. 787; *E. Rotheray & Sons Ltd.* v. *Carlo Bedarida & Co.* [1961] 1 Lloyd's Rep. 220 (material documents in a foreign language placed before arbitrator who decides without knowing the foreign language and without proper translations); *Giacomo Costa Fu Andrea* v. *British Italian Trading Co. Ltd.* [1963] 1 Q.B. 201 (only misconduct of arbitration appeal board, but not of arbitrator of first instance, is relevant).

former procedure, which has been abolished by the Arbitration Act 1979, s. 1, it was also misconduct if, on a bona fide and reasonable application by a party to state a case on a point of law for the decision of the court or to delay his award until the party had obtained a direction of the court to that effect, the arbitrator refused to comply and made his award at once in order to prevent the party from applying to the court.[27]

If a party to an arbitration agreement commences proceedings in court, contrary to his undertaking to submit to arbitration, the question arises whether the court has jurisdiction to allow the court proceedings to continue, thus breaking the arbitration agreement. Here the distinction between domestic and non-domestic arbitrations is relevant. In domestic arbitrations the court has discretion to order a stay of court proceedings, thus allowing the arbitration to proceed, or to refuse a stay, thus breaking the arbitration agreement and allowing the court proceedings to continue (s. 4(1)). Normally the English courts will hold the parties to the arbitration agreement[28] but in exceptional cases they will break it.[29] In non-domestic arbitrations the court is bound to stay the court proceedings unless satisfied that the arbitration agreement is null and void, inoperative or incapable of being performed, or that there is not in fact any dispute between the parties with regard to the matter referred to arbitration (Arbitration Act 1975, s. 1(1)).[30]

As regards the judicial review of arbitration awards, the Arbitration Act 1979[31] has introduced a far-reaching reform. Under the original provisions of the Arbitration Act 1950, s. 21, if a question of law arose in arbitration, a party could request the arbitrator to state a special case for the decision of the court and, if the arbitrator refused, the court could order him to do so. The Arbitration Act 1979 s. 1(1) has abolished the special case procedure[32] and further provides that the court shall no longer have jurisdiction to set aside an award on the ground of error of fact or law on the face of the award. The Act further provides that, if the award does not set out its reasons, the court may order the arbitrator to state reasons for his award in sufficient detail to enable the court to decide whether it should allow the appeal to the court on a point of law.[33] The court may allow such an appeal if it considers that its determination may substantially affect the rights of the parties.[34] However, the parties may abrogate the judicial

---

[27] *Re Fischel and Mann* [1919] 2 K.B. 431; *General Rubber Co. Ltd.* v. *Hessa Rubber Maatschappij* (1927) 28 Ll.L.R. 362; *G. W. Potts Ltd.* v. *Macpherson, Train & Co.* (1927) 27 Ll.L.R. 445; *Halfdan Grieg & Co. A/S* v. *Sterling Coal & Navigation Corpn.*; *The Lysland* [1973] Q.B. 843.

[28] *Unterweser Reederei GmbH* v. *Zapata Off-Shore Co.* [1968] 2 Lloyd's Rep. 158; *The Eleftheria* [1969] 1 Lloyd's Rep. 237, 242.

[29] *The Fehmarn* [1958] 1 W.L.R. 159.

[30] That the provisions of s. 1(1) of the Arbitration Act 1975 are mandatory was decided in *Roussel-Uclaf* v. *G. D. Searle & Co. Ltd.* [1978] 1 Lloyd's Rep. 225.

[31] The Act applies only to England and Wales.

[32] It is provided that s. 21 of the Arbitration Act 1950 shall cease to have effect.

[33] Arbitration Act 1979, s. 1(5).

[34] *Ibid.* s. 1(4).

review procedure by making an *exclusion agreement* which must be in the written form.[35] Such an agreement is admissible in the following cases:

(*a*) in domestic and non-domestic arbitrations *after* the commencement of the arbitration;
(*b*) in non-domestic arbitrations, *before* the commencement of the arbitration, unless the arbitration falls within one of the special categories listed under (*c*);
(*c*) in special category arbitrations governed by the laws of England or Wales the position is the same as in domestic arbitrations. Special category arbitrations are arbitrations concerning—
(i) a question or claim falling within the Admiralty jurisdiction of the High Court, or
(ii) a dispute arising out of a contract of insurance, or
(iii) a dispute arising out of a commodity contract.[36]

In the result, in domestic and special category arbitrations the parties cannot exclude the judicial review on points of law before the commencement of the arbitration. The parties can, however, provide that no action shall be brought in court until an award is made.[37] Such clause, known as the *Scott* v. *Avery* clause, is commonly stipulated in submissions to commercial arbitration in England. If the High Court enters into a judicial review of the award, *i.e.* if it admits an appeal, its decision is final unless:

(*a*) the High Court or the Court of Appeal gives leave; and
(*b*) it is certified by the High Court that the question of law to which the decision relates either is one of general public importance or is one which for some other special reason should be considered by the Court of Appeal.[38]

Disputes covered by the arbitration agreement

An arbitration clause does not cover all disputes that may arise in connection with a contract. Although it is usual for these clauses to be widely worded, as is illustrated by the examples on p. 414, *ante*, they cannot be invoked when the validity of the contract of which they form part is challenged because, as Lord Macmillan expressed it,[39] "if there has never been a contract at all, there has never been as part of it an agreement to arbitrate. The greater includes the less." Consequently, a claim that the contract is void on the grounds of fraud, duress or essential error cannot be submitted to arbitration. Likewise, if the parties agree to rescind their contract with retrospective effect and to treat it as if it had never been concluded, the arbitration clause perishes with the contract. On the other hand, the clause remains alive if a party maintains that the contract has come to an end by repudiation, or under the terms of the agreement, or on the ground of frustration or for other reasons. In these cases, the arbitration clause remains binding on both parties and, if one party claims damages in a court of law for an alleged breach of contract, the defendant

[35] *Ibid.* s. 3(1).
[36] *Ibid.* s. 4(1). The Act provides that the exception to the non-domestic regulation in the case of special category arbitrations may be discontinued if an order is made to that effect by the Secretary of State (s. 4(3)).
[37] *Scott* v. *Avery* (1856) 25 L.J.Ex. 308.
[38] Arbitration Act 1979, s. 1(7).
[39] In *Heyman* v. *Darwins Ltd.* [1942] A.C. 356, 371.

can obtain a stay of the court proceedings and compel the plaintiff to submit the dispute to arbitration[40]; in the case of frustration the arbitrator may make an adjustment under the Law Reform (Frustrated Contracts) Act 1943.[41] An arbitrator has discretion under the Misrepresentation Act 1967, s. 3, as amended by the Unfair Contract Terms Act 1977, s. 8, to admit an exemption clause excluding liability for misrepresentation only if it satisfies the requirement of reasonableness, as stated in the Unfair Contract Terms Act, and the onus of showing that it does is on the party claiming the exemptions.

Unless it is clear from the arbitration agreement that the parties intended to refer an issue pertaining to the jurisdiction of the arbitrator to his decision, the arbitrator cannot decide his own jurisdiction but has to leave this decision to the court.[42]

The award

The arbitration award should normally state the reasons for the award. It may be expressed in a foreign currency.[43] It normally carries reasonable interest.[44]

On principle the arbitrator should award the costs of arbitration to the successful party. If he wishes to depart from this rule, he should set out the reasons which caused him to depart from the usual order.[45]

The law governing the arbitration procedure

The adoption of an English arbitration clause supports, in general, the assumption that the parties intended to submit their contract to the rules of English law,[46] but the law applicable to the arbitration procedure may be different from the law governing the contract; thus, in a case[47] in which the law governing the contract was English law, the parties held their arbitration in Scotland in accordance with the Scots law applicable to arbitration; the House of Lords decided that Scots law regulated the

---

[40] *Heyman* v. *Darwins Ltd.* [1942] A.C. 356. *The Tradesman* [1961] 2 Lloyd's Rep. 183. See also *Mackender, Hill and White* v. *Feldia A.G.* [1966] 2 Lloyd's Rep. 449, 455, 458 (insurance contract voidable).

[41] *Government of Gibraltar* v. *Kenney* [1956] 2 Q.B. 410. (If the arbitration clause is wide enough to cover claims "arising out of the contract" (see p. 414, *ante*) the arbitrator may also deal with a quasi-contractual claim, such as a claim for *quantum meruit*, incidental to frustration.)

[42] Sellers J. in *Getreideimport GmbH* v. *Contimar S.A. Compania Industrial Commercial y Maritima* [1953] 1 W.L.R. 207, 219; affd. *ibid.* p. 793 (C.A.); see further *Kruse* v. *Questier & Co. Ltd.* [1953] 1 Q.B. 669.

[43] *Jugoslavenska Oceanska Plovidba* v. *Castle Investment Co. Inc.* [1974] Q.B. 292.

[44] *Panchaud Frères S.A.* v. *R. Pagnan & Fratelli* [1974] 1 Lloyd's Rep. 394, 411.

[45] *Smeaton Hanscomb & Co. Ltd.* v. *Sassoon I. Setty, Son & Co.* (*No.* 2) [1953] 1 W.L.R. 1481; *Lewis* v. *Haverfordwest Rural District Council* [1953] 1 W.L.R. 1486.

[46] See p. 132, *ante*.

[47] *Whitworth Street Estates (Manchester) Ltd.* v. *James Miller & Partners Ltd.* [1970] A.C. 583; *International Tank and Pipe S.A.K.* v. *Kuwait Aviation Fuelling Co. K.S.C.* [1975] Q.B. 224. See also *Dalmia Dairy Industries Ltd.* v. *National Bank of Pakistan* [1978] 2 Lloyd's Rep. 223, 228.

arbitration procedure whilst the arbitrator had to apply English law as the law governing the contract.

International arbitration

The various national laws of arbitration[48] differ in material aspects; in Dutch law an arbitration clause appointing arbitrators in even numbers is invalid; in French law an appeal to the ordinary courts is admitted unless that right is expressly excluded or the arbitrators are appointed *amiable compositeurs*; in Belgian law arbitrators can be appointed as *amiable compositeurs* only after the dispute has arisen; in Italian law a distinction is drawn between *arbitrato rituale* (formal arbitration) and *arbitrato libero* (informal arbitration) which has features of its own; further, in Italian law an arbitration clause printed in the general conditions on a business letter is not binding on the addressee unless he expressly agrees thereto; and so forth.

Various attempts have been made to devise an international procedure of commercial arbitration which commands wide acceptance. The most important of them will be considered here under the following headings[49]:

The UNCITRAL Arbitration Rules;
The London Court of Arbitration;
The ICC Court of Arbitration;
The European Convention on International Commercial Arbitration;
Arbitration in countries of state-planned economy;
Arbitration in investment disputes.

The UNCITRAL Arbitration Rules

These Rules were published by the United Nations Commission on International Trade Law on April 28, 1976 and approved by the General Assembly on December 15, 1976. They represent one of the most important and successful contributions of UNCITRAL to the unification of international trade law.

The UNCITRAL Arbitration Rules are not contained in an international convention and do not have the force of law in any country. They may be adopted by the contracting parties. The following model clause is recommended for their adoption:

> Any dispute, controversy or claim arising out of or relating to this contract, or the breach, termination or invalidity thereof, shall be settled by arbitration in accordance with the UNCITRAL Arbitration Rules as at present in force.

---

[48] See *Handbook of National and International and Commercial Arbitration*, issued by E.C.E. (1958); *International Commercial Arbitration*, edited by the International Union of Advocates, Vol. 1 (Paris, Dalloz et Sirey, 1956), Vols. 2 and 3 (Martinus Nijhoff, 1960 and 1965); *International Trade Arbitration* (Martin Domke, ed.) (American Arbitration Association, 1958). See further *International Arbitration* (Liber Amicorum for Martin Domke, ed. Pieter Sanders, 1967). Martin Domke, *The Law and Practice of Commercial Arbitration*, 1968; Commercial Arbitration Yearbook (Pieter Sanders, ed., since 1976); *International Commercial Arbitration* (Clive M. Schmitthoff, ed.) (2nd ed., Oceana, 1979).

[49] Another attempt which is not treated here is the European Convention providing a Uniform Law on Arbitration, sponsored by the Council of Europe; European Treaty Series No. 56, opened for signature on January 20, 1966.

Note— Parties may wish to consider adding:

(*a*) The appointing authority shall be . . . (name of institution or person);

(*b*) The number of arbitrators shall be . . . (one or three);

(*c*) The place of arbitration shall be . . . (town or country);

(*d*) The language(s) to be used in the arbitral proceedings shall be. . . .

The UNCITRAL Rules have also been incorporated into the arbitration rules of other organisations or used as models for them. Thus the London Court of Arbitration Rules (1978 ed.) adopt the UNCITRAL Rules as subsidiary rules of procedure or, if the parties so desire, as primary rules. The amended rules of procedure of the Inter-American Commercial Arbitration Commission (effective from January 1, 1978) incorporate substantially the UNCITRAL Rules, and the Asian–African Legal Consultative Committee (AALCC), at its Doha session in January 1978, has recommended the insertion, in any arbitration clause, of a reference to the UNCITRAL Rules and has included such references in its standard contract forms. Many organisations have indicated their willingness to act as appointing authorities under the UNCITRAL Rules, among them the London Court of Arbitration, the American Arbitration Association and the Stockholm Chamber of Commerce, also the regional arbitration centres in Kuala Lumpur and Cairo of the AALCC.

The main characteristic of the UNCITRAL Arbitration Rules is that no arbitration shall fail on the ground that the parties cannot agree on an arbitrator or for any other reason no arbitrator can act. If no appointing authority has been agreed by the parties or if the appointing authority refuses to act or fails to appoint an arbitrator within 60 days of the receipt of a party's request, either party may request the Secretary-General of the Permanent Court of Arbitration at the Hague to designate an appointing authority.[50] Unless the parties have agreed upon the place where the arbitration is to be held, such place is determined by the arbitration tribunal.[51] It is further provided by Article 21(1) and (2) that the arbitration tribunal shall have the power to rule on objections that it has no jurisdiction and to determine the existence or the validity of the contract of which an arbitration clause forms part; for the purposes of this provision the arbitration clause is treated as independent of the other terms of the contract and a decision that the contract is null and void shall not entail *ipso facto* the invalidity of the arbitration clause. It is doubtful whether the English courts will uphold an agreement of the parties enabling the arbitrator to decide on his own jurisdiction, and it is likely that they will treat as invalid the provision that an arbitration clause shall survive even if the contract in which it is contained is void ab initio.[52]

---

[50] UNCITRAL Arbitration Rules, Art. 6(2).

[51] *Ibid.* Art. 16(1).

[52] See p. 418, *ante* and pp. 424 and 425, *post.*

The London Court of Arbitration

Among the permanent arbitration institutions the London Court of Arbitration holds a prominent position and is regarded with particular esteem by the international business world. It is a tri-partite organisation, sponsored by the London Chamber of Commerce, the City of London Corporation, and the Chartered Institute of Arbitrators, and is administered by the latter.

The 1978 edition of the London Court of Arbitration Rules contains a Part which deals specifically with international arbitrations.[53] It greatly reduces the possibility of judicial review of the arbitration proceedings.[54] As already observed, the London Court of Arbitration Rules adopt the UNCITRAL Arbitration Rules as ancillary rules[55] and, if the parties so desire, as primary rules.[56]

The Court recommends the adoption of the following arbitration clause which, at the same time, is a satisfactory arrangement for the choice of English law as the law governing the contract[57]:

The validity, construction and performance of this contract (agreement) shall be governed by the law of England* and any dispute that may arise out of or in connection with this contract (agreement), including its validity, construction and performance, shall be determined by arbitration under the Rules of the London Court of Arbitration** at the date hereof, which Rules with respect to matters not regulated by them incorporate the UNCITRAL Arbitration Rules. The parties agree that service of any notices in reference to such arbitration at their addresses as given in this contract (agreement) (or as subsequently varied in writing by them) shall be valid and sufficient.

*Alter, if the parties agree that the law of another country shall apply. (Reference to the law to apply is unnecessary if provided for in another clause of the contract or agreement).
**If desired, insert here either of the following:
"applicable to international Arbitrations"
or
"applicable to Small Claims Arbitrations."

The London Court of Arbitration is open to members of the London Chamber of Commerce and non-members and is available both for reference by the parties and by the courts which might wish to remit a case to commercial arbitration. The Court of Arbitration has prepared a *London Panel of International Arbitrators* which contains the names of many prominent international personalities. The reference is usually to a single arbitrator unless the parties expressly stipulate otherwise. A scale of arbitration fees is provided which are within moderate limits. The powers of the arbitrator under the rules of the London Court of Arbitration are con-

---

[53] In addition, the 1978 edition of the London Court of Arbitration Rules contain two other Parts, one dealing with ordinary, *i.e.* domestic, arbitrations and the other dealing with small claims arbitrations. An international arbitration is defined in those Rules as an arbitration between parties of whom one at least does not carry on business in the U.K.

[54] London Court of Arbitration Rules (1978 ed.), R. 19.

[55] *Ibid.* Rule 2(8).

[56] *Ibid.* Rule 2(9).

[57] *Ibid.* Sched. I(1).

siderably wider than those conferred upon him by the provisions of the Arbitration Acts 1950 to 1979.

Where the parties agree to arbitrate under the rules of a chamber of commerce and the arbitrator is chosen because of his knowledge and experience of the trade, he may give his award as to the quality of goods or to damages on his own knowledge without hearing expert evidence unless any party or both of them call expert evidence.[58]

A number of trade associations provide their own machinery for international commercial arbitration.[59] The most important are those listed earlier[60] when the standard contract forms issued by trade associations were discussed; these standard contracts normally embody an arbitration clause providing for arbitration under the rules of the association in question.

The ICC Court of Arbitration

It is the merit of the International Chamber of Commerce[61] to have devised a procedure for international commercial arbitration which commands the confidence of businessmen living in different countries and being of different nationality and which is also used increasingly in East-West trade. The International Chamber has created a Court of Arbitration which administers a code of rules especially adapted to the settlement of international commercial disputes.[62] This procedure should be adopted whenever the arrangement of English arbitration does not appear appropriate. The present arbitration rules have been in force as from June 1, 1975.[63] The following arbitration clause has been recommended by the International Chamber of Commerce when it is intended to submit differences to arbitration by its Court of Arbitration[64]:

> All disputes arising in connection with the present contract shall be finally settled under the Rules of Conciliation and Arbitration of the International Chamber of Commerce by one or more arbitrators appointed in accordance with the said Rules.
>
> *Note:*
>
> Attention is called to the fact that the laws of certain countries require that parties to contracts expressly accept arbitration clauses, sometimes in a precise and particular manner.

---

[58] *Mediterranean and Eastern Export Co. Ltd.* v. *Fortress Fabrics (Manchester) Ltd.* [1948] 2 All E.R. 186.

[59] See *e.g.* Lord Goddard C.J. in *Mediterranean and Eastern Export Co. Ltd.* v. *Fortress Fabrics (Manchester) Ltd.* [1948] 2 All E.R. 186, 188; Diplock J. in *Wessanen's Koninklijke Fabrikien* v. *Isaac Modiano Brother & Sons Ltd.* [1960] 1 W.L.R. 1243, 1246; Lord Wilberforce in *Compagnie d'Armement Maritime S.A.* v. *Compagnie Tunisienne de Navigation S.A.* [1971] A.C. 572, 600.

[60] See p. 51, *ante*.

[61] The offices of the British National Committee of the International Chamber of Commerce are at 6–14 Dean Farrar Street, London, SW1H 0DT.

[62] E. J. Cohn, "The Rules of Arbitration of the International Chamber of Commerce" (1965) 14 I.C.L.Q. 132; F. Eisemann, "Arbitration under the International Chamber of Commerce Rules" (1966) 15 I.C.L.Q. 726.

[63] ICC Brochure No. 291.

[64] In *International Tank and Pipe* v. *Kuwait Aviation Fuelling Co.* [1974] 3 W.L.R. 721 the parties had adopted a clause allowing ICC arbitration.

The parties may—if they so desire—stipulate, in the arbitration clause itself, the national law applicable to the contract. The parties' free choice of the place of arbitration is not limited by the ICC.

Arbitration under the Rules of the International Chamber of Commerce is open to members and non-members. A procedure for optional conciliation may be adopted. An Administrative Commission for Conciliation is constituted at the ICC and for each dispute a Conciliation Committee of three members is set up by the President of the ICC. The party requesting conciliation may apply either through his National Committee or to the International Headquarters of the ICC directly.

If no request for conciliation is made or the conciliation has failed, the dispute proceeds to arbitration. No person having sat on the Conciliation Committee for the settlement of the dispute in question may be appointed as arbitrator. The Court of Arbitration does not itself settle disputes but if the parties have not agreed on the arbitrator(s), the Court chooses a National Committee of the ICC and requests it to propose the arbitrator(s); usually the National Committees have lists of competent and suitable persons to serve in that capacity. The sole arbitrator or the chairman of an arbitration tribunal shall be chosen from a country other than those of which the parties to the dispute are nationals. The arbitration is initiated by a request for arbitration to the secretariat of the ICC Court of Arbitration, either through the National Committee of the applicant or to Headquarters directly, and the date when the request is received by the secretariat is deemed to be the date of the commencement of the arbitral proceedings.[65] Article 8(3) and (4) of the ICC Court of Arbitration Rules provides:

(3) Should one of the parties raise one or more pleas concerning the existence or validity of the agreement to arbitrate, and should the Court be satisfied of the prima facie existence of such an agreement, the Court may, without prejudice to the admissibility or merits of the plea or pleas, decide that the arbitration shall proceed. In such a case any decision as to the arbitrator's jurisdiction shall be taken by the arbitrator himself.

(4) Unless otherwise provided, the arbitrator shall not cease to have jurisdiction by reason of any claim that the contract is null and void or allegation that it is inexistent provided that he upholds the validity of the agreement to arbitrate. He shall continue to have jurisdiction, even though the contract itself may be inexistent or null and void, to determine the respective rights of the parties and to adjudicate upon their claims and pleas.

These provisions constitute an agreement of the parties to empower the arbitrator to decide on his own jurisdiction and to have jurisdiction even if the contract containing the arbitration clause is "inexistent," *i.e.* void *ab initio* or invalid or illegal when he gives his award. The first of these provisions was considered in *Dalmia Dairy Industries Ltd.* v. *National Bank of Pakistan*,[66] a case concerning Indian law which on the relevant issues was held by the Court of Appeal to be the same as English law.

---

[65] IIC Court of Arbitration Rules (1975), Art. 3(1). A—prior—nomination of the arbitrator does not "commence" the arbitration: *Offshore International S.A.* v. *Banco Central S.A.* [1976] 2 Lloyd's Rep. 402, 407.

[66] [1978] 2 Lloyd's Rep. 223. In that case the provisions of Article 13(3) and (4) of the 1955 Rules were considered by the court; they are substantially the same as those of Article 8(3) and (4) of the 1975 Rules.

Kerr J. held that the parties could empower the arbitrator to decide on his own jurisdiction but the Court of Appeal unanimously disagreed with the learned judge and held that in Indian and English law the arbitrator could not be allowed finally to determine his own jurisdiction. It is respectfully thought that the decision of Kerr J. is preferable as being in harmony with modern principles of international commercial arbitration.[67]

The arbitrator shall make every effort to make his award enforceable in law. With this end in view, before signing the award, he has to submit it in draft form to the Court of Arbitration. The Court may lay down modifications as to the form, without affecting the arbitrator's liberty of decision, and may also draw his attention to points of substance. The arbitral award is deemed to be made at the place of the arbitration proceedings and on the date when it is signed by the arbitrator. The award is final, whether it is partial or definitive.

In December 1976 the ICC constituted an *International Centre for Technical Expertise.*[68] The need for this Centre arises primarily in cases where a technical dispute has become unavoidable during the performance of an international contract, such as a long term contract for the construction of works and installations. A neutral expert can be appointed by the Centre and may assist in the solution of the problems which have arisen. Such assistance is not in the nature of an arbitration.

The ICC has established an *ICC Liason Committee with Chambers of Commerce in Socialist Countries*. The Liason Committee is under the joint chairmanship of an Eastern and Western representative. Terms of reference of the Liason Committee were published in April 1975.[69]

As a new source of the *lex mercatoria*, the ICC intends to publish extracts from past awards given in arbitration proceedings held under the rules of the ICC Court of Arbitration. The published extracts will be carefully edited to ensure the anonymity of the parties.

---

[67] In the *Dalmia* case the question was whether certain guarantees which the Bank of Pakistan had given to Dalmia in 1962 and 1964 were enforceable although allegedly a state of war existed between India and Pakistan in 1965 and 1971. The guarantees provided for ICC arbitration. The Swiss arbitrator made two awards in favour of the plaintiffs Dalmia who brought an action in the English courts for the enforcement of these awards. Kerr J. and the Court of Appeal decided in favour of the plaintiffs. The Court of Appeal ruled that in English law an arbitration clause between "enemies" was not abrogated on the outbreak of war, if the main contract in which it was contained was not abrogated and if no dispute requiring arbitration had then arisen.

[68] ICC Brochure No. 307 (1977).

[69] ICC Brochure No. 297 (1975).

European arbitration

A *European Convention on International Commercial Arbitration* was signed on April 21, 1961, in Geneva and came into force on January 7, 1964.[70] The Convention has been ratified or adhered to by

Austria, Belgium, Bulgaria, Byelorussian S.S.R., Czechoslovakia, Cuba, Denmark, France, Germany (Democratic), Germany (Federal), Hungary, Italy, Poland, Romania, Spain, Ukrainian S.S.R., Upper Volta, U.S.S.R. and Yugoslavia.

The United Kingdom has neither signed nor ratified the Convention. The Convention which is sponsored by the United Nations Economic Commission for Europe attempts to overcome difficulties in the constitution of arbitral tribunals and in arbitration procedure, particularly in trading relations between countries of free market and state-planned economy. The Convention provides that the parties to an arbitration agreement shall be free to submit their dispute to a permanent arbitral institution or to an *ad hoc* constituted tribunal. It further contains detailed rules for the arrangement of arbitration if the parties cannot agree on the composition or venue of the arbitral tribunal or one party fails to co-operate with the other in making the necessary arrangements for the arbitration. In particular, a *Special Committee* is constituted which consists of three members, one designated by the International Chamber of Commerce, the other by the countries in which no national committees of the ICC exist, *i.e.* mainly the socialist countries, and the chairman being a member of one of these two groups in rotation; the chairmanship changes every two years. The function of the Special Committee is to appoint the arbitrator or umpire and to settle procedural details of the arbitration if the contract is silent or the parties cannot agree. The Special Committee constitutes a bridge between Eastern and Western arbitration.

Other provisions of the Convention which should be mentioned are that foreign nationals may be designated as arbitrators, that the arbitrators shall act as amiable compositeurs if the parties so decide and if they may do so under the law applicable to the arbitration, and that "legal persons of public law," such as foreign trade corporations of the countries of state-planned economy, have the right to conclude valid arbitration agreements.

The United Nations European Commission for Europe has also sponsored the *Economic Commission for Europe's Arbitration Rules* of January 20, 1966. These Rules may be adopted by the parties to a contract. The Rules,[71] like the Convention of 1961, aim at assisting the parties to constitute an arbitration tribunal if there exists uncertainty or the defendant fails to co-operate. They designate certain "Appointing Authorities" which on principle are national chambers of commerce. They provide that if within a specified period the arbitration tribunal is not constituted, the claimant

[70] The Convention was complemented by the *Agreement relating to the Application of the European Convention on International Commercial Arbitration*, signed in Paris on December 17, 1962.

[71] United Nations reference: Ref. E/ECE/625/Rev. 1 (1970).

may apply to the competent Appointing Authority for the appointment of the arbitrator or umpire. The competent Appointing Authority is that designated in the contract, failing such designation the one operating at the place of arbitration defined in the contract, and if the contract neither designates an Appointment Authority nor defines the venue of arbitration, the claimant may apply to the Special Committee constituted under the Convention of 1961 for the appointment of the arbitrator or umpire. In the United Kingdom the Association of British Chambers of Commerce has been designated as Appointing Authority.

Arbitration in countries of state-planned economy

In the countries of state-planned economy in which the state has a monopoly of foreign trade, *foreign trade arbitration commissions* are constituted for dealing with commercial disputes between the state organisations to whom the foreign trade monopoly is delegated and the foreign businesses with which they enter into export and import transactions.[72] These arbitration commissions exist in Soviet Russia where two tribunals, both attached to the All-Union Chamber of Commerce in Moscow, operate, *viz.* the Foreign Trade Arbitration Commission and the Maritime Arbitration Commission, and in Poland, Czechoslovakia, East Germany, Romania, Hungary, Yugoslavia and China. In their negotiations with businesses in the countries of free economy, the foreign trade organisations of countries with planned economy will attempt to obtain agreement to clauses submitting disputes to the arbitration commission of their own country. Since these commissions have a reputation for fair and impartial dealings in purely commercial matters,[73] some exporters in countries of free economy do not object; others who object will normally find that the foreign trade organisation with which they negotiate is willing to agree to arbitration under the rules of the Court of Arbitration of the International Chamber of Commerce, or to "neutral" arbitration, *e.g.* in Sweden or Switzerland. In Yugoslavia there is no difficulty in obtaining the consent of the foreign trade corporations, which enjoy considerable independence from the state, to arbitration outside the country.

---

[72] See *International Commercial Arbitration*, 2nd. ed., Vol. I, Pt. III; Clive M. Schmitthoff, "A New Approach to East-West Trade" [1958] J.B.L. 141; Harold J. Berman, "The Legal Framework of Trade between Planned and Market Economies," *Law and Contemporary Problems*, "State Trading," Part II, 1959, p. 493 *et seq.*; Samuel Pisar, "Soviet Conflict of Laws in International Commercial Transactions" (1957) 70 Harv. Law Rev. 593, 607; A. Goldštajn, "Le Réglement des litiges par voie d'arbitrage en Yougoslavie" in *Aspects juridiques du commerce avec les pays d'économie planifiée*, Paris, 1961, p. 103 *et seq.*; on foreign trade arbitration in China, see (1957) 3 *Ost-Europa-Recht* 121 *et seq.*; on Hungary, see L. Faragó in (1960) 9 I.C.L.Q. 682. Also D. F. Ramzaitsev and Denis Tallon on "The Law applied by Arbitration Tribunals" in *The Sources of the Law of International Trade*, (Schmitthoff, ed.) (London, 1964), pp. 138 *et seq.*

[73] See Berman, *op. cit.* p. 493; Stephen Schafer in [1958] J.B.L. 56.

The legal principles on which the Soviet Foreign Trade Arbitration Commission acts, are explained by Dmitri Ramzaitsev in "F.O.B. and C.I.F. in the Practice of the Soviet Foreign Trade Organisations" [1959] J.B.L. 315, and "The Application of Private International Law in Soviet Foreign Trade Practice" [1961] J.B.L. 343.

Arbitration in the countries of state-planned economy differs in some respects from that in the countries of free economy. The arbitration commissions are permanent arbitration tribunals, created by the state, usually by way of legislation. They combine judicial and arbitral functions and it is not very easy to define their true character; in some respects they resemble state courts dealing with commercial matters, in others true arbitration tribunals.[74] Since their jurisdiction is exclusively founded on voluntary submission by the parties, *i.e.* on an arbitration agreement, it is thought that, in spite of the peculiarities of their constitution, they are proper arbitration tribunals. In Soviet Russia, the Foreign Trade Arbitration Commission is the tribunal to which are submitted all disputes between Soviet foreign trade organisations and foreign firms, whereas the Maritime Arbitration Commission has jurisdiction over claims arising from contracts of carriage by sea, bills of lading, charterparties, marine insurance policies, and further, speaking generally, over claims which in England would fall within the province of Admiralty jurisdiction.[75] In the China People's Republic the Foreign Trade Arbitration Commission is established within the China Council for the Promotion of International Trade in Peking.[76]

The rules governing the constitution and procedure of the various foreign trade arbitration commissions are published and most of them are available in English. In most instances the arbitrators must be nationals of the country in question. In Soviet Russia the commissions sit as boards which include, or are advised by, members of the legal profession; in the other countries a panel of arbitrators exists and each party may choose his arbitrator therefrom. The arbitrators are normally managers of commercial or industrial enterprises not concerned in the dispute, or eminent professors of law or economics who are experts in international trade.[77] Usually the parties are entitled to be represented by foreign counsel. The arbitrators normally give full reasons for the award and where they differ from the majority decision they often state their dissenting opinions. In Russia, as in England, the award is subject to the supervision of the court although, of course, the typically English review procedure is unknown; the decisions of the Russian Foreign Trade Arbitration Commission may be overruled in compulsory enforcement proceedings by the People's Courts, and those of the Maritime Arbitration Commission may be set aside on appeal by the Supreme Court of the U.S.S.R., if in violation of the law.[78] In most other countries of state-planned economy, on the other hand, the award is final and the position is, in that respect, similar to that in Scotland and the Western countries of the Continent of Europe. The countries of the

[74] See Pisar, "Treatment of Communist Foreign Trade Arbitration in Western Courts" in *International Trade Arbitration* (ed. Domke), 1958, pp. 101, 106; Berman, *loc. cit.* p. 494.

[75] Similar is the jurisdiction of the mixed Polish, East German and Czechoslovakian Maritime Arbitration Commission in Gdynia (Poland).

[76] *International Commercial Arbitration* (Schmitthoff, ed., 2nd. ed.), Vol. I, No. IV. B.(a)(1).

[77] Berman, *loc. cit.* p. 493.

[78] Pisar, "Soviet Conflict of Laws" (1957) 70 Harv.Law Rev. 593, 607.

Council of Mutual Economic Assistance (CMEA) adopted on May 26, 1976 a revised *Convention on the Settlement by Arbitration of Civil Law Disputes resulting from Economic, Scientific and Technical Co-operation.* Further, in 1975 the Executive Committee of CMEA approved revised *Uniform Rules for Arbitration Tribunals* of the CMEA countries.[79]

The particular character of foreign trade arbitration in the countries of planned economy has raised difficult problems in the courts of the Western countries. In the Swiss courts the question arose[80] whether awards of the Arbitration Court of the Czechoslovak Chamber of Commerce in Prague were enforceable in Switzerland under the Geneva Convention of 1927[81] to which both Czechoslovakia and Switzerland were parties; the Federal Supreme Court of Switzerland held that the fact that the members of the arbitration court were nominated by the President of the Czechoslovak Chamber of Commerce was not against Swiss public policy and that the enforcement of the Czech award could not be refused on that ground. In the English and American courts proceedings have been stayed so that arbitration in Moscow could proceed.[82] The Soviet Foreign Trade Commission itself had to consider the plea that the Soviet tribunal and the Soviet party were, in fact, one and the same person and rejected it.[83] In all these cases the courts attached decisive importance to the fact that the defendant, when accepting the arbitration clause, had voluntarily submitted to the jurisdiction of a tribunal in a country of planned economy; to relieve him of that obligation on the ground that the tribunal was composed in a particular manner, would be contrary to the principle that contracts have to be performed (*pacta sunt servanda*). Differences in legal concepts between countries of planned and free economy have been considered by the English courts in another connection[84] and have been held not to infringe English public policy.

Arbitration of investment disputes

A Convention on the Settlement of Investment Disputes between States and Nationals of Other States was concluded in Washington in 1965. Effect was given to this Convention in the United Kingdom by the *Arbitration (International Investment Disputes) Act 1966.*

---

[79] Jersey Rajski, *Basic Principles of International Trade Law of Certain Socialist States and of East-West Trade Relations* [1978] D.P.C.I. 13.

[80] *Ligna Aussenhandelsunternehmen* v. *Baumgartner & Co. A.G.*, BGE 1958 (84), I, 39; *Compagnie Continentale d'Importation* v. *Eberle,* BGE 1958 (84), I, 56; see H.-P. Friedrich in [1960] J.B.L. 468.

[81] See p. 431, *post.*

[82] In England: *May & Hassell Ltd.* v. *Exportles* (1940) 66 Ll.L.R. 103. In U.S.A.: *Amtorg Trading Corpn.* v. *Camden Fibre Mills Inc.* (1952) 304 N.Y. 519.

[83] *Exportles* v. *Compagnie Commerciale de Bois à Papier*, quoted by Pisar in "Treatment of Communist Foreign Trade Arbitration in Western Courts," *International Trade Arbitration* (Domke, ed.), 1958, 101, 104. That the Polish State and a Polish foreign trade corporation were different persons was decided in *C. Czanikow Ltd.* v. *Roliwfeer* [1978] 3 W.L.R. 274; see p. 113, *ante.*

[84] *Luther* v. *Sagor* [1921] 3 K.B. 532, 539; *Re Trepca Mines Ltd.* [1960] 1 W.L.R. 1273, 1278.

This Convention and the Act of 1966 are treated earlier in the section dealing with Foreign Investment Laws.[85]

Enforcement of awards

The decision of the arbitrator or umpire is called the award. In many cases the award is carried out faithfully by the parties, but sometimes it is necessary to ascertain the means by which the award can be enforced in law.

In England an English award is normally enforced in the same manner as a judgment; the only difference is that leave of the court must first be obtained for the execution of an award. Leave is granted by a master of the court in a simple and inexpensive procedure which is commenced by originating summons. In exceptional cases, *e.g.* when the submission was oral, an action for the enforcement of the award has to be brought which is heard by the judge.

More important for the exporter is the question whether an English award can be enforced in a foreign country where property of the debtor is situate, or, vice versa, whether a foreign award can be enforced in the English jurisdiction. As matters stand at present, it can be stated that in many cases the enforcement of a foreign award is possible, but the legal method of enforcement varies. As far as the enforcement of a foreign award in England is concerned—and the same applies to the enforcement of an English award in the respective foreign countries—one distinguishes between the enforcement under the Geneva Convention and that under the New York Convention. Both aim at making the enforcement of a foreign award as simple as that of an award made within the jurisdiction and to admit it to execution under the same conditions. Enforcement under the Geneva documents is regulated by the Arbitration Act 1950 and these awards are known as *foreign awards*. Enforcement under the New York Convention is possible under the Arbitration Act 1975 and these awards are referred to as *Convention awards*. The New York Convention is designed to supersede the Geneva Protocol and Convention by one instrument and, at the same time, to make more effective the international recognition of arbitration agreements and foreign arbitraral awards and the enforcement of the latter. At present these two methods of enforcement overlap with respect to some countries. Where that is the case, the enforcement as Convention award is preferable because it is the easier method of enforcement. Both methods will be considered below.

An arbitration award can be enforced against foreign state property for the time being in use or intended for use for commercial purposes.[86]

---

[85] p. 203, *ante*.
[86] State Immunity Act 1978, s. 13; see p. 135, *ante*.

The Geneva Protocol and Convention

Two international agreements have been concluded in Geneva, the Protocol on Arbitration Clauses of 1923, and the Convention on the Execution of Foreign Arbitral Awards of 1927. Both agreements have been ratified by a number of countries, amongst them the United Kingdom. By the Arbitration Act 1950 statutory effect is given in the United Kingdom to the Protocol on Arbitration Clauses of 1923 by sections 4(2) and 35, and to the Convention on the Execution of Foreign Arbitral Awards of 1927 by section 35. The Protocol is contained in the First Schedule and the Convention in the Second Schedule to the Act of 1950.

Under the Convention a foreign award can be enforced in the English jurisdiction in the same manner as an English award provided the arbitration agreement is valid under its proper law and certain other requirements have been satisfied, but the enforcement will be refused if the award is contrary to English public policy. The application of these provisions depends on reciprocity being granted by the country where the award is made. Awards are mutually enforceable in the following countries[87]:

Austria, Belgium, Belize, British Virgin Islands, Cayman Islands, Czechoslovakia, Denmark, Falkland Islands, Finland, France, Germany (West), Germany (East), Gibraltar, Greece, Grenada, Hong Kong, India, Ireland, Israel, Italy, Japan, Kenya, Luxembourg, Mauritius, Montserrat, Netherlands, New Zealand, Pakistan, Portugal, Romania, Spain, Sweden, Switzerland, Tanzania, Thailand, Turks and Caicos Islands, United Kingdom, West Indies, Yugoslavia.

The New York Convention

On June 10, 1958, a *Convention on the Recognition and Enforcement of Foreign Arbitral Awards* was approved by a United Nations Conference at New York.[88] The New York Convention has been given effect in the United Kingdom by the Arbitration Act 1975. The following 52 States have agreed to be bound by the Convention[89] but some states have ratified or acceded subject to reservations, notably specifying that the Convention's application is subject to reciprocity or that it is limited to business and commercial transactions:

Australia, Austria, Belgium, Benin, Botswana, Bulgaria, Byelorussian SSR, Central African Empire, Chile, Cuba, Czechoslovakia, Denmark (also for Faeroe Islands and Greenland), Ecuador, Egypt, Finland, France (with all overseas territories), Germany (Democratic Republic), Germany (Federal Republic), Ghana, Greece, Holy See, Hungary, India, Israel, Italy, Japan, Kampuchea, Korea (Republic), Madagascar, Mexico, Morocco, Netherlands (also for Netherlands Antilles and Surinam), Niger, Nigeria, Norway, Philippines, Poland, Romania, South Africa, Spain, Sri Lanka, Sweden, Switzerland, Syria, Tanzania, Thailand, Trinidad and Tobago, Tunisia, Ukrainian SSR, Union of Soviet Socialist Republics, United Kingdom (also for Gibraltar), United States of America.

The New York Convention undoubtedly represents great progress in the field of international arbitration, when compared with the Geneva pro-

---

[87] Arbitration (Foreign Awards) Order 1978 (S.I. 1978 No. 186).

[88] The text of the Convention is reproduced in [1958] J.B.L. 396, and its provisions are explained by Samuel Pisar, "The United Nations Convention on Foreign Arbitral Awards," in [1959] J.B.L. 219.

[89] According to the United Nations Office of Public Information, as of May 1977.

visions. They were founded on the requirement of reciprocity which made it necessary to conclude bilateral agreements between States before the Geneva provisions could become operative in their jurisdictions. The requirement of reciprocity is abandoned by the New York Convention which applies, on principle, to every foreign award, *i.e.* an award made in the territory of any State other than that in which its recognition and enforcement is sought, but, as already observed, when ratifying the Convention or acceding to it some States have limited the application of the Convention to awards made in the territory of other Member States (Art. I).[90] It has rightly been said[91] that that reservation is self-liquidating since its effect will abate as more and more states ratify the Convention.

Further, whilst the application of the Geneva Protocol of 1923 depended on the parties to the agreement being subject to the jurisdiction of different States which were members of the Protocol, the New York Convention no longer stipulates that requirement and applies to all agreements in writing under which the parties undertake to submit to arbitration (Art. II).

The Arbitration Act 1975 provides[92] that, on principle, enforcement of a Convention award shall not be refused. Exceptionally the enforcement may be refused if the person against whom it is invoked proves[93]:

(*a*) that a party to the arbitration agreement was (under the law applicable to him) under some incapacity; or

(*b*) that the arbitration agreement was not valid under the law to which the parties subjected it or, failing any indication thereon, under the law of the country where the award was made; or

(*c*) that he was not given proper notice of the appointment of the arbitrator or of the arbitration proceedings or was otherwise unable to present his case; or

(*d*) . . . that the award deals with a difference not contemplated by or not falling within the terms of the submission to arbitration or contains decisions on matters beyond the scope of the submission to arbitration; or

(*e*) that the composition of the arbitral authority or the arbitral procedure was not in accordance with the agreement of the parties or, failing such agreement, with the law of the country where the arbitration took place; or

(*f*) that the award has not yet become binding on the parties, or has been set aside or suspended by a competent authority of the country in which, or under the law of which, it was made.

Enforcement of a Convention award may also be refused if the award is in respect of a matter which is not capable of settlement by arbitration, or if it would be contrary to public policy to enforce the award.[94] A Convention award which contains decisions on matters not submitted to arbitration may be enforced to the extent that it contains decisions on matters submitted to arbitration and separable from the matters not so submitted.[95] A Convention award is enforceable in the manner provided for by section 26 of

---

[90] References are to the New York Convention.
[91] By Samuel Pisar, *loc. cit.*, p. 225.
[92] Arbitration Act 1975, s. 5(1).
[93] *Ibid.* s. 5(2).
[94] *Ibid.* s. 5(3).
[95] *Ibid.* s. 5(4).

the Arbitration Act 1950, *i.e.* by leave of the master or the judge, in the same manner as an English judgment.[96]

Enforcement of awards in the absence of international regulation

In countries which do not adhere to the international regulation, the position is the following: where the country forms part of the Commonwealth, the English award is enforceable upon registration in the same manner in which an English judgment may be admitted to execution in that country.[97] This method likewise is satisfactory because it is inexpensive and requires the observation of few formalities. The method of registration is available in Australia, New Zealand,[98] the Canadian Provinces of Newfoundland[98] and Saskatchewan and Gibraltar,[98] and many other parts of the Commonwealth. In those parts which do not admit the system of registration, *e.g.* in Canada (with the exception of Newfoundland and Saskatchewan), and in the foreign countries outside the Commonwealth which have not ratified the Geneva or New York Conventions with effect to the United Kingdom, the enforcement of English awards depends entirely on private international law and might meet with considerable difficulties.

The EEC Treaty provides in Article 220 that the Member States of the European Community shall conclude a convention for the simplication of formalities governing the reciprocal recognition and enforcement of arbitral awards. Such a convention has not been proceeded with because the New York Convention of 1958 attempts such regulation on a global level.

LITIGATION

If the exporter feels compelled to take court proceedings against a customer abroad, he is faced with a difficult choice. His first inclination will be to commence proceedings in the debtor's country and to obtain a judgment which he can execute into the debtor's assets situate there. He has, however, an alternative course. If certain conditions which will be considered below are satisfied the English courts are prepared to assume jurisdiction over persons and companies not resident in England and Wales even if they are unwilling to submit to the English jurisdiction; if these conditions are satisfied, the exporter may consider obtaining a judgment in the English courts and trying to enforce it against the debtor's assets in the United Kingdom or abroad.

It depends on the circumstances, such as the situation of the debtor's assets and the accessibility of the foreign courts and lawyers, which course to choose. Unless he is sufficiently experienced, the exporter will be wise,

---

[96] *Ibid.* s. 3(1)(*a*).

[97] Under the Administration of Justice Act 1920 (see p. 437, *post*). s. 12(1) extends the application of the Act to awards.

[98] Alternatively with the method admitted by the Geneva Convention of 1927.

before deciding on the course which he will pursue, to obtain competent legal advice in his own country.[99]

Submission to jurisdiction

Where a foreign defendant in an action for breach of contract voluntarily submits to the jurisdiction of a local court, the court is normally prepared to exercise jurisdiction over him. It is doubtful whether, if the defendant appears before the court solely to protest against its jurisdiction, that has to be regarded as a voluntary submission.[1] There may be various reasons why he wishes to do so, *e.g.* in order to protect his property situate in the jurisdiction of that court. The better view is to hold that an appearance solely to protest against jurisdiction does not constitute a voluntary submission because there is clearly no intention to submit. But if the defendant does more than merely protesting against the jurisdiction, if, *e.g.* he asks the court to exercise its discretion in his favour or takes a procedural step beyond the mere protest, he has clearly submitted to the jurisdiction of the court.[1]

Service out of the jurisdiction

In the following cases the English courts are empowered to assume jurisdiction over persons or companies not present in England and who have not submitted to the English jurisdiction:

(1) Where an action is brought on a contract which is governed by English law, or concluded or broken in the English jurisdiction, or is made by or through an agent resident in the jurisdiction (Rules of the Supreme Court 1965, Ord. 11, r. 1(1)(*f*) and (*g*)).[2]

(2) Where the contract contains a term that the English High Court shall have jurisdiction to hear and determine the case (*ibid.* Ord. 11, r. 2).[3]

(3) Where the defendant abroad is joined with a defendant within the jurisdiction as a necessary and proper party (*ibid.* Ord. 11, r. 1(1)(*j*)).

(4) Where the action arises under the Carriage by Air Act 1961, the Carriage by Air (Supplementary Provisions) Act 1962, or the Carriage of Goods by Road Act 1965 (*ibid.* Ord. 11, r. 1(1)(*l*)).

(5) Where a foreign partnership is sued which carries on business within the jurisdiction (*ibid.* Ord. 81, r. 1).

(6) Where a foreign limited company is sued which either has an established place of business within Great Britain (in this case it has to register a person authorised to accept

---

[99] It should be noted that the limitation period in the foreign country may be shorter than in England; the judgment of the foreign court that an action is time-barred may be regarded as conclusive by the English courts in subsequent English proceedings: *Black-Clawson International Ltd.* v. *Papierwerke Waldhof-Aschaffenburg A.G.* [1974] 2 W.L.R. 789.

[1] *Henry* v. *Geoprosco International Ltd.* [1976] Q.B. 726. The adoption of English law as the proper law of the contract does not necessarily mean submission to the jurisdiction of the courts of this country: *Dundee Ltd.* v. *Gilman & Co. (Australia) Pty. Ltd.* [1968] 2 Lloyd's Rep. 394 (Sup.Ct. of N.S.W.). Where a foreign plaintiff has commenced proceedings in the English courts, he is regarded as having submitted to a counterclaim by the defendant: *Derby & Co. Ltd.* v. *Larsson* [1976] 1 W.L.R. 202.

[2] If the representative is doing his business in the jurisdiction, and not the principal's, he is not an agent within the meaning of this provision: *Vogel* v. *R. and A. Kohnstamm Ltd.* [1973] Q.B. 133.

[3] Where the contract is governed by English law, service out of the jurisdiction may be granted for a claim for relief under the Law Reform (Frustrated Contracts) Act 1943: *B.P. Exploration Co. (Lybia) Ltd.* v. *Hunt* [1976] 1 W.L.R. 788.

service of legal process in accordance with section 407 of the Companies Act 1948 as amended by the Companies Act 1976), or which carries on business within the jurisdiction if the company is here by its chairman, president, secretary, "similar officer" or other person who carries on business for the company in this country (*ibid.* Ord. 65, r. 3).[4]

The assumed jurisdiction of the court is discretionary; the court is "exceedingly careful before it allows a writ to be served out of the jurisdiction."[5] Even where the application is clearly within the terms of the assumed jurisdiction of the court, the court will refuse the application when, in the circumstances of the case, it thinks that it is not proper that a foreigner should be put to the inconvenience of contesting his rights in this, instead of his own, country.[6] In every case, a full and fair disclosure of all surrounding circumstances is demanded by the court, and the order for service out of the jurisdiction will be set aside when afterwards material facts transpire which were not disclosed in the application for the order.[7]

Where the English courts assume jurisdiction over persons or companies abroad, leave may be obtained of the court to serve a writ, or notice of the writ, on the defendant residing in a foreign country, and when the service is duly effected, the defendant is in the same position as a defendant within the jurisdiction; he may appear before the court by counsel or in person and defend the case, or he may not appear, in which case the plaintiff will sign judgment by default against him, if able to establish his case.

The Mareva injunction

If the English courts have jurisdiction over the dispute, whether original or assumed jurisdiction, it is possible to obtain an interlocutory injunction against the defendant ordering him not to remove specified assets from the jurisdiction.[8] That type of injunction is known as the *Mareva* injunction.[9] It is granted on the balance of convenience. A *Mareva* injunction is only ancillary to other proceedings; it cannot be granted in order to found a jurisdiction which the English courts would not have otherwise. "It cannot stand on its own. It is dependent upon there being a pre-existing cause of action against the defendant arising out of an invasion, actual or threatened by him, of a legal or equitable right of the plaintiff for the enforcement of which the defendant is amenable to the jurisdiction of the court."[10]

---

[4] See Palmer's *Company Law* (22nd ed., 1976), para. 8–12.

[5] *Per* Pearson J. in *Société Générale de Paris* v. *Dreyfus Bros.* (1885) 29 Ch.D. 239, 243, and du Parcq L.J. in *George Monro Ltd.* v. *American Cyanamid & Chemical Corporation* (1944) 60 T.L.R. 265; also *Aaronson Bros. Ltd.* v. *Maderera del Tropico S.A.* [1967] 2 Lloyd's Rep. 159, 162.

[6] See *The Atlantic Star* [1973] 2 W.L.R. 795 (H.L.).

[7] *Bloomfield* v. *Serenyi* [1945] 2 All E.R. 646.

[8] *Siskina* (*Cargo Owners*) v. *Distos Compania Naviera S.A.* [1977] 3 W.L.R. 818 (H.L.).

[9] Named after *Mareva Compania Naviera S.A.* v. *International Bulkcarriers S.A.; The Mareva* [1975] 2 Lloyd's Rep. 509 (C.A.); see David G. Powles, "The Mareva Injunction" [1978] J.B.L. 11. See also *Third Chandris Shipping Corp.* v. *Unimarine S.A.* [1979] 2 All E.R. 972.

[10] *Per* Lord Diplock in *Siskina*, p. 829.

The *Mareva* injunction is particularly useful against a defendant residing abroad against whom the English courts, in the exercise of their assumed jurisdiction, have granted service out of the jurisdiction.[11] It prevents such a defendant from removing assets out of the jurisdiction and thus rendering an English judgment against him difficult to enforce.

Enforcement of English judgments abroad

There are two methods of enforcing a judgment outside the jurisdiction of the court which pronounced it: a new action may have to be commenced in the foreign country; this action has to be based on the judgment which has been obtained and not on the original contract between the parties; or it may be possible to register the judgment in the foreign country where it is sought to be executed and then to enforce it directly in the same manner as a judgment given in the courts of that country. The method of bringing an action upon the judgment is dilatory and cumbersome because the plaintiff is compelled to conduct two lawsuits in order to obtain satisfaction; the method of direct enforcement is more satisfactory and much favoured in modern law.

The method of direct enforcement is not regulated by general international agreement like the conventions on the execution of foreign arbitral awards,[12] but the EEC Treaty provides in Article 220 that the Member States shall conclude a convention on this subject, and, pursuant to that provision, a *Convention on Jurisdiction and the Enforcement of Judgments in Civil and Commercial Matters* was concluded by the original Member to which the three new Member States, including the United Kingdom, will have to accede; more will be said about the Judgments Convention of the EEC later on.[13]

The direct enforcement of foreign judgments is admitted in the United Kingdom by a number of bilateral treaties which are based on the principle of reciprocal treatment. Where a foreign country grants substantial reciprocity to the United Kingdom, the benefits of the Foreign Judgments (Reciprocal Enforcement) Act 1933 are extended to it by Order in Council. Under this Act foreign judgments are admitted to direct enforcement in England upon registration in the English courts or compliance with certain conditions. In fact, enforcement upon registration is in these cases the only way in which the foreign judgment can be executed in England (s. 6) and

---

[11] The injunction is founded on R.S.C. Order 11, r. 1(1)(i).
[12] See p. 431, *ante*.
[13] See p. 438, *post*.

bankruptcy proceedings may be instituted on the basis of a registered judgment.[14] The Act has so far been applied to

the Australian Capital Territory, Austria, Belgium, France, Germany (West) and Berlin (West), Guernsey, Jersey, India, Israel, Italy, Malta, Man (Isle of), Netherlands, Norway, Pakistan.

Judgments given by the superior courts of those countries are admitted to direct enforcement in England and, vice versa, judgments of the High Court in England, the Court of Session in Scotland and the High Court in Northern Ireland can be enforced upon registration in those countries. A Draft Convention for the Reciprocal Recognition and the enforcement of Judgments in Civil Matters between the United Kingdom and the United States was published in 1977 but has not been signed or ratified yet[15]; as regards the United States it is still necessary to bring an action upon the judgment.

The direct method of enforcement of judgments is further widely though not universally admitted within the Commonwealth, in so far as the Act of 1933 has not been extended to those countries. Under the Administration of Justice Act 1920, money judgments given in British territories outside the United Kingdom can be enforced in the United Kingdom upon registration, provided the British territory in question has extended reciprocity to England. Under this arrangement, English judgments are enforceable in Australia, New Zealand, the Canadian Provinces of Newfoundland and Saskatchewan, Ghana, Malawi, Nigeria, Zambia and Rhodesia, the West Indies, Gibraltar, and other parts of the Commonwealth. Notable exceptions are the other Provinces of Canada.

The account that has been given of the enforcement of an award or judgment outside the jurisdiction reveals considerable imperfections in a branch of law which is of great practical importance for international trade. It is firmly believed that unification of this aspect of the law can, and ought to, be achieved on the international level.

Judgments in foreign currency in the English courts

It has already been discussed[16] that in appropriate cases the English courts are prepared to give judgment in a currency other than pounds sterling.

---

[14] *Re a Judgment Debtor* (No. 2176 of 1938) (1939) 160 L.T. 92. A foreign judgment which is registrable is entitled to recognition in the U.K. and is conclusive between the parties in all proceedings on the same cause of action: Foreign Judgments (Reciprocal Enforcement) Act 1933, s. 8(1) and *Black-Clawson International Ltd.* v. *Papierwerke Aschaffenburg A.G.* [1974] 2 W.L.R. 789. A French judgment awarding damages as *résistance abusive* is registrable under the Foreign Judgments (Reciprocal Enforcement) Act 1933 because the award is for compensatory damages and not for a penalty and its enforcement is not against English public policy: *S.A. Consortium General Textiles* v. *Sun & Sand Agencies Ltd.* [1978] Q.B. 279.

[15] Cmnd. 6771 (1977).

[16] See p. 133, *ante*.

The EEC Judgments Convention

On September 27, 1968 the six original Member States of the EEC concluded the *Convention on Jurisdiction and the Enforcement of Judgments in Civil and Commercial Matters.*[17] The Convention, which is also called the Full Faith and Credit Convention and which was signed in Brussels, came into operation on February 1, 1973. The three new members of the EEC, Denmark, Ireland and the United Kingdom, undertook to accede to the Convention. A Convention of Accession, amending the original Convention, was signed on October 9, 1978.[18] At present[19] the Accession Convention has not been given effect in English law yet.

The EEC Judgments Convention pursues two aims: to reduce the possibility of forum shopping, *i.e.* the multiplicity of jurisdictions in which a plaintiff, according to his choice, may commence proceedings; and to make the judgments to which it applies enforceable in all Member States of the EEC.

The Convention applies in civil and commercial matters, whatever the nature of the court or tribunal, but the Convention does not extend to revenue, customs or administrative measures. It also does not apply to[20]:

1. the status or legal capacity of natural persons, rights in property arising out of matrimonial relationship, wills and succession;
2. bankruptcy, proceedings relating to the winding up of insolvent companies or other legal persons, judicial arrangements, compositions and analogous proceedings;
3. social security;
4. arbitration.

Jurisdiction clauses

The Convention admits a contract clause conferring exclusive jurisdiction on a particular court of a Contracting State but requires that[21]:

> such an agreement conferring jurisdiction shall be either in writing or evidenced in writing or, in international trade or commerce, in a form which accords with practices in that trade or commerce of which the parties are or ought to have been aware.

The Court of the European Communities held[22] that the requirement that there should be "an agreement in writing" was not satisfied by the mere insertion of a jurisdiction clause into the general conditions of one of the parties but that it was necessary that "the contract signed by both parties contain[ed] an express reference to those general conditions." But it would, according to the European Court,[23] be otherwise "where an oral agreement forms part of a continuing trading relationship between the parties, provided also that it is established that the dealings taken as a whole are governed by the general conditions of the party giving the confirmation,

[17] The Convention is founded on Art. 220 of the EEC Treaty.
[18] *Official Journal,* 1978, No. L.304/1–102.
[19] Position: September 1, 1979.
[20] EEC Judgment Convention, as amended by the Accession Convention, Art. 1.
[21] *Ibid.* Art. 17.
[22] In *Colzani* v. *RÜWA Polstereimaschinen GmbH* [1977] 1 C.M.L.R. 345, 356.
[23] *Galeries Segoura Sprl* v. *Firma Rahim Bonakdarian* [1977] 1 C.M.L.R. 361, 372; see also p. 54, *ante*.

and these conditions contain a clause conferring jurisdiction." The wording of the Accession Convention mentioned earlier attempts to give effect to these decisions of the European Court.

If the exclusive jurisdiction clause was inserted for the benefit of only one of the parties, he may waive that benefit and bring proceedings in any other court which has jurisdiction by virtue of the Convention.

Jurisdiction where there is no jurisdiction clause

The Convention[24] provides that, on principle, a person "domiciled"[25] in a Contracting State shall, whatever his nationality, be sued in the courts of that State and that the courts of other Contracting States shall declare of their own motion that they have no jurisdiction over the claim in question.[26] As regards matters relating to a contract, proceedings may also be instituted in the courts of the place where the obligation in question has to be performed.[27] Here the Convention appears to admit forum shopping because the plaintiff has the choice between two jurisdictions, that of the domicile of the defendant and that of the place of performance of the contract.

In a claim arising from, or in connection with, an insurance contract proceedings may be taken in the courts of the State in which the insurer is domiciled or in those of another Contracting State where the policy-holder is domiciled.[28] Similarly in instalment sales (or loans) the seller (or lender) can, on principle, be sued in the seller's (or lender's) or the buyer's (or borrower's) courts.[28a]

Recognition

A judgment given in a Contracting State shall be recognised in the other Contracting States without any special procedure being required.[29]

However, a judgment shall not be recognised[30]:

1. if such recognition is contrary to public policy in the State in which recognition is sought;
2. where it was given in default of appearance, if the defendant was not duly served with the document which instituted the proceedings or with an equivalent document in sufficient time to enable him to arrange for his defence;
3. if the judgment is irreconcilable with a judgment given in a dispute between the same parties in the State in which recognition is sought;
4. if the court of the State in which the judgment was given, in order to arrive at its judgment, had decided a preliminary question concerning the status or legal capacity of natural persons, rights in property arising out of a matrimonial relationship, wills or succession in a way that conflicts with a rule of the private international law of the State in which the recognition is sought, unless the same result would have been reached by the application of the rules of private international law of that State;
5. if the judgment is irreconcilable with an earlier judgment given in a non-Contracting State involving the same cause of action and between the same parties, provided that

[24] EEC Judgment Convention, amended by the Accession Convention, Art. 22.
[25] "Domiciled" is not used here in the common law sense but means "habitually resident."
[26] EEC Judgment Convention, amended by the Accession Convention, Art. 19.
[27] *Ibid.* Art. 5(1). The place of performance has to be determined according to the rules of private international law of the national court seized with the matter: *Industrie Tessili Italiana Como* v. *Dunlop A.G.* [1977] 1 C.M.L.R. 26, 52.
[28] *Ibid.* Art. 8. [28a] Arts. 13–15.
[29] *Ibid.* Art. 26.
[30] *Ibid.* Art. 27.

this latter judgment fulfils the conditions necessary for its recognition in the State addressed.

Under no circumstances may a foreign judgment be reviewed as to its substance.[31]

Enforcement

A judgment given in one Contracting State shall be enforced in another Contracting State by order for enforcement made in the latter; in the United Kingdom the proper procedure will be to have the foreign judgment registered for enforcement in the relevant part of the United Kingdom[32] In brief, the enforcement procedure of the judgment of another court in the EEC will be similar to the well-established registration procedure under the Foreign Judgments (Reciprocal Enforcement) Act 1933.

Judgments of the Court of the European Communities

The judgments of the Court of the European Communities at Luxembourg, other Community judgments and orders of the Community institutions are directly enforceable in the United Kingdom, subject to certain conditions.[33] Such enforcement is done by registration in the High Court but it is necessary that first the Secretary of State appends an order of enforcement. These European measures are then enforceable in the United Kingdom, subject to the Treaties, as if they were judgments or orders of the court in which they are registered.

---

[31] *Ibid.* Art. 29.
[32] *Ibid.* Art. 31.
[33] European Communities (Enforcement of the Community Judgments) Order 1972 (S.I. 1972 No. 1590), made under the European Communities Act 1972.

PART FOUR

LONG TERM CONTRACTS

Chapter 27

THE CONSTRUCTION OF WORKS AND INSTALLATIONS ABROAD

THE contract for the construction of works and installations abroad has certain typical characteristics. The parties to this international contract are often a foreign government department or government corporation as *employer* and a company—or several companies jointly—incorporated in another country as *contractor*. Often, but not necessarily, the employer is an organisation in a country in the course of development and the contractor is incorporated in an industrialised country. Legally, this type of international contract is a contract for work or the supply of goods or a combination of both; economically, it is a contract for the transfer of technology from one country to another. Illustrations of this type of contract are the undertaking of a contractor to build and equip in the country of the employer a hospital, a factory, an airport or a pipeline but in some cases contractors are known to have undertaken to build whole ports or cities for the employer. The contract may be a turn-key contract under which the contractor undertakes to hand over the installation ready for use, or it may proceed by stages when each stage has to be tested and accepted by the employer.

Another feature of an international procurement contract is that it involves usually considerable amounts of money.[1] Often the employer, particularly if he is an organisation in a developing country, cannot or will not finance the undertaking out of his own resources and it has to be financed by public international bodies, such as the International Bank for Reconstruction and Development (the World Bank), the International Development Association (IDA), both in Washington, D.C., or the European Development Fund (EDF) of the EEC in Brussels. While these financial institutions are loath to decree the terms on which their borrower, the employer, has to contract, they have established guidelines which they expect the parties to the international procurement contract to respect. Another aspect of the financial magnitude of these transactions is that they have given rise to various kinds of contract guarantees, such as tender guarantees, performance guarantees, repayment guarantees and payment guarantees,[2] some of which have attracted the attention of the International

[1] In the Department of Trade an *Overseas Projects Group* has been set up to provide an identifiable central point to which industrialists, bankers and consultants can look for co-ordination on government and official support for capital projects overseas. The Group administers the Overseas Projects Fund from which contributions may in certain circumstances be made towards the cost of a wide range of activities preceding the main contract, but such contributions are repayable in the event of the contract being secured.

[2] See p. 81, *ante*.

Q

Chamber of Commerce and are dealt with in their brochure on *Uniform Rules for Contract Guarantees.*[3]

A third feature of international procurement contracts is that their performance often extends over a considerable period of time. During that time the economic situation may change. For that reason it is usual to insert into this type of contract, in addition to the ordinary currency and *force majeure* clauses, special clauses aimed at reducing the economic risk inherent in long-term contracts, such as price adjustment and hardship clauses.

Types of Procurement

From the legal point of view, there exist two methods of international procurement, *viz.* by inviting tenders from companies prepared to contract with the employer (*appels d'offres*) or by negotiating the contract of work or supply with the contractor directly or through agents, without previously requiring competitive bids from intending contractors (*marchés de gré à gré*). Of these two methods, procurement by tender, *i.e.* by competitive bid, is the preferred method. It has been said[4]:

> Competitive tender has certain obvious advantages over other methods of contractor selection. . . Not only is it an effective means of getting the needed goods or service at lowest cost, but the resulting fixed price contract, under which increased cost must normally be absorbed by the contractor, is easy to administer. Competitive tender also diminishes the risk of bias or favouritism in contract awards and tendering firms will feel that they have an equal chance of getting the contract.

It is therefore understandable that the World Bank requires that method as the normal method of procurement; it is stated in the Bank's *Guidelines*[5]:

> The Bank is required by its articles of agreement to ensure that the proceeds of its loans are used with due attention to economy and efficiency. The Bank considers that international competitive bidding is the most economic and efficient method for procuring most of the goods and works required for the projects it finances. International competitive bidding has the further advantage of ensuring that manufacturers, suppliers and contractors from all Bank member countries have an opportunity to compete in providing goods and works financed by the Bank. In most cases,[6] therefore, the Bank requires that the goods and works which it finances be procured through international competitive bidding, open to suppliers and contractors in all of its member countries and Switzerland.

There are two types of tender: the open and the selective. Under the open (or public) procedure "tenders are invited through advertisements or other forms of public notice from any eligible contractor. In the case of selective tenders only those parties who have been invited to tender by the [employer's] contracting agency can submit offers. The agency can select the tenders either through its previous knowledge of the market or after a prequalification procedure, in which elegible firms are invited to

---

[3] ICC Brochure No. 325 (August 1978).

[4] Colin Turpin, *Government Contracts* (London, Penguin, 1972), 135.

[5] *Guidelines for Procurement under World Bank Loans and IDA Credits* (August 1975), 1.

[6] The Bank admits, in appropriate cases other forms of procurement, see *ibid.* 16–18.

provide evidence of their ability to perform the services or produce the goods desired by the agency "[7] The prevalent method is selective competitive bidding preceded by a prequalification procedure.

If the procurement is done without competitive bidding, the observation discussed in the previous chapters apply to the contract between the employer and the contractor, but sometimes some of the special clauses noted in this chapter, *e.g.* the hardship clause, are added.

The following observations deal only with the procurement by competitive tender.

PROCUREMENT BY TENDER

The course of dealing

Where a foreign government department or corporation intends to invite tenders, the normal course of business is as follows. The employer, *i.e.* the foreign government organisation, publishes *an announcement of preliminary selection* in leading newspapers of the world. This advertisement states, apart from the nature of the work, the name and address of the employer and the time limit for the applications, the conditions of the *prequalification procedure, i.e.* the conditions of technical and financial capability which applicants have to satisfy in order to be allowed to tender; normally the applicants are required to pay a small fee for the tender documents. Interested firms from various parts of the world, which think that they satisfy the prequalification conditions, will then apply to the employer for the *tender documents*. The employer will send the documents to those applicants who in his opinion satisfy the prequalification conditions. The tender documents are usually voluminous, setting out the technical specifications, the contract terms, the amount of the tender guarantee and the instructions on how and when to submit the tender. The employer will also appoint a *consulting engineer*, if he has not done so before; his function is to advise him impartially on the suitability of the tenderers; he is not one of the competing bidders. The firms which have received the tender documents will consider them and, if they are interested, submit a formal *tender*. Sometimes formalities are prescribed for such a submission, *e.g.* it has to be submitted in a sealed envelope in order to safeguard the confidentiality of the tender. At the same time the tenderers will provide a *tender guarantee* (*tender bond*) in the prescribed amount. The tender guarantee is usually provided by means of a bank guarantee. It indicates to the employer that the tenderer is seriously interested in the proposition and that his submission is not frivolous.

The next step is the *opening of the tenders by the employer*. In some cases this is done in a ceremonious manner: all tenders, which are contained in sealed envelopes, are opened on the same day and publicly read out. In other cases a less formal procedure is followed and the tenders are

[7] Gösta Westring, *International Procurement*, (Revised 1977) (UNITAR, New York), 9.

opened and read as they are received. The employer then proceeds to the *evaluation of the tenders*, on the advice of his consulting engineer. At this stage, under the terms of the tender documents, he may negotiate with one or the other of the tenderers, but that should be done only to clarify points in their tenders; it would be unfair if the terms of the other tenders were disclosed at this stage. The employer will then decide to accept the most advantageous tender, which need not be the lowest, and send a *letter of acceptance* to the contractor whom he has selected. Eventually the formal *contract* is signed by both parties. It is normally a short document, referring to, and embodying, the tender, the drawings, the conditions of contract, the specifications, the bills of quantities, the letter of acceptance, etc. Often the tender guarantees are released only after the signature of the formal contract, because before that event there is no certainty that a binding contract has been concluded.

The parties will then proceed to the *performance of the contract*. The contractor will usually give the employer a *performance guarantee* from a bank and in some cases the employer will give the contractor a *payment guarantee* of a bank. Under some contracts the employer will appoint the so-called *engineer*; he is a technical expert whose duty it is to resolve any differences which may arise in the course of performance; he is not an arbitrator and he may be a person other than the consulting engineer who advised in the evaluation of the tenders. The contract usually provides for the rough work to be done by local labour and for the technical work to be executed by the contractor's staff, but it is important that a representative of the contractor be present at the site from the beginning to supervise the co-ordination of the foundations and the installation of the machinery. The contract also sometimes provides for the training of the employer's personnel in the country of the contractor and for the adequate housing of the contractor's personnel employed on the site in the country of the employer.

The terms of payment vary according to the nature of the work to be done or the goods to be supplied. Sometimes, when goods have to be supplied, they are the terms usual in c.i.f. or other contracts concluded on the familiar trade terms,[8] but in other cases they depend on the progress of the work and payment is made in stages, on the certificate of the engineer. Here complicated procedures are sometimes arranged for the *acceptance of the work* and it is not unusual to distinguish between provisional and final acceptance. The contract may also provide for the payment of liquidated damages in cases of delayed performance and bonus payments in case of performance in advance of the stipulated time.

When the work or installation is completed, it is unusual for the employer to release the final balance of the price at once. Normally he is entitled to *retention money*, *i.e.* he may retain the balance for a specified time, sometimes as long as a year, in order to be assured that the installation operates satisfactorily.

[8] See p. 8, *ante*.

The standard contract forms

Contracts for the construction of works and installations abroad are usually concluded in the form of standard forms which are adapted to the requirements of the transaction in question. The most important of these standard contract forms were listed earlier[9] but reference may be made again to those whose terms will be considered here from time to time. They are:

1. *Conditions of Contract (International) for Works of Civil Engineering Construction, with Forms of Tender and Agreement* (3rd ed., March 1977). This standard form is sponsored by FIDIC, the *Fédération Internationale des Ingénieurs-Conseils*. This form is known as the *FIDIC Contract.*[10]
2. *The Guidelines for Procurement under World Bank Loans and IDA Credits* (August 1975), known as the *World Bank Guidelines.*[11]
3. *General Conditions for Public Works and Supply Contracts* financed by the European Development Fund of the EEC (Brussels, February 14, 1974). These Conditions are known as the *EDF Conditions.*[12]

The FIDIC Contract

Of particular importance is the FIDIC Contract because it is approved by professional organisations in 73 countries, *viz.* 29 of which are members of FIDIC itself[13] and 44 which are members of other organisations.[14]

The FIDIC Contract is arranged in—

Part I General Conditions,
Part II Conditions of Particular Application,
Part III Conditions of Particular Application to Dredging and Reclamation Work,
Form of Tender,
Form of Agreement.

The General Conditions of Part I include 71 clauses. They are intended to be of universal application and do not contain any reference to the names of the parties or the particular work in hand. The Conditions of Particular Application in Part II contain the terms which apply to the particular transaction in question. They are variable and are intended as an *aide-memoire* for the adaptation of Part I to the particular contract. The clauses of Part II are linked to those of Part I by the same numbers.

---

[9] See p. 53, *ante*; other standard contract forms are set out in Gösta Westring, *op. cit.*

[10] The FIDIC contract can be obtained from the Association of Consulting Engineers, Hancock House, 87 Vincent Square, London, SW1P 2PH.

[11] Obtainable from the Headquarters of the World Bank, 1818 H Street, N.W., Washington D.C. 20433, U.S.A.

[12] Obtainable from the Commission of the European Communities, Directorate-General for Development, Finance and Administration Unit, rue de la loi 200, Brussels, Belgium. These conditions are at present subject to revision. Three sets of General Conditions are being prepared: for works, services and supplies. In addition, Rules of Arbitration for EDF-financed contracts are being prepared. At the date of writing, (January 1, 1979), the drafts of these documents have not been finalised yet.

[13] The headquarters of FIDIC are at Carel van Bylandtlaan 9, The Hague, The Netherlands.

[14] The other organisations are: the *Fédération Internationale Européene de la Construction*, International Federation of Asian and Western Pacific Contractors Associations, Inter-American Federation of the Construction Industry, and the Associated General Contractors of America.

They contain, *inter alia*, the names of the employer and contractor, as well as that of the engineer, the language(s) of the contract and the ruling language, and the law to which the contract shall be subject.

The form of the tender suggested by the FIDIC contract is quite brief. It will be considered later on. Appended to the tender are the financial details, such as the amount of the performance guarantee, of liquidated damages or a bonus, of the retention money, and the time limits, *e.g.* the period for the commencement of the work, of completion, of maintenance, and the time within which payment is to be made after the issue of the certificate issued by the engineer. The FIDIC contract does not provide a standard form for the letter of acceptance by the employer.

The form of agreement set out in the FIDIC contract is also extremely short. It contains only four clauses but it incorporates by reference:

(*a*) the tender,
(*b*) the drawings,
(*c*) the conditions of Contract (Pts. I, II and III where applicable),
(*d*) the specification,
(*e*) the bill of quantities,
(*f*) the schedule of rates and prices (if any),
(*g*) the letter of acceptance.

The FIDIC Contract suggests that the agreement is executed in the form of a deed, duly signed, sealed and delivered by both parties in the presence of witnesses.

A typical feature of the FIDIC Contract is that it requires the employer to appoint *an engineer* whose name is inserted into Part II of the Conditions of Contract. He is a technical expert whose function includes the decision of disputes which may arise in the execution of the work, the issue of certificates of satisfactory completion of certain stages or of the whole work, and the giving of orders, particularly with respect to alterations, additions and omissions of the agreed work.

The pre-contractual stage

The prequalification procedure

There exists no standard procedure for prequalification requirements. Sometimes the requirements are kept in general terms, *e.g.*:

> In order to obtain the necessary application form, interested companies which can prove their fitness, technical and financial capacity, experience and tradition in such field of the . . . industry, are requested to contact. . . .

Sometimes the employer, if so requested, sends applicants a prequalification questionnaire. Where tenders are invited for work already begun, it is usual to exempt applicants who have already prequalified for previous stages from further prequalification.

Transactions financed by World Bank loans or IDA credits will normally require a prequalification procedure for bidders. The World Bank Guidelines provide[15]:

---

[15] World Bank Guidelines, Art. 1.3.

Prequalification is normally advisable for large or complex contracts to ensure in advance of bidding that invitations to bid are confined to capable firms. The loan agreement with the Bank will specify whether prequalification is required in respect of particular contracts. Prequalification should be based entirely on the ability of the interested firm to perform the particular work satisfactorily, taking into account, *inter alia*: (i) experience and past performance on similar contracts, (ii) capabilities with respect to personnel, equipment and plant, and (iii) financial position.

The World Bank and IDA will normally wish to review prequalification procedures and to be notified of the list of prequalified firms and any reasons for exclusion of any applicant for prequalification. This has to be done before the applicants are notified.[16] These international financial institutions thus wish to safeguard industry against arbitrary exclusion from prequalification and to ensure that fair play is observed.

The invitation to tender

The contracting agency of the employer will send those applicants who have qualified the tender documents. From the legal point of view they constitute an invitation to bid, *i.e.* to make an offer. Although in the legal context this is still a preliminary step, the tender documents are of the utmost importance because they constitute the basis of any contract which may result. They are usually incorporated into the tender and again the contract is made by reference to them.

The tender documents are usually divided into three parts, one which contains the conditions of contract, another which contains the technical details, such as the drawings, specifications and bill of quantities, and a third one which contains detailed instructions to the intending bidder on how to submit his tender.

Four clauses which are often found in invitations to bid may be mentioned here.

First, the invitation will state that the employer is not bound to accept the lowest bid or any bid at all. Even without the addition of this clause the employer would not be bound to do so. Secondly, the employer may reserve the right to seek clarification of the bid from a bidder. The principle which applies here is defined in the World Bank Guidelines thus[17]:

The [employer] may ask any bidder for a clarification of his bid but should not ask any bidder to change the substance or price of his bid.

Thirdly, if it is intended to give certain bids preference for non-commercial reasons, *e.g.* where domestic, political or regional preference is intended to be given, that should be stated clearly in the invitation to tender. Fourthly, the invitation should state that the employer shall be entitled to avoid the contract if it is proved that the contractor or any of his employees were engaged or involved in any form of bribery or corruption in connection with the contract.[18]

---

[16] *Ibid.* Annex 1.
[17] *Ibid.* Art. 3.3.
[18] ICC Brochure No. 315 (1977) on *Extortion and Bribery in Business Transactions*, 10–11.

Furthermore, since bids are usually invited from tenderers in different countries, the tender documents should clearly state the currency or currencies in which bid prices may be expressed and the contract price will be paid.[19]

The tender

This is the offer made by the contractor to enter into a binding contract with the employer on the terms of the tender documents. In English law and the laws of many other countries the tender can be withdrawn by the contractor before it is accepted but normally the right of withdrawal is restricted. The EDF Conditions restrict it to the end of the tendering time[20]:

> Any tender may be withdrawn, supplemented or amended prior to the date fixed for the receipt of tenders.

The FIDIC Contract goes further than that and its form of tender excludes the right of withdrawal for a specified time after the expiration of the tendering time[21]:

> We agree to abide by this tender for the period of . . . days from the date fixed for receiving the same and it shall remain binding upon us and may be accepted at any time before the expiration of that period.

In English law these restrictions of the right of withdrawal do not prevent the tenderer from withdrawing the tender after the expiration of the specified period, provided that the withdrawal communication reaches the employer's contracting agency before acceptance. Here, however, the mechanism of the tender guarantee operates: if the tenderer withdraws the tender contrary to his undertaking to be bound by it, it is thought that the bond is forfeit.

The tender incorporates the tender documents by reference and consequently both the conditions of contract and the technical details become part of the tender. The form of tender suggested by the FIDIC Contract also contains the following significant provision which excludes the "subject to (formal) contract" interpretation:

> Unless and until a formal agreement is prepared and executed this tender, together with your written acceptance thereof, shall constitute a binding contract between us.

The tender guarantee

It is customary to ask the tenderer to support his tender by a tender guarantee (tender bond) given by a bank, insurance company or other third party. The object of the tender guarantee is twofold: to indicate to the employer that the tenderer is in earnest and to protect the employer against the breach of any obligations which the tenderer undertakes by

[19] World Bank Guidelines, Art. 3.9.
[20] EDF Conditions, Art. 40(1).
[21] FIDIC Contract, p. 26.

submitting his tender. As far as the banks, insurance companies and other third parties are concerned, the *Uniform Rules for Contract Guarantees*, published by the ICC,[22] provide a useful regulation which applies, however, only if adopted by the parties. The Uniform Rules define a tender guarantee thus[23]:

"tender guarantee" means an undertaking given by a bank, insurance company or other party ("the guarantor") at the request of a tenderer ("the principal") or given on the instructions of a bank, insurance company, or other party so requested by the principal ("the instructing party") to a party inviting tenders ("the beneficiary") whereby the guarantor undertakes—in the event of default by the principal in the obligations resulting from the submission of the tender—to make payment to the beneficiary within the limits of a stated sum of money.

Under the Uniform Rules the tender guarantee expires:

(*a*) six months from the date of the guarantee[24]
(*b*) on acceptance of the tender by the employer by the award of a contract to the tenderer[25]
(*c*) by the award of the contract to another tenderer[26]
(*d*) if the employer expressly declares that he does not intend to place a contract.[27]

According to the Uniform Rules, a tender guarantee is valid only in respect of the original tender and does not cover any amendments not approved by the guarantor.[28] The Rules further provide that the employer who wishes to make a claim under the tender guarantee has to submit documentation supporting his claim within a specified time.[29] If the guarantee does not specify the documentation, a declaration from the employer is required that the contractor's tender has been accepted but he has failed either to sign the contract or to submit a performance guarantee. In addition, a declaration is required, addressed to the contractor, to have any dispute settled by arbitration, if not otherwise specified, in accordance with the Rules of the ICC Court of Arbitration or the UNCITRAL Arbitration Rules, at the option of the contractor. The Uniform Rules for Contract Guarantees fail to deal with a claim under the guarantee by the employer if the contractor withdraws the tender contrary to his undertaking to be bound by it. The Uniform Rules provide[30] that if a guarantee does not indicate the law applicable, it shall be governed by the law of the guarantor's place of business, and if he has several places of business by the law of the place of the branch which issued the guarantee.

The World Bank Guidelines provide[31] that bid bonds or guarantees shall be released to unsuccessful bidders as soon as possible after it is determined that they will not be awarded the contract.

---

[22] ICC Brochure No. 325 (1978).
[23] *Ibid.* Art. 2(*a*).
[24] *Ibid.* Art. 4(*a*).
[25] *Ibid.* Art. 5(2)(*a*).
[26] *Ibid.* Art. 5(2)(*b*).
[27] *Ibid.* Art. 5(2)(*c*).
[28] *Ibid.* Art. 7(1).
[29] *Ibid.* Arts. 8 and 9.
[30] *Ibid.* Art. 10.
[31] World Bank Guidelines, Art. 2.3.

Evaluation of tenders

Both the World Bank Guidelines[32] and the EDF Conditions[33] require the bids which are formally in order to be opened in public session, but the EDF Conditions do so only with respect to contracts for the supply of goods and not with respect to contracts for work. The World Bank Guidelines state:

Bids should normally be opened in public. The name of the bidder and the total amount of each bid and of any alternative bids, if they have been requested or permitted, should, when opened, be read aloud and recorded.

It has already been observed that the employer normally reserves in the tender documents the right not to accept the lowest or any bid and to negotiate with tenderers about the clarification of their bids or even to invite alternative bids. That is necessary in order to have a basis for comparison. The FIDIC Contract form of tender provides expressly:

We understand that you are not bound to accept the lowest or any tender you may receive.

The contract

The international contract for the construction of works and installations abroad contains many of the terms which have been discussed in the previous chapters, particularly as far as the supply of machinery and equipment for the installations to be built is concerned. However, some terms peculiar to construction contracts require attention.

Inspection and acceptance

The acceptance of the progressive stages of the work or the completed work is an important incident in the performance of the contract because often payment, or part payment, is made dependent on it. This topic is usually regulated in the contract with some particularity. Sometimes the contract provides for provisional acceptance and final acceptance. According to the arrangement of the parties, the engineer will issue his certificate on provisional or final acceptance of part of the works, and on such certificate a further instalment of the price will become payable.

Great difficulty arises in practice with respect to alterations, additions and omissions because it is rarely possible to execute a major building operation strictly according to the original drawings. Here the FIDIC Contract provides[34]:

All extra or additional work done or work omitted by order of the engineer shall be valued at the rates and prices set out in the contract if, in the opinion of the engineer, the same shall be applicable. If the contract does not contain any rates or prices applicable to the extra or additional work, then suitable rates or prices shall be agreed upon between the engineer and the contractor. In the event of disagreement, the engineer shall fix such rates or prices as shall, in his opinion, be reasonable and proper.

---

[32] World Bank Guidelines, Art. 3.2.

[33] EDF Conditions, Art. 4.2.

[34] FIDIC Contract, cl. 52. This contract form contains further more detailed rules on the fixing of rates and prices.

Sub-contracting

While the contractor is prohibited to assign the contract or any part of it without the prior consent of the employer,[35] it is not unusual to allow him to sub-contract certain parts of the contract. Where, *e.g.* a hospital has to be built by a construction firm, it is probable that they will sub-contract x-ray and other clinical equipment to specialists. The FIDIC Contract refers to sub-contractors, who are approved by the employer or the engineer as "nominated sub-contractors"[36] and provides that, before the engineer issues his certificate of completion of work or a stage thereof, he may ask the contractor to furnish proof that the sub-contractors in question have been paid and, failing such proof, the employer may pay the sub-contractors directly.[37] The parties may, of course, agree that the employer shall pay the sub-contractors directly in any event, *e.g.* on the certificate of the engineer or the main contractor.

The FIDIC Contract further provides[38] that the main contractor shall be responsible for the acts, defaults or neglects of any sub-contractor, his agents, servants or workmen.

The financial arrangement

It is usual for the contractor to provide a *performance guarantee* which is issued by a bank, insurance company or other third party. The guarantee is intended to safeguard the employer against the failure of the contractor to perform his obligations under the contract. That type of guarantee is sometimes combined with a *repayment guarantee*, *viz.* if the employer has paid advances on the contract price and fears that the contractor may not fulfil the terms of the contract. Sometimes the employer will be asked to provide a *payment guarantee*, *e.g.* by a bank in a neutral country such as Switzerland, in order to safeguard any claims by the contractor against the employer, but where the employer is a public authority and in the last resort, the credit of a foreign State is involved, payment guarantees are rarely demanded. These types of contract guarantees have been considered earlier.[39]

It is usual in international construction contracts to provide for *retention money*. The employer is entitled, under the terms of such a contract, to retain, *e.g.* 5 to 10 per cent. of the total price for a specified length of time, *e.g.* six or 12 months, in order to be satisfied that the installation works as promised. The World Bank Guidelines provide[40]:

> Contracts should normally provide for a certain percentage of the total payment to be held as retention money to secure compliance by the contractor.

---

[35] *Ibid.* cls. 3 and 4. The FIDIC Contract requires the employer's consent to be given in writing.
[36] *Ibid.* cl. 59(1).
[37] *Ibid.* cl. 59(5).
[38] *Ibid.* cl. 4.
[39] See p. 81, *ante*.
[40] World Bank Guidelines, Art. 2.13.

In the FIDIC Contract, the percentage of the retention money and its limit is stated in the appendix to the form of tender.

Particular attention has to be paid to the *currency clauses*, especially if the employer has to make payment to joint contractors in different countries or to sub-contractors carrying on business in countries other than that of the main contractor. Both the World Bank Guidelines[41] and the FIDIC Contract[42] contain elaborate provisions relating to payment in foreign currency. In appropriate cases the separation of the money of account and the money of payment, which was discussed earlier,[43] may provide a solution. The contract price would be expressed in the employer's currency which is the money of account, and payment is made in the various currencies of the joint contractors or the main contractor and the sub-contractors, and these are the currencies of payment. Where this device is used it has to be stated at which rate the exchange shall be carried out, *e.g.* the rate governing the exchange shall be that ruling at the date of payment.

Insurance and indemnity clauses

The contract will also have to make provision for insurance and indemnity. The World Bank Guidelines require the types and terms of insurance already to be specified in the tender documents.[44] According to the FIDIC Contract, the contractor has to take out insurance of workmen and for third party risks,[45] but if he fails to do so the employer may insure himself for the account of the contractor.[46]

The FIDIC Contract also provides for indemnities to be given by the contractor as well as by the employer.[47]

Post-contractual problems

An international construction contract normally incorporates many of the clauses discussed earlier[48] in this work, in particular:

the price escalation clause,[48]
the force majeure clause,[49]
the choice of law clause,[50]
the arbitration clause,
the waiver of immunity clause.[50a]

Some of these clauses, such as the arbitration clause, have to be adapted to the special requirements of a long-term construction contract.

---

[41] World Bank Guidelines, Art. 2.10.
[42] FIDIC Contract, cls. 60(3) and 72.
[43] See p. 133, *ante*.
[44] World Bank Guidelines, Art. 2.14.
[45] FIDIC Contract, cl. 24.
[46] *Ibid.* cl. 15.
[47] *Ibid.* cls. 22, 24(1), 65(1).
[48] See p. 53, *ante*.
[49] See p. 121, *ante*.
[50] See p. 128, *ante*.
[50a] State Immunity Act 1978, ss. 2(2) and 9; see p. 134, *ante*.

The arbitration clause

The position with respect to arbitration is complicated by the fact that many of these contracts, particularly those concluded in the FIDIC Contract form, provide for the office of an engineer, an official mediator or intervener who is not an arbitrator but whose functions include the duty of resolving difficulties of technical and similar nature which may arise almost daily. The FIDIC Contract, in its clause on the settlement of disputes,[51] adopts the following procedure. Any dispute or difference between the employer and the contractor or the engineer and the contractor shall be settled by the engineer within 90 days after being requested by either party to do so. If the engineer fails to communicate his decisions in writing within those 90 days to the employer and the contractor, or if either party is dissatisfied with his decision, the matter may be referred to arbitration, but the reference must be made within 90 days from the expiration of the first period of 90 days, or from the date after receiving the engineer's decision, as the case may be. The arbitration shall be held under the Rules of Conciliation and Arbitration of the Court of Arbitration of the ICC.[52] If, after the engineer has given his decision, no application is made for arbitration, the engineer's decision becomes final. As far as possible, work on the installations shall continue, despite the arbitration.

The European Development Fund (EDF) has drafted a detailed *Regulation on the Arbitration of Public Contracts financed by the EDF*,[53] which, however, has not been adopted by the EEC yet. This Draft Regulation does not adopt ICC arbitration but proposes the setting up of an arbitration board, the President of which shall be the President of the Court of Justice of the European Communities at Luxembourg, and the secretary of which shall be an official of that Court. It is proposed that there shall be a panel of arbitrators from which the arbitrator(s) in a particular dispute shall be elected. A sole or a third arbitrator shall not be of the same nationality as the parties to the proceedings. An application may be made in certain circumstances to have the award set aside; such application is made to an arbitration court consisting of three members chosen from the panel of arbitrators and appointed by the President of the arbitration board.

Third person intervention

Experience has shown that in long-term contracts the intervention of a third person mediator, such as the engineer appointed under a FIDIC Contract, can be helpful. A contract may, in the light of circumstances appearing after it has been signed, show defects. There may be lack of precision, the existence of gaps, the possibility of different interpretations, and similar deficiencies. The ICC proposes to set up procedure enabling the parties to a contract to call upon a third person to facilitate the

[51] FIDIC Contract, cl. 67.
[52] See p. 423, *ante*.
[53] EEC Doc. VIII/119/77-E.

implementation of their contract. These proposals are contained in an ICC Brochure entitled *Adaptation of Contracts*.[54] A Standing Committee for the Regulation of Contractual Relations is constituted at the ICC. At any time during their contractual relations, the parties may ask the Standing Committee for the appointment of a third person or a board of three, to fulfil the task which has been contractually assigned to them. These third person interveners do not act as arbitrators. The third person or board must formulate a recommendation or take a decision within 90 days after the file is delivered to them.

In order to make this facility available, the parties have to insert into their contract an appropriate clause. Before so doing, they have to ascertain the legality and effectiveness of the third person's intervention under the law which is applicable. They have also to agree on whether they wish the third party to make only a recommendation or to give a decision. The following are the two model standard clauses suggested by the ICC:

> In the event that the parties are unable to agree to apply all or any of the provisions of article . . . of this contract (or any other appropriate wording chosen by the parties in the particular circumstances of the contract) . . , they shall apply to the Standing Committee for the Regulation of Contractual Relations of the International Chamber of Commerce (ICC) in order that a third person* who shall be appointed in accordance with the Rules on the Regulation of Contractual Relations of the ICC, and who shall carry out his mission in accordance with the said Rules—
>
> *may issue a recommendation***
>
> or
>
> *may on their behalf make a final decision which shall be binding on the parties and shall be deemed to be incorporated in the contract.***
>
> *Should the parties wish to have the decision or recommendation made by a board of three persons instead of by one person, they should make this clear in the clause.
>
> **Only one of these alternatives can be adopted.

Hardship clauses

A problem which is typical for international long-term contracts is this: After the conclusion of the contract, there may have been a fundamental change in the economic or political circumstances, which occurred beyond the control of the parties, and yet the parties are anxious to continue their contractual relations. This fundamental change in the situation is similar to that which gives rise to frustration[55] or the application of a *force majeure* clause,[56] but the intention of the parties is different: they do not wish to dissolve the contract but, on the contrary, wish to continue it. Sometimes the parties are compelled by economic circumstances to consider the continuation rather than the dissolution of their contract, in spite of the changed circumstances. The construction of the factory has to be completed, or the supply of crude oil or natural gas has to be continued, in spite of those changes.

---

[54] ICC Brochure No. 326 (1979).

[55] See p. 109, *ante*.

[56] See p. 121, *ante*.

To meet this situation, the parties sometimes insert into their contract a so-called *hardship clause.*[57] Under this clause the parties are obliged, if such change in circumstances occurs, to enter into negotiations and to seek an adaptation of their contract to them, such as an adjustment of the price, an extension of time for the completion of the work, or other changes in the contract terms as originally arranged. Legally the hardship clause is merely an agreement to agree and, as such, without legal effect, except that it obliges the parties to negotiate. It has therefore to be complemented by a further clause which provides for the contingency of the parties not reaching agreement within a specified time. This complementary clause usually provides for arbitration but it would also be possible to provide that in that contingency either party shall be entitled to give notice of termination of the contract or for another resolution of the deadlock.

The following is an illustration of a hardship clause which is contained in a contract for the supply of natural gas[58]:

> Substantial hardship shall mean if at any time or from time to time during the term of this agreement, without default of the party concerned, there is the occurrence of an intervening event or change of circumstances beyond the said party's control, when acting as a reasonable and prudent operator, such that the consequences and effects of which are fundamentally different from what was contemplated by the parties at the time of entering into this agreement . . . the party claiming that it is placed in such a position as aforesaid may by notice request the other for a meeting to determine if said occurrence has happened and, if so, agree upon what, if any, adjustment in the price then in force under this agreement and/or other terms and conditions thereof is justified in the circumstances, in fairness to the parties to alleviate said consequences and effects of said occurrence. . . .
>
> If the seller(s) and the buyer(s) have not agreed a mutually acceptable solution within 60 days after the notice requesting a meeting . . . either party may request the matter to be submitted to arbitration. . . . The arbitrators shall determine whether the aforesaid occurrence has happened, and if so what adjustments, if any, in the said price or in the other terms and conditions should be made . . . having due regard to the interest of the other party, and any revised prices or other conditions so determined by said arbitrators shall take effect on the date when notice of arbitration was first given. . . .

Liquidated damage and bonus clauses

International construction contracts often contain clauses providing for the payment of liquidated damages by the contractor if the work is not carried out within the stipulated times. The amount of the liquidated damages should be a reasonable estimate of the loss likely to be suffered; it should not be of punitive character because in that case it would be a penalty and may be set aside as such. Further, the clause should provide that no liquidated damages are payable if the contractor is prevented by an event beyond his control from completing the work. The FIDIC Contract also states[59] that if, before the completion of the whole of the works, any part or section of the works has been certified by the engineer as completed

---

[57] B. Oppetit, *L'adaptation des contrats internationaux aux changements de circonstances: la clause 'hardship'*, in *Journal du droit international* (1974), pp. 794 *et seq.*; M. J. Bonell, *Arbitration as a means for the Revision of Contracts*, in Italian National Reports to the Xth International Congress of Comparative Law, Budapest 1978, Milan, Giuffré, 1978, 221; M. Fontaine, "Hardship Clauses" in (1976) 2 P.D.C.I.51.

[58] Oppetit, *loc. cit.*, 812; Bonell, *loc. cit.*, 226.

[59] FIDIC Contract, cl. 47(2).

and occupied or used by the employer, the liquidated damages for delay shall be reduced in the proportion which the value of the part or section so certified bears to the value of the whole of the works.

That a clause stipulating liquidated damages is appropriate in this type of contract, is indicated in the World Bank Guidelines[60]:

> Liquidated damage or similar clauses for an appropriate amount should be included in bidding documents when delays in completion of works or delivery of goods, or failure of the works or goods to meet performance requirements, would result in extra cost, loss of revenues or loss of other benefits to the borrower. Provision may also be made for a bonus to be paid to contractors for completion of contracts ahead of the times specified in the contract when such earlier completion would be of benefit to the borrower.

Clauses providing for bonus payments to the contractor, if he completes the work before the time agreed, are less frequently found than clauses stipulating liquidated damages; they are not provided for in the General Conditions (Pt. I) of the FIDIC Contract but have always to be specified in the Conditions of Particular Application (Pt. II) and in the Form of Tender.

---

[60] World Bank Guidelines, Art. 2.15.

PART FIVE

CUSTOMS LAW

CHAPTER 28

GOVERNMENT REGULATION OF EXPORTS

THE United Kingdom regulation of exports extends to three topics:

(1) the requirement of export licences for the exportation of certain goods,
(2) customs formalities to be complied with on the exportation of goods, and
(3) EEG regulation of free movement of goods.

In addition, the British exporter had to comply with the regulations of the United Kingdom exchange control when it was still in operation.[1] Further, the exporter has to bear in mind the provisions applying to value added tax (VAT) which are likewise administered by customs and excise. These provisions are explained in certain Customs Notices.[2] Goods exported direct by a taxable person to a customer overseas are relieved from VAT by zero-rating. Further, retail export schemes, notably the Personal Export Scheme and the Over-the-Counter Scheme, are admitted.

EXPORT LICENSING

The legislation relating to export licensing deals with "goods" only. This term does not include banknotes, treasury bills, bills of exchange, promissory notes, shares, stock, debentures and similar things in action, and gold bullion, which were exclusively governed by exchange control regulations.[3]

The present system of export licensing comprises the *general control* of exports which applies to the exportation, from the United Kingdom, of specified goods, and the *control of strategic goods* which prohibits, except by licence of the Department of Trade, the disposal of specified goods situate outside the United Kingdom to governments, government agencies, bodies or persons in certain specified countries.

The general control of exports

The general powers of the Department of Trade to regulate the exportations of goods are based on the Import, Export and Customs Powers (Defence) Act 1939, which authorises the Department to make "such provisions as the Department think expedient" for the regulation of the importation into, or exportation from, the United Kingdom of all goods of a specified description. In exercise of these powers the Department of Trade has issued the Export of Goods (Control) Order 1978.[4]

---

[1] Exchange Control was repealed in the U.K. on October 23, 1979.
[2] The most important of them are Customs Notices No. 703 on Value Added Tax—Exports and No. 704 on Value Added Tax—Retail Export Schemes, the former revised October 1975 and the latter July 1976.
[3] Exchange Control Act 1947, s. 22.
[4] S.I. 1978 No. 796; this Order is amended from time to time.

The provisions of the Export of Goods (Control) Order apply to goods intended to be exported from the United Kingdom but, unlike the control of strategic goods,[5] have no extraterritorial effect.

The exporter who wishes to ascertain whether an export licence is required in respect of the particular goods which he intends to export, should obtain a copy of the Order and all amendments to date, or inquire of the Export Licensing Branch of the Department of Trade[6] or his trade association.

The regulation provided by the Order may be summed up as follows:

Goods—this expression includes used and unused goods unless otherwise specified (Art. 1(2))—are divided by the Order into two categories:

1. Goods which do not require an export licence. Hereunder fall most types of consumer goods of ordinary character.
2. Goods, the exportation of which is prohibited or restricted and which require an export licence if their export is intended. Here it is provided (Art. 2):—
   (i) scheduled goods[7] indicated by the letter "A" are prohibited to be exported to any destination;
   (ii) scheduled goods indicated by the letter "T" are prohibited to be exported to any destination except that when in relation to such goods the provisions of Regulation (EEC) 223/77,[8] as amended by Regulation (EEC) 1601/77,[9] relating to the use of Community transit documents requiring anything to be done at or before the time of exportation have been complied with, the goods may be exported to a destination in another Member State;
   (iii) scheduled goods indicated by the letter "E" are prohibited to be exported to any destination except a destination in another Member State;
   (iv) scheduled goods indicated by the letter "C" are prohibited to be exported to any destination except a destination in any country named, or included in a country named, in Schedule 2 hereto;
   (v) scheduled goods consisting of classes of ships indicated by the letter "S" are prohibited to be exported to any destination after delivery, or for the purpose of delivery, directly or indirectly, to a person in Albania, Bulgaria, China, Czechoslovakia, the German Democratic Republic, Hungary, Democratic Kampuchea, the Lao People's Democratic Republic, Mongolia, North Korea, Poland, Romania, the Union of Soviet Socialist Republics and the Socialist Republic of Vietnam;
   (vi) all goods in relation to the export of which from any country an international import certificate has been issued and which have been imported into the United Kingdom are prohibited to be exported to any destination; and
   (vii) goods of any description are prohibited to be exported to any destination in Southern Rhodesia.

Schedule 1, also known as the prohibition list, is too lengthy and technical to be produced here and, besides, is subject to frequent amendments; it is arranged as follows:

Part I	Group A	Goods Specified by Reference to Headings in the common customs tariff of the European Economic Community
	Group B	Documents, Photographic Material and Antiques
Part II	Group 1	Aircraft, Arms and related material, Ammunition, Military Stores and Appliances, and Para-military Police Equipment

---

[5] See p. 464, *post*.

[6] Address: Sanctuary Buildings, 16–20 Great Smith Street, London SW1P 3BD.

[7] "Scheduled goods" are goods described in Sched. 1 to the Export of Goods (Control) Order 1978, as amended.

[8] O.J. No. L38, 9.2.77, p. 1.

[9] O.J. No. L182, 22.7.77, p. 1.

Group 2	Atomic Energy Minerals, Materials and Appliances
Group 3A	Metal Working Machinery and Associated Equipment
Group 3B	Chemical and Petroleum Equipment
Group 3C	Electrical and Power-Generating Equipment
Group 3D	General Industrial Equipment
Group 3E	Compasses, Gyroscopic Apparatus, Marine Equipment and Ships (other than Warships and Naval Equipment)
Group 3F	Electronic Equipment including Communications and Radar
Group 3G	Scientific Instruments and Apparatus, Servo-Mechanisms and Photographic Equipment
Group 3H	Metals, Minerals and their Manufactures
Group 3I	Chemicals, Metalloids and Petroleum Products
Group 3J	Synthetic Film and Synthetic Rubber

The Export Licensing Branch of the Department of Trade will advise whether an export licence is required and provide the appropriate application form.

Even in case of goods which, as a rule, require an export licence, exceptions are admitted. They are stated in article 3 of the Export of Goods (Control) Order 1978, as amended.

Any licence or other permission for the exportation of goods may be modified or revoked at any time by the Department of Trade (Art. 8).

Goods are exported within the Order although, when they are taken out of the country, it is intended to bring them back later. Thus, a traveller in possession of jewellery which she intends to wear abroad, "exports" them and has to declare them on leaving the country, in compliance with what is now article 1(2), although she intends to bring them back and has insured them for the return journey.[10]

The exporter is not entitled to assign the authority to export goods which he is granted by the licence, unless he is expressly authorised by the licence to do so. Normally the licence is not transferable, but in case of bulk shipments or similar exceptional cases the licence may be granted to "X Y or any person or firm authorised in writing by them."

Antiques are works of art manufactured or produced more than 100 years before the date of exportation; they are subject to the requirement of export licensing. But documents, manuscripts and archives, photographic positives and negatives already require a licence if produced more than 70 years before the date of exportation; there exist, however, exceptions, when the 100 year time limit is restored; they extend to:

(i) printed books, printed pamphlets and similar printed matter;
(ii) newspapers, periodicals and magazines;
(iii) postage stamps and other articles of philatelic interest;
(iv) birth, marriage or death certificates or other documents relating to the personal affairs of the exporter or the spouse of the exporter; and
(v) letters or other writings written by or to the exporter or the spouse of the exporter.[11]

The export licence does not authorise the exporter to do an act prohibited by other enactments or regulations such as regulations relating to exchange control, customs or postal matters. The grant of the export licence in the

[10] *R.* v. *Berner* (1953) 37 Cr.App.R. 113.
[11] Group B of Sched. 1 to the Export of Goods (Control) Order 1978, as amended.

United Kingdom does not relieve the exporter from his duty to obtain an import licence in the country of importation if such licence is required there and he has undertaken, by the contract of sale, to procure the import licence.

Control of strategic goods

This control goes beyond the general control of exports in so far as it has extraterritorial effect. Its regulation is contained in the Strategic Goods (Control) Order 1967.[12]

The Order provides that, on principle, no person in the United Kingdom or ordinarily residing therein shall dispose of the goods specified in Schedule I and situate outside the United Kingdom to the government, a government agency or other authority or person in any of the countries specified in Schedule II to the Order. Moreover, such disposal is prohibited "to any person whatsoever" if the United Kingdom resident has reasonable cause to believe that the goods may be imported directly or indirectly into a country specified in that Schedule (Art. 1).

The countries listed in Schedule II are:

Albania, Bulgaria, China, Czechoslovakia, East Germany (Soviet Zone of Germany), Hungary, North Korea, North Vietnam, Poland, Romania, Tibet, U.S.S.R.

The general prohibition of Article 1 does not apply to the disposal of—

(*a*) any goods disposed of under a licence of the Department of Trade, provided that the conditions of the licence are complied with (Art. 2(*a*));
(*b*) direct supplies of ships' stores or stores for an aircraft (Art. 2(*b*));
(*c*) turbine engine fuel supplied directly to any aircraft as fuel (Art. 2(*c*)).

Disposal, within the meaning of the Order, is the

disposal whether inside or outside the United Kingdom and includes disposal of
(*a*) ownership or any proprietary interest; or
(*b*) the right to possession; or
(*c*) possession whether or not accompanied by any disposal of ownership or any proprietary interest or of the right to possession;
but does not include disposal by a carrier (otherwise than by way of sale) in the course of his business as such (Art. 4).

The goods specified in Schedule I to the Strategic Goods (Control) Order are arranged in the same groups as those in Schedule 1 to the Export of Goods (Control) Order but the latter Schedule contains many goods which do not appear in that to the Strategic Goods Order. A dual control of strategic goods is thus provided: if the exportation from the United Kingdom is in question, the Export of Goods (Control) Order applies but if the disposal outside the United Kingdom is in issue the provisions of the Strategic Goods (Control) Order have to be complied with.

[12] S.I. 1967 No. 983. The Strategic Goods (Control) Order is made in pursuance of the powers conferred upon the Board of Trade under ss. 3(1) and 22(3) of the Emergency Laws (Re-anactments and Repeals) Act 1964.

Powers of inquiry and search, penalties

The customs authorities which are charged with the execution of the export licensing regulations exercise wide powers of inquiry and search.[13]

Contraventions of the licensing control may constitute criminal offences.[14]

Transhipment licences

Where goods are brought from overseas to the United Kingdom for transhipment or transit to another overseas country, the regulations in force for transhipment licences have to be complied with.

The then Board of Trade issued an Open General Transhipment Licence, dated April 30, 1965,[15] according to which, subject to certain formalities, the following goods may be imported for transhipment and subsequently exported:

(*a*) goods which are not subject to export control;
(*b*) goods which, though subject to export control, are expressly referred to in the Schedule to the Open Licence.
(*c*) goods (other than aircraft, arms and military stores and appliances) which are to be exported to destinations in the Commonwealth, Ireland, South Africa, South West Africa or the U.S.A.
(*d*) aircraft, arms and military stores and appliances which are to be exported to destinations in the Commonwealth, Ireland or the U.S.A. (goods falling into this category and destined to South Africa or South West Africa require individual licences).

One of the formalities which the Open Licence requires is that the goods are, at the time of their importation, entered with the Commissioners of Customs and Excise for transit or transhipment and exportation; a transhipment bond note and a transhipment shipping bill must be completed and produced to the customs authorities at the place of importation.

Where a licence is required, application should be made to the Import Licensing Branch[16] of the Department of Trade, from which application forms for transhipment licences can be obtained. Application should be made before shipment and must be made by a firm or individual responsible in the United Kingdom.

Customs Regulations

The principal purpose of customs legislation is to secure the payment of customs duties in the interest of the revenue. This explains why the customs formalities, which have to be observed on the exportation of goods from the United Kingdom, depend to some degree on the dutiable character of the goods intended to be exported. Where the exportation does not involve the payment or refund of customs duties, these formalities are relatively simple, but, where the payment or refund of customs duties is involved,

[13] Export of Goods (Control) Order 1978, Arts. 4 and 6.
[14] *Ibid.* Art. 5.
[15] Obtainable from HMSO.
[16] Address: Sanctuary Buildings, 16–20 Great Smith Street, London SW1P 3DB.

as in the case of bonded and drawback goods, the procedure is more complicated. In addition to the task of collecting and safeguarding customs duties, the customs authorities are charged with the executive side of export licensing and exchange control; in the cases in which these regulations apply, the customs requirements are normally, likewise, strict.

The customs requirements to be complied with on exportation of goods from the United Kingdom are laid down in the Customs and Excise Act 1979[17] and in the statutory instruments having effect thereunder. The customs authorities have published a number of important *Customs Notices* which give detailed information on special subjects and can be obtained from the Secretary, Customs and Excise,[18] and any officer of customs and excise.

An "exporter," according to the Customs and Excise Management Act 1979, s. 1(1) includes "the shipper of . . . goods and any person performing in relation to an aircraft functions corresponding with those of a shipper."

Entry and pre-entry of goods

The exporter is required, on exportation of goods which are not community transit goods,[19] to deliver to the proper customs officer a document giving particulars of the goods exported. Where nothing else is required than the delivery of such document on or after the exportation of the goods, the procedure is called "the entry" of goods, but it would be more correct to call it "post-entry" as it need only be completed after exportation of the goods. Where the document has to be delivered before the exportation of the goods and the goods must not be exported until the customs authorities have approved of it, the procedure is called "the pre-entry" of goods. The clearance for entry is effected by the signature of the proper customs officer on the document in question.

The document, which the exporter has to deliver to the Customs authorities on entry or pre-entry of the goods, is a "specification" or a "shipping bill," according to the nature of the intended exports. The first form is less detailed than the latter; both types of returns have to be made on prescribed Customs Forms. On principle, a specification is required for exports that have to be post-entered, while a shipping bill is required for exports which have to be pre-entered.

---

[17] The "Customs and Excise Act 1979" is defined in section 1(1) of the Customs and Excise Management Act 1979 as meaning—
that Act,
the Customs and Excise (General Reliefs) Act 1979,
the Alcoholic Liquor Duties Act 1979,
the Hydrocarbon Oil Duties Act 1979,
the Matches and Mechanical Lighters Duties Act 1979, and
the Tobacco Products Duty Act 1979.

[18] Address: King's Beam House, Mark Lane, London, E.C.3.

[19] For the definition of "Community transit goods" see p. 473, *post*.

Pre-entry

The Customs and Excise Management Act 1979, s. 52, requires "dutiable and restricted goods" to be pre-entered. It defines these goods as follows:

(*a*) goods from warehouse, other than goods which have been kept, without being warehoused, in a warehouse by virtue of section 92(4) below;
(*b*) transit goods;
(*c*) any other goods chargeable with any duty which has not been paid;
(*d*) drawback goods;
(*e*) goods with respect to the exportation of which any restriction is for the time being in force under or by virtue of any enactment;
(*f*) any goods required by or under any provision of this Act other than a provision of this Part or by or under a provision of any other Act to be entered before exportation or before shipment for exportation or as stores.

"Other" provisions of the Act of 1979 which require the pre-entry of goods are sections 75 and 76. The goods referred to therein are explosives within the meaning of the Explosives Act 1875.

Entry

In all cases in which a pre-entry is not required, a post-entry after exportation of the goods is sufficient. The Customs and Excise Management Act 1979 provides in section 54(2) that "the form of entries . . ., the particulars to be contained therein and the manner of their delivery shall be such as the Commissioners may from time to time direct."

Goods exported by post need not be entered or pre-entered by means of a specification or shipping bill but are subject to special rules,[20] unless a drawback is claimed in respect of them.[21]

The entry and pre-entry of goods should not be confused with the entry outwards of the ship. This is a declaration which the master of the ship has to make to the customs authority on a prescribed form before commencing to load an export cargo. The purpose of the entry outwards of the ship is to warn the customs authorities of the intended departure of the ship. The exporter has nothing to do with the completion of that form.

Tariff requirements for exports

The exporter is required to enter or pre-enter exported goods on the specification or shipping bill in accordance with the description of the goods in the Tariff and Overseas Trade Classification of the United Kingdom and Northern Ireland, briefly known as the *Tariff*.[22]

The *Tariff* is based on the internationally agreed *Brussels Nomenclature* which is also the basis of the *Common Customs Tariff* (CCT) of the EEC. The Brussels Nomenclature was devised by the Customs Co-operation

---

[20] See p. 471, *post*.
[21] See p. 469, *post*.
[22] HMSO (loose leaf, with frequent Supplements). The present Tariff came into force on July 1, 1977. Each item has a Tariff/Trade Code Number which is unique to that commodity and serves to identify imported and exported goods on customs documents. The same identification number is used for statistical purposes, and also for re-exports.

Council (CCC) which was established by a Convention in 1950 and has its seat in Brussels, but is not connected with the EEC. The Brussels Nomenclature is based on a Convention of December 15, 1950, and was revised with effect from January 1, 1965. It is a highly successful measure aiming at the international unification of the classification of goods for customs purposes.[23] Certain minor changes in the wording of the published international text of the Brussels Nomenclature have been made in the United Kingdom Tariff for legal reasons but these do not affect the practical scope of the headings. This Nomenclature provides a systematic classification of all the goods of international commerce, designed to ensure, with the aid of general Interpretative Rules and Notes to the sections and chapters, that each article falls to be classified in one place and in one place only within the Nomenclature Tariff.[24]

In the introductory part of the *Tariff* the general requirements of customs export documentation are explained. Reference is made to the Customs Assigned Number (CAN) which the exporter can obtain and the use of which greatly simplifies the customs procedure.[25] That part of the *Tariff* gives detailed information on trade statistics, the forms to be used and the significance of CAN, mixed goods, the particulars to be given on the forms, where to lodge export documents, Common Agricultural Policy (CAP) licences, and CAP export refunds and export levies.

Under particulars to be given on the customs forms the following items are explained: CAN, Tariff heading number, EEC trade, ship/flight etc., country of destination, final destination, description of goods, port/airport of export, inland clearance depot (ICD), goods in containers, roll on/roll off road traffic (known as ro/ro), packages, marks and numbers etc., Tariff/Trade Code number, quantities, value, licence particulars.

The value to be declared on export documents is the f.o.b. value of the goods although it is no longer described as such.[26] The description which the *Tariff* gives is this:

> The value to be declared on customs documents is the cost, to the nearest pound sterling, of the goods to the purchaser abroad (or if there is no sale, the price which the goods would fetch if sold to a purchaser abroad), including packing, inland and coastal transport in the United Kingdom, dock dues, loading charges and all other costs, profits, charges and expenses (*e.g.* insurance and commission) accruing up to the point where the goods are deposited on board the exporting vessel or aircraft or at the land boundary of Northern Ireland. For goods re-exported after process in the United Kingdom the value to be declared must include the charge for the process and the value of the goods when imported.
>
> In all cases, outwards sea or air freight and marine or air insurance should be excluded, and cash and trade discounts to the purchaser abroad deducted.

---

[23] Approximately 120 countries use Brussels-type tariffs.

[24] There exists also a *Guide to the Classification for Overseas Statistics*, 1974, HMSO.

[25] Customs and Excise Management Act 1979, s. 55. Customs Notice No. 275 explains how a CAN number can be obtained and used.

[26] The import value of goods traded in the United Kingdom under a trade name includes the "uplift": *Rolex Watch Co. Ltd.* v. *Commissioners of Customs and Excise* [1956] 1 W.L.R. 612.

Goods other than bonded or drawback goods[27]

It has been seen that these goods were, and in some instances still are, privileged in comparison with bonded or drawback goods in so far as they require merely an entry and not a pre-entry.

The specification has to be given on a prescribed customs form which can be obtained from the local offices of H.M. Customs.[28] The form most frequently used for the post-entry relating to the produce and manufactures of the United Kingdom is Customs Form C.273. For the pre-entry, normally Forms C.63 and 63A are required; where no export licence is required, Form C.63 should be used; where the goods have to be pre-entered by reason of export licensing requirements,[29] Form C.63A has to be completed. In the case of pre-entry, the shipping bill is produced to the customs officer at the port of exportation before the shipment of the goods. The goods have likewise to be produced; the customs officer examines the goods and documents, enters particulars of examination on the bill, and certifies that the goods may be shipped; the goods together with the shipping bill are then taken aboard ship; the master, mate or other authorised person acknowledges receipt on the bill which is returned to the customs house.

The re-exportation of imported goods, on which customs duties have been paid or which were imported free of duty and for which no drawback is claimed, is entered by specification (Customs Form C.273) unless an export licence is required in which case the appropriate Form C.63A has to be completed.

Bonded and drawback goods

Bonded goods are goods liable to import duties which are imported without payment of duties and kept in an approved warehouse until payment of the duties; the keeper of the warehouse gives a bond to the customs authorities as a security for his obligations. Many dutiable commodities are stored in such bonded warehouses where they can be inspected by customers of the importer; when the goods are sold for home consumption, duties are paid and they are released from bond; when they are unsaleable in this country, the importer tries to export them to another country. No manufacturing process is allowed on the goods while lying in a bonded warehouse.

Drawback goods are goods on which import duties or excise duties have been paid but which are entitled to a refund of the whole or part of the duties when the goods are exported in accordance with certain conditions. In some cases drawback is granted where the goods are exported in the same state as imported or have undergone a process which has not changed their form or character. In other cases, drawback is granted when the

---

27 Export goods other than bonded or drawback goods are sometimes referred to as "free goods," but this term is avoided here because, in present-day circumstances, it is liable to be misunderstood.

28 For these addresses, see the *Tariff*.

29 See p. 461, *ante*.

goods have been used for a specified purpose of manufacture, *e.g.* leather has been used for the manufacture of shoes for export, or sugar for beer brewed for export. The law relating to drawback is contained in the Import Duties Act 1958,[30] s. 9 and Sched. 5, and general provisions relating to drawbacks are contained in the Customs and Excise Management Act 1979, ss. 119 *et seq*. The rates of drawback for the various species of goods are stated in the *Tariff*. General information as to the procedure to be followed by exporters claiming drawback for exported goods is published in various Customs Notices obtainable from any collector of customs and excise.

The customs requirements for the exportation of goods ex bonded warehouse or subject to drawback claims are much stricter than those applying to other goods. Numerous forms of shipping bills and other official forms are in use when these goods are exported, and the exporter, when carrying out these transactions for the first time, might experience difficulties in ascertaining the correct customs form required for the contemplated transaction, unless he asks the customs office for guidance, but after the first few transactions a routine will develop. As a rule, the exporter has to give a bond for due shipment or, if a series of transactions is contemplated, has to give a general bond. The exporter can withdraw goods from a bonded warehouse only on a "bond warrant"; attached to this document is the "warehouse keeper's order" which has to be signed by the proper customs officer; the duly signed order is produced to the warehouse keeper who releases the goods to a licensed carman or lighterman for conveyance to the exporting ship. The goods have to be pre-entered for exports on the appropriate shipping bill and proper clearance has to be obtained.

Special arrangements are made for an examination of goods, for which drawback is claimed, on the premises of the exporter. The exporter has to give the customs officer "notice to pack" in writing at least twenty-four hours before the packing is to commence and has to enclose with the notice the shipping bill and other documents. A printed notice to pack forms part of many shipping bills. Although the goods have been examined and sealed at the premises of the exporter, they have to be produced—though, as a rule, not to be opened—at the port of shipment together with the shipping bill because the customs officer in attendance at the port has to certify the exportation of the goods as a condition precedent to the drawback claim.

In case of drawback goods, the shipping bill contains the drawback claim of the exporter, including particulars of his claim and his duly signed declaration that the goods to which the drawback claim refers do not contravene export control regulations and that, if called upon, documentary proof of the correctness of the statements in the shipping bill will be produced.

---

[30] The Import Duties Act 1958 is, in part, repealed by the Customs and Excise (General Reliefs) Act 1979 but the provisions referred to in the text are not repealed.

Goods exported by parcel post

Goods other than drawback goods may be exported by parcel post without being pre-entered or post-entered for customs. A customs declaration has to be completed which can be obtained from a post office. The form, together with the postal dispatch note, has to be handed to the post office when the goods are posted. The exporter has to state, on the customs declaration, whether the goods are exported under an export licence (in which case the licence has to be attached), whether the goods are exported under a general licence (number and date of which has to be given), or whether they are not prohibited to be exported.

Two kinds of customs declarations are in use, namely,

(*a*) an adhesive form which is affixed to the parcel; an alternative tie-on version of the adhesive form may be used in appropriate cases. This form is mainly used for parcels to destinations in the EEC, in Commonwealth countries and the Irish Republic[31];

(*b*) a non-adhesive form. This form is prescribed for most foreign countries. It requires more details of the consignment than the adhesive form; thus, the description of outer packing and of any special marks and the country of production or manufacture have to be stated on the non-adhesive form, and a postal despatch note has to be sent with it.

The adhesive form thus simplifies the customs requirements and where it is possible to use it the exporter has to complete one form only instead of two. For letters and small parcels the green label statement of contents is sufficient.

Where goods on which drawback is claimed are sent by parcel post, shipping bills have to be completed.

Return of unused imports

An importer is entitled[32] to claim from the Commissioners repayment of any import duty, subject to such conditions as the Commissioners may impose, where it is shown—

(*a*) that goods were imported in pursuance of a contract of sale and that the description, quality, state or condition of the goods was not in accordance with the contract or that the goods were damaged in transit; and

(*b*) that the importer with the consent of the seller either—

(i) returned the goods unused to the seller and for that purpose complied with the provisions of section 53 of this Act as to [pre-entry] in like manner as if they had been dutiable or restricted goods for the purposes of Part V of this Act; or

(ii) destroyed the goods unused.

No repayment of import duties can be claimed for goods imported on approval, or on sale or return, or on similar terms.[33]

---

[31] The countries for which the adhesive form may be used are listed in the current *Post Office Guide*.

[32] By virtue of the Customs and Excise Management Act 1979, s. 123.

[33] In the case of a non-trader, the value of goods for import duties is the price paid abroad by a non-trader for such goods, plus freight and expenses, see *Salomon* v. *Customs and Excise Commissioners* [1967] 2 Q.B. 116.

Goods in transit

Special provisions exist for goods consigned from an overseas destination to another place overseas and being in transit in the United Kingdom. If the goods are Community transit goods,[34] the observations made later[35] apply. But goods in transit may also be goods which have not been imported from another Community country or are not destined for such a country. Often these goods are shipped on a through bill of lading, sometimes they are exported in the same vessel that imported them, but sometimes they are transhipped in the same port or another port. These provisions likewise apply where goods in transit pass through an approved airport or over the land frontier of Northern Ireland. Goods imported for transit or transhipment are not liable to import duty.

Strict customs formalities are provided to ensure that the same goods that were imported are, in fact, exported. Lighters and cars which are licensed to carry transhipment goods are secured by Crown locks and accompanied by customs officials, and transit goods removed from one port to another have to be conveyed in bonded railway trucks or lorries. Goods must be removed from the place of importation to that of exportation with all reasonable dispatch, and a time limit may be set for this. As a general rule, transit and transhipment operations should be completed within one month of the importation of the goods, but an extension may be granted if sufficient cause is shown.

In some instances, an export licence is required for transhipment goods.[36] The licence has to be produced together with the shipping bill and bond note which have to be prominently marked with the number and date of the licence on the top left-hand corner of these documents.

FREE MOVEMENT OF COMMUNITY GOODS

The EEC Treaty of May 25, 1957, to which the United Kingdom acceded on January 22, 1972 with effect from January 1, 1973, provides for the free movement of goods in the Community territory.[37] This aim entails the operation of a customs union. Within the territory of that customs union there shall be a free circulation (*libre pratique*) of Community goods from one member country to another which shall not be impeded by internal tariffs or other obstacles and the whole territory of the union is protected against imports from other countries by a common external tariff (CET), usually referred to as the Common Customs Tariff (CCT).

Following a transitional period which terminated on July 1, 1977, the customs union has been accomplished with effect to all nine member countries of the EEC. The main measures concerning Community transit of goods are:

---

[34] For a definition of Community transit goods see p. 473, *post*.
[35] See p. 473, *post*.
[36] See p. 465, *ante*.
[37] EEC Treaty, Arts. 9–37.

Council Regulation of December 13, 1976 on Community Transit (222/77),[38] and
Council Regulation of December 22, 1976 on provisions for the implementation of the Community transit procedure and for simplifications of that procedure (223/77).[39]

The Customs and Excise Duties (General Reliefs) Act 1979, s. 1(2), provides that goods may be relieved from customs duty in the United Kingdom if that is necessary or expedient with a view to:

(*a*) conforming with any Community obligations; or
(*b*) otherwise affording relief provided for by or under the Community Treaties or any decisions of the representatives of the governments of the member States of the Coal and Steel Community meeting in Council.

Customs and Excise have published a series of informative Customs Notices on Community transit.[40]

Central concepts

The free movement of goods in the EEC is founded on three central concepts which require further consideration, *viz.* those of Community goods, the free circulation of goods, and the Common Customs Tariff.

Community goods

They are defined[41] as:

(*a*) goods which wholly originate in the Community, and
(*b*) goods other than those of (*a*) which are in free circulation.

Community goods are entitled to Community treatment in any Member State of the EEC.

There exists a definition of Community transit goods.[42] The term means:

(*a*) in relation to imported goods,
  (i) goods which have been imported under the internal or external Community transit procedure for transit through the United Kingdom with a view to exportation where the importation was and the transit and exportation are to be part of one Community operation; or
  (ii) goods which have, at the port or airport at which they were imported, been placed under the internal or external Community transit procedure for transit through the United Kingdom with a view to exportation where the transit and exportation are to be part of one Community transit operation;
(*b*) in relation to goods for exportation,
  (i) goods which have been imported as mentioned in paragraph (*a*)(i) of this definition and are to be exported as part of the Community transit operation in the course of which they were imported; or

---

[38] O.J. 1977/L 38/1.

[39] O.J. 1977/L 38/20. A Draft Export Directive of the EEC has been published. It aims at the simplification of Community transit procedures. This measure will require certain changes in the U.K. customs procedure relating to Community transit; see *Trade and Industry*, April 13, 1979.

[40] The most important of these Customs Notices are: No. 750 (Community Transit), No. 750A (List of Community Transit Offices), No. 751 (1) Completion of Community Transit forms, (2) Use of loading lists as parts of Community Transit documents), No. 755 (Special Control Procedures), No. 827 (EEC Exports Preference Procedures), No. 828 (EEC Preferences; Rules of Origin).

[41] In Customs Notice No. 750, Appendix C.

[42] Customs and Excise Management Act 1979, s. 1(1). Community transit goods do not require a customs pre-entry or entry; see *ante*.

(ii) goods which have, under the internal or external Community transit procedure, transited the United Kingdom from the port or airport at which they were imported and are to be exported as part of the Community transit operation which commenced at that port or airport.

Free circulation

This means:

the ability of goods to move within the EEC without liability to customs import charges. Goods imported into the Community are in free circulation if all the import formalities in the Member State where they are imported are completed and all the customs import charges due are paid and not repaid in whole or part.[43]

By applying the concept of free circulation status the Community avoids, in the great majority of cases, the need for certificates of origin for Community goods—a considerable simplification of export documentation.[44]

The Common Customs Tariff

The CCT is founded on the Brussels Nomenclature which has been considered earlier.[45] The Nomenclature is accepted by all Member States and the Community itself.

Community Transit Certificates

The movement of goods in the Community across the frontiers of the Member States is carried out on the basis of Community Transit Certificates.[46] The purpose of these certificates[47] is to prove to the customs authorities of the importing country that the goods are entitled to free circulation status. These documents must, therefore, be certified by the customs of the exporting member State. The movement certificates are issued on so-called T Forms. Goods which pass between member States without T Forms are regarded as not being in free circulation and are charged duty at the full rate under the CCT and any agricultural levy.

Forms T1 and T2

These forms are appropriate in the following cases:

T1 status is attributed to

(*a*) goods for which an export refund is claimed under the Common Agricultural Policy (CAP) provisions; and

---

[43] Customs Notice No. 750, Appendix C.

[44] There exists Council Regulation 802/68 of June 27, 1968 on the Common Definition of the Concept of the Origin of Goods (J.O. 1968 L 148/1; O.J. 1968, 165).

[45] See p. 467, *ante*.

[46] The law regulating the movement of goods in the EEC is contained in Regulations and decisions of the Community authorities. The most important of them are Regulations 222/17, 223/77, and 1617/69 and 1461/73. The movement procedure is explained in the Customs Notices referred to in n. 40, *ante*. See also A. G. Walker, *Export Practice and Documentation* (2nd ed., 1977), Chap. 12.

[47] "Movement Certificates" are also used in connection with other EEC procedures, *e.g.* when a preferential rate of duty is allowable in respect of goods traded with certain non-Community countries. These should not be confused with CT Movement Certificates.

(*b*) goods which are, or which include, imported goods which
(i) have not completed the appropriate United Kingdom import formalities, and/or
(ii) either have not borne the appropriate charges or are, or will be the subject of a claim for repayment of all or part of such charges to which they are liable.

T2 status is attributed to goods for which a T1 declaration is not obligatory.

It appears, therefore, that the T2 Form is the one applicable for most Community goods.

CT movement certificates

In addition, there exist CT movement certificates. Their only function is to provide evidence of Community status. Despite their name, they do not affect normal customs requirements for the movement of goods and need not accompany goods during their movement. They do not replace any customs entry document. Normally they cannot be used if the goods are moved under the full CT procedure.

There are three types of CT movement certificates: Forms T2L, DD3 and DD5. Form DD5 is used only by Community fishing vessels.

Form T2L may be used only for movements of Community goods directly transported, *i.e.* if they do not pass through the territory of a non-Community country, except Austria and Switzerland, or if they pass through the territory of a non-Community country under cover of a single transport document made out in a member state; further, Form T2L can only be used if the use of the full CT procedure is not obligatory.

Form DD3 is used for Community goods (with certain exceptions) consigned to a non-Community country, other than Austria or Switzerland, and expected to be reconsigned to a Member State. This form is valid for six months only. No process may be carried out on the goods and they must be reimported into the Community in exactly the same state in which they were exported. This form may be issued in conjunction with a T form if the goods are to travel under the full CT procedure to the point at which they leave Community territory.

TIR and ATA carnets

The full CT procedure need not be used for goods travelling under ATA carnet. It must not be used for goods covered by TIR carnet.

The TIR procedure must not be used for movements wholly within the Community territory. It may be used for movements involving Member States if:

(i) the movement begins or ends outside the Community, Austria or Switzerland; or
(ii) the goods leave and re-enter the Community in the course of the movement; or
(iii) the consignment is for split delivery to destinations in the Community and in Austria or Switzerland; or
(iv) the consignment is for split delivery to destinations both in the Community, Austria or Switzerland and in another non-Community country.

A TIR movement must be covered by a Form T2L if delivery of the goods is intended in a Community country, Austria or Switzerland, but no

CT movement certificate will be issued for goods travelling under TIR carnet in the circumstances of (i) or (iii) above.

The full CT procedure

The full CT procedure is an intra-Community transit procedure to facilitate the movement of goods between Member States by reducing border formalities and avoiding the use of different national transit procedures. Forms T1 or T2, which are used here, act both as transit documents and as evidence as to whether or not the goods are entitled to intra-Community rates of import charge. If it is used for goods which are not entitled to intra-Community rates but are entitled to some other preferential rate (*e.g.* under a Free Trade Agreement with a non-Community country) the appropriate evidence of entitlement, such as a certificate of origin, must be produced with the Form when customs entry is made for the goods in the Member State of destination. The use of the full CT procedure as a transit system is on principle obligatory, but in some circumstances, which are explained in Customs Notice No. 750, its use is optional.[48]

In the full CT procedure the T Forms are used in the following manner. Each of the T Forms is issued in a set of four copies. Copy 1 is retained by the customs office of departure. Copies 2, 3 and 4 are returned to the exporter after authentication by that office and must eventually be produced with the goods at the customs office of destination. The latter returns copy 3 to the customs office of departure as proof of the export and retains copy 4. In certain circumstances a control copy T Form must accompany the other copies as copy 5. The usual purpose of the control copy is to provide proof of arrival and/or evidence that the goods have been put to a particular use.

There also exists the article 41 procedure.[49] It is available when export entry is made before exportation at the point of exit from the United Kingdom and the goods are to be entered through customs at the point of importation into the next Member State. This procedure is used instead of the normal Form T2 but only two copies are completed.

Full CT procedure guarantees

Exporters starting an operation under the full CT procedure must, except in the cases listed in Customs Notice No. 750,[50] have guarantee cover in respect of the duty and similar charges which may become payable on the goods in the course of the transit operation as the result of any irregularity. This is required whether or not the goods are in free circulation. The guarantee will normally take the form of a written contract of guarantee

[48] Customs Notice No. 750, para. 16.

[49] The name is derived from Art. 41 of Reg. 542/22, now repealed.

[50] Customs Notice No. 750, para. 36. These exceptions include passage by sea and passage by air by an approved airline (most airlines operating frequent flights between the U.K. and other member States are approved for this purpose; if in doubt, the customs office should be consulted).

given by a person or organisation other than the exporter. Where a CT guarantee covers the movement of the goods in the United Kingdom any security which might normally be required for that movement under a United Kingdom national procedure need not be provided.

Various types of guarantees are in use, such as individual guarantees, comprehensive guarantees, and flat-rate guarantees.[51]

Transit through Austria and Switzerland

The Community Transit (CT) system and its various subsidiary and simplified procedures are available for movements of goods which:

(*a*) cross Austria or Switzerland during a movement between two points in the Community, or
(*b*) are reconsigned from Austria or Switzerland after deposit, up to a limited period in a bonded warehouse, or
(*c*) move to Austria or Switzerland from a point in the Community, or vice versa.

These arrangements are intended to facilitate the passage of goods which cross Austria or Switzerland en route from one point in the Community to another or which cross part of the Community to or from Austria or Switzerland. Austria and Switzerland are not members of the European Community and the use of Community transit documentation for trade through or with these two countries does not confer any entitlement to preferential duty rates upon Community goods entering Austria or Switzerland or on Austrian or Swiss goods entering the Community.[52]

EEC preference arrangements

Some countries which are not members of the EEC grant imports from an EEC country preferential tariff treatment. These countries are:

(*a*) the EFTA countries which have not joined the EEC, *viz.* Austria, Finland, Iceland, Norway, Portugal (including the Azores and Madeira), Sweden and Switzerland (including Liechtenstein);
(*b*) Cyprus;
(*c*) Israel;
(*d*) Malta;
(*e*) Spain; and
(*f*) those countries which receive preferences from the EEC and which, though not required to do so, give a preference to EEC originating goods.

The exporter in the EEC country has to comply with certain requirements to enable his customer in the preference-giving non-EEC country to claim preferential treatment.[53] The basic condition is that the exported goods must comply with the origin rules governing the particular preference. Those origin rules vary in the preference-giving countries and the exporter must satisfy himself that the goods he is exporting comply with the rules for the particular country of destination. The rules of origin are set out in

[51] The U.K. flat-rate guarantors are listed in Appendix E of Customs Notice No. 750.
[52] See Customs Notice No. 750B.
[53] These requirements are stated in Customs Notice No. 827.

Customs Notice No. 828. The exporter has to supply his customer with a prescribed certificate of origin which will normally be movement certificate EUR1 (C1299); that form is endorsed by the customs authority of the exporting country. A different form can be used for certain low-value or postal exportations; in those cases Form EUR2 (C1297), which does not require endorsement by the customs authority, is sufficient. In the case of private exportations of small value no form is required at all. It should, however, be emphasised that the use of forms is not obligatory. Their use is necessary only if the exported goods qualify as originating and preferential admission into the importing country is to be claimed. Often the certificate of origin can be certified by the local chamber of commerce. A movement certificate must normally be produced for the customs authorities of the importing country within a specified period after endorsement in the exporting country. For Spain certificates are valid for two months, for the EFTA countries four months, and for Cyprus, Israel and Malta five months.[54]

The exporter may be called upon to give supporting evidence showing that the particulars of the certificate of origin are correct. Untrue information given to Customs and Excise may in certain circumstances be a customs offence. If no verifying evidence is forthcoming, when required, the customs authorities of the importing country will normally require the importer to pay the full non-preferential duties and may also impose a penalty.

The range of goods admissible for preference in the preference-giving countries, the preferential rates of duty, the application of quota requirements and the consignment rules vary considerably in the preference-giving countries. Information about the availability of a preference and the preferential rate should, if required by the exporter, be sought from the customer in the country concerned or from the Department of Trade, Overseas Tariffs and Regulations Section (OTAR).[55]

As a general rule there can be no entitlement to both export relief in the EEC and preferential tariff treatment, at least not in an EFTA country. Such export relief is sometimes available in the EEC; it means the suspension or reimbursement of import duties on goods which are exported in the form of compensating products from an inward processing relief arrangement but it does not include relief from CAP levies and variable charges, payment of export refunds, or relief from, or repayment of, excise duties.[56] As an exception to the general rule, export relief can be claimed as follows:

(a) *Exports to EFTA countries.* When the relief claim is restricted to:
(i) materials originating in the EEC or the EFTA countries and imported from those countries;

[54] *Ibid.* para. 19.
[55] Address: Export House, 50 Ludgate Hill, London EC4M 7HU (Tel. 01-248 5757).
[56] Customs Notice No. 827, para. 7.

(ii) materials imported from other countries of a kind which are not covered by the EEC-EFTA Agreements; and

(iii) packing regarded as forming a whole with the goods it contains, except packing in which goods are put up for retail sale.

(*b*) *Exports to other countries.* A declaration that goods are originating can be made even if export relief is being claimed.

CUSTOMS OFFENCES

The Commissioners of Customs and Excise administer, in addition to the regulation of the customs, the executive provisions of the law relating to exchange control, export and import licensing, European Community regulation of the free movement of goods, and VAT taxation. The measures dealing with these topics contain in many instances criminal provisions requiring that offences against them should have consequences similar to customs offences. The concept of the customs offence is thus much wider than merely constituting an infringement of the Customs and Excise Acts and the regulations made thereunder.

The Customs Acts provide heavy fines and terms of imprisonment for persons contravening the Customs regulations.[57] The goods in respect of which the offence is committed may be treated as "prohibited goods" and declared as forfeited.[58] In particular, section 68 of the Customs and Excise Management Act 1979 provides that a person who exports, or brings to any place in the United Kingdom for the purpose of export, goods, the exportation of which is prohibited or restricted, shall be liable to a penalty of three times the value of the goods[59] or £100, whichever is the greater, and the goods shall be liable to forfeiture. If the offence is committed knowingly, the penalty may be imprisonment.[60]

Section 68(2) extends criminal liability to any person knowingly "concerned in the exportation" of goods which require an export licence. Activities which amount to being "concerned in the exportation" are not limited to those of actually taking the goods out of the country, but a person can be "concerned in the exportation" by doing things in advance of the time when the ship or aircraft leaves, *e.g.* by handing over the goods to the buyer's agent the night before the ship or aircraft leaves, knowing

---

[57] On the burden of proof in Customs prosecutions, see p. 480, *post*.

[58] On service abroad in condemnation proceedings under what is now Sched. 3 to the Customs and Excise Management Act 1979, see *Commissioners of Customs and Excise* v. *I.F.S. Irish Fully Fashioned Stockings Ltd.* [1957] 1 W.L.R. 397. Forfeiture proceedings are procedures *in rem*; this means that the only question is whether the goods are liable to forfeiture; it is irrelevant who has imported them or whether they were unsolicited goods; *Denton* v. *Jones* [1971] 1 W.L.R. 1426 (Rhodesian stamps).

[59] On the calculation of the value of the goods, see *Byrne* v. *Low* [1972] 1 W.L.R. 1282.

[60] What is now s. 68 (then s. 56 of the Customs and Excise Act 1952) was applied to an illict export to Rhodesia, when exportation to that country became prohibited, but in the case before the court the offence was not committed knowingly: *Super-heater Co. Ltd.* v. *Commissioners of Customs and Excise* [1969] 1 W.L.R. 858. This provision also applies to Exchange Control offences, as the Exchange Control Act 1947 refers to Customs offences; it was applied to a person engaged in smuggling banknotes out of the United Kingdom: *R.* v. *Goswami* [1969] 1 Q.B. 453.

that the agent will take the goods out of the country without licence.[61] If a conspiracy to commit an offence in England is committed abroad, the English courts have jurisdiction to convict a conspirator who in pursuance of the conspiratorial intent, and without having abandoned it, comes to England.[62]

Where patented goods, without being licensed by the owner of the patent, are imported into the United Kingdom, the customs authorities must disclose the names of the importers to the owner of the patent because the illicit importation constitutes a tort against the owner of the patent and every person who, though innocently, becomes involved in tortious acts of others, comes under a duty to assist the injured person by giving him full information by way of discovery, although he personally may not be liable in damages to the third person.[63] Where whisky worth £7000 (not including excise duty) in transit to a destination abroad was stolen from the transporting vehicle in the United Kingdom, the owner had to pay the (unpaid) excise duty of some £30,000.[64]

The burden of proof that the goods have been lawfully imported and Customs duties have been paid on them, rests on the importer[65]; he has to establish his innocence in all cases where he is prosecuted, and not merely in those cases where the goods have been seized by the Customs authorities.[66] The offence of dealing with uncustomed goods with intent to defraud the revenue of import duties or purchase tax can be committed anywhere in the realm and not merely at the port of entry.[67] But if on importation of goods a customs officer mistakenly undervalues the goods, without having been misled by an untrue statement of the importer (who realises that the officer made a mistake), no customs offence is committed.[68]

---

[61] *Garrett* v. *Arthur Churchill* (*Glass*) *Ltd.* [1970] 1 Q.B. 92.

[62] *R.* v. *Doot* [1973] A.C. 807.

[63] *Norwich Pharmacal Co.* v. *Customs and Excise Commissioners* [1974] A.C. 133.

[64] *James Buchanan & Co. Ltd.* v. *Babco Forwarding and Shipping* (*U.K.*) *Ltd.* [1978] A.C. 141.

[65] Customs and Excise Management Act 1979, s. 154(2).

[66] *R.* v. *Fitzpatrick* [1948] 1 All E.R. 769.

[67] *Beck* v. *Binks* [1949] 1 K.B. 250.

[68] *Customs and Excise Commissioners* v. *Tan* [1977] A.C. 650 (Customs officer asked importer at airport what two jade pendants which she had bought in China for £8,300 were worth and she replied that she did not know. The officer valued them £50 and charged the duty at £12.50. She sold one pendant for £8,400. No customs offence was committed).

APPENDICES

APPENDIX 1

INSURANCE OF EXPORTS[1]

Marine Insurance Act 1906

FIRST SCHEDULE

FORM OF POLICY[2]

BE IT KNOWN THAT as well in own name as for and in the name and names of all and every other person or persons to whom the same doth, may, or shall appertain, in part or in all doth make assurance and cause and them, and every of them, to be insured lost or not lost, at and from Upon any kind of goods and merchandises, and also upon the body, tackle, apparel, ordnance, munition, artillery, boat, and other furniture, of and in the good ship or vessel called the whereof is master under God, for this present voyage, or whosoever else shall go for master in the said ship, or by whatsoever other name or names the said ship, or the master thereof, is or shall be named or called; beginning the adventure upon the said goods and merchandises from the loading thereof aboard the said ship,
upon the said ship, &c.
and so shall continue and endure, during her abode there, upon the said ship, &c. And further, until the said ship, with all her ordnance, tackle, apparel, &c., and goods and merchandises whatsoever shall be arrived at upon the said ship, &c., until she hath moored at anchor twenty-four hours in good safety; and upon the goods and merchandises, until the same be there discharged and safely landed. And it shall be lawful for the said ship, &c., in this voyage, to proceed and sail to and touch and stay at any ports or places whatsoever without prejudice to this insurance. The said ship, &c., goods and merchandises, &c., for so much as concerns the assured by agreement between the assured and assurers in this policy, are and shall be valued at

Touching the adventures and perils which we the assurers are contented to bear and do take upon us in this voyage: they are of the seas, men of war, fire, enemies, pirates, rovers, thieves, jettisons, letters of mart and countermart, surprisals, takings at sea, arrests, restraints, and detainments of all kings, princes, and people, of what nation, condition, or quality soever, barratry of the master and mariners, and of all other perils, losses, and misfortunes, that have or shall come to the hurt, detriment, or damage of the said goods and merchandises, and ship, &c., or any part thereof. And in case of any loss or misfortune it shall be lawful to the assured, their factors, servants and assigns, to sue, labour, and travel for, in and about the defence, safeguards, and recovery of the said goods and merchandises, and ship, &c., or any part thereof, without prejudice to this insurance; to the charges whereof we, the assurers, will contribute each one according to the rate and quantity of his sum herein assured. And it is especially declared and agreed that no acts of the insurer or insured in recovering, saving, or preserving the property insured shall be considered as a waiver, or acceptance of abandonment. And it is agreed by us,

---

[1] p. 288, *ante*.
[2] p. 308, *ante*.

the insurers, that this writing or policy of assurance shall be of as much force and effect as the surest writing or policy of assurance heretofore made in Lombard Street, or in the Royal Exchange, or elsewhere in London. And so we, the assurers, are contented, and do hereby promise and bind ourselves, each one for his own part, our heirs, executors, and goods to the assured, their executors, administrators, and assigns, for the true performance of the premises, confessing ourselves paid the consideration due unto us for this assurance by the assured, at and after the rate of

IN WITNESS whereof we, the assurers, have subscribed our names and sums assured in London.

N.B.—Corn, fish, salt, fruit, flour, and seed are warranted free from average, unless general, or the ship be stranded—sugar, tobacco, hemp, flax, hides and skins are warranted free from average, under five pounds per cent., and all other goods, also the ship and freight, are warranted free from average, under three pounds per cent. unless general, or the ship be stranded.

RULES FOR CONSTRUCTION OF POLICY

The following are the rules referred to by this Act for the construction of a policy in the above or other like form, where the context does not otherwise require:—

1. Where the subject-matter is insured "lost or not lost," and the loss has occurred before the contract is concluded, the risk attaches unless, at such time, the assured was aware of the loss, and the insurer was not.

2. Where the subject-matter is insured "from" a particular place, the risk does not attach until the ship starts on the voyage insured.

3.—(*a*) Where a ship is insured "at and from" a particular place, and she is at that place in good safety when the contract is concluded, the risk attaches immediately.

(*b*) If she be not at that place when the contract is concluded the risk attaches as soon as she arrives there in good safety, and, unless the policy otherwise provides, it is immaterial that she is covered by another policy for a specified time after arrival.

(*c*) Where chartered freight is insured "at and from" a particular place, and the ship is at that place in good safety when the contract is concluded the risk attaches immediately. If she be not there when the contract is concluded, the risk attaches as soon as she arrives there in good safety.

(*d*) Where freight, other than chartered freight, is payable without special conditions and is insured "at and from" a particular place, the risk attaches pro rata as the goods or merchandise are shipped; provided that if there be cargo in readiness which belongs to the shipowner, or which some other person has contracted with him to ship, the risk attaches as soon as the ship is ready to receive such cargo.

4. Where goods or other movables are insured "from the loading thereof," the risk does not attach until such goods or movables are actually on board, and the insurer is not liable for them while in transit from the shore to the ship.

5. Where the risk on goods or other movables continues until they are "safely landed," they must be landed in the customary manner and within a reasonable time after arrival at the port of discharge, and if they are not so landed the risk ceases.

6. In the absence of any further licence or usage, the liberty to touch and stay "at any port or place whatsoever" does not authorise the ship to depart from the course of her voyage from the port of departure to the port of destination.

7. The term "perils of the seas" refers only to fortuitous accidents or casualties of the seas. It does not include the ordinary action of the winds and waves.

8. The term "pirates" includes passengers who mutiny and rioters who attack the ship from the shore.

9. The term "thieves" does not cover clandestine theft or a theft committed by any one of the ship's company, whether crew or passengers.

10. The term "arrests, &c., of kings, princes, and people" refers to political or executive acts, and does not include a loss caused by riot or by ordinary judicial process.

11. The term "barratry" includes every wrongful act wilfully committed by the master or crew to the prejudice of the owner, or, as the case may be, the charterer.

12. The term "all other perils" includes only perils similar in kind to the perils specifically mentioned in the policy.

13. The term "average unless general" means a partial loss of the subject-matter insured other than a general average loss, and does not include "particular charges."

14. Where the ship has stranded, the insurer is liable for the excepted losses, although the loss is not attributable to the stranding, provided that when the stranding takes place the risk has attached and, if the policy be on goods, that the damaged goods are on board.

15. The term "ship" includes the hull, materials and outfit, stores and provisions for the officers and crew, and, in the case of vessels engaged in a special trade, the ordinary fittings requisite for the trade, and also, in the case of a steamship, the machinery, boilers, and coals and engine stores, if owned by the assured.

16. The term "freight" includes the profit derivable by a shipowner from the employment of his ship to carry his own goods or movables, as well as freight payable by a third party, but does not include passage money.

17. The term "goods" means goods in the nature of merchandise, and does not include personal effects or provisions and stores for use on board.

In the absence of any usage to the contrary, deck cargo and living animals must be insured specifically, and not under the general denomination of goods.

APPENDIX 2

CARRIAGE OF EXPORTS BY SEA AND AIR[1]

Carriage of Goods by Sea Act 1971[2]

SCHEDULE

THE HAGUE RULES AS AMENDED BY THE BRUSSELS PROTOCOL 1968

ARTICLE I

In these Rules the following words are employed, with the meanings set out below—

(*a*) "Carrier" includes the owner or the charterer who enters into a contract of carriage with a shipper.
(*b*) "Contract of carriage" applies only to contracts of carriage covered by a bill of lading or any similar document of title, in so far as such document relates to the carriage of goods by sea, including any bill of lading or any similar document as aforesaid issued under a pursuant to a charter party from the moment at which such bill of lading or similar document of title regulates the relations between a carrier and a holder of the same.
(*c*) "Goods" includes goods, wares, merchandise, and articles of every kind whatsoever except live animals and cargo which by the contract of carriage is stated as being carried on deck and is so carried.
(*d*) "Ship" means any vessel used for the carriage of goods by sea.
(*e*) "Carriage of goods" covers the period from the time when the goods are loaded on to the time they are discharged from the ship.

ARTICLE II

Subject to the provisions of Article VI, under every contract of carriage of goods by sea the carrier, in relation to the loading, handling, stowage, carriage, custody, care and discharge of such goods, shall be subject to the responsibilities and liabilities, and entitled to the rights and immunities hereinafter set forth.

ARTICLE III

1. The carrier shall be bound before and at the beginning of the voyage to exercise due diligence to—

(*a*) Make the ship seaworthy.
(*b*) Properly man, equip and supply the ship.
(*c*) Make the holds, refrigerating and cool chambers, and all other parts of the ship in which goods are carried, fit and safe for their reception, carriage and preservation.

2. Subject to the provisions of Article IV, the carrier shall properly and carefully load, handle, stow, carry, keep, care for, and discharge the goods carried.

3. After receiving the goods into his charge the carrier or the master or agent of the carrier shall, on demand of the shipper, issue to the shipper a bill of lading showing among other things—

---

[1] See p. 329, *ante*.
[2] See p. 346, *ante*.

(*a*) The leading marks necessary for identification of the goods as the same are furnished in writing by the shipper before the loading of such goods starts, provided such marks are stamped or otherwise shown clearly upon the goods if uncovered, or on the cases or coverings in which such goods are contained, in such a manner as should ordinarily remain legible until the end of the voyage.

(*b*) Either the number of packages or pieces, or the quantity, or weight, as the case may be, as furnished in writing by the shipper.

(*c*) The apparent order and condition of the goods.

Provided that no carrier, master or agent of the carrier shall be bound to state or show in the bill of lading any marks, number, quantity, or weight which he has reasonable ground for suspecting not accurately to represent the goods actually received, or which he has had no reasonable means of checking.

4. Such a bill of lading shall be prima facie evidence of the receipt by the carrier of the goods as therein described in accordance with paragraph 3(*a*), (*b*) and (*c*). However, proof to the contrary shall not be admissible when the bill of lading has been transferred to a third party acting in good faith.

5. The shipper shall be deemed to have guaranteed to the carrier the accuracy at the time of shipment of the marks, number, quantity and weight, as furnished by him, and the shipper shall indemnify the carrier against all loss, damages and expenses arising or resulting from inaccuracies in such particulars. The right of the carrier to such indemnity shall in no way limit his responsibility and liability under the contract of carriage to any person other than the shipper.

6. Unless notice of loss or damage and the general nature of such loss or damage be given in writing to the carrier or his agent at the port of discharge before or at the time of the removal of the goods into the custody of the person entitled to delivery thereof under the contract of carriage, or, if the loss or damage be not apparent, within three days, such removal shall be primâ facie evidence of the delivery by the carrier of the goods as described in the bill of lading.

The notice in writing need not be given if the state of the goods has, at the time of their receipt, been the subject of joint survey or inspection.

Subject to paragraph 6*bis* the carrier and the ship shall in any event be discharged from all liability whatsoever in respect of the goods, unless suit is brought within one year of their delivery or of the date when they should have been delivered. This period may, however, be extended if the parties so agree after the cause of action has arisen.

In the case of any actual or apprehended loss or damage the carrier and the receiver shall give all reasonable facilities to each other for inspecting and tallying the goods.

6*bis*. An action for indemnity against a third person may be brought even after the expiration of the year provided for in the preceding paragraph if brought within the time allowed by the law of the Court seized of the case. However, the time allowed shall be not less than three months, commencing from the day when the person bringing such action for indemnity has settled the claim or has been served with process in the action against himself.

7. After the goods are loaded the bill of lading to be issued by the carrier, master, or agent of the carrier, to the shipper shall, if the shipper so demands, be a "shipped" bill of lading, provided that if the shipper shall have previously taken up any document of title to such goods, he shall surrender the same as against the issue of the "shipped" bill of lading, but at the option of the carrier such document of title may be noted at the port of shipment by the carrier, master, or agent with the name or names of the ship or ships upon which the goods have been shipped and the date or dates of shipment, and when so noted, if it shows the particulars

mentioned in paragraph 3 of Article III, shall for the purpose of this article be deemed to constitute a "shipped" bill of lading.

8. Any clause, covenant, or agreement in a contract of carriage relieving the carrier or the ship from liability for loss or damage to, or in connection with, goods arising from negligence, fault, or failure in the duties and obligations provided in this article or lessening such liability otherwise than as provided in these Rules, shall be null and void and of no effect. A benefit of insurance in favour of the carrier or similar clause shall be deemed to be a clause relieving the carrier from liability.

Article IV

1. Neither the carrier nor the ship shall be liable for loss or damage arising or resulting from unseaworthiness unless caused by want of due diligence on the part of the carrier to make the ship seaworthy, and to secure that the ship is properly manned, equipped and supplied, and to make the holds, refrigerating and cool chambers and all other parts of the ship in which goods are carried fit and safe for their reception, carriage and preservation in accordance with the provisions of paragraph 1 of Article III. Whenever loss or damage has resulted from unseaworthiness the burden of proving the exercise of due diligence shall be on the carrier or other person claiming exemption under this article.

2. Neither the carrier nor the ship shall be responsible for loss or damage arising or resulting from—

(*a*) Act, neglect, or default of the master, mariner, pilot, or the servants of the carrier in the navigation or in the management of the ship.
(*b*) Fire, unless caused by the actual fault or privity of the carrier.
(*c*) Perils, dangers and accidents of the sea or other navigable waters.
(*d*) Act of God.
(*e*) Act of war.
(*f*) Act of public enemies.
(*g*) Arrest or restraint of princes, rulers or people, or seizure under legal process.
(*h*) Quarantine restrictions.
(*i*) Act or omission of the shipper or owner of the goods, his agent or representative.
(*j*) Strikes or lockouts or stoppage or restraint of labour from whatever cause, whether partial or general.
(*k*) Riots and civil commotions.
(*l*) Saving or attempting to save life or property at sea.
(*m*) Wastage in bulk or weight or any other loss or damage arising from inherent defect, quality or vice of the goods.
(*n*) Insufficiency of packing.
(*o*) Insufficiency or inadequacy of marks.
(*p*) Latent defects not discoverable by due diligence.
(*q*) Any other cause arising without the actual fault or privity of the carrier, or without the fault or neglect of the agents or servants of the carrier, but the burden of proof shall be on the person claiming the benefit of this exception to show that neither the actual fault or privity of the carrier nor the fault or neglect of the agents or servants of the carrier contributed to the loss or damage.

3. The shipper shall not be responsible for loss or damage sustained by the carrier or the ship arising or resulting from any cause without the act, fault or neglect of the shipper, his agents or his servants.

4. Any deviation in saving or attempting to save life or property at sea or any reasonable deviation shall not be deemed to be an infringement or breach of these

Rules or of the contract of carriage, and the carrier shall not be liable for any loss or damage resulting therefrom.

5. (*a*) Unless the nature and value of such goods have been declared by the shipper before shipment and inserted in the bill of lading, neither the carrier nor the ship shall in any event be or become liable for any loss or damage to or in connection with the goods in an amount exceeding the equivalent of 10,000 francs per package or unit or 30 francs per kilo of gross weight of the goods lost or damaged, whichever is the higher.

(*b*) The total amount recoverable shall be calculated by reference to the value of such goods at the place and time at which the goods are discharged from the ship in accordance with the contract or should have been so discharged.

The value of the goods shall be fixed according to the commodity exchange price, or, if there be no such price, according to the current market price, or, if there be no commodity exchange price or current market price, by reference to the normal value of goods of the same kind and quality.

(*c*) Where a container, pallet or similar article of transport is used to consolidate goods, the number of packages or units enumerated in the bill of lading as packed in such article of transport shall be deemed the number of packages or units for the purposes of this paragraph as far as these packages or units are concerned. Except as aforesaid such article of transport shall be considered the package or unit.

(*d*) A franc means a unit consisting of 65·5 milligrammes of gold of millesimal fineness 900. The date of conversion of the sum awarded into national currencies shall be governed by the law of the Court seized of the case.

(*e*) Neither the carrier nor the ship shall be entitled to the benefit of the limitation of liability provided for in this paragraph if it is proved that the damage resulted from an act or omission of the carrier done with intent to cause damage, or recklessly and with knowledge that damage would probably result.

(*f*) The declaration mentioned in sub-paragraph (*a*) of this paragraph, if embodied in the bill of lading, shall be primâ facie evidence, but shall not be binding or conclusive on the carrier.

(*g*) By agreement between the carrier, master or agent of the carrier and the shipper other maximum amounts than those mentioned in sub-paragraph (*a*) of this paragraph may be fixed, provided that no maximum amount so fixed shall be less than the appropriate maximum mentioned in that sub-paragraph.

(*h*) Neither the carrier nor the ship shall be responsible in any event for loss or damage to, or in connection with, goods if the nature or value thereof has been knowingly mis-stated by the shipper in the bill of lading.

6. Goods of an inflammable, explosive or dangerous nature to the shipment whereof the carrier, master or agent of the carrier has not consented with knowledge of their nature and character, may at any time before discharge be landed at any place, or destroyed or rendered innocuous by the carrier without compensation and the shipper of such goods shall be liable for all damages and expenses directly or indirectly arising out of or resulting from such shipment. If any such goods shipped with such knowledge and consent shall become a danger to the ship or cargo, they may in like manner be landed at any place, or destroyed or rendered innocuous by the carrier without liability on the part of the carrier except to general average, if any.

Article IV bis

1. The defences and limits of liability provided for in these Rules shall apply in any action against the carrier in respect of loss or damage to goods covered by a contract of carriage whether the action be founded in contract or in tort.

2. If such an action is brought against a servant or agent of the carrier (such servant or agent not being an independent contractor), such servant or agent shall

be entitled to avail himself of the defences and limits of liability which the carrier is entitled to invoke under these Rules.

3. The aggregate of the amounts recoverable from the carrier, and such servants and agents, shall in no case exceed the limit provided for in these Rules.

4. Nevertheless, a servant or agent of the carrier shall not be entitled to avail himself of the provisions of this article, if it is proved that the damage resulted from an act or omission of the servant or agent done with intent to cause damage or recklessly and with knowledge that damage would probably result.

Article V

A carrier shall be at liberty to surrender in whole or in part all or any of his rights and immunities or to increase any of this responsibilities and obligations under these Rules, provided such surrender or increase shall be embodied in the bill of lading issued to the shipper. The provisions of these Rules shall not be applicable to charter parties, but if bills of lading are issued in the case of a ship under a charter party they shall comply with the terms of these Rules. Nothing in these Rules shall be held to prevent the insertion in a bill of lading of any lawful provision regarding general average.

Article VI

Notwithstanding the provisions of the preceding articles, a carrier, master or agent of the carrier and a shipper shall in regard to any particular goods be at liberty to enter into any agreement in any terms as to the responsibility and liability of the carrier for such goods, and as to the rights and immunities of the carrier in respect of such goods, or his obligation as to seaworthiness, so far as this stipulation is not contrary to public policy, or the care or diligence of his servants or agents in regard to the loading, handling, stowage, carriage, custody, care and discharge of the goods carried by sea, provided that in this case no bill of lading has been or shall be issued and that the terms agreed shall be embodied in a receipt which shall be a non-negotiable document and shall be marked as such.

Any agreement so entered into shall have full legal effect.

Provided that this article shall not apply to ordinary commercial shipments made in the ordinary course of trade, but only to other shipments where the character or condition of the property to be carried or the circumstances, terms and conditions under which the carriage is to be performed are such as reasonably to justify a special agreement.

Article VII

Nothing herein contained shall prevent a carrier or a shipper from entering into any agreement, stipulation, condition, reservation or exemption as to the responsibility and liability of the carrier or the ship for the loss or damage to, or in connection with, the custody and care and handling of goods prior to the loading on, and subsequent to the discharge from, the ship on which the goods are carried by sea.

Article VIII

The provisions of these Rules shall not affect the rights and obligations of the carrier under any statute for the time being in force relating to the limitation of the liability of owners of sea-going vessels.

Article IX

These Rules shall not affect the provisions of any international Convention or national law governing liability for nuclear damage.

Article X

The provisions of these Rules shall apply to every bill of lading relating to the carriage of goods between ports in two different States if:

(*a*) the bill of lading is issued in a contracting State, or
(*b*) the carriage is from a port in a contracting State, or
(*c*) the contract contained in or evidenced by the bill of lading provides that these Rules or legislation of any State giving effect to them are to govern the contract,

whatever may be the nationality of the ship, the carrier, the shipper, the consignee, or any other interested person.

[*The last two paragraphs of this article are not reproduced. They require contracting States to apply the Rules to bills of lading mentioned in the article and authorise them to apply the Rules to other bills of lading.*]

[*Articles* 11 *to* 16 *of the International Convention for the unification of certain rules of law relating to bills of lading signed at Brussels on 25th August* 1924 *are not reproduced. They deal with the coming into force of the Convention, procedure for ratification, accession and denunciation, and the right to call for a fresh conference to consider amendments to the Rules contained in the Convention.*]

Appendix 3

EXCHANGE CONTROL[1]

Exchange Control Act 1947

Part IV

IMPORT AND EXPORT

21.—(1) The importation into the United Kingdom of—

(*a*) any notes of a class which are or have at any time been legal tender in the United Kingdom or any part of the United Kingdom; and
(*b*) any such other notes as may be specified by order of the Treasury, being notes issued by a bank or notes of a class which are or have at any time been legal tender in any territory; and
(*c*) any Treasury bills; and
(*d*) any certificate of title to any security, including any such certificate which has been cancelled, and any document certifying the destruction, loss or cancellation of any certificate of title to a security.

is hereby prohibited except with the permission of the Treasury.

(2) In this section the expression "note" includes part of a note and the expression "security" includes a secondary security.

22.—(1) The exportation from the United Kingdom of—

(*a*) any notes of a class which are or have at any time been legal tender in the United Kingdom or any part of the United Kingdom or in any other territory; and
(*b*) any Treasury bills; and
(*c*) any postal orders; and
(*d*) any gold; and
(*e*) any of the following documents (including any such document which has been cancelled), that is to say—
  (i) any certificate of title to a security and any coupon; and
  (ii) any policy of assurance; and
  (iii) any bill of exchange or promissory note expressed in terms of a currency other than sterling; and
  (iv) any document to which section four of this Act applies not issued by an authorised dealer or in pursuance of a permission granted by the Treasury;

  and any document certifying the destruction, loss or cancellation of any of the documents aforesaid; and
(*f*) any such articles exported on the person of a traveller or in a traveller's baggage as may be prescribed.

is hereby prohibited except with the permission of the Treasury.

(2) In this section, the expression "note" includes part of a note, the expression "security" includes a secondary security and the expression "coupon" shall be construed in accordance with the meaning of "security."

23.—(1) The exportation of goods of any class or description from the United Kingdom to a destination in any such territory as may be prescribed is hereby

[1] See p. 71, *ante*.

prohibited except with the permission of the Treasury, unless the Commissioners of Customs and Excise are satisfied—

(*a*) that payment for the goods has been made to a person resident in the United Kingdom in such manner as may be prescribed in relation to goods of that class or description exported to a destination in that territory, or to be so made not later than six months after the date of exportation; and

(*b*) that the amount of the payment that has been made or is to be made is such as to represent a return for the goods which is in all the circumstances satisfactory in the national interest.

Provided that the Treasury may direct that, in cases to which the direction applies, paragraph (*a*) of this subsection shall have effect as if for the reference to six months there were substituted a reference to such longer or shorter period as may be specified in the direction, or as if the words "or is to be so made not later than six months after the date of exportation" were omitted.

(2) For the purpose of satisfying themselves in the case of any goods as to the matters specified in subsection (1) of this section, the Commissioners of Customs and Excise may require the person making entry of the goods for export to deliver to the collector or other proper officer together with the entry such declarations signed by such persons as the Commissioners may require, and where any such declaration has been so required the goods shall not be exported until it has been delivered as aforesaid.

(3) Where the Commissioners of Customs and Excise are not satisfied in the case of any goods as to the matters specified in paragraph (*b*) of the said subsection (1), they shall give their reasons to the person making entry of the goods for export and shall take into consideration any representations made by him.

(4) Any reference in this section to the destination of any goods includes a reference to the ultimate destination thereof.

APPENDIX 4

FREIGHT FORWARDERS[1]

Standard Trading Conditions
sponsored by

The Institute of Freight Forwarders Ltd.
[*1978 Edition*]

1. (i) All and any business undertaken, including any advice, information or service provided whether gratuitously or not by .... (name and style of Company) (hereinafter called "the Company") is transacted subject to the Conditions hereinafter set out and each Condition shall be deemed to be incorporated in and to be a Condition of any agreement between the Company and its Customers. The Company is not a common carrier and only deals with goods subject to these Conditions. No agent or employee of the Company has the Company's authority to alter or vary these Conditions.

(iii) If any legislation is compulsorily applicable to any business undertaken, these Conditions shall as regards such business be read as subject to such legislation and nothing in these Conditions shall be construed as a surrender by the Company of any of its rights or immunities or as an increase of any of its responsibilities or liabilities under such legislation and if any part of these Conditions be repugnant to such legislation to any extent such part shall as regards such business be void to that extent but no further.

2. Customers entering into transactions of any kind with the Company expressly warrant that they are either the owners or the authorised agents of the owners of any goods to which the transaction relates and further warrant that they are authorised to accept and are accepting these Conditions not only for themselves but also as agents for and on behalf of all other persons who are or may thereafter become interested in the goods.

3. Any instructions or business accepted by the Company may in the absolute discretion of the Company be fulfilled by the Company itself by its own servants performing part or all of the relevant services or by the Company employing or instructing or entrusting the goods to others on such conditions as such others may stipulate to perform part or all of the services.

4. Subject to express instructions in writing given by the Customer, the Company reserves to itself absolute discretion as to the means, route and procedure to be followed in the handling, storage, and transportation of goods. Further, if in the opinion of the Company it is at any stage necessary or desirable in the Customer's interests to depart from those instructions, the Company shall be at liberty to do so.

5. Pending forwarding or delivery, goods may be warehoused or otherwise held at any place or places at the sole discretion of the Company and the cost thereof shall be for the account of the Customer.

6. Except where the Company is instructed in writing to pack the goods the Customer warrants that all goods have been properly and sufficiently packed and/or prepared.

---

[1] See p. 179, *ante*. These Standard Trading Conditions are © The Institute of Freight Forwarders Ltd. and are reproduced by kind permission of the Institute.

7. The Company is entitled to retain and be paid all brokerages, commissions, allowances and other remunerations.

8. Quotations are given on the basis of immediate acceptance and are subject to withdrawals or revisions. Further unless otherwise agreed in writing the Company shall be after acceptance at liberty to revise quotations or charges with or without notice in the event of changes occurring in currency exchange rates, rates of freight, insurance premiums or any charges applicable to the goods.

9. The customer shall be deemed to be bound by and to warrant the accuracy of all descriptions, values and other particulars furnished to the Company for Customs, Consular and other purposes and he undertakes to indemnify the Company against all losses, damages, expenses and fines whatsoever arising from any inaccuracy or omission, even if such inaccuracy or omission is not due to any negligence.

10. The Customer shall be liable for any duties, taxes, imposts, levies, deposits or outlays of any kind levied by the authorities at any port or place for or in connection with the goods and for any payments, fines, expenses, loss or damage whatsoever incurred or sustained by the Company in connection therewith.

11. When goods are accepted or dealt with upon instructions to collect freight, duties, charges or other expenses from the consignee or any other person the Customer shall remain responsible for the same if they are not paid by such consignee or other person immediately when due.

12. No insurance will be effected except upon express instructions given in writing by the Customer and all insurances effected by the Company are subject to the usual exceptions and conditions of the policies of the insurance company or underwriters taking the risk. The Company shall not be under any obligation to effect a separate insurance on each consignment but may declare it on any open or general policy. Should the insurers dispute their liability for any reason the insured shall have recourse against the insurers only and the Company shall not be under any responsibility or liability whatsoever in relation thereto notwithstanding that the premium upon the policy may not be at the same rate as that charged by the Company or paid to the Company by its Customer.

13. (i) The Company shall only be responsible for any loss of or damage to goods or for any non-delivery or mis-delivery if it is proved that the loss, damage, non-delivery or mis-delivery occurred whilst the goods were in the actual custody of the Company and under its actual control and that such loss, damage, non-delivery or mis-delivery was due to the wilful neglect or default of the Company or its own servants.

(ii) The Company shall only be liable for any non-compliance or mis-compliance with instructions given to it if it is proved that the same was caused by the wilful neglect or default of the Company or its own servants.

(iii) Save as aforesaid the Company shall be under no liability whatsoever however arising, and whether in respect of or in connection with any goods or any instructions, business, advice, information or service or otherwise.

(iv) Further and without prejudice to the generality of the preceding subcondition, the Company shall not in any event, whether under sub-conditions (i) or (ii) or otherwise, be under any liability whatsoever for any consequential loss or loss of market or fire or consequence of fire or delay or deviation however caused.

14. In no case whatsoever shall any liability of the Company however arising and notwithstanding any lack of explanation exceed the value of the relevant goods or a sum at the rate of £800 per tonne of 1000 kilos of the gross weight of the goods whichever is the less, with a maximum of £9,600 per claim.

15. In any event the Company shall be discharged from all liabilty—

(*a*) for loss from a package or an unpacked consignment or for damage or mis-delivery (however caused) unless notice be received in writing within seven days after the end of the transit where the transit ends in the British Isles or within fourteen days after the end of the transit where the transit ends at any place outside the British Isles;

(*b*) for loss or non-delivery of the whole of a consignment or any separate package forming part of the consignment (however caused), unless notice be received in writing within twenty-eight days of the date when the goods should have been delivered.

16.(*a*) The Company shall not be obliged to make any declaration for the purpose of any statute or convention or contract as to the nature or value of any goods or as to any special interest in delivery, unless expressly instructed by the Customer in writing.

(*b*) Where there is a choice or rates according to the extent or degree of the liability assumed by carriers, warehousemen or others, goods will be forwarded, dealt with, etc., at Customer's risk or other minimum charges, and no declaration of value (where optional) will be made, unless express instructions in writing to the contrary have previously been given by the Customer.

17. Perishable goods which are not taken up immediately upon arrival or which are insufficiently addressed or marked or otherwise not readily identifiable, may be sold or otherwise disposed of without any notice to the Customer and payment or tender of the net proceeds of any sale after deduction of charges and expenses shall be equivalent to delivery. All charges and expenses arising in connection with the sale or disposal of the goods shall be paid by the Customer.

18. The Company shall be entitled to sell or dispose of all non-perishable goods which in the opinion of the Company cannot be delivered either because they are insufficiently or incorrectly addressed or because they are not collected or accepted by the Consignee or any other reason, upon giving 21 days notice in writing to the Customer. All charges and expenses arising in connection with the storage and sale or disposal of the goods shall be paid by the Customer.

19. Except under special arrangements previously made in writing the Company will not accept or deal with any noxious, dangerous, hazardous or inflammable or explosive goods or any goods likely to cause damage. Should any Customer nevertheless deliver any such goods to the Company or cause the Company to handle or deal with any such goods otherwise than under special arrangements previously made in writing, he shall be liable for all loss or damage whatsoever caused by or to or in connection with the goods however arising and shall indemnify the Company against all penalties, claims, damages, costs and expenses whatsoever arising in connection therewith and the goods may be destroyed or otherwise dealt with at the sole discretion of the Company or any other person in whose custody they may be at the relevant time. If such goods are accepted under arrangements previously made in writing, they may nevertheless be so destroyed or otherwise dealt with on account of risk to other goods, property, life or health. The expression "goods likely to cause damage" includes goods likely to harbour or encourage vermin or other pests.

20. Except under special arrangements previously made in writing the Company will not accept or deal with bullion, coins, precious stones, jewellery, valuables, antiques, pictures, livestock or plants. Should any Customer nevertheless deliver any such goods to the Company or cause the Company to handle or deal with any such goods otherwise than under special arrangements previously made in writing the Company shall be under no liability whatsoever for or in connection with the goods however caused.

21. Without prejudice to Condition 2 the Company shall have the right to enforce any liability of the Customer under these Conditions or to recover any sums to be paid by the Customer under these Conditions not only against or from the Customer but also if it thinks fit against or from the sender and/or consignee and/or owner of the goods. All sums shall be paid to the Company in cash immediately when due without deduction and payment shall not be withheld or deferred on account of any claim, counterclaim or set-off.

22. All goods (and documents relating to goods) shall be subject to a particular and general lien and right of detention for monies due either in respect of such goods, or for any particular or general balance or other monies due from the Customer or the Sender, consignee or owner to the Company. If any monies due to the Company are not paid within one calendar month after notice has been given to the person from whom the monies are due that such goods are being detained, they may be sold by auction or otherwise at the sole discretion of the Company and at the expense of such persons, and the net proceeds applied in or towards satisfaction of such indebtedness.

23. In addition to and without prejudice to the foregoing Conditions the Customer undertakes that he shall in any event indemnify the Company against all liabilities whatsoever suffered or incurred by the Company arising directly or indirectly from or in connection with the Customer's instructions or their implementation of the goods, and in particular the Customer shall indemnify the Company in respect of any liability whatsoever it may be under to any servant, agent or sub-contractor or any haulier, carrier, warehousemen, or other person whatsoever at any time involved with the goods arising out of any claim made directly or indirectly against any such party by the Customer or by any sender, consignee or owner of the goods or by any person interested in the goods or by any other person whatsoever.

24. All agreements between the Company and its customers shall be governed by English Law and be within the exclusive jurisdiction of the English Courts.

INDEX

(References in **bold** *type indicate the page where the subject is treated fully)*